AMERICAN
GOVERNMENT

A PANORAMA OF WASHINGTON extends across the cover of this book onto the title page. The title page shows, also, the Seal of the United States as it appears in a ceiling of the Federal Reserve Building.

Panorama and Seal are from photographs by Horydczak.

MAGRUD

AMERICAN

Revise

ALLYN AND BACON

BOSTON   NEW YORK   CHICAGO   ATLAN

R'S

GOVERNMENT

y WILLIAM A. McCLENAGHAN

DEPARTMENT OF POLITICAL SCIENCE
OREGON STATE COLLEGE

1958

ic.

LLAS SAN FRANCISCO

★

AMERICAN GOVERNMENT, *first published in 1917, is an enduring symbol of the author's faith in American ideals and American institutions. The life of Frank Abbott Magruder (1882–1949) was an outstanding example of Americanism at its very best. His career as teacher, author, and tireless worker in civic and religious undertakings remains an inspiring memory to all who knew him.*

PREFACE

Magruder's *American Government,* 1958, is a carefully rewritten edition of this national leader. The new format, the new illustrations, the new open typography, and the new supplementary features all speak for themselves. No effort has been spared to make this book the most usable and effective book in its field.

Like earlier editions, this new edition continues the practice of reporting on up-to-the-minute events while maintaining its primary emphasis on the basic structure of American Government. At the same time, it throws into bold relief those simple pioneering precepts of government which have made us a strong, a productive, a free America.

The many teachers who have used this book in their classes for years will recognize that the time-tested topics — our Government's origin, its growth, its organization, its powers, and its truly functional character — are basic elements to be thoroughly mastered during the course. The text continues to point out, also, that there is a substantial amount of civic principle and thought which never changes, yet is an essential to a thorough comprehension of a citizen's responsibility to his Government.

In recent years, this book has sounded anew its warnings against threats to our American way of life. Our Declaration of Independence, our Constitution, and other documents of our liberties set forth our rights, our privileges, and our duties as American citizens. So, once again, let students, teachers, everyone, be urged to know our Government, to take a constant interest in it, and to be a part of it.

Class Activities and Study Aids

A course in American Government provides an abundance of resource materials for class projects and supplementary reading programs. The carefully developed suggestions that follow will aid the teacher in discovering and selecting those activities which are particularly suited to the needs and interests of the class.

Field trips are always of keen interest to the students. Schedule them as a regular part of the year's activities, and plan definitely on trips to local and county agencies of government. Trips to the State and National capitals would be of special interest. Plan on having local, State, and National legislators discuss their work before the class or school assembly, or even before a community group if that is necessary in order to justify taking the officials' time. Be sure to publicize such lectures and forums on subjects closely related to the work of the class.

The importance of the reading program as part of the course in American Government should be stressed, no matter what the research facilities are in a community. As a prerequisite of the year's work, every student should read and study for quick reference the Constitution of the United States, reprinted with annotations in this book. The bibliographies provide guidance to excellent resource materials. Every effort should be made to use them to the fullest extent.

Shostal

DOCUMENTS OF OUR LIBERTIES

The Declaration of Independence, the Constitution, and the Bill of Rights, those historic documents which embody the basic principles of our democracy, are now in the Document Room of the National Archives in Washington.

CONTENTS

THE BETTERMENT OF SOCIETY 621

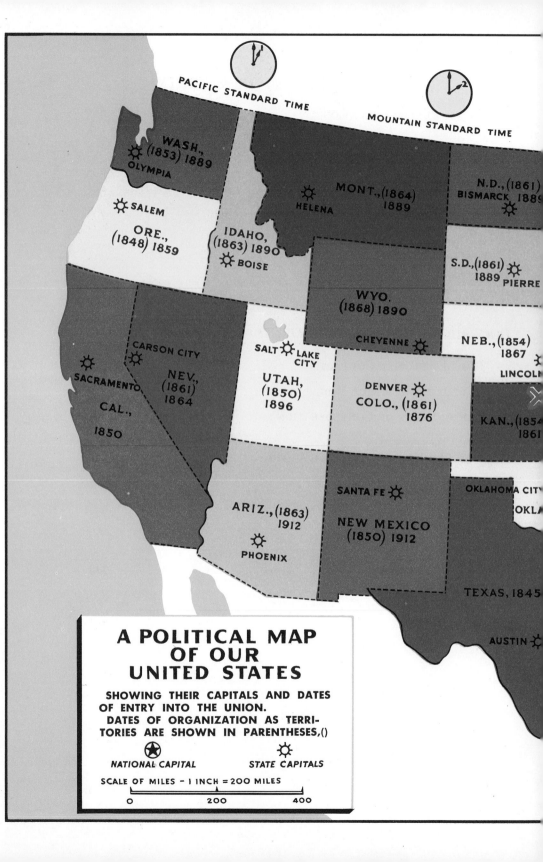

PACIFIC STANDARD TIME

MOUNTAIN STANDARD TIME

WASH., (1853) 1889
OLYMPIA

SALEM
ORE., (1848) 1859

IDAHO, (1863) 1890
BOISE

MONT., (1864) 1889
HELENA

N.D., (1861)
BISMARCK 1889

WYO. (1868) 1890

CHEYENNE

S.D., (1861) 1889 PIERRE

NEB., (1854) 1867

LINCOLN

CARSON CITY
NEV, (1861) 1864

SACRAMENTO
CAL., 1850

SALT LAKE CITY
UTAH, (1850) 1896

DENVER
COLO., (1861) 1876

KAN., (1854) 1861

ARIZ., (1863) 1912
PHOENIX

SANTA FE

NEW MEXICO (1850) 1912

OKLAHOMA CITY
OKLA

TEXAS, 1845

AUSTIN

A POLITICAL MAP OF OUR UNITED STATES

SHOWING THEIR CAPITALS AND DATES OF ENTRY INTO THE UNION.
DATES OF ORGANIZATION AS TERRITORIES ARE SHOWN IN PARENTHESES,()

NATIONAL CAPITAL   STATE CAPITALS

SCALE OF MILES – 1 INCH = 200 MILES

0   200   400

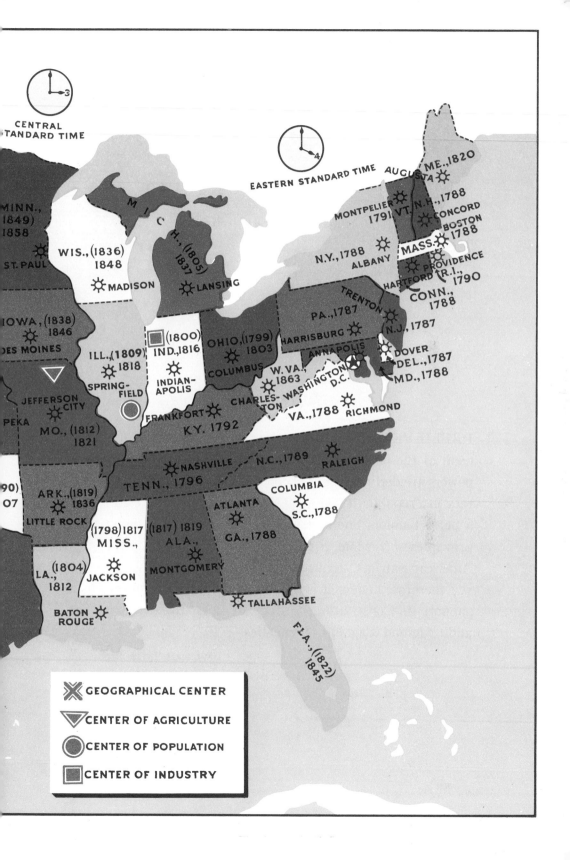

IN GOD WE TRUST

THE NATIONAL MOTTO

The American's Creed

I BELIEVE IN THE UNITED STATES OF AMERICA as a government of the people, by the people, for the people, whose just powers are derived from the consent of the governed; a democracy in a republic, a sovereign Nation of many sovereign States; a perfect union, one and inseparable, established upon those principles of freedom, equality, justice, and humanity for which American patriots sacrificed their lives and fortunes.

I therefore believe it is my duty to my country to love it, to support its Constitution, to obey its laws, to respect its flag, and to defend it against all enemies.

WILLIAM TYLER PAGE

UNIT I
DEVELOPMENT
OF GOVERNMENT

The Washington Monument, Seen from the Lincoln Memorial

1

"RESOLVED, That these United Colonies are, and of right ought to be, Free and Independent States."

In this mural of the Continental Congress, meeting in Independence Hall, Philadelphia, July 2, 1776, Benjamin Franklin is shown, seated at the left. At his left stands John Adams; at his right, Thomas Jefferson. Benjamin Harrison has just read the Independence Resolve to the assembly, and the vote is about to be taken.

Sail on, O Ship of State!
Sail on, O Union, strong and great!
Humanity with all its fears,
With all the hopes of future years,
Is hanging breathless on thy fate!
— *Henry Wadsworth Longfellow*

★

Chapter 1

STRENGTH THROUGH UNION

Our American Heritage. The United States of America was born with these bold lines:

We hold these truths to be self-evident: that all men are created equal; that they are endowed by their Creator with certain unalienable Rights; that among these are Life, Liberty, and the pursuit of Happiness.

These words form the very heart of the Declaration of Independence. The words are simple ones; yet, what they say is of deep and lasting significance. They express a faith: in individualism, in freedom, and in equality.

It is this faith which has made America the greatest nation on earth. This faith is our American heritage.

Ours is a nation with the highest standard of living ever known to man. Look about you; it is easy to see the material things that make it so: automobiles, skyscrapers, radios and television sets, busy factories, airplanes,

mighty dams, electric lights, and fertile farms; the list is endless.

But these things are only the material evidences of America's greatness. They may *show* that we are great, but in themselves they do not *make* us great.

We are a great nation and a great people today because we have carried forward the spirit of the Declaration of Independence. We are great because we have built and maintained a " government of the people, by the people, for the people."

It remains true, no matter how many times it is said, that the future of America rests upon its youth. America will remain great *only* to the extent to which *you* believe in the American heritage. Our nation will remain great *only* to the extent that *you* and *all* of your generation are willing to dedicate yourselves to the high purpose of carrying forward the heritage which is ours.

"To Form a More Perfect Union"

(From the Preamble to the Constitution)

Meeting in Philadelphia in the summer of 1787, our forefathers wrote the Constitution of the United States in order

to form a more perfect Union, establish justice, insure domestic tranquillity, provide for the common defense, promote the general welfare, and secure the blessings of liberty to ourselves and our posterity.

The fifty-five men who wrote the Constitution showed the rest of mankind that independent states could unite through peaceful agreement. They did this by creating a kind of government never before tried: a Federal Government — a Union in which the powers of general national concern are vested in the National Government, while authority over local matters is held by the States.

Our struggle for an ever-closer Union has not always been easy. Occasionally political strife and sometimes physical violence have marred our progress. Yet these growing pains have not kept us from moving ahead to the pinnacle that we occupy today.

In Union There Is Strength. The United States stretches some 3000 miles from the Atlantic on the east to the Pacific on the west and some 1500 miles from Canada on the north to Mexico and the Gulf on the south. Within this area of 3,022,387 square miles lies one of the largest and richest of lands on earth.

We have a climate that varies from semi-tropical to arctic and produces everything from tropical oranges to arctic furs. Our long coast lines are dotted with magnificent harbors. Inland there are towering mountains, mighty rivers, great lakes, and tremendous expanses of rolling plains.

We are blessed with a wealth of natural resources. We have iron, oil, coal, timber, and power in abundance. Each year we find new and better ways to use and conserve this wealth.

Because our forty-eight States are united in one great nation, we have a huge market that includes 173,000,-000 people stretching across the continent. And within this market are none of the trade barriers and petty international jealousies which plague other parts of the world.

An Ever-Closer Union. The formation of a Federal Union provided a tool with which to build a stronger nation. This tool, the Constitution, has made possible the co-operation of our present forty-eight States and of our people to the best interests of all.

Because we were united we were able to build railroads over almost uninhabited plains to connect the West with the more populous East. We were able to join our highways into a network linking every corner of the land. And we were able to connect all parts of the country by airways.

Telegraph and telephone lines were built so that we might talk from New

JET TRAVEL

Passengers board a jet transport at Los Angeles International Airport. As one of the chief means of overcoming time and space, the airplane is another reason for our ever-closer Union.

York to New Orleans or from Washington to Walla Walla with the same ease as when calling the neighborhood grocer. Radio and television have given every American a ringside seat at the important events of the world — an address by the President, United Nations proceedings, political party conventions, or on-the-scene broadcasts from trouble-spots around the globe.

Press, radio, and television coverage of the 1956 presidential campaign was the most extensive in our history. More than 100,000,000 witnessed the national conventions on television, and millions more followed the proceedings by radio.

Our Union, and indeed the whole world, seems almost a neighborhood because time and space have been conquered by man's ingenuity.

"To Establish Justice"

(From the Preamble to the Constitution)

We have defined the American heritage as a faith in individualism, in freedom, and in equality. It is a belief in the dignity and worth of every human being. The Framers of our Constitution recognized that an ordered system of justice is essential to the maintenance of this belief. They agreed with Thomas Jefferson that the establishing and maintaining of justice is " the most sacred of the duties of a government."

Federal Courts Provided. Until the Constitution was established, we had only State courts to decide disputes between States and between citizens of different States. The Constitution provided for a Supreme Court and authorized Congress to create other federal courts.

The first bill considered in the Senate of the new Congress of the United States in 1789 was a measure which set the basic pattern of our national court system. Since that beginning, the national judiciary has acted as the guardian of the rights and liberties of the American people.

It is the duty of all branches and agencies of the National Government to operate within the limits of the Constitution. But it is the special function of the courts to safeguard the people against arbitrary actions by the Government.

The Bill of Rights was added to the Constitution in 1791 to guarantee the people against injustices by the National Government such as those suffered under George III.

REVOLUTIONARY JUSTICE

The Green Mountain Boys administer the " high chair treatment " to the holder of a questionable land grant. We have outgrown individually imposed justice.

Courtesy National Life Insurance Company, Montpelier, Vt.

Unit I. DEVELOPMENT OF GOVERNMENT

The Bill of Rights lists our basic civil liberties. For example, it guarantees to all freedom of speech, press, and religion. Everyone is entitled to his " day in court," with full opportunity to present evidence and witnesses in his behalf when accused of crime. Our law insists that any accused person must be presumed innocent unless and until he is proved guilty.

Justice and the Citizen. The American system of justice is the product of centuries of opposition to injustice and oppression. The United States itself was born in rebellion against wrongs.

Our Constitution and the courts give strength to our system of justice. But, in the last analysis, it must depend for its life upon the everyday actions and attitudes of the American people. Those who abide by the law and respect it maintain law and make it stronger. Those who have little respect for the rights of others and try to " get away " with as much as they can only weaken it.

"To Insure Domestic Tranquillity"
(From the Preamble to the Constitution)

The Government Guarantees Order. Order is essential to the well-being of any society, and keeping the peace at home has always been one of the major functions of government. This responsibility was very much in the minds of the men who framed the Constitution.

As we shall see, the economic difficulties of the 1780's in the United States was one of the reasons for the drafting of the new Constitution. The strained conditions of the period (known as the Critical Period in American history) even led to open violence in some instances.

One of the most spectacular of these incidents, Shays' Rebellion, took place in Massachusetts. As in most States at that time, the farmers and merchants were ranged against one another over the question of " hard " or " soft " money. For six months (1786–1787) an armed band of several hundred farmers and debtors under the command of Daniel Shays defied the State Government. They prevented many of the county courts from sitting in debt cases and even threatened to lay siege to Boston. Their attempt to capture the arsenal at Springfield had to be repulsed with grapeshot. Only when the State militia took the field were the " rebels " finally dispersed.

If rebellion or riots occur in any State today, the President can use his power as Commander-in-Chief of the armed forces to send troops to restore order. When the trouble is purely local, the President will furnish protection if asked to do so by the State legislature or the governor.

Man-made violence is much less disruptive than the rampages of nature. Here, too, the Government stands ready to come to the aid of the stricken areas. Thus when disastrous floods hit the States of Missouri, Oklahoma, and Texas in the spring of 1957, the armed forces were used to aid flood victims and protect their property. Medical supplies, food, clothing, temporary shelter and other necessities were rushed to the critical areas. Order was very quickly restored.

"To Provide for the Common Defense"
(From the Preamble to the Constitution)

National Defense. In addition to keeping the peace at home, defense against foreign enemies has always been one of the major functions of government. The men who drafted the Constitution well understood this fact. George Washington was President of the Constitutional Convention and many of its members had served in his Revolutionary armies.

Two World Wars and the threat of a third have sharply emphasized the importance of national defense. No sooner had Hitler's warmaking dictatorship been defeated than the Soviet Union, through its military and political expansion, became another threat to the democracies of the world. Today Congress appropriates some $40,000,000,000 a year for national defense. Since World War II we have sent more than $60,000,000,000 in military and economic aid to our Allies in the Cold War against world communism. Our armed forces are more powerful than ever before in our peacetime history.

A Nonmilitaristic People. As a people, we hate and deplore war. We cherish a strong nonmilitaristic tradition. The armed forces are controlled by civilian authorities — the President and Congress. The law even requires that the Secretary of Defense must not have served in the armed forces for at least ten years before his appointment. Control by militarists has usually gone hand-in-hand with dictatorship, as it did in Germany and Japan.

Increasing Cost of Wars. The costs of wars and of national defense have mounted steadily throughout our history. The first World War cost the United States about $25,000,000,000; but the second one cost us about $300,000,000,000. Interest on the World War II debt alone costs the United States over $7,000,000,000 a year — more than half of the total cost of public school education. National defense and foreign aid in the Cold War have cost us some $300,000,000,000. Much more important than the cost in dollars and resources were the deaths of 300,000 youth of our land and the disabling of nearly twice that number in World War II. To that sad total must be added the 142,000 dead and wounded in the Korean war.

Increasing Destructiveness of Wars. The mere mention of atomic weapons, the hydrogen bomb, rockets, and bacteriological warfare emphasizes the fact that war today means *total war*. The atomic ruins of Hiroshima and Nagasaki, the war-scarred face of Europe, and the awesome destruction wrought in Korea, all bear eloquent testimony to the increasing destructiveness of war. No nation can " win " a third world war — the entire world would be the loser.

Military Defense. To say that no nation can possibly " win " a third world war does not mean that one may not come. To guard against that possibility, and to be so strong as to discourage any attack, is the basic pattern of our military policy. In a world as unsettled as ours, we must be prepared to meet any eventuality. We work for peace, but we keep our powder dry.

The Army, Navy, Marines, and Air Force are stationed around the globe. In addition to the billions now being spent on our own arms and on aid to our Allies, we have forged a system of *defensive* alliances in both Europe and Asia.

Industrial Defense. The tremendous productive capacity of American industry is a trump card in our defense hand. A modern war can be won or lost in the factory, on the farm, or in the laboratory just as assuredly as on the battlefield.

The war against Japan was shortened by the perfection of the atomic bomb — a laboratory product of Allied scientists. Since the end of the war scientific research has continued at a rapid pace — indeed, many claim

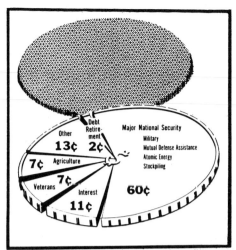

Source: Bureau of the Budget

THE BUDGET DOLLAR

Wars and fear of future wars have resulted in heavy defense spending.

that American scientific achievement has been the major reason that a third world war has not come.

But we cannot rest on past laurels. Scientific research, industrial development, agricultural improvements must continue if we are to maintain our superiority. Thus when the Russians launched the first earth satellite, the " Sputnik," in 1957, the United States intensified its own efforts in that field. The Russian achievement also prompted increased effort in the closely-related work on the intercontinental ballistics missile, the ICBM, a weapon capable of carrying an atomic warhead to any point in the world with deadly accuracy.

Physical Welfare for Defense. Millions of American men were rejected from service in World War II because they were physically unfit.

COCOONS OF WAR

Big guns, protected from the weather by their casings, appear to the observer as cocoons standing for review.

Today many men are being rejected for the same reason. Local, State, and National governments, through Departments of Health and otherwise, contribute in many ways to the good health of our citizens. Periodic physical examinations are part of every school program.

Educational Defense. The United States spends four times as much on military defense as we spend on education. Yet in modern warfare educated scientists are as important as soldiers. A highly educated nation has the advantage in diplomacy and in propaganda. Today the communists are trying to give the rest of the world a false and distorted picture of the United States, to turn our allies away from us, and even to make the American people lose faith in themselves and in the Government. To prevent this we must know the facts and present them to the world.

Patriotic Defense. Many people thought Great Britain was doomed when in 1940 the Germans bottled the British Army at Dunkirk; but intangible patriotism plus an abhorrence of dictators caused sturdy British civilians to swarm to the rescue. In little gasoline launches they braved the waves of the rough Channel, the bombs from the German planes that swarmed over them, and even the flaming seas, because of this intangible something called patriotism.

Patriotism can be aroused by patriotic teachers, editors, radio news interpreters, film producers, and Gov-

Unit I. Development of Government

ernment propaganda; but patriotism whose roots grow deepest comes from a just Government that promotes equal opportunities for all — a Government of, for, and by the people. Such a Government is our own, " established upon those principles of freedom, equality, justice, and humanity for which American patriots have sacrificed their lives and fortunes." Thus it is our privilege as well as our duty to love our country, support its Constitution, obey its laws, respect its flag, and defend it against all its enemies.

All Types of Defense Depend upon High Moral Standards. The shocking report of the Senate Crime (Kefauver) Committee indicates that organized crime operates on a large scale in the United States today. Illegal gambling, narcotics, political bribery, labor and business racketeering, and gangsterism in all forms can undermine the moral strength of the nation. Yet, according to FBI Director J. Edgar Hoover, most crime could be eliminated in two days by vigorous action at the local level all over the country.

Religion as a Foundation of Strength. As the dignity and worth of the individual lies at the very heart of the American heritage, so it lies at the very heart of religion. Over a century ago, a visitor from Europe is said to have remarked that he sought for the greatness and genius of America in her harbors and her ample rivers; in her fertile fields and boundless forests; in her rich mines and her

vast world commerce; in her public schools and institutions of learning; in her democratic Congress and her matchless constitution; and it was in none of these. Not until he went to the churches of America and heard her pulpits flame with righteousness did he understand the secret of her genius and power. He concluded:

America is great because America is good, and if America ever ceases to be good, America will cease to be great.

The Good-Neighbor Policy as a Source of Strength. The greatest law in the world is the Golden Rule; and if a Government adopts this rule

THE PROTECTION OF DIVINE PROVIDENCE

From the beginning, America's greatness has been based on an enduring belief in God. In the words of our new Pledge of Allegiance, we firmly face the future as " one nation under God."

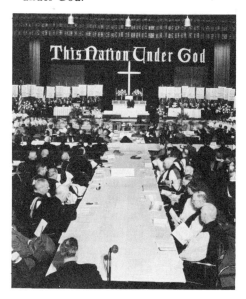

This Nation Under God

in its foreign policy most countries will respond and be neighborly. The United States applied the good-neighbor policy to Canada and Latin America, and when we became involved in war they became our Allies. We are now applying the good-neighbor policy to Western Europe, and in case of war these countries would almost certainly be our allies.

How to bring about peaceful and neighborly relations between the free nations led by the United States and the communist nations led by Russia is the big question that confronts people today. As we have said before, so long as Russia has powder we must keep our own powder dry; but this should not mean that war is inevitable. The only *sure* way to win a third world war is to prevent its ever breaking out.

Defense through Co-operation with the United Nations. The United Nations was founded " to save succeeding generations from the scourge of war." Its Charter was ap-

proved by the United States Senate by a vote of 89 to 2. In some ways, and especially because of obstructions by Russia, it has not accomplished all that it was hoped it might. But the United States supports it as a genuine and in many ways an effective international organization for peace.

Armed forces of the United States fought aggression in Korea with other United Nations troops as their allies. Thus, for the first time in the history of man, an international organization met aggression with armed force.

We have peace in our cities because we have agreed to local laws and have police to enforce them. We have peace in our States because we have agreed to State laws and have State police to enforce them. We have peace in the United States because we have agreed to federal laws and have an army to enforce them. If we could have definite international laws and means to enforce them, perhaps we might then have international peace, as well.

"To Promote the General Welfare"
(From the Preamble to the Constitution)

Government as Servant. Centuries ago the chief task of government was felt to be that of defending the people against foreign invasion and domestic violence. Defense is still one of the main functions of government, but gradually through the years government has assumed a much broader role. Especially in democratic countries, such as the United

States, it has become the *servant* as well as the protector of the people.

Few people realize the many and varied ways in which our government at all levels — National, State, local — serves them, providing them with services they could hardly live without.

All through life the citizen is served by his local, State, and National governments. The food that he eats is inspected to guarantee its purity and protect his health. He may receive much of his education at public expense. The hours and conditions under which he works, the quality of the clothing he wears, and the home he lives in, all are protected in a great many ways by governmental regulations meant for his safety and well-being.

His automobile must be licensed and must meet certain safety standards set by government, and he must pass a driving test to secure an operator's license. The roads that he drives on are built, maintained, and protected by government, also. Employment service, on-the-job training, unemployment compensation, injury bene-fits, collective bargaining rights, and social security for old age are a few among the many ways in which government serves its citizens.

Government regulates public utilities such as electric power companies, bus, railway, and air lines in order to insure safe and adequate service. It guarantees bank deposits and, in times of national emergency, it may regulate wages and prices. Dope peddlers, gamblers, criminals of all sorts are hunted down and prosecuted by government. Property is protected by fire departments against fire, by police agencies against theft, and by various other services against the ravages of nature. In these and countless other ways, government serves the people — " to promote the general welfare."

"To Secure the Blessings of Liberty to Ourselves and Our Posterity"

(From the Preamble to the Constitution)

Liberty versus Authority. This country was founded by men who loved liberty and prized it above all earthly possessions. For it they pledged their lives, their fortunes, and their sacred honor. Patrick Henry electrified the colonists with his stirring cry " Give me liberty or give me death! " Thomas Jefferson declared that " The God who gave us life, gave us liberty at the same time." Benjamin Franklin wrote " They that can give up essential liberty to obtain a little temporary safety deserve neither liberty nor safety." The desire for liberty for their country and for the individual was the prime force governing the leaders of our Revolution, and these objectives have remained our goal throughout our history. We are opposing communist aggression in the world today in order " to secure the blessings of liberty to ourselves and our posterity."

For us liberty is *relative*, not absolute. We recognize that absolute liberty is impossible in an ordered society. Each individual cannot do exactly as he pleases because in so doing he would inevitably interfere with the rights of his neighbors. So liberty by its very nature is a mutual privilege. Justice Oliver Wendell Holmes once emphasized the fact that liberty is relative and not absolute in a case in which he remarked that " the most stringent protection of free speech will not protect a man in falsely shouting ' Fire! ' in a theatre and causing a panic."

While liberty must be exercised with due regard for others, authority must be limited also. If a government is able to do anything it pleases, individual liberty cannot exist at all. The Soviet Union and her satellites ruth-

TOWN MEETING

Citizens of Milton, Massachusetts, meet to discuss plans for a new school building. Here townsmen think and speak freely on matters of common concern. Milton is now too large for everyone to attend the town meeting; 300 elected members represent the people instead.

© C. L. Fasch, 1950

lessly suppress individual freedom because they fear popular revolt. It is estimated that there are between twelve and twenty million so-called " political prisoners " in Russian slave-labor camps. Only those things which are " acceptable " to the Soviet government may be taught, spoken, or written in Russia today.

By sharp contrast, our government is subject to the will of the people. In other words, we have taken the middle ground between absolute liberty and absolute authority and strive for a just balance between the interests of the individual and those of society as a whole.

In brief, liberty is a thing of the spirit — to be free to worship, to think, and to speak without fear — free to challenge wrong and oppression with surety of justice. Liberty conceives that the mind and the spirit of men can be free only if the individual is free to choose his own calling, to develop his talents, to win and to keep a home sacred from intrusion, to rear children in an orderly society. It holds that man must be free to earn, to spend, to save, and to accumulate property that may give protection and security to himself and to his loved ones.

Our Task. Because America has been the melting pot of all the nations of the world, our national thought represents the hopes and the aspirations of liberty-loving people everywhere. These people are our close neighbors today because modern communication and travel have made them so. They

14

have the right to take the same steps that we have taken as a nation " to secure the blessings of liberty to ourselves and our posterity." So we have fought, and will fight again if need be, " for the things which we have always carried nearest our hearts — for a democracy, for the right of those who submit to authority to have a voice in their own governments, for the rights and liberties of small nations, for a universal dominion of right by such a concert of free peoples as shall bring peace and safety to all nations and make the world itself at last free." Thus Woodrow Wilson phrased the goal which only the good citizenship of every American can safeguard.

More than two thousand years ago, Aristotle wrote that " If liberty and equality are chiefly to be found in democracy, they will be best attained when all persons alike share in the government to the utmost." So you, your teachers, and all of us who have America's welfare at heart must study to know our government in order that we may protect it from all its enemies both at home and abroad. " Eternal vigilance is the price of liberty."

WHAT THIS CHAPTER IS ABOUT

Our American heritage — a faith in individualism, in freedom, and in equality — has made us the greatest nation on earth. Our task is to maintain and carry on that heritage.

The purposes for which our government exists are stated in the Preamble to the Constitution. The Constitution established a type of government never before tried: a Federal Government, one in which power over national matters is vested in the National Government and authority over local matters is held by the States.

Our Union, blessed with much physical wealth, is becoming ever closer through the wonders of modern transportation and communication.

An ordered system of justice is essential to the American heritage. The courts stand as the guardians of the people's rights. But, in the last analysis, our system of justice must depend for its life on the actions and attitudes of the American people.

Keeping the peace at home, against both man-made and natural violence, is one of the major functions of government. So is defense against foreign enemies.

As a people, we hate war. But we must remain strong to discourage attack and to defend ourselves in case of another war. A third world war is not inevitable, but we must be prepared should it come.

In the modern world, industrial strength, physical welfare, education, patriotism, and high moral and religious standards can be as important as military strength for defense. We have based much of our foreign policy on the Golden Rule.

In a democracy like the United States, government is the *servant* as well as the protector of the people. Few realize the many and varied ways in which government serves the people today.

Both liberty and authority are essential to a democracy, but they must be in proper balance. If one outweighs the other, democracy itself is lost.

QUESTIONS ON THE TEXT

1. What is the American heritage?

2. List the purposes of our Government as stated in the Constitution.

3. How large, in length, width, and area is the United States?

4. Why is an ordered system of justice essential to the maintenance of the American heritage?

5. Upon what, in the last analysis, does the American system of justice depend?

6. What is our basic military policy? Why must we keep our powder dry?

7. How much did World War II cost us in casualties? How many casualties did the Korean war cost? How much interest do we pay on the war debt? How does this compare with the cost of public school education?

8. Give an example of how each of the following kinds of national defense adds to our national security:

a. Industrial   e. Moral
b. Physical welfare   f. Religious
c. Educational   g. Good-Neighbor
d. Patriotic   Policy

9. Explain what is meant when we say that government is our servant.

10. Why, in a democracy such as ours, must liberty be relative and not absolute? Why must authority be limited?

11. Why is eternal vigilance the price of liberty?

PROBLEMS FOR DISCUSSION

1. A century and a half ago a young English economist named Malthus figured that the population was increasing more rapidly than the food supply, and that an overcrowded world would soon be stricken with famine unless large numbers of the people died from plagues or were killed off by wars. What has science done about preventing starvation because of overpopulation? How has the formation of a strong Union helped to prevent it in the United States? How might science and an international organization prevent it on a world-wide scale?

2. What new inventions made World War II more destructive than World War I? In what ways could another war be even more destructive than World War II?

3. Christian A. Herter of Massachusetts has stated: " Eighty-five cents out of every dollar spent by the Federal Government since the beginning of this Republic has been spent on wars, or preparation for wars, or repairing the damages caused by wars." The Second World War cost the world about $1,000,000,000,000. If this had been borne equally by each of the two and a half billion people in the world, how much would each man, woman, and child have paid as his share of the cost?

THINGS YOU MIGHT DO

1. Write a short essay on why it is so necessary that, if at all possible, we prevent a third world war. (And remember Patrick Henry's comment that peace is not to be bought at the price of chains and slavery.)

2. Explain in your own words what Thomas Jefferson meant when he wrote that " It is to secure our rights that we resort to government at all."

3. Make a list of as many as you can of the ways in which each level of government in the United States serves the people.

Unit I. Development of Government

WORDS AND PHRASES YOU SHOULD KNOW

American heritage   Liberty
Bill of Rights   Nonmilitaristic tradition
Federal Government   Preamble to the Constitution
Justice

SELECT BIBLIOGRAPHY

ARONSON, J. HUGO, " What America Means to Me," *American,* August, 1956.

CARR, ROBERT K., and others, *American Democracy in Theory and Practice,* Chapters 1 and 2. Rinehart, 1955.

DAVENPORT, RUSSELL W., *U.S.A.: The Permanent Revolution.* Prentice-Hall, 1952.

DRUCKER, PETER F., " America's Next Twenty Years," *Harper's,* March, 1955, and following issues.

JESSUP, JOHN K., " Western Man and the American Idea," *Life,* November 5, 1951.

LINDBERGH, CHARLES A., " But How about Man? " *Reader's Digest,* April, 1954.

LINDSEY, FRED B., " 44 Million More Americans in 1975," *Nation's Business,* February, 1955.

McEVOY, J. P., " America through the Eyes of a Japanese War-Bride," *Reader's Digest,* April, 1955.

SARNOFF, DAVID, " Preview of the Next Twenty-five Years," *Reader's Digest,* March, 1955.

SEVAREID, ERIC, " Why Did They Fight? " *Reader's Digest,* October, 1953.

SMITH, T. V., *The Bill of Rights and Our Individual Liberties.* League of Women Voters, 1954.

Man is by nature a political animal.

— *Aristotle*

★

Chapter 2

GOVERNMENTS AND POLITICAL IDEAS IN THE WORLD TODAY

In this book we are especially concerned with governments in the United States — National, State, and local. But we do not live, and the United States does not exist, in a vacuum. There are other governments and other political ideas in the world, of course — and many of them are quite different from our own.

In this day and age, when man can travel two and three times the speed of sound, what exists and what happens anywhere in the world is of vital concern to us and to our country.

We can better understand the world of the late 1950's if we know at least something of the governments and the political philosophies of other peoples. And, with this knowledge, we can better support our friends and oppose our enemies. How effective can we be in opposing communism, for example, if we don't really know what communism is?

Governments in the World Today

The State. A state [1] is an organized body of people living within a defined territory and having the power

[1] *State* is a technical or legal word for what is commonly called a " country " or a " nation." Throughout this book the word *state* printed with a small " s " denotes an independent state belonging to the family of nations, as Great Britain, France, the United States; the word *State* printed with a capital " S " refers to one of the members of the United States of America, as Maine, Texas, California, and so on.

to make and enforce *law* without the consent of any higher authority. There are more than ninety states in the world today and they vary greatly in size and importance.

But each of them meets the four basic requirements:

(1) *Population.* Obviously there must be people. The number of people is not essential to existence as a state, however. The smallest state

Courtesy Swiss National Tourist Office

A SWISS "TOWN MEETING"

Switzerland has made democracy work for over 700 years. Some areas still use the ancient Citizen's Assembly for public business.

in the world, population-wise, is one few people have ever heard of — tiny San Marino.[2] Nestled in the Apennines and bounded on all sides by Italy, its population is less than 14,000.

The largest state in the world, from the population standpoint, is China with some 600,000,000 people. Because of the high birth rate, if the Chinese people were to line up and march four abreast into the Yellow Sea they would never stop coming.

---

[2] Stamp collectors are often familiar with San Marino because it raises a large share of its annual budget by issuing postage stamps of many kinds.

(2) *Territory.* Just as there must be people, there must also be territory with definite and known boundaries. But, again, the amount of territory is not important. San Marino, with only 38 square miles, is the smallest. The Soviet Union, the largest, has some 6,800,000 square miles, or about one-sixth of the land surface of the earth. The United States is 3,022,387 square miles in area.

(3) *Sovereignty.* Every state is sovereign; that is, it has supreme and absolute power to chart its own policies, both foreign and domestic. It is not responsible to any higher authority. Hence, as a sovereign state, the

United States can determine its own form of government, its own economic system, its own foreign policies, and all other matters for itself.[3]

The *location* of sovereignty within the state, that is, who actually *holds* the sovereign power, determines the nature of that state, democratic or dictatorial. If the people are sovereign, as in the United States, a democracy exists. If one person or a small group is sovereign, as in Russia, a dictatorship exists.

(4) *Government.* Every state has a government. But there are many different kinds of governments in the world.

Government Defined. Government is the agent through which the state exerts its will and accomplishes its ends. It consists of the machinery and the personnel through which the state is ruled (governed). In effect, the government may be likened to the engine that keeps the entire machine (the state) moving.

Forms of Government. Since governments are the product of human experience, human needs, and conditions, no two are exactly alike. But, because of certain basic features, all governments may be classified in a variety of ways. The most important classifications are (A) according to the distribution of the powers of government, (B) according to the type

of executive the government has, and (C) according to how many participate in the governmental process.

A. *According to Distribution of Powers.* Under this method of classification there are three forms of government to be considered — *unitary, federal,* and *confederate.*

(1) *Unitary.* A unitary government is one in which all *governmental* powers are concentrated in the hands of a single central government. Although local governments exist, they are only administrative agents of the central government; they are created by and for the convenience of the central government and from it derive such powers as they have.

Great Britain is the outstanding example of a unitary government today. All of the powers that the British government possesses are held by one central organ, the Parliament. Local governments exist to relieve Parliament of a burden it could perform only with extreme difficulty. But, if it wished to, Parliament could wipe out all local government tomorrow.

Be careful *not* to confuse a unitary government with a dictatorship. Again, in the unitary form *all the powers that government possesses* are concentrated in the central government. But government might not possess *all* power. In Great Britain, for example, government has no power to interfere with freedom of speech, of the press, and of religion.

(2) *Federal.* A federal government is one in which the powers of government are divided between a cen-

[3] Thus States in the Union are not states in the international legal sense. They are not sovereign because the Constitution of the United States is over them. Hawaii, Alaska, Hong Kong, and other dependent areas of the world are not states, either.

tral and several local governments. This division of powers is made by an authority superior to both the central and the local governments and cannot be changed by either acting alone.

For example, in the United States certain powers belong to the National Government and others to the States. The sovereign people have made this division of powers through the Constitution — which cannot be altered unless the people, acting through both the National and State governments, approve such a change. Canada, Australia, and Switzerland also have the federal form of government.[4]

(3) *Confederate.* A confederation is a very loose form of federalism with very little real power placed in the hands of the central government. It is more an alliance of independent states, usually for defensive purposes. The United States under the Articles of Confederation (1781–1789) and the Confederate States of America during the War Between the States (1861–1865) afford examples. The confederate form was most widely used among the ancient Greek city-states.

B. *According to Executive Types.* Here there are two major forms of government to be considered: *presidential* and *parliamentary.*

(1) *Presidential.* The presidential form of government is character-

Combine Photos

QUEEN ELIZABETH

The British Queen rules through parliamentary government. Elizabeth, here attending the Royal Film Show, is also a symbol of the free association of states in the Commonwealth of Nations.

ized by a chief executive (president) elected by the voters for a fixed term of office. Hence, the chief executive is independent of the legislature. He cannot be removed except by the cumbersome and difficult process of impeachment. Usually, as in the United States and each of the forty-eight States, a written constitution provides for a separation of powers among the executive, legislative, and judicial branches. Although each branch has its own distinct set of powers, all three are equal and work together for smooth and effective government.

---

[4] It is sometimes said that the 1936 Constitution of the U.S.S.R. created a federal government in Russia, but this is true only on paper. Virtually all power is concentrated in the hands of the central government in Moscow despite the provisions of the 1936 Constitution.

(2) *Parliamentary.* Under a parliamentary form of government the executive is composed of a prime minister and his cabinet, and they are themselves members of the legislative branch (parliament). The prime minister is the leader of the majority party in the parliament and is chosen to his office by that body. With majority approval, he in turn selects the members of his cabinet from among the members of parliament. The prime minister and his cabinet are thus chosen by the legislative branch and are subject to its control. They hold office only so long as their policies and administration retain the confidence of at least a majority in parliament. If they are defeated on an important measure (a " vote of confidence "), they must resign. Then a new " government " must be chosen. Either parliament chooses a new prime minister and cabinet or, as often happens, a general election is held and all of the seats in parliament go before the voters. Great Britain, most European states, and the members of the British Commonwealth have governments of this type.

C. *According to How Many Rule.* The most meaningful and realistic classification of governments is based upon the number of people actually participating in the governing process. Formal legal institutions are important to the successful mechanical operation of government, but the degree of popular participation is the vital heart of the matter. Here we consider *dictatorship* and *democracy.*

(1) *Dictatorship.* When unlimited political authority rests with one person or with a very few persons, a dictatorship is said to exist. Examples of modern dictatorships are Nazi Germany, Fascist Italy, and the Soviet Union. A dictatorial government is often in the hands of a single all-powerful individual, but not always. Nikita Khrushchev is a dictator, yet he must rule with the aid of the small, potent Presidium of the Communist Party of the U.S.S.R. The primary characteristic of any dictatorship is that *it is not responsible to the people and cannot be limited by them.*[5] Freedom of speech, press, thought, and association, so vital in a democratic system, are not permitted in a dictatorship; the individual exists for the state, not the state for the individual. Mussolini spoke for all dictators in saying: " All is in the state and for the state; nothing outside the state, nothing against the state." [6]

(2) *Democracy.* Democracy is a form of government in which supreme power rests with the people. In other words, the people govern themselves. Democracy may be either *direct* or *indirect.* In a *direct democracy* the will of the state is formulated directly and

---

[5] The formal elections of the Soviet Union and other communist countries do not mean that these governments are responsible to the people. The only " candidates " on the ballot are those of the communist party; the voter has no real choice.

[6] A *totalitarian* state is one in which *all* (total) power is held by the government. Dictatorships are usually, but not always, totalitarian dictatorships.

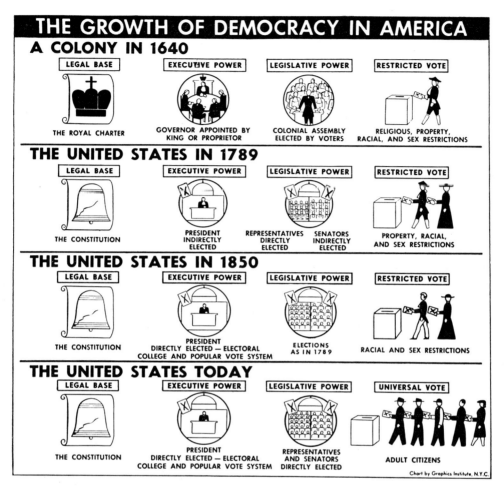

THE GROWTH OF DEMOCRACY IN AMERICA

A COLONY IN 1640

LEGAL BASE	EXECUTIVE POWER	LEGISLATIVE POWER	RESTRICTED VOTE
THE ROYAL CHARTER	GOVERNOR APPOINTED BY KING OR PROPRIETOR	COLONIAL ASSEMBLY ELECTED BY VOTERS	RELIGIOUS, PROPERTY, RACIAL, AND SEX RESTRICTIONS

THE UNITED STATES IN 1789

LEGAL BASE	EXECUTIVE POWER	LEGISLATIVE POWER	RESTRICTED VOTE
THE CONSTITUTION	PRESIDENT INDIRECTLY ELECTED	REPRESENTATIVES DIRECTLY ELECTED — SENATORS INDIRECTLY ELECTED	PROPERTY, RACIAL, AND SEX RESTRICTIONS

THE UNITED STATES IN 1850

LEGAL BASE	EXECUTIVE POWER	LEGISLATIVE POWER	RESTRICTED VOTE
THE CONSTITUTION	PRESIDENT DIRECTLY ELECTED — ELECTORAL COLLEGE AND POPULAR VOTE SYSTEM	ELECTIONS AS IN 1789	RACIAL AND SEX RESTRICTIONS

THE UNITED STATES TODAY

LEGAL BASE	EXECUTIVE POWER	LEGISLATIVE POWER	UNIVERSAL VOTE
THE CONSTITUTION	PRESIDENT DIRECTLY ELECTED — ELECTORAL COLLEGE AND POPULAR VOTE SYSTEM	REPRESENTATIVES AND SENATORS DIRECTLY ELECTED	ADULT CITIZENS

Chart by Graphics Institute, N.Y.C.

immediately through a mass meeting of the people.[7] In the United States, we have an *indirect*, or *representative, democracy* — or, as it is sometimes called, a *republic*. The will of the state is formulated and expressed through a relatively small body of persons chosen by the people to act as their representatives. These representatives are responsible to the people for the day-to-day operation of government and must face periodic election. The ultimate source of all political authority is in the people; the people are sovereign. Democracy in a republic, then, is " government of the people, by the people, for the people."

[7] Direct democracy is practicable only in small communities where it is physically possible for the entire citizenry to assemble in a given place and where the problems of government are few and simple. It does not exist anywhere on a national level today. However, the New England town meeting and the *Landsgemeinde* in five of the smaller Swiss cantons are excellent examples of direct democracy in action. In a limited sense, law-making by initiative petition is a form of direct democracy (see pages 486–89).

Capitalism versus Socialism and Communism

Capitalism. Our economic system, founded as it is on free enterprise and private ownership of production, distribution, and exchange, is known as capitalism (or free or private enterprise). In a capitalistic society factories, mines, stores, farms, banks, and the like are the private property of individuals or companies formed by individuals. These owners run their businesses largely at their own discretion, hire labor, and compete with one another to provide goods and services at a profit.

The life-blood of the free enterprise system is competition — providing the best product at the lowest possible cost. In other words, capitalism means economic freedom and the incentive to do one's best. Generally speaking, anyone may start a business, large or small, and the risks and the rewards are his.

Most large and many small businesses in the United States are actually owned by millions of individual stockholders — people who own shares in the business itself. The American Telephone and Telegraph Company, for example, now has well over one million stockholders. In our system, if a company makes money, part of its earnings is paid out as dividends (interest) to the stockholders, and part

STAKE IN AMERICA
    The profits and risks of most American business enterprises are shared by many persons. Shares of stock represent their participation.

Charles Phelps Cushing

Unit I. Development of Government

is "plowed back" into the business. Thus business expands, more jobs are created, people buy more things, and a higher living standard results.

Unregulated capitalism may result in monopolies and other injustices. To prevent this, the National Government and the States increasingly regulate our economy by such means as anti-trust, labor-management relations, and, in times of crises, price and wage control laws. Competition also acts as a business regulator.

We have discovered that some activities are better carried on by society as a whole acting through the government. Free public education, the postal system, and help for the aged are familiar examples of long standing in the United States. As Abraham Lincoln expressed it: "The legitimate object of government is to do for the community of people whatever they need to have done, but cannot do so well for themselves, in their separate and individual capacities."

One needs only to look at the great achievements and the standard of living in the United States to see the advantages of the free enterprise system. Freedom of choice is inherent in a democracy — and in our economic system. We view trends toward nationalization and socialism in other countries with misgivings. We stand for a well-regulated capitalism as the best guarantee of the better life for all mankind.

Socialism. Socialism is an economic philosophy which advocates government ownership and control of the *major* instruments of production, distribution, and exchange, such as industry, transportation, and banking.

Most socialists are "evolutionary" — that is, they feel that they can bring about socialism gradually and peaceably, by lawful means. They believe that they can accomplish their goal by working within the established framework of government in their own particular country. This is well-illustrated by the Labour party in Great Britain today.

To the socialist, his philosophy is just because it attempts to accomplish a fair distribution of wealth among men. The economy would be managed, says the socialist, for the good of the entire community.

Socialism's opponents condemn it because they say that it stifles the individual's initiative. They also argue that the increased governmental regulation and bureaucracy will inevitably lead to a police state. Some opponents also contend that socialism is merely a step along the road to communism.[8]

The complexities of modern industrial society have led to vastly expanded governmental functions in most states, including the United States. Many of these newer governmental activities are attacked by op-

[8] Socialism is often identified with communism, primarily because the followers of Karl Marx often refer to themselves as socialists. While the socialists believe and preach many of the things the Marxists do, most of them today reject the Marxian ideas of the class struggle, the necessity of a violent revolution, and the dictatorship of the proletariat. These features of communism are discussed next.

ponents on the grounds that they are "socialistic."

Communism. Communism is *both* an economic and a political doctrine. As we know it today, communism was born in 1848 with the publication of the *Communist Manifesto*. This brief document was written by the founder of modern communism, Karl Marx, with the aid of his friend Friedrich Engels.

In the *Manifesto,* Marx and Engels laid down the cardinal premises of what they called " scientific socialism," or communism. Since then, these theories have been interpreted and expanded by Marx's followers. The most important of these " high priests of communism " have been V. I. Lenin and Joseph Stalin.

The *four central features* of communist theory are: (1) the communist theory of history, (2) the labor theory of value, (3) the communist theory of the nature of the state, and (4) the dictatorship of the proletariat.

(1) *The Communist Theory of History.* According to Marx, all of the history of mankind has been a story of " class struggle." The communists say that there have always been two opposing classes in society — one an oppressor (dominating) class and the other an oppressed (dominated) class. In feudal times the two classes were the noblemen and the serfs. Today, say the communists, the capitalists (the *bourgeoisie*) and the workers (the *proletariat*) are the contending classes. Workers in capitalistic countries are described by the communists as " wage-slaves " who are paid barely enough to permit them to eke out a starvation living. The communists claim that this alleged situation must be changed by a mass revolt of the workers and the " liquidation " of the capitalists.

(2) *The Labor Theory of Value.* According to communist theory, the value of any commodity is determined by the amount of labor necessary to produce that commodity. In other words, a pair of shoes is worth so much because it takes so much labor to produce the shoes. Because the laborer produced the shoes and thus created their value, the communists claim that he should receive that value in full. They maintain that all income should come from work. They are violently opposed to the free enterprise profit system and condemn profits as " surplus value." They claim that this " surplus value " should go to the worker.

(3) *The Communist Theory of the Nature of the State.* To the communists the state is the instrument or " tool " of the dominant class — a tool with which the bourgeoisie keeps the proletariat in bondage. Because the capitalists are so firmly entrenched and control the power of the state, said Lenin, it is only through " a violent and bloody revolution " that the situation can be altered. (The communists claim that other institutions are also used as " tools." Marx described religion as " the opiate of the people " — a drug fed to the proletariat as a hoax through which the

26   *Unit I.* DEVELOPMENT OF GOVERNMENT

Sovfoto

Courtesy South Carolina State Chamber of Commerce

FARMING — EAST AND WEST

Russian cotton growers, wearing medals for their achievements, inspect the crop of a collective farm. At right, two Americans harvest their own crops, using their own machines.

people are led to tolerate their supposed harsh lot in this life in order to gain a " fictional " afterlife.)

The " violent and bloody revolution " envisioned by Lenin would wipe out the capitalist class and place its holdings in the hands of the state.

(4) *The Dictatorship of the Proletariat.* The communists do not see a proletariat able to govern themselves after a revolution. They would need " guidance " and " education " from the communist party. So communist dogma calls for a " dictatorship of the proletariat " to accomplish this. The dictatorship would " educate " the people to the place where each individual would work not for himself but for society. Then the state would " wither away " and the communist

goal of a " free classless society " would be realized. In this society the cardinal principle would be: " From each according to his ability, to each according to his need."

Evaluation of Communism. The Soviet Union presents the outstanding example of communism in action. Strictly speaking, the Russians do not have pure communism today, but a peculiar type of socialism.[9] After the

---

[9] According to Marx, the guiding economic principle of communism is " From each according to his ability, to each according to his need." Compare this with Article 12 of the Soviet Constitution of 1936: " In the U.S.S.R. work is a duty and a matter of honor for every able-bodied citizen in accordance with the principle: 'He who does not work, neither shall he eat.' The principle applied in the U.S.S.R. is: 'From each according to his ability, to each according to his work.' "

1917 Revolution Lenin attempted to establish communism, but it failed. The inefficient and the lazy were paid as much as the efficient and the industrious. The lazy became indifferent and the industrious disgruntled. Workers and peasants refused to work to support the ne'er-do-wells, and the government executed many for disobedience. Finally the Soviet leaders turned to socialism and now claim that they are working toward communism.

Communism destroys the individual's incentive to produce. He knows that he will get only so much no matter how hard or how little he works. If the state owns everything, there is no opportunity for the inventive and the enterprising to strike out on their own to create new and better things.

The dictatorship of the proletariat, the stage of communist development Russia is now in, denies to its subjects the benefits of a free and democratic life. Freedom of speech and press, for example, cannot be tolerated by the dictatorship, lest the people examine and question the policies of the rulers. And what guarantee is there that the dictatorship will ever end? With all power gathered in the hands of a few at the top, what is to prevent the few from perpetuating their rule?

The class struggle theory of communism is disproven many times over by the American way of life. One of the basic differences between our system and theirs is that while we strive to promote *equality of opportunity,* the communists argue for *equality of condition.*

We are an individualistic people. We do not have sharp division of classes, and our standard of living is the highest the world has ever seen. In effect, the American way of life has made socialism obsolete and has shown communism to be a stagnant pool of violence and reaction.

Man is independent and creative by nature. By suppressing these traits, communism is surely signing its own death warrant.

Fascism. Yet another challenge to our democratic system is fascism. The defeat of Hitler's Germany and Mussolini's Italy in World War II left fascism without a home state from which to operate on the world scene. But fascism remains a danger to the free world.

Politically, fascism rests upon two tenets utterly contrary to those upon which democracy is based: (1) the leadership principle (the *Führer prinzip*) and (2) state socialism (*etatism*). Under the leadership principle, absolute and final power is held by the leader to whom all must pay allegiance and obedience. *Etatism* is an extreme form of totalitarianism — the state embodies everything and everybody.

In fascism, as in communism, force and terror, combined with all-out propaganda, are used to further the interests of the state as determined by the leader. A fascist state usually retains the outward forms of representative government, but inside it is a totalitarian dictatorship. The only political party allowed is composed of the " elite," the privileged few.

WHAT THIS CHAPTER IS ABOUT

Today it is essential that we understand the nature of government and the many different forms of government that exist in the world.

The *state* is an organized body of people living within a defined territory and having the power to make and enforce its own laws. There are over eighty states in the world today. Each of them possesses four characteristics: (1) population, (2) territory, (3) sovereignty, and (4) government.

No two governments are exactly alike, but all fall into classifications. A *unitary* government is one in which all the powers government possesses are held by a single central organ, as in Great Britain. A *federal* government is one in which all the powers government possesses are divided between a central and several local governments, as in the United States. A *confederate* government is a very loose form of federalism with a very weak central government, as in the United States under the Articles of Confederation from 1781–1789.

A *presidential* government is one in which the executive (president) is independent of and equal with the legislature, as in the United States. A *parliamentary* government is one in which the executive (prime minister) is a member of and subject to the control of the legislature (parliament), as in Great Britain.

Democracy is that system of government in which the people rule — are sovereign, as in the United States. *Dictatorship* is that form of government in which one or a few rule, as in Russia.

Capitalism is an economic system based upon free enterprise, private ownership of the instruments of production, distribution, and exchange, and individual initiative. *Socialism* is an economic system based upon government ownership of the major instruments of production, distribution, and exchange.

Communism goes further than socialism and is both an economic and a political system. Founded by Karl Marx in 1848, its four central ideas are: (1) the communist theory of history, (2) the labor theory of value, (3) the communist theory of the nature of the state, and (4) the dictatorship of the proletariat. Communism can be criticized on many grounds, among them, its dictatorial nature, its denial of individual incentive, and the falseness of the class-struggle idea.

Fascism is, like communism, a dictatorial philosophy placing the state before the people.

QUESTIONS ON THE TEXT

1. What is a *state?* What is a *government?* Distinguish clearly between a state and a government.

2. Distinguish between *state* and *State* as used in this text.

3. What are the four essential characteristics of a state?

4. Define *sovereignty.* Why is the location of sovereignty within a state so important?

5. Which three of the following words can be used to describe the United States? Presidential, unitary, confederate, parliamentary, federal, dictatorial, democratic.

6. Distinguish between a federal and a unitary government; presidential and parliamentary; democratic and dictatorial.

7. What is capitalism? How does it provide for incentive?

8. What is socialism?

9. What is the communist theory of history? The labor theory of value? The communist theory of the nature of the state? The dictatorship of the proletariat?

10. List as many criticisms of communism as you can.

PROBLEMS FOR DISCUSSION

1. What did Dwight D. Eisenhower mean when he said, " Tyrannies must feed on new conquests or wither "?

2. Thomas Paine wrote: " Those who expect to reap the blessings of freedom must undergo the fatigues of supporting it." Has indifference been the main reason for the rise of dictatorships? Have there been other reasons?

3. In 1952 Galo Plaza, who was born in New York and once played football for the University of California, completed a constitutional four-year term as President of Ecuador. He thus became the first man in 32 years to turn the trick. Prior to Plaza, Ecuador had 23 chiefs of state in 28 years. Some of them were constitutionally elected presidents, but most were acting presidents and dictators. Each of these 23 was deposed by revolutions or military coups. The man who succeeded Plaza and is now President, Velasco Ibarra, has held the post twice before, 1934–1935 and 1944–1947. Both times he was overthrown by army officers who felt that he had become a dictator. What reasons would you give for this marked difference between Ecuador and the United States?

4. Explain why you agree or disagree with these lines from Alexander Pope's " Essay on Man ":

For forms of government let fools contest;
Whate'er is best administer'd is best.

THINGS YOU MIGHT DO

1. Have several members of the class study the governments of other countries and report their findings to the class. In addition to the library, foreign consulates (located in most major cities) and embassies in Washington, D.C., can provide information.

2. Invite a local businessman to address the class and have him describe his business and how it operates.

3. List as many as you can of the ways that government entered directly into your life today. Be sure to include your activities at school.

WORDS AND PHRASES YOU SHOULD KNOW

Bourgeoisie	Dictatorship	Parliamentary form
Capitalism	Dictatorship of the	Presidential form
Class struggle	proletariat	Proletariat
Communism	Fascism	Socialism
Communist theory of the	Federal form	Sovereignty
state	Government	State — state
Confederate form	Incentive	Unitary form
Democracy	Labor theory of value	Vote of confidence

Unit I. DEVELOPMENT OF GOVERNMENT

SELECT BIBLIOGRAPHY

ALLEN, F., " The Unsystematic American System," *Reader's Digest*, August, 1952.

ANGELL, NORMAN, " The British Commonwealth Has Not Learned the American Lesson," *Reader's Digest*, April, 1954.

EBENSTEIN, WILLIAM, *Today's Isms: Communism, Fascism, Capitalism, Socialism.* Prentice-Hall, 1954.

FINER, HERMAN, *The Government of Great European Powers.* Holt, 1955.

——, " How Big Is Too Big? " *Time,* October 25, 1954.

GALLERY, DANIEL V., " We Can Baffle the Brainwashers! " *Saturday Evening Post,* January 22, 1955.

JOHNSTON, ERIC, " The Dollar Is a Fighting Word," *Collier's,* March 18, 1955.

LIPPMANN, WALTER, " Democracy's Sickness — and a Way to Cure It," *United States News,* April 22, 1955.

MUNRO, WILLIAM B., and AYEARST, MORLEY, *The Governments of Europe.* Macmillan, 1954.

ROCHE, JOHN P., and STEDMAN, MURRAY S., *The Dynamics of Democratic Government.* McGraw-Hill, 1954.

ROSTOW, W. W., " Marx Was a City Boy, or Why Communism May Fail," *Harper's,* February, 1955.

SALISBURY, HARRISON E., " The Fatal Flaws of Dictatorship," *New York Times Magazine,* February 20, 1955.

SNYDER, LOUIS L., *The World in the Twentieth Century.* D. Van Nostrand, 1955.

" The Continuing American Revolution," *Life,* May 16, 1955 and *Reader's Digest,* August, 1955.

" The Good Man," *Time,* September 24, 1956.

THOMAS, NORMAN, " The ' Isms ' Are Out," *The Reporter,* February 24, 1955.

U.S. STATE DEPARTMENT, *The Kremlin Speaks.* Washington, D.C.

We hold these truths to be self-evident: that all men are created equal; that they are endowed by their Creator with certain unalienable Rights; that among these are Life, Liberty and the pursuit of Happiness.

— The Declaration of Independence

★

Chapter 3

THE BEGINNINGS OF GOVERNMENT IN THE UNITED STATES

The roots of American government reach deep into the past. Our system of government did not suddenly spring into being as at the wave of some political magician's wand. Nor was it pulled out of thin air by the Founding Fathers at Philadelphia in the summer of 1787. Rather, it has developed through long centuries of experience, tradition, thought, and deed. We shall now review the high points of these beginnings.

The Colonial Period

Our English Heritage. The French, Spanish, Dutch, Norwegians, and other Europeans settled in parts of what was to become the United States. But it was the English who came in the largest numbers. And it was the English who came to control the thirteen colonies that stretched for 1300 miles along the Atlantic seaboard.

These early pioneers who cleared the wilderness and fought off the Indians had to hack out their own economic future in the New World. But they came here in search of greater freedom and they brought much of their political future with them, ready-made. They brought with them the knowledge of a governmental system that had been working and developing in England for hundreds of years.

Three political ideas or concepts that came to us from England were especially important to the shaping of government in the United States.

(1) *The Concept of Ordered Government.* These first English settlers recognized the absolute necessity for government. They established units and officers of local government, many

Unit I. Development of Government

THE FIRST REPRESENTATIVE LEGISLATURE

With the meeting of the Virginia Assembly in 1619, representative government was born in America. Its slow growth led finally to the Declaration of Independence and the Constitution.

of which are to be found today — county, borough, jury, sheriff, coroner, and justice of the peace, for example. And all of these were well-known in England long before the first Englishman ever heard of America.

(2) *The Twin Concepts of Limited Government and Civil Liberties.* They brought with them, too, the twin ideas of limited government and civil liberties. That is, that government is *not* all-powerful, that government is limited in what it may do, and, especially, that it is limited in the sense

that each man has certain rights that government cannot injure or take away. These great principles of freedom were proclaimed in such historic English documents as the Magna Carta in 1215, the Petition of Right in 1628, and the Bill of Rights and the Act of Toleration of 1689.

(3) *The Concept of Representative Government.* A third vitally important concept brought to America in English ships was that of representative government. For centuries there had been developing in England the

idea that government exists to serve the people and that the people should have a voice in shaping the policies of government. As with limited government and civil liberties, representative government found fertile soil in America and flourished quickly.

While we have changed, developed, and added to the institutions and ideas that came to us from England, there is much in the American governmental system that bears the stamp of our English heritage. Is this so strange when we recall that the colonial period of American history lasted for 168 years (1607–1775) and that the United States of America has not existed as a nation for a very much longer time?

Government in the Colonies. The first permanent English settlement in America was made at Jamestown, Virginia, in 1607. The other twelve colonies were established over the next century and a quarter, the last being Georgia in 1732.

Jamestown was founded by colonists sent out from England by a commercial corporation, the London Company. The Company, acting under a royal charter, founded the Virginia colony as a money-making venture.

At first there was little local government in Virginia; a governor and council were set up but tight control was held by the Company in London. In 1619 the Company did permit the creation of a legislature of burgesses [1] elected from each settlement.

---

[1] The term " burgesses " was used because it was expected that the settlements would

This assembly, the first representative legislature to meet in America, met on July 30, 1619, in the chancel of the church at Jamestown. It passed laws to aid the farmers of the colony, to regulate women's dress, and to curb gambling and drunkenness.

Because the London Company had failed to create a prosperous colony, the King withdrew its charter in 1624. From then until it became independent in 1776, Virginia was a *royal colony.*

Three Types of Colonies. According to the form of government in each, especially the way in which the governor was chosen, there were three types of colonies: *royal, proprietary,* and *charter.*

(1) *The royal colonies* were the most numerous. By the beginning of the Revolution they included New Hampshire, New York, New Jersey, Virginia, North Carolina, South Carolina, Georgia, and (after 1691) Massachusetts. For each of these colonies a royal governor and a council, or " upper house," were appointed by the King, and a popular assembly, or " lower house," was elected in the colony. The governor, together with his council and the assembly, ruled the colony according to written instructions issued from time to time by the Crown. The royal governors most often ruled with a stern hand, and

develop into boroughs (towns). After 1634 the " burgesses " represented counties, and in 1776 the name was changed to " assemblymen." Virginia called its colonial representatives " House of Burgesses "; South Carolina, " House of Commons "; Massachusetts, " House of Representatives."

much of the resentment that finally led to the Revolution originated in these royal colonies.

(2) *The proprietary colonies* were Pennsylvania, Delaware, and Maryland. These three got the name " proprietary " from the term *proprietor*. He was an individual to whom the King had made a grant of land which could be settled and governed as the proprietor (owner) saw fit, subject only to the general supervision of the Crown. The proprietor appointed the governors and established a legislature, court system, and local governments. He was, in effect, a " little king." The " frames of government " (constitutions) that William Penn drew up for Pennsylvania were, for that day and age, exceedingly democratic.

(3) *The charter colonies* were Rhode Island and Connecticut. A real charter existed between each of these colonies and the King. They were written documents outlining certain rights of self-government which could be withdrawn by the King if he chose to do so. The governor was elected annually by the freemen of the colony, and although the King's approval was required, it was seldom asked. The council and assembly were also elected annually, and the governor had no veto over the assembly's acts.

The Connecticut and Rhode Island charters were so liberal that after independence the charters continued to serve as State constitutions until 1818 and 1842 respectively.

The Colonies and England. The colonists were British subjects and they owed allegiance to the Crown. In the minds of the King and his ministers, the colonies existed as handmaidens to serve the mother country. They were regarded as sources of raw materials and as markets for finished products. They were far-off territories to be held and ruled for the benefit of England.

In theory, the colonies were controlled in all important matters from London. But London was 3000 miles away. It took almost two months to sail from England to North America. So, in practice, the colonists became quite used to doing pretty much as they pleased. They made their own laws, and the few regulations imposed by Parliament, having to do mainly with trade, were generally ignored.

But, in the early 1760's, matters changed. When George III ascended the throne in 1760 Britain began to deal more firmly with her North American dependencies. The King's ministers felt that the time had come to enforce and expand the restrictive trading acts; and they felt, too, that the colonists should be required to pay a larger share for the support of British troops stationed in America.

The colonists took strong exception to these moves. They could see no need for the troops — the power of the French had been broken in the French and Indian War (1756–1763). They objected to taxes they had no part in levying — it was " taxation without representation." They recog-

Metropolitan Museum of Art

BENJAMIN FRANKLIN

Franklin was a widely respected political philosopher, although he is probably better known for his scientific experiments and advice on the handling of money. To him goes the credit for the Albany Plan of Union, a forerunner of our Constitution.

nized the sovereignty of the King, but they flatly refused to recognize any right of Parliament to control colonial affairs. In short, the colonists maintained that they possessed the same rights as Englishmen at home and that they had the right to manage their own local affairs as they saw fit.

The King's ministers were poorly informed and stubborn. They pushed ahead with their plans despite the resentment their policies stirred in America. Within a very few years, the colonists found themselves faced with a fateful choice — to submit to England or revolt against her.

The Colonies Unite. Long before the 1770's, attempts had been made to bring the colonies together for collective action.

Early Attempts. In 1643 the Massachusetts Bay, Plymouth, Connecticut, and New Haven settlements had joined in the New England Confederation — a " league of friendship " for defense against Indian attacks. But as the Indian danger passed and frictions developed, the Confederation soon lost importance and finally died in 1684.

William Penn proposed an elaborate plan for colonial co-operation, especially in trade and criminal matters, in 1696, but nothing came of it.

The Albany Plan, 1754. In 1754 the Lords of Trade called a conference of seven of the northern colonies at Albany to consider the problems of colonial trade and the threat of French and Indian attacks. Here Benjamin Franklin proposed what came to be known as his Albany Plan of Union.

Franklin would have created an annual congress (conference) consisting of one delegate from each of the thirteen colonies. This body was to have power to raise military and naval forces, to make war and peace with the Indians, to regulate trade with the tribes, and to collect customs and levy taxes.

Franklin's plan was ahead of its time, but it was to be remembered later when independence came. Although it was adopted by the Albany meeting, it was rejected by each of the colonies as a *surrender of too much* local power. And, at the same time, it was opposed in London as a *grant of too much* power to the colonies.

The Stamp Act Congress, 1765. As we know, the harsh tax and trade policies of the 1760's fanned colonial resentment. A series of new laws had been passed by Parliament including the Stamp Act of 1765. This law required a stamp tax to be paid on all legal documents and agreements, and on newspapers circulating in America.

Immediately, a Stamp Act Congress met in New York. Delegates from nine of the colonies drafted a Declaration of Rights and Grievances protesting the Stamp Tax and other stern policies of the King's ministers. This was the first time that a large number of the colonies had co-operated against England and it warned of more drastic things to come.

Parliament repealed the Stamp Tax, but events were moving rapidly toward the final break. Resentment and anger were expressed in wholesale evasion of the laws; mob violence took place at the ports; English goods were boycotted; and such outbreaks as the Boston Tea Party of 1773 occurred.

Independence

The First Continental Congress, 1774. In the spring of 1774 Parliament passed yet another set of laws, this time intended to punish the colonists for the disturbances in Boston and elsewhere. The " Intolerable Acts," as the new laws were called in America, prompted the Massachusetts and Virginia assemblies to call a general meeting of the colonies.

Fifty-six delegates, from every colony except Georgia, assembled in Philadelphia on September 5, 1774. Many of the leaders of the day were there men like Patrick Henry, Samuel Adams, and George Washington. For nearly two months the members of this First Continental Congress debated the strained and critical situation with England.

A Declaration of Rights protesting the British attitude was drafted and sent to George III. The delegates also urged each of the colonies to refuse to trade with Great Britain. They called for the creation of local committees to enforce the boycott and take stern action against anyone who bought, sold, or consumed English goods. Later, the assemblies in each of the colonies, including the one in Georgia, approved the actions of the Congress.

Before they adjourned on October 26, the delegates called for a second Congress the following May.

Events moved rapidly. The British did nothing to satisfy the colonists. Instead, they applied even stricter measures. Then it happened. Open and armed conflict came a little over two weeks before the Second Continental Congress assembled. The battles of Concord and Lexington were fought, the " shot heard round the world " was fired, on April 19, 1775.

The Second Continental Congress, 1775. All thirteen colonies sent delegates to the Second Continental Congress which convened at Philadelphia on May 10, 1775. Most of those who had attended the earlier meeting were again present in Independence Hall. Especially notable among the new members were Benjamin Franklin and John Hancock.

Hancock was chosen president of the Congress and almost immediately a " continental army " was organized with George Washington as its commander-in-chief. Thomas Jefferson then replaced Washington as a delegate from Virginia.

This Second Continental Congress became the first government of the United States. Although it had no constitutional basis, it served as our first National Government for six years, that is, until the Articles of Confederation went into effect in March, 1781.

The Declaration of Independence, 1776. On June 7, 1776, Richard Henry Lee of Virginia proposed to the Congress:

Resolved, That these United Colonies are, and of right ought to be, free and independent States, that they are absolved from all allegiance to the British Crown, and that all political connection between them and the State of Great Britain is, and ought to be, totally dissolved.

A committee of five of the ablest men in the Congress — Benjamin Franklin, John Adams, Roger Sherman, Robert Livingston, and Thomas Jefferson — was appointed to draft a

statement to proclaim independence. Their momentous product, the Declaration of Independence,[2] was almost wholly the work of the young and brilliant Jefferson.

On July 2 the final break came. By unanimous vote the delegates adopted Lee's resolution. Two days later, on the 4th of July, the Declaration itself was adopted and announced to the world.

What the Declaration Says. Most of the great document deals with the grievances the colonists felt toward England and the King. Its real heart, the lines which have made it our most precious charter, are found in the second paragraph:

We hold these truths to be self-evident: that all men are created equal; that they are endowed by their Creator with certain unalienable Rights; that among these are Life, Liberty, and the pursuit of Happiness. That to secure these rights, Governments are instituted among Men, deriving their just powers from the consent of the governed; That whenever any Form of Government becomes destructive of these ends it is the Right of the People to alter or abolish it, and to institute a new Government, laying its foundation on such principles and organizing its powers in such form, as to them shall seem most likely to effect their Safety and Happiness.

With these brave words the United States of America was born. The thirteen former colonies were now free and independent States. The

---

[2] The text of the Declaration appears on pages 722–24.

COMPOSING THE DECLARATION

Thomas Jefferson, standing with pen in hand, was chairman of the committee appointed by Congress to draft the Declaration. Jefferson has just handed the written sheets to Benjamin Franklin, who is reading them to John Adams.

fifty-six men who gave birth to the new nation sealed the Declaration of Independence with this final sentence:

And for the support of this Declaration, with a firm reliance in the Protection of a divine Providence, we mutually pledge to each other our Lives, our Fortunes, and our sacred Honor.

Jefferson wrote his wife:

It is a heavenly comfort to see that these principles of liberty are so strongly felt. I pray God they may be eternal.

The First State Governments

In January, 1776, New Hampshire adopted a constitution to replace royal control. Two months later South Carolina did the same. Then, on May 10, 1776, the Congress urged that each of the States adopt " such governments as shall, in the opinion of the representatives of the people, best conduce to the happiness and safety of their constituents."

Most of the States adopted written constitutions in 1776 and 1777. With minor changes, Connecticut and Rhode Island transformed their charters into State constitutions. Assemblies or conventions were commonly used to draft and approve the new documents. Massachusetts completed the list, and set a lasting precedent, when it submitted its new fundamental law to the voters for approval. This Massachusetts Constitution of 1780 is still in force, the oldest of our present State constitutions.

Nature of the New State Constitutions. These new documents differed widely in detail. But they had many important features in common — and in a few years they were to have a marked effect on the drafting of the Constitution of the United States. Four of these important features should be noted:

(1) *Popular Sovereignty.* The

COLONIAL VOTING

In the colonies the right to vote was held by less than ten per cent of the whole population. Votes could be cast only by those adult males who owned a specified amount of property or paid a certain tax.

Courtesy National Life Insurance Company, Montpelier, Vt.

Unit I. DEVELOPMENT OF GOVERNMENT

people were recognized as the sole source of governmental authority — all power held by government could come from one, and *only* one, fountain: the people themselves.

(2) *Limited Government.* Government could exercise *only* those powers granted to it by the people. Because of the oppression of colonial days, these new constitutions granted powers very sparingly.

(3) *Civil Liberties.* Seven of the new documents began with bills of rights containing the " unalienable rights " of the people. In every State it was made clear that the sovereign people had rights that government must at all times respect.

(4) *Separation of Powers, Checks and Balances.* The powers that were given to the new State governments were purposely divided among three distinct branches — the executive, the legislative, and the judicial. Each branch was given powers to " check " the others.

These first State constitutions were very short compared to those of today. The memory of royal governors was fresh and the new State governors were given strictly limited powers. Most of the authority was vested in the legislatures. The right to vote was severely limited to adult males who met property ownership and other rigid suffrage qualifications.

The Confederation and the Critical Period

Our First National Constitution. The First and Second Continental Congresses rested on no legal base. They were called in haste to meet an emergency and they were intended to be temporary. Something more regular and permanent was needed.

When Richard Henry Lee introduced his resolution which led to the Declaration of Independence, he also called for " a plan of confederation." Off and on for seventeen months the Congress debated and considered a scheme to unite the States. Then, on November 15, 1777, the Articles of Confederation were approved.

But the Articles did not go into effect immediately — indeed, not until 1781. All thirteen States had to approve them first and, although eleven

States ratified in 1778 and Delaware agreed in 1779, Maryland did not go along until March 1, 1781.

The Articles established " a firm league of friendship " among the States. Each State retained " its sovereignty, freedom, and independence, and every Power, Jurisdiction, and Right . . . not . . . expressly delegated to the United States, in Congress assembled." The States came together " for their common defense, the security of their Liberties, and their mutual and general welfare."

The government established by the Articles was exceedingly simple. A Congress, composed of delegates appointed annually by the States in whatever manner their legislatures might direct, was the single organ created.

Each State had one vote in the Congress, regardless of its population or wealth. There was no executive and no judicial branch. These functions were handled by committees of the Congress, and civil officers (postmasters, for example) were appointed by Congress.

The powers of Congress appear, at first glance, to have been considerable. Its more important powers included those to make war and peace, send and receive ambassadors, enter into treaties, borrow money, raise and equip a navy, maintain an army by requesting troops from the States, request funds from the States to meet the costs of government, regulate Indian affairs, fix standards of weights and measures, and establish post offices. But all was not as at first appears.

Fatal weaknesses soon crippled the new government and showed it to be inadequate for the pressing needs of the times.

The new National Government had no power to tax. It could raise needed funds in only two ways: by borrowing and by requesting money from the States. Heavy borrowing had been necessary to finance the Revolution, so this source was at best none too good. And throughout the period of the Articles not one of the States met its financial obligations to the central government.

The lack of a power to tax was bad enough, but, beyond that, the Congress had no power to regulate trade between the States. It could not even

levy export or import duties. The results, as we shall see, were chaotic.

And, still worse, the Congress had no power to force either the States or the people to obey the Articles or its own laws. All that the Congress could do was to *advise* and *request* the States to do this or that. In effect, all it could do was say " please " and wait with hat in hand — often in vain.

Finally, most of the important powers that Congress did have could be exercised only with the consent of delegates from *nine* of the thirteen States, and no changes could be made in the Articles unless *all* of the States agreed.[3]

The Critical Period, 1781–1787. On October 10, 1781, a British band played the old air, " The World Turned Upside Down " as Lord Cornwallis surrendered his army to General Washington. Victory had come to the United States and it was confirmed by the Treaty of Paris in 1783.

The coming of peace brought the political, social, and economic difficulties of the new nation into sharp focus. With a central government powerless to act, the States bickered among themselves and became increasingly jealous of one another. They levied tariffs on one another's goods

---

[3] To get all thirteen jealous and increasingly unfriendly States to agree on anything seemed hopeless. In 1785 Congress made a final attempt to solve its financial problems by proposing an amendment to the Articles to provide for import duties. But New York was reaping a handsome return from its own tax on imports and so refused to approve the proposal, and the measure died.

Unit I. Development of Government

and even banned some trade. They negotiated directly with foreign governments, even though this was forbidden in the Articles. They often refused to obey laws and treaties made by the Congress, and most even raised armies and navies of their own. They stamped their names on paper and called it money. Prices soared skyhigh. Debts, public and private, went unpaid. And the States refused to support the central government, financially and in almost every other way.

George Washington was moved to complain:

We are one nation today and thirteen tomorrow. Who will treat with us on such terms?

And James Madison wrote this of the situation:

New Jersey, placed between Philadelphia and New York, was likened to a cask tapped at both ends; North Carolina, between Virginia and South Carolina, to a patient bleeding at both arms.

John Fiske thus described existing commercial conditions:

The city of New York with a population of 30,000 souls had long been supplied with firewood from Connecticut, and with butter and cheese, chickens and garden vegetables from the thrifty farms of New Jersey. This trade, it was observed, carried thousands of dollars out of the city and into the pockets of the detested Yankees and despised Jerseymen. " It was ruinous to domestic industry," said the men of New York. " It must be stopped by . . . a navigation act and a protective tariff." Acts were accordingly passed, obliging every Yankee sloop which came down through Hell Gate and every

Courtesy of the Bowdoin College Museum of Fine Arts

JAMES MADISON

One of the younger Founders, Madison has been called the " Father of the Constitution." Besides taking a leading part in the framing of the Constitution, he kept careful and exhaustive notes on the work of the Constitutional Convention.

Jersey market boat which was rowed across from Paulus Hook to Cortlandt Street to pay entrance fees and obtain clearances at the custom house, just as was done by ships from London and Hamburg; and not a cart-load of Connecticut firewood could be delivered at the back door of a country house in Beekman Street until it should have paid a heavy duty. Great and just was the wrath of the farmers and lumbermen. The New Jersey legislature made up its mind to retaliate. The city of New York had lately bought a small patch of ground on Sandy Hook, and had built a lighthouse there. This lighthouse was the one weak spot in the heel of Achilles where a hostile arrow could strike, and New Jersey gave vent to her indignation by laying a tax of $1800 a year on it. Connecticut was equally prompt. At a great meeting of business men, held at New London, it was unanimously agreed to suspend all commercial intercourse with New York. Every merchant signed an agreement, under a penalty of $250 for the first offence, not to send any goods whatever into the hated State for twelve months.[4]

Such distressing conditions as these led the more conservative groups, including the merchant and creditor classes, to yearn for a stronger central government better able to cope with the situation.

The Conventions at Mount Vernon and Annapolis. Maryland and Virginia, in an attempt to settle disputes over the navigation of the Potomac River and Chesapeake Bay, held a meeting at Alexandria in 1785. At Washington's invitation the meeting was moved to Mount Vernon. This meeting proved to be such a success that on January 21, 1786, the Virginia Assembly called for a " joint meeting of . . . the States to recommend a federal plan for regulating commerce."

When this meeting convened at Annapolis in September, 1786, only five States were represented — Virginia, New York, New Jersey, Pennsylvania, and Delaware. Discouraged, but not completely, the Annapolis Convention proposed another meeting of the States

at Philadelphia on the second Monday in May next . . . to devise such further provisions as shall appear to them necessary to render the constitution of the Federal Government adequate to the exigencies of the Union . . .

By February of 1787 seven of the States had named delegates to the Philadelphia meeting. And on the 17th, Congress, which had been hesitating, also called upon the States to send delegates to Philadelphia

for the sole and express purpose of revising the Articles of Confederation and reporting to Congress and the several legislatures such alterations and provisions therein as shall when agreed to in Congress and confirmed by the States render the [Articles] adequate to the exigencies of Government and the preservation of the Union.

The Constitutional Convention

The Philadelphia Convention began its work on Friday, May 25.[5] In all, twelve States participated — Rhode Island not attending.[6]

The Founding Fathers. Seventy-four men were chosen as delegates by the various legislatures, but only fifty-

[4] *The Critical Period of American History*, p. 146.

[5] Not enough States were represented on the original date, Monday, May 14. Those delegates who were present met and adjourned each day until the 25th when a majority of the States were on hand. The Convention met in Independence Hall.

[6] The Rhode Island legislature was controlled by the so-called " soft-money " group — mainly debtors and farmers who benefited by inflation and were thus against the creation of a stronger central government. Their opponents in Rhode Island did send a letter of encouragement to Philadelphia, however.

New Hampshire had similar difficulties but her delegation finally reached Philadelphia in late July.

44

five made the journey to Philadelphia. The average daily attendance ran about thirty.

Never before or since has so remarkable a group of men met under one roof. From Virginia came George Washington, Edmund Randolph, and James Madison; Pennsylvania sent Benjamin Franklin, Gouverneur Morris, and James Wilson. Alexander Hamilton was there from New York, William Livingston and William Paterson from New Jersey, Elbridge Gerry and Rufus King from Massachusetts, Luther Martin from Maryland, Oliver Ellsworth and Roger Sherman from Connecticut, John Dickinson from Delaware, and John Rutledge and the two Pinckneys from South Carolina.

These were men of wide knowledge and public experience, men of wealth and prestige. Many of them had served in the Revolution, in the Continental and Confederate Congresses, and in their own State governments. Eight had signed the Declaration of Independence. Two were to become President of the United States; one became Vice-President. Eighteen were later Senators and eight became Representatives.[7]

Is it any wonder that the product

_____

[7] Some prominent men were notable by their absence. Patrick Henry " smelt a rat " and refused to attend. Samuel Adams and John Hancock also refused to serve. Thomas Jefferson was in France on a diplomatic mission. Thomas Paine was in France, too. John Adams was our minister to England. Richard Henry Lee and John Marshall weren't there, either.

of such a gathering was described by the English statesman Gladstone nearly a century later as " the most wonderful work ever struck off at a given time by the brain and purpose of man "?

Here is a remarkable thing — the average age of the delegates was only forty-two and half of them were in their thirties! The real leaders were all in that age bracket — Madison was thirty-six, Morris thirty-five, Randolph thirty-four, and Hamilton thirty-two. Benjamin Franklin, at eighty-one, the oldest member, was ill and unable to attend many of the sessions. Washington at fifty-five was one of the older active members.

The Convention organized itself on the 25th and George Washington was unanimously chosen president. It was decided that each State should have one vote in the sessions and all of the delegates pledged themselves to the strictest secrecy. The Convention naturally attracted a great deal of public attention, and the members were anxious to protect themselves as much as possible against outside pressures.

The Great Agreement. Almost at once a momentous decision was made. The Founding Fathers agreed that they were meeting in Independence Hall to create a *national* government.

Resolved, . . . that a national government ought to be established consisting of a Supreme Legislative, Judiciary, and Executive.

These men had been appointed to " recommend revisions " in the Articles. But, with this decision, they set about writing a whole new Constitution.

This meant the creation of a vastly expanded government with extensive new powers — a government with powers supreme over the States and able to reach the people directly.

The debates were often bitter and at times the Convention even seemed to be on the verge of collapse. Once this decision was made, however, the determination of the majority never wavered.

The Virginia Plan. On May 29, Edmund Randolph introduced the so-called " Virginia Plan," largely drafted by Madison. It proposed a Congress of two houses (bicameral) with power to legislate on all national matters and to compel obedience by the States. Representation in each house was to be based on population, thus giving the larger States control of both branches of the legislature. Further, since the President, judges, and other officers were to be appointed by Congress, the whole administration would be controlled by the larger States.

The Virginia Plan, sometimes called the " Large State Plan " or " Randolph Plan," served as model. But some of its features, especially the matter of representation, were stoutly opposed by delegates from the smaller States.

The New Jersey Plan. On June 15, William Paterson introduced the so-called " New Jersey Plan," or as it is also known, the " Small State Plan " or " Paterson Plan." It would

have provided some increase in the powers of the central government; but it was more a piecemeal revision of the Articles than a new constitution.

The major point of difference between the Virginia and the New Jersey Plans had to do with representation in Congress. The smaller States wanted a one-house (unicameral) Congress in which all States would be equally represented.

For weeks the debate on this point raged. The result was a compromise — one of the Great Compromises of the Convention.

The Great Compromises. Many of the Constitution's provisions we take for granted today were the result of compromises reached only after long and intense discussion — provisions like those relating to the structure of Congress, an independent court system, the President's term, and the commerce power. The main compromises were as follows:

The Connecticut Compromise. The dispute over representation in Congress was finally settled by a compromise first suggested by Roger Sherman of Connecticut. It was agreed that Congress should consist of two houses, a Senate and House of Representatives. In the smaller Senate the States were to be equally represented, thus satisfying the small States. In the House, representation would be in accord with population; thus satisfying the large States.

The Three-Fifths Compromise. When it was agreed that the lower house should be based on population, another conflict arose. Should the southern States be permitted to count their slaves in figuring population? The argument was fierce. But, finally, the delegates agreed that all " free persons " would be counted and so would " three-fifths of all other persons." Of course, this strange compromise disappeared from the Constitution at the end of the War Between the States.

The Commerce and Slave Trade Compromise. Much of the agitation that led to the calling of the Constitutional Convention came from those who were most interested in a stricter and more regularized control of commerce. But if the new National Government controlled commerce, the Southerners were afraid that Northerners might shut off the profitable cotton trade with England and force Southern products to the less profitable markets of the North.

So another compromise was made. Congress was given the power to regulate interstate and foreign commerce and trade with the Indians. But, to satisfy the South, it was forbidden to tax exports, favor one port over another, or to interfere with the slave trade, except by a small head tax, until at least 1808.

Other Compromises. These were the major compromises. But there were many others. Some delegates preferred a long and some a very short term for the President. Many felt that the President should be chosen by Congress while others wanted direct popular election. The matter of voting qualifications was left to each State because the delegates could not agree.

And so it went. In many ways, and perhaps very important to its great and lasting strength, the Constitution is a " bundle of compromises."

In addition to the many compromises, much that went into the Constitution came directly — sometimes word-for-word — from the Articles of Confederation and from the various State constitutions.

The Convention Completes Its Work. The delegates worked on through the hot summer months. By the end of July a series of resolutions was tailored into an organized text and the next several weeks were spent in analyzing and perfecting this remarkable document.

BUILDING BLOCKS

The Constitution was the end result of much experience in the ways of sound government.

1789 CONSTITUTION

ARTICLES OF CONFEDERATION 1781

DECLARATION OF INDEPENDENCE 1776

SECOND CONTINENTAL CONGRESS 1775

FIRST CONTINENTAL CONGRESS 1774

On September 8, a Committee on Style was named to " revise the style and arrange the articles which had been agreed to by the house." This group, headed by Gouverneur Morris, put the Constitution in its final clear, concise form.

Then, at long last, on September 17, 1787, thirty-nine men signed the finished product.[8]

Probably none of the Framers was *completely* satisfied with what had been done. Wise old Ben Franklin spoke for most of them when he said:

I agree to this Constitution, with all its faults, if they are such; . . . I doubt whether any other Convention we can obtain may be able to make a better Constitution. For when you assemble a number of men to have the advantage of their joint wisdom, you inevitably assemble with those men all their prejudices, their passions, their errors of opinion, their local interests, and their selfish views. From such an assembly can a perfect production be expected? It therefore astonishes me, Sir, to find this system approaching so near to perfection as it does; and I think it will astonish our enemies . . .

While the Constitution was being signed, Madison tells us:

Doct[r] Franklin looking towards the Presidents Chair, at the back of which a rising sun happened to be painted, ob-

---

[8] Forty-two men were present. Edmund Randolph, who had introduced the Virginia Plan, refused to sign. But he later supported ratification in Virginia and served as Attorney-General and Secretary of State under Washington. Elbridge Gerry of Massachusetts, later Vice-President under Madison, and George Mason of Virginia also refused to sign.

served to a few members near him, that Painters had found it difficult to distinguish in their art a rising from a setting sun. I have, said he, often and often in the course of the Session . . . looked at that behind the President without being able to tell whether it was rising or setting: But now at length I have the happiness to know that it is a rising and not a setting sun.

Ratification. The new Constitution was intended to replace the Articles of Confederation. The Articles provided that changes could be made *only* with the approval of *all* of the States. But the Founding Fathers had seen how crippling this requirement had been. So the new Constitution provided (Article VII) that the ratifications " of nine States shall be sufficient for the establishment of this Constitution between the States so ratifying the same."

The Confederate Congress agreed to this irregular procedure when it sent the new document on to the States on September 28, 1787.

Two factions sprung up in most of the States: The *Federalists* who favored the new Constitution and the *Anti-Federalists* who opposed it. It was out of these two factions that the first political parties in the United States developed.

Objections Raised. Many of the Anti-Federalists, including men like Patrick Henry, Richard Henry Lee, and John Hancock, thought it too undemocratic. Henry said: " I look on that paper as the most fatal plan that could possibly be conceived to enslave a free people."

Unit I. DEVELOPMENT OF GOVERNMENT

DEFECTS IN THE ARTICLES	CORRECTED BY THE CONSTITUTION
1. One vote for each State, regardless of size.	1. States represented according to population in the House of Representatives and equally in the Senate.
2. Congress had no power to lay and collect taxes or duties.	2. Congress given power to lay and collect taxes, and duties on imports.
3. Congress had no power to regulate foreign and interstate commerce.	3. Congress given power to regulate foreign and interstate commerce.
4. No executive to enforce acts of Congress.	4. A President and administration to enforce acts of Congress.
5. No national court system.	5. A national system of courts.
6. Amendment only with consent of all of the States.	6. Proposal by national convention or ⅔ of both houses of Congress and ratification by ¾ of State legislatures or conventions.
7. 9/13 majority required to pass laws.	7. Simple majority required in each house of Congress.
8. Articles only a "firm league of friendship."	8. Constitution the "supreme law of land."

Many small farmers and debtors opposed it because it prohibited the States from printing paper money. Others objected to the lack of a bill of rights listing such fundamental liberties as freedom of speech, press, and religion and trial by jury — an objection that was satisfied almost at once with the addition of the Bill of Rights in 1791.

Success! The contest was bitter in many States, but by June, 1788, the Federalists prevailed.[9] The Constitu-

tion was ratified by the several States on these dates and by these votes in their State conventions:

1. Del.	Dec.	7, 1787	30–0
2. Pa.	Dec.	12, 1787	46–23
3. N.J.	Dec.	19, 1787	38–0
4. Ga.	Jan.	2, 1788	26–0
5. Conn.	Jan.	9, 1788	128–40
6. Mass.	Feb.	6, 1788	187–168
7. Md.	Apr.	28, 1788	63–11
8. S.C.	May	23, 1788	149–73
9. N.H.	June	21, 1788	57–46
10. Va.	June	25, 1788	89–79
11. N.Y.	July	26, 1788	30–27
12. N.C.	Nov.	21, 1789	194–77
13. R.I.	May	29, 1790	34–32

[9] Special note must be made of the *Federalist Papers*, a series of eighty-five remarkable essays written by Alexander Hamilton, James Madison, and John Jay. Though written as an argument for ratification in New York and published at the rate of two or three a week, they remain one of the best commentaries ever written on the original Constitution.

The Inauguration of the New Government. On September 13, 1788, with eleven of the thirteen States "under the federal roof," the

INAUGURATION, 1789

Surrounded by admiring countrymen, George Washington takes the oath of office as our first President. Washington had traveled to New York City, the first seat of government, from Mount Vernon. Part of the journey was by horseback, part on a special barge.

old Confederate Congress paved the way for its successor. It chose New York as the temporary capital; provided for the selection of presidential electors in the States; set the first Wednesday in February as the day on which they would vote; and decided that the new government should be inaugurated on March 4.

The new Congress met on March 4, 1789, in Federal Hall on Wall Street.

But, because a quorum (enough members to conduct business) was lacking, this First Session of the First Congress did not count the electoral vote until April 6.

Then on April 30, after a memorable trip from Mount Vernon to New York, George Washington, the unanimous choice of the electors, was sworn in as the first President of the United States of America.

Unit I. DEVELOPMENT OF GOVERNMENT

WHAT THIS CHAPTER IS ABOUT

Government in the United States did not suddenly spring into being. It is the product of centuries of development.

The English, who settled the thirteen colonies, contributed much to the shaping of our governmental system: especially, the pattern of early government in America, the twin concepts of limited government and civil liberties, and the concept of representative government.

Beginning with the founding of Jamestown in Virginia, 1607, all thirteen colonies were established by 1732. Three types of colonies existed: royal, proprietary, and charter. The eight royal colonies were ruled by a royal governor under the King. The three proprietary colonies were governed under a proprietor who was in turn responsible to the King. The two charter colonies were the most nearly democratic and governed themselves much as they saw fit.

England's control over her colonies was tightened in the 1760's, and the resentment this created led to the Revolution. England looked on the colonies as hand-maidens to serve the mother country — the colonists demanded the right to manage their own affairs. The colonists did attempt to head off the break, especially in the First Continental Congress in 1774.

By the meeting of the Second Continental Congress in 1775, the Revolution had actually begun. This body functioned as our first National Government until 1781. It proclaimed the Declaration of Independence on July 4, 1776, and drew up our first national constitution, the Articles of Confederation, which went into effect in March, 1781.

The government set up under the Articles, mainly a Congress, proved too weak for the times. The chaos of the Critical Period led to the meeting of the Constitutional Convention in 1787.

From May 25 to September 17, 1787, the Founding Fathers worked to produce the Constitution. It replaced the Articles of Confederation in 1789 when George Washington was inaugurated as the first President of the United States of America.

QUESTIONS ON THE TEXT

1. What were the chief political ideas that the English colonists brought to America?

2. Name the three kinds of colonies and briefly describe each.

3. What was the English attitude toward the colonies? The colonists' attitude toward their relationship with the mother country?

4. What body became our first national government?

5. The Declaration of Independence was drafted by whom?

6. Which part of the Declaration is most important? Why?

7. Describe *briefly* the nature of the first State governments.

8. What were the Articles of Confederation? When were they framed? By whom? When ratified?

9. What were the major powers of the Congress under the Articles? What were the three major weaknesses?

10. Why is the period 1781–1787 known as the Critical Period of United States history?

11. When and where was the Constitution framed?

12. Name five of the outstanding members of the Constitutional Convention.

13. What great decision did the Founding Fathers make at the outset of the Convention?

14. What was the Virginia Plan? The New Jersey Plan?

15. List the three major compromises at the Philadelphia Convention.

16. List two of the objections raised against the new Constitution.

17. When did the new government begin functioning?

PROBLEMS FOR DISCUSSION

1. What did the individual State gain by entering the federal union? What did it lose?

2. If our thirteen States had not united, what nation would probably control northern New England today? Florida? Louisiana? Texas? California? Washington? Wisconsin? Minnesota?

3. The Constitutional Convention met in Independence Hall in Philadelphia (probably in a room directly above the one in which the Declaration of Independence had been signed eleven years before). On the first day, May 25, 1787, the delegates unanimously elected George Washington as presiding officer. Why was this particular choice so significant? What was Washington's standing with the people of the day? Could the fact that Washington had presided at the Convention have had any effect in the ratification controversy?

4. Several of the leaders of the Revolutionary period were conspicuous by their absence at the Philadelphia Convention. Thomas Jefferson was at the time on a diplomatic mission to France and John Adams was in England. Samuel Adams and John Hancock declined to serve. Patrick Henry also refused to attend saying that he " smelt a rat." Richard Henry Lee, the man who had introduced in the Continental Congress the resolution proposing a Declaration of Independence and Articles of Confederation, was not appointed in Virginia. Thomas Paine was in Paris where he shortly would take a part in the French Revolution. Why has it been said that it was perhaps a fortunate thing that some of these men (especially Patrick Henry, Samuel Adams, and Thomas Paine) were not in Philadelphia? In what way was their absence unfortunate?

THINGS YOU MIGHT DO

1. Make an outline of the Articles of Confederation and the Constitution, reprinted at pages 724–727 and 728–741.

2. Prepare brief biographical sketches of the outstanding Revolutionary leaders and framers of the Constitution.

3. Write short essays describing such things as life in the colonies, the causes of the Revolution, the major battles of the Revolutionary War, the Critical Period, and the formation of the new government under the Constitution.

4. Stage a debate on this subject: Resolved, That the colonists would have been better off had they stayed in the British Empire.

Unit I. DEVELOPMENT OF GOVERNMENT

WORDS AND PHRASES YOU SHOULD KNOW

Albany Plan of Union
Anti-Federalists
Boycott
Charter Colony
Civil Liberties
Commerce
Critical Period
Federalist Papers

Federalists
First Continental
  Congress
Founding Fathers
Great Agreement
Great Compromises
Intolerable Acts
Limited Government
New Jersey Plan

Proprietary Colony
Proprietor
Ratification
Royal Colony
Second Continental
  Congress
Stamp Act Congress
Virginia Plan

SELECT BIBLIOGRAPHY

CARR, ROBERT K., and others, *American Democracy in Theory and Practice,* Chapter 3. Rinehart, 1955.

DeVOTO, BERNARD, " The Louisiana Purchase," *Collier's,* March 21, 1953.

HANDLIN, OSCAR, " The Louisiana Purchase," *The Atlantic,* January, 1955.

LAGEMANN, JOHN K., " How Jefferson Spent the First Fourth," *Collier's,* July 4, 1953.

LEE, HENRY, " Our Lives, Our Fortunes, and Our Sacred Honor," *Collier's,* July 9, 1954.

MALONE, DUMAS, " The Men Who Signed the Declaration," *New York Times Magazine,* July 4, 1954.

" Men Who United the United States," *Life,* July 4, 1955.

MORISON, SAMUEL E., " The Battle That Set Us Free," *Saturday Evening Post,* July 7, 1956.

NICHOLSON, ARNOLD, " Ben Franklin: Wit Was His Weapon," *Saturday Evening Post,* January 21, 1956.

PADOVER, SAUL K., " The Message of Washington," *The Reporter,* February 24, 1955.

SWARTHOUT, JOHN M., and BARTLEY, ERNEST R., *Principles and Problems of American National Government,* Chapter 2. Oxford University Press, 1955.

TUNLEY, ROUL, " Street of Freedom, Philadelphia," *American Magazine,* April, 1955.

VAN DOREN, CARL, *The Great Rehearsal.* Viking, 1948.

" George Washington: A Man to Remember," *Time,* July 6, 1953, also, *Reader's Digest,* July, 1956.

> The Constitution, in all its provisions, looks to an indestructible Union, composed of indestructible States.
>
> — *Chief Justice Salmon P. Chase*, in *Texas* v. *White*, 1868

★

Chapter 4

OUR FEDERAL SYSTEM OF GOVERNMENT

The Fundamental Bases of American Government. Government in the United States is firmly based on two essential propositions: the twin doctrines of popular sovereignty and limited government.

Popular Sovereignty. All political power in the United States belongs to the people. The people are sovereign and *from them* must flow any and all powers of government. Here the people rule. Government is conducted only with the consent of the governed. Note, then, the tremendously important meaning of these words from the Preamble to the Constitution:

We, the people of the United States, . . . do ordain and establish this Constitution for the United States of America.

Limited Government. While *all* governmental power must flow from the people, government may exercise *only* those powers that the people have seen fit to vest in government. The National Government may exercise only those powers granted to it by the people through the National Constitu-tion, and the States may exercise only those powers the people have given them through the National and their own State constitutions.

As we shall see, there are many areas in which the people have not authorized government to act. And there are many others in which government is severely restricted.

In describing the limited character of governmental power under the Constitution, George Washington wrote to his friend Lafayette in 1788 that it is " provided with more checks and barriers against the introduction of tyranny . . . than any government hitherto instituted among mortals hath possessed."

The United States Has a Federal Government. The Constitutional Convention of 1787 was faced with many difficult and perplexing problems. One of the thorniest of these was this — How were they to provide for a new national government of real authority and, at the same time, preserve the already existing States?

" The powers not delegated to the United States by the Constitution, nor prohibited by it to the States, are reserved to the States respectively, or to the people " — Amendment 10

POWERS OF GOVERNMENT

FEDERAL [1] . .
- Expressed [2] — (Article I, Section 8, Clauses 1–17; Amendment 16)
- Implied [3] — (Article I, Section 8, Clause 18)
- Denied — (Article I, Section 9; Amendments 1–11; 13)

CONCURRENT [4] (Examples: taxation, eminent domain)

STATE . . .
- Reserved [5] — (Amendment 10) — Example: police powers — Health, Morals, Safety, Welfare
- Denied — (Article I, Section 10; Amendments 13–15, 17, 19)

[1] The terms " national " and " delegated " mean the same as " federal " in this connection.

[2] The term " enumerated " (numbered) means the same as " expressed " in this connection.

[3] The term " resultant power " is used when a power is not clearly implied from any one " expressed power " but results from several expressed powers. The term " inherent in sovereignty " is sometimes used for powers neither clearly expressed nor clearly implied but necessarily belonging to a sovereign state. Recognizing new sovereign states and deporting aliens are examples of powers inherent in sovereignty.

[4] The term " concurrent power " means one which may be exercised by either the Federal Government or the State Government or both.

[5] The term " residual " is often used in the sense of " reserved."

Few if any of the Founding Fathers favored a strong centralized (unitary) government in the British pattern. They knew how stoutly the people had fought for their rights of local self-government. And they knew how much the people would distrust a strongly centralized national government.

Somehow they had to create a national government adequate for the needs of the country and at the same time preserve local self-government in the States.

The solution they hit upon was a *federal* system, something new in state-making, a type of government never before tried.

The Advantages of Federalism. Our federal system provides all of the advantages of local self-government for the States and, as well, the great strength which results from union. While this system of state-making is the most complicated of all methods, it is at the same time the most stable.

Local needs vary and the federal system gives consideration to the wishes of the people in the various States. The people are able to protect their liberties through representation in Congress. In such matters as

Chapter 4. OUR FEDERAL SYSTEM OF GOVERNMENT   **55**

religion, education, and voting — subjects which produce determined sentiments — the States can adapt their own laws to their own particular conditions.

Texas can tax church property or not as it thinks best; South Carolina can provide free textbooks if it wishes to do so; New York can have an educational test to bar illiterates from voting. If the peace of Texas should be disturbed by Mexican invaders, Texas knows she can count on the help of the remaining forty-seven States in her defense. If yellow fever in Cuba should threaten the Southern States, the efforts of the entire nation would be exerted to prevent it.

Division of Powers between the Nation and the States

The Constitution outlines the basic scheme of the American federal system. It provides for a *division of powers* on a territorial basis; that is, governmental powers in the United States are divided between the National Government on the one hand and the States on the other. This division of powers is most clearly stated in the 10th Amendment:

The powers not delegated to the United States by this Constitution, nor prohibited by it to the States, are reserved to the States respectively, or to the people.

The National Government Is a Government of Delegated Powers. The National Government possesses only those powers *expressly delegated* (granted) to it in the Constitution and those which may be reasonably *implied* from the *expressed powers*.[1]

The *expressed powers,* those that are stated in so many words in the Constitution, include, among others, the powers to —

Declare war and make peace
Maintain armed forces
Make treaties and conduct foreign relations
Regulate foreign and interstate commerce
Lay and collect taxes
Establish post offices and post roads
Issue coins and paper money
Borrow money
Grant patents and copyrights
Establish a federal court system
Regulate bankruptcy and naturalization
Do anything " necessary and proper for carrying into execution the foregoing powers "

The *implied powers* are those that can be reasonably " implied " from the " Necessary and Proper Clause." [2]

---

[1] Most of the expressed powers are found in Article I, Section 8.

[2] " Congress shall have power . . . to make all laws which shall be necessary and proper for carrying into execution the foregoing powers, and all other powers vested by this Constitution in the government of the United States, or in any department or officer thereof." Article I, Section 8, Clause 18. This clause is also known as the " Elastic Clause "; through congressional and court interpretation the words " necessary and proper " have come to mean " convenient and appropriate." See pages 106–110.

For example, the regulation of labor-management relations, the building of power dams, river and harbor improvements, flood control, punishment as a federal crime the transporting of stolen goods across a State line — these and many other powers are exercised by the National Government because they may be *reasonably implied* from the *expressed* power to regulate foreign and interstate commerce.

Powers Denied to the National Government. While the Constitution delegates certain powers to the National Government, it also denies it certain powers.[3] For example, the Constitution forbids it the power to levy export duties, to restrict freedom of religion, and to grant titles of nobility.

Some powers are also denied the National Government simply because the Constitution is silent as to them. Thus the National Government has no power over public education or marriage and divorce.

The States Are Governments of Reserved Powers. The Constitution *reserves* (leaves) to the States those powers which are not granted to the National Government and at the same time not denied to the States.[4] Thus the State of Alabama, or any other State, may require police consent for the holding of religious services in the streets. She could forbid

persons under twenty-one to marry or to vote; could prohibit the carrying, or even owning, of firearms; and could charter and control corporations. She may also establish public school systems and units of local government and legislate concerning marriage and divorce.

Alabama can do all these things and more because there is nothing in the Constitution of the United States which prohibits her from doing so. The National Government cannot do these things because, as we have seen, it has not been delegated the power to

CO-OPERATION

The States and the National Government co-operate in a wide variety of undertakings. A notable example is the national system of interstate and defense highways. Ninety per cent of the construction cost will be borne by the National Government, but the States will be responsible for maintenance of the system.

Caterpillar Tractor Co.

---

[3] Most of these are found in Article I, Section 9, and Amendments 1–8.

[4] Most of the powers denied to the States are found in Article I, Section 10. One must always remember that a State's *own* constitution may further restrict the powers of the State government.

do so. Thus the power to do these things is *reserved* to the States.

Powers Denied to the States. The Constitution also forbids the States to do several things. For example, no State may enter into any treaty, alliance, or confederation, nor may it coin money, make any law impairing the obligation of contracts, grant titles of nobility, or deprive any person of life, liberty, or property without due process of law.

Exclusive and Concurrent Powers. Some of the powers delegated to the National Government are denied to the States by the Constitution. For example, the power to coin money is expressly granted to the National Government and denied to the States. Thus, the power to coin money is an *exclusive power* of the National Government, as are the powers to make treaties, raise armed forces, etc.

But some of the delegated powers are not denied to the States.[5] While

---

[5] The Supreme Court has held that those delegated powers which are of such a character that the exercise of them by the States would be, under any circumstances, inconsistent with the general theory of a *National* Government, may be exercised only by the United States.

Those delegated powers not of this character may be exercised by the States until the United States sees fit to exercise them. To illustrate, the Constitution delegates to Congress the power to enact bankruptcy laws. From 1878 to 1898 Congress did not desire a national bankruptcy law. All States enacted them. When a new national bankruptcy act was passed in 1898 any details of State laws inconsistent therewith became void. Therefore, while the States have a certain amount of power, the National Government is supreme in the field of concurrent powers.

the National Government may lay and collect taxes, so may the States. Hence, the power to tax is a *concurrent power* (that is, a power held by both the National and State Governments).

The Supreme Law of the Land. The division of powers between the National and State governments is, as we have just seen, a rather complicated arrangement. It produces what has been called a " dual system of government.'' In other words, there are two governments operating over exactly the same people and the same area at one and the same time.

In such a situation there are bound to be conflicts. There are bound to be times when national law and State law conflict. Because of this, the Framers wrote into the Constitution, in Article VI, a provision declaring the supremacy of national law:

This Constitution and the laws of the United States which shall be made in pursuance thereof, and all treaties made or which shall be made under the authority of the United States, shall be the supreme law of the land. . . .

This section, then, makes the Constitution and acts and treaties of the United States the highest forms of law. The Constitution stands at the top; immediately under it are the acts and treaties of the United States.

California, or any other State, could not prohibit Chinese born in the United States from voting at regular elections, as this would violate the 15th Amendment to the United States Constitution. Nor could California hold regular elections for Congressmen in June because an act of Congress prescribes the month of November. Or, if the United States should make a treaty with China agreeing to guarantee to all Chinese citizens living in the United States the same privileges as our own citizens, California could not place a higher license fee upon laundries run by alien Chinese than that upon similar laundries run by Americans.

By the same token, local laws, such as city charters and city and county ordinances, must square with the supreme law of the land. For example, city ordinances which forbid the use of public halls to particular groups simply because local officials disapprove of them, are unconstitutional. They conflict with the 14th Amendment's guarantee of liberty.

The Supreme Court as " Referee " in the Federal System. The final authority in cases of conflict between State and national law is the United States Supreme Court. Thus when the State of Oregon passed a law requiring all children of school age to attend *public* schools, the Supreme Court knocked it down as unconstitutional. The Court held that the State law violated the 14th Amendment's guarantee of liberty by denying parents the right to send their children to church-supported (parochial) schools if they chose to do so.

The decisions of the Supreme Court are binding on private persons, on States (and their local governments), and even on the Congress and President if they do something contrary to the Constitution.

Judicial Review. The power of the courts to determine the constitutionality of acts of Congress or of State legislatures and the actions of the executive agencies of National or State Governments is known as the power of *judicial review.* Every court in the land has this power, but the highest court, the United States Supreme Court, has the final word.

This power of judicial review is not granted to the courts by the Constitution in so many words. Rather, it was first announced by the Supreme Court in the case of *Marbury* v. *Madison* (1803).

Late the night of March 3, 1801, President John Adams had signed commissions of office appointing several new federal judges. (Because this was done so late at night, these men are known to history as the " midnight justices.")

On the next day Thomas Jefferson was inaugurated President and he immediately ordered his new Secretary of State, James Madison, not to deliver the commissions. One of the appointees, William Marbury, then applied to the Supreme Court for a *writ of mandamus* (a court order) to force Madison to make delivery. Marbury based his request on a provision in the Judiciary Act of 1789 which empowered the court to issue writs in such cases.

But, in a unanimous decision written by Chief Justice John Marshall, the high court refused his request. It refused because it held that section of the Judiciary Act empowering the Court to issue the writ to be unconstituitional. It was unconstitutional, said the Court, because Congress had no power under the Constitution to make such a law.

Thus, for the first time, the Supreme Court declared an act of the Congress to be in violation of the Constitution and, hence, unenforceable. Since 1803, it has held some eighty congressional statutes, in part or whole, invalid. The first State law to be held unconstitutional was one from Georgia in 1810. Since then it has invalidated parts or all of more than 500 State laws.

Obligations of the National Government to the States

The Constitution imposes several obligations on the National Government for the benefit of the States. Most of them are to be found in Article IV.

The Guarantee of a Republican Form of Government. The National Government is required to " guarantee to every State in this Union a republican form of government." [6] Although the phrase " republican form of government " has never been defined by the courts, it is generally understood to mean a representative democracy.

President John Tyler acted under this constitutional guarantee when he moved to put down " Dorr's Rebellion " in Rhode Island (1841-1842). The followers of Thomas Dorr attempted to force the conservative ruling group in the State to adopt a new constitution and ease the voting laws. They proclaimed a new constitution and named Dorr governor. However, when Dorr attempted to put his new government into operation, the legally elected governor appealed to President Tyler for help. When the President took steps to put down the rebellion, it collapsed. But a new and more liberal State constitution was adopted in 1842.

In a case growing out of this incident, the Supreme Court held in 1849 that the question of whether or not a State has a republican form of government is a *political* and not a *judicial* one and is to be decided by the political branches of the Government (the President and Congress).

The Court repeated this holding in a 1912 case. An Oregon corporation had refused to pay a tax enacted by the voters of the State. The company claimed that the use of the initiative and referendum, " direct legislation " by which voters propose and enact laws at the polls, meant that Oregon lacked a republican (representative) government.

Protection against Invasion and Domestic Violence. In addition to guaranteeing to each State a republican form of government, the National Government is required to ". . . pro-

---

[6] Article IV, Section 4.

60

tect each of them against invasion; and on application of the legislature, or of the executive (when the legislature cannot be convened), against domestic violence." [7] Today, of course, an invasion of one State would be considered an attack upon the United States as a whole.

The President, as commander-in-chief of the armed forces, may use federal troops to quell domestic violence, such as riots and looting. Normally, he sends troops only when requested to do so by the governor or legislature of the State involved. However, when a federal question is involved, he need not wait for such a request.[8]

In recent years, domestic violence has come to mean more than man-made violence. Thus the armed forces and other federal agencies are used to render emergency aid in such disasters as those caused by the hurricane which struck Louisiana and a slice of East Texas in the summer of 1957.

Respect for Geographic Identity. The National Government is further obliged to respect the geographic identity or integrity of each of the States. Thus Congress may not create a new State from territory belonging to one or more of the existing States unless it first has the consent of the State legislatures involved.[9] Nor may a State be denied its equal representation in the Senate without its own consent.[10]

Federal-State Co-operation

More and more, as you will see as you read through this book, the National Government and the States are working together in many fields.

Perhaps the best known example of this co-operation is found in the so-called *grant-in-aid* system. Each year the National Government grants more than $3,000,000,000 to the States. This money is given to the States for particular programs, such as highway building, aid to dependent children, unemployment insurance, school-lunch programs, hospital construction, cancer control, wildlife conservation, extension services, agricultural colleges, forest-fire work, and veterans' training.

Often the States are required to " match " the federal funds, usually dollar-for-dollar. And the States must

---

[7] Article IV, Section 4. Remember, the States themselves cannot maintain armies or navies (Article I, Section 10, Clause 3).

[8] President Cleveland sent federal troops to restore order in the Chicago railyards during the Pullman Strike of 1894, *acting over the express objections* of Governor Altgeld of Illinois. The Supreme Court upheld his action in 1896 because rioters had threatened federal property and impeded the mails and interstate commerce. Since then, several Presidents have acted without a request: as President Eisenhower did in 1957 in sending troops to Little Rock to halt the unlawful obstruction of a school integration order which had been issued by a United States District Court.

[9] Article IV, Section 3, Clause 1.
[10] Article V.

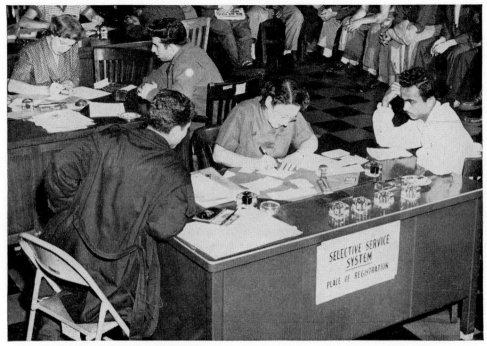

UNCLE SAM CALLS

Selective Service is specifically a federal function. State and local governments, however, administer this important law by operating draft boards. This is another way in which the States and the National Government work together for the common good.

also meet certain requirements in order to use the federal money. For example, highway construction specifications are often attached to a grant-in-aid for highway building.

But there are many other fields in which the two levels of government work together. The Federal Bureau of Investigation aids State and local police in numerous ways. State and local draft boards help administer the selective service system. The United States Department of Agriculture works with State agricultural agencies and colleges.

To help States enforce their crim-inal laws the Congress has made it a federal crime to transport stolen goods, such as an automobile, across a State line; to flee from justice in one State to another; to kidnap across a State line; to travel from one State to another with a woman for an immoral purpose. The FBI conducts a "police academy" at which State and local police officers are trained in the most effective ways of fighting crime. The Federal Civil Defense Administration works with State and local civil defense agencies. The list of activities in which National and State and local governments cooperate is almost endless.

Interstate Relations

The States Are Legally Separate.
Each State is legally separate from every other State in the Union. When the States are acting within the sphere of their reserved powers they stand toward one another as independent and wholly separate. Each State has no jurisdiction outside its own boundaries.[11] But given the interwoven nature of the American scene, the States must of course have dealings with one another. In several important respects these interstate relationships are covered by the United States Constitution.

Interstate Compacts.
As we have seen, no State may enter into any treaty, alliance, or confederation. But States may, with the consent of Congress, enter into *compacts* or agreements among themselves and with foreign states.[12]

In the last several years an increasing number of compacts have been concluded and today well over one hundred are in force. Oregon and Washington have protected fish in boundary waters; New York and New Jersey created the Port of New York Authority to provide wharves, tunnels, bridges, street approaches, bus terminals, and airports; every State in the Union belongs to the Parole

As a matter of course, however, practically all agreements are submitted for congressional action.

INTERSTATE CO-OPERATION
The States of New Jersey and New York created the Port of New York Authority by treaty in 1921. The bus terminal, largest in the world, is one of the many buildings and facilities used to develop the commerce of the port district.

The Port of New York Authority

---

[11] " Hot pursuit " agreements are an exception here. Most States now permit police officers from an adjoining State to pursue lawbreakers across the State line, arrest them, and turn them over to local authorities. But this can be done only when the police are in actual " hot pursuit " of their quarry.

Air travel provides another exception. Washington and Minnesota, for example, now permit adjacent counties in neighboring States to acquire and operate airports within their States, provided the neighboring State does the same.

[12] Article I, Section 10, Clauses 1 and 3. The Supreme Court has ruled that congressional consent need not be had for compacts which do not " tend to increase the political power of the States." Thus, some years ago, New York, New Jersey, and Connecticut, without going to Congress at all, settled among themselves a long-standing dispute over sewage pollution of New York harbor.

and Probation Compact which provides for interstate supervision of parolees and probationers. Among the compacts Congress approved in 1957 was one which had been drawn up by the States of Massachusetts and New Hampshire to enable them to promote more adequate flood control and the greater use of the water resources in the basin of the Merrimack River and its tributary streams.

Most compacts relate to the common use of natural resources, as the Hoover Dam Compact involving the States of the Colorado River Basin. This compact was the first great attempt to bring several of the States together as political units for the development, control, and management of a regional river in which they all are interested.

Many other compacts have been used to settle interstate disputes while still others have been instrumental in promoting interstate co-operation in the handling of common problems that have arisen.

The Full Faith and Credit Clause. Each State is required to give " full faith and credit . . . to the public acts, records, and judicial proceedings of every other State." [13]

The words " acts, records, and judicial proceedings " as used here refer to such matters as acts, ordinances, records of births, marriages, divorces, wills, deeds, contracts, and the decisions, judgments, and decrees rendered by courts. For instance, if a man dies in Baltimore and his will disposes of

---
[13] Article IV, Section 1.

property in Chicago, Illinois must give full faith and credit to the will probated under Maryland law.

One may prove age, marriage status, or title to land by obtaining a certificate from the State where the record was made. Or, suppose that A secures a judgment for $1000 against B in a New York court, in which State both men reside. B moves to New Jersey, taking all his property with him before it can be attached for the debt. A follows him and shows the New York judgment in the proper New Jersey court. The New Jersey court, without re-examining the merits of the original claim, will give full faith and credit and have its officer collect the debt for A.

Two exceptions to the rule of full faith and credit must be noted. First, it applies only to civil matters; that is, one State will not enforce another State's criminal laws. Second, and for the present at least, full faith and credit need not be given, in certain cases, to a divorce granted by courts of one State to citizens of another.

This confusing situation in the matter of " interstate divorces " came about as the result of a 1945 Supreme Court decision. The Court held that a Nevada divorce granted to *bona fide* (good faith) Nevada residents must be recognized in all other States. But a Nevada divorce granted to citizens of another State need not be. The Court felt that the forty-two days required by Nevada's divorce law is not long enough to establish *bona fide* residence. In order to become a resident of a State one must intend to reside there permanently. This decision and several others which have followed have cast a dark cloud of doubt over the validity of thousands of interstate divorces.

Privileges and Immunities. The Constitution specifically provides that " the citizens of each State shall be entitled to all privileges and immunities of citizens in the several States." (Art. IV, Sec. 2.) This means that a citizen of one State may go to another State and there enjoy the same civil rights [14] that citizens of the latter State enjoy, and likewise be subject to the same restrictions.[15]

As an example of the rights a citizen of one State may enjoy in another State, the legislature of Maryland passed a law (1868) imposing a license on the privilege of selling articles not manufactured in Maryland. For citizens of Maryland the license was not to exceed $150, but for citizens of other States the license was to be $300. Mr. Ward of New Jersey refused to pay more than $150, and the Supreme Court of the United States decided that he could not be required to pay more than citizens of Maryland.

As an illustration of a restriction upon a citizen of one State while in another State, a citizen of Washington State cannot marry in Oregon unless he is physically and mentally examined as required by the Oregon law.

The courts have never given a complete list of privileges and immunities, but the following are some of them: the right to pass through or reside in any other State for the purpose of trade, agriculture, professional pursuits, or otherwise; to demand the writ of *habeas corpus;* to bring suit in the courts of the State; to make contracts; to buy, sell, and own property; to pay no higher taxes than the citizens of the State; to marry.

A State is not required to grant *public* or political privileges to nonresidents. It may require one to live in a State a specified period before voting or holding office.

A State may require a period of residence in a State before it grants licenses to practice medicine or dentistry, and may restrict the practice of law to citizens of the State. The State has the right to take time to observe the moral character of a person who desires to enter an occupation of great importance to the general public.

Wild fish and game are property of the State, therefore a nonresident may

---

[14] *Civil rights* are those of person and property.

[15] Under the " privileges and immunities " clause a corporation is not a citizen. Therefore a State may refuse a corporation chartered in another State the privilege of conducting business in its borders. For instance, outside insurance companies may enter a State only on such conditions as the State may impose; *e.g.*, that premiums collected in a State be invested there. But a State cannot interfere with interstate commerce without the consent of Congress, and a corporation has the same privileges of interstate commerce as a natural person. It may ship commodities into a State under the same conditions as a natural person, and may likewise become an interstate common carrier.

be compelled to pay a higher fee for a hunting or fishing license than a resident, who pays taxes to help maintain game and fish hatcheries. Likewise a State school may charge higher tuition to nonresidents than to residents.

Extradition.[16] The Constitution provides that " a person charged in any State with treason, felony, or other crime, who shall flee from justice and be found in another State, shall on demand of the executive authority of the State from which he fled be delivered up to be removed to the State having jurisdiction of the crime." (Article IV, Section 2.)

A man, and a woman who posed as his sister, operated a racket in New York in which the man made love to wealthy widows, obtained money from them, and then jilted them. The couple killed one suspicious woman to prevent her exposing them, and moved to Michigan. In Michigan they likewise killed a woman and her child to cover their tracks, and were caught. The governor of New York requested extradition of the couple and the governor of Michigan complied because Michigan does not have capital punishment for murder. In New York the couple was sentenced to death.

The return of a fugitive is usually a routine matter. Occasionally, however, a governor will refuse to surrender a wanted man. Despite the fact that the Constitution says " shall," the Supreme Court has consistently held that the Constitution imposes only a *moral* duty on a governor. As the National Government cannot force a governor's hand, when one governor refuses the request of another, whether the reasons be good, bad, or indifferent, there the matter ends.

Several years ago, ex-Governor Taylor of Kentucky was implicated in the murder of Governor Goebel and he fled to Indiana. The governor of Indiana, feeling that Taylor, a Republican, would not receive a fair trial with the Democrats then in control in Kentucky, refused to extradite him. Recently, the governor of Oregon refused a West Virginia request based on a crime committed in 1903 because the wanted man had lived as a respected member of his Oregon community for nearly half a century.

Congress, acting under the commerce power, has made it a federal crime to flee across a State line to avoid arrest, prosecution, or imprisonment. This means that State and local police have the invaluable assistance of the FBI in such cases.

The Admission of New States

Congress Admits New States. Only Congress has the power to admit new States to the Union. But it may not create a new State by taking territory from an existing State without

---

[16] Extradition has been carried on between sovereign states from early times, and the word *extradition* has been the popular term used in the United States for what is more technically known as *interstate rendition.*

the consent of that State.[17]   In addition to the thirteen original States, Congress has so far admitted thirty-five additional ones.[18]

The normal process of admission is relatively simple.   The area desiring Statehood petitions (applies to) Congress for admission.   If Congress is favorable it passes an ." enabling act " which directs the framing of a constitution.   After the document is drafted and approved by the people, it is submitted to Congress.   If Congress is still agreeable, it passes a resolution of admission.   Hawaii (1950) and Alaska (1956) have already drafted constitutions and each stands ready and waiting for the passage of the necessary enabling act.

Before finally admitting a new State, Congress usually imposes certain conditions.   Thus, in 1896, Utah was admitted on condition that its new constitution outlaw polygamy; and, in 1802, Ohio was required not to tax for five years any public lands sold within her borders by the United States.

Courtesy LIFE Magazine: © Time, Inc.

A NEW STATE?

Citizens of Hawaii prepare a 500-foot-long sheet, signed by some 10,-000 people.   The petition asks Congress to admit the Territory as a new State in the Union.

[17] Article IV, Section 3, Clause 1.

[18] Although North Carolina (November 21, 1789) and Rhode Island (May 29, 1790) ratified the Constitution after the new Government had been organized (April 30, 1789), they are, of course, included among the original thirteen.   Five States (Vermont, Kentucky, Tennessee, Maine, and West Virginia) were created from parts of already existing States.   Texas was an independent republic before admission.   California was admitted after being ceded by Mexico.   The other twenty-eight States were admitted after a period as organized territories of the United States.

But each State enters the Union on an *equal footing with each of her sister States*.   When Oklahoma was admitted in 1907, Congress required that the State capital not be moved from Guthrie prior to 1913.   In 1910 the legislature moved the capital to Oklahoma City.   When this step was challenged, the Supreme Court declared that Congress may impose conditions as it sees fit, but they cannot be enforced when they compromise the independence of a State to manage its own internal affairs. Again, President Taft vetoed a resolution admitting Arizona in 1911. He objected to the constitutional provision permitting the popular recall of judges. Arizona was admitted by a new resolution in 1912, but without the recall provision. Almost immediately thereafter the people of Arizona added the recall provision to their new State Constitution.

Separation of Powers in the National Government

In addition to a *division of powers* between the National Government and the States, the Constitution also provides for a *separation of powers* within the National Government. That is, the powers of the National Government are separated (distributed) among three distinct branches of the National Government — the legislative, the executive, and the judicial.

In defense of this unusual arrangement, James Madison, the " Father of the Constitution," wrote:

The accumulation of all powers, legislative, executive, and judiciary, in the same hands, whether of one, a few, or many, and whether hereditary, self-appointed, or elective, may justly be pronounced the very definition of tyranny.

Legislative Branch. The Constitution vests *all* of the legislative (lawmaking) powers of the National Government in Congress. This body cannot authorize any other persons to make laws in its stead. But it often passes acts which outline general policies and set certain standards while leaving the actual details of day-to-day administration to some governmental agency. For instance, Congress has provided for the regulation of freight rates and created the Interstate Commerce Commission to fix the actual rates in a given case. If Congress were to fix the rates in each case, it would have no time for other business.

Executive Branch. The Constitution provides that all executive (law-executing, law-enforcing, law-administering) powers shall be vested in the President. Of course, he is assisted by all of the departments and agencies of the vast executive branch, but he alone is personally responsible for its actions.

Judicial Branch. The Constitution vests the judicial (law-interpreting, law-applying) powers in the Supreme Court and such lower courts as Congress may create. The courts interpret and apply the law in actual cases as these are brought before the courts.

Check and Balance System. Thus, three *separate and distinct* branches of the National Government exist. But these three branches are not *completely* independent of one another. While each branch has its own distinct field of powers, it is subject to a series of constitutional checks which the other branches may exercise against it. For example, the President may veto acts of Congress; Congress may override a veto by a two-

68

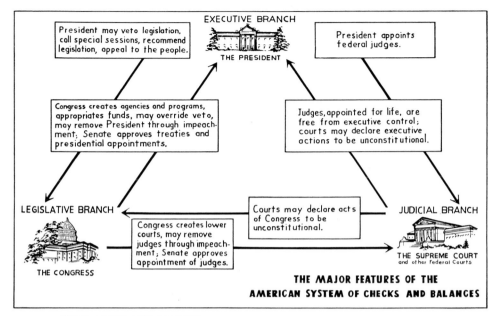

EXECUTIVE BRANCH

President may veto legislation, call special sessions, recommend legislation, appeal to the people.

THE PRESIDENT

President appoints federal judges.

Congress creates agencies and programs, appropriates funds, may override veto, may remove President through impeachment; Senate approves treaties and presidential appointments.

Judges, appointed for life, are free from executive control; courts may declare executive actions to be unconstitutional.

LEGISLATIVE BRANCH

Congress creates lower courts, may remove judges through impeachment; Senate approves appointment of judges.

Courts may declare acts of Congress to be unconstitutional.

JUDICIAL BRANCH

THE CONGRESS

THE SUPREME COURT
and other Federal Courts

THE MAJOR FEATURES OF THE AMERICAN SYSTEM OF CHECKS AND BALANCES

THE SHIP OF STATE

To keep our National Government on an even keel, each of its three branches has separate powers. The balance of power is maintained through the system of constitutional checks.

thirds vote in each House. Or Congress may refuse to appropriate funds requested by the President, or may impeach the President, judges, and other civil officers. The courts have assumed the power to pass on the constitutionality of acts of Congress or actions of the President (judicial review).

As a concrete illustration, when in 1952 President Truman seized the steel industry to prevent a strike, he claimed that such a strike would endanger the nation's security and that, as Commander-in-Chief of the armed forces, he had the constitutional authority to act. But the Supreme Court, saying that " this is a job for the Nation's lawmakers, not for its

military authorities," declared that the President's seizure action exceeded his powers under the Constitution and was, therefore, unconstitutional.

The Founding Fathers intended the check and balance system to prevent " an unjust combination of the majority." And, on the whole, the system has worked well. The people have learned, however, that while mistakes or evil designs of one department may be checked by another, so also can well-planned, honest policies of one be checked by another for political reasons.

When both houses of Congress are controlled by the President's supporters the system works well. But when one or both houses are in the hands of the opposing party it is exceedingly difficult for the National Government to operate smoothly. In such instances the National Government does not fail completely, of course. But it is often stalled over vital policy decisions.

The check and balance system makes compromise necessary, and compromise is of the essence in a democratic system. Dictatorships are based upon the usurping of power by one man or a small group. Thus the check and balance system prevents the rise of an all-powerful dictator in the National Government.

Our Changing Constitution

Formal Amendment. The methods for amending the Constitution are set forth in Article V. Of the four methods there provided, only two have thus far been used.

First, an amendment may be proposed by a two-thirds vote of each house of Congress and ratified by the legislatures of three-fourths of the States. Twenty-one amendments have been adopted in this manner.

Second, an amendment may be proposed by a two-thirds vote of each house of Congress and ratified by conventions in three-fourths of the States. The convention method has been used only once, in the case of the 21st Amendment. The disadvantage of

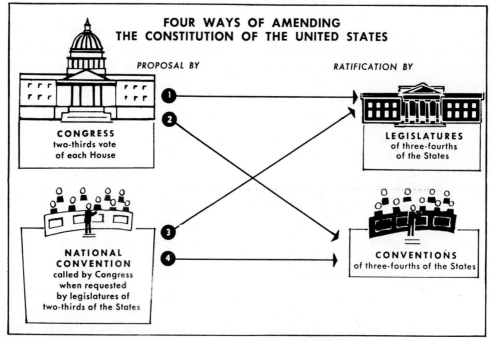

FOUR WAYS OF AMENDING THE CONSTITUTION OF THE UNITED STATES

PROPOSAL BY

RATIFICATION BY

CONGRESS
two-thirds vote
of each House

LEGISLATURES
of three-fourths
of the States

NATIONAL CONVENTION
called by Congress
when requested
by legislatures of
two-thirds of the States

CONVENTIONS
of three-fourths of the States

CHART BY GRAPHICS INSTITUTE, N. Y. C.

Unit I. DEVELOPMENT OF GOVERNMENT

this method lies in the fact that there is only one opportunity in each State for ratification; whereas, under the first method, if a legislature refuses to ratify at one session, a subsequent one might do so. But once a legislature does ratify, it can never rescind that action. The 21st Amendment was ratified by convention because Congress felt that the people would be more favorable to it than the State legislators.[19]

Third, an amendment may be proposed by a national convention, called by Congress at the request of two-thirds of the State legislatures, and ratified by the legislatures of three-fourths of the States.

Fourth, an amendment may be proposed by a national convention, called by Congress when requested by the legislatures of two-thirds of the States, and ratified by conventions in three-fourths of the States. The Constitution was originally adopted in this manner.

Referendum Denied. In 1920 the United States Supreme Court ruled that State legislatures may not refer federal amendments to the people but must pass upon them themselves. However, a legislature may be influenced by an advisory vote of the people.

The Twenty-Two Amendments. The first ten amendments, the Bill of Rights, were added to the Constitu-

tion in 1791.[20] They define most of the rights guaranteed to individuals against acts of the National Government. For example, the guarantees include freedom of speech, press, religion, petition, and assembly; protection from unreasonable searches and seizures; freedom from double jeopardy and self-incrimination; protection from the depriving of life, liberty, or property without due process of law; and numerous other guarantees of fair treatment before the law. (See Chapter 22, " Civil Rights.") But it must always be remembered that the Bill of Rights restricts *only* the National Government, and not the States. Amendment X reserves to the States those powers not granted to the National Government.

The 11th Amendment (1798) provides that a State may not be sued by a citizen of another State without its consent. The 12th (1804) deals with the election of the President and Vice-President. No more amendments were added for the next 61 years. The War Between the States resulted in the adoption of the 13th (1865), the 14th (1868), and the 15th (1870). These amendments abolished slavery,

---

[19] Congress determines whether an amendment is to be ratified by State legislatures or by State conventions.

[20] Many people, including Thomas Jefferson, agreed to support the adoption of the original Constitution only on condition that a listing of the rights of the people against the National Government be added immediately. These amendments were proposed by the First Congress in 1789 and ratified in 1791. They are known as the Bill of Rights because they contain many of the rights gained by the British people in their Bill of Rights passed by Parliament in 1689.

defined citizenship and thus extended it to former slaves, and prohibited any voting restrictions "on account of race, color, or previous condition of servitude." The 14th also extended the "due process clause" to the States. (See Chapter 22.)

After 43 more years, in 1913, both the 16th Amendment, providing for a federal income tax, and the 17th, for the popular election of United States Senators, were ratified.

The 18th Amendment (1919) established national prohibition, and the 19th (1920) provided for woman suffrage. The 20th, providing that Congress shall meet January 3d and that the President shall take office January 20th, and the 21st, repealing the 18th, were adopted in the same year, 1933. The 22nd Amendment, adopted in 1951, limits a President to two full terms or not more than ten years in office.

Thus is the Constitution formally amended. Because the formal process is so difficult, the Supreme Court has been led to give an "elastic" construction to the Constitution; in effect, informally amending it.

Informal Amendment. In the nearly 170 years that the Constitution has been in force, great changes have taken place. In 1789, the young Republic was a small agricultural nation of some 4,000,000 souls scattered along the eastern edge of the continent. Today, she is the most powerful nation on earth. The nation spans the continent and has many far-flung dependents and commitments; some

170,000,000 people live within the borders of her modern, highly industrialized and technological domain.

How has the Constitution kept pace with this astounding growth and change? A glance will show that the twenty-two formal amendments, important as they are, have not been responsible for the document's adaptability and vitality.

Rather, the changes have come about through a process of what might be called "informal" amendment. That is, they are the result of developments in the day-to-day, year-to-year experience of government.

To understand the true nature of our government and constitutional system as it exists today, one must consider five methods whereby the Constitution has developed, aside from formal amendment — basic legislation, executive action, court decisions, party practices, and custom.

1. *Basic Legislation.* Many portions of the Constitution are vague and skeletal in nature. The Framers purposely left it to Congress to fill in the details as circumstances required. For example, the entire federal court system, except the Supreme Court itself, has been created by acts of Congress. So have all of the dozens of departments and agencies of the executive branch, save the offices of President and Vice-President. The question of who shall act as President should both the Presidency and Vice-Presidency become vacant, is answered by an act of Congress, not by the Constitution.

72

POLICY TALK

President Eisenhower is shown here with the king of Saudi Arabia, Ibn Saud, and his young son. Sometimes the President, in his meetings with foreign heads of state, makes executive agreements which are binding upon the United States.

2. *Executive Action.* The manner in which the various Presidents have exercised their powers has contributed to this " informal " development of the Constitution. Although only the Congress may declare war, the armed forces have been used by various Presidents (acting as Commander-in-Chief) for military action abroad on no fewer than 127 occasions, without a declaration of war by Congress.

Among the many other examples, the device of " executive agreements " is typical. Recent Presidents have made such agreements rather than use the cumbersome process of treaty-making outlined in the Constitution.

Executive agreements are agreements made personally by a President with the head of a foreign state, and the courts consider them as binding as treaties.

3. *Court Decisions.* Under the American doctrine of judicial review, as we have seen, the Supreme Court is the ultimate interpreter of the Constitution. In short, the Constitution means what the Court says it means. This is what Chief Justice Charles Evans Hughes meant when he described the Court as " a continuous Constitutional Convention."

Again, judicial review (the power of the courts to determine the constitutionality of some governmental action) is not expressly bestowed upon the courts by the Constitution. The Supreme Court established the practice in *Marbury* v. *Madison*, 1803. It is based upon logic rather than on any specific constitutional provision, and it has come to constitute one of the most notable features of the American system of government.

In expanding the Constitution through judicial interpretation, the Court has leaned most heavily on the Necessary and Proper Clause, the Commerce Power, and the Taxing Power, all to be found in Article I, Section 8.

4. *Party Practices.* Political parties themselves have grown up *extra-constitutionally*. Not only does the Constitution not even mention parties, but most of the Founding Fathers were opposed to their growth. In his Farewell Address in 1796, George Washington warned the people against " the baneful effects of the spirit of party." Yet, in many ways today, government in the United States is government by party.

As an illustration, the electoral college system has become a " rubber stamp " for party action. The national convention system for selecting party candidates for the Presidency is not provided for in the Constitution; the device was originated by the parties. Actions and policies of the House of Representatives are largely determined by party caucuses. The President makes major federal appointments with an eye to party politics.

5. *Custom.* Unwritten custom may be as strong as written law. When a President dies in office the Vice-President becomes President. Read carefully the *exact* wording of Article II, Section 1, Clause 6.

It is a well-established custom for the Senate to reject an appointment by the President if it is opposed by a Senator of the majority party from the State where the appointee is to serve. The most recent dramatic example of the application of this custom, known as *senatorial courtesy,* occurred in 1951. President Truman had appointed two new U.S. district judges for Illinois. Senator Douglas of Illinois objected and the Senate refused to confirm the President's appointments by a vote of 89–0. This practice practically shifts the power to appoint many federal officers from the President to the Senators.

The strength and importance of unwritten customs is well illustrated by the rare instance in which one of them was nullified. From the time George Washington refused a third term as President in 1796, there had existed the so-called " no-third-term tradition " in American politics. But, in 1940 and 1944, Franklin D. Roosevelt sought and won not only a third term but a fourth as well. Since then the 22nd Amendment has been added to the Constitution, thus making an unwritten custom a part of the written Constitution. It would be impossible, then, to gain a realistic picture of the American political system simply by reading the Constitution.

WHAT THIS CHAPTER IS ABOUT

Government in the United States rests upon two basic ideas: (1) *popular sovereignty* — that is, that the people are sovereign and are the *only* source for governmental power, and (2) *limited government* — that is, that government is limited to *only* those powers the people grant to government.

The United States is a *federal* system of government. This system was created by the Framers of the Constitution in order to provide a National Government and, at the same time, to preserve the rights of local self-government in the States. Under it, national matters are the concern of the National Government, and State and local matters are chiefly the concern of each State.

The Constitution sets up a division of powers between the Nation and the States. The National Government possesses the powers *delegated* to it by the Constitution. These *delegated powers* are of two kinds: (1) *the expressed powers* — those that are delegated in so many words in the Constitution, and (2) the *implied powers* — those that may be reasonably implied from the expressed powers. The Constitution also *denies* certain powers to the National Government.

The States possess the *reserved powers*. These are the powers not delegated to the National Government and not denied to the States by the Constitution. The States are also denied certain powers in the Constitution.

The *exclusive powers* are those that belong only to the National Government. The *concurrent* powers are those that may be exercised by both the National and State Governments.

The Constitution makes itself the " supreme law of the land." Immediately under it are acts of Congress and treaties of the United States. All provisions of State constitutions and State and local laws must not conflict with these acts and treaties.

The U.S. Supreme Court is the " referee " in the federal system. It is the final interpreter of the constitution. The power of *judicial review,* established in the Court's decision in *Marbury* v. *Madison,* 1803, is the power of any court in the land to test the constitutionality of any governmental action.

The National Government has certain obligations toward the States under the Constitution. It must guarantee to each State a republican form of government, protect each State against foreign invasion and domestic violence, and respect the geographic integrity of every State in our Union.

The States and the National Government co-operate with one another in many ways, from the grant-in-aid program to the selective service system.

Each of the States is legally separate from all the others in their dealings. But the Constitution requires them to co-operate with one another in the matters of giving full faith and credit to one another's public acts, records, and judicial proceedings, granting one another's residents the privileges and immunities of their own residents, and extradition (the return of fugitives from one State to another). The States may, with the consent of Congress, enter into compacts (agreements) among themselves.

New States may be admitted by Congress, and Congress often imposes requirements on States as they come into the Union. But each State enters the Union on an equal footing with her sister States.

Chapter 4. OUR FEDERAL SYSTEM OF GOVERNMENT

There is a *separation of powers* in the National Government between the legislative (Congress), executive (President), and judicial (courts) branches. Each has its own set of powers and is equal to the other. But all three are tied together by the *check and balance system.*

There are four ways in which the Constitution may be amended, but only two of them have ever been used. The Constitution has been formally amended twenty-two times since the Founding Fathers drafted it.

In addition to the formal amendments our Constitution has been changed and has kept pace with the changing times by " informal amendment." This has come about in five ways — by (1) basic acts of Congress, (2) precedent-setting actions of the various Presidents, (3) decisions of the Supreme Court, (4) political party practices, (5) custom.

QUESTIONS ON THE TEXT

1. Define federalism. What are the advantages secured by the American Federal System?

2. List the more important powers granted by the Constitution to the National Government. What powers are prohibited to the National Government?

3. Distinguish between " delegated " and " reserved powers." " Concurrent " and " exclusive powers." Give examples of each.

4. If a State law conflicts with a National law, which must yield? A provision in a State constitution with an act of Congress?

5. With whom does the ultimate interpretation of the Constitution rest?

6. Explain the Supreme Court's decision in *Marbury* v. *Madison.*

7. Who has the sole power to admit new States? What is the usual process of admission?

8. What is meant by the Full Faith and Credit Clause? Privileges and Immunities? Interstate Rendition?

9. What relation do States bear to one another except as specifically provided in the Constitution? Under what conditions may they enter agreements among themselves? Give examples.

10. Explain the meaning of the doctrine of separation of powers. What are the three great departments? What is the check and balance system?

11. In what ways may the Constitution be formally amended? How has it been developed otherwise? Illustrate with examples.

PROBLEMS FOR DISCUSSION

1. What do you think conditions might be like here if there were no federal system and the thirteen States had become independent states?

2. Give reasons why the powers to declare war and to regulate foreign and interstate commerce are exclusive powers of the National Government.

3. Some people view our Constitution as a sacred document that should not be changed, but Thomas Jefferson expresses the contrary view in the following words: " Some men ascribe to the men of the preceding age a wisdom more than human, and suppose what they did to be beyond amendment. I knew that age [of the Revolution] well. I belonged to it and labored with it. It deserved well

76

of its country. It was very like the present, but without the experience of the present; and forty years of experience is worth a century of book reading; and this they would say themselves were they to arise from the dead." Are these words more or less true today than when they were spoken?

4. Congress defeated a proposed Constitutional amendment which would have allowed the Constitution to be amended by a bare majority vote of Congress and a bare majority of popular votes at an election. The makers of the Constitution were unwilling to trust every Tom, Dick, and Harry voter with the amendment of the Constitution. Were they right or wrong?

THINGS YOU MIGHT DO

1. Prepare a large chart showing the powers of government under our federal system. The accompanying figure designed by Professor Frank H. Garver can be enlarged. Circle I represents all possible powers of the National Government and circle II all possible powers of State governments. Area *A* represents powers delegated to the National Government and area *B* those reserved to the State governments; segment *C* concurrent powers; segment *D* powers prohibited to the National Government; segment *E* powers prohibited to the State governments; and segment *F* powers prohibited to both governments. Space can be economized by the use of figures. I.8.3. in area *A* would mean Article I, Section 8, Clause 3; Am. X in area *B* would mean Amendment X.

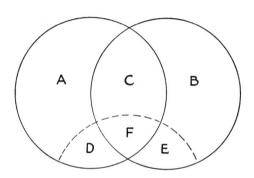

2. Make an outline of the Constitution, article by article, section by section, clause by clause.

3. Have your local county agent, chief of police, or other official talk to the class on the ways in which, in his work, the National Government co-operates.

WORDS AND PHRASES YOU SHOULD KNOW

Checks and balances	Full faith and credit	*Marbury* v. *Madison*
Concurrent powers	Grants-in-aid	Popular sovereignty
Delegated powers	Implied powers	Privileges and immunities
Enabling Act	Informal amendment	Republican form of government
Exclusive powers	Interstate compacts	Reserved powers
Expressed powers	Judicial review	Resolution of admission
Extradition	Limited government	Separation of powers
Federalism		Supreme law of the land

SELECT BIBLIOGRAPHY

BURNS, JAMES M., and PELTASON, JACK W., *Government by the People,* Chapters 4, 5, and 6. Prentice-Hall, 1954.

CORWIN, EDWARD S., *The Constitution and What It Means Today.* Princeton, 1954.

"Dilemma of Empire," *Current History,* entire issue, December, 1955.

FERGUSON, JOHN H., and MCHENRY, DEAN E., *The American System of Government,* Chapters 4, 5, and 6. McGraw-Hill, 1956.

GOSNELL, CULLEN B.; LANCASTER, LANE W.; and RANKIN, ROBERT S., *Fundamentals of American Federal Government.* McGRAW-HILL, 1955.

"The Government of the U.S.A.," *Fortune,* February, 1952. Entire issue.

"John Marshall's Legacy," *Life,* August 29, 1955.

KENNEDY, SENATOR JOHN F., "A Great Day in American History," *Collier's,* November 25, 1955.

MACDONALD, AUSTIN F., *State and Local Government in the United States,* Chapters 1, 2, and 4. Crowell, 1955.

PADOVER, SAUL K., *The Living U.S. Constitution.* Praeger, 1953.

SWARTHOUT, JOHN M., and BARTLEY, ERNEST R., *Principles and Problems of American National Government,* Chapters 2, 3, and 4. Oxford University Press, 1955.

"The Civil War," *Time,* June 4, 1956.

UNIT II
LEGISLATIVE
POWERS

Horydczak

The Capitol

LIKE A VAST PICTURE thronged with figures of equal prominence and crowded with elaborate and obtrusive details, Congress is hard to see satisfactorily and appreciatively at a single view and from a single standpoint. Its complicated forms and diversified structure confuse the vision and conceal the system which underlies its composition. It is too complex to be understood without an effort, without a careful and systematic process of analysis. Consequently, very few people do understand it, and its doors are practically shut against the comprehension of the public at large.

WOODROW WILSON
Congressional Government, 1885

Congress is a mighty good cross section of the American people.

— *Representative Sam Rayburn of Texas*

★

Chapter 5

THE LEGISLATIVE DEPARTMENT

Congress — the Law-Making Branch. Article I, Section 1, of the Constitution declares: " All legislative powers herein granted shall be vested in a Congress of the United States, which shall consist of a Senate and House of Representatives." Congress, then, is the law-making branch of the National Government. It is the branch which, in our representative democracy, is responsible for translating the popular will into public policy.

Bicameralism. Congress is bicameral (composed of two houses) for several reasons: *Historically,* the British Parliament had consisted of two houses (Lords and Commons) since the thirteenth century; most of the colonial legislatures and all but two (in 1787) of the State legislatures were bicameral. *Practically,* the compromise between the Virginia and New Jersey plans in the Constitutional Convention solved the most serious dispute there and dictated a two-chambered Congress. *Theoretically,* the Founding Fathers leaned toward a bicameral Congress in order that one house might act as a check on the other.

Thomas Jefferson, who possessed great faith in " the voice of the people," was in France when the Constitution was framed. Upon his return, while taking breakfast with Washington, he opposed the two-body form of legislature, and was disposed to twit Washington about it. At this time Jefferson poured his coffee from his cup into his saucer. Washington asked him why he did so. " To cool it," he replied. " So," said Washington, " we will pour legislation into the Senatorial saucer to cool it."

A bicameral Congress has worked extremely well because: (1) A bill passed in the heat of passion by one house can be submitted to the cool judgment of the other. (2) The urban and industrial North and East control the House, and the rural and agricultural South and West control the Senate. (3) One large house elected for a short term can express the wishes of the people, while the other, smaller house elected for a long term can weigh and consider

MR. SPEAKER

Sam Rayburn has been Speaker of the House since 1940, with the exception of two terms, when his friend Joseph W. Martin was Speaker.

them. (4) The press, TV, radio, groups especially affected, and the general public have a better opportunity to examine a bill and affect its fate when the two houses rather than one must act on it.

It has been argued that the equal representation of the States in the Senate should be scrapped as undemocratic.[1] Some argue it is unfair, for example, that Nevada, the State with

the smallest population (160,083), should have as many Senators as the largest, New York (with 14,830,192). Those who argue this ignore the fact that Senators were never intended to represent people as such. The Senate represents the States as coequal members and partners in the Federal Union. Besides, had not the States been equally represented in the Senate, there might never have been a Constitution!

Terms of the Congress. Each term of Congress, lasting two years, is numbered consecutively beginning with the first term, which began March 4, 1789. The term of the Eighty-Fifth Congress began at noon, January 3, 1957, and will end at noon, January 3, 1959.

Sessions of the Congress. There are two regular sessions to each term of Congress. The first session begins on January 3 following the election of Congressmen in November of each even-numbered year. The second session begins the next January 3.

Congress adjourns its sessions when it sees fit. In the past it met for no more than four or five months in a year. But the many important, pressing issues of today force Congress to remain in session most of the year.

In an attempt to streamline its operations, Congress provided in 1946 that it should adjourn each of its regular sessions no later than July 31, unless it should decide otherwise or a national emergency exist. Since then, Congress has actually met its deadline only twice, in 1952 and 1956.

---

[1] The prospects for any such change are so slim as to be nonexistent. Article V of the Constitution provides, in part: " and that no State, without its consent, shall be deprived of its equal suffrage in the Senate." In the face of this, the physical impossibilities of securing a change are obvious.

The Constitution allows the President to adjourn Congress whenever the two houses cannot agree upon a date for adjournment; but no President has ever been called upon to exercise this power.

Special Sessions. The President may call special sessions of Congress. President Roosevelt called an extra session in 1939 at the outbreak of World War II; the last one was called by President Truman in 1948 to consider such matters as high prices and social legislation. On some forty occasions Presidents have called only the Senate in special session to consider treaties and appointments. The House has never been called alone.

THE HOUSE OF REPRESENTATIVES

Membership. The House of Representatives, with its 435 members, is the larger chamber in Congress. The Constitution requires that its seats be apportioned (distributed) among the States on the basis of population. But each State is entitled to at least one member, regardless of how small its population. Today four States, Delaware, Nevada, Vermont, and Wyoming, have only one member each. (Alaska and Hawaii are each represented by a Territorial Delegate, and Puerto Rico by a Resident Commissioner. They are entitled to most of the privileges of members of the House, but have no vote.)

Reapportionment of the House. The Constitution directs Congress to reapportion the seats in the House among the States after each census. Before the First Census in 1790, the House in the First Congress had only sixty-five members. The 1790 Census showed a national population of 3,929,214 and the size of the House was raised to 106.

As the nation's population grew and the number of States increased, so did the size of the House. After the census in 1910, the membership stood at 435. After the 1920 census, Congress did not want to add more seats; the House was already too large for effective floor action. But to reapportion the seats without increasing the total number meant that some States would have had to lose seats. And, in effect, some members would have been voting themselves right out of Congress. So, despite the constitutional provision, nothing was done.

Inevitably the problem arose with the next census. So, in 1929, Congress passed the Reapportionment Act. This law provides for a sort of " automatic " reapportionment every ten years. It provides:

(1) The " permanent " size of the House shall be 435 members (but any future Congress could change this).

(2) The Census Bureau figures the number of seats to which each State is entitled.

(3) The President sends this information to Congress.

(4) If, within sixty days, neither house turns down the Census Bureau's

plan, it takes effect. Based on the 1950 census, each State now has, in round numbers, one member for every 345,000 persons.

Election of Representatives. Congress determines the time, place, and manner of electing Representatives, but the Constitution provides for a two-year term of office and that any person whom a State permits to vote for members of the " most numerous branch " of its legislature may vote for Representatives. In 1872 Congress enacted that congressional elections should be held on the same day throughout the country — the Tuesday following the first Monday in November of every even-numbered year.[2] In the same year it decreed that Representatives should be chosen by written or printed ballots. The use of voting machines has been permitted since 1899. When a vacancy occurs in the House, the Constitution provides that the governor of the State involved call a special election to fill the seat.[3]

During the first fifty years of our Union the States were permitted to elect their Representatives as they chose. The method of electing them by districts early became popular, but some States elected all members at large,[4] which made it possible, for example, for a State with a small majority of one party to elect all the members from that one party.

This was clearly unrepresentative, and in 1842 Congress prescribed that thenceforth all members should be chosen by districts.[5] The district system tends to give representation to the minority party; but, as the States were laid out into districts by the State legislatures, the districts were generally so arranged that the majority party continued to have a great advantage.

By an Act passed in 1872, Congress required that the districts be of contiguous territory and contain as nearly equal populations as practicable.

In 1911 Congress amended the Act to read " contiguous and compact territory." But in 1932 the United States Supreme Court held that the 1929 Reapportionment Act does not require contiguity and compactness of territory or equality of population; and populations vary greatly. For example, in Michigan at the time of the 1950 census, the Twelfth Congressional District had a population of only 177,360, while the Seventeenth District in the same State had a population of 724,717.

---

[2] For 137 years, until the voters amended the State's constitution in 1957, Maine held its congressional elections in September.

[3] United States Constitution, Article I, Section 2, Clause 4. Congress controls State election officials in the execution of State election laws when national officials are being chosen. All corrupt election practices automatically become federal offenses.

[4] *At large* means from the entire State. Each voter votes for all in the State.

[5] If the reapportionment following a decennial census increases the representation of a State, the additional Representatives may be elected at large until the State is reapportioned. If the representation of a State is reduced, *all* of the remaining Representatives must be elected at large until the districts are redrawn.

Unit II. Legislative Powers

1	2
50,000 REP. 25,000 DEM.	60,000 REP. 15,000 DEM.
3	**4**
40,000 DEM. 35,000 REP.	38,000 DEM. 37,000 REP.

FIGURE A

1	2	3	4
45,000 REP.	40,000 REP.	50,000 REP.	47,000 REP.
30,000 DEM.	35,000 DEM.	25,000 DEM.	28,000 DEM.

FIGURE B

Gerrymandering.[6] The scheme resorted to by an unfair legislative body to lay out congressional or other districts so as to secure a majority of voters for the party in power in the greatest possible number of them is known as " gerrymandering." This can sometimes be done by collecting as many voters of the minority party as possible into one district so as to make other bordering districts safe for the majority party.

For instance, Figure *A*, on this page, represents a State with four congressional districts, each consisting of 75,000 voters. In districts 1 and 2 the Republicans have a majority, whereas in districts 3 and 4 the Democrats have a majority, but in the entire State the Republicans have a majority of voters and therefore elect the majority of the members of the State legislature. This Republican State legislature redistricts the State as shown in Figure *B,* having gerrymandered it so that the Republicans have a majority of voters in districts 1, 2, 3, and 4.

The map below shows how the districts of South Carolina were skillfully arranged in 1890 so as to throw large blocks of the Republican Negro

---

6 The scheme of unfair apportionment of districts is called " gerrymandering " from Elbridge Gerry of Massachusetts. In 1812, when Gerry was governor of Massachusetts, the Republican legislature re-districted the State in such a manner that one district had a dragonlike appearance. It was indicated on a map of Massachusetts which hung over the desk of a Federalist editor. A celebrated painter added with his pencil a head, wings, and claws, and exclaimed, " That will do for a salamander! " " Better say Gerrymander," growled the editor.

vote together, the populations varying from 134,000 in the first district to 217,000 in the seventh.

Qualifications of Representatives. According to the Constitution, a member of the House must be a man or woman at least twenty-five, at least seven years a citizen [7] of the United States, and an inhabitant of the State in which he is chosen. Political custom dictates that a Representative should reside in his district. This district custom dates from colonial days and is based on the feeling that the Representative should be a man who knows the local problems. It often means, as we shall see later, that a Congressman is regarded by many of his constituents as an " errand boy " — that is, someone sent to Washington to do favors for the people back home.

Some people claim that the district custom also means that the voters cannot always select the best man possible. Only in rare instances is a man from outside a district chosen to

[7] Ruth Bryan, daughter of William Jennings Bryan, married a British subject named Owen in 1910 and became a British citizen. She lived in England until 1919, when she and her husband returned to the United States. In 1925 Ruth Bryan Owen became a naturalized citizen. In 1928 she was elected to Congress from Florida. Her election was contested on the ground that she had not been seven years a citizen just before election. In 1930 the House decided that *any* seven years in a person's life fulfilled the requirement, and she was allowed to keep her seat.

BUSY CONGRESSIONAL SCHEDULE

A modern congressman has many demands upon his time, not the least of which is public relations. Senator Morse of Oregon is shown with a group of students after an appearance on " Youth Wants to Know."

Courtesy of NBC–TV

Unit II. Legislative Powers

represent it. In the 81st, 82nd, and 83rd Congresses, Franklin D. Roosevelt, Jr., represented New York's 20th District on Manhattan Island, but he did not live in the district.

In cases of contest, the House is the judge of elections, returns, and qualifications of its members; it has excluded persons for various reasons.[8] Two-thirds of the House may expel a member for any reason it thinks fit, but no one has been expelled in recent years.

THE SENATE

Membership. The Senate is a much smaller body than the House and is composed of two members from every State. As there are now forty-eight States, there are ninety-six Senators.

Terms of Senators. Senators serve a six-year term, three times as long as the two-year term of Representatives. Where the short term of the Representatives makes the House closer to the people, the longer term makes the Senate a more conservative body.

One-third (thirty-two) of the Senators' terms end every two years. By dividing the seats into three classes this way, the presence of too many new and inexperienced members is avoided.

---

[8] This means, in effect, that the House can add " informal qualifications," in addition to those provided by the Constitution. In 1901, for example, the House refused to seat Brigham H. Roberts of Utah on grounds he had been a polygamist. In 1919 the House excluded Victor L. Berger, a Socialist from Wisconsin, on grounds of sedition and " un-Americanism " during World War I. The Supreme Court later cleared Berger of the sedition charge and, finally, after being elected from his Milwaukee district for the third time, the House gave him his seat.

Election of Senators. Senators are popularly elected. Until the adoption of the 17th Amendment in 1913 they were chosen by State legislatures. Now, at the November election every even-numbered year, they are elected by the people and are sworn into office when the new Congress assembles in January.[9] Each Senator is chosen from the whole

---

[9] Only one Senator is elected from a State at any one election, except when the other Senate seat has been vacated because of death or resignation. The 17th Amendment provides that a vacancy may be filled by a special election called by the governor, or that the legislature may authorize the governor to make a temporary appointment until the people fill the vacancy at a regular election. The State legislatures decide which method is to be used and most States follow the latter practice. At the 1954 election, Nebraska voters actually elected *three* Senators! Both regular Senators had died and the Governor appointed two Senators to serve until the November election. One of the seats was normally up at the 1954 election. But someone also had to be elected to fill that seat from November until January. A third Senator also had to be chosen to fill out the remaining four years of the unexpired term of the other seat. Altogether, because of vacancies that occurred as the result of death and resignation, thirty-eight Senators were elected across the country in the 1954 elections and thirty-five in 1956.

State and all persons who are qualified to vote for members of the House of Representatives may vote for members of the Senate.

Qualifications of Senators. A Senator must meet higher qualifications than those prescribed for a Representative. He or she must be at least thirty years of age, at least nine years a citizen of the United States, and a resident of the State which sends him to Congress. Like members of the House, a Senator cannot hold any other federal office.

The Senate, like the House, is the judge of the qualifications of its members and may exclude a person by majority vote.[10] Also like the House, the Senate may expel a member by a two-thirds vote.

The Personnel of Congress

Who are the members of Congress? What are they like? What is their job? How well do they do it? These and dozens of other such questions should be asked and the answers should be learned by every informed citizen. After all, it is the members of Congress who decide such vital matters as how large our armed forces should be, at what age a young man may be drafted, how heavy our taxes should be, how labor-management relations should be regulated. These and the hundreds of other decisions Congress makes affect all of our lives intimately every day.

The Background of the Members. Several studies have been made of various Congresses in recent years. They show that members of the House average fifty-two years of age and Senators fifty-seven. Over half of the members are lawyers and most of the rest are, in order, businessmen, insurance men, career public servants, farmers, journalists, teachers, bankers, and doctors. Over three-fourths have college degrees. Most of them were born in the States they represent and only a bare handful were born outside the United States. There are a few millionaires sprinkled here and there.

Most Congressmen have had some political experience. About a third of the Senators were once members of the House and about a sixth of them governors of their home States. Some have been members of a President's Cabinet or held other high national or State offices. The House includes

[10] In 1912 Mr. Lorimer of Illinois was excluded by a majority vote, being elected as a result of bribes paid to Illinois legislators in behalf of his election. He had been seated, although under protest, and had voted on many measures before the committee on elections could investigate. In 1928 Mr. Smith of Illinois was excluded because $203,-000 expended in his behalf in the primary election was contributed by officials of public utility corporations whose rates were regulated by the Illinois Commerce Commission, of which Mr. Smith was a member. In 1947, Mr. Bilbo of Mississippi was temporarily excluded because he urged the use of "any means" to keep the Negro away from the polls and allegedly accepted illegal gifts from war contractors. Mr. Bilbo's death precluded any final Senate action in the case.

many former State legislators, public prosecutors, and the like.

Nearly all Congressmen are married, few are divorced, and they have, on the average, two children. Few of them claim no church membership.

In short, Congress is made up of typical upper-middle-class Americans. And, on the whole, Congressmen are able and hard-working people. The few " rotten apples " that come along now and then simply prove the old saying that the people get what they vote for.

The Job of a Congressman. The *primary* job of the Senator or Representative is to make law, translate the will of the people into public policy. But that is not the whole picture at all.

Let former Representative Luther Patrick of Alabama tell us about it:

A Congressman has become an expanded messenger boy, an employment agency, getter-outer of the Navy, Army, Marines, ward heeler, wound healer, trouble shooter, law explainer, bill finder, issue translator, resolution interpreter, controversy oil pourer, gladhand extender, business promoter, convention goer, civic ills skirmisher, veterans' affairs adjuster, ex-serviceman's champion, watchdog for the underdog, sympathizer with the upper dog, namer and kisser of babies, recoverer of lost luggage, soberer of delegates, adjuster for traffic violators, voters straying into Washington and into toils of the law, binder up of broken hearts, financial wet nurse, good samaritan, contributor to good causes — there are so many good causes — cornerstone layer, public building and bridge dedicator, ship christener — to be sure he does get in a little flag waving — and a little constitutional hoist-

The New York Times Magazine

CAMPAIGN KISSES

Cartoonist Gordon Hake points up one of the less serious sides of political life.

ing and spread-eagle work, but it is getting harder every day to find time to properly study legislation — the very business we are primarily here to discharge, and that must be done above all things.

And here is how Senator Paul Douglas of Illinois once described a typical day when the Senate is *not* in session: [11]

7–8:30 A.M. Rise, breakfast, read two morning papers and study memoranda for hearings.

8:30–9:30 A.M. Look over mail, answer some of the most important letters and block out today's policy with the staff.

9:30–11 A.M. Hearings on the Taft-Hartley repeal.

11–12. Hearings on the housing bill.

12–1 P.M. Work on correspondence and see visitors.

1–2 P.M. Lunch with constituents.

2–2:30 P.M. See delegations and telephone Government departments.

2:30–5 P.M. Hearings on the Taft-Hartley repeal.

5–6:30 P.M. Sign 250 pieces of mail, send telegrams on pressing matters of business.

6:30–7:30 P.M. Dinner with group which wants to consult on legislation.

7:30–10 P.M. Hearings on the Taft-Hartley repeal.

10–12. Read two evening papers and several weekly journals. Clean up correspondence and study more material on Taft-Hartley law and housing problems, block out radio speech for next day.

12:30 A.M. Go to bed.

The "Errand-Boy" Concept. As we know, members of Congress represent the people. But some of the people take this to mean that a Congressman is in Washington especially to do personal favors. The average

member is plagued with many requests — as Mr. Patrick points out — from the time he enters until he leaves office: help in securing government contracts, appointments to West Point, free sight-seeing tours in Washington, even help in marital disputes or requests for personal loans. The Congressman knows that to refuse most of these requests would mean to lose votes at the next election.

The Congressman has a tremendous responsibility for the welfare of the United States. Though many of them are often criticized for this or for that, it is in some ways a wonder that we are able to find so many men of ability willing to take the job.

Compensation of Congressmen. Congressmen, unlike other officers and employees of the government, fix their own salary, and the only limits on the amount are the President's veto and the possibility of not being re-elected.

Except in the year 1795, Senators and Representatives have always received equal salaries.[12] Today each receives:

(1) a salary of $22,500 per year;

(2) 20 cents a mile going and com-

---

[11] "Report from a Freshman Senator." *New York Times Magazine.* March 20, 1949.

[12] From 1789 to 1795 members of each house were paid $6 per day. In 1795 Senators received $7 per day and Representatives $6. From 1796 to 1816 the salary for both was again $6 per day. In 1816 it was raised to $15, but in 1817 went back to $6. From 1818 to 1856, $8 per day; 1856 to 1866, $3000 per year; 1866 to 1873, $5000; 1873, $7500; 1874 to 1907, $5000; 1907 to 1925, $7500; 1925 to 1933, $10,000; 1933 to 1936, $8663; 1936 to 1946, $10,000; 1946 to 1955, $12,500 plus $2500 "expense account"; 1955 to date, $22,500.

ing by the shortest route for each regular session, and usually for special sessions; [13]

(3) publications and free distribution of speeches; [14]

(4) free postage for official business (the " franking privilege ");

(5) an office in Washington (plus one at home for a Senator or two in his district for a Representative);

(6) an allowance for stationery, long-distance telephone and telegrams;

(7) an allowance for hiring an assistant and office help;

(8) a pension (to which members contribute) at age sixty-two after at least six years service and retirement from Congress; and

(9) a $3000 tax exemption because of the need to maintain a place in Washington as well as one at home.

Then, too, there are additional items that cannot be measured in terms of dollars and cents. One is the matter of the prestige that one has as a member of Congress. Another is the opportunity to make democracy work through the most direct way in which any citizen can participate in the governing process. Then, too, a member of Congress is able to do many things that private citizens cannot ordinarily do — for example, travel about the country and to many parts of the world at public expense as a part of his official duties.

At $22,500 a year plus the other allowances they receive, members of Congress are reasonably well paid today. Still, many persons in private life receive much higher salaries — and have far lighter responsibilities. It certainly would be wrong to say that our Congressmen are overpaid.

Before the 1955 salary increase, Cabell Phillips of the *New York Times* wrote:

Although there is an unmistakable glamour surrounding the job and the person of a member of Congress, the cold fact is that many statesmen spend long and melancholy evenings with the family account books, trying to balance their payables with their receivables. Like citizens of lesser stature, they are beset by debts, mortgages, installment payments and all the other vicissitudes of trying to make ends meet. For not a few it is an unequal and exasperating contest, and one that is not made any easier by the lack of popular understanding. . . . Figured either on the importance and responsibility of the job, or on what it actually costs a member of Congress to live in reasonable comfort, his pay and perquisites fall short by at least $3000 a year.

Mr. Phillips added that " an outside income — whatever the source — is an almost indispensable requirement for congressional service these days," and he quoted Senator Hubert Humphrey of Minnesota on that point:

---

[13] When a special session of Congress merged into a regular session, Theodore Roosevelt allowed mileage for both sessions; but under like conditions Wilson denied it. Congressmen have since insured their mileage for special sessions by adjourning before the regular session.

[14] Many speeches which are not actually delivered on the floor of Congress are published in the *Congressional Record*, of which each congressman receives sixty copies free. He may obtain any number of reprints of his speech by paying the Government Printing Office the actual cost of reprinting.

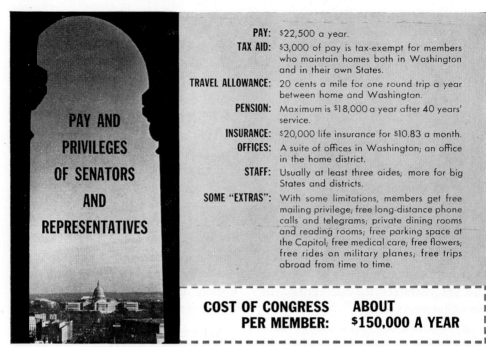

PAY:	$22,500 a year.
TAX AID:	$3,000 of pay is tax-exempt for members who maintain homes both in Washington and in their own States.
TRAVEL ALLOWANCE:	20 cents a mile for one round trip a year between home and Washington.
PENSION:	Maximum is $18,000 a year after 40 years' service.
INSURANCE:	$20,000 life insurance for $10.83 a month.
OFFICES:	A suite of offices in Washington; an office in the home district.
STAFF:	Usually at least three aides; more for big States and districts.
SOME "EXTRAS":	With some limitations, members get free mailing privilege; free long-distance phone calls and telegrams; private dining rooms and reading rooms; free parking space at the Capitol; free medical care; free flowers; free rides on military planes; free trips abroad from time to time.

PAY AND PRIVILEGES OF SENATORS AND REPRESENTATIVES

COST OF CONGRESS PER MEMBER: ABOUT $150,000 A YEAR

Reprinted from "U.S. News & World Report," an independent weekly news magazine published at Washington. Copyright 1957 United States News Publishing Company.

" To do my duty as a Senator I have to go back home at least once a month. Each trip costs me from $200 to $250. But every time I go I have to scrounge the countryside like the Russian army, making speeches and lectures along the way. I simply can't afford it out of my salary."

It should be obvious that simply paying better salaries is not going to attract automatically the best people to Congress. But the evidence indicates that it might help to make the job more appealing.

Privileges of Congressmen. The Constitution makes members of Congress free from arrest while going to, attending, and returning from sessions of Congress " in all cases, except treason, felony, and breach of the peace." This provision dates from colonial days when the King's officers arrested legislators for little or no reason simply to keep them from their official duties. It has not been important in our national history. But it does save a Congressman now and then from a minor traffic ticket, should he elect to use it.

Another and much more important privilege is also provided in the Constitution. For what he says in Congress, a member " shall not be questioned in any other place." This means that a member cannot be sued for any statement made on the floor of Congress. And this immunity (freedom from suit) extends also to what he says in committee or in any printed official document such as a committee report or the *Congressional Record*. But he is not privileged to defame another person in a newspaper article or in conversation.

The object of this provision is to protect and encourage freedom of debate. And the privilege imposes a truly grave responsibility.

The Nonlegislative Powers of Congress

As we know, the main job of the Congress is legislative, to make law. But the Constitution also assigns certain " nonlegislative " powers to the House and Senate:

(1) **Electoral.** Under the Constitution, the President and Vice-President are elected by the people through the Electoral College. This process will be discussed later when we consider the Presidency. But whenever no person receives a majority (at least one over half) of the electoral votes for President, the House, voting by States, must choose a President from among the three highest candidates in the Electoral College.

Whenever no person receives a majority of the votes for Vice-President, the Senate must choose one from among the two highest candidates.

The House elected Thomas Jefferson in 1801 and John Quincy Adams in 1825. It was necessary for the Senate to elect Richard M. Johnson as Martin Van Buren's Vice-President in 1837.

(2) **Constituent.** As we have already seen, Congress may propose amendments to the Constitution by a two-thirds vote in each house. Or it may call a national convention to propose amendments whenever this is requested by two-thirds of the State legislatures. As in the case of choosing a President or Vice-President, when Congress does this it is not making law but exercising a nonlegislative power.

(3) **Judicial.** The Constitution provides that the President, the Vice-President, and all civil officers of the United States may be removed from office " on impeachment for, and conviction of, treason, bribery, or other high crimes and misdemeanors." [15] The House impeaches (brings charges) and the Senate sits as a court to try the case.

A two-thirds vote of the Senators present is necessary for conviction and the Chief Justice presides when a President is being tried. The penalty for conviction is removal from office, and if it desires, the Senate may add a provision against the holding of any future federal office. After removal,

---

[15] Article II, Section 4. Military officers are not " civil officers " and are removed by court martial; and members of Congress are not so considered here. When the House impeached Senator Blount of Tennessee in 1798 the Senate refused to try the case on grounds that it had the power to expel its own members if it saw fit. Blount was later expelled and this precedent is followed today.

criminal charges may be brought in the regular courts, if necessary.

To date there have been but twelve impeachments and four convictions. On several other occasions officers have resigned under the threat of impeachment.[16] When the House impeached President Andrew Johnson in 1868 the Senate failed by only one vote to convict him.

(4) **Executive.** The Senate has two " executive " powers, one in the matter of appointments made by the President and the other in treaties. Both of these matters we will consider later, but they must be at least mentioned here.

As a part of the system of checks and balances, the Constitution makes the approval of the Senate necessary to all major appointments made by the President. Such nominations to office are referred to the Committee on Appropriations by the Vice-President, unless the Senate orders otherwise. The committee's report may be considered by the Senate in secret (" executive ") session.

The appointments of Cabinet officers and other top officials in the President's " official family " are seldom rejected by the Senate. But the un-

written rule of " senatorial courtesy " enters the picture in the appointments of federal officers who serve in the various States. This custom provides that the Senate will not approve appointments if a majority party Senator from the State involved objects to the person named by the President. In practice, this means that the majority party Senators often dictate such appointments as those of postmasters, federal judges, federal attorneys, and customs collectors.[17]

Treaties are made by the President " by and with the advice and consent of the Senate . . . provided two-thirds of the Senators present concur." For a while after the adoption of the Constitution the advice of the Senate was asked before the President prepared a treaty, but now he merely consults with the Senate Committee on Foreign Relations and with influential members of both parties. The Senate may reject a treaty in full or may suggest amendments to it. Treaties may be considered in " executive session." [18] Because the House has a

---

[16] The four removed were all judges. One other judge resigned after the House impeached him but just before the Senate began his trial, and the case was dropped. Four other judges were acquitted. Aside from Senator Blount and President Johnson, W. W. Belknap, who was President Grant's Secretary of War, was impeached and acquitted in 1876 on the ground that the Senate no longer had jurisdiction because Belknap had resigned.

[17] See page 74. Those who criticize the practice often forget that a Senator is much more likely to know more about affairs in his own State than does the President.

[18] Previous to 1929, appointments and treaties were regularly considered in closed sessions. But a Senate rule adopted that year reads, in part: " Hereafter all business in the Senate shall be transacted in open session unless the Senate in closed session by a majority vote shall determine that a particular nomination, treaty, or other matter shall be considered in closed executive session. . . . Provided that any Senator may make public his vote in a closed executive session."

MEMBERS	HOUSE OF REPRESENTATIVES 435	SENATE 96
Qualifications	25 years of age, 7 years a citizen of the United States, inhabitant of State where elected. Other qualifications determined by the House.	30 years of age, 9 years a citizen of the United States, inhabitant of State where elected. Other qualifications determined by the Senate.
Elected by	Votes of Congressional Districts.	Votes of State.
Term	Two years.	Six years.
Salary.	$22,500 and allowances.	$22,500 and allowances.
Sole Powers.	(1) To impeach civil officers. (2) To originate revenue bills. (3) To elect a President if no candidate has a majority of the electoral votes.	(1) To try persons impeached. (2) To confirm appointments made by the President. (3) To approve treaties. (4) To elect a Vice-President if no candidate has a majority of the electoral votes.
Convene (in regular session)	Third of January every year.	Third of January every year.

PRESIDING OFFICER	SPEAKER	VICE–PRESIDENT [19] OF THE UNITED STATES CALLED " PRESIDENT OF THE SENATE "
Qualifications	Member of House.[20]	The same as for President.
Elected by	Members of the House.	Presidential electors or Senate.
Term	Two years (often re-elected).	Four years.
Salary	$35,000 + $10,000 expenses.	$35,000 + $10,000 expenses.
Vote	The same as any other member of the House.	Only in case of a tie vote.

[19] A president *pro tempore* of the Senate is elected by the Senate to preside in the absence of the Vice-President.   [20] According to custom based on parliamentary and colonial precedents.

Chapter 5. THE LEGISLATIVE DEPARTMENT   95

hold on the governmental purse strings, influential House members are frequently consulted in treaty matters, too.

(5) **Investigative.** Congress, through its committees, has the power to investigate (look into matters) for three purposes: (1) to gather information that may be of use to Congress in the making of law, (2) to see how laws already enacted are working out and whether they need changing or not, and (3) to determine whether or not programs provided by Congress are actually being administered in the way that Congress intended they should be. As in the case of the other four nonlegislative powers, the investigative functions of Congress are considered again in this book.

WHAT THIS CHAPTER IS ABOUT

Congress is the legislative (law-making) branch of the National Government. It is composed of two houses — the Senate and the House of Representatives.

Congress is *bicameral* (composed of two houses) for several reasons: because of the familiarity of the Framers with the bicameral British Parliament and the fact that all but two of the State legislatures in 1787 were bicameral, the Connecticut Compromise at the Convention, and the feeling that one house could check the other. Bicameralism has worked out extremely well in Congress.

A *term* of Congress lasts two years. There are two *regular sessions* to each term, one a year. *Special sessions* may be called by the President.

Members of the House serve a two-year term and are popularly elected. The Congress reapportions the seats in the House among the States on the basis of population after every ten-year census, but each State is guaranteed at least one Representative. The "permanent" size of the House is fixed by law at 435. Members are elected from districts within each State. These districts are drawn by the State legislature and, occasionally, they are *gerrymandered* — that is, drawn to the advantage of the majority party in the State.

A Representative must be at least twenty-five years old, seven years a citizen of the United States, and a resident of the State from which chosen. Political custom has added that he or she must also live in the district from which chosen. Both the House and the Senate have the power to decide contests over the qualifications of their own members and both have at times added " informal " qualifications. Each house may expel a member by a two-thirds vote.

Each State has two seats in the Senate and Senators serve a six-year term. One third of the Senate seats are up at each November election. Since 1913 (the 17th Amendment), our Senators are popularly elected. They must be at least thirty years old, nine years a citizen of the United States, and residents of the State from which chosen.

Members of Congress fix their own salaries by law. Today they receive $22,500 a year along with various other compensations. If you consider their heavy duties and the demands made upon them, they are by no means overpaid. They enjoy freedom from arrest for petty offenses while going to, attending, and returning from sessions of Congress. And they cannot be sued for what they say in the course of their official duties.

Congress performs several nonlegislative functions — choosing a President or Vice-President when the Electoral College fails to do so; proposing constitutional amendments or calling a national convention for this purpose; impeaching and trying officers of government; approving or rejecting, by the Senate, appointments and treaties made by the President; and investigating, through its various standing and special committees, projected laws and enacted legislation.

QUESTIONS ON THE TEXT

1. What Article of the Constitution treats of Congress?

2. Congress consists of what two houses? Each represents what?

3. Why has bicameralism worked so well in Congress?

4. When do regular sessions of Congress begin? Who may call extra sessions?

5. How is the membership of the House of Representatives determined? Of how many members does it now consist? Each represents approximately how many people?

6. Do any States have more Senators in the Senate than Representatives in the House?

7. Explain *gerrymandering*.

8. When are Representatives elected? Senators? How long is it after the election until they take their seats? What are their terms of office?

9. What are the qualifications for membership in the House? In the Senate?

10. Of how many members does the Senate consist?

11. By what vote of either house may a member be excluded? Expelled?

12. What business of the Senate is sometimes transacted behind closed doors? Why?

13. What salary do Congressmen receive? What further compensation?

14. What is a Congressman's primary job?

15. What special privileges has a Congressman? May he defame the character of a person in a newspaper article?

16. What are the nonlegislative functions of Congress?

PROBLEMS FOR DISCUSSION

1. It may seem at times that popularity is the only requisite for Congressmen aside from age, citizenship, and residence in the State. What additional qualifications would you add?

2. Many times a Congressman finds himself faced with a conflict between his own thinking on a particular piece of legislation and that of his constituents, upon whom he must depend for re-election. Do you think that Congressmen should respond to public opinion or should they investigate, debate, and decide according to their convictions? Consider the words of one of the foremost statesmen in British history, Edmund Burke, in 1774:

". . . Parliament is not a congress of ambassadors from different and hostile interests; which interests each must maintain, as an agent and advocate, against other agents and advocates; Parliament is a deliberative assembly of one nation, with one interest, that of the whole; where not local purpose, not local prejudices ought to guide, but the general good. You choose a member, indeed. But when you have chosen him he is not a member of Bristol, but he is a member of Parliament."

3. In order to do what the people want

them to do, Congressmen must know what it is the people want. How can private citizens inform their Congressmen?

4. Bicameralism is criticized by some for allowing stalls and delays. Why has it worked out so well in the Congress?

THINGS YOU MIGHT DO

1. Invite your Representative and/or Senator to address the class or the entire student body. Ask him about his work as well as current questions.

2. What is the background of your Congressmen? (See *Who's Who* and the *Congressional Directory*.) Draw up a list of current topics and find out how your Congressmen feel on these issues.

3. Prepare a class report on the impeachment of President Johnson.

4. Make a map showing the congressional districts in your State. Is your State gerrymandered?

WORDS AND PHRASES YOU SHOULD KNOW

Bicameral
Census
Congressman-at-large
Errand-boy concept

Franking privilege
Gerrymandering
Impeachment
Legislative

Nonlegislative powers
Reapportion
Session of Congress
Term of Congress

SELECT BIBLIOGRAPHY

BENDINER, ROBERT, " The Hard Life of a New Congressman," *Saturday Evening Post*, November 14, 1953.

COUGHLAN, ROBERT, " Joe Martin and Sam Rayburn: Proprietors of the House," *Life*, February 14, 1955, and *Reader's Digest*, May, 1955.

DIES, MARTIN, " The Truth about Congressmen," *Saturday Evening Post*, October 30, 1954.

GALLOWAY, GEORGE B., *The Legislative Process in Congress*, Chapters 9, 10, 11, 14, 15, 16, 20, 25. Crowell, 1953.

GROSS, BERTRAM M., *The Legislative Struggle*. McGraw-Hill, 1953.

JAVITS, JACOB J., " Congress Wants to Hear from You," *American Magazine*, June, 1952.

JOHNSON, CLAUDIUS O., *American National Government*, Chapter 12. Crowell, 1955.

MACKAYE, MILTON, " The Congress," *Holiday*, February, 1950.

PHILLIPS, CABELL, " A Profile of Congress," *New York Times Magazine*, January 10, 1954.

REYNOLDS, JOHN A., " Private Laws for Private Citizens," *Reader's Digest*, February, 1956.

SWARTHOUT, JOHN M., and BARTLEY, ERNEST R., *Principles and Problems of American National Government*, Chapters 10, 11. Oxford, 1955.

WHITE, WILLIAM S., " The Pressures That Drive a Congressman," *New York Times Magazine*, June 6, 1954.

All legislative powers herein granted shall be vested in a Congress of the United States. . . .

— *Constitution of the United States,*
Article I, Section 1

★

Chapter 6

THE POWERS OF CONGRESS — EXPRESSED AND IMPLIED

As we have seen, Congress may exercise only those powers granted to it by the Constitution. And the Constitution gives Congress only those powers *expressed* in the document plus those powers that may be reasonably *implied*, that is, those " necessary and proper " to carrying out the expressed powers.

Liberal v. Strict Construction.
Hardly had the Constitution come into force when a dispute arose as to just how broad the powers granted to Congress actually are.

The *strict-constructionists*, led by Thomas Jefferson, favored retaining as much power as possible in the States and a weaker National Government.

They agreed with Jefferson that " that government is best which governs least." In short, they wanted to restrict Congress to those powers actually stated in the Constitution.

The *liberal-constructionists,* led by Alexander Hamilton, favored a stronger National Government and, therefore, a liberal or broad interpretation of the Constitution in order to widen the powers of Congress.

As we shall see, those who favored a liberal interpretation prevailed. Decisions of the Supreme Court have been most responsible for the liberal construction. But the other two branches and the people have played their part in the process, too.

EXPRESSED POWERS

Interpretation of Expressed Powers. The expressed powers of Congress are enumerated very briefly;

and without courts to decide exactly what they mean and what they include, Congress would often be tempted to exceed its authority. To illustrate, the Constitution (Art. I, Sec. 8, Cl. 3) provides that " Congress shall have power to regulate commerce with foreign nations and among the several States, and with the Indian tribes." These words are very general, and federal courts have decided thousands of cases in explanation of them, and several hundred of these cases have been appealed and decided and supported by lengthy opinions of the Supreme Court of the United States.

Power to Tax and Power to Regulate Interstate Commerce. These are the most important expressed powers of Congress. They are so important and require so much space and time to do justice to them that a separate chapter is given for each of them.

Power to Make Money. Congress has power to coin money and to issue paper money, but the States are forbidden to do either.[1]

Before the Revolutionary War the English shilling was the recognized unit of value, and the restraining hand of the Mother Country kept issues of depreciated paper money within bounds. But with the coming of independence, the legislatures of several States printed the States' names on paper and called it money.[2] As always happens, bad money drove good money from circulation; and each State had paper money of an uncertain and declining value. This variety of money made local business uncertain and interstate business intolerable.

Because of these conditions the makers of the Constitution gave Congress the exclusive right to coin money, and the United States Supreme Court has upheld its right to issue paper money, as implied in its power to borrow.

---

[1] The Constitution forbids the States to coin money, emit bills of credit (paper money), or make anything but gold and silver coin a tender in the payment of debts. Congress can make coins or paper money legal tender. ("Legal tender" is any kind of money which a creditor is required by law to accept in payment of a monetary debt.)

[2] The Rhode Island Legislature of 1786 issued a large amount of paper money, and in six months a dollar was passing for 16 cents. John Fiske thus describes the situation: " The farmers from the inland towns were unanimous in support of the measure. They could not see the difference between the State making a dollar out of paper and a dollar out of silver. The idea that the value did not lie in the government stamp they dismissed as an idle crotchet, a wire-drawn theory, worthy only of ' literary fellows.' What they could see was the glaring fact that they had no money, hard or soft; and they wanted something that would satisfy their creditors and buy new gowns for their wives, whose raiment was unquestionably the worse for wear. On the other hand, the merchants from Providence, Newport, and Bristol understood the difference between real money and the promissory notes of a bankrupt government, because they had to pay real money to European firms from whom they bought their stocks of goods."

The penalty for not accepting this paper money in payment for goods or debts was a fine of $500 and the loss of suffrage. When a merchant refused to accept the paper the matter came to court, and the Act was declared contrary to the State constitution and hence void. A special session of the legislature dismissed the judges, but their decision remained.

From the beginning, the United States has issued coins — in gold (until 1933) and silver. In 1791, Congress chartered the first United States Bank with the power to issue bank notes; but this paper money was not made legal tender. During the War Between the States, however, Congress did provide for a national paper currency as legal tender in payment of debts.[3]

At first, these new notes (" greenbacks ") could not be redeemed for

coin at the Treasury and their worth fell to less than half their face value on the open market. In 1870, the Supreme Court held the issuance of these notes to be unconstitutional. Said the Court, " to coin " meant to stamp metal and this could not be held to include paper money. But the Court soon reversed itself. In 1871 and 1884 it upheld the issuing of paper money as legal tender as a proper exercise of the congressional powers to coin money and regulate its value, to borrow money on the credit of the United States, and to make war.

Power to Borrow Money. The Constitution gives Congress power to " borrow money on the credit of the

---

[3] Congress soon found that this paper money was being interfered with by notes issued by State-chartered private banks. When Congress placed a tax of ten per cent on the issuance of private bank notes, the latter soon disappeared from circulation.

POWER TO MAKE MONEY

Employees of the Bureau of Engraving and Printing carefully examine currency before it is placed in circulation. The life of the average dollar bill is only about a year.

Harris & Ewing

United States." When there are unusual undertakings, like the Panama Canal, World Wars, or relief for unemployed, the usual revenues are not adequate and Congress borrows. There is no constitutional limit on the amount the Government may borrow, but the current ceiling placed by Congress is $280,000,000,000. At the start of fiscal year 1958 the debt stood at $270,527,171,896.

The most common method of governmental borrowing is through the sale of bonds. Bonds used by governments or corporations when they borrow money are like promissory notes (" I.O.U.'s ") given by individuals when they borrow — a promise to pay a certain sum at a specified time.

These government bonds are purchased as investments by individuals, business concerns, and especially by insurance companies and banks. The National Government could borrow all the money it needs from banks — or it could simply print all the money it wants. But to do either of these would mean placing more money in circulation and thus contributing to inflation.

The constitutional right to borrow makes borrowing a federal function; hence federal bonds cannot be taxed by the States. The right to borrow also implies the right to establish national banks to assist the Government in securing loans. It would have been very difficult to finance World War II had not the banks bought most of the bonds.

Bankruptcy. Congress has power to pass " uniform laws on the subject

PROMISE TO PAY

Strong governments can raise needed money by borrowing from the citizens. Bonds are the most common method used for governmental borrowing. United States Savings Bonds are considered by many to be the finest investment that a person could make. Recently the interest rates were changed to make these bonds a more attractive investment.

Printed by special permission, Chief, U.S. Secret Service, Treasury Department. Further reproduction, in whole or in part, is strictly prohibited.

Unit II. LEGISLATIVE POWERS

of bankruptcies throughout the United States." Bankruptcy is a legal proceeding for the distribution of a debtor's assets among his creditors when he is unable to pay his bills in full. When a person has been declared a bankrupt he is no longer legally responsible for any debts made before his bankruptcy.

The National Government and the States both have power in the field of bankruptcy. It is, then, a concurrent power. Except for three brief periods, Congress left the matter entirely under State control for more than a hundred years. But, in 1898, Congress passed a general bankruptcy law and today the law on the subject is so all-inclusive as practically to exclude the States from the field.

Bankruptcy proceedings are usually handled by the United States District Court in the district in which the bankrupt lives. The court generally appoints an officer (referee) to handle the details of the case. The referee investigates and advises the judge. After a hearing, the judge either declares the person a bankrupt or dismisses the case.

Today, any individual or corporation, except railroads, banks, building and loan associations, insurance companies, and cities, may voluntarily begin bankruptcy proceedings. Creditors may begin proceedings against any individual or corporation, except those just listed, and wage earners.

Depending on State law, a bankrupt is allowed to keep certain kinds of property, such as tools or land, so that he can support himself and his family. In some instances, it is possible for one to be declared a " debtor " and have his debts adjusted downward without actually becoming a bankrupt.

Naturalization. Naturalization is the process by which citizens of one country become citizens of another, and Congress has the power " to establish a uniform rule of naturalization." Under our immigration laws certain persons are not allowed to enter the United States and naturally such persons are not permitted to become naturalized citizens. The whole subject of citizenship is treated later in Chapter 13, pages 246–54.

Postal Service. Congress has power to establish post offices and post roads. Post roads are all letter carrier routes including railroads and the waters of the United States during the time that mail is carried thereon.

The postal service is a monopoly. No State may establish one nor may an individual. Thus express companies cannot make a business of carrying first class mail. Congress has established some 37,500 post offices, most of them in buildings leased from private owners. These offices conduct a more than $2,000,000,000-a-year business. The 500,000 postal workers handle some 60,000,000,000 pieces of mail each year.

Under its power to establish post roads, Congress has made it a federal crime to obstruct the passage of the mails " knowingly and willfully."

Thus, if someone were purposely to wreck a train carrying mail, he would have committed a federal as well as a State offense. After the great Pullman strike in Chicago in 1894, Eugene V. Debs was sent to the federal penitentiary because he persuaded the strikers not to move the trains.

States cannot interfere unreasonably with the mails. For example, they cannot require trains carrying mail to make an unreasonable number of stops; nor can they require a license for cars owned by the United States nor tax gasoline used in mail trucks. But those who contract to carry mail can be taxed.

No person can use the mails to commit a federal or State crime. And articles which are banned by a State's laws, like whiskey or firecrackers, cannot be sent into a State through the mails. Such things as obscene literature and lottery tickets cannot be mailed.

Copyrights and Patents. Congress is given the power " to promote the progress of science and of useful arts, by securing for limited times to authors and inventors the exclusive right to their respective writings and discoveries."

A *copyright* is the exclusive right of an author or his assignee to print and publish his literary or artistic work. The copyright laws, administered by the Copyright Office in the Library of Congress, guarantee an author or an artist the exclusive right to publish, sell, or reproduce his work for a twenty-eight-year period. This protection is renewable for an additional twenty-eight years. A copyright covers all products of literary and artistic efforts like books, magazine articles, musical compositions, photographs, paintings, maps, cartoons, and motion pictures.

If an author's copyright is infringed upon by another person, he may sue for damages in the federal courts. We have several treaties with foreign nations extending the protection of the copyright laws to their citizens and, in return, they do the same for us.

A *patent* is a grant of the exclusive right to manufacture, use, or sell " any new and useful art, machine, manufacture, or composition of matter, or any new and useful improvement thereof." A patent is good for a varying period of years — seventeen on a patent of invention. The term of a patent may be extended only by a special act of Congress. We have patent agreements with several foreign states. The Patent Office is in the Department of Commerce.

Weights and Measures. Congress has established the pound, gallon, bushel, yard, and their subdivisions as standards of weights and measures, and has made the metric system optional. The basic standards of these measures, by which all other measures throughout the United States are tested and corrected, are deposited in the Bureau of Standards in Washington, D.C.

In 1901 Congress established the Bureau of Standards, which has become a wonderful laboratory. It determines the measures for our groceries, the specifications of the doctor's thermometer, and the strength of concrete and steel. It can accurately weigh the penciled crossing of a " t " on a sheet of paper, and it tests and corrects surveyors' instruments. It has developed a clock verified from star observations, and can send an electric impulse each second by wire to any laboratory for research time precision. It now has an atomic clock.

The Bureau does not act as an agency of compulsion, but of service. For instance, it encourages the standardization of such things as bolts that will fit machines of all makes, and of different sizes of bed springs and mattresses to make them fit the corresponding beds.

Power over Federal Territories and Other Areas. Congress has power to acquire, govern, and dispose of various federal areas. The importance of this power can be seen in the fact that it includes a good deal more than such areas as the District of Columbia and possessions outside the United States such as Hawaii, Alaska, and Puerto Rico. It also includes hundreds of military and naval stations, forts, arsenals, dockyards, post offices, parks and forest preserves, prisons, hospitals, asylums, agricultural experiment stations, and other holdings throughout the country.

The National Government may acquire property by *eminent domain.* The power of eminent domain is the power a government exercises when

National Bureau of Standards

ATOMIC CLOCK

An ordinary clock connected to this instrument would vary no more than one second in three hundred years. This is the most precise instrument for measuring time known to man.

it takes private property for public use. Of course, the owner must be paid a fair price for his property.

Territory may also be acquired from a foreign state as the result of the power to admit new States, the war powers, and the President's treaty-making power. Under international law, any sovereign state may acquire unclaimed territory by discovery.

Judicial Powers. Congress has the power to create all federal courts below the Supreme Court and to provide for the organization and composition of the federal judiciary. Congress also has the power to define and provide for the punishment of federal crimes. And, as we know, it may impeach any civil officer of the United States.

Powers over Foreign Relations. The National Government has greater power in the field of international relations than in any other field. Here Congress shares its powers with the President, who is primarily responsible for the conduct of our foreign relations. The States are not sovereign and are, hence, unrecognized in international law; and the Constitution forbids them to participate.

Authority for the powers over foreign relations arises from two sources. *First,* from the delegated powers which include the power to make treaties, to regulate foreign commerce, to send and receive diplomatic representatives, and to define and punish piracy and other crimes committed on the high seas and offenses against the law of nations. The war powers and the power to acquire and govern territories are also the basis for action in the field of international relations.

Second, power to act in this field arises from the fact that the United States is a sovereign member of the world community. As such, it has the authority to deal with matters which affect the interests of the United States.

War Powers. Several of the powers provided for in Article I, Section 8, deal exclusively with war and national defense. Although the President is Commander-in-Chief of the armed forces, Congress has power to declare war, to grant letters of marque and reprisal,[4] to make rules concerning captures on land and water, to raise and support armies, to provide and maintain a navy, to make rules governing the land and naval forces, to provide for calling out the militia, and to provide for organizing, arming, and disciplining the militia.

Congress cannot appropriate money for " armies " for longer than a two-year period. This does not apply to the Navy, but is intended to ensure that the Army will always be subordinate to the civil authorities.

IMPLIED POWERS

The " Necessary and Proper " Clause. Thus far we have considered the expressed powers of Congress, most of which are found in Article I, Section 8, Clauses 1–17. Clause 18, is the so-called " necessary and proper " or " elastic " clause:

The Congress shall have power . . . To make all laws which shall be necessary and proper for carrying into execution the

foregoing powers, and all other powers vested by this Constitution in the government of the United States, or in any department or officer thereof.

The amazing vitality and adaptability of the Constitution can be traced

---

[4] These are commissions authorizing private citizens to fit out vessels to capture or destroy in time of war. They are forbidden by the Declaration of Paris, 1856, of which the United States is a signatory.

to this clause and the Supreme Court's interpretation of it. Indeed, the implied or " necessary and proper " powers that Congress exercises today are far more extensive than the expressed powers.

Liberal v. Strict Construction. The Constitution had barely come into force when the meaning of Clause 18 became the subject of one of the most famous and important disputes in American political history. Thomas Jefferson and the strict-constructionists were ranged against Alexander Hamilton and the liberal-constructionists. The central issue: Was the Constitution to be so construed that Congress could exercise only those powers *expressly* stated in so many words in that document; or could Congress exercise additional powers which could be reasonably *implied* as necessary and proper?

The dispute came to a head almost immediately. Hamilton, as Secretary of the Treasury, proposed in 1790 that Congress create a Bank of the United States. The Jeffersonians stoutly opposed the plan, saying that the Constitution gave Congress no power which would allow the creation of such a bank. The Hamiltonians replied that such a step was necessary and proper to the execution of such powers as those to borrow, to coin money and regulate its value, and to tax.

This the Jeffersonians refuted by claiming that such reasoning would give the National Government almost unlimited powers and practically destroy the States' reserved powers.[5]

Logic and practical necessity won the dispute for Hamilton and the liberal-constructionists. In 1791 Congress chartered the First Bank of the United States. The Bank's charter expired in 1811 with the Bank's constitutionality and the basis upon which it was created (the implied powers doctrine) unchallenged in the courts.

McCulloch v. Maryland. In 1816 Congress issued a charter to the Second Bank of the United States. This action was taken only after another struggle over the extent of the powers of Congress.

Several States attempted to limit the new Bank's authority in various ways. In 1818 Maryland imposed a tax upon all notes issued by any bank doing business in that State but not chartered by the State legislature. This tax was aimed directly at the Bank's branch in Baltimore. McCulloch, the Bank's cashier, purposely issued notes on which no tax had

---

[5] When, in 1800, a bill was introduced in Congress to incorporate a company to mine copper, Jefferson, as Vice-President, ridiculed the proposal with this sarcastic comment: " Congress is authorized to defend the nation. Ships are necessary for defense; copper is necessary for ships; mines necessary for copper; a company necessary to work the mines; and who can doubt this reasoning who has ever played at ' This Is the House That Jack Built '? "

While Jefferson himself was President (1801–1809), he and his party were many times forced to reverse their earlier position. For example, it was only on the basis of the implied powers doctrine that the Louisiana Purchase in 1803 and the embargo on foreign trade in 1807 could be justified.

Chief Justice Marshall delivered one of the Court's most important and far-reaching decisions in this case. Here, for the first time, the Court was squarely faced with the thirty-year-old question of the constitutionality of the implied powers doctrine.

The Court upheld the constitutionality of the Bank as a necessary and proper step in the execution of such expressed powers as to borrow, to coin and regulate the value of money, and to tax. But, far more important, the Court thereby upheld the doctrine of implied powers. The decision is so important that we quote its central passage:

JOHN MARSHALL

As a constitutional lawyer, Marshall stands without a rival. In his court opinions, the great Chief Justice set the pattern for the development of our strong constitutional system.

been paid in order to challenge the Maryland law. Maryland brought suit to collect the tax and the United States, in McCulloch's behalf, then carried the case to the Supreme Court in 1819.

Maryland based its case on the argument that Congress had no constitutional authority to incorporate a bank. The United States, represented by such able men as the great Daniel Webster, defended the doctrine of implied powers and further argued that Maryland had no right to tax an instrumentality of the United States.

We admit, as all must admit, that the powers of the Government are limited, and its limits are not to be transcended. But we think the sound construction of the Constitution must allow to the national legislature that discretion, with respect to the means by which the powers it confers are to be carried into execution, which will enable that body to perform the high duties assigned to it, in the manner most beneficial to the people. Let the end be legitimate, let it be within the scope of the Constitution, and all means which are appropriate, which are plainly adapted to that end, which are not prohibited, but consistent with the letter and spirit of the Constitution, are constitutional.[6]

---

[6] The decision also invalidated the Maryland tax law. Because the power to tax involves the power to destroy (tax out of existence), said the Court, Maryland could not be permitted to tax the United States. The problem of intergovernmental taxation is treated later.

This broad interpretation of the powers granted to Congress has become firmly fixed in our constitutional system. Indeed, it is difficult to see how our nation could have developed as it has under the Constitution without it.

Examples of Implied Powers. There are literally thousands of examples of the use of the doctrine of implied powers. Decisions of the Supreme Court and the way in which Congress has regarded and used its powers have made Article I, Section 8, Clause 18, truly the " elastic clause." Today the words " necessary and proper " really read " convenient and useful," especially when applied to the power to regulate commerce and to tax.

The original Constitution gave the National Government the express power to punish only four specific crimes — counterfeiting, felonies committed on the high seas, offenses against the law of nations, and treason. But many other laws which Congress has the express power to enact, as for example tax laws, would be worthless

if it were not a crime to break them. Therefore, Congress has the *implied* right to define and provide the punishment for all offenses against the United States.

The Constitution does not expressly provide for river and harbor improvements, but the power is *implied* from the expressed powers to regulate commerce and maintain a navy.

The words *Air Force* do not appear in the Constitution, but should anyone ever question the constitutionality of its existence, the courts could imply it from the right to raise armies.

The power of eminent domain is not expressly granted in the Constitution. But the Congress has the expressed power to establish post offices and to create courts. Therefore, the United States can condemn land for post office and courthouse sites.

Such a list as this could go on and on. It is plain that the idea of implied powers is an important and essential part of our governmental system. *But, remember,* the basis for *any* implied power must *always* be found among the expressed powers.

WHAT THIS CHAPTER IS ABOUT

Congress may exercise only those powers (1) *expressly* granted to it in the Constitution, and (2) those that may be reasonably *implied* from the expressed powers.

Early in our history the question of whether the powers granted to the National Government were to be strictly or liberally interpreted became an issue. It

was finally resolved in the great Supreme Court decision in *McCulloch* v. *Maryland* (1819). The Court ruled that the powers were to be liberally construed, thus upholding the doctrine of implied powers. It is difficult to see how the United States could have developed as it has under the Constitution without the idea of implied powers.

THE POWERS VESTED IN CONGRESS
by Article I, Section 8
EXPRESSED POWERS

I. PEACE POWERS:

1. To lay taxes.
   a. Direct (not used since the War Between the States, except income tax).
   b. Indirect.
      Customs = Tariff
      Excises = Internal revenue.
2. To borrow money.
3. To regulate foreign and interstate commerce.
4. To establish naturalization and bankruptcy laws.
5. To coin money and regulate its value; to regulate weights and measures.
6. To punish counterfeiters of federal money and securities.
7. To establish post offices and post roads.
8. To grant patents and copyrights.
9. To create courts inferior to the Supreme Court.
10. To define and punish piracies and felonies on the high seas; to define and punish offenses against the law of nations.
11. To exercise exclusive jurisdiction over the District of Columbia; to exercise exclusive jurisdiction over forts, dockyards, national parks, federal buildings, etc.

II. WAR POWERS:

12. To declare war; to grant letters of marque and reprisal; to make rules concerning captures on land and water.
13. To raise and support armies.
14. To provide and maintain a navy.
15. To make laws governing land and naval forces.
16. To provide for calling forth the militia to execute federal laws, suppress insurrections, and repel invasions.
17. To provide for organizing, arming, and disciplining the militia, and for governing it when in the service of the Union.

IMPLIED POWERS

18. To make all laws necessary and proper for carrying into execution the foregoing powers.
    For example — To punish the breaking of federal law.
    To establish national banks.
    To improve rivers, harbors, and canals.
    To condemn property by eminent domain.

QUESTIONS ON THE TEXT

1. Where in the Constitution are most of the expressed powers to be found?

2. Upon what clause is the theory of *implied* powers based?

3. What was the nature of the dispute between the liberal- and the strict-constructionists? Who were the leaders on each side?

4. What are the two most important expressed powers of Congress?

5. Why was Congress given the exclusive power to coin money?

6. What experience did Rhode Island have with paper money in the 1780's? How did Congress get its right to issue paper money?

7. What is meant by *bankruptcy?*

Naturalization? What are post roads? How may the United States acquire sites for post offices?

8. What is a copyright? A patent? What is the Bureau of Standards?

9. What powers do Congress have in the field of foreign relations? What are its war powers? Why are they so important?

10. Under what authority may Congress acquire and govern territory? Does the United States own much territory? Illustrate.

11. What is meant by *implied powers?* Give examples. Give the facts in the case in which the Court upheld the doctrine of implied powers.

PROBLEMS FOR DISCUSSION

1. Britain has no written constitution and Parliament may enact any law it believes is necessary. Why has Congress only those powers enumerated in the Constitution plus those necessary and proper to carry the enumerated powers into execution?

2. Would commercial progress in the United States be promoted if each of the States had its own monetary system? Weights and measures?

3. A century ago in Pennsylvania it was found that the annual cost of keeping debtors in prison was more than the total debts they owed. Which is the more just, debtors' prisons or bankruptcy? Why?

4. In his decision in *McCulloch* v. *Maryland,* Chief Justice Marshall wrote that " the power to tax involves the power to destroy." What did he mean by this?

5. Why must the source for each and every exercise of an implied power be found in an expressed power? Has this anything to do with the doctrine of limited government?

THINGS YOU MIGHT DO

1. Explain why Congress was given each of the expressed powers it possesses. Each of the powers might be the subject of a short class report.

2. One student might prepare a short biography of John Marshall. Another student might write a short paper on the extent of implied powers today.

3. If Congress is in session, discover from the newspapers what laws have been passed in the current session and what bills are now being considered. How many of these are examples of expressed and how many of implied powers? Of the latter, from what expressed powers are they implied?

WORDS AND PHRASES YOU SHOULD KNOW

Bankruptcy	Implied powers	*McCulloch* v. *Maryland*
Copyright	Legal tender	Naturalization
Counterfeit	Letters of marque and	Patent
Eminent domain	reprisal	Post roads
Expressed powers	Liberal construction	Strict construction

SELECT BIBLIOGRAPHY

BARTHOLOMEW, PAUL C., *American Government under the Constitution*, Chapter 5. Brown, 1954.

CORWIN, EDWARD S., *The Constitution and What It Means Today*, Pages 3–87. Princeton, 1954.

FERGUSON, JOHN H., and McHENRY, DEAN E., *The American System of Government*, Chapters 19, 25–31. McGraw-Hill, 1956.

GALLOWAY, GEORGE B., *The Legislative Process in Congress*, Chapters 1, 2. Crowell, 1953.

KELLY, ALFRED H., and HARBISON, WINFRED A., *The American Constitution*. Norton, 1955.

Taxes are what we pay for civilized society.
— *Justice Oliver Wendell Holmes*

★

Chapter 7

THE TAXING POWER

The power to tax is absolutely necessary to the existence of government. It must have the power to raise the revenues with which to support its functions. The Supreme Court once said:

The power to tax is the one great power upon which the whole national fabric is based. It is as necessary to the existence of a nation as is the air he breathes to a natural man.

We have already seen that the lack of an adequate taxing power was one of the fatal weaknesses of the Articles of Confederation. Some idea of the importance of the power can be seen in the fact that it heads the list of the powers granted to Congress in the Constitution.

Article I, Section 8, Clause 1, provides:

The Congress shall have power to lay and collect taxes, duties, imposts, and excises, to pay the debts and provide for the common defense and the general welfare of the United States; but all duties, imposts, and excises shall be uniform throughout the United States.

The power to tax is almost absolute. However, as the chart on the next page shows, the Constitution does impose four *expressed* and two *implied* limitations.

Taxes Must Be for Public Purposes. According to the Constitution, taxes may be levied only " to pay the debts and provide for the common defense and general welfare of the United States." This means that taxes may be used only for *public* purposes, not private benefit. Thus one of the reasons the Supreme Court invalidated the first Agricultural Adjustment Act in 1936 was because the proceeds from processing taxes under the Act were earmarked to benefit farmers who agreed to reduce production. The Court held that one group was being taxed to benefit another and, hence, that the tax was invalid as not levied for a public purpose.

What is meant by " public purposes " is something for Congress and the Court to decide. The power to tax (*i.e.*, to raise money for public purposes) is much broader than the other congressional powers. For example, Congress has no power to establish colleges across the country, but it does give federal money to the States for the support of land-grant colleges.

The Congress shall have power to lay and collect taxes, duties, imposts, and excises, to pay the debts and provide for the common defense and general welfare of the United States. — *Article I, Section 8, Clause 1.*

Taxing Power of Congress Subject to Six Limitations

Four Expressed Limitations

1. Taxes must be " to pay the debts and provide for the common defense or the general welfare." [1]
2. No taxes may be laid on exports.
3. Direct taxes (except the income tax) [2] must be apportioned among the several States on the basis of population.
   - Head tax
   - Land tax
   - Property tax
4. Indirect taxes must be uniform throughout the United States.
   - Excise tax
   - Tariffs
   - Estate tax
   - Corporation tax

Two Implied Limitations

1. The National Government may not tax the instrumentalities of States or their subdivisions — cities, counties, districts. [3]
2. Congress *may* be denied the power to tax purely for the purpose of social regulation, if the tax act clearly shows on its face that it is not intended for the purpose of raising revenue. [4]

Export Taxes Are Prohibited. The reason for the Constitutional prohibition against the export tax is plain. American farmers did not want to be handicapped in competing with farmers of other countries. For instance, suppose Congress could levy an export tax of five cents a pound on cotton.

The English cotton buyers would pay no more to American cotton growers than to growers in other countries. So, in order to compete, the American grower would have to pay the tax.

[1] The Supreme Court has held that Congress has very extensive discretion, however, in determining what expenditures are for the " general welfare."

[2] The 16th Amendment gives the National Government the right to tax incomes without apportioning such taxes among the States on the basis of population.

[3] Congress can neither tax real estate belonging to a State or its subdivision, nor State or city bonds or the income therefrom.

[4] Thus, in 1922, the Supreme Court held unconstitutional a 10% tax on the profits of concerns employing child labor and a special tax on liquor dealers operating in violation of State law. But, in 1904, it upheld a prohibitive tax on colored oleomargarine (repealed in 1950); on traffic in narcotics (1919); on the sale of sawed-off shotguns (1937); on professional gambling (1953).

Unit II. LEGISLATIVE POWERS

Equal Apportionment of Direct Taxes. Those taxes which are actually borne by the person upon whom they are imposed, such as capitation (poll) taxes and taxes on land and buildings, are *direct* taxes. This provision means, for example, that a tax which raised $1,000,000,000 would have to produce approximately $100,000,000 from New York and $10,000,000 from Oregon. This is so because New York has about 10 per cent and Oregon about one per cent of the total national population.

Since wealth is not evenly distributed among the States a direct tax levied in proportion to population would be unjust to the people in certain States. Except for an income tax, Congress has not levied a direct tax outside the District of Columbia since the War Between the States.

Federal Income Tax. This is a direct tax permitted by the 16th Amendment regardless of population. Congress varies the rates according to the needs of the government. The tax has always been " progressive "; that is, the higher one's net income, the higher the rate.

The tax on individual incomes is the largest single source of federal revenue today. The first year's take under the 16th Amendment came to only $28,000,000. Under the current 1958 rates, the tax brings in nearly $40,000,000,000. Federal taxes are close to the highest level in our peacetime history. Commenting on high taxes, Congressman Doughton of North Carolina once said: " You can

shear a sheep once a year; you can skin him only once." [5]

The income tax rates effective in 1958 vary from about twenty per cent on the first $2000 of taxable income to about ninety per cent on all over $200,000. Payment is made on " taxable income " — that is, total income minus certain exemptions and deductions.

A tax exemption of $600 is allowed for each dependent, including the taxpayer himself. Thus, a man with a wife and two children has dependency exemptions totalling $2400. An exemption can be taken for any person who lives with the taxpayer and receives at least half of his support from him. An additional $600 is allowed for each person sixty-five or older or blind.

Deductions are permitted for many things. For example: business expenses, interest on debts, most State and local taxes, medical expenses above three per cent of taxable income, charitable contributions up to 30 per cent, up to $600 for working wives or widows who must hire baby sitters, etc.

By April 15 everyone who earns $600 or more must file a tax return; husbands and wives may file a joint re-

---

[5] Many economists claim that taxes are a *deflationary* influence (draining off " excess purchasing power ") up to the rate of 25 per cent of the national income. Beyond that, it is held, they become *inflationary*, especially if taxes do not fully cover governmental spending. Federal, State, and local taxes today take some 30 per cent of the national income.

Courtesy " U.S. News & World Report "

LAST–MINUTE RETURNS

Each year many thousands of people crowd the offices of the Internal Revenue Service. These government workers help the taxpayer to complete his tax return before the legal deadline, now April 15.

turn. It is sent to the nearest Director of Internal Revenue. Two kinds of income tax returns are now used: Form 1040 and Form 1040A.

Form 1040A is a small card the size of a bank check. It is designed for anyone with less than $5000 income from wages or salary and who has no other income over $100. On it, the taxpayer enters his total income and dependency exemptions, plus any tax already " withheld." High-speed machines process the return, allowing a standard deduction of ten per cent for such things as State taxes paid, interest, etc. He sends no money with his return. Once the machines figure his tax he receives a bill for taxes owed or a refund for overpayment.

Form 1040 is longer and more com-plicated. It *must* be used by anyone with over $5000 income or over $100 from any source other than wages or salary. On this form a person figures his own tax. He lists his income, subtracts his dependents and deductions and finds the tax due in a table which accompanies the form. If he chooses, he can take a standard ten per cent deduction, but it usually pays him to itemize his deductions (as it sometimes also does the taxpayer with less than $5000 in annual income).

Under the " pay-as-you-go " plan, the law requires each employer to withhold a certain amount from each employee's paycheck. The employer sends this withholding tax to the Treasury where it is credited to the taxpayer's account. Because most people receive their income from salaries or wages, this arrangement means that the tax blow falls a little easier; the total tax is not due in one large payment, but has been paid in several smaller ones.

A single person with an income over $5000 — or a married couple with over $10,000 — must make an annual estimate of income for the coming year and pay the tax in quarterly installments beginning April 15. A special allowance is made for farmers: they are allowed to file an estimate and pay their taxes after the year is over, after having had time to harvest and market their crops.

Income Tax on Corporations. A corporation organized for profit is a company owned by stockholders; and all earned above the expenses of the business is taxable. On this income the progressive tax runs as high as fifty-two per cent on all earnings above $25,000.

Nonprofit organizations, such as churches, colleges, lodges, co-operatives, and labor unions, are exempted from the income tax. The corporation income tax produces over $20,000,-000,000 in revenue each year.

Enforcement of the Tax Laws. The overwhelming number of taxpayers are honest, of course. Some people quite honestly under-figure their taxes; but others often over-figure them, too.

The Treasury has a " conscience fund " into which goes all the money — several thousand a year — that people send to ease their consciences

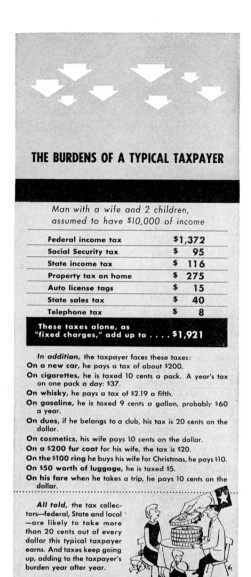

THE BURDENS OF A TYPICAL TAXPAYER

Man with a wife and 2 children, assumed to have $10,000 of income

Federal income tax	$1,372
Social Security tax	$ 95
State income tax	$ 116
Property tax on home	$ 275
Auto license tags	$ 15
State sales tax	$ 40
Telephone tax	$ 8

These taxes alone, as "fixed charges," add up to $1,921

In addition, the taxpayer faces these taxes:
On a new car, he pays a tax of about $200.
On cigarettes, he is taxed 10 cents a pack. A year's tax on one pack a day: $37.
On whisky, he pays a tax of $2.19 a fifth.
On gasoline, he is taxed 9 cents a gallon, probably $60 a year.
On dues, if he belongs to a club, his tax is 20 cents on the dollar.
On cosmetics, his wife pays 10 cents on the dollar.
On a $200 fur coat for his wife, the tax is $20.
On the $100 ring he buys his wife for Christmas, he pays $10.
On $50 worth of luggage, he is taxed $5.
On his fare when he takes a trip, he pays 10 cents on the dollar.

All told, the tax collectors—federal, State and local —are likely to take more than 20 cents out of every dollar this typical taxpayer earns. And taxes keep going up, adding to the taxpayer's burden year after year.

NOTE: State and local taxes used in the figures above are based on rates that apply in Montgomery County, Md., which is taken as a fairly typical area.

Reprinted from "U.S. News & World Report," an independent weekly news magazine published at Washington. Copyright 1957 United States News Publishing Company.

THE INDIVIDUAL TAX BURDEN

Taxes are an individual's way of contributing to the maintenance of government. Some of these taxes are apparent; others are hidden and included in the price of a purchase.

over past "mistakes." Not long ago, a retired businessman sent in $5000 *just in case* he had made any mistakes through the years. After checking his returns, the Internal Revenue Service not only returned his $5000 but $17,000 besides for overpayments he had made in the past.

But there are always a few chiselers and the law provides for them. Those who intentionally fail to report part or all of their taxable income may be fined up to $10,000, imprisoned for as long as five years, charged a penalty of fifty per cent of the amount not re-ported, or all three. Honest mistakes are excused if not found within three years. But the Government has six years in which to catch and prosecute those who make a false return or none at all. Whenever fraud is involved, additional taxes may be collected at any time, even when an estate is being settled after death. Income tax evasion charges have sent many known criminals to federal prison when State and local police have been unable to gather enough evidence to convict them of their other crimes.

The files of the Internal Revenue Service are filled with cases of tax-cheating. A woman in Alabama claimed her mule "William" as a dependent for three years before agents caught her. A man in California claimed nine children on five annual returns; actually he had none.

One agent heard a man voicing some especially low opinions of income tax laws and decided to check the man's returns. He had never filed any. In the end he paid $76,000 in penalty and interest.

Indirect Taxes Must Be Uniform Throughout the United States. Indirect taxes are those that, although paid by one person, are actually passed on to another and are therefore *indirectly* paid by the second person. For example, the excise tax on cigarettes is paid by the producer; he passes it on to the wholesaler and distributor who in turn pass it on to the retailer. The retailer includes it in the price he charges for the cigarettes and so the consumer actually pays the tax. Cus-

VICIOUS CIRCLE

When John Q. Citizen spends his money without regard to real values, the cost of what he buys goes up and inflation results.

TASTY IMPORT

South American workers load bags of coffee bound for American tables. Since the United States does not grow coffee, we allow it to be shipped in free of duty.

toms are another good example. They are paid by the importer but ultimately are passed on to the purchaser.

The constitutional requirement that indirect taxes must be uniform throughout the United States means that these taxes must be the same on the same commodities in all parts of the country. Thus the federal excise tax on the manufacture of tobacco, playing cards, or alcoholic beverages must be the same in New York as it is in New Mexico. The import duty on cut diamonds, which is now 10 per cent *ad valorem* (of their value), must be the same at the port of New York as it is at the port of New Orleans.

Excises, popularly known as internal revenue duties, are taxes on com-

modities produced or services performed in the United States. The producer pays the tax, but usually passes it on to the consumer. As evidence of payment a revenue stamp is placed on such commodities as cigarettes, playing cards, and alcoholic drinks. The Federal Government taxes many nonessentials, but not food, housing, or basic clothes.

Customs, popularly known as tariff duties, are taxes on commodities imported from foreign countries. The most recent tariff act is that of 1930, but it has been amended frequently. The rates vary on different articles, now being as high as 80 per cent on some. Articles entering the United States without tariff are said to be on the " free list " — *e.g.,* Bibles, raw

CUSTOMS INSPECTION

Americans returning from abroad have their baggage looked over. The knowledge of routine check-ups stops many persons from trying to evade the legal duties on certain goods.

silk, coffee, bananas, and agricultural implements. All articles imported solely for display at the International Trade Fairs held periodically in various parts of the United States are permitted to enter the country duty free. Articles taxed at a low rate are said to be taxed " for revenue only " — *e.g.*, diamonds, chamois skins, and raw hair. Articles taxed at a high rate are said to be taxed " for protection " — *e.g.*, sugar at $\frac{1}{2}$ cent a pound, tomatoes at $1\frac{1}{2}$ cents a pound, beef at 3 cents a pound, eggs at $3\frac{1}{2}$ cents a dozen, wool at from 11 to 28 cents a pound, wheat

at 21 cents a bushel, shoes at 20 per cent of their value, silk at 25 per cent, articles of knit rayon at 25 cents per pound plus 65 per cent of their value, and jewelry at 30 to 55 per cent.

The tax is often so high that certain articles are not shipped into this country at all. Then, of course, no revenue is collected, but the manufacturer of the articles in this country can charge more for these articles than otherwise, since foreign competition is removed. The tax is " for protection " to home industry.

Free Foreign Trade Zones may be established by cities, where importers can hold imports for reshipment to foreign countries without the payment of tariff to the United States Government.

A United States resident returning from a short trip abroad is allowed to bring home duty free $200 worth of goods for personal or household use once within 31 days; or $500 on 12-day trips once in six months. Only one gallon of an alcoholic beverage and 100 cigars are exempt.

The *United States Tariff Commission* [6] was created in 1916 to investigate the difference in cost of production here and abroad so as to determine the effects of the customs laws of the United States on industry. This information was supposed to prevent the log-rolling method of framing tariff laws; but when the last general tariff

---

[6] The Commission is composed of six members appointed by the President and Senate. Not more than three of the six may be of the same political party.

law was enacted in 1930 the old methods of log-rolling were not greatly modified. However, the information collected by the Commission is of value to Congress, to the President, and during time of war to the various war agencies.

The *estate (inheritance) tax*[7] varies from 5 per cent on a net estate not exceeding $5000 to 77 per cent on that portion of a net estate in excess of $10,000,000. " Net estate " means what remains after the payment of debts, bequests to governmental, religious, charitable, and educational institutions, the cost of settling the estate, and an exemption of $60,000. The exemption does not apply if the deceased was not a resident or citizen of the United States at death.[8]

If a husband leaves an estate to his wife, or vice versa, the tax is levied on only half of the estate's net value. But when the survivor dies the tax applies to all of the original estate left by the deceased.

An estate or inheritance tax (or both) is usually paid to a State. A partial credit for this is allowed on the federal estate tax. The Supreme Court calls the estate tax an indirect tax — on the *privilege* of bequesting.

---

[7] The tax upon the estate of one who dies might be levied upon the entire net estate before it is divided, and that is an " estate tax "; or the tax might be levied upon the portion inherited by each heir, and that is an " inheritance tax." The present federal tax is an *estate tax*. Most States have *inheritance taxes*. Some States have both taxes.

[8] If a nonresident alien dies owning property in the United States, the exemption allowed is only $2000.

A *gift tax* (about three-fourths as high as the estate tax) is also collected. It prevents a person from evading the estate tax by making gifts before death. Gifts to governmental, religious, charitable, and educational institutions are not taxed. Gifts within the year to any one individual amounting to not more than $3000 and gifts to all individuals taken together of not more than $30,000 are exempt.

When a husband or wife makes a gift to the other, the gift tax applies to only one half of the value of the gift because only one half is considered as coming from the giver. The other half is considered as already belonging to the spouse.

Social security taxes, collected under the social security system, now provide more than $7,000,000,000 a year in federal revenue. Old-age and survivors insurance is financed by a $2\frac{1}{4}$ per cent tax on an employee's wages (up to $4200 a year) and an identical tax on the employer's payroll. The employer deducts the tax from the employee's paycheck and sends the combined $4\frac{1}{2}$ per cent tax to the Treasury. Self-employed persons pay a $3\frac{3}{8}$ per cent tax on their first $4200 of income.

State unemployment insurance programs are financed in part from federal grants which are financed by a 3 per cent tax on the payrolls of businesses with four or more employees.

These payroll taxes all go into the general Treasury, and Congress appropriates money as it is needed under the social security system.

Congress Does Not Tax the Instrumentalities of States unless Engaged in Nongovernmental Functions. Because the power to tax is the power to destroy, the Supreme Court forbade the United States to tax the real estate, bonds, or other governmental machinery of the States, counties, districts, cities, or towns; and likewise forbade the States and local governments to tax the United States.

However, the Federal Government may tax State activities of a nongovernmental character, that is, activities which are not necessarily or ordinarily engaged in by a State or its subdivisions. Such activities are considered in competition with private businesses. For example, in 1893 South Carolina set up a liquor monopoly selling liquor at government dispensaries and claiming exemption from the federal saloon license tax. But the United States Supreme Court required the State to pay the tax for each dispensary because the sale of liquor is not a necessary or usual governmental activity.[9]

Congress May Sometimes Exercise the Right to Tax Merely for the Purpose of Regulation. During the War Between the States Congress established a National banking system, and desired to get rid of paper money issued by State banks. So it imposed an annual tax of 10 per cent on the circulation of such money, a rate so high as to drive it out of circulation.[10]

In 1902 Congress levied a tax of ten cents a pound on oleomargarine artificially colored to look like butter. When the manufacturers of oleomargarine protested that it was not a tax but was practically destroying an industry over which Congress did not constitutionally have control, the Supreme Court upheld the constitutionality of the law. The Court refused to go into the motives behind the law, but upheld it as a valid exercise of the taxing power. (The tax was repealed in 1950.)

The white or yellow phosphorous used in the manufacture of the old-fashioned match is very poisonous. Workmen in match factories often had their teeth fall out or their jawbones decay. Many died from the poison. Matches made from other materials were a little more expensive. The Constitution does not give Congress power to regulate labor conditions directly; therefore, in 1912 Congress imposed a stamp tax of two cents a hundred on matches of white or yellow phosphorous. As matches sold for one cent a hundred, the phosphorous match industry was destroyed.

In 1941 Congress laid a tax of $300

---

[9] It has not as yet been judicially determined whether the States can tax those activities of the Federal Government which may be classed as nongovernmental. See Chapter 31, "State Finance," and the discussion of *McCulloch* v. *Maryland,* pages 107–109.

[10] In upholding the law the Supreme Court said: "Having, in the exercise of undisputed constitutional powers, undertaken to provide a currency for the whole country, it cannot be questioned that Congress may, constitutionally, secure the benefits of it to the people by appropriate legislation."

British Information Services

COMPETING CARS

These British-built automobiles are subject to duty when imported into the United States. Rather than revenue, the main purpose of this tax is to protect American manufacturers from foreign competition.

a pound on the manufacture of opium used for smoking and thus destroyed the industry by taxation.

It looked as though there were no limit on the power of Congress to regulate through taxation those industries which fall under State control and could not otherwise be regulated by Congress. So, in 1919, Congress passed a law imposing a ten-per-cent tax on any person or corporation employing child labor. But this was encroaching too far upon States' rights, and in the Child Labor Case decided in 1922 the Supreme Court said: " Taxes do not lose their character as taxes because of the incidental motive. But there comes a time in the extension of the penalizing feature of the so-called tax when it loses its character as such and becomes a mere penalty with the characteristics of regulation and punishment. Such is the case in the law before us." The Court declared this law unconstitutional.

In 1934 Congress imposed a tax of $200 on the transfer of each sawed-off shotgun. The purpose of the statute is not revenue but a record of criminals who buy such guns. The Court upheld the Act in 1937; and in 1953 it also upheld a $50 stamp tax imposed on gamblers.

High tariff is largely for protection of American industries; high estate taxes are intended to destroy large estates; yet they are legal. In recent years, Congress has used the interstate commerce clause more than its power to tax for regulatory purposes. This practice is discussed more fully in the following chapter.

WHAT THIS CHAPTER IS ABOUT

The power to tax is absolutely necessary to the existence of government. The lack of an adequate taxing power was one of the chief weaknesses of the Articles of Confederation.

Article I, Section 8, Clause 1 of the Constitution gives Congress the power to tax, subject to four expressed and two implied limitations.

The four expressed limitations: (1) Taxes must be levied for a public purpose, not for private benefit. (2) Congress cannot levy any export taxes. (3) Direct taxes, except the income tax, must be apportioned among the States on the basis of population. (4) Indirect taxes must be uniform throughout the United States.

A direct tax is one that is borne directly by the person upon whom it is imposed, for example a head tax. An indirect tax is one that may be shifted to another person.

The income tax is a direct tax provided by the 16th Amendment and need not be levied in proportion to population. It is a progressive tax and produces nearly $40,000,000,000 a year. The tax is laid on total income minus certain deductions and exemptions.

The corporation income tax, levied on corporations organized for profit, produces over $20,000,000,000 a year.

Most taxpayers are honest, but the penalties for dishonesty are stiff. Excises are taxes on goods produced or services performed in the United States. Customs duties are taxes levied on imported goods. The Tariff Commission advises the President and Congress on tariff matters.

An estate tax is levied on the estate of the deceased and a gift tax is levied on expensive gifts made. Social security taxes are levied on employers, employees and the self-employed.

The *two implied limitations* are: (1) Congress may not tax the governmental functions of State and local governments — but it may tax the *non*-governmental (business) functions, like admission tickets or liquor stores. (2) Congress may be denied the power to tax for purposes of social regulation, but it seldom is.

QUESTIONS ON THE TEXT

1. What restrictions are placed upon Congress as to its power of taxation?

2. Why are export taxes prohibited?

3. Does the constitutional requirement that taxes must be for the general welfare really impose much of a restriction upon Congress?

4. Why has not the United States levied any direct tax, except the income tax, since the War Between the States?

5. Why is the income tax, which is direct, constitutional even though it is not apportioned among the States?

6. How much income does a single person have to earn before he is taxed? How much exemption is there for each dependent?

7. What are indirect taxes? What kinds of indirect taxes are there?

8. What is meant by the requirement

that indirect taxes must be uniform throughout the United States?

9. Give examples of the *excise tax*.

10. Why is the federal inheritance tax constitutionally considered an indirect tax? Why is it called an *estate tax?*

11. Name an article that enters the United States free of duty; one on which tariff for revenue is imposed; one on which tariff for protection is imposed.

12. Explain to what extent Congress may tax for the purpose of regulation.

PROBLEMS FOR DISCUSSION

1. The United States pays subsidies to certain American steamship lines running between the United States and countries that otherwise would not have American lines. Is this money spent for the " general welfare "?

2. Are direct taxes or indirect taxes more just? Which are easier to collect?

3. When a high internal revenue tax was placed on tobacco, the people of Virginia, who manufactured large quantities of tobacco, felt that they were being unjustly taxed. The tax has not been reduced, but complaints are no longer heard. Why?

4. Even at today's high rate of taxation, the National Government does not always live within its income. Why? How does the Government secure the additional money necessary to finance its operations? Suggest various ways in which federal expenditures might be reduced. Discuss and evaluate each of these suggestions.

5. In November, 1951, Congress required all professional gamblers to purchase a $50 federal tax stamp or face possible fine and imprisonment. By January, 1952, the Internal Revenue Bureau estimated that 90 per cent of the nation's illegal gambling business had been choked off. (After " the heat was off," many gamblers were back at the same old stand, but with a wary eye peeled for federal agents.) The stamp tax does not provide much in revenue, but is intended as a regulatory measure. In purchasing the tax stamp, gamblers are forced to reveal their illegal operations to State and local police, the general public, and the press. If they do not buy the stamps, they face federal action.

During 1952 the tax was declared unconstitutional by two United States District Courts and upheld in another. The cases were appealed by the Justice Department and, in 1953, the Supreme Court upheld the tax as a proper exercise of the congressional power to tax. If you were on the Supreme Court, how would you have ruled? Explain your answer.

6. The power to tax is a concurrent one enjoyed by both the National and State (and local) Governments. Many items, such as individual and corporation incomes, gasoline, liquor, and tobacco are taxed by the United States and by all or most of the States, too. A steadily increasing number of local governments also tax these items. Approximately 90 per cent of all National and State tax collections come from the same sources. Why have authorities in the field of public finance repeatedly urged the development of a co-ordinated tax policy for the nation? What particular problem does the high rate of federal taxation create for the States?

7. Should Congress be given power to tax State, county, and city bonds? As these bonds are exempt from the federal income tax and from most or all State and

local taxes, they are issued at a very low interest rate. Learn what rate of interest your State, county, or city pays on bonds it has issued in recent years.

8. The University of Georgia and Georgia Institute of Technology claimed that taxing admissions to their football games was in fact taxing the State and hence was unconstitutional. In 1938 the Supreme Court of the United States decided that the taxes can be collected. Why?

THINGS YOU MIGHT DO

1. Secure copies of the latest income tax returns and make them out as though they were actually to be filed. The Internal Revenue Service will supply forms and instruction booklets.

2. If your State has an income tax compare it with the federal tax.

3. Make a list of as many tariffs as you can that directly affect your locale.

Several students might present a panel discussion on the question of higher or lower tariffs.

4. See how many different federal excise taxes you can discover by consulting local automobile dealers, service station operators, grocers, appliance store owners, and various other people in your own community.

WORDS AND PHRASES YOU SHOULD KNOW

Ad valorem	Gift tax	16th Amendment
Customs duties	Income tax	Tariff
Direct tax	Indirect tax	Tariff Commission
Estate tax	Internal Revenue	Taxable income
Excises	Internal Revenue Service	Withholding tax

SELECT BIBLIOGRAPHY

HAWLEY, CAMERON, " Our Tax Laws Make Us Dishonest," *Saturday Evening Post,* July 14, 1956, also *Reader's Digest,* October, 1956.

HEALY, PAUL F., " So You Hate the Tax Collector! " *Saturday Evening Post,* March 6, 1954.

LASSER, J. K., *Your Income Tax.* Simon and Schuster, annual, $1.50.

LEAR, JOHN, " Some People Do the Craziest Things for Income Tax Refunds," *Collier's,* March 19, 1954.

STARR, JOHN, " Big-Time Bootlegging Is Back," *Collier's,* June 13, 1953.

SWARTHOUT, JOHN M., and BARTLEY, ERNEST R., *Principles and Problems of American National Government,* Chapter 21. Oxford, 1955.

" Taxes: The Big Bite," *Time,* March 10, 1952.

The prosperity of commerce is now perceived and acknowledged by all enlightened statesmen to be the most useful as well as the most productive source of national wealth, and has accordingly become a primary object of their political cares.

— *Alexander Hamilton*

★

Chapter 8

COMMERCIAL POWERS OF CONGRESS

In Chapter 3, we saw that the weak Congress under the Articles of Confederation had no power to regulate commerce among the States. It had very little real authority over foreign commerce. The Critical Period of the 1780's was marked by intense commercial rivalries and jealousies among the newly independent States.

High trade barriers and spiteful State laws created confusion and chaos in both interstate and foreign commerce. Indeed, the situation was so grave that George Washington was moved to remark: " We are one nation today and thirteen tomorrow. Who will treat with us on such terms? "

Because of these conditions, no group was more responsible for the calling of the Philadelphia Convention of 1787 than the merchants and creditors. They had an obvious interest in orderly commerce and a stabilized economy. To accomplish this, they favored the creation of a National Government with power adequate to control foreign and interstate commerce.

The Constitution, then, gives Congress the power to

regulate commerce with foreign nations, among the several States, and with the Indian tribes.[1]

This " Commerce Clause " has done more to develop a loose confederation into a strong Union than has any other part of the Constitution. Along with the power to tax, it has contributed most to the tremendous growth of the power of the National Government since 1789.

---

[1] Article I, Section 8, Clause 3. The Constitution's framers viewed the Indian tribes very much as they did foreign nations, and so they gave Congress the power to regulate trade with them. They also realized the importance of keeping " firearms " and " firewater " from them. Later, when the transcontinental railroads were built, Congress had the power to grant rights of way through Indian lands for railroads.

A Free Market at Home. In many parts of Europe a traveler is annoyed every few hundred miles at a national boundary. His train is delayed while he and his fellow passengers show their passports (for which the visa may have cost several dollars). His baggage is inspected and may be taxed.

When he comes to America, passes the Statue of Liberty, and "goes through customs," he can travel through the forty-eight States without delay, without a passport, and without inspection or taxation of his luggage.

If an American wants to sell automobiles or other items in Europe, he must pay a high duty in each of several countries. And he must fight all sorts of other annoying regulations imposed to give advantages to home-made goods. In our United States, the American dealer finds a public with a purchasing power far superior to that of all of Europe, without a cent of tariff to pay, and free of other discriminatory regulations.

In short, the Commerce Clause has made for the citizens of the United States the greatest unrestricted market in the world.

What Is Commerce?

No Precise Definition Possible. As it is used in the Constitution, the word "commerce" cannot be exactly and precisely defined. What it includes and what it does not include is being continuously determined by (1) the Congress, when it passes laws regulating commerce, and (2) the Supreme Court, when it decides cases involving the Commerce Clause.

Like so many parts of the Constitution, the meaning of the Commerce Clause has changed and expanded as the nation has developed. In 1787 wagons and stagecoaches called for very little regulation, and sailing ships presented few interstate problems. The chief and perhaps the only purpose of the Commerce Clause in the minds of the Founding Fathers was to prevent the States from interfering with the free flow of goods among themselves. It referred to *articles to be transported* rather than to *means of transporting them.*

A Broad Interpretation. Both Congress and the Court have given a very liberal interpretation to the meaning of the Commerce Clause.

Under its commerce power, Congress has enacted thousands of statutes dealing with such subjects as radio and television broadcasting, the telephone and telegraph, railroads, steamships, airplanes, automobiles, buses, trucks, bridges, ferries, rivers, canals, harbors, and pipelines. It has regulated the transmission of electric energy, the building of dams, and the setting of freight rates.

It has regulated the interstate transportation of firearms, firecrackers, alcoholic beverages, stolen cars and stolen goods of various kinds, kid-

128

Official Coast Guard Photo

OCEAN LINERS
Seven liners, among them some of the world's largest, are moored at New York piers. The S.S. *United States* is the fastest of these ships.

naped persons, women for immoral purposes, and foods, drugs, and cosmetics.

It has controlled immigration, levied tariffs, and forbidden the importation of certain goods; provided for minimum wages, maximum hours, and safe working conditions; guaranteed the rights of employees to join unions and bargain collectively; and built highways and aided the States to build others.

Gibbons v. Ogden, 1824.   In 1807 Robert Fulton's steamboat made its first successful run from New York to Albany; and the New York legisla-

ture gave Fulton and his partner, Robert Livingston, an exclusive long-term grant to navigate the waters of the State by steamboat. From this monopoly, Aaron Ogden secured a permit for steam navigation between New York City and the Jersey shore.

Thomas Gibbons, operating under a coasting license granted by the United States Government, began a competing line. Upon Ogden's petition, the New York courts ordered Gibbons to discontinue his business.

Gibbons appealed to the United States Supreme Court. He claimed that the New York grant conflicted with the Constitution's grant to Congress of the power to regulate commerce.

The decision in this case was bound to have far-reaching effects.[2] It was the first case involving the Commerce Clause to come before the Court. And even Congress itself could not agree upon the extent of its powers over commerce.

The Court ruled unanimously in favor of Gibbons. It held the New York law in violation of the Constitution's grant of the commerce power to Congress. In reply to Ogden's argument that " commerce " should be narrowly defined as " traffic " or the mere buying and selling of goods, Chief Justice John Marshall wrote:

Commerce, undoubtedly, is traffic, but it is something more — it is intercourse.

It describes the commercial intercourse between nations, and parts of nations, in all its branches, and is regulated by prescribing rules for carrying on that intercourse.

The Court's decision was immensely popular because it dealt a death blow to the steamboat monopolies. But it had a much broader significance, which became apparent only with the passage of time.

The Court had given a sweeping definition of commerce and had thus greatly increased the powers of Congress to regulate — and promote — it. Freed from restrictive State regulation, steam navigation increased at an amazing rate on all the country's waterways. And in a few years, steam railroads, freed from similar restrictions, revolutionized the nation's domestic transportation.

Foreign Commerce

The Commerce Clause gives Congress the power to " regulate commerce with foreign nations." This power is even broader than that over interstate commerce, as the States have no power whatever in the field.

---

[2] Other States, like Massachusetts, New Hampshire, Pennsylvania, Georgia, Tennessee, and Louisiana, had made exclusive grants similar to New York's. This decision would affect them, too. And New York's neighbors, New Jersey and Connecticut, had passed retaliatory measures against New York's steamboat monopoly laws. In closing his argument against the monopoly, United States Attorney-General William Wirt said: " It is a momentous decision which this Court is called on to make. Here are three States almost on the eve of war."

Exclusion of Imports. Congress has prohibited the importation of many items. Here are only a few of them: diseased animals and plants, opium except for medical purposes, obscene literature, literature advocating the forceful resistance to any law of the United States, lottery tickets, adulterated and misbranded foods, articles having names or emblems simulating domestic trade-marks, convict-made articles, white or yellow phosphorus matches, firearms except to dealers licensed to receive them, and sugar in quantities that exceed the quotas as assigned by the Secretary of Agriculture.

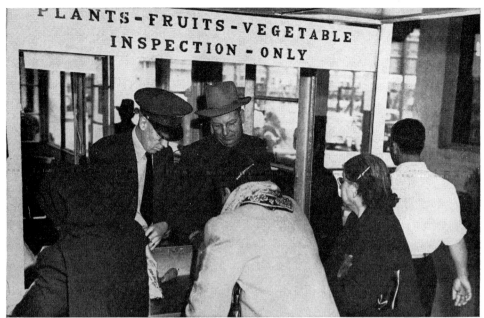
USDA Photo

QUARANTINE INSPECTION
Officers of the United States Department of Agriculture inspect a bag of fresh vegetables about to be brought into the country from Mexico. Only diseased items will be kept out. This station is at El Paso, Texas.

Embargo on Exports. Congress also has power under the Commerce Clause to forbid the export of commodities. Thus, since the end of World War II, the exportation of war materials and certain heavy machinery has been controlled by a strict licensing system. We do not want to help build war machines in Russia, Red China, and other countries behind the Iron Curtain.

Protection against State Interference. In 1827 the Supreme Courts announced the *Original Package Doctrine.* This rule forbids a State to tax or exercise its police pow-

ers [3] over imports from foreign countries until the original package has " come to rest " — that is, has reached the importer in this country and is broken open, sold, or used by him. Thus a State cannot interfere with the sale of cigars from Cuba until the importer opens the shipping packages or sells them.

If a State could interfere with the commodities in their original packages, coastal States could by collecting

---

[3] The *police power* is the power of the State to protect, promote, and regulate the public health, safety, morals, and general welfare of its citizens. See pages 387–389.

revenues and setting up other hindrances prevent imports from reaching inland States.

Regulation of Navigation. Congress regulates shipping; determines numerous conditions under which vessels may fly the American flag, such as requiring wireless equipment, life preservers, lifeboats, a definite limit to the number of passengers, and inspection of the ships; and prescribes how ships must enter and leave ports. To protect our seaports from possible atom bomb attacks, Congress provided that foreign ships entering American waters may be searched.

Regulation of Foreign Communication. The courts have interpreted " commerce " to include the communication of ideas as well as the exchange or transportation of commodities. Therefore Congress regulates cables, telegraph, and telephone wires extending to foreign countries, all kinds of foreign wireless communications, and the importation of printed matter.

Regulation of Immigration. The Constitution does not in so many words give Congress power to regulate immigration except under the power to regulate foreign commerce. But since the courts consider the movement of people to be commerce, Congress excludes certain classes of aliens altogether, prescribes conditions under which others may enter and whether they may enter permanently or only temporarily, and provides for the deportation of undesirable aliens.

Interstate Commerce

Commerce Includes Navigation. As we know, the Supreme Court held commerce to include navigation in the Gibbons case. Thus Congress has the power to regulate vessels in interstate trade and also the use of the waters in which these vessels navigate. Congress requires that the vessels be inspected as to seaworthiness and that they carry life preservers and other safety devices. The number of passengers a ship may carry is limited, and minimum working conditions for crews are also prescribed.

Congress appropriates money for dredging rivers and harbors, constructing canals, marking channels, and operating lighthouses. It forbids obstructions in navigable streams; and a bridge, causeway, or dam cannot be built across navigable streams without the consent of the Secretary of the Army.

Without the express permission of Congress, foreign vessels cannot carry freight or passengers from one port in the United States to another. In this way Congress protects Americans engaged in interstate shipping against the competition of foreign vessels.

The regulatory power of Congress extends to all navigable waters which are used or are susceptible of being used for interstate commerce. Congress has authority over navigable streams running through two or more

States, and also over those located wholly within one State but connecting with other navigable waters so as to form a continuous channel of communication with other States.[4]

The authority of Congress also has been extended to navigable waters wholly within a State and connected with no exterior water if these waters are actually navigated by boats which connect with interstate common carriers. Thus, a box of fish shipped across a lake wholly within a State is interstate commerce if consigned to a party outside the State and delivered by an interstate railroad. Therefore the little lake boat carrying this interstate box of fish is subject to regulation by Congress.

---

[4] Streams that are not navigable were not originally considered within the power of Congress. However, in 1893 Congress created the California Débris Commission to prevent such hydraulic mining in nonnavigable streams as would cause débris to float into navigable streams and fill their channels. The United States Circuit Court of Appeals sustained this Act.

Power plants built on nonnavigable streams at first came under State rather than federal authority. A 1935 Act of Congress, however, gives the Federal Power Commission power to refuse licenses for dams on navigable streams, and on nonnavigable streams if they affect interstate commerce.

In 1931 the Federal Power Commission claimed supervision over a power plant on New River, Virginia — a nonnavigable stream which flows into a navigable stream and thus affects the flow of the navigable stream. A United States District Court sustained the Commission in its claim to federal control over nonnavigable streams. Nine years later the Supreme Court sustained the right of the Federal Government to control such dams.

Commerce Includes Transportation on Land. The first railroads were built about 1830. Until the War Between the States, their building was encouraged by the States. Then, under the Granger movement in the Middle West, they were rather drastically regulated. States even interfered with interstate rates. In 1886 the Supreme Court checked this interference, and in 1887 Congress created the Interstate Commerce Commission. The courts justified the regulation of interstate railroads under the commerce clause, saying that commerce means " traffic," " intercourse," and also " transportation."

Under this power to control interstate " transportation " the Federal Government regulates rates for articles or persons carried from one State to another, limits the number of hours that employees are permitted to work, requires safety appliances, and compels roads to pay damages to employees actually engaged in carrying on interstate commerce, or their assignees, if the employees are injured or killed through the negligence of a railroad employee. Also, it is a federal crime to wreck an interstate train.

Commerce between the States is called *interstate commerce* and includes the movement of passengers and freight from one State to another, and the agencies and facilities by which the transfer is accomplished. Commerce within a State is called *intrastate commerce*. As a general rule, the Federal Government controls interstate commerce, and each State controls intrastate commerce within its borders.

The simple rule that the States have control over intrastate commerce is modified by some court decisions. In fact, there has been a tendency to narrow the power of the States and to broaden those of the Federal Government. When State regulation of intrastate commerce directly interferes with interstate commerce, the State regulation must yield to federal law.

For example, Shreveport, Louisiana, which is near the Texas border, and Dallas, Texas, competed for the trade of the Texas towns between these two cities. The freight rates from Dallas to these towns had been fixed by the Texas Railway Commission, and they were much lower per mile than the rates from Shreveport to these towns which had been fixed by the Interstate Commerce Commission. The dealers of Shreveport complained that they were discriminated against because they happened to be located across a State line and were regulated by the federal Interstate Commerce Commission. The Interstate Commerce Commission heard their complaint and decided that the intrastate rates from Dallas were too low, and ordered them to be raised on a par with the interstate rates from Shreveport. The case was taken to the United States Supreme Court. Here it was decided in 1914 that the order of the Interstate Commerce Commission was valid; that *the authority of the Federal Government to regulate interstate commerce carries with it the right to regulate intrastate commerce when it is necessary for the protection of interstate commerce.*

In 1935 Congress gave the Commission control of interstate common or contract carrier motor vehicles, and in 1940 of common or contract carriers by water.

Commerce Includes the Communication of Ideas. The first telegraph line was built in 1842, and the first telephone was exhibited at the Centennial Exposition in the year 1876. Both, when extending from one State to another, are regulated by the Federal Government, inasmuch as the courts have said " commerce includes the transmission of messages." Likewise, television and radio broadcasting are commerce, and in 1934 Congress created the Federal Communications Commission to control interstate wire and wireless communications. It is a federal crime to threaten to injure a person, property, or reputation, or to request a reward for the release of a kidnaped person across a State line.

Commerce Includes the Movement of Persons. Vehicles carrying persons across a State line for business or pleasure are engaged in interstate commerce. Even persons walking across a State line are considered interstate commerce. In 1941 the Supreme Court held unconstitutional a California statute which forbade a nonresident indigent (poor) person to enter the State. This restriction violated the interstate commerce clause, over which the Federal

Courtesy R. F. Fuquay

READY TO ROLL

This moving van operates in about a fourth of our States. It displays the licenses of the States through which it passes as well as those of the Interstate Commerce Commission.

Government, and not the State, has control.

Under the White Slave Act any person who knowingly transports or assists in obtaining the transportation of a female from one State to another or from a foreign country or in the District of Columbia for immoral purposes, or persuades her to come, is punishable by a fine not exceeding $5000 or imprisonment not exceeding five years or both.

Recently a movie actor was tried for paying the fare of and accompanying a single woman from Hollywood to New York. And in the District of Columbia a woman taxi driver who knowingly transported a woman four blocks to a hotel for an immoral appointment was convicted.

It is also a federal crime to kidnap across a State line, to flee to another State to avoid prosecution, or to cross a State line to avoid testifying in felony cases.

Commerce Includes Securities. Many State laws give inadequate protection to investors, and billions of dollars invested in stocks and bonds have been lost through lack of information or outright fraud. In 1934 Congress created the Securities and Exchange Commission (SEC) to help protect investors.

Commerce Includes Insurance. In 1944 the Supreme Court declared fire insurance (and life insurance by inference) to be commerce.

The Right to Regulate Interstate Commerce Includes the Right to Protect It. In interstate commerce, it is a federal crime to obstruct trucks by violence or threatened violence, to break into a car or station or steal shipments, knowingly to receive them, or to rob passengers or steal their baggage.

The Right to Regulate Interstate Commerce Includes the Right to Prohibit It. Congress excludes from interstate commerce such things as lottery tickets, obscene publications, game killed in violation of State laws, goods manufactured by child labor, liquor for dry States, diseased cattle, dangerous explosives, firearms shipped by unlicensed persons, disease-infected goods and persons, and impure or misbranded foods and drugs.

It had become difficult for an honest man to compete because dishonest producers indulged in every dishonest device — from misrepresenting the quantity in a package to selling fraudulent remedies for cancer. The homely squash, when doctored, flavored, colored, and attractively packed, became " canned peaches "; the apple with a little seed added became " preserved strawberries"; oleomargarine dyed yellow took the name of " butter "; veal became " potted chicken "; and even mineral earths have been mixed with cheap meals to produce " flour." Therefore, Congress enacted laws prohibiting the circulation in interstate trade of foods, beverages, drugs, and cosmetics that are misbranded as to quantity, quality, or place of production and that are injurious to health.

It is a federal crime knowingly to transport stolen firearms, cattle, aircraft or other vehicles of any value; stolen money, securities, or other goods of $5000 or more value; or to cause those items to be transported or to receive them across a State line. It is likewise a federal crime to steal interstate freight, express, baggage, fares, or to steal from passengers in a station, railroad car, aircraft, or other vehicle; or knowingly to buy, receive, or have possession of such stolen articles.

Protection against Unreasonable State Interference. A package in interstate commerce retains federal protection against State taxation until it is delivered to its consignee or comes to rest. Moreover, it retains federal protection against other State regulations until the original package is once sold, broken, or used. Thus a State cannot tax cigarettes as they cross the State border but must wait until they are delivered, or come to rest. Moreover, a State must wait until the package is once sold, broken, or used before regulating the sale of the cigarettes.[5]

---

[5] The original package which has federal protection is one which the trade ordinarily uses for transportation. Thus a ten-pound package of oleomargarine was held to be an original package; but paper cartons containing a pound of oleomargarine are not original packages. The original package is the tub or

If the States could tax or otherwise interfere unreasonably with goods being shipped in interstate commerce, the whole value of the Commerce Clause would be lost. We would, in effect, find ourselves living under the same conditions which plagued the original States before the adoption of the Constitution.

A State may, under its police powers, require interstate commerce to comply with *reasonable* State regulations pertaining to health, morals, safety, and general welfare. For example, States may require proper heating of all passenger cars as well as the supplying of sanitary drinking cups. They may forbid gambling on all trains, require crews of sufficient size to protect the public against accident, require all trains to slow down when going through cities, and require them to make a reasonable number of stops within the State. Of course even reasonable regulation of interstate commerce must yield to federal regulation whenever it comes in conflict with a general federal law.

Protection against Monopolies. By 1890 most of the major industries in the country were dominated by

___

box in which the pound packages are shipped.

Goods brought into a State by peddlers and sold in the original package cease to have the federal protection given to consigned commodities. Peddlers' goods are subject to State taxation and regulation as soon as brought into the State. This exception to the original package doctrine is justified because the retail transactions begin at once and the transaction is not analogous to the ordinary wholesale transaction with a jobber who stores his goods in a warehouse.

such combinations as the Sugar Trust, the Whiskey Trust, the Beef Trust, and the Standard Oil Trust.[6] Many supposedly competing companies made agreements with one another to limit production or fix prices. Sometimes they agreed not to compete in certain sections of the country assigned to one or another of them. Often the same persons sat on the boards of directors of competing companies (interlocking directorates) and were thus able to regulate and restrict competition.

State regulation proved largely ineffective against these powerful interstate combinations and federal regulation became necessary. Acting under the commerce power, Congress passed the famous Sherman Antitrust Act of 1890. This Act remains the basic law against monopolies today. It prohibits " every contract, combination in the form of a trust or

___

[6] The *trust* was originally a device by which several corporations engaged in the same line of business would combine to eliminate competition and regulate prices. This was done by creating a central board composed of the presidents or general managers of the different corporations and transferring to them a majority of stock from each of the corporations to be held " in trust " for the stockholders who thus assigned their stock. The stockholders received in return " trust certificates " showing that they were entitled to receive dividends on their assigned stock, though the voting power of it had been passed to the trustees. This enabled the trustees to elect all the directors of all the corporations and thus prevent competition and insure better prices. Though the " trust " has been superseded by " holding companies," any monopolistic combination is today called a " trust."

otherwise, or conspiracy in restraint of trade or commerce among the several States, or with foreign nations." It also provides penalties for violations.

Because of the very general wording and inadequate enforcement of the law, little was accomplished until 1911. In that year the Supreme Court decided two cases involving monopoly prosecutions of the American Tobacco Company and the Standard Oil Company of New Jersey. In forcing the dissolution of the two monopolies, the Supreme Court announced the so-called "rule of reason."

Although the act prohibits *every* agreement in restraint of trade, the Court interpreted this to mean *every unreasonable* agreement.

In 1914 Congress passed the Clayton Act making four specific practices illegal: (1) the purchase by one corporation of the stock of another; (2) interlocking directorates; (3) "exclusive agreements" requiring a dealer to sell the products of only the one company; and (4) price discriminations in the sale of the same product to different purchasers (expanded by the Robinson-Patman Act of 1936).

INTERSTATE COMMERCE

Baggage loaded on trains is entered thereby into interstate commerce. Federal laws regulate and protect it until delivery. It is a federal crime to steal or obstruct the movement of property in interstate commerce.

Several economic groups have been specifically exempted from the provisions of the Sherman and Clayton Acts by Congress. For example, under the Transportation Act of 1920 railroads are allowed to agree to the division of traffic or earnings with the approval of the Interstate Commerce Commission. Labor unions are exempt on the grounds that " labor is not a commodity of commerce." Some utilities, farmer and dairy cooperatives, and exporters are exempted.

Examples of Antitrust Law Violations. The Pullman Company, which had a practical monopoly in the manufacture of sleeping cars and which operated practically all sleeping cars throughout the country, was required either to dispose of its sleeping car factories or to dispose of its sleeping cars. It chose to dispose of the cars; and in 1947 fifty-seven railroad companies purchased all the sleeping cars and facilities.

The Associated Press was required to refrain from imposing any restrictions on the admission of new members because the papers of the applicants competed with the papers of existing members. Such restrictions were declared to be in restraint of trade.

The Ethyl Gasoline Corporation was held to be restraining trade by requiring users of its patents to sell Ethyl gasoline only to jobbers who were licensed by the Ethyl Corporation. Jobber licenses had been granted only to those who followed price policies of the Ethyl Corporation.

The Federal Trade Commission

The Sherman Antitrust Act was indefinite, and a corporation was often uncertain as to whether it was violating the law. This was unfair to business. On the other hand, the law was not systematically enforced and the public was not protected against high prices caused by monopolistic restraint of trade. To help correct both evils the Federal Trade Commission was created (1914) to warn a business of violation without prosecution, if the business seems honestly endeavoring to obey the law; but if necessary, to proceed against the accused, impose penalties, and issue an order of " cease and desist " if found guilty of violating a law. (Appeals may be taken from the Commission to the United States Court of Appeals and in many cases may be taken from there to the Supreme Court.)

Organization. The Commission is composed of five members appointed by the President with the approval of the Senate for seven-year terms.

Duties. The duties of the Commission have been expanded by several Acts of Congress; but, in brief, its duty is to prevent persons, partnerships, or corporations from using unfair business practices in matters that the Federal Government can control under its interstate and foreign commerce powers,[7] and to recommend needed legislation to the President and Congress.

The Commission's work can be best illustrated by citing actual examples: In order to enhance sales, some fur dealers were in the habit of giving fancy foreign-sounding names or glamorous fictitious names to common furs. Thus rabbit furs went under at least thirty different commercial aliases — " French Chinchilla," " Electric Beaver," " Baltic Fox," etc. On the FTC's recommendation, Congress enacted legislation designed to end this misleading practice. Now all furs must be sold under their actual names. The FTC has issued regulations requiring that rabbit be called rabbit, that skunk fur be called just that. Only furs actually produced in the Middle East may be sold as Persian Lamb. If a coat is made from ordinary cat's fur it must be labeled as Domestic Cat.

Some firms have simulated well-known trade names, labels, or slogans in attempts to capitalize on another concern's good name. Thus the FTC issued a cease-and-desist order against the " Westinghouse Union Company " in order to protect consumers and the Westinghouse Electric Company. The " Goodwear Tire and Rubber Company " was found to be too much like Goodyear.

On several occasions the Commission has had to issue orders to forbid combinations and conspiracies in restraint of trade through price-fixing agreements to restrict competition. For instance, 45 manufacturers of book paper who produced 86 per cent of the total volume of book paper were prosecuted because of a price agreement intended to suppress competition and increase the price of paper.

The FTC's regulations forbid price discriminations where the effect is to lessen competition and promote monopoly. For instance, it forbids buying supplies at excessive prices to " freeze out " a competitor, or systematically selling below cost to suppress competition.

Manufacturers are not allowed to give discounts, rebates, and other similar allowances to chain stores if they give these large corporations undue advantages over small independent dealers. (Chain stores may still have an advantage by manufacturing their own goods, by buying the entire supply of a factory at a low price, or by buying a large supply when prices are low.) Differential prices are legal when quantity buying reduces the cost of manufacturing, selling, or delivery.

The FTC holds " Trade Practices Conferences " where members of an entire industry (e.g., fur, appliances, etc.) meet with the Commission to define and promote fair trade practices.

---

[7] It is more exact to say that the Federal Trade Commission's duty is to restrict unfair practices other than those in fields assigned to other bodies. For instance, the Interstate Commerce Commission regulates railroads and other common carriers, the Federal Reserve Board regulates banks, and the Securities and Exchange Commission regulates stocks and bonds and stock exchanges.

The Fair Trade Controversy

So-called " Fair Trade Acts " have produced a very interesting and most complicated problem in the regulation of interstate commerce. This problem stems from the fact that many manufacturers of nationally advertised brand-name products attempt to set the price at which retailers may sell those products. Commonly, they require a dealer to sign a contract binding him to sell at a " fair trade " price set by the manufacturer, and making him liable for damages if he does not abide by the agreement.

However, signing all dealers is a very cumbersome, costly procedure. And many dealers refuse to sign such agreements. So business groups began persuading States to enact so-called " Fair Trade Acts." By 1958 some forty had done so. These statutes legalize " fair trade pricing " by manufacturers. And most of them provide that when one or a few dealers in the State have signed " fair trade " contracts, the contracts become binding on all dealers selling the particular item in the State — whether or not they themselves have actually signed such contracts.

Of course, these State laws cannot bind those who deal in *inter*state commerce — only in *intra*state commerce. But in 1937 Congress passed the Miller-Tydings amendment to the Sherman Antitrust Act. This amendment permits " interstate price-fixing " in those States in which such a practice is permitted in *intra*state commerce. The Miller-Tydings amendment, however, did not mention nonsigners.

The question of the legality of the nonsigner provisions of State laws insofar as interstate commerce was concerned reached the Supreme Court in 1950. The Calvert Corporation, a liquor concern, had signed several " fair trade " contracts with dealers in Louisiana. Louisiana's law binds both signers and nonsigners. Schwegmann Brothers Giant Supermarkets, Inc., of New Orleans, did not sign a contract and was selling Calvert's liquor at cut-rate prices. Calvert sued, but in 1950 the Supreme Court held that by the Miller-Tydings amendment Congress did not intend to bind nonsigners.

So, in order to bind nonsigners, business groups persuaded Congress to amend further the Sherman Act to that effect. In 1952 Congress passed the McGuire Act, which provides that if a State's laws decree that both signers and nonsigners are bound in *intra*state commerce by " fair trade " contracts, then the federal law binds them in *interstate* commerce just as well.

Now, with manufacturers attempting to force nonsigners to comply as provided in the McGuire Act, literally dozens of court cases have been instituted across the country.

It seems probable that the Supreme

Court will rule on the legality of the McGuire Act in the near future. Several cases involving the act have been appealed to it. One of the principal cases involved Schwegmann Brothers, this time against Eli Lilly & Co. Lilly & Co. obtained an injunction against Schwegmann Brothers in the U.S. District Court in Louisiana. This injunction directed Schwegmann Brothers to halt the sale of Lilly & Co.'s products below the " fair trade " price. In 1953 the U.S. Court of Appeals upheld the injunction (and thus upheld the McGuire Act), and the Supreme Court refused to review.

In the first Schwegmann case (1950) the question was *had* Congress (in the Miller-Tydings amendment) included nonsigners. The question in the second Schwegmann case (and in those cases still to be heard) is *could* Congress (in the McGuire Act) include nonsigners.

The Pro Argument. " Brand name " manufacturers, thousands of small independent merchants, the drug trade, and some department stores support " fair trade " laws. They argue that such laws prevent big department and chain stores from offering " fair traded " items at cut-rate prices the small merchants can-

not meet. They also contend that the larger stores used the reduced price on brand-name goods to lure customers into the store. These customers also buy other merchandise, it is said, and the profits lost on cut-rate items are more than offset by the overall increase in business.

Manufacturers supporting these laws claim that they protect their products and good name from being " cheapened and debased " by retail price-cutting. And they say that the manufacturer should be allowed to set the price to be charged for his product, adding that if the price is too high the customer will turn to a competitor.

The Con Argument. The opponents of these laws argue that they violate the basic principles of free enterprise. The large retailers believe that they are in a better position than the manufacturer to determine what the retail price of any item they sell ought to be.

Macy's of New York, the world's largest department store, claims that " fair trade " is a " misleading title — the real title is ' price-fixing.' The simple truth is that no group fights for price-fixing privileges except to make prices higher than they would be under free and open competition."

WHAT THIS CHAPTER IS ABOUT

In order to establish orderly commerce and a stabilized economy, the Constitution places the control of foreign and interstate commerce in the hands of the National Government. The Commerce Clause has done more to create a strong

Union than has any other part of the Constitution.

No exact definition of " commerce " is possible. It is being continually defined and enlarged by Congress and the Supreme Court. Both Congress and the

Court have given it a very broad interpretation.

In its first case on the subject (*Gibbons* v. *Ogden,* 1824), the Supreme Court held commerce to be more than mere traffic in goods; it held it to be " intercourse . . . in all its branches."

Under its powers over foreign commerce, Congress has excluded many things from importation. It has regulated shipping, provided for protection from State interference, and regulated immigration and foreign communications.

Under its powers over interstate commerce, Congress regulates most aspects of navigation and also regulates transportation on land and in the air, communications, the movement of persons across State lines, securities, and insurance.

Congress may and does protect interstate commerce and prohibits the shipping of certain articles. Unreasonable State interference is prohibited. Monopolies in restraint of trade are prevented under the commerce power.

The Federal Trade Commission restricts unfair trade practices in most phases of interstate commerce. So-called " Fair Trade Acts " allowing a manufacturer to set the retail price of his product have produced an interesting and complicated controversy in interstate commerce.

QUESTIONS ON THE TEXT

1. Why was the " Commerce Clause " written into the Constitution? What does it provide?

2. Why is an exact and precise definition of " commerce " impossible? By whom is it being constantly defined?

3. Outline the case of *Gibbons* v. *Ogden.* What was its broad significance?

4. Why is the power over foreign commerce broader than that over interstate commerce?

5. Distinguish between *interstate* and *intrastate* commerce.

6. Does a body of water necessarily have to communicate with another State to come under the regulation of Congress?

7. Under what condition does the Federal Government regulate intrastate rates? Explain by the Shreveport case.

8. Are bus lines engaged in interstate commerce?

9. What does Congress regulate under its power to regulate interstate communication of ideas?

10. Is a person walking across an interstate bridge interstate commerce according to the Commerce Clause?

11. Can one caught taking a stolen car from one State to another be prosecuted in a federal court?

12. Give some examples of the regulation of interstate commerce by States under their police power.

13. What is a monopoly? What is a trust?

14. What exceptions are there to the original meaning of the Sherman Anti-Trust law?

15. Why was the Federal Trade Commission created? What are some unfair practices announced by it?

PROBLEMS FOR DISCUSSION

1. A ranchman was driving his sheep from Oregon to Montana through Idaho on the day that annual property taxes were assessed in Idaho. The tax assessor in Idaho endeavored to tax these sheep, but was unsuccessful because the owner appealed to the federal courts, basing his case upon Article I, Section 8, Clause 3,

of the United States Constitution. Explain.

2. A loaded freight truck, en route from New York to Portland, Maine, was put in a garage in Boston on the evening of March 31st. The next morning it was assessed for taxation by the Boston assessors under the provisions of the Massachusetts law which permits the levy of a tax on all tangible personal property within the State on the first day of April each year. Why was this unconstitutional?

3. Can a State tax an " original package " from a foreign country? From another State? Can it regulate it under its police power if from a foreign country? If from another State? Do you think this wise? Explain.

THINGS YOU MIGHT DO

1. Make a list of as many federal activities as you can that stem from the commerce power.

2. Prepare a short report on the Critical Period and deliver it to the class.

3. Stage a class debate or forum on the question: " *Resolved,* That Fair Trade Acts should be abolished."

WORDS AND PHRASES YOU SHOULD KNOW

Clayton Act	*Gibbons* v. *Ogden*	Navigable waters
Commerce Clause	Intercourse	Original Package Doctrine
Critical Period	Interstate commerce	Police Power
Embargo	Intrastate commerce	Sherman Antitrust Act
" Fair Trade " Acts	Monopoly	Trust

SELECT BIBLIOGRAPHY

BARTHOLOMEW, PAUL C., *Summaries of Leading Cases on the Constitution.* Littlefield, Adams, 1954.

BURNS, JAMES M., and PELTASON, JACK A., *Government by the People,* Chapters 24–25. Prentice-Hall, 1954.

CORWIN, EDWARD S., *The Constitution and What It Means Today,* Pages 31–53. Princeton, 1954.

FERGUSON, JOHN H., and McHENRY, DEAN E., *The American System of Government,* Chapters 25, 26, and 27. McGraw-Hill, 1956.

JOHNSON, CLAUDIUS O., *American National Government,* Chapters 18, 19. Crowell, 1955.

KELLY, ALFRED H., and HARBISON, WINFRED A., *The American Constitution.* Norton, 1955.

SEIB, CHARLES B., " Fair Trade Acts: Pro and Con," *Nation's Business,* March, 1955.

SWISHER, CARL B., *American Constitutional Development.* Houghton Mifflin, 1954.

" The Revolution on Our Railroads," *Newsweek,* November 21, 1955.

THRUELSEN, RICHARD, " They Deliver the Goods — And Fast! " *Saturday Evening Post,* December 3, 1955.

> For this reason the laws are made: that the stronger may not have the power to do all that they please.
>
> — *Ovid*

★

Chapter 9

CONGRESS IN ACTION

Many of the thousands of Americans who visit the House and Senate chambers each year leave with the feeling that all is not quite as it should be. They go fully expecting to see a most impressive scene, steeped in tradition, dignified and dramatic.

Occasionally, that is exactly what they do see. But a typical moment on the floor finds only a half dozen or so Senators or perhaps thirty-five to forty Representatives present. The visitor wonders where all the other members are and why they aren't "tending to business." Much of what is done on the floor seems to the visitor in the galleries to be done in utter confusion, or to be so dull and boring as to be a complete waste of time.

It is not at all unusual for a Senator or Representative to be speaking away while his few colleagues present are chatting with one another, reading newspapers, or working at their desks.

Is this Congress in action? Hardly. The picture one gets from the galleries is a very, very incomplete one. If we could observe the committees in session and Congressmen at their daily duties, we certainly would get a much different view of Congress at work.

Woodrow Wilson once said that "the making of laws is a very practical matter." It is also a very complicated — and a very important — matter. Let us see, then, just what is involved in the day-by-day work of the United States Congress.

The Opening of a New Congress

Opening Day in the House of Representatives. When the 435 men and women who have been chosen in their States as Representatives assemble at the Capitol on January 3, they are, in effect, just so many Representatives-elect. Because all 435 seats are refilled every two years, the House has no sworn members, no rules, no organization until the official opening-day ceremonies are held.

The Clerk of the preceding House presides at the beginning of the first day's session. He calls the roll of members-elect as furnished by the several States.

THE PRESIDENT REPORTS

Mr. Eisenhower delivering a State of the Union message to a new Congress. When the President appears before Congress, the two houses meet in joint session in the House chamber.

The members-elect then choose a Speaker, the permanent presiding officer. The new Speaker is always a member of the majority party, and his election on the floor is a mere formality. The majority party caucus (conference of party members) has really chosen him beforehand.

The new Speaker is then sworn in by the " Father of the House " — the member-elect longest in point of service. After he takes the oath, the Speaker proceeds to swear in the rest of the members as a body. The Democrats take their seats to the right of the center aisle and the Republicans to the left.

Next, the House chooses a Clerk, a Chaplain, a Sergeant-at-Arms, a Doorkeeper, and a Postmaster. As in the case of the Speaker, their selections are little more than a formality. The majority party caucus has already decided whom they shall be. They are never members of Congress.

Following the election of officers, the House adopts its rules. The rules, which have developed over more than 150 years, are usually taken over from those of the preceding House with little or no change. Then the House committees are appointed by vote of the members and the House of Representatives is fully organized.

Opening Day in the Senate. Because only one-third of its members face election every two years, the Senate does not have the problems the House has on opening day. The Senate is a continuous body; that is, it has been continuously organized since its first session in 1789. Its new members must be sworn in, vacancies in its organization and on committees must be filled, and a few minor details must be attended to; then the Senate is ready to proceed.

The President's State of the Union Message. When the Senate is notified that the House is organized, a joint committee of the two informs the President that the Congress of the United States is in session and prepared to receive any communications from him.

Within a day or two the President delivers his " State of the Union Message " to Congress. Recent Presidents, including Mr. Eisenhower, have delivered this message in person. Whenever the President personally addresses Congress, the two houses meet in joint session in the House chamber.

In this message the President gives Congress his observations on the state of the nation in all its concerns, foreign and domestic, and he makes specific recommendations concerning laws he feels should be passed. When he has finished, the two houses adjourn their joint session and each turns to the first order of business before it.

The Organization of Congress

Our national legislature is a much bigger operation than most people realize. Each year it costs more than $100,000,000 to run. Only $11,947,-500 of this is spent to pay the salaries of the 531 members of the two houses. More than $24,000,000 goes to hire office assistants for members and the annual stationery bill runs to nearly $1,000,000.

There are some 3500 congressional employees. We have already mentioned a few of them, the Clerk of the House, for example. There are hundreds of committee assistants, office clerks, research experts, guards, maintenance men, shorthand reporters, page boys, and grounds-keepers. Each of these, in his or her own way, is important to the successful working of Congress.

Presiding Officers of Congress. The *Speaker of the House* is by far the most important member of that body. His post as presiding officer is provided in the Constitution and, although the Constitution does not require it, the House always selects him from its own members.

The Speaker is the leader of the majority party and is usually a long-time member. The present Speaker, Sam Rayburn of Texas, has been a member of the House since 1913.

All of his powers revolve about two duties: to preside and to maintain order; and he often uses his powers for the benefit of his own party and its program. No member may speak until he is "recognized" by the Speaker. He refers bills to committee, appoints the members of special and conference committees, and signs all bills and resolutions passed by the House. He may order the galleries cleared if the spectators become too noisy. If a member strays from the subject at hand the Speaker may rule him out of order and force him to sit down.

When the House is in session, the mace, symbol of the Speaker's authority, rests in a stand to his right. If the Speaker cannot maintain order on the floor, he directs the Sergeant-at-Arms to approach an unruly member with the mace and demand order in the name of the House. If the display of the mace fails to quiet the disturbance, the Speaker may order the Sergeant-at-Arms to arrest the unruly member.

Because he is himself a Representative, the Speaker may debate and vote on any question, but he is required to vote only to break a tie. When he engages in floor debate, he must vacate the chair and appoint a temporary presiding officer to take his place.

The importance of the office of Speaker may be seen in the fact that, after the Vice-President, he is next in the line of succession to the presidency.

The *President of the Senate,* who is also the Vice-President of the United States, is a much less important presiding officer. Since he is not himself a member of the Senate, he cannot debate and may (must) vote only in case of a tie. He recognizes members, puts motions to a vote, and generally acts as an impartial chairman.

Whatever influence the Vice-President has over Senate business comes chiefly from his own personality. The three most recent Vice-Presidents, Messrs. Truman, Barkley, and Nixon, all previously served in the Senate and thus gained considerable influence.

The Senate has another presiding officer, the *President pro tempore,* who presides in the absence of a Vice-President. The Vice-President is often absent because of other duties. And seven times in our history fate has suddenly made the Vice-President the President of the United States. The President *pro tem* is always a leading majority party Senator and, of course, has much influence in his own right.

Committee Chairmen. Next to the presiding officers in each House, the most important congressional officers are the chairmen of the standing (regular, permanent) committees. A large bulk of the actual work of Congress, especially in the House, is done in committee. The chairman of each committee is chosen by the majority party caucus, and he is always a ranking member of his party.

The chairman decides when his committee will meet, whether or not it will even consider a bill, if public hearings are to be held, and what witnesses should be called. When his committee has reported a bill to the floor, he manages the debate and attempts to steer it to final passage.

In a moment we shall see how the committees operate in the legislative process and refer to the chairmen again. But here we should examine a rather controversial matter — the so-called " rule of seniority."

The *rule of seniority* is an unwritten custom rigidly followed in each house. Under it, the most important posts in congressional organization and in the organization of each party go to the members who have served the longest in Congress. The rule is applied most strictly in the case of committee chairmanships, and it makes no difference what the particular member's experience, interests, or abilities might be.

Those who attack the rule have a strong case. They claim that it ignores ability, puts a premium on mere length of service, and discourages younger members. They also note that the rule means that a committee chairman almost always comes from a " safe " constituency — that is, a State or district where, election after election, he and his party have no effective opposition. Because the play of fresh and contending forces is almost nil, committee chairmen are often out of touch with current public opinion.

Those who defend the rule argue that it means that a powerful and experienced member will head each committee. They also cite the fact that because the rule is easy to apply, it practically eliminates feuds within the party.

Although the weight of the argument is against the rule, there is little prospect for change. Those who have the power to alter it are the very ones who benefit from its operation.

The *Majority and Minority Floor Leaders* are the managers of their party's program on the floor in each house. They are not *official* officers of the House or Senate; rather, they are *party* officers chosen by the party caucus. Though their positions are unofficial, each is given a huge desk on his own side of the center aisle.

Each of these " quarterbacks " watches over and attempts to control floor action to the benefit of his party. He must try to persuade the members to vote in accord with the wishes of the party leadership — and this is often a difficult task. The Majority Leader is more important than the Minority Leader for the simple reason that his party has the most seats (votes) in the house.

The *Party Whips* assist the Floor Leaders. Each Floor Leader appoints a Whip and he and his assistants sound out party sentiment, try to see that the members vote with the party's leadership, and see that members are present when an important vote is to be taken. If a member is away from Washington, his Party Whip sees that he is " paired " with a member of the other party who is also absent or who agrees not to vote on certain measures.

The *Party Caucus* is a closed meeting of the members of each party in each house. It meets just before the beginning of each session in January and occasionally during the session itself.

The caucus decides such questions as the candidate for Speaker and who the Floor Leaders shall be and attempts to secure united party action on certain measures. Often the work of the caucus is to determine the attitude of the members on pending legislation. Neither party imposes an ironclad acceptance of caucus decisions on its members — nor can it.

In recent years, the Republicans have called their caucus the *party conference.*

The *Policy or Steering Committees* in each party consist of a dozen or so leading members who function as an " executive committee " for the caucus. The Majority Policy Committee, a party group, tells the official Rules Committee what to do.

The Committee System

Both houses of Congress have become so large and the scope of business is so great that measures cannot be handled by all of the members acting together. So each house has divided itself into several standing (permanent) committees and many temporary ones.

Standing Committees. Originally, the House and Senate appointed a special committee to consider each bill introduced. But by 1794 each house had over 300 committees. So both chambers began creating permanent groups, called " standing committees," to which all bills of like character could be referred.

Through the years the number of committees has varied. By 1946 the number stood at forty-eight in the House and thirty-three in the Senate. Many members of Congress were forced to spend practically all of their time in committee work; on the average, each Senator was serving on five committees and each Representa-

tive on at least two. So, by the Legislative Reorganization Act of 1946, an act which streamlined many congressional procedures, the number of committees was sharply reduced.

Today the House has nineteen standing committees and the Senate fifteen. The size of each committee varies from nine to fifty members in the House and from thirteen to twenty-one in the Senate. The rules of the lower house limit Representatives to service on one major committee and Senate rules allow members to serve on only two.

HOUSE COMMITTEES

Agriculture
Appropriations
Armed Services
Banking and Currency
District of Columbia
Education and Labor
Government Operations
Foreign Affairs
House Administration
Interior and Insular Affairs
Interstate and Foreign Commerce

Judiciary
Merchant Marine and Fisheries
Post Office and Civil Service
Public Works
Rules
Un-American Activities
Veterans' Affairs
Ways and Means

SENATE COMMITTEES

Agriculture and Forestry
Appropriations
Armed Services
Banking and Currency
District of Columbia
Finance
Foreign Relations
Government Operations
Interior and Insular Affairs
Interstate and Foreign Commerce
Judiciary
Labor and Public Welfare

Post Office and Civil Service
Public Works
Rules and Administration

The Speaker and the President of the Senate refer bills to the appropriate standing committee. For instance, the Speaker refers tax bills to the House Ways and Means Committee, and the President of the Senate refers them to the Senate Finance Committee. A bill to amend the Selective Service Act would go to the Armed Services Committee in either house.

We have already seen how the committee chairmen are selected by the House and Senate according to the rule of seniority. Each house also formally elects the other members of

CONGRESSIONAL INVESTIGATION
Flashbulbs pop as an important witness takes the oath before a Senate investigating committee.

its committees.[1] The majority party controls each committee, but the minority party also has a substantial representation on each.

In fact, party membership on each committee is proportionate to party strength in the entire house. Thus, if the Republicans have 220 seats in the House and the Democrats 215, the party split in committee seats is also very close — on a 25-member committee the division would be thirteen Republicans and twelve Democrats.

Except for the House Committee on Rules and the Senate Committee on Rules and Administration, each of the standing committees is a " subject-matter " group. That is, each deals with bills relating to particular subjects, as for example, the Senate Committee on Foreign Relations or the House Committee on Agriculture.

---

[1] Though the committee members are *formally* elected by each house, they are *actually* chosen in a much different manner. In the House, the Democratic caucus first selects its members for the Ways and Means Committee and these then act as a " committee on committees " to fill the seats on the rest of the standing committees. The Republicans in their House caucus select a Committee on Committees consisting of one member from each State with G.O.P. representation. Each member of this group has as many votes as there are Republican Representatives from his State. This body fills *all* the Republican committee seats.

Each party in the Senate has a Committee on Committees chosen by the caucus. But, because only one-third of the Senate is reelected every two years, all the committee seats do not have to be refilled at the first of every term. When there is a change in party control, however, much reshuffling is necessary.

We shall discuss the standing committees again when we trace a bill from its introduction to final enactment. But for now special note should be made of one of them.

The House Committee on Rules. Until 1880, the Rules Committee was simply a special (temporary) committee set up at the beginning of each term of Congress. Its function was to propose the adoption of the rules of the preceding House and to offer whatever changes, if any, the committee might wish. But since it was made a standing committee in 1880, the Rules Committee has grown in power to the place where today it has life-and-death say over most bills in the House.

So many bills are introduced in the House each year — an average of 4000 to 5000 — that some sort of screening process is needed. Most bills die in the committees to which they are referred, and a large number of them deserve to. But, still, many more than the House can handle are reported out by the committees. Before these can get to the floor for debate they must first pass through the Rules Committee.

Working in co-operation with the House leadership, the Rules Committee schedules the appearance of bills on the floor. It has the power to bring in a *special rule* to consider a bill out of its regular order, or to limit the length of debate on a bill, or to determine which sections of a bill may or may not be amended in debate. Thus it has the power to hasten, delay, or prevent action on a bill.

JOINT COMMITTEE ON ATOMIC ENERGY

Major General Frederick Smith of the Air Force testifies before an executive session of this important joint committee, composed of nine Senators and nine Representatives.

The decisions of this twelve-member committee are, in effect, the decisions of the Majority Policy Committee and are very rarely reversed on the floor. The minority party often cries " Gag rule! " when a special rule is brought in. But each party uses the practice to its own advantage when it is in the majority.

The Senate, a much smaller body, has much less strict rules than the House, and its Committee on Rules and Administration is really only a pale shadow of its counterpart in the lower house.

Special Committees. From time to time each house creates special committees. These special committees (also known as *select commit-*

tees) are temporary and exist only until they accomplish a particular purpose. The members are appointed by the Speaker or by the President of the Senate. The best-known special committee in recent years has been the Senate Select Committee on Improper Activities in the Labor or Management Field, popularly known as the McClellan or Senate Rackets Committee.

Joint Committees. A joint committee is a permanent committee composed of members of both houses of Congress. The Senators and Representatives are appointed to the committee by the presiding officer in their own house and act together in this single body. To date, except for the Joint Committee on Atomic Energy, the Congress has used joint committees only for routine and somewhat minor matters — for example, the Joint Committee on Printing and the Joint Committee on the Library of Congress. Because the standing committees in each house often duplicate one another's work, many people urge a much wider use of the joint committee device.

Conference Committees. Before a bill may be sent to the President for his action it must be passed by each house in identical form. When the two houses pass differing versions of the same bill, a temporary " conference committee " is created.

A conference committee is composed of an equal number of Senators and Representatives appointed by the President of the Senate and the Speaker of the House. They meet to try to iron out the differences in the House and Senate versions and reach a compromise acceptable to the two houses.

Investigating Committees. Congress must have the power to investigate. It needs to inform itself on matters before it. It must check on laws already passed and see whether or not they need changing. And it must look into government programs it has already provided for to be sure that they are being administered the way the Congress intended.

Each house uses one of its standing committees, or a subcommittee thereof, a special committee, or a joint committee to investigate a given matter.

The most widely known investigating committees today are those which have been investigating communist activities, like the House Un-American Activities Committee and the Investigations Subcommittee of the Senate Government Operations Committee.

But congressional investigations really cover a much wider variety of subjects. In recent years some of the major investigations have included one which uncovered fraud in the Internal Revenue Service and another which found that a Congressman was " padding " his office payroll and requiring members of his staff to " kick back " part of their salaries to him. In the latter case, the Congressman was later tried in court and sentenced to a federal penitentiary.

Most congressional investigations, those of which the public seldom is aware, are less spectacular. Examples of these would include instances when the House Committee on Agriculture looks into the question of providing price supports for a particular farm commodity or when the Senate Interior and Insular Affairs Committee tries to determine the need for access roads in national forest lands.

How a Bill Becomes a Law

Some 15,000 bills are introduced during each term of Congress. Less

than ten per cent ever become law. Where do these bills originate? Why

154

do so few of them become law? What steps are involved in the making of a law?

We shall first trace a bill through the House and, then, because in many respects procedure in the two houses is quite similar, note the differences found in the procedure followed in the Senate.

Authorship and Introduction. Very few of the bills introduced in either house are actually written by the Congressmen themselves. Many are prepared in the executive departments and handed to a member to introduce. Business, labor, agriculture, education and other pressure groups often draft bills. Some come from private citizens and many are drafted by the standing committees of the House and Senate.

The Constitution provides that all bills for the raising of revenue must originate (be first introduced) in the House of Representatives.[2] But once a revenue bill passes the House and is sent to the Senate, the upper house may amend it just as it may any other measure.

Only a member may introduce a bill. He does this by dropping the bill in the " hopper." [3] As many as 2500 bills have been introduced on opening day in the House.

Types of Bills and Resolutions. Some measures introduced in Congress take the form of bills while others are called resolutions.

Public bills are measures of general application, such as the Selective Service Act or an income tax law.

Private bills are those that apply to specific persons or places. For example, Congress recently passed an act to pay a man $1229.52, the amount he would have made on a government contract if a Wyoming post office had handled his mail promptly.

Joint resolutions differ very little from bills, but they usually deal with a single and simple matter. They have the same force and effect as bills do when they become law. A typical joint resolution would be one naming a certain week as Boy Scout Week.

Concurrent resolutions deal with matters in which joint action of the Senate and House are necessary but for which a law is not needed. The setting up of a joint committee is usually handled by this device.

Simple resolutions are passed by only one or the other house and deal with matters relating only to that branch of Congress. For example, special committees are set up by simple resolution.

A bill usually relates to only one subject. But sometimes a " rider " dealing with an entirely different matter is included. A rider [4] is a pro-

---

[2] Article I, Section 7, Clause 1.

[3] The " hopper " is a large box hanging at the end of the Clerk's desk. In the Senate a bill is introduced by addressing the Chair.

[4] The term " rider " probably comes from the field of music. A musical string vibrates in sections, and if you pinch a strip of paper and hang it over the string at an interval where the string vibrates least the paper will *ride* the string; if at the wrong interval it will bounce off.

vision which rides through a legislative body attached to a more important act certain to pass. For instance, some years ago the barrooms in the Capitol Building were abolished by a short sentence tucked in an annual appropriation bill — which Congress was practically obliged to pass and the President obliged to sign.

Reference to Committee. The Clerk gives each bill a number: H.R. 216, for example, would be the 216th bill introduced in the session. (Bills originating in the Senate get the prefix " S." — as S. 216.)

Here the bill gets what is known as its " first reading." Each bill that finally passes in either house is read three times along the legislative route. The second reading comes during debate, if the bill gets that far; and the third reading occurs just before the final vote.[5] Each of these readings is usually by title only — " A bill to . . ." — and not in full, except in the case of important or controversial measures. These are usually read in full, line-by-line, on second reading.

The Speaker then refers the bill to the appropriate standing committee. The bill is also recorded in the House *Journal*[6] and in the *Congressional Record*[7] for the day.

---

[5] All bills introduced are immediately printed and distributed to the members. The three readings are somewhat unnecessary now, but were quite important in the days when some members could not read.

[6] The *Journal* contains the minutes of the daily proceedings and these are read at the opening of each day's session, unless dispensed with.

The Committee Stage. The standing committees have been described as " sieves " — sifting out most bills and considering and reporting only the more important or worthwhile ones. Woodrow Wilson once wrote that " Congress in its committee rooms is Congress at work."

Most bills die right here. They are " pigeonholed "[8] and never see the light of day. Many of the bills killed in committee deserve their fate. But occasionally, for political or personal reasons, the majority on a committee will pigeonhole a measure the majority of the House wishes to consider. The bill may be " blasted " out of committee under the " discharge rule,"[9] but this is seldom done successfully.

The bills that a committee, or at least the chairman, does wish to con-

---

[7] The *Congressional Record* is a word-for-word record of the debates, motions, votes, and disposition of bills in each house. The next morning each Congressman has a temporary copy of the previous day's proceedings on his desk. The official reporters often correct the grammar in speeches and give them a more elegant finish without changing the meaning. A Congressman may also " dress up " his remarks before permanent copies of the *Record* are printed.

[8] The term comes from the old-fashioned rolltop desks with pigeonholes into which papers were often put and promptly forgotten. A great number of " by request " bills are regularly killed in each committee. These are bills that Congressmen introduce only because some person or group at home has asked them to do so.

[9] The Discharge Rule provides that after a bill has been in committee for at least thirty days a petition signed by at least half (218) of the total House membership can force a House vote on whether or not the bill should be discharged from the committee.

"IT HAPPENS EVERY YEAR"

White, "The Akron Beacon Journal"

sider are discussed and considered at times indicated by the chairman. Most committees work through sub-committees, which are actually " committees within committees." When more important measures come up, committees may decide to hold public hearings on them. Interested persons, private organizations and pressure groups, and government officials are invited to give testimony in these hearings.[10]

Occasionally, subcommittees make trips (" junkets ") to particular areas affected by a measure. Thus some members of the House Agriculture Committee may journey to the Southwest to look into drought conditions or members of the Senate Interior and Insular Affairs Committee may visit the Pacific Northwest to gather information on a public power bill.

These " junkets " are made at public expense and Congressmen are sometimes criticized for taking them. But an on-the-spot investigation often proves to be the best way a committee may inform itself.

After examining a bill the full committee may do one of several things. It may:

(1) Report the bill favorably, with a " do pass " recommendation. It is then the chairman's job to steer the bill through debate.

(2) Refuse to report the bill, pigeonhole it. In the past some committee chairmen refused to report bills they opposed even though a majority of committee members favored it. The Legislative Reorganization Act now requires a chairman to report a bill " promptly " after committee approval.

(3) Report the bill in amended form. Many bills are changed in

----
[10] If necessary, a committee has the power to *subpoena* a witness. A subpoena is an order compelling one to appear or produce evidence under penalty of contempt for failure to comply.

committee and several on the same subject may be combined before they are reported out.

(4) Report the bill with an unfavorable recommendation. This does not often happen, but sometimes a committee feels that the House should have a chance to consider a bill or the committee does not want to take the responsibility for killing it.

(5) Report a " committee bill." In effect, this is an entirely new bill which the committee has substituted for one or more referred to it. The chairman reports this new bill and it goes on from there.

The Rules Committee and the Calendars. From the standing committee, and before it goes to the floor for consideration, the bill is placed on one of several " calendars." A calendar is a schedule of the order in which bills will be considered on the floor. There are five of these calendars in the House:

(1) *The Calendar of the Whole House on the State of the Union,* commonly known as the *Union Calendar* — for all bills relating to revenues, appropriations, or government property.

(2) *The House Calendar* — for all other public bills.

(3) *The Calendar of the Committee of the Whole House,* sometimes called the *Private Calendar* — for all private bills.

(4) *The Consent Calendar* — for all bills from the Union or House Calendar which are taken up out of order by unanimous consent of the

House. These are usually minor bills to which there is no opposition.

(5) *The Discharge Calendar* — for petitions to discharge bills from committee.

Theoretically, bills are taken from the calendars on a first-come-first-served basis. But, as we have seen, the Rules Committee has the power to bring in a special set of rules to consider a bill out of its regular order — and this is often done. Too, the Rules Committee can prevent a bill from getting to the floor by failing to bring in a special set of rules. It is no wonder that the Rules Committee is sometimes known as the " traffic cop of the House."

The Rules Committee is often criticized and it is true that some members use it for personal or political advantage. But it must also be remembered that despite the great number of bills that die in committee, many more than the House could possibly consider are reported.

For certain bills, definite days are assigned. Bills from the Consent Calendar are considered on the first and third Mondays of each month. District of Columbia measures on the second and fourth Mondays, and private bills on Fridays. On " Calendar Wednesdays " the various committee chairmen may call up any bills their committees have acted on.

But none of these arrangements is followed too closely. What generally happens is rather complicated. Some bills are " privileged " — that is, they may be called up at almost any time, interrupting other business less privileged. Privileged bills include general revenue and appropriations measures, reports of conference committees, and special rules. And on some days, often the first and third Mondays, a two-thirds vote of the House may suspend all rules. When this happens, the House departs so far from its established rules that a major bill can go through all the necessary steps, including final passage, in a single day.

The House calendars and the complicated order of business developed for several reasons. The large size of the House and the wide variety of measures demanded a set order of business. In addition to the House rules, custom has played a part in the development of procedure as we know it today.

Consideration on the Floor. When and if a bill finally manages to reach the floor, it receives its " second reading." It is this part of congressional procedure that is usually seen by the visitor in the galleries.

Many of the bills that Congress enacts are minor ones to which there is little or no opposition. Bills of this sort are usually called from the Consent Calendar, get their second reading by title only, and are quickly disposed of.

About ninety per cent of the more important measures are dealt with in a much different manner, however. They are considered in *Committee of the Whole,* an old parliamentary device for speeding business.

The Committee of the Whole [11] is the House sitting not as itself but as one large committee. Its rules are much less strict and debate is freer. A *quorum* (a majority, 218) must be present to permit the House to conduct business, but in Committee of the Whole only 100 members need be on hand.

When the House resolves itself into Committee of the Whole, the Speaker steps down and the mace is removed for the House is not legally in session. Another member takes the chair and presides.

General debate is held and then the bill receives its second reading, section-by-section. As each section of the bill is read, amendments may be offered. Under the "five-minute rule" the supporters and opponents of each amendment have just five minutes to present their case.

Votes are taken on each section and its amendments as the reading proceeds. When the entire bill has been gone through, and some are as long as a book, the Committee of the Whole has completed its work. It adjourns, the House is back in session, and the work of the committee is formally adopted.

---

[11] Technically, there are two committees of the whole: the Committee of the Whole House, which considers private bills, and the Committee of the Whole House on the State of the Union, which considers public bills, but both are simply the House sitting as a committee of itself. The device has not been used in the Senate, except to consider treaties, since 1930. Because of the Senate's smaller size, all types of committees are less important or necessary than in the House.

Debate. Because of the large size of the House, debate must be and is severely limited. A rule adopted in 1841 limits each member to no more than one hour on any point unless he has unanimous consent to speak longer. If he strays from the subject, the Speaker may force him to sit down.

The Majority and Minority Floor Leaders usually decide in advance how much time will be spent on a bill. And at any time a member may "move the previous question." That is, he may call for a vote, and then the Speaker allows each side another twenty minutes, after which the vote is taken.

As we shall see, this is in sharp contrast to Senate procedure.

Methods of Voting. Four methods of voting are used in the House: (1) *Voice votes* are the most common with the members shouting "Yea" or "Nay." (2) If any member thinks the Speaker has erred in judging which side has the most voice votes, he may call for a *standing vote,* technically known as a "division of the House." All in favor and then all opposed stand and are counted by the Clerk. (3) One-fifth of the members present may demand a *teller vote.* Each of the members voting passes between two tellers, one from each party, and is counted for or against. (4) Finally, a *roll-call* (or *record*) *vote* may be demanded by one-fifth of the members present. Here the Clerk reads the roll and the members are recorded for or against.

Roll-call votes take about forty-five minutes and are sometimes called for by those who want to delay matters while gathering their strength. Throughout a session all of the roll-call votes taken total about *three months* of working time in the House! If the House had an electrical voting system, as half the State legislatures do, a great deal of time could be saved.

Voting procedures in the Senate are quite similar but take much less time because of the fewer members involved.

Final Steps in the House. Once a bill is approved at second reading it is *engrossed* — printed in final form with all changes made in it. Then it is read a third time, by title, and the final vote is taken.

If the bill is defeated, it must begin all over again if it is ever to pass the House. If it is approved, as most bills which reach this stage are, it is signed

Acme Photo

PAGE AT WORK

Page boys serve their Senator sponsors in many ways. Here a boy picks up copies of a report at the document room. They will be placed on the Senator's desk before Congress convenes.

by the Speaker and taken to the Senate by a page boy who lays it on the Vice-President's desk.

The Bill in the Senate

Proceedings in each house are much the same, and so it is not necessary to trace a bill in the Senate as we did through the House. Bills are introduced by Senators, given a title and number, and referred to standing committees. In committee they are dealt with much as they are in the House.

The Senate has only one calendar for all bills reported out of committee, and bills are taken up in the order desired by the Majority Floor Leader. Senate business is conducted in a less formal manner and its rules are more liberal than the rules in the lower house.

Free Debate and the Filibuster. The chief distinction between Senate and House procedures comes in debate. Debate is strictly limited in the House. In the smaller Senate, it is almost unlimited. Because of this, the Senate has been called " the greatest deliberative body in the world " and its members are intensely proud of their right to carry on free debate.

The Filibuster. Occasionally, however, this privilege is abused by a "filibuster." A filibuster is the practice of "talking a bill to death." Under Senate rules, once a member gets the floor he may hold it for as long as he chooses. One or more Senators "filibuster" by talking on and on until the Senate either agrees to drop the bill involved or change it in some manner.

In one famous filibuster several years ago, Senator Huey Long of Louisiana stalled along by reading from the Washington telephone directory and a mail-order catalogue. No rule requires members to speak only on the subject at hand, so filibusterers usually supply themselves with several documents, books, dictionaries, and the like. The filibuster record is now held by Senator Strom Thurmond of South Carolina who spoke against the Voting Rights Act of 1957 for 24 hours and 18 minutes.

The Closure Rule. The Senate does have one rule, adopted in 1917, with which it can limit debate. But the rule is weak and it has been successfully invoked only four times since it was adopted.

The closure rule provides that a petition to close (end) debate on a bill may be signed by sixteen Senators. On the second day after the petition is filed, a vote to end debate must be taken. A full two-thirds (sixty-four) is necessary to approve closure. If it is passed, each Senator has only one hour in which to discuss the bill, and when discussion is finished, a final vote on it is taken.

In addition to using this rule, the Senate tries to beat a filibuster by holding continuous day and night sessions to wear down the participants, but this seldom works. When the Senate adjourns for the day, the member holding the floor has it when the next day's session begins.

The Final Stages

The Conference Committee. Before a bill may be sent to the White House, each house must pass it in exactly the same form. But the two houses often disagree on certain sections in important bills. If one house will not accept the other's changes, a *conference committee* is appointed.

Here, an equal number of Senators and Representatives attempt to "iron out" the differences and draw up a compromise version. The compromise is then submitted to each house and,

if this new version is approved, signed by the Speaker and the President of the Senate.

Most routine bills go through both houses in the same form and, therefore, a conference committee is not necessary.

The President's Action. After passing both the House and Senate in the same form, a bill is sent to the President. He has ten days, not counting Sundays, in which to act. If he signs it, it becomes the law of the land. If he does not act within the ten-day period, it becomes law without his signature.

But if Congress adjourns within the ten days and he does not sign it, the bill dies — the so-called " pocket veto " has been applied.

If the President does not approve of a bill, he may veto it. In this case, he must send it back to the house in which it was first introduced, together with his objections to it.

Congress may, but seldom does, pass a bill over the President's veto. This may be done by a two-thirds vote in each house.

Lobbyists and Pressure Groups

No consideration of Congress in action would be complete without some mention of *lobbyists*. Practically every organized interest in the country — business, labor, agriculture, the professions, veterans, " drys," churches, and a host of other groups — maintain *lobbies* in Washington.

Nearly a thousand well-paid persons are regularly employed as lobbyists. Their task is to work for or against legislation in which their groups are interested. They spend millions each year in their activities.

Some lobbyists are former Congressmen who " know the legislative ropes " and have intimate contacts with many members. Others are lawyers, former journalists or experts in special fields. Government officials also lobby for appropriations and for particular laws.

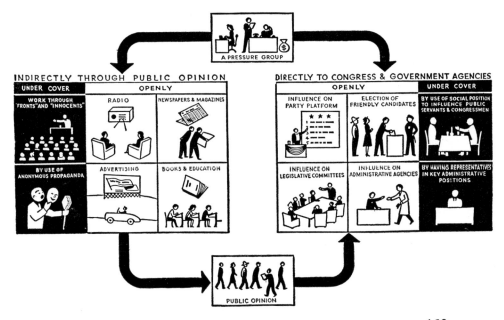

The lobbyist employs numerous and varied methods in his work. Quite often he offers expert (or biased) information to committees and to individual Congressmen. When a committee is considering a bill on agriculture, for example, one of its best sources of information is an organization like the Farm Bureau Federation or the Grange. The so-called " social lobby " affords opportunities for more intimate contacts through parties, dinners, excursions, and the like.

The *pressure group* is wider in scope than the lobby. It exerts pressure on Congress through campaigns to create a favorable public opinion. It encourages letters and telegrams to impress Congressmen with its point of view. Pressure groups work at the " grass-roots " level while lobbyists might be called their Washington arm.

The public generally regards lobbies as " bad," but many are definitely " good." One such group is the Citizens Committee for the Hoover Report which works for " better government at a better price."

The lobbies have been called the " third house of Congress." Lobbying involves the expression of the views of organized groups and, as such, is a part of the democratic process. Abuses do occur, but lobbying is vital to the give-and-take so necessary in a representative government.

Congressional Reforms

Much of the internal organization and rules of procedure in Congress are in sore need of streamlining. Congress itself has recognized the problem. The Legislative Reorganization Act of 1946 was passed to bring about many of the badly needed reforms. But it did not go far enough.

That act reduced the number of standing committees in each house, furnished committees with expert professional staffs, and expanded the Legislative Reference Service to aid Congressmen. It further provided for the registration of lobbyists, attempted to reduce the number of private bills, and removed many petty tasks from the shoulders of Congress.

But much still remains to be done.

Indeed, many Congressmen were surprised that so much was accomplished in 1946. Petty politics and vested interests have several times blocked further improvement.

The seniority rule for committee chairmanships still vexes both houses. At the end of each session a " logjam " of unpassed bills always piles up; many of these are then passed with inadequate consideration while other more worthy bills are lost in the shuffle. Filibustering in the Senate continues to be a matter for debate (pages 161–162).

Many Congressmen have long complained of the need for closer contact with the executive branch of the Government. Several members think that

164

this can be accomplished by allowing members of the President's Cabinet and other officials to appear on the floor of each house at regularly scheduled times for questioning and debate.

Many constituents make unreasonable demands on their Congressman, who feels obligated to meet these demands if he is to keep good will at home. Some Congressmen spend more time with their private affairs than with the nation's business. It is up to Congress, supported by public opinion, to solve these problems.

The Library of Congress

The Library of Congress is the largest library in the world. It occupies two buildings with 35 acres of floor space and shelving for 20,000,-000 books, pamphlets, maps, pieces of music, manuscripts, and bound volumes of papers. The two buildings are on adjoining blocks, and books are carried from the center of one building to the center of the other at the rate of 25 feet a second. The Library has 200 research rooms — many of them air-conditioned. The Library's Legislative Reference Service compiles information and makes studies to aid Congress in its deliberations. The Copyright Office is also within the Library.[12]

WHAT THIS CHAPTER IS ABOUT

Opening day in the House of Representatives is filled with ceremony. A Speaker must be chosen, the members sworn in, employees selected, the rules adopted, and committee posts filled. The Senate's first day is much more simple because it is a continuous body and does not require such wide reorganization.

After organizing, the two Houses await the President's State of the Union Message. In this speech the Chief Executive reports on the condition of the country and makes recommendations. The Congress then turns to its work.

The Speaker is the most important member of the House. His chief duties are to preside and to maintain order. He uses his powers in a partisan way. The Vice-President presides over the Senate, but has little real power.

Committee chairmen, chosen under the controversial rule of seniority, are powerful individuals with almost life-and-death power over bills in their commit-

---

[12] Subordinate to the Librarian of Congress is the Register of Copyrights, whose office is in the annex Library of Congress building in Washington. When a book is published, the notice of copyright should be printed on the title page or the page following. Promptly after publication two copies of the best edition must be sent to the Register with an application for registration and a money order for four dollars payable to the Register of Copyrights. Application forms will be furnished upon request. For a work of art a photograph is sent. Any print or label used for an article of merchandise may be copyrighted for a fee of $6. Lectures, dramas, and music, published or not, may be copyrighted for a fee of $4.

tees. Much of the actual work of Congress is done in committees.

The Majority and Minority Floor Leaders manage their parties' programs on the floor, assisted by the Party Whips. The party caucus consists of all the party's members in each house and has an " executive committee " known as the Policy or Steering Committee.

Congress does a great deal of its work in committees, especially in the House. Standing committees are permanent and bills introduced are referred to them for consideration. One, the House Rules Committee, is " the traffic cop of the legislative process." Special committees are temporary, and joint committees, consisting of members of each house, permanent. Conference committees " iron out " differences in bills passed by both houses. Investigating committees provide information to Congress.

Bills may be introduced only by Senators or Representatives, though they usually originate with another source, the executive branch, for example. After introduction they are referred to committee, where most of them die. Bills reported out go on one of five calendars in the House to be called up through the Rules Committee. There is only one calendar in the Senate and bills are called up by the Majority Floor Leader. The House Rules Committee, through its power to bring in special rules, is very important.

Bills are debated in the House at the second of the three readings. The House, but not the Senate, considers most important bills in Committee of the Whole.

Debate is sharply limited in the House but not in the Senate. Filibustering, talking a bill to death, may be prevented in the Senate, but seldom is, through the closure rule.

Bills passed in different form by the two houses go to a conference committee. Then the bill goes to the President who may sign it, allow it to become law without his signature, veto it, or pocket veto it. Congress may override a veto by a two-thirds vote in each house.

Lobbies, the legislative arm of pressure groups, are a vital part of the democratic process. Lobbyists work for and against those bills in which their clients are interested.

Congress still needs many reforms, as in the rule of seniority, but political considerations many times block badly needed changes.

The Library of Congress, largest library in the world, is intended especially for the use of members but does much for the general public, too.

QUESTIONS ON THE TEXT

1. Describe and contrast the opening day in the House and Senate. How is the Speaker *actually* chosen?

2. Who presides in the House? In the Senate? Why does the Senate have an alternate presiding officer?

3. How do committee chairmen get their posts? Why are they so powerful?

4. What are the jobs of the Floor Leaders? The Whips? What is the caucus?

5. Distinguish: standing, special, joint, and conference committees. What role does the Rules Committee play in the House?

6. Give three reasons why Congress must have the power to investigate.

7. List three sources for bills. Who may introduce bills? About what propor-

tion of the bills which are introduced finally become law?

8. Who refers bills to committee in the House? What is meant by *pigeonholing?*

9. What is a calendar? Why is the House Rules Committee so important?

10. What is a Committee of the Whole?

11. Explain how debate is limited in the House. What is a *filibuster* in the Senate?

12. What four methods of voting are used in Congress? Which is most common?

13. What alternatives has the President when the Congress sends a bill to him for his action?

14. What do lobbyists do?

15. Why hasn't Congress made many of the reforms that it recognizes and obviously needs?

PROBLEMS FOR DISCUSSION

1. Many Congressmen are reluctant to vote on a roll-call vote. Why? Would you favor or oppose an electrical voting system which would provide a " score card " on each Congressman for the information of his constituents?

2. One of the most famous filibusters in Senate history occurred in March, 1917. President Wilson had asked Congress for a law authorizing him to arm merchant vessels for protection against German submarines. The bill passed the House 403–13. Nearly all members of the Senate favored it. But a small handful managed to filibuster it to death. The public was outraged and President Wilson wrote: " A little group of willful men, representing no opinion but their own, have rendered the great government of the United States helpless and contemptible."

As a result of this episode, the Senate passed the closure rule. But the rule is a weak one. What is your own attitude toward filibusters? What arguments can you give to counter your own?

3. Such surveys as the Gallup Poll and the Roper Poll and those conducted by various newspapers and magazines indicate public opinion. Should a Congressman vote in accordance with these even when he personally disagrees? Should he vote for the national good even when this conflicts with what might be best for his own locale? Explain.

4. Do you think, as many do, that sessions of Congress should be broadcast and televised? Why?

THINGS YOU MIGHT DO

1. Stage a debate on the question: *Resolved,* That the practice of filibustering should be abolished in the Senate.

2. If possible, invite your Senator or Representative to address the class or student body on the work of Congress.

3. Trace a current bill as it goes through the legislative mill. Follow it in the newspapers and ask your Congressmen how they feel about it. Also, ask them for the committee reports relating to the measure.

4. Draw up a list of eight or ten questions on current topics. Ask your Congressmen for their opinions on each one and compare the answers.

5. One or more students could prepare a short essay on the work of the Rules Committee, the methods of voting used in Congress, the office of Speaker, the rule of seniority, or needed congressional reforms.

WORDS AND PHRASES YOU SHOULD KNOW

Calendar
Closure rule
Committee of the
  Whole
Conference committee
Congressional Record
" Father of the House "
Filibuster
Hopper
Joint committee
Junket

Legislative Reorganization
  Act
Lobbyist
Majority Floor Leader
Minority Floor Leader
Party caucus
Party Whip
Pigeonhole
Pocket veto
President pro tem
Rider

Roll-call vote
Rule of seniority
Speaker of the House
Special Committee
Standing committees
Standing vote
State of the Union
  Message
Teller vote
Veto
Voice vote

SELECT BIBLIOGRAPHY

BAILEY, STEPHEN K., and SAMUEL, HOWARD D., *Congress at Work.* Holt, 1952.

BOYD, EDWARD, " Mr. Speaker — the Dynamo of Capitol Hill," *American Magazine,* April, 1955.

BURNHAM, JAMES, " Tribunes of the People," *Reader's Digest,* February, 1955.

CARR, ROBERT K., and others, *American Democracy in Theory and Practice,* Chapters 19, 21, and 22. Rinehart, 1955.

CARR, ROBERT K., *The Constitution and Congressional Investigating Committees.* League of Women Voters, 1954.

" Congressional Elections," *Current History,* October, 1954.

GALLOWAY, GEORGE B., *The Legislative Process in Congress.* Crowell, 1953.

——, " To Break the Congress Log-Jam," *The New York Times Magazine,* July 26, 1953.

" Inside a Senate Investigation," *U.S. News and World Report,* October 22, 1954.

JOHNSON, CLAUDIUS O., *American National Government,* Chapter 13. Crowell, 1955.

KENNEDY, SENATOR JOHN F., " Ross of Kansas: The Man Who Saved a President," *Harper's,* December, 1955.

NEUBERGER, SENATOR RICHARD L., " Washington Lobbyists: the Third House of Congress," *Coronet,* August, 1956.

PRINGLE, HENRY F. and KATHERINE, " The ' Terrible Twelve ' of Capitol Hill," *Saturday Evening Post,* June 19, 1954.

SHALLETT, SIDNEY, " The Loneliest Man in Washington," *Saturday Evening Post,* January 8, 1955.

" The Lobbyists," *Time,* January 30, 1956.

WILSON, H. HUBERT, *Congress: Corruption and Compromise.* Rinehart, 1951.

UNIT III
THE EXECUTIVE
DEPARTMENT

The White House

Wide World Photo

ENERGY IN THE EXECUTIVE is a leading characteristic in the definition of good government. It is essential to the protection of the community against foreign attacks; it is essential to the steady administration of the laws . . . A feeble executive implies a feeble execution of the government. A feeble executive is but another name for a bad executive; and a government ill-executed, whatever it may be in theory, must be, in practice, a bad government.

ALEXANDER HAMILTON
The Federalist, No. 70, 1788

He is the Chief of State, and he is the symbol of the American people.

— *The Hoover Commission*

★

Chapter 10

THE PRESIDENCY

In 1953 and again in 1957, Dwight D. Eisenhower placed his left hand on a Bible, raised his right hand, and solemnly swore that he would " preserve, protect and defend the Constitution of the United States." With this pledge he began each of his terms as the thirty-fourth President of the United States. As President, he occupies the most powerful and the most important office in the world.

His powers in both domestic and foreign affairs are vast. The manner in which he uses them is of the greatest importance to people everywhere. And the problems he faces are as complex and difficult as his powers are great.

The burdens of the presidential office are tremendously heavy. Every day he must make decisions, small ones and big ones, that can and often do shape the course of history. He is the official spokesman for the United States and its government, and his words and actions are closely watched here and abroad.

Admiral George Dewey, when he announced that he was a candidate for the presidential nomination in 1900, said that " the office of the President is not such a very difficult one to fill, his duties being mainly to execute the laws of Congress." Let us see why this is one of the most ridiculous comments ever made in our public life.

The Election of the President

The Constitutional Convention spent more time on the question of choosing the President than on any other matter. It was, said James Wilson, " the most difficult of all on which we have had to decide."

Direct election by the people was opposed by nearly all of the delegates for two reasons: (1) because they felt

that it would lead, as Alexander Hamilton said, to " tumult and disorder " and " mob rule," and (2) because they did not believe that the people, scattered over so large an area, could know enough about the various candidates to make a wise decision.

Election by Congress was favored at first. But the Framers later changed their opinion. Most of them felt that this would destroy the check and balance system and put the President " too much under the legislative thumb."

The original plan, as outlined in Article II, is a rather simple one. The Constitution set up an indirect scheme under which the President is chosen by a " college of electors."

Briefly, it was provided that each State would have as many electors as Senators and Representatives in Congress. These electors would be chosen in each State in whatever manner the legislature might direct. Each elector would cast two electoral votes, each for a different person. The man receiving the highest number of votes, if that amounted to a majority, would become President and the runner-up would be Vice-President. If no one received a majority or if there was a tie for President, the House would decide the matter. The Senate would settle any similar dispute over the vice-presidency.

Flaws in the system began to appear in 1796 when John Adams was elected President and his arch rival, Thomas Jefferson, was elected Vice-President.

The system collapsed in the election of 1800. Two well-defined political parties had developed — the Federalists and the Republicans (later called Democrats). Both parties put forth candidates in 1800 and the electors were chosen with the understanding that they would vote for their own party's nominees.

All seventy-three of the Republican electors voted for Thomas Jefferson and Aaron Burr. Of course, this produced a tie. And the tie was possible because each elector casts *two* ballots, each for a different man but each for President.

Although popular opinion clearly favored Jefferson for President and Burr for Vice-President, the House had to take thirty-six separate ballots before Jefferson was finally chosen.

The 12th Amendment was added to the Constitution in 1804 to prevent this from happening again. The electors now cast one ballot for President and a second and separate one for Vice-President.

The Electoral College System Today. Each State chooses as many electors as it has Senators and Representatives. Texas, for example, has twenty-two Representatives and two Senators, hence twenty-four electors. At first the legislatures chose electors, but after a few years they were elected by the people.[1]

---

[1] In only three States (California, Massachusetts, and Oregon) are the electors *legally* bound to vote for the candidate who carries their State. But, because electors are themselves party men, they almost always vote for their party's candidate. Except in the three States just noted, it is quite possible, however, for an elector to vote for some one other than the candidate of his party. Only five times has any elector ever done so, however: in 1796, 1824, 1912, 1948, and 1956. In 1956 an Alabama elector voted for State Circuit Judge Walter B. Jones, even though the Democratic party had carried Alabama and the State's ten other electors voted for Adlai Stevenson.

Today in each State the electors are chosen on a general state-wide ticket. Thus in a State with a Democratic majority, all the electors will be Democrats; in a State in which Republican voters are in the majority, all the electors will be Republicans. The election of 1884 provides an unusual illustration of this.

In 1884 the Democrats in New York had a majority of less than 600 out of a total vote of more than 1,000,-000. But all of the State's thirty-six electors were Democrats because of that handful of votes. And they all cast their electoral ballots for the Democratic candidate, Grover Cleveland. In the same election, the Republicans had a majority of 81,000 in a total Pennsylvania vote of 886,-000. All thirty of Pennsylvania's electors were Republicans and cast their ballots for James G. Blaine.

In other words, in these two States Blaine received some 80,000 more popular votes than Cleveland. But Cleveland received six more electoral votes. (If Blaine had carried New York, he, not Cleveland, would have been President.)

In brief, the President is elected as follows: Each major party nominates a candidate for the presidency at a national convention held in July or August of the " presidential year." At about the same time, the various parties in each State nominate their candidates for electors, in whatever manner is provided by State law. The electors are then chosen by the voters in each State on the Tuesday follow-ing the first Monday in November of every fourth year. Thus in 1956 the electors were chosen on November 6th.

A third of the States still print the names of the electors on the ballot, but more and more States are simply listing the names of the presidential and vice-presidential candidates. Regardless of what the ballot looks like, the fact remains that the people do not vote for a President and Vice-President. They vote for electors who in turn choose them.

To illustrate the election process, if a Republican in Wisconsin votes for

34th PRESIDENT

President Eisenhower smiles as he sits at his desk in the White House. This picture was taken January 21, 1953, the day after his inauguration as the thirty-fourth President of the United States. His second term expires January 20, 1961.

United Press Photo

SAMPLE

Official Presidential Ballot

Make a cross (X) or other mark in the square opposite the names of the candidates for whose electors you desire to vote. Vote in ONE square only.

DWIGHT D. EISENHOWER .... President ⎱ Republican
RICHARD M. NIXON .... Vice President ⎰   ☐

ADLAI E. STEVENSON .... President ⎱ Democrat
ESTES KEFAUVER .... Vice President ⎰   ☐

T COLEMAN ANDREWS .... President ⎱
  (Better Government Under the Constitution)   ⎱ Independent   ☐
THOMAS HAROLD WERDEL .... Vice President ⎰
  (Better Government Under the Constitution)

FARRELL DOBBS .... President ⎱
  (Socialist Workers Party)   ⎱ Independent   ☐
MYRA TANNER WEISS .... Vice President ⎰
  (Socialist Workers Party)

ERIC HASS .... President ⎱
  (Socialist Labor Party)   ⎱ Independent   ☐
GEORGIA COZZINI .... Vice President ⎰
  (Socialist Labor Party)

DARLINGTON HOOPES .... President ⎱
  (Socialist Party)   ⎱ Independent   ☐
SAMUEL H. FRIEDMAN .... Vice President ⎰
  (Socialist Party)

WISCONSIN BALLOT

In the 1956 Presidential election the Eisenhower-Nixon ticket carried Wisconsin's twelve electoral votes with a popular plurality of 367,823. In this record-breaking Presidential election more voters went to the polls than ever before in the history of the United States.

the twelve Republican electors, he places an X after the name of the Republican presidential candidate on the official ballot. Then, if after the State election board has received all of the returns of the election from the various local election boards, it is found that the Republican electors have received more votes than any other set of electors, they assemble at the capital city,[2] Madison, and cast

[2] The law provides that the electors shall meet "at such place in each State as the legislature of such State shall direct." All of the legislatures have designated their State capitals.

their votes the first Monday after the second Wednesday in December. The votes are signed by each elector, sealed, and sent by registered mail to the president of the Senate in Washington.[3] The same method is followed in all States today.

On the sixth of January, the president of the Senate opens the returns from each State and counts them in the presence of both houses of Congress. The candidate who receives a majority of the votes for President is declared elected. The same process is gone through for the Vice-President.

If no one has a majority for President (at least 266 of the 531 electoral votes), the election is thrown into the House. This happened as we saw, in 1800, and it happened again in 1824. The House chooses a President from among the top three candidates in the Electoral College. Each State delegation has one vote and it takes a majority (twenty-five) to elect.[4] If the House fails to choose a President

[3] Two lists of votes are sent to the State Secretary of State, two to the Archivist of the United States, one to the president of the Senate, and one to the local U. S. District Judge. If the president of the Senate, or the Archivist of the United States, does not receive the votes of any State and cannot obtain them from the State Secretary of State by the 4th Wednesday of December, he sends a special messenger for the votes filed with the District Judge.

[4] Two vital objections have been raised against electing the President in the House: (1) a small State like Nevada has the same vote as a large State, like New York; and (2) if the House members from a State divide equally, the State loses its vote.

by January 20th, the newly elected Vice-President is inaugurated as President.

If no man receives a majority for Vice-President, the Senate decides between the top two candidates. It takes a majority of the whole Senate to elect. The Senate has had to choose a Vice-President only once, in 1837.

Criticisms of the Electoral College System have been heard almost from the beginning. One of the most common complaints involves so-called "minority presidents." Several men have been chosen President by receiving a majority of the *electoral* votes but at the same time receiving *less* than a majority of the *popular* votes.

The most striking example of this occurred in the election of 1888. Benjamin Harrison received a majority of the electoral votes even though Grover Cleveland actually received almost 100,000 more popular votes. This happened because Cleveland piled up big majorities in the Southern States (with less electoral votes) while Harrison carried most of the Northern States by smaller majorities.

In 1860 Abraham Lincoln received *more* popular votes than any of his rivals but still had 500,000 less than a majority of all the votes cast. In 1912 Woodrow Wilson had some 2,000,000 more popular votes than his nearest competitor, Theodore Roosevelt; still Wilson received only forty-two per cent of all votes cast.

In short, the record shows that the electoral voter bears only a very indirect relationship to the people's choice as shown by the popular vote. Using the 1956 vote as an illustration, note how inexact the electoral vote is as a barometer of national preference:

	ELECTORAL VOTE	%	POPULAR VOTE	%
Eisenhower	457	86.1	35,582,236	57.2
Stevenson	73	13.7	26,028,887	41.9
Jones	1	0.2	——	

Two other criticisms of the Electoral College System have already been mentioned. The first of these is that there is no provision in the Constitution, or in any federal statute, requiring electors to vote for the candidate favored by the popular vote. As we noted on page 172, electors have "broken their pledges" on five different occasions. The other criticism (see page 174) is that in *any* presidential election it is *possible* that the contest will be decided in the House of Representatives rather than by a vote of the people.

Current proposals for change revolve around two generally supported moves. Both would require amendment of the Constitution: (1) Retain the electors and continue to choose two at large in each state (i.e., one for each Senator) plus one for each representative-at-large (if any) and choose all others from the congressional districts. (2) Discard the electors and allow the people to vote directly on the presidential and vice-presidential candidates, then apportion each State's total electoral vote among the candidates on the basis of the popular vote, with a plurality of 40 per cent the minimum for election.

Direct popular election (which would mean discarding both electors and electoral votes) would mean that a State with unrestricted suffrage requirements would have an unfair advantage over those States that require higher educational attainments for their voters.

Qualifications, Term, Compensation, Succession

The President's Qualifications. Whatever else he must be to gain this highest of offices, the Constitution provides that the President must (1) be a natural-born citizen of the United States, (2) be at least thirty-five years of age, and (3) have been at least fourteen years a resident within the United States.

Compensation of the President. The President's salary is set by Congress, and it cannot be changed during his term of office. He receives a salary of $100,000 yearly plus a $50,000 " expense account," both of which are taxable.

The Constitution forbids him " any other emolument from the United States or any of them." [5] But this provision is not construed to forbid such supplementary funds as are necessary to provide the White House (with its 16 acres of grounds including a swimming pool, theater, tennis courts), a large suite of offices, a large official staff, a private railway car, several airplanes and automobiles, a yacht, medical and dental care for himself and his family, a very liberal travel and entertainment fund, and similar perquisites. The total of his salary and perquisites comes to about $3,000,000 a year. Still his actual income is well below that of many persons in private life.

Term of the President. Upon his inauguration on January 20 following his election, the President serves a four-year term. Until the 22nd Amendment, there was no constitutional limitation on the number of terms a President might serve, provided he could gain the necessary votes.[6] The 22nd Amendment, added in 1951, now provides that no President may serve more than ten years — a maximum of two elected terms of his own plus not more than two years of a term to which he had previously succeeded from the vice-presidency.

Succession to the Presidency. Should a President die in office, resign, be removed by impeachment, or otherwise be unable to continue in office, the Constitution says that the

---

[5] At the Constitutional Convention, Benjamin Franklin argued that, since money and power might corrupt a man, the President should receive nothing beyond his actual expenses. But Franklin's suggestion was never brought to a vote.

[6] Several Presidents, beginning with George Washington, refused to run for more than two terms. Soon the so-called " no-third-term tradition " became an unwritten custom. Franklin Roosevelt, however, broke with tradition when he sought and won third and fourth terms in 1940 and 1944. The 22nd Amendment made the old unwritten custom a part of the written Constitution.

powers and duties of the office " shall devolve on the Vice-President." [7]

The Constitution leaves to Congress the power to determine the order of succession after the Vice-President. The Presidential Succession Act of 1947 places the Speaker of the House next in line. He is followed by the President *pro tem.* of the Senate and then by the Secretary of State and by the other members of the Cabinet in order.

The Vice-President

When Thomas Jefferson was elected Vice-President in 1796 he wrote:

It will give me philosophical evenings in the winter and rural days in the summer. The second office of the Government is honorable and easy.

Throughout our history the vice-presidency has been regarded as something of a " fifth-wheel." John Adams, the first to hold the office, called it " the most insignificant office that ever the invention of man contrived or his imagination conceived." While he was President, Theodore Roosevelt, who had himself been Vice-President, was annoyed by the tinkling of a huge chandelier in his study. He ordered it removed and said, " Take it to the office of the Vice-President. He doesn't have anything to do. It will keep him awake."

Despite the jokes, the vice-presidency is important if for no other reason than the fact that the occupant is " only a heart beat away from being President." So far in our history seven Presidents have died in office.

Too often when the national conventions are selecting the vice-presidential candidates they forget this important fact. Candidates are usually nominated with an eye to politics — to help carry a doubtful State or appease

MR. NIXON AT WORK

Among the varied duties of the Vice-President of the United States is that of interviewing the many persons who have business to conduct with the Executive Branch. Mr. Nixon here takes notes on a conference at his White House office.

Courtesy LIFE Magazine: © *Time, Inc.*

[7] But, strictly speaking, the Constitution (Article II, Section I, Clause 5) does *not* say that the Vice-President shall become President. Only tradition dictates this — beginning with John Tyler's succession in 1841.

a disappointed faction in the party, to replenish the party treasury or appeal to a particular section of the country, to reward a faithful party workhorse, or for some similar reason.

The qualifications for the Vice-President are the same as those for the President whom he might have to replace. As we have seen, his only constitutional duty, unless he succeeds to the presidency, is to preside over the Senate. Most of our Vice-Presidents have been men with years of legislative experience and, because of this, they have often proven to be valuable links between the White House and Capitol Hill.

The Vice-President's salary is $35,-000 a year plus $10,000 for " personal expenses." Many have suggested that he be given more responsibility in the executive branch. In this manner he would be more aware of the problems of the office should the President die. Too, he could be used to relieve the President of some of the tremendous burden the Chief Executive carries. From all reports, Vice-President Nixon is more of a " working Vice-President " than any before him.

Presidential Assistants

The Executive Office of the President is the Chief Executive's right arm. It is an agency directly under him staffed by his closest official advisers and his chief assistants. Actually, the Office consists of five agencies:

(1) *The White House Office* includes the immediate assistants to the President: secretaries and administrative assistants who assist the President in such matters as public relations, personnel problems, relations with Congress, foreign affairs and the like. There are several others, too, including a physician, military aides, the Secretary to the Wife of the President, and dozens of clerks and stenographers.

(2) *The National Security Council* has been called " America's cold-war general staff." It advises the President on all matters relating to national security. The President is chairman and the other members include the Vice-President, the Secretaries of State and Defense, the Director of the Office of Defense Mobilization, and certain other officers whom the President might choose to appoint. The Central Intelligence Agency, under the Council, makes recommendations to that body and is the clearing house for national security information from all governmental agencies.

(3) *The Office of Defense Mobilization* is responsible for planning the emergency steps we must take in the event of war. For example, it has blueprinted a price and wage control program and, if such controls become necessary again, will administer them. The Office also has charge of the stockpiling of scarce strategic materials.

(4) *The Council of Economic Ad-*

178

PRESS CONFERENCE

Flashbulbs and careful notes accompany the President's words as he answers newsmen's queries. The press conference is an important means for presidential communication with the country at large.

visers is composed of three expert economists who advise the President on economic matters, report to him on the state of the national economy, and assist him in the preparation of his economic reports to Congress.

(5) *The Bureau of the Budget* is a sort of "handy man" for the President. Its major job is to direct the preparation of the annual budget which the President submits to Congress. But it also studies and recommends changes in the organization and procedures of the whole executive branch, keeps the President informed on the work of the various agencies, aids other agencies with almost any kind of problem, supervises the expenditure of funds, and attempts to establish better working relationships with the State governmental agencies.

The Cabinet

The Cabinet is not provided for by the Constitution,[8] nor was it created by an act of Congress. It is one of many examples of ways in which our governmental system has devel-

---

[8] The closest thing in the Constitution is found in Article II, Section 2, Clause 1, where the President is authorized to "require the opinion, in writing, of the principal officer in each of the executive departments upon any subject relating to the duties of their respective offices."

oped through custom in the course of the years.

The First Congress created the posts of Secretary of State, Secretary of the Treasury, Secretary of War, and Attorney-General in 1789. By his second term, President Washington was seeking the advice of these three officers — and so the Cabinet was born.

Today there are ten Cabinet members. These secretaryships were established over the years, as shown in the following list:

1. The Secretary of State	1789
2. The Secretary of the Treasury	1789
3. The Secretary of Defense [9]	1947
4. The Attorney-General	1789
5. The Postmaster-General	1794
6. The Secretary of the Interior	1849
7. The Secretary of Agriculture	1889
8. The Secretary of Commerce	1903
9. The Secretary of Labor	1913
10. The Secretary of Health, Education and Welfare	1953

These ten secretaries are appointed by the President to serve at his pleasure. As the Cabinet they serve as a sort of advisory council. Its meetings are secret, but other officials are often invited to attend. For example, Vice-President Nixon attends and often conducts Cabinet meetings.

Some Presidents have had unofficial advisory groups besides the Cabinet. Andrew Jackson had such a group and it usually met in the kitchen of the White House. Of course, it came to be known as the " Kitchen Cabinet."

The President usually meets with the Cabinet once a week in a room in the executive offices which adjoin the White House. He does not have to take their advice unless he wants to. Abraham Lincoln once brought a proposition he favored before his Cabinet, but every member voted against it. Lincoln then announced the vote: " Seven nays, one aye; the ayes have it."

The President's Powers

Article II of the Constitution begins with the statement: " The executive power shall be vested in a President of the United States of America." And then it lists specific powers: for example, to execute the law, make treaties, approve or veto acts of Con-

gress, convene and adjourn Congress, and command the armed forces.

As in so many of its provisions, the Constitution provides only an outline of presidential power. Nearly 170 years of history have added much to that outline. Several factors have contributed to the growth of the office. The manner in which strong Presidents like Washington, Jackson, Lincoln, Cleveland, and the two Roosevelts used their powers has helped to shape the presidency. Acts of Congress and court decisions have done

[9] In 1947 the Congress created the Department of Defense and included the old War Department (1789) and Navy Department (1798) and a new Air Force Department (1947) within it. The Secretaries of the Army, the Navy, and the Air Force are without Cabinet rank. By law, they must be civilians.

it, too, and much of the real nature of the office is overlooked by those who forget that the President is also the leading power in his political party.

Power of Appointment. The Constitution provides that the President

by and with the advice and consent of the Senate, shall appoint ambassadors, other public ministers, and consuls, judges of the Supreme Court, and all other officers of the United States whose appointments are not otherwise herein provided for, but the Congress may by law vest the appointment of such inferior officers, as they think proper, in the President alone, in the courts of law, or in the heads of departments.[10]

There are some 2,300,000 civilian employees of the National Government. Of these, the President unaided appoints very few; with the consent of the Senate he appoints about 26,000 of the most important; perhaps half are selected by competitive civil service examinations; and the rest, many of whom are laborers, are appointed by the department heads or their assistants.

The *President alone* appoints the members of his personal staff and such others as officers for secret missions.

With the *consent of the Senate* he appoints the most important officers, for example: ambassadors, Cabinet members and their chief assistants, federal judges, military and naval officers, heads of such agencies as the

Interstate Commerce Commission, most postmasters, and district attorneys and marshals.

The unwritten rule of *senatorial courtesy* plays an important part in the appointment process. This custom requires the President to confer with the Senator or Senators of his party from a State before making an appointment in that State. The Senate will approve only those appointments which are approved by the majority party Senators from the State involved. In many instances this practice means that the *actual* appointment is made by a Senator. (See page 94.)

The *Civil Service Commission* examines applicants for more than 1,000,000 positions, such as clerks, postmasters, letter carriers, Internal Revenue Service agents, and the like. The President and other high officers make appointments based on the civil service ratings.

Removal Power. Except for the cumbersome impeachment process, the Constitution is silent on the power to remove appointive officers. But the First Congress gave the President the power to remove any officer he appoints, except judges. Without such a power, the President could be saddled with misfits and political opponents in his administration.

In the postwar fight between President Johnson and Congress, the Tenure of Office Act of 1867 was passed. It prohibited the President from removing certain officers without Senate consent. Though Johnson and his

[10] Article II, Section 2, Clause 2. Those whose appointments are "otherwise provided for" are the President, Vice-President, Senators, Representatives, electors, and employees of Congress.

supporters charged that the law was unconstitutional, it was never challenged in the courts. The act was finally repealed in 1887.

The question of the removal power did not reach the Supreme Court until the *Myers Case* in 1926. In 1876 Congress had passed a law requiring Senate consent before the President could remove any first-, second-, or third-class postmaster. In 1920, without consulting the Senate, President Wilson removed one Frank S. Myers as postmaster at Portland, Oregon. Myers sued for the salary he claimed was due him for the remaining portion of his four-year term, basing his claim on the fact that he had been removed in violation of the 1876 law.

The Supreme Court held the act of 1876 unconstitutional. Chief Justice Taft, himself a former President, declared that the removal power was essential to the carrying out of the President's constitutional duty to " take care that the laws be faithfully executed."

In the 1935 *Humphrey Case* the Supreme Court limited the President's removal power slightly by holding that *quasi-legislative* and *quasi-judicial* officers [11] could be removed only for the reasons provided by Congress. This decision grew out of President Roosevelt's removal of a Federal Trade Commissioner who had been ap-

pointed for a seven-year term which still had five years to run.

Generally then, the President may remove those he appoints. Those who enter office through civil service may be removed in any cause " for the good of the service."

Powers in Foreign Affairs. In the field of foreign affairs the scope of the President's power is well-nigh immeasurable. This is particularly evident in today's world.

Receiving Diplomatic Representatives. The President receives ambassadors and ministers sent to the United States. Upon an appointed day the Secretary of State escorts a new minister or ambassador to the White House, where the latter delivers a short ceremonial address to which the President responds. The minister or ambassador is then recognized as the official organ of communication between the United States Government and the government represented. When the independence of a country is in doubt, or the representative is personally objectionable to the United States Government, the President may refuse to receive him; and the President may request a foreign country to recall a representative, or dismiss one for conduct offensive to the Government. Recognition does not necessarily indicate favor of a particular regime; and the withdrawing or withholding of diplomatic recognition has occasionally been used to indicate official displeasure.

Treaty Power. If the United States desires to enter into commercial

---

[11] That is, officers whose duties are *partly* legislative and *partly* judicial. For example, members of the FTC *make rules* and *decide controversies;* they have *quasi-legislative* and *quasi-judicial* powers.

Unit III. THE EXECUTIVE DEPARTMENT

Wide World Photo

WHITE HOUSE "HELIPORT"

In the interests of speed and efficiency the President has taken to the air, using helicopters. This fast "taxi" service is also safer, in ordinary times and especially in times of national crises. In a matter of minutes the President can be at the airport and out of the city.

compacts, define its boundaries, make peace, or enter into any other compacts appropriate for international agreements, the President, with the assistance of the State Department, may negotiate a treaty with the other state or states concerned. Given Senate approval, it is then signed by his representative, usually the Secretary of State. The Constitution provides that a vote of two thirds of the Senate present is necessary before the treaty may be signed by the President and become binding.[12]

[12] As a treaty is merely a law, Congress may repeal it by passing a law contrary to its provisions; or an existing law may be re-

The small original Senate of twenty-six members was considered a suitable council to advise the President as to foreign relations. Secrecy was then considered necessary in debating foreign relations, and it was not believed that secrecy could be maintained in a

pealed by the terms of a treaty. In other words, when a treaty and a law of Congress conflict, a court will consider the one last enacted to be the law. A treaty which is contrary to the Constitution is void, but the courts have, as yet, never declared one to be contrary to the Constitution.

Money cannot be appropriated by a treaty, but in practice whenever the Senate has agreed to a treaty providing for the payment of money, the House has concurred on a bill appropriating it.

group as large as the House; and the two-thirds requirement compensated the House for exclusion from treaty-making deliberations.

Turn the two-thirds rule around and it becomes a one-third rule. In other words, one third of the members plus one is all that is necessary to defeat a treaty — no matter how popular it might be with the people generally. Because of this, many have criticized the rule and suggested change to a simple majority.

John Hay, one of our greatest Secretaries of State, once remarked: " The irreparable mistake of our Constitution puts it into the power of one third plus one of the Senate to meet with a categorical veto any treaty negotiated by the President, even though it might have the hearty approval of nine tenths of the people of the nation."

After World War I, the Treaty of Versailles, which included the creation of the League of Nations, was rejected by our Senate even though 49 senators voted for it and only 35 against it. This was 7 votes short of the necessary two thirds. More than once, the President has been forced to bow to a small minority in the Senate in order to secure passage of a treaty — even when this involved concessions opposed by the majority.

On other occasions, Presidents have had to resort to round-about methods. When a Senate minority rejected a treaty to annex Texas, President Polk accomplished annexation by a *joint resolution* of both houses — a

move which required only a majority in each. Hawaii was likewise annexed by a joint resolution after a treaty had failed.

Executive Agreements. Agreements entered into with a foreign state do not always take the form of treaties. More and more, our international agreements, especially routine ones, are made as *executive agreements*. These agreements are concluded between the President and the chief executive of the foreign state or states involved — but do not require senatorial approval. Such agreements are sometimes submitted, however, for approval (by simple majority) by *both houses* of Congress. But this is not the common practice — usually being done only when appropriations are needed to implement the agreement.

The Supreme Court has held executive agreements to be as legally binding as treaties, and a part of the supreme law of the land. Indeed, some argue that executive agreements can be used instead of treaties in any and all cases.

One of the most notable of executive agreements came in 1940. Then, President Roosevelt gave 50 over-age destroyers to Great Britain in exchange for 99-year leases to several island bases extending from Newfoundland to South America.

Hundreds of executive agreements are made each year. For example, over 10,000 have been made to spell out the terms of the North Atlantic Treaty alone.

The President's Military Powers.
The Constitution makes the President Commander-in-Chief of the Armed Forces. His military powers are shared with the Congress because that body makes rules for the governance of the Armed Forces, must appropriate the funds for defense as well as for all other purposes, and has the power to declare war. The Senate must confirm the appointments (commissions) of military officers.

But the President's position here is as dominant as in the related field of foreign affairs. He may literally force Congress to act. Thus, in 1907, President Theodore Roosevelt sent the Navy around the world in order that the men might gain experience and that other nations might be impressed with its strength. Some Congressmen objected to the cost and threatened to withhold the necessary appropriation. Mr. Roosevelt is said to have replied: " Very well, the existing appropriation will carry the Navy half way around the world and if Congress chooses to leave it on the other side, all right." President Polk brought on the Mexican War by ordering troops across the Nueces River, and President Truman, acting in support of the United Nations, sent elements of the Army, Navy, Marines, and Air Force to Korea in 1950. Presidents have used the armed forces in combat at least 127 times without a congressional declaration of war.

The President directs campaigns and could take personal command of the Army or Navy if he wished. So long as he acts within the rules of international law he may do anything to weaken the power of the enemy. In the exercise of this power President Lincoln issued the Emancipation Proclamation during the War Between the States, freeing the slaves in certain Southern States.

Whenever the enforcement of federal law is prevented by combinations too strong to be suppressed by the courts with their marshals, the President may send United States regular troops to protect the mails and interstate commerce, as Cleveland did in 1894 during the Pullman strike at Chicago; or he may call out State militia, as Roosevelt did in 1940. When the army occupies the enemy's territory, the President, as commander-in-chief, may assume control of the enemy government, as President McKinley did in Puerto Rico and in the Philippines, or as Mr. Truman did in Japan, in a part of Germany, and elsewhere.

In case of domestic violence, the legislature of a State, or the governor, if the legislature is not in session, may request the President to send regular troops into the State with commands to restore order.

Legislative Powers. The Constitution makes the President the chief *executive* officer of the government. As a part of the check and balance system, it also gives him certain legislative powers. These powers make it possible for him to exert considerable influence over Congressional legislation.

Power to Recommend Legislation. The Constitution requires that the President

from time to time, give to the Congress information of the State of the Union, and recommend to their consideration such measures as he shall judge necessary and expedient.

At the beginning of each session the President delivers his State of the Union Message to the Congress. This is quickly followed by the proposed budget and an economic report. He also submits occasional special messages on particular subjects. In all of these he recommends laws that he considers necessary.

In a sense, the President has become the leader in lawmaking. In fact, Congress spends a good share of its time considering the measures that he has requested.

The Chief Executive has several ways in which to influence Congress in behalf of the administration's legislative program. He has considerable influence as the leader of his party. Most Presidents have tried to ease the way for their program by maintaining rather intimate friendships with congressional leaders.

One of the most useful devices is the so-called " patronage " power, the practice of doing or refusing to do favors for individual Congressmen. Abraham Lincoln once allowed a Congressman to name the appointee to a $20,000 position in the Custom House in New York. The Congressman's vote was needed to admit Nevada to the Union and Nevada was needed to ratify the 13th Amendment. Appointments are often withheld until an important bill is passed by Congressmen who want a favor for themselves or a friend.

The press, radio, and television follow everything the President does very closely. His weekly press conferences and public speeches affect public opinion which is keenly felt in Congress, especially in an election year.

The Veto Power. As we know, every bill or joint resolution [13] passed by Congress must be sent to the President for his action. When a bill is presented to him, he sends a copy of it to the department or agency which must enforce it. If he signs it, it becomes law. If he vetoes it, he must send it back to the house in which it originated, with his reasons for the veto. (See pages 162–163.)

The veto power enables the President, who is the only representative of *all* the people, to act as a check on the Congress. The word " veto " comes from the Latin and means " I disapprove." Many times the mere threat of a presidential veto is enough to defeat a bill.

Bills must be vetoed in their entirety. The President does not have the power to veto only certain items in an appropriation bill, as most State governors do. If he had, needless and wasteful projects might be eliminated.

---

[13] Except those proposing amendments to the Constitution which, by custom, are not sent to the White House.

But, on the other hand, he might use the " item veto " as a political weapon with which to punish an opponent.

The President also has the power to call Congress into special session as we saw in Chapter 5. And too, he has the power to adjourn Congress whenever the two Houses cannot agree on a date for adjournment.

The Direction of Administration. The President might be called the " Chief Administrator " as well as the Chief Executive. He heads the vast executive branch and is responsible for the execution and the administration of the laws passed by Congress.

Congress plays a part with the President in the control of the administrative agencies and the operations of the executive branch. All of the vast executive branch below the President and Vice-President has been created by congressional action. Through investigations and its control of the purse strings, Congress exerts considerable influence on administration. And, of course, Congress is the policy-making branch of the Government.

Executive Ordinances. Congress makes the laws and the President is responsible for executing them. But in making laws, Congress sets out the broad policies to be followed and usually leaves the details of administration to the executive branch.

These details are spelled out by the President (or his subordinates acting for him) in the form of executive ordinances or orders. For example, the Immigration and Nationality Act of 1952 lists certain grounds upon which

an alien may be refused admission to the United States. The procedures to be followed in examining immigrants and in actually determining which aliens are to be denied admission under the law must, for practical reasons, be established by the executive branch — specifically in this case by the Immigration and Naturalization Service within the Department of Justice. Reductions under the Tariff Reciprocity Acts are accomplished by executive orders, and many reforms urged by the Hoover Commission (page 188) have been brought about by executive ordinance. The President issues these orders under constitutional or congressional authority. They are printed in the *Federal Register*.

Pardoning Power. The pardoning power of the President is absolute for all offenses against the United States, except in cases of impeachment, where a pardon may never be granted. Of course he cannot pardon offenses against State laws; but for crimes committed in territories or the District of Columbia, or offenses against federal laws such as the postal, revenue, or banking laws, the accused may be pardoned either before or after conviction.

If an individual is involved, a pardon is seldom granted before conviction. But in 1889 President Harrison issued a proclamation of *amnesty* (group pardon), which pardoned Mormons who had violated the antipolygamy laws applying to the territories of the United States. The President may pardon conditionally provided the condition is reasonable, or he may *commute* a sentence by decreasing the penalty. He may reduce a fine or cancel it before it is paid.

A central Board of Parole has authority to release federal prisoners on parole with the assent of the Attorney-General.

Independence of the President. The President, as head of one of the three branches of government, must have a degree of independence of the other two branches, else he would not remain a check upon them. So long as the President is in office — and he may be removed only by impeachment — he may not be arrested. But as soon as he is out of office he may be punished for any crime committed by him while in office. The courts can neither restrain nor compel him to perform any act. When Aaron Burr was tried for treason in 1807, Chief Justice Marshall issued a subpoena requiring President Jefferson to produce a certain paper relating to Burr's acts. Jefferson refused to obey. He reasoned that the duties of a President could not be performed if he could be compelled to obey court writs.

Reorganization of the Executive Branch

Beginning with President Taft in 1911, every President has asked Congress to grant him authority to reorganize the Executive Branch. The need for such reorganization became especially acute with the rapid expansion of the Government in the 1930's. It became even more acute with the tremendous expansion brought about by World War II.

The First Hoover Commission. Congress made some attempts to meet the problem (especially with the Reorganization Act of 1939), but little concrete progress was made up to 1947. In that year Congress created the Commission on Organization of the Executive Branch of the Government. Its purpose was to study the organization of the Executive Branch and to recommend ways in which waste and inefficiency could be eliminated and efficiency and economy could be secured in this part of the National Government.

This "Hoover Commission" (named for its chairman, former President Herbert Hoover) worked through twenty-four "task forces" employing some 300 of the nation's ablest authorities in the various fields of governmental activity. It took a year and a half to complete the job.

Some indication of the problems the Commission faced can be seen in the fact that it found that there were 1,816 component parts of the Executive Branch, employing well over 2,000,-000 people in 9 departments, 104 bureaus, 12 sections, 108 services, 51 branches, 460 offices, 631 divisions, 19 administrations, 6 agencies, 16 areas, 40 boards, 6 commands, 20 commissions, 19 corporations, 5 groups, 10 headquarters, 20 units, 3 authorities, 263 miscellaneous parts.

The Commission found that it could not even be certain just how many agencies reported directly to the President, but that there were at least 65. Obviously, no President could handle so many subordinates adequately — even if he spent only one hour a week on each and neglected all his other duties.

In 1949 the Hoover Commission reported to Congress. Its studies revealed a vast amount of waste, duplication, confusion, and inefficiency — arising from causes within the Executive Branch, from the haphazard way in which Congress had created the various agencies, and from the greatly expanded functions of the National Government. As typical examples of duplication, the Commission found 75 agencies dealing in the field of transportation, 93 in government lending,

37 in foreign trade, and 64 in business relations.

The *Reorganization Act of 1949* gave the President authority to reorganize the Executive Branch provided neither house of Congress rejected his plans within 60 days. So far, about three-fourths of the Hoover recommendations have become fact, some by executive orders not rejected within the statutory 60 days, some by direct Congressional legislation. Most of the Executive Branch has been reorganized at least to some extent, but much remains to be done.

The *Second Hoover Commission* was created in 1953. Its task was to take up where the first group stopped. And, beyond that, it investigated the whole range of governmental functions and specified those it felt the Government should not be engaged in.

OUTLINE OF THE EXECUTIVE DEPARTMENT

I. PRESIDENT

Qualifications: (1) Natural-born citizen of the United States.

(2) Thirty-five years of age.

(3) Fourteen years a resident of the United States.

Elected: By Electoral College, or by House of Representatives.

Oath: Taken when inaugurated.

Term: Four years.

Vacancy: Filled by Vice-President, by Speaker of the House, or by President *pro tem.* of the Senate, according to law of succession.

Salary: (1) $100,000 + $50,000 " expenses " and allowances for traveling and official entertainment.

(2) White House, servants, autos, etc.

Powers and Duties: (1) Executes the laws of the nation.

(2) Appoints ambassadors, consuls, judges, postmasters, other officers.

(3) May remove officers and fill vacancies.

(4) Receives foreign ministers, etc.

(5) May make treaties with the consent of two-thirds of Senate.

(6) Commander-in-Chief of the Army, Navy, and Air Force.

(7) Delivers a message to Congress each January and at other times.

(8) May call a special session of Congress or of either House.

(9) Signs or vetoes bills passed by Congress.

(10) May grant reprieves and pardons.

Removal: (1) May be impeached by majority of House.

(2) May be tried and convicted by two-thirds of Senate.

II. VICE-PRESIDENT

Qualifications: The same as required for President.

Elected: By the Electoral College, or by the Senate.

Term: Four years.

Vacancy: Not filled until next presidential election.

Salary: $35,000 + $10,000 " expenses."

Duty: Presides over Senate and votes only in case of a tie. Becomes President if President dies or is in any way disqualified.

III. CABINET MEMBERS (nonofficial)

Qualifications: None prescribed.

Appointed: By President with consent of Senate.

Term: Indefinite.

Salary: $25,000.

Duty: To advise President and administer their respective departments according to the will of the President and statutes.

WHAT THIS CHAPTER IS ABOUT

The President occupies the most powerful and important office in the world. The problems he faces are as complex and difficult as his powers are great.

The President is not elected by a direct popular vote. Rather, he is chosen indirectly through electors who are chosen by the people in each of the States. If no candidate wins a majority of the electoral votes for President, the House decides the question. The Vice-President is chosen in the same manner, except that the Senate elects if the Electoral College fails to do so.

This system is often criticized especially because of " minority Presidents " and the fact that electoral votes bear only a very indirect relationship to actual popular votes.

The Constitution provides that a President must be a natural-born citizen at least thirty-five years of age who has lived in this country for at least fourteen years. He receives a salary of $100,000 a year plus a $50,000 expense account and other items which amount to about $3,000,000 annually. He serves a four-year term and the 22nd Amendment limits him to two full terms or not more than ten years in office.

In case of a vacancy in the presidency, the Vice-President succeeds, followed by the Speaker of the House, the President *pro tem.* of the Senate and the Cabinet members in order.

The vice-presidency has been regarded as something of a " fifth-wheel," but is quite important because its occupant might become President at any moment. The Vice-President presides over the Senate and many think he could be used to relieve some of the constantly growing presidential burden.

The President's principal advisors and chief assistants are contained in the Executive Office of the President. The Cabinet, an unofficial body, composed of the heads of the ten executive departments, also advises the President.

The powers of the Chief Executive are vast. They arise from the Constitution, and various strong Presidents have shaped the office. Acts of Congress, court decisions, custom, and the President's position as party leader have also contributed to the growth of presidential power.

He appoints, alone, with the consent of the Senate, or through his subordinates, most of the approximately 2,300,000 civilian employees of the National Government. Generally speaking, those he appoints he may remove.

His powers are great in the closely related fields of foreign relations and national defense. He has the power to recognize other governments, make treaties with the consent of two thirds of the Senate, and make executive agreements. While Congress has the power to declare war, he is the Commander-in-Chief of the Armed Forces.

The President's legislative powers make him a legislative leader. He has the message power, can call special sessions, and veto legislation. And he has various informal weapons that may be used in behalf of his legislative program.

As head of the administration he executes the laws passed by Congress and has the power to issue executive ordinances. He also has the power to pardon, grant amnesty, or commute sentences.

The continuing problem of reorganization of the executive branch was very successfully handled by the first Hoover Commission. The second one carried on the work.

QUESTIONS ON THE TEXT

1. Explain in detail how the President is elected.

2. What are the formal qualifications for the presidency? Compensation?

3. What is the term of office? May he succeed himself?

4. Explain the President's powers of appointment and removal.

5. Who makes treaties? If a treaty and statute conflict, which will the courts enforce? Who appoints diplomatic officers? Receives them?

6. What are the President's powers as Commander-in-Chief?

7. Explain the President's power over legislation by means of messages; special sessions; ordinances; the veto; informal methods.

8. What is the President's pardoning power?

9. Can a court compel the President to perform a duty? Can he be punished after he is out of office for a crime committed while in office?

10. How is the Vice-President chosen? Term? Qualifications? Salary? Duties?

11. Name the Cabinet offices. Term?

PROBLEMS FOR DISCUSSION

1. Explain how Mr. Harrison was elected President in 1888 although Mr. Cleveland received more popular votes.

2. Would a State with a large population or one with a small population gain influence by the popular direct election of the President? Would you vote for or against it if you lived in Nevada? In New York?

3. Would the direct popular election of the President be an incentive for honest or dishonest elections in a one-party State? In the direct election every vote would count. Would it be to the advantage of urban or rural States?

4. Enlarge on the following statement: " The presidency involves the most grinding administrative work in the world. Every major decision, every major squabble comes inexorably to the big presidential desk. Whenever that desk gets cluttered up, trouble ensues. The man who sits at that desk cannot pass the time of day swapping stories, snatching catnaps, whittling sticks or dreaming mystical dreams. It is a place for decisiveness, clear thinking, efficiency and dispatch." — Raymond Moley. *27 Masters of Politics,* page 82. Funk & Wagnalls. New York. 1949.

THINGS YOU MIGHT DO

1. Draw up a list of the qualifications, in addition to those stated in the Constitution, that you feel a President should possess.

2. Stage a class debate or forum on the question: *Resolved,* That the President should be elected by a direct vote of the people of the United States.

3. From the *World Almanac* compare the electoral and popular votes cast in the last several presidential elections. What conclusions might be drawn from such a study?

4. Through the newspapers and other periodicals follow the President's day-to-day activities over a two-week period and from this material make a report on his typical day.

WORDS AND PHRASES YOU SHOULD KNOW

Amnesty	Executive Office of the	Patronage
Budget Bureau	President	Presidential Succession
Cabinet	Hoover Commission	Act
Civil Service Commission	Inauguration	Quasi-judicial
Commute	National Security Council	Quasi-legislative
Council of Economic Advisers	Office of Defense Mobilization	Recognition
Electoral College	Ordinance	12th Amendment
Electoral Vote	Pardon	22nd Amendment
		White House Office

Unit III. THE EXECUTIVE DEPARTMENT

SELECT BIBLIOGRAPHY

BENDINER, ROBERT, "How Presidents Are Made," *The Reporter,* February 9, 1956.

——, "The Changing Role of the Vice-President," *Collier's,* February 17, 1956.

BURNS, JAMES M., and PELTASON, JACK W., *Government By the People,* Chapters 16, 17, 18, 20. Prentice-Hall, 1954.

"Cabinet in Action: A Look Behind the Scenes," *U.S. News,* November 5, 1954.

CARR, ROBERT K., and others, *American Democracy in Theory and Practice,* Chapters 17, 22, 23, 24. Rinehart, 1955.

COUGHLAN, ROBERT, "How to Ease the Burdens of World's Most Burdensome Job," *Life,* February 27, 1956, and *Reader's Digest,* May, 1956.

DANIELS, JONATHAN, "Mr. President," *Holiday,* February, 1950.

HASSETT, WILLIAM D., "The President Was My Boss," *Saturday Evening Post,* October 10, 1953 through November 28, 1953.

HYMAN, SYDNEY, *The American President.* Harper, 1954.

——, "What Makes a 'Strong' President?" *New York Times Magazine,* December 13, 1953.

JOHNSON, CLAUDIUS O., *American National Government,* Chapters 10, 11. Crowell, 1955.

MEANS, CYRIL C., "Is Presidency Barred to Americans Born Abroad?" *U.S. News,* December 23, 1955.

"Presidential Elections," *Current History,* entire issue, October, 1952.

SHALETT, SIDNEY, "We Bring You Now the President," *Saturday Evening Post,* May 21, 1955.

SMITH, MERRIAM, *Meet Mr. Eisenhower.* Harper, 1955.

STEVENSON, ADLAI E., "A Candidate's Story," *Life,* March 2, 1953.

SWARTHOUT, JOHN M., and BARTLEY, ERNEST R., *Principles and Problems of American National Government,* Chapters 13, 14. Oxford, 1955.

TAYLOR, ROBERT, "A Week Inside the White House," *Collier's,* February 19, and March 5, 1954.

"The Presidency," *Current History,* entire issue, September, 1953.

TRUMAN, HARRY S., "The Truman Memoirs," *Life,* September 26, October 3, 10, 17, 24, 1955; January 23, 30, February 6, 13, 20, 1956.

WHARTON, DON, "How the Secret Service Protects the President," *Reader's Digest,* August, 1956.

"When a President is too Ill to Handle the Job," *U.S. News,* March 9, 1956.

WILLIAMS, IRVING G., *The American Vice-Presidency: New Look.* Doubleday, 1954.

> Observe good faith and justice toward all nations. Cultivate peace and harmony with all.
>
> — *George Washington*

★

Chapter 11

THE DEPARTMENT OF STATE

It would be impossible to over-emphasize the importance of our foreign relations. The United States is the most powerful nation on earth and the leader of the free world against the tyranny of communism. The way in which American power is used — that is, the way in which America's foreign relations are conducted — affects the fate of all mankind.

The way in which other nations conduct themselves is of vital concern to us, too. In this age of ultra-rapid travel and communication, we live, physically, in " one world," whether we like it or not.

As we have learned in Chapter 10, the President is primarily responsible for the conduct of our foreign relations. But he cannot do the job singlehanded; the Department of State is his " right hand."

Organization and Functions

The Secretary of State. The Secretary of State is appointed by the President with the consent of the Senate and is the President's chief aide in the conduct of foreign relations. He ranks first among the Cabinet officers by tradition and because his was the first Department created by Congress in 1789.

Many distinguished Americans have served as Secretary of State. The entire list reads like a roll call of the nation's great, including such men as Thomas Jefferson, John Marshall, James Madison, James Monroe, John Quincy Adams, Henry Clay, Martin Van Buren, Daniel Webster, John C. Calhoun, William Seward, James G. Blaine, John Hay, Elihu Root, William Jennings Bryan, and Charles Evans Hughes.

Recent Secretaries have been Cordell Hull (1933–1944), Edward Stettinius (1944 1945), James F. Byrnes (1945–1947), George C. Marshall (1947–1949), Dean Acheson (1949–

194

1953), and John Foster Dulles
(1953–   ).

Some Presidents have entrusted foreign affairs largely to the Secretary while others have held the reins in their own hands. But, in either case, the Secretary has been important.

His duties are partly connected with domestic affairs, but to a much greater extent with foreign affairs.

Domestic Duties. The Secretary attends to all correspondence between the President and the governors of the several States. Thus, if the President calls a State's National Guard into federal service, or if a governor requests the extradition [1] of a criminal who has fled to another country, the correspondence takes place through the Secretary of State. The Secretary also has custody of the Great Seal of the United States. Many of his former domestic functions, like the safekeeping of the laws passed by Congress,

---

[1] Extradition means the handing over by one state to another of fugitives from justice. The United States has extradition treaties with the leading nations of the world. When a person accused of crimes flees from an American State to a foreign country, the governor of the State applies to the Secretary of State for the return of the fugitive, furnishing evidence of probable guilt. The governor also names a person who will go for the fugitive. The proper papers are sent to our diplomatic representative, and he is instructed to request the extradition of the fugitive. The "President's Warrant" is given the agent whom the governor has designated to bring back the accused. Frequently an application is made by telegraph for the provisional arrest and detention of the fugitive in advance of the presentation of formal evidence.

" HIS MOST PROMISING PUPIL — IF PROPERLY GUIDED "

One of the many problems facing the Secretary of State is the future of atomic energy. Sound international controls will help to insure peace and security for all.

have now been transferred to others, especially the Archivist of the United States.

Foreign Duties. He is the President's chief aide in the conduct of American foreign relations and the " caretaker " of American interests abroad. Merely to mention such matters as Korea, Berlin and West Germany, the United Nations, the North Atlantic Treaty Organization (NATO), threats of international aggression, the seething and oil-rich Middle East, foreign economic and military aid, international control of atomic energy, the Point 4 policy, Russia's earth satellite "Sputnik," hemispheric solidarity and the Good Neighbor Policy, the protection of American property abroad, aid and advice to American importers and exporters, passports and visas, shipping, and tariffs, is to suggest the wide range of activities of the Department of State.

Organization of Department. The Secretary's chief assistant and principal adviser is the Under Secretary of State, who takes over as Acting Secretary of State in the absence of the Secretary. He is assisted by three Deputy Under Secretaries: one for Political Affairs who works with the Secretary and coordinates the Department's foreign policy activities, one for Economic Affairs who concentrates on the economic aspects of our foreign policy, and one for Administration who supervises the internal organization and working of the Department and the Foreign Service. The Counsellor, who corresponds in rank with the Assistant Secretaries, is an intimate adviser to the Secretary.

There are nine Assistant Secretaries, for: Public Affairs, Congressional Relations, Policy Planning, Inter-American Affairs, European Affairs, Far Eastern Affairs, Near Eastern, South-Asian, and African Affairs, International Organization Affairs, and Economic Affairs. Also at the Assistant Secretary level are the Legal Adviser, the Administrator of Security and Consular Affairs, the Special Assistant for Intelligence, and the Assistant Secretary-Controller for the Department.

Under the Assistant Secretaries there are several "Offices," such as the Office of Chinese Affairs under the Assistant Secretary for Far Eastern Affairs. Each of the Offices is in turn divided into "Divisions," as the Public Services Division in the Office of Public Affairs.

It is to this organizational structure that our diplomatic agents abroad must look for instructions and information. And it is here that (with the President) the responsibilities for formulating and implementing foreign policy belong.

The Foreign Service. The Foreign Service of the United States represents this nation abroad. Included within its ranks are positions ranging from that of ambassador down to the lowliest alien clerk or employee in some distant outpost.

Under international law every nation has the "right of legation" (the sending and receiving of diplomatic representatives); and the severing of diplomatic relations is usually a step towards war. We send such representatives to nearly all states, and most states have representatives in Washington. The practice is ancient, history indicating that the Egyptians followed it over 6000 years ago. Benjamin Franklin is said to have been our first professional Foreign Service officer, having been elected Minister to France by the Continental Congress in 1778.

Ambassadors are sent to most foreign capitals and ministers to some of

196

the lesser ones.[2] We now have seventy-seven embassies and three legations around the world.

Ambassadors are appointed by the President and Senate and they serve at the pleasure of the President. There is no prescribed term of office and there are numerous changes

---

[2] The exact titles are *Ambassador Extraordinary and Plenipotentiary* or *Envoy Extraordinary and Minister Plenipotentiary.*

When there is a vacancy in the office of ambassador or minister, or during his absence, his post is usually filled by a secretary of the embassy or legation. This officer temporarily in charge of his country's affairs is called the *chargé d'affaires.*

whenever there is a change of the party in power.

An ambassadorship is a much-to-be-desired political plum. Too often mere amateurs have been appointed because of their social position or party service. Fortunately, an increasing number are now being named from the ranks of our career diplomats in the Foreign Service. President Truman appointed our first woman ambassador, to Denmark; President Eisenhower has named ambassadoresses to Italy, Norway, and Switzerland.

The President may refuse to receive an ambassador from another state who

GOOD FOREIGN REPRESENTATION

The problem of appointing good ambassadors and ministers is difficult because of the inadequate salaries. We should not only build attractive embassies, such as this model of the embassy to be built in Bangkok, but we should try to have the best possible men in them.

Hesse in " St. Louis Globe Democrat "

Louis Checkman

'If You Need More—Spend Your Own'

is for any reason objectionable to the United States. He is declared *persona non grata*. In order to avoid having this happen to our own appointees, the State Department inquires beforehand about the acceptability of the person we propose to send. Any country may demand the recall of any diplomatic official it finds undesirable.

Under international law,[3] ambassadors and ministers and their staffs enjoy the special privileges of diplomatic immunity. They cannot be taxed, nor may they be arrested. When a war breaks out between two countries they are given safe conduct home. They send and receive mail and other communications in a diplomatic pouch safe from any inspection. Important messages are usually sent in code and the code is changed frequently to preserve secrecy. Embassies and legations are not subject to the jurisdiction of the state in which they are located.

The duties of an ambassador are to

(1) transmit official communications;

(2) give information to foreigners concerning American institutions, laws, and customs;

(3) keep his government advised of the progress of events in the country where he lives;

(4) protect American citizens;

(5) negotiate treaties and other agreements if requested to do so by the President; and

---

[3] *International law* consists of the treaties, practices, and customs that are followed by states in their dealings with one another.

(6) promote American interests in every way.

To perform these duties efficiently an ambassador must be on terms of friendly intimacy with the leading men in the country to which he is sent. A knowledge of the language, history, customs, and culture also helps, of course.

The following extracts from a letter written by Walter Hines Page, when he was our ambassador to Great Britain, give a close-up view of an ambassador's day-to-day job:

If you think it's all play, you fool yourself; I mean this job. There's no end of the work. It consists of these parts: Receiving people for two hours every day, some on some sort of business, some merely to "pay respects"; attending to a large (and exceedingly miscellaneous) mail; going to the Foreign Office on all sorts of errands; looking up the oddest sort of information that you ever heard of; making reports to Washington on all sorts of things; then the so-called social duties — giving dinners, receptions, etc., and attending them. I hear the most important news I get at so-called social functions. Then the court functions; and the meetings and speeches! The American Ambassador must go all over England and explain every American thing. You'd never recover from the shock if you could hear me speaking about Education, Agriculture, the observance of Christmas, the Suffrage, Medicine, Law, Radio-Activity, Flying, the Supreme Court, the President as a Man of Letters, the Hookworm, the Negro — just get down the Encyclopædia and continue the list!

I forgot, there are a dozen other kinds of activities, such as American marriages, which they always want the Ambassador to attend; getting them out of jail when they are jugged (I have an American woman on my hands now, whose children come to see me every day); looking after the American insane; helping Americans move the bones of their ancestors; interpreting the income-tax law; receiving medals for Americans; hearing American fiddlers, pianists, players; sitting for American sculptors and photographers, sending telegrams for property owners in Mexico; reading letters from thousands of people who have shares in estates here; writing letters of introduction; getting tickets to the House Gallery; getting seats in the Abbey; going with people to this, that and t'other; getting tickets to the races, the art-galleries, the House of Lords; answering fool questions about the United States put by Englishmen. With a military attaché, a naval attaché, three secretaries, a private secretary, two automobiles, Alice's private secretary, a veterinarian, an immigration agent, consuls everywhere, a despatch agent, lawyers, doctors, messengers — they keep us all busy. A woman turned up dying the other day. I sent for a big doctor. She got well. As if that wasn't enough, both the woman and the doctor had to come and thank me (fifteen minutes each). Then each wrote a letter!

Then there are . . . Rhodes Scholars from Oxford . . . women who wish to go to court . . . Negroes from Liberia . . . passports, passports to sign . . . opera singers going to the United States; artists who have painted some American portraits — don't you see?

Special Diplomats. Besides the men regularly stationed in major foreign capitals, there is one Ambassador-at-Large who acts as a sort of " international troubleshooter " for the Secretary. On various occasions, men are appointed to the *personal* rank of

UNITED NATIONS DIPLOMAT
As our chief delegate to the United Nations, Mr. Henry Cabot Lodge, shown on the right talking to Secretary General Dag Hammarskjold, holds ambassadorial rank.

ambassador to undertake special assignments. The American member of the North Atlantic Treaty Council and our chief delegate to the UN each hold the rank of ambassador.

Ministers are sent to the governments of the less important countries. Ministers are officially outranked by ambassadors, and the official residence is called a legation. Today the United States is gradually elevating most of its legations to embassies as a gesture of international friendship.

Until recently, *Chiefs of Missions* (Ambassadors or Ministers) received salaries much smaller than those paid by other great nations. Even today it is impossible for one without a private fortune to represent us, for example, in London. The salaries paid today range from $20,000 to $27,500 plus fairly liberal allowances.

Assistants. At most embassies and at some legations there is a counselor who gives technical advice in matters of international law and diplomatic practice. Embassies and legations have technical experts, secretaries, clerks, and interpreters. The more responsible of these are drawn from the Foreign Service of the United States, but some are alien employees recruited on the scene. Most embassies and legations have one or more military attachés assigned from the Army and Air Force Departments, and, in those nations which are naval powers, there are naval attachés assigned from the Navy Department. These attachés and those from other departments, as from the Commerce Department, are subject to the orders of their own departments.

Let us take a military attaché to illustrate the duties performed by a departmental attaché. He is military adviser to the ambassador or minister, he collects information on the military situation in the country to which he is accredited, he is constantly on the alert for new ideas which can be applied to his own army, and he makes confidential reports, through secret diplomatic mail bags, to the Army Department where Information Digests of world conditions are kept.

While ambassadors and ministers are sometimes political appointees of the President, more than ten thousand highly trained career men assist these diplomats and man the consulates. It is from this group of Foreign Service officers that the candidates for the top positions are increasingly being drawn. Many are now serving as ambassadors and ministers. Entrance examinations for the Foreign Service are difficult, but promotion is on the merit basis. Salaries range as high as $17,000, plus generous allowances, leaves, and contributory retirement and disability annuities.

It might be added that the diplomatic staffs of the Great Powers have increased in size because secret service work and propaganda are today carried on under the protection of diplomatic immunity.

Consular Service. The Consular Service is a part of the Foreign Service. Its agents are appointed by the President, with the consent of the Senate, from those who have passed civil service examinations. They are commercial agents, or " America's lookouts on the watchtowers of international trade." The United States maintains some two hundred consular offices in cities through the world.

Consular Duties. Consuls perform a great variety of duties, primarily commercial in nature. Their chief task lies in the promotion of American trade and commerce abroad by discovering new promised lands of commercial opportunity. They answer inquiries addressed to them by American exporters and importers, and send reports regarding foreign markets for American products to the State

Department.[4] This information includes the special demands of local markets due to prevailing customs or prejudices or to unusual shortage of crops; includes changes in foreign laws bearing on commerce, such as customs regulations, patent laws, and food laws; and includes foreign methods of doing business.

Consuls also enforce customs regulations of the United States, assist in excluding prohibited classes of immigrants, and aid stranded or wrecked vessels and shipwrecked American seamen. They visa (approve) passports for aliens coming to the United States, and some may issue passports to Americans abroad. They assist American citizens in legal transactions of all sorts, taking oaths and depositions, and even acting as witnesses to marriages.

Consular Jurisdiction. The consul has some jurisdiction over whatever relates to the internal economy of American vessels. He settles disputes among masters, officers, and men.

Consular officials are not entitled to diplomatic immunity, but treaties usually exempt them from arrest in civil cases and also guarantee the protection of their archives. An American consulate in a weak state is a fairly safe place in times of disturbances. An embassy or a legation is usually a place of safety (*asylum*).

Foreign Service Institute. In 1946 Congress established the Foreign Service Institute to provide further training for the Service officers. This has tended to break down the " old school " concept of diplomacy. For instance, before World War II, Ambassador Dodd had to contend with the stiff formalities of his staff in Berlin. They wanted him to travel by special train, and not in his own Chevrolet; they could not see why it was necessary for him to be in his office at nine o'clock rather than coming leisurely in at noon; and they thought that he should pretend to admire Nazism.

Passports. The Passport Office regulates the issuing of passports. A passport is a certificate used to identify a citizen of one country when he is traveling or living in another country. It permits him to enjoy all the privileges that international law, treaties, or the prestige of his native country can insure.

An American citizen who wants to obtain a passport may apply to the Passport Office in Washington, at one of the passport agencies maintained in a few principal cities, or to a clerk of a United States District Court or any State court of record. The application must be accompanied by a certificate from a creditable witness, by two photographs, and by a $10 fee.

Within the United States passports are granted by the Passport Office, in

---

[4] The *Foreign Commerce Weekly* is published by the Bureau of Foreign Commerce for American businessmen who subscribe for it at $3.50 a year. Items like the following are published in it:

No. 16363. Agency wanted for spark plugs for airplanes. Madrid.

(Names are not published because foreign competitors might use them.)

the territories by the governor, and abroad by the higher ranking consuls. Passports are valid for two years and may be renewed by an American consul for two more years.

A *visa* should not be confused with a passport. A visa is a permit to enter another country and must be obtained from the country a person wants to enter.

Agencies Outside the State Department

Although the State Department is the department primarily concerned with the conduct of our foreign relations, there are several other agencies which also participate.

The Department of Defense, for example, is directly concerned with foreign policy. It is charged with protecting national security, and foreign policy and national defense are but two sides of the same coin. (See Chapter 13.) The National Security Council, the Office of Defense Mobilization, and the Cabinet advise the President, as we learned in Chapter 10. Congress, through its powers in the field of foreign affairs, through its power of the purse, and through its committees, also enters the field.

A large number of other agencies participate in our foreign relations, too. For example: the Immigration and Naturalization Service in the Department of Justice deals with citizens of other countries; the Bureau of Customs in the Treasury Department deals with imports from other nations and maintains agents abroad to detect smuggling; the Coast Guard, also in the Treasury Department, has an iceberg patrol in the North Atlantic to protect the shipping of all nations; the Public Health Service in the De-

partment of Health, Education and Welfare works with other governments and international organizations on world health problems; and the Bureau of Foreign Commerce in the Commerce Department promotes American trade abroad.

As a matter of fact, it is not stretching matters *too* much to say that *all* our governmental agencies are in some way involved in foreign relations. This is so because more and more today it is impossible to draw a clear and distinct line between foreign affairs on the one hand and domestic affairs on the other.

Take the Interstate Commerce Commission as a simple example. Its major function is to regulate freight rates in interstate commerce. The costs for shipping a carload of cashmere sweaters made in Portland, Oregon, to a department store in Dallas, Texas, enter into the price the store charges for each sweater. And the price charged for each domestically produced cashmere sweater has a direct bearing on the sales of cashmere sweaters imported from Scotland.

Special mention should be made of two agencies directly and immediately concerned with foreign affairs: the super-secret Central Intelligence Agency and the United States Information Agency.

The CIA, our chief "cloak-and-dagger" agency, functions under the National Security Council (page 178). It collects and evaluates the information which is so vital to the making of foreign policy decisions. Its data is gathered by its own secret agents and from all other federal agencies, our allies, refugees, foreign journals, and every other possible source.

The *USIA* operates the "Voice of America" and conducts other programs to combat the Russian campaign of hate and propaganda against the United States. In co-operation with the State Department it broadcasts the official views of our Government, presents news and feature programs on the American way of life, and attempts to promote our friendship with other peoples. Its short-wave broadcasts go out from New York in twenty-odd languages through transmitters in the United States and relay stations in Manila, Honolulu, and Munich. It also operates a floating transmitter to help broadcast behind the Iron Curtain.

Motion pictures, libraries, and the exchange of persons also are used to promote international understanding and good will. For example, we are engaged in a vast international student exchange program. Thousands

SPREADING THE TRUTH
This United States Information Service Center in Greece, like many others around the world, makes it possible for these foreign citizens to learn the truth about American democracy and way of life. The pictures show United States scenes, with Greek captions.

United States Information Agency

of foreign students are now studying in American colleges and observing various phases of our national life. At the same time, thousands of Americans are studying abroad. This exchange program is intended to spread understanding between the United States and our world neighbors.

American Foreign Policies and Problems

Our Policies in the Past. American foreign policy is — and always has been — based on two fundamental concerns: *peace* and *national security*.

The Early Years. Until recently, American foreign policy was characterized by our refusal to become generally involved in the affairs of the rest of the world. *Isolationism,* as this policy was called, began with George Washington's administration. In his Farewell Address in 1796, he advised the young republic to have " as little *political* connection as possible " with foreign nations. In 1801, Thomas Jefferson warned against " entangling alliances."

Isolationism seemed a wise policy for several reasons: we were a young and relatively weak nation, with problems of our own, a continent to settle, and the Atlantic and Pacific to separate us from the rest of the world.

The United States began its westward expansion, and at the same time the elimination of European influences on this continent, almost at once. The Louisiana Purchase of 1803 doubled the size of the country and gave us the whole area drained by the Mississippi. The Florida Purchase of 1819 completed our continental expansion to the South.

The *Monroe Doctrine* gave new expression to our policy of isolationism. It was announced by President Monroe in a message to Congress in 1823. Monroe declared it to be our intention to remain out of the affairs of Europe and he warned the European powers (and Russia in Alaska) that any attempt to extend their systems to this hemisphere would be regarded " as dangerous to our peace and security." He also declared that the New World was no longer open to further European colonization.

The Monroe Doctrine is not a law; rather, it is a self-defense policy that opposes any non-American encroachment on the independence of any country in the Western Hemisphere. We had a sympathetic interest in the new Latin-American republics, but especially we wanted to keep European powers away from our doorstep. And, like us, the British wanted to share in the lucrative Latin-American trade that Spain had formerly succeeded in monopolizing.

At first, most Latin Americans paid little attention to the Doctrine. They knew that it was the British fleet and not Monroe's paper pronouncement that protected them. Later, as the United States became more powerful, they considered it a selfish doctrine;

204

they felt we were more concerned with our own protection than with their independence.

Continued Expansion. While the United States remained aloof from the affairs of Europe, we continued to fill out the continent. We gained the Oregon Country by treaty with Great Britain in 1846. Texas was annexed in 1845, and Mexico ceded California and the land between after her defeat in the Mexican War of 1846–1847. The continental limits of the United States were rounded out by the Gadsden Purchase in 1853. In that year we bought from Mexico a strip of territory in what is now the southern part of Arizona and New Mexico as the best rail route to the Pacific.

In 1867 we purchased Alaska from the Russians and began to become a colonial power. In that same year, the Monroe Doctrine got its first real test. While we were occupied with the War Between the States, French troops had established the Emperor Maximilian in Mexico. We backed the Mexicans in forcing the withdrawal of France and the downfall of the Maximilian regime.

The United States a World Power. The United States emerged as a first-class world power just be-

SEAL PUPS AT REST

When the United States purchased Alaska in 1867, it acquired vast natural resources. The profitable fur seal industry was part of the bargain. Many other resources have been discovered.

U.S. Fish and Wildlife Service

Wide World Photo

NATIONALIST CHIEF

Chiang Kai-shek, leader of Nationalist China, salutes American naval personnel after watching war maneuvers off the Formosa coast. We recognize the Nationalist Government of China.

fore the end of the nineteenth century. American feeling against Spain's mistreatment of her colonial possessions in the Caribbean had produced an explosive situation. When the U.S.S. *Maine* was mysteriously sunk in Havana Harbor on February 15, 1898, the United States and Spain went to war.

The Spanish-American War was over in less than a year; Spain was decisively beaten. We gained the Philippines and Guam in the Pacific and Puerto Rico in the Caribbean. Cuba became independent, under American protection, in 1899.

By 1900, then, the United States

had become a colonial power with interests extending 3000 miles across the continent, to Alaska and the Arctic, to the tip of Latin America, and clear across the Pacific to the Philippines.

The Open Door in China. While our interests were directed toward Europe and Latin America, we also had an interest in the Far East. Forty-five years before the United States acquired territory in the far Pacific, Admiral Matthew C. Perry had opened Japan to American trade (1854).

In 1899 we found our commercial interests in the Orient seriously threatened. Britain, France, Germany, and Japan were on the verge of grabbing slices of the coast of China as their own private trading preserves.

Our Secretary of State, John Hay, announced American insistence on an " open door " to all nations in trade with China and our insistence on the preservation of China's independence and sovereignty over her own territory.

The other powers came to accept the American position although our relations with Japan worsened from then until the climax at Pearl Harbor in 1941. The Chinese remained grateful to us and two World Wars strengthened the Open Door idea. But, since the communists took over in China, our relations there have sunk to the lowest depths. We do not recognize the Chinese Reds as constituting the lawful government of China. We recognize the Nationalist Government of Chiang Kai-shek on the island of Formosa.

The Good Neighbor Policy. Our relations with Latin America have ebbed and flowed. The Monroe Doctrine has always served two purposes: on the one hand, it has guaranteed the independence of Latin America; on the other, it has protected our position in the New World.

The threat of European intervention, which gave rise to the doctrine, declined in the last half of the nineteenth century. It was replaced by problems within the hemisphere. Political instability, revolutions, unpaid debts to foreign countries, and injuries to citizens and property of the United States and other countries, plagued Latin America.

Under the " Roosevelt Corollary " of 1904, the United States began to police the Western Hemisphere. For example, in 1902 British and German ships blockaded the Venezuelan coast to force that country to pay debts it owed. The United States stepped in and forced a settlement. Carrying a " big stick " the United States used the Marines to police customhouses and trouble spots throughout Central America. We stabilized political and financial conditions, settled boundary disputes, protected foreign lives and property, paid off foreign debts through customs collections, and generally maintained order in the area.

In 1903 Panama revolted and became independent of Colombia, with our blessings. In the same year we gained the right to construct a canal across the Panamanian Isthmus. The Canal was opened in 1914. In 1917 we purchased the Virgin Islands from Denmark.

The Latin Americans were resentful and suspicious of our actions, even though they benefited greatly. They complained about " Yankee imperialism " and " dollar diplomacy."

In the late 1920's and early 1930's our Latin-American policies took a decisive turn. We began a conscious effort to " win friends and influence people " to the south. The " Roosevelt Corollary " was abandoned, and what Franklin Roosevelt termed the " Good Neighbor Policy " was begun. New life was breathed into the Pan American Union (first founded in 1890 and now also known as the Organization of American States).

Today, we and our Latin-American neighbors are partners in " hemispheric solidarity." The Monroe Doctrine is now enforced by all twenty-one American republics. Our policy of helpful friendship has paid ample dividends.

World War I and the Return to Isolationism. Germany's submarine campaign against American shipping forced the United States out of its isolationist cocoon in 1917. We entered World War I to " make the world safe for democracy."

But after the defeat of Germany and the Central Powers we returned to our former isolationist policy. We refused to join the League of Nations. Europe's problems and those of the rest of the world, so many Americans thought, were no direct concern of ours.

The rise of Mussolini in Italy, of Hitler in Germany, and of the militarists in Japan cast a dark cloud on the horizon. But in the twenty years after World War I we continued to " wrap our two oceans around us " in isolation.

World War II. It took the coming of World War II to really awaken us to the fallacies of isolationism in this day and age. We know now that we cannot, even if we wanted to, shut ourselves away from the rest of the world.

Most Americans were pro-Ally at the start of the war in 1939, but our policy was to stay out of the war if at all possible. While our official position was one of neutrality, we nevertheless aided the Allies through such policies as the Lend-Lease Act. Under this 1941 law, the President was authorized to " sell, transfer title to, exchange, lease, lend, or otherwise dispose of defense articles " to any countries vital to our own security.

With the sudden Japanese attack on Pearl Harbor, December 7, 1941, all thoughts of neutrality vanished. From then until the war ended in 1945, the United States fought side-by-side with her allies in Europe and the Pacific. American forces fought and defeated the Axis Powers on battlefields around the world. During the war we were the " arsenal of democracy." By Lend-Lease our allies received nearly $50,000,000,000 in food, munitions, and other supplies.

Our Policies Today. The years since 1945 have been marked by a fundamental change in the role of the United States in world affairs. And with this shift has come a transformation in American foreign policy.

In little more than a decade, this country has grown from a position as *one* of the world's major powers to its present role as *the* responsible leader of the world's free nations. Until recently, our policy was characterized by our refusal to become generally involved in the affairs of the rest of the world. Now it is characterized by our *global*, all-out participation in international affairs.

Yet, while specific American foreign policies reflect this great change, the goal of our foreign policy remains the preservation of peace and the maintenance of national security.

We Keep Our Powder Dry. One of the basic planks in current American foreign policy is that of making ourselves and our allies so strong that our very strength will deter aggression. We hope that our military and economic might will make the Soviet Union, or any other potential aggressor, realize that it would be sheer suicide to attack us. As the President has said: " Our economic and our military strength are our nation's shields — without which peace could never be preserved, nor freedom defended." In effect, we have taken a leaf from the pages of our own Revolutionary history: " Put your trust in God, my boys, but keep your powder dry."

Peace Through Collective Security and the United Nations. We live in " one world " in the sense that no nation can live in peace and prosperity while others are at war or in want. Hence, *collective security,* that is, the preserving of international order through the united efforts of free nations, has become a cornerstone in our foreign policy. Thus in 1945 we were determined not to repeat our basic error of 1919–20 when the United States refused to join the League of Nations. We took the lead in creating the United Nations, dedicated " to save succeeding generations from the scourge of war . . . and to maintain international peace and security." Today we support and work through the UN because, as President Eisenhower has said, it is " the living sign of all people's hope for peace." (See Chapter 40.) In our search for collective security we have also concluded a number of regional alliances with our allies around the globe.

Resisting Communist Aggression is another of the pillars of American policy. We had hoped to work with the Russians through the UN to build a just and lasting peace after World War II. But it was soon clear that the communists had not abandoned their plans to dominate the world.

At the Big Three Conferences at Yalta and Potsdam in 1945, Stalin had guaranteed free elections in occupied East Germany and the nations of Eastern Europe. Instead, puppet communist regimes were quickly established and an iron curtain was clamped around an empire of Soviet satellites.

By 1949, when the Chinese Communists succeeded in overrunning the mainland of China, postwar communist aggression had brought over 700,-000,000 people and 7,500,000 square miles of territory under its control.

The Truman Doctrine. The critical turning point in American policy toward the designs of the USSR came in the early months of 1947. Greece and Turkey were in desperate straits; without immediate and substantial aid from the United States they were certain to fall under Soviet control.

The response was immediate. At President Truman's request the Congress quickly provided for economic and military aid to both nations. In his message to Congress, Mr. Truman declared that it was

. . . the policy of the United States to support free peoples who are resisting attempted subjugation by armed minorities or outside pressures.

This statement and the actions which followed it came to be known as the *Truman Doctrine.* It is clear now that its enunciation, March 12, 1947, marked the beginning of the policy the United States has followed consistently ever since in combatting communist aggression around the world.

The Eisenhower Administration has several times applied the Truman Doctrine. Thus when communist intrigues made war likely in the Middle East in 1957, the President restated the Doctrine and applied it specifically to that area. Under what has been called the *Eisenhower Doctrine,* the United States has pledged aid to any nation in the Middle East threatened by communist-inspired aggression.

The Korean War provides an excellent illustration of our policies of supporting the UN and resisting communist aggression. The war began on June 25, 1950, when communist North Korea attacked the UN-sponsored Republic of South Korea. The UN called upon its members to aid in repelling the invaders, and American forces went into action at once.

The war pitted the United Nations Command (composed largely of American and South Korean forces, but with troops from sixteen nations altogether) against the Russian-trained and -equipped North Korean and Chinese Red armies.

The fighting was ended by a truce signed on July 27, 1953. The communists have thus far refused to agree to permanent peace terms acceptable to the UN nations which fought against them, and so, to date, there has been no final settlement of the Korean problem.

The thirty-seven months and two days of bitter fighting did not end in a clear-cut UN victory in the sense that the communists were beaten to their knees. The war cost the United States more than 140,000 casualties, including some 28,000 dead or missing, and over $20,000,000,000. The South Koreans suffered untold thousands of civilian casualties, and practically all

of Korea lay wasted and barren.

Still, much was accomplished. The enemy was repulsed and with far heavier losses. *For the first time in history* armed forces fought under an international flag to resist aggression. In the hope of preventing a third world war, communist aggression had to be stopped with force somewhere; and there is no way of telling how far it might have gone, had South Korea not been defended.

The Korean War, with its tremendous cost to the communists, told them in no uncertain terms that the free world, led by the United States, is ready to fight for peace and security. They know that we most earnestly want a just and lasting peace; but they know, too, that we prize our freedom far above mere peace.

Only history can judge how effective the Korean war was in preventing another global conflict, but the war aroused and united the free world. We and our allies are strong today, and are growing stronger all the time.

President Eisenhower stated the basic reason for our opposition to communism when he said in his inaugural address: " Americans, indeed all free men, remember that in the final choice a soldier's pack is not so heavy a burden as a prisoner's chains."

Foreign Aid to our friends abroad is another vital part of our foreign policy. Since the end of World War II we have given some $60,000,000,000 in economic and military aid to other nations. At first this aid was primarily economic. Under the Marshall

210

Plan we sent food, fuel, farm machinery, and the like to help rebuild war-devastated nations. Now because of the successes achieved through economic aid we are able to concentrate on military aid. Still, economic aid is important; the stomach often rules the head. Thus in 1957, in addition to aid to our allies, we provided aid for the refugee victims of the anti-communist revolts behind the iron curtain. The Point 4 program is another form of economic aid. Under it we are providing technical, industrial, and scientific " know-how " to underdeveloped and backward areas of the world. In this way we are helping people to help themselves to produce more and better food, clothing, and shelter, and to develop their own natural and industrial resources.

President Eisenhower has put the case for foreign aid in these very practical terms: " We need allies, and these allies must be bound to us in terms of their own enlightened self-interest, just as in like terms we are bound to them."

Regional Security Treaties help to spell out collective security and our resistance to communism. They are based on the realization that distance and the oceans are no longer guarantees against foreign attack. Atomic and hydrogen bombs and other modern weapons of mass destruction have pushed our defensive frontiers to the far corners of the earth. Because of this the United States has now concluded eight " regional security " treaties with forty-two nations. Each of

these is defensive in nature. They pledge the parties to aid one another in case of attack. The objective of each treaty is clear — security for us and for the rest of the free world. And each bolsters and implements the UN Charter and the principle of collective security.

(1) *The North Atlantic Treaty*, signed in 1949, now includes the United States, Canada, Great Britain, France, Italy, Portugal, Belgium, the Netherlands, Luxembourg, Denmark, Norway, Iceland, Greece, Turkey, and (since 1955) West Germany. The member nations have agreed that " an armed attack against one or more of them in Europe or North America shall be considered an attack against them all." The purpose of the alliance is the mutual defense against attack from any quarter, but particularly from Russia, of course. The North Atlantic Treaty Organization (NATO), set up under the treaty, is building a unified armed force to discourage aggression — but prepared to fight in case of attack. In addition to the billions of dollars in aid we have given the pact members, several United States Army, Navy, and Air Force units are stationed in Europe as part of the NATO forces. Supplementing the NATO pact, we have an agreement with Spain giving us air and sea bases there in return for economic and military aid.

(2) *The Rio Pact* (Inter-American Treaty of Reciprocal Assistance), signed in 1947, binds the United States and the twenty Latin-American

Republics to aid one another in case of an attack in this hemisphere. Our neighbors to the south are essential to our own defense; they are, in effect, our own backyard. Through the Good Neighbor Policy and the Organization of American States (the Pan American Union), we are promoting ever closer ties with Latin America.

(3) *The Anzus Pact,* signed in 1951, unites Australia, New Zealand, and the United States in a defensive alliance. If any of the three is attacked in the Pacific area, the others agree to come to its aid.

(4) *The Japanese Pact,* signed in 1951, involves Japan and the United States. After seven years of American occupation, we and our World War II allies (but not Russia) concluded a peace treaty with Japan. At the same time we also signed a mutual defense pact with the Japanese. In return for American protection, we are permitted to maintain land, sea, and air forces in and about Japan. We are adding to our own security by converting a former foe into a friend.

(5) *The Philippines Pact,* signed in 1951, serves notice on any potential aggressor that the United States and the Philippines will stand together in the Pacific area.

(6) *The Korean Pact,* signed in 1953, pledges the United States to come to the aid of South Korea should she be attacked again. (In addition to this pact, the sixteen UN members whose troops fought in Korea have promised prompt action should the communists renew the war.)

(7) *The Southeast Asia Treaty* (SEATO), signed in 1954, is patterned after the NATO pact. It pledges eight nations — the United States, Great Britain, France, Australia, New Zealand, the Philippines, Pakistan, and Thailand — to guarantee the security of one another in Southeast Asia.

(8) *The Formosa Pact,* signed by the United States and Nationalist China in 1954, pledges each to come to the aid of the other in the event either is attacked in the Formosa area. The United States does not recognize the Chinese Communist Government at Peking, and we oppose the admission of the Chinese Reds to the UN. We are committed to the defense of the Nationalist stronghold on the island of Formosa, and the United States Seventh Fleet guards the Strait between it and the mainland.

Our most important ally is Great Britain. Our two nations are closely tied by history and tradition and by a common stake in freedom. The resources and strategic locations of the far-flung parts of the British Empire are key factors in the East-West struggle. Without Britain we should find our task of world leadership much more difficult.

Our most powerful foe is the Soviet Union. Since 1945 the U.S.S.R. has brought more than 700,000,000 people and 7,500,000 square miles of new territory under its control. Some of this vast empire was taken by the Red Army during and immediately after World War II. But most of it has been taken by native communist parties — trained, controlled, and directed by Moscow. International communism thus serves as a " right arm " for Russian foreign policy. If a third world war is to be averted, Russia must be made, in one way or another, to seek the paths of peace.

Every nation in the world is important to us. *Germany,* for example, is the key to much of the future of all of Europe. Thus we are working for a strong, peaceable, and united Germany. So long as the USSR prevents this by keeping East Germany in bondage as a satellite and refusing to permit free, all-German elections, we are pledged to support the free, democratic government of the Federal Republic of (West) Germany.

India, with her resources and teeming millions, is the key to the future of much of Asia. Thus we are attempting to work with her for the peaceful, noncommunist development of that whole vast region.

The Middle East is the land bridge connecting Europe, Africa, and Asia and is immensely rich in oil. The fields in Iraq, Iran, and Saudi Arabia contain more than two-fifths of the world's proved oil reserves. When the Egyptian-Israeli war broke out anew in 1956 and Britain and France attacked and occupied the Suez Canal Zone, we turned at once to the UN to head off the crisis. Its oil and its location make the Middle East a rich prize and could easily provide the spark for World War III. We seek to prevent Soviet influence and control in the region. Under the Eisenhower Doctrine of 1957, the United States has pledged itself to provide economic and military aid to any Middle Eastern nation threatened by a communist-inspired attack.

As a nation, we lead the free world in the search for a just and lasting peace. The search thus far has not been an easy one — nor does it promise to be an easy one in the future. Still, we know we must carry it forward. To shirk our duty now would be to doom the world as we know it and as we would like it to be.

WHAT THIS CHAPTER IS ABOUT

The conduct of our foreign relations affects the fate of all mankind. The State Department, headed by the Secretary of State, is the President's " right hand " in this vital field.

The Secretary, who is appointed by the President and Senate, has a few domestic duties but his chief concern is with foreign affairs.

Our diplomatic agents abroad look to the Secretary and his staff in Washington for instructions and information. The Foreign Service, from ambassadors and ministers down to the lowest clerks, execute our policies on the scene and generally look after American interests. Ambassadors and ministers are appointed by the President and Senate, and more and more of them are now being chosen from the career service rather than for political reasons. They are assisted by staffs of experts and enjoy the special privileges of diplomatic immunity.

We also have special diplomats who

serve at the UN or undertake other special assignments. Consuls are maintained in most of the principal cities of the world to promote our economic relations with other states. Passports are issued by the State Department and must be visaed by the country one wants to enter.

Agencies outside the State Department are also concerned with foreign policy, especially the Central Intelligence Agency and the United States Information Agency. It is so difficult to draw a sharp line between foreign and domestic matters today that it can be said that practically all governmental agencies operate in some way in the field of foreign affairs.

Our foreign policies have always been aimed toward protecting the United States and securing world peace. We began our history with a policy of isolationism dictated by our relative weakness, internal problems, and geographic position. In the Monroe Doctrine we warned Europe out of the New World. As we expanded we became more powerful and became a first-class world power with the Spanish-American War. By 1900 our interests extended throughout this hemisphere and clear across the Pacific.

World War I brought us out of isolation for a brief moment, but we returned to it until World War II. The Good Neighbor Policy has supplanted the original applications of the Monroe Doctrine, and we now work in partnership with Latin America.

World War II convinced us of the fallacies of isolationism in today's world. Through the United Nations, aid to the free world, and collective security agreements we oppose Soviet communist aggression and work to prevent a third global war.

QUESTIONS ON THE TEXT

1. How is the Secretary of State chosen? Why does he rank first among the Cabinet officers?

2. What is the Secretary's chief function?

3. How are ambassadors and ministers chosen? What are their duties? An increasing number of them are being drawn from where?

4. Explain the term *persona non grata*.

5. What is a consul?

6. What is a passport? A visa?

7. Why is it becoming increasingly difficult to draw a sharp line between foreign and domestic affairs?

8. Explain the meaning of isolationism. Why did it seem a wise policy in the early years?

9. What is the Monroe Doctrine? How has it changed through the years?

10. Describe briefly the continental expansion of the United States.

11. About when did the United States become a first-class world power? What was the Open Door Policy?

12. What major event finally forced the United States to abandon a policy of isolationism?

13. What are the basic purposes of our foreign policies today?

PROBLEMS FOR DISCUSSION

1. The United States refused to join the League of Nations but took a leading role in the forming of the United Nations. How do you explain this shift in policy?

2. Some people oppose our participation

in the UN. Why? How do you feel in the matter?

3. Communist parties in other countries are directed and controlled from Moscow. How do they serve as the " international arm of Soviet foreign policy "?

THINGS YOU MIGHT DO

1. Make an attractive wall map illustrating the territorial growth of the United States since 1789.

2. Stage a debate or forum on the question: *Resolved,* That the Soviet Union and its satellites should be expelled from the United Nations.

3. Select a particular Secretary of State and write a brief report on our history during his term of office.

4. Select a particular problem in our current foreign relations, for example our policy toward Nationalist China and Red China, and write a brief report on it.

WORDS AND PHRASES YOU SHOULD KNOW

Collective Security
Consul
Embassy
Extradition
Foreign Service
Good Neighbor Policy

International law
Isolationism
Legation
Lend-Lease
Marshall Plan
Monroe Doctrine
North Atlantic Treaty

Open Door Policy
Passport
Persona non grata
Regional security treaties
Visa
Voice of America

SELECT BIBLIOGRAPHY

" ABC's of Middle East Oil," *U.S. News,* October 12, 1956.

ACHESON, DEAN, " What A Secretary of State Really Does," *Harper's,* December, 1954.

ALSOP, JOSEPH, and STEWART, " What We Must Do to Stay Free," *Saturday Evening Post,* March 26, 1955.

KENNAN, GEORGE, " The Soviet Will Never Recover," *Saturday Evening Post,* November 24, 1956.

" Paris Close-up: Embassy in Action," *U.S. News,* August 10, 1956.

PETERS, C. BROOKS, " Why Not a Foreign Service Career? " *Reader's Digest,* October, 1956.

" Price of World Leadership Goes Up," *U.S. News,* August 10, 1956.

RUSSELL, BEATRICE ANN, " We Like the Foreign-Service Life," *Saturday Evening Post,* June 18, 1955.

SONDERN, FREDERIC, " They Carry Our Top Secrets," *Reader's Digest,* May, 1956.

SWARTHOUT, JOHN M., and BARTLEY, ERNEST R., *Principles and Problems of American National Government,* Chapters 18, 19, 20. Oxford, 1955.

Money is, with propriety, considered as the vital principle of the body politic; as that which sustains its life and motion, and enables it to perform its most essential functions.

— *Alexander Hamilton*

★

Chapter 12

THE TREASURY DEPARTMENT

The National Government today takes in some $70,000,000,000 a year and it spends approximately the same amount each year. On the average, then, it costs every man, woman, and child in the country over $400 a year to support the functions and services of the National Government. It means, too, that the National Government accounts for twenty cents out of every dollar of our total national income. The Treasury Department is charged with the major responsibility for the collection, disbursement (paying out), and safekeeping of these tremendous sums.

The Secretary of the Treasury

The *Secretary of the Treasury,* like all other Cabinet officers, is appointed by the President and the Senate. His Department was created by the First Congress in 1789 to " supervise and manage the national finances."

Through the years a variety of other functions have been added, as we shall see. In addition to his domestic duties, he is responsible for our policies and programs in the field of international finance. He works closely with the Secretary of State in these matters, as, for example, in the granting of loans to other governments.

Revenue Collection

In Chapter 7 we discussed the Congress' power to levy taxes. The collection of the sixty-odd taxes it levies is made through the Internal Revenue Service and the Bureau of Customs.

The large bulk of all federal revenues is funneled through these two agencies. Lesser amounts, so-called " nontax revenues," reach the Treasury through other channels, as we shall see.

Some idea of the job involved in the collection of federal revenues can be gained from this consideration: If, on the day that Christ was born, a machine had been invented that ground out a one-dollar bill every second of every hour of every day of every year since then, the machine would not yet have produced what the National Government now collects in revenue *each year!*

The *Bureau of Customs* is headed by a Commissioner of Customs appointed by the President and Senate. Under him, the United States and its possessions are divided into forty-seven Customs Districts. Each District is administered by a Collector of Customs who is also appointed by the President and Senate. The Bureau's principal duties are to assess and collect import tariffs, guard against smuggling, and arrest those who violate the customs laws.

The *Internal Revenue Service* is under a Commissioner of Internal Revenue appointed by the President and Senate. He directs the over-all operation of the agency. Under him, the Service is organized on a geographic basis. There are nine Internal Revenue Regions, each headed by a Regional Commissioner. These areas are further divided into Internal Revenue Districts, sixty-four in all and each headed by a Director. The Regional Commissioners and the Directors are appointed under civil service rules. The Service collects billions of dollars from millions of citizens each year and guards against tax evasion.

The *income tax* on individuals and corporations produces more than eighty per cent of all federal revenues.

The Government has various methods of checking upon the honesty of those who should pay income taxes. It requires the keeping of records of business; it requires employers to withhold and turn in the tax due from employees; it requires corporations to report dividends and interest, and those paying royalties on patents and copyrights to report the sums of money paid; it exchanges information with State income tax collectors; it compels witnesses to testify; and it employs secret service agents. The Government can inspect bank accounts, records, and, to some extent, safe deposit boxes. It even has international treaties granting inspection privileges in other countries.

Those who fail to report all of their taxable income may be imprisoned, may be fined, and may have a penalty added equal to 50 per cent of the amount not reported. For example, it was discovered that a movie star had shortchanged the Government $118,364. For this fraud he was required to pay the $118,364, plus a penalty of 50 per cent of the $118,364, plus a $3000 fine; or a total of $180,546. In 1931 " Scarface Al " Capone was indicted for evading an income tax on $1,000,000 obtained over a period of six years. He was given an eleven-year prison sentence, fined $50,000, and his property was seized for the taxes and penalty. Evasions may be detected even after death.

Information comes from all kinds of sources. In one interesting case, a man told the woman he was engaged to how cleverly he had cheated the tax collector. But he later jilted her and she then reported him for spite. So years after he thought he had "got by," he paid the price of dishonesty.

RECEIPTS AND EXPENDITURES OF THE UNITED STATES GOVERNMENT
(In Millions of Dollars)

	Fiscal Years				
	1953	1954	1955	1956	1957
BUDGET RECEIPTS					
Individual Income Taxes	$32,768	$32,383	$31,650	$35,334	$39,012
Corporation Income Taxes	21,595	21,523	18,265	21,299	21,531
Excise Taxes	9,934	10,014	9,211	10,004	9,176
All Other (*inc.* customs; estate and gift taxes; mineral, oil, forest leases; canal tolls; court fines; interest; etc.)	3,646	4,112	4,690	5,212	5,187
Gross Budget Receipts	$67,943	$68,032	$63,816	$71,849	$74,906
Less Refunds and Receipts (*esp.* income tax and customs)	−3,118	−3,377	−3,426	−3,684	−3,917
NET BUDGET RECEIPTS	$64,825	$64,655	$60,390	$68,165	$70,989
BUDGET EXPENDITURES					
National Security:					
Defense Department — military	$43,610	$40,335	$35,533	$35,791	$38,377
Foreign Economic and Military Aid	5,656	4,882	4,219	4,201	3,912
Atomic Energy Commission	1,791	1,895	1,857	1,651	1,994
Stockpiling and Other Defense	1,008	1,045	944	588	490
Total National Security	$52,065	$48,157	$42,553	$42,231	$44,773
Interest on the Public Debt	6,583	6,470	6,438	6,486	7,312
Veterans' Programs	4,333	4,249	4,405	4,731	4,805
Agricultural Programs	3,217	2,915	4,636	5,177	5,021
Health, Education, and Welfare Programs	2,122	2,184	2,187	2,302	2,544
Post Office	659	312	356	463	522
All Other Expenditures	5,295	3,485	3,995	5,450	4,367
TOTAL EXPENDITURES	$74,274	$67,772	$64,570	$66,540	$69,344
SURPLUS (+) or DEFICIT (−)	−$9,449	−$3,117	−$4,180	+$1,626	+$1,645

Standard Oil Co. (N.J.)

FILL 'ER UP

The price of gasoline includes a State tax, which varies, and a uniform federal excise of three cents per gallon which helps to finance the Government's road-building program.

Other internal revenue is derived from taxes on inheritances, liquor, cigarettes, automobiles, gasoline, playing cards, etc. Most of these taxes are collected by means of stamps attached so that they will be torn when the package is opened.

Most taxpayers are honest, but there are enough dishonest ones to necessitate a Secret Service within the Treasury. " T-men " rival the FBI in excellence, and work with Treasury agencies to enforce tax laws.

Customs (tariffs, import duties) were the major source of federal revenue for more than a century. Today they produce only a minor fraction of the total — $754,461,000 in 1957.

Ewing Galloway

WORLD SERIES

Another pleasant way to pay taxes is to buy a ticket to a baseball game. All admissions tickets which cost more than ninety cents are subject to a ten per cent federal tax.

All articles brought into the country must enter at specified points, " ports of entry." The ports of entry are located along the Atlantic, Pacific and Gulf coasts and include several inland cities, like St. Louis and Chicago. More than half of all customs are collected at the port of New York.

Customs on about 2000 taxable articles are of three kinds — *specific, ad valorem,* and *mixed. Specific* means so much per unit, as half a cent a pound on sugar or eggs at $3\frac{1}{2}$ cents per dozen. *Ad valorem* means " in proportion to value," as 55% on mesh bags valued at less than $5 per dozen and 35% if valued at more. *Mixed* means that both a *specific* duty and an *ad valorem* duty are imposed upon the same article.

As the determination of values is very difficult, persons exporting to the United States articles valued at over $100 are required to have invoices certified by an American consul; when valued at $100 or less an oral statement is accepted. If the consul is not certain of the value, he may demand three samples, one for himself, one for the United States Customs Court in New York, and one for the appraiser at the port to which the merchandise is sent.

To prevent fraud when merchandise is received at a port, ten per cent of the packages, taken at random, are opened and examined; and all personal baggage is examined. To prevent smuggling, detectives are at work here and abroad, and the Treasury Department maintains a Coast Guard. Recently, customs inspectors at Long Beach, California, seized 700 bales of clothing which had been fraudulently listed as rags. Any person, except an officer of the United States, who gives original information leading to conviction of smugglers may be rewarded by the Commissioner of Customs.

Not long ago, an employee of the Cunard Steamship Company received a reward of $17,119. His tip to a

ART EXPERT

An art examiner, employed by the Bureau of Customs, inspects an oil painting. An original oil painting is admitted duty-free. A copy of an original, though, is subject to payment of customs.

Wide World Photo

FALSE–BOTTOM

Alert inspectors spotted this false-bottom trunk at the port of New York. Customs thus was able to collect duty on the very valuable but tiny watch movements hidden in the false bottom.

Wide World Photo

Unit III. The Executive Department

customs agent led to the discovery of $171,197.60 worth of gold bullion concealed in a car and about to be smuggled out of the country aboard the *Queen Elizabeth.*

Nontax Revenues. These monies come from sources other than taxation. They amount to more than $2,000,000,000 a year and include such things as fines imposed by the courts, interest and principal on loans, Panama Canal tolls, fees for patents and passports, sale or lease of public lands, forestry grazing permits, etc. One interesting source is the profit obtained from the minting of coins. The profit (about $30,000,000 a year) is the difference between the value of the metals used in minting and the face value of the minted coins. Also, the Government gains income through borrowing (the issuing of bonds).

Safekeeping and Disbursement of the Revenues

The *Treasurer of the United States* (not to be confused with the Secretary) is the officer responsible for every penny of the billions involved in our national finance.

The Constitution provides that " no money shall be drawn from the Treasury but in consequence of appropriations made by law." (Article I, Section 9, Clause 7.) The money is paid out by the Treasurer upon the presentation of a warrant (an order to pay such as a check) drawn by the Secretary and approved by the Comptroller-General.

The *Currency Redemption Division* is located within the Treasurer's Office. Some 45,000 persons bring burned or mutilated currency to the Division's experts each year. The " money surgeons " examine it and redeem as much as possible. When a man brought in a large stack of bills that had rotted underground, experts were able to redeem $53,000 worth. But $48,000 of it had to go to the tax collector; the man was a professional gambler who had never reported his winnings.

A man in North Carolina put $600 in an electric heater for " safekeeping." He forgot about the money and months later the Redemption Division was able to identify $570 from his handful of ashes. The experts were also able to save $8500 out of a $9000 lump of black char belonging to a South Dakota farmer who didn't trust banks.

The *Comptroller of the Currency* exercises general supervision over the operations of National Banks. (See pages 330–335.)

The *Fiscal Service* is the general bookkeeping office in the Treasury. It performs accounting functions and maintains the financial records.

The *Comptroller-General,* who heads the General Accounting Office, is often called the " Watchdog of the Treasury." His agency's principal job is to see that all expenditures are made in the way and for the purpose Congress intended.

Actually, the Comptroller-General and the GAO are not located within the Treasury at all. The office was set up in 1921 in order that Congress might have a check on the spending of funds it appropriates and is independent of the executive branch. The Comptroller-General is appointed by the President and Senate. His independence is guaranteed by the fact that he serves a fifteen-year term and may be removed only by Congress.

In 1934 when it seemed that the prairie States were becoming a dustbowl President Roosevelt ordered that $15,000,000 of the $525,000,000 drought relief fund authorized by Congress be used for planting strips of trees to stop soil erosion. (See page 280.) The Comptroller-General ruled that the drought relief fund was intended for *direct* and *immediate* relief — not for projects whose results lay so far in the future — so he allowed only $1,000,000 of the fund to get the scheme started. This was all that could be efficiently spent on those employed to plant the young trees available.

The General Accounting Office also superintends the recovery of debts owed to the United States. For example, a military officer received an extra allowance for his dependent mother. When it was discovered that his mother was worth $42,500, the Accounting Office took steps to recover the excess payment.

The Public Debt

The cost of government has mounted rapidly in the last few decades. National expenditures have risen from less than $500,000,000 in 1900 to very close to $70,000,000,000 in 1957. The Government now spends more *each year* than it did during all of the first 150 years of our history!

When the Government's spending exceeds its income it must borrow and thus go into debt. Congress has the power to borrow, as we learned in Chapter 6.

The public debt today is over $270,000,000,000. It is mainly due to the depression of the 1930's, the First and Second World Wars and the present defense program.

The average interest on the debt is now two and seven-tenths per cent and amounts to more than $7,000,000,000 a year. Since 1930 the public debt has risen in every fiscal year except five: 1947, 1948, 1951, 1956, and 1957. The debt was reduced by $2,223,641,-753 during fiscal 1957. Most economists deplore " deficit spending " and urge that the debt be reduced in these prosperous days. As outstanding bonds come due today, new ones are sold to raise the needed funds. The debt for selected fiscal years was:

1916, pre-World War I	$ 1,225,000,000
1919, post-World War I	25,482,000,000
1930, start of Depression	16,185,000,000
1940, decade of Depression	42,968,000,000
1941, pre-World War II	48,961,000,000

1946, post-World War II	$269,422,000,000
1950, pre-Korean War	257,357,000,000
1953, post-Korean War	266,071,000,000
1956, latest fiscal year	270,527,171,896

How the United States Borrows Money. The Federal Government uses both the " short-term " and the " long-term " types of borrowing. Short-term borrowing uses notes, bills, and certificates of indebtedness, which run anywhere from thirty days to four years. Long-term borrowing is through the sale of bonds which usually run ten years or more — often for twenty or thirty years. For short-term borrowing the rate of interest now ranges from $1\frac{1}{2}$ to a little over 3 per cent; but for long-term bonds the rate now runs over 3 per cent and in some cases as high as 4 per cent.

The Federal Government issues both bearer bonds and registered bonds. The former may be passed around like money, and the interest is collected every six months by clipping and cashing at any bank the coupons attached to the bottom of each bond. The latter are registered at the Treasury in the name of the owner and can-not to be disposed of without having ownership transferred. The interest is paid by checks from the Treasury. The bearer bonds are more convenient for quick sale, but the latter are safer because, if lost or stolen, they can-not be sold by finder or thief.

Series E Savings Bonds are the most popular bonds issued by the Treasury. The E bond now matures in eight years and eleven months and pays $3\frac{1}{4}$ per cent, compounded semi-annually, when held to maturity. E bonds bought before 1957 mature in nine years, eight months and pay three per cent. The maturity period was re-duced and the interest rate raised in 1957 in order to make the bonds more attractive to today's small investor. The bonds may be registered in the name of one person, two persons as co-owners, or one as owner and another as beneficiary (heir). If lost or stolen, the Treasury will replace them. They may be cashed at a bank any time after sixty days from date of issue. They are issued in denominations from $25 to $10,000, but no one may pur-chase more than $10,000 worth in any one year.

Currency

Currency, that is, money issued by the Government, is of two kinds — metallic and paper.

Metallic Currency. United States coins are stamped by the Bureau of the Mint. There are three United States Mints, located in Philadelphia, Denver, and San Francisco. The San Francisco Mint no longer produces coins but serves as a storage house. The Bureau also has a depository for gold at Fort Knox, Kentucky, and one for silver at West Point.

Gold. Until 1933, the double eagle ($20), the eagle ($10), and the half eagle ($5) were coined by the mints.

When the financial crisis came in 1933, many people hoarded these gold coins, and others shipped them out of the country. To prevent these practices and pave the way for revaluing gold, the Government required all gold coins held by individuals or by banks to be turned into the United States Treasury in exchange for paper money. Gold coins are no longer allowed to circulate in this country, and the mere holding of them is illegal under heavy penalties. But gold may be purchased from the Government and exported to pay trade balances.

From 1834 until 1934 the gold content of the dollar was set at $25\frac{4}{5}$ grains nine-tenths fine; but in 1934 it was reduced to $15\frac{5}{21}$ grains nine-tenths fine. Thus by making a " sixty-cent dollar " (or 59.06 to be exact) the Government caused prices to rise, which helped people who were in debt. Previous to the revaluation of the dollar, gold sold for $20.67 per ounce. At present the Government is paying $35 in paper for an ounce of the metal; and at this artificially high price we have accumulated about $23,000,000,000 or 70 per cent of the gold money of the world.

In 1934 Federal Reserve Banks were required to desposit all their gold with the U.S. Treasurer, for which certificates of the re-valued (59.06) gold dollar were given. These Gold Certificates do not circulate, but are security for Federal Reserve Notes.

Silver. The mints now pay 90.5 cents an ounce for silver newly mined in the United States. No silver dollars have been minted since 1935, but they are still legal tender, as are half dollars, quarters, and dimes, which the mints continue to issue. Silver coins of the United States contain 90 per cent silver and 10 per cent copper.

Minor Coins. The five-cent piece is made of three parts copper and one part nickel, and the one-cent piece is made of bronze (95% copper and 5% tin or zinc). Metal for these coins is purchased from the lowest bidder by the superintendent of the mint, with the approval of the Director of the Mint. The profit on these coins is even greater than that on silver coins. Minor coins worn smooth are recoined at Government expense. During World War II substitute metals were used for minor coins.

Legal Tender. Money which the law requires a creditor to accept in payment of a debt when tendered by a debtor is known as *legal tender*. Congress has provided " all coins and currencies of the United States shall be legal tender for all debts, public and private."

Paper Currency. The paper currency issued today is of three kinds:

(1) *Federal Reserve Notes* issued by any one of the twelve Federal Reserve Banks (see pages 335–336) in denominations of $5 and upward. They are direct obligations of the United States Government and the most common type of currency in circulation today. They are backed by 25% Gold Certificates and 75% Government bonds or 75% commercial paper (notes or drafts on local banks).

HOW TO MAKE MONEY

The foundry worker (*upper left*) pours a molten blend of silver and copper into ingot coinage molds. An operator (*upper right*) inspects finished nickels as they pass before her on a belt at the Philadelphia Mint. An official (*below*) counts parcels of paper currency being stored in the United States Treasury at Washington.

The amount in circulation can be increased or decreased as needed to supply local banks and affect economic conditions.

(2) *United States Treasury Notes* which are in circulation only in small quantity.

(3) *Silver Certificates* issued mostly in $1 denominations.

National Bank Notes, once issued by National Banks, are being retired whenever deposited in banks.

Mutilated paper money may be redeemed if the Government's experts can identify it.

The *Bureau of Engraving and Printing* designs, engraves, and prints all federal money and bonds, all customs, postage, revenue, and savings stamps, checks and all other forms of engraved documents used by the Government. (A roundhouse, located under the Bureau's building, houses the President's special railway car.)

The Purchasing Power of the Dollar

The purchasing power of the dollar, how much a dollar will buy (or, to put it another way, how much a dollar is worth), varies from time to time. Quite obviously, when prices are low a dollar will buy more (is worth more) than when prices are high. A family with a $5000 income can maintain a higher standard of living in a period of lower prices than it can on the same income in a period of higher prices. The 1920 dollar was worth 65% of the 1926 dollar because of the soaring price level in the period immediately after World War I. Today's dollar is worth about 49¢ as compared with the dollar of 1935–1939.

Inflation is a more rapid increase in the amount of money or purchasing power in the hands of the people than in the supply of goods and services they want to purchase. For instance, during the hard times of 1932 the income of all the people of the United States was only $40,000,000,000.[1]

When the United States entered World War II, however, and the requirements of our armed forces had to be produced, good times returned and nearly everybody got a job, usually at high wages. The necessity for de-

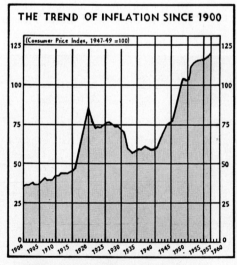

THE TREND OF INFLATION SINCE 1900

(Consumer Price Index, 1947-49 =100)

THE SHRINKING DOLLAR
Since 1900 the major price trend has been gradually upward.

000,000,000 — more than eight times that of 1932.

---

[1] The annual income now is over $350,-

Unit III. The Executive Department

voting so much of our production to war requirements made it impossible to supply many of the things needed by civilians. As people had plenty of money the tendency was to pay almost any price for a desired article, thus bringing on inflation.

To control this condition, the Government put " ceiling prices " on most commodities, thus saving the American people billions of dollars. But following the war, price controls were removed from most items and world-wide scarcities shot prices sky-high.

The resulting inflation reduced the purchasing power of wages, salaries, and savings, and increased defense costs and the amount of war debt.

Price controls were re-imposed after the start of the Korean war but were soon eliminated by the Eisenhower Administration.

Deflation is the opposite of inflation. It is just as dangerous because people stop buying whatever they can get along without — in the hope that prices will go lower and lower. The Government tries to prevent deflation through buying surplus goods, providing employment on public projects, and putting more money into circulation.

Bureau of Narcotics

Our law holds that the only legitimate uses for narcotics are in medicine and other scientific fields and that their sale should be limited to those purposes only. Dope addiction has become one of our most serious problems, especially among those of high-school age.

The Bureau of Narcotics, under a Commissioner, administers and enforces federal laws on the subject. With the Public Health Service, the Bureau sets the amount of narcotics that may be legally imported in any year. It licenses those who may lawfully sell them and arrests those who violate the laws. All States have anti-narcotics laws and the Bureau's agents work in co-operation with State law-enforcement officers.

Most illegal narcotics are smuggled into the country by plane or ship and the Bureau works closely with Customs agents and the Coast Guard. Narcotics agents recently seized a ship's steward who attempted to smuggle more than $1,000,000 worth of dope into San Francisco.

Red China is the world's largest producer of opium and most of it peddled here comes from there. The communists use it to get American dollars and to weaken our moral fiber.

The Coast Guard

The Coast Guard is one of our military services, but it operates under the Treasury Department in peacetime.

When we are at war, it is transferred to the Navy Department.

The Coast Guard is commanded by

a Commandant and is organized much like the Navy. It is primarily a police agency enforcing the maritime laws (those relating to the sea) and preventing smuggling. It also performs a large number of other duties — operates life-saving stations, aids vessels in distress, patrols the North Atlantic to warn ships against icebergs, suppresses mutinies on merchant ships, breaks ice in frozen channels, enforces the fishing and sealing laws in Alaskan waters, maintains lighthouses, lightships, radio beacons, fog signals, and buoys, licenses merchant marine personnel, inspects all classes of vessels for seaworthiness and safety, and brings ill seamen or passengers to land hospitals by plane or fast cutter.

The Coast Guard also patrols the coasts to prevent piracy, the operation of gambling ships, and the smuggling of dutiable goods, narcotics, liquor, and undesirable persons. In wartime it escorts convoys, operates landing craft in invasions, and guards against enemy landings. It also maintains the Coast Guard Academy at New London, Connecticut, to train new officers for the service.

WHAT THIS CHAPTER IS ABOUT

The Treasury Department is charged with the major responsibility for the collection, safekeeping, and disbursement of the tremendous sums involved in national finance. The Secretary of the Treasury heads the Department and is appointed by the President and Senate.

The Internal Revenue Service and the Bureau of Customs collect most of the federal revenue. The personal and corporate income tax produces over eighty per cent of all federal funds. Other internal revenue comes from such sources as taxes on liquor, gasoline, and playing cards. Customs duties are of three kinds: *specific* (so much per unit), *ad valorem* (in proportion to value), and *mixed* (a combination of the two).

Nontax revenues are those that come from sources other than taxation — Panama Canal tolls and court fines, for example.

The Treasurer of the United States is responsible for the safekeeping and disbursing of the revenues. The Currency Redemption Division redeems mutilated and burned currency. The Comptroller of the Currency supervises National Banks, and the Fiscal Service is the Treasury's bookkeeping agency.

The Comptroller-General and his General Accounting Office are independent of the Treasury and the executive branch, acting as a watchdog for Congress.

Our public debt of some $270,000,000,000 has been created by two world wars, a depression, and the current defense program. Metallic currency (coins) is stamped by the Bureau of the Mint. Paper currency is put out by the Bureau of Engraving and Printing.

The purchasing power of the dollar varies from time to time. Inflation is a more rapid increase in purchasing power than in goods and services available. Deflation is the opposite.

The Bureau of Narcotics enforces the federal narcotics laws, and the Coast Guard enforces the maritime laws and prevents smuggling.

Unit III. The Executive Department

QUESTIONS ON THE TEXT

1. Approximately how much does the National Government spend each year?

2. Who heads the Treasury Department?

3. What taxes produce over eighty per cent of all federal revenues? List three other internal revenue taxes.

4. Identify the three kinds of import duties levied.

5. What are nontax revenues? Examples?

6. What are the functions of the Treasurer of the United States? The Currency Redemption Division? The Comptroller of the Currency? The Fiscal Service?

7. Who heads the General Accounting Office? How is the GAO made independent of the executive branch?

8. Why does the Government borrow? How large is the national debt? The interest on the debt?

9. What denominations of coins are now in circulation? What agency produces them?

10. What three types of paper money are now in circulation? What agency produces them?

11. What is meant by inflation? Deflation?

12. What is the main function of the Bureau of Narcotics? The Coast Guard?

PROBLEMS FOR DISCUSSION

1. If you buy a United States Savings Bond, Series E, for $18.75, it will increase in value each year. At maturity, 8 years and 11 months, it will be worth $25. What per cent interest would this be? How does owning bonds make you more loyal to your country? List reasons why people should buy bonds.

2. Some people, especially big-time gamblers and racketeers, operate on a strictly cash basis. They keep no records and do not deposit their profits in regular bank accounts. Thus it is very difficult for the Internal Revenue Service to check on possible tax evasions. Former Congressman Sutton of Tennessee proposed that the United States change the color of its paper money and require that all " greenbacks " be exchanged for the newly colored currency within a specified time or become worth-

less. How would such a move help in uncovering tax-evaders who might not otherwise be caught?

3. Some people propose that the Constitution be amended to limit federal income taxes to a maximum 25 per cent, except in wartime emergencies. Assuming a continued high rate of federal expenditures (which seems certain), what changes would be necessary in the Government's tax program if such an amendment were adopted? Why would you favor or oppose such an amendment?

4. It is unconstitutional for the United States to tax State, county, or municipal bonds, or the income from them. Would you favor having the Supreme Court reverse itself on this? What effect would this have on the interest rates State and local governments would have to pay?

THINGS YOU MIGHT DO

1. Invite a local banker to speak to the class on his bank's relations with the

Treasury and the Federal Reserve System. Ask a local businessman and others in your community how federal taxes affect their lives.

2. The entire class might begin and continue a list of the federal agencies in your area and descriptions of their work.

3. Write an editorial for the school paper on the subject of those who cheat on their tax returns.

4. Stage a class debate or forum on the question: *Resolved,* That the National Government should adopt a sales tax.

WORDS AND PHRASES YOU SHOULD KNOW

Appropriation	Expenditure	Public debt
Currency	Federal Reserve Notes	Receipt
Customs	Fiscal year	Revenue
Deficit	Inflation	Silver Certificates
Deflation	Internal revenue	Surplus
Disbursement	Nontax revenue	Tariff
Duties		U.S. Treasury Notes

SELECT BIBLIOGRAPHY

ANDREWS, T. COLEMAN, " Whose Income Tax Are You Paying?" *American Magazine,* February, 1954.

——, " Why the Income Tax is Bad," *U.S. News,* May 25, 1956.

CARR, ROBERT K., and others, *American Democracy in Theory and Practice,* Chapters 26, 27. Rinehart, 1955.

CLARK, NEIL M., " Money By the Ton," *Saturday Evening Post,* September 15, 1956.

JOHNSON, CLAUDIUS O., *American National Government,* Chapter 17. Crowell, 1955.

" Lower Tariffs: Other Nations Do Not Follow U.S. Lead," *Time,* December 3, 1955.

MARGOLIUS, SYDNEY, " The Art of Taxmanship," *Harper's,* March, 1955.

MILLS, REP. WILBUR D., " Keep the Income Tax But Make it Fair," *U.S. News,* July 27, 1956.

ROSS, IRWIN, " Red China: The World's Biggest Dope Peddler," *Reader's Digest,* February, 1955.

SONDERN, FREDERIC, " The World War Against Narcotics," *Reader's Digest,* January, 1956.

" U.S. Tax Policy," *Current History,* entire issue, August, 1954.

U.S. Treasury Department, *Know Your Money.* Washington, D.C.

" Who Owns the Gold at Fort Knox? " *U.S. News,* February 24, 1956.

YODER, ROBERT, " The Money Surgeons," *Saturday Evening Post,* July 4, 1953.

——, " The Things You Can Deduct! " *Saturday Evening Post,* October 20, 1956.

Americans, indeed all free men, remember that in the final choice
a soldier's pack is not so heavy a burden as a prisoner's chains.

— Dwight D. Eisenhower

★

Chapter 13

THE DEPARTMENTS OF DEFENSE AND JUSTICE

THE DEPARTMENT OF DEFENSE

One of the major purposes for the establishing of the Constitution, as noted in the Preamble, was to "provide for the common defense."

The American people earnestly desire to live in a world at peace. As we have seen, peace is one of the primary goals of our foreign policy. It is also one of the primary goals of our defense policy. Indeed, foreign policy and national defense are but two sides of the same coin — national security.

The United States maintains huge and powerful defense forces (1) to defend us against foreign attack and (2) to discourage any such attack by making it plain to any potential aggressor that to attack us would be to commit suicide.

The citizens of our democracy have many duties and obligations to perform. One of the most important of these is to serve in the nation's defense. This is as true today when we face the threat of international communism as it was in the days of the minutemen.

The "War Powers"

Defense a National Function. The Constitution makes defense a national function, as we learned in Chapter 4.[1] For example, the States are

[1] See Article I, Sections 8 and 10; Article II, Section 2.

forbidden to "keep troops or ships of war" except with the consent of Congress. They cannot make war "unless actually invaded or in such imminent danger as will not admit of delay."

The State Militia. Each State may and does have a militia. This force is intended to preserve the peace at home and, since an act of 1795, may be called into federal service by the President. In 1916 the Congress defined the militia (unorganized) as consisting of all able-bodied males between the ages of eighteen and forty-five.

The *National Guard* is the *organized* part of the militia. It is maintained and supported by federal grants-in-aid, may be called into federal service by the President, and is " a nationally organized body of State troops auxiliary to the Regular Army."

Congress is vested with the so-called " war powers." They are found in Article I, Section 8, and we discussed them in Chapter 6. The major war powers are those to declare war and to raise and maintain the armed forces.

The power to determine the amounts of money to be spent for national defense is also an important congressional " war power." The " power of the purse " can be and is used to decide such basic military questions as the size of the armed forces and whether the air, land, or sea forces are to be our most powerful.

The President is made Commander-in-Chief of the armed forces, as we learned in Chapter 10. If he cares to do so, he may take actual command of troops in the field as President Washington did during the Whisky Rebellion in 1794. But later Presidents have exercised broad control and placed the actual direction of the armed forces in the hands of professional military and naval officers.

Defense Organization

The Department of Defense has existed only since 1947. It was created to " unify " the armed forces and so replaced the old War Department, created in 1789, and the old Navy Department, created in 1798.

It includes three other Departments — not of Cabinet rank: the Departments of Army, Navy, and Air Force.

The *Secretary of Defense,* who must be a civilian, is appointed by the President and Senate and heads the entire Defense Department. Under the President's direction, he establishes general policies, directs the De-partment, and co-ordinates the activities of the three service departments. His authority over the defense establishment has been strengthened under the Eisenhower administration, and his staff assistance is now centered around a Deputy Secretary and eight Assistant Secretaries.

The *National Security Council,* of which the President is chairman, has among its members the Secretary of Defense and the three service secretaries. It is " America's Cold War General Staff." (See page 178.)

The *Joint Chiefs of Staff* consists of a Chairman and the three military

232

heads of the armed services: the Army Chief of Staff, the Air Force Chief of Staff, and the Chief of Naval Operations (plus the Marine Commandant when Marine Corps matters are involved.) These officers are appointed by the President and Senate and serve as principal military advisers to the President and the Secretary.

The *Armed Forces Policy Council* is composed of the Secretary, the Deputy Secretary, the three service secretaries (Army, Navy, and Air Force) and the members of the Joint Chiefs of Staff. The Council advises the Secretary of Defense on matters of broad policy relating to the armed forces and their functions.

Functions of the Armed Forces. Our defense forces carry out the orders of the President, that is, of the Commander-in-Chief.

In brief, the services perform these major duties: (1) support and defend the Constitution against all enemies, foreign and domestic; (2) maintain the security of the United States, its possessions, and all other areas vital to its protection; (3) uphold the national policies of the United States; and (4) safeguard the internal security of the United States.

Army Department

Functions of the Army. Of the three major services, the United States Army has primary interest in all military operations on land. Its main duties are to defend the United States, to defeat enemy land forces, to seize and occupy enemy territory, to train and equip its forces, and to perform whatever other duties the Commander-in-Chief may see fit to assign to it.

The Army also administers the Panama Canal Zone, land bases and fortifications, and river and harbor improvements in the United States and the territories.

The *Secretary of the Army*, the civilian chief appointed by the President and Senate, heads the Army and is under the Secretary of Defense.

The *Chief of Staff* is the chief military adviser and executive to the Secretary. He is assisted by the General Staff and the Special Staff.

The *Army* consists of a permanent force and several reserve components.

The *Regular Army* is the heart of our land forces. Just before World War II it had an authorized strength of 375,000 officers and men. During the war it jumped to between seven and eight million out of the approximately twelve million in the armed forces. Today there are about 900,-000 men on active duty in the Army.

Reserve and National Guard units provide a reservoir of trained personnel who may be called to active duty in time of national emergency.

Enlistments, for periods ranging up to six years, and Selective Service (see page 242) are used to provide manpower for the Army. Any physically qualified young man may enlist

RECEPTION CENTER

Young men called up under Selective Service report first of all to a Reception Center. Here they are outfitted, are tested, and so on. Within a few weeks they will be in basic training.

at age eighteen, or at seventeen with his parents' consent. Young women too may enlist in the armed services.

Our military manpower problem is a crucial one. *Universal Military Training* for all eligible youth seems to many to be the only practical solution (see pages 242–243).

The GI, whether he enlists or is drafted, has tremendous educational opportunities. He may equip himself for one or more of many civilian occupations while he is serving his country. The Army maintains various technical schools, and regular high school and college courses are offered through the Armed Forces Institute.

Commissioned officers, all of whom are appointed by the President, come from West Point (the United States Military Academy), the National Guard, Officers' Candidate Schools within the Army, and the Reserve Officers Training Corps (ROTC) in colleges and universities.

Units of the Army. The infantry, artillery, and armored cavalry are the combat arms of our land forces. The foot soldiers of the infantry engage the enemy directly in small-arms combat. The artillery, including the field artillery, the antiaircraft artillery, and the coast artillery, supports the infantry and smashes enemy concentrations with its heavier guns. The cavalry also supports the infantry, and with its tanks often spearheads the breaking of enemy lines.

Other units provide the services essential to combat. The infantry, artillery, and cavalry could not fight without the services of the engineers, the military police, and the chemical, signal, ordnance, quartermaster, transportation, and medical corps. Modern combat conditions often demand that the men in these services fight alongside regular combat troops.

Chaplains corps in the Army, Navy, and Air Force minister to spiritual needs of our men.

Effect of Recent Inventions on the Army. The invention of atomic and hydrogen bombs, of guided missiles and long-range rockets, and of other weapons of mass destruction have made war a task for specialists. But the age of " push-button warfare " has not arrived. Though one of our great needs now is for research and scientific development, troops are still the basic part of the Army.

We have always needed the Army as a police force to keep the peace at home and to guard the country against foreign attack. Today the Army also mans our overseas defense posts, occupies former enemy territory, and guards against renewed aggression in Korea. Until we have lasting world peace we must maintain a large standing army to protect our freedoms and to discourage attacks by the military dictatorships of communism.

H–BOMB MUSHROOM CLOUD

The almost incredible devastation wrought by the hydrogen bomb has revolutionized the weapons and defenses of our Army. We pray that the atom's use, as we plan, will be restricted to peaceful purposes. Yet we must always be prepared to protect ourselves against its use in war.

U.S. Air Force

Navy Department

Functions of the Navy. The United States Navy includes naval combat and service forces, naval aviation, and the United States Marine Corps. It is organized, trained, and equipped to offer prompt and sustained combat at sea and to co-operate with and support the other services.

The *Secretary of the Navy*, the civilian chief who directs the Navy, is subordinate to the Secretary of Defense.

The *Chief of Naval Operations* is the principal naval adviser to the President and to the Secretary of the Navy. He is the Navy's top-ranking officer, responsible for its use in war and its preparation and readiness for war. He has direct command of the Operating Forces of the Navy: the sea-going forces and the related shore activities. The Marines are under the separate command of the Marine Corps Commandant.

The Army's basic fighting unit is the soldier, trained as an efficient fighter. The basic fighting unit in the Navy is not the sailor but the warship. The sailor seldom fights hand to hand. His major duty is to make

WORLD'S FIRST ATOMIC–POWERED SUBMARINE
The 2800-ton U.S.S. *Nautilus*, launched in January, 1955, heads out from its base at Groton, Connecticut. It has since been joined by its even mightier sisters, the *Sea Wolf* and the *Skate*.

the warship an efficient fighting machine.

Enlistments in the Navy are for as long as six years. Any sailor may reenlist, of course, and the real backbone of each of our armed services is found in the " career men " — those who spend their lives in the service of the country. The Navy's minimum enlistment age is 17.

A young man who wants to enlist must first satisfy the Navy's physical, mental, and moral requirements. Then he goes through an intensive eight weeks of training in " boot camp." Here he learns basic naval courtesy, drill, and the regulations. He learns to salute, to say " aye, aye, sir! " instead of " yes, sir " or " okay." He also learns the basic elements of sailing, how to handle a rifle, and how to signal.

As in the other services, women are now a part of the Navy, too.

As in the Army, there are many educational opportunities available to the " gob." He may attend such schools as those for —

Mechanics
Woodworkers
Electricians
Ordnance men
Clerical personnel
Musicians
Hospital corpsmen
Cooks and bakers
Fire controlmen
Gyrocompass electricians
Motion-picture technicians
Torpedomen
Aerographers
Aviators
Deep-sea divers
Dental technicians
Parachute materielsmen
Pharmacist mates
Photographers
Radio men
Submarine personnel
Metalsmiths

Each of these schools provides trained specialists for the Navy. They also give sailors special skills they can put to use in civilian life.

Commissioned officers come from the Naval Academy at Annapolis, the reserves, the Naval ROTC, and the ranks. There are now some 650,000 officers and men in the Navy.

Ships of the Fleet. We have three major fleets; namely, the Atlantic Fleet, the Eastern Atlantic and Mediterranean Fleet, and the Pacific Fleet.

Battleships are heavily armored and carry huge guns mounted in groups of three in turrets. Watertight compartments along the outer hulls at the water line enable them to resist torpedo attack and take and inflict severe damages in combat. Their larger guns permit them to inflict damage on the enemy from great range.

Heavy and light cruisers are more lightly armored and have fewer guns than battleships. But this permits greater speed.

Aircraft carriers as large as or larger than battleships carry as many as 100 planes. Pacific action against the Japanese in World War II, and later action against the Communists in Korea, demonstrated their great value.

FLOATING AIR BASE

The aircraft carrier, *U.S.S. Forrestal*, one of the largest warships afloat, is one of the cornerstones of our modern navy. The helicopters are in readiness to be used as plane guards, should a mishap occur when the jets are being catapulted or soon thereafter.

Destroyers, or " tin cans," carry very little armor and lighter guns. Their torpedoes are deadly weapons, and the ships are designed for " hit and run " attacks.

Submarines of the " silent service " operate mostly beneath the sea on long and dangerous patrols torpedoing enemy shipping.

Smaller combat vessels include motor torpedo boats, minelayers, subchasers, and patrol craft.

Noncombat vessels include such types as tankers, supply and ammunition ships, transports, mine sweepers, hospital ships, and destroyer, submarine, and seaplane tenders. The President may order the arming of merchant vessels in time of emergency.

There are also task forces for special duties — especially in time of war. These duties are to convoy our troop ships, to convoy supplies, to attack enemy convoys, or to bombard an enemy base.

" Mothballing " Surplus Ships. At the end of World War II we found ourselves with about a thousand naval vessels not needed in peacetime. Rather than destroy them, as we did after World War I, they were " mothballed " in a number of harbors. The ships were stripped and sealed against the effects of weather and time.

Their interiors are kept so dry to prevent rust that a little moisture is added to prevent dry rust. The " mothball fleet " gives us a reserve that can be made ready for active duty on very short notice.

Modern Warfare has made many changes in the Navy, just as it has in the other services. Atomic weapons, submarines powered by atomic energy, planes which fly faster than sound, warning and navigation devices like radar, sonar, and loran, are only a few examples of these changes.

Today the Navy places the greatest emphasis on its aircraft carriers and submarines. By 1958 not a single battleship was on active service. All the combat vessels built in recent years are armed with guided missiles and most carry nuclear weapons. The carriers are equipped with atomic bombs and long-range planes to deliver them. Many of our submarines, operating all over the world, can rise to the surface, launch an atomic missile in a matter of minutes, and submerge quickly — while the missile speeds to its target hundreds of miles away. And the Navy is now using atomic depth charges as one of its many anti-submarine weapons.

We now have three atomic-powered submarines and several more are on the ways. In 1957, one of them, the *U.S.S. Nautilus*, gave an apt demonstration of the capabilities of our modern Navy. It traveled for over five days *submerged under* the Arctic ice pack and penetrated to within 180 miles of the North Pole itself.

The Marine Corps. " First to Fight " is the watchword of our Marines, called the " soldiers of the sea." The Japanese learned to fear the fighting fury of the " Leathernecks " in World War II — and the communists have learned the same lesson in Korea.

The 190,000 Marines act as a land force for the fleet, fortify land bases from which the fleet can operate, man antiaircraft guns aboard capital ships, and serve as garrisons for naval establishments.

The Raider Battalions are trained for surprise attacks in rubber boats, amphibian landing boats, or other craft. The Defense Battalions are designed to protect advance bases of the Navy. The Paramarines land behind enemy lines to capture or destroy ammunition dumps, airports, railheads, and highway junctions. Garbed in heavy cloth jumpers, loose-fitting trousers tucked into leather boots, and three pieces of headgear — leather, plastic, and steel helmets — the Marines bail out from their carrier plane at the rate of two a second. Marines are also trained to operate gliders and helicopters.

Not long ago the Marines provided a good demonstration of one of the many ways in which the armed services help the nation other than in defense. Two convicted murderers had escaped a southern penitentiary and had hidden in a farmhouse. The sheriff and his men were unable to go in after them because the convicts held hostages.

A Marine helicopter hovered directly over the house so that the fugitives were unable to see what happened. A Marine was lowered to the roof, climbed in an attic window, and singlehandedly surprised and captured the convicts.

The *Coast Guard* performs a wide variety of important duties along our coasts in time of peace (see page 227). In wartime it operates as a part of the Navy to defend our coasts, operates landing craft, and performs many other war missions.

Air Force Department

Functions of the Air Force. The United States Air Force includes all military aviation not assigned to the Army and Navy. It is organized, trained, and equipped for prompt and sustained air operations in peace and war. It is responsible for preparation for war and for such peacetime duties as may be assigned to it — such as the ferrying of food and supplies to our occupation forces and German civilians of blockaded Berlin in 1948–1949. In time of war its primary functions are to repel enemy air attacks, to gain and hold air supremacy over the enemy, to support land and sea action, and to bombard enemy industrial and military centers.

The *Secretary of the Air Force,* the civilian chief of the Air Force, is subordinate to the Secretary of Defense. The Chief of Staff of the Air Force is the military commander, under the Secretary of the Air Force, of our new air arm.

Enlistments in the Air Force. Enlistments are accepted on the same basis as for the Army and the Navy, but Air Force men must pass more rigid physical examinations. The work of our airmen demands that they be in excellent physical condition. Aviation Cadet training is open to all qualified men between the ages of 20 and 26½ who have had two years of college training or the equivalent. As in the Army, Navy, and Marine Corps, there is a reserve force called the Air Reserve.

Commissioned officers come from the Air Force Academy at Colorado Springs, the Reserves, the Air ROTC, and the ranks. The Air Force has a strength of about 875,000 men.

Air Force in Action. The crippling blows dealt by our Air Force to the German and Japanese industrial centers during World War II shortened that war by untold months or even years. The atomic bombs which ended the war in the Pacific were delivered to Hiroshima and Nagasaki by the Air Force. And the USAF played a leading role in the United Nations operations in Korea. Its planes include heavy and light bombers, dive bombers, attack bombers, conventional and jet fighters, transport planes, hospital ships, and observation planes.

The major emphasis in our over-all defense strategy is placed on the Air

AIR FORCE ACADEMY

The Air Age made necessary the establishment of an academy to train men as officers for our expanding air force. This is a model of the academy as it will look when construction is completed.

Force today. This is not to say that the Army and the Navy are being neglected — far from it. But it is the Air Force that is looked to as our first line of defense against sudden enemy attack to deliver the first crushing, retaliatory blows against an aggressor and his home bases.

The strength of the Air Force today is truly awesome. And its great power is being added to and improved upon constantly. Very few of the aircraft now in the combat units of the Air Force were in them even as late as the Korean conflict. Today the huge B–47 jet bomber is our standard long-range (*i.e.,* "strategic") bomber.

President Eisenhower recently told the nation that *just one* of these planes can carry an atomic bombload with as much destructive power as that delivered by *all* the bombs dropped by all the bombers in all of World War II. Even so, the President added, mightier planes will soon add to the Air Force's incredible striking power.

All of our fighter and interceptor aircraft are now equipped with air-to-air missiles for use against attacking planes or missiles. All of our " tactical " (*i.e.,* shorter-range attack and dive) bombers also carry missiles for use against ground targets.

Like the Army and the Navy, the

Air Force has many types of surface-launched missiles. Most of the USAF missiles are used especially for flight research or for defense against attacking enemy planes. Research missiles have been fired as high as 4000 miles into space. Some of the newest missiles are capable of seeking out and destroying flying targets many miles from their launching points.

Selective Service and U.M.T.

The Draft. World War II and conditions since have convinced us that small standing armed forces are no longer adequate for national defense. Accordingly, Congress has authorized the induction (drafting) of eligible men into the armed forces.

Those eligible include all males between the ages of 18½ and 26, but one must register at 18. Draftees must serve for 24 months of active duty plus an additional period (up to six years) in an active reserve unit.

Exemptions and Deferments. Members of the armed forces, most reservists and veterans, and ministers and theological students are exempted from (not liable to) the draft. High school students (until graduation or age 20), college students (so long as their work is satisfactory), all elected officials, those in essential occupations, " hardship " cases, and those physically, mentally, or morally unqualified are deferred. Anyone deferred remains liable for service until age 35.

Rights and Benefits. All draftees receive the same pay and benefits as others in service, including government life insurance and civil service preference. Those who held a job before being drafted are guaranteed the same job upon return to civilian life.

Universal Military Training. As early as 1790 George Washington proposed a program of compulsory military training for all of the nation's able-bodied young men. Similar proposals have been heard periodically ever since. Woodrow Wilson advanced such a plan at the end of World War I. And interest has been especially acute since World War II.

Congress approved U.M.T. in principle in 1951, creating a National Security Training Commission to prepare a concrete plan. The Commission's plan called for drafting all fit youths at 18. They would receive six months of basic training at camp or on shipboard and spend another six months in service schools or other training. Then they would spend several years in the reserves — ready to serve should the need arise. Altogether some 400,000 would be in training at any one time. (Several similar plans have been advanced by many private persons and organizations.)

Congress enacted a *restricted* version of the Commission's plan in 1955: A *limited* number of youths between 17 and 18½ may now enlist in the reserves for eight years. They are draft-exempt and must serve six months on active training duty and then serve for seven and a half years in the active reserves.

Many groups favor U.M.T. Most patriotic and veterans organizations and some periodicals and newspapers lead the campaign in its behalf. Basically, they argue that because of the continued possibility of another war we must be " fully prepared." The best way to do this, they say, is to maintain a large, trained " citizen reserve " rather than a large standing army. It is claimed, too, that a U.M.T. program would help to promote vigorous and effective citizenship.

Many groups oppose U.M.T. The major opponents include most religious, educational, farm, and labor groups. Basically, they argue that such a program might easily lead to the " militarization " of our society and perhaps even to military dictatorship. It is claimed, too, that U.M.T. could not provide an adequately trained reserve that could be called up at a moment's notice in this age of atomic warfare.

Atomic Energy Commission

The atomic bomb dropped on Hiroshima August 6, 1945, heralded a new age in warfare. American scientists, with the help of outstanding British and Canadian scientists, had unleashed the most fearful power man has known.

The splitting of the atom also marked the beginning of a new age in man's peaceful pursuits. We are only now beginning to scratch the surface of the wonders atomic energy can bring. We know that atomic weapons can destroy the world. We also know that atomic energy can help all of the earth's peoples to a fuller life.

The *Atomic Energy Commission,* created in 1946, is an independent body responsible directly to the President. Its five civilian members are appointed by the President and Senate.

The Commission controls atomic energy in the United States. Gradu-ally private industry is being permitted to take over and develop some aspects of this mighty force.

The AEC maintains huge laboratories and works with our colleges and private industry to develop the potentials of the atom. Because of the tense international situation, major emphasis is placed on military uses. But a great deal of work has already been done and is still being done to develop more humane uses. For example, radioactive isotopes are now widely used in the medical field.

It is illegal to produce, possess, or transfer fissionable materials without the consent of the AEC. If a person violates the law with intent to injure the United States, he may be sentenced to death.

Atomic energy is released through " fission " — the splitting apart of the parts of the atom. Prospecting for uranium, the major source for atomic power, is greatly encouraged by the AEC. Modern " gold rushes " have started again in the West.

The United States stands ready to share its atomic knowledge with the rest of the world as soon as the other nations will co-operate to prevent its use for war. (See pages 712–714.)

THE DEPARTMENT OF JUSTICE

The *Attorney-General* heads the Justice Department. His office was created by Congress in 1789, but the Department was not established until 1870. He is the chief legal adviser to the President and to the rest of the Government.

The Attorney-General and his aides, especially the Solicitor-General, are the Government's prosecuting attorneys. Under him the Department investigates alleged violations of federal law, directs the federal prison system, and administers the operation of the federal courts.

As prosecuting attorney the Attorney-General seldom appears in court in person. His numerous assistants prepare cases and represent him in court. For example, one group represents the Government in all suits brought against the United States in the Court of Claims; another has charge of cases arising out of the administration of our tax laws; while another is known as the " trust busters."

As director of the federal court system the Attorney-General is consulted by the President in the appointment of federal district attorneys and federal district marshals. After these officers are appointed by the President they are under the direction of the Attorney-General.

The *Bureau of Prisons* has charge of all nonmilitary federal penal and correctional institutions. At Atlanta, Georgia; Lewisburg, Pennsylvania; Leavenworth, Kansas; McNeil Island, Washington; Terre Haute, Indiana; and Alcatraz, California, are federal penitentiaries. Alcatraz ("the rock"), in San Francisco Bay, is for very dangerous criminals.

There are three reformatories for male first offenders over 17, and one reformatory for women guilty of federal offenses. Seven correctional institutions are provided for males serving short-term sentences. Also short-term male offenders may be sent to the four federal prison camps where they are used for roadbuilding and other construction work. Prisoners soon eligible for release are often transferred to these camps. Juvenile delinquents guilty of federal crimes are sent to the National Training School for Boys, at Washington, D.C.

The prison hospital at Springfield, Missouri, cares for prisoners who are insane, tubercular, or otherwise chronically ill.

The Federal Government contracts with county jails and State institutions for " boarding " federal prisoners awaiting trial or serving short terms; but in such cities as New York,

244

Detroit, New Orleans, and El Paso it operates its own jails.

The Commissioner of Prison Industries, under the Federal Prison Industries Incorporated, uses prison labor to manufacture materials for Government use only; or he can work prisoners on federal roads, levees, forests, lands, and the like.

A Police Academy is conducted in the Department and is open to State and city police free of charge.

The *Board of Parole* consists of eight members appointed by the President. It acts in his name and has sole authority to grant or revoke paroles for United States prisoners.

Probation Officers may be appointed by United States District Court Judges — with or without salary. These officers aid persons on probation and bring about improvements in their conduct and condition. They must perform such duties for persons on parole as the Attorney-General may request.

The *Federal Bureau of Investigation* is the most famous and efficient law-enforcement agency in the world. It investigates all violations of federal law except those specifically assigned to other agencies — *e.g.,* counterfeiting, postal violations, and internal revenue matters.

PRINT COMPARISON

A Department of Justice man uses the master file of fingerprints to link a forged signature on a bank check with the prints of a known criminal. Fingerprinting is an important weapon against crime.

The FBI investigates alleged violations of more than 140 federal statutes, such as the Federal Kidnaping (Lindbergh) Act, the National Motor Vehicle Theft (Dyer) Act, the White Slave (Mann) Act, the Atomic Energy Act, and the National Bank Act.

The G-men, under FBI Director J. Edgar Hoover, co-operate closely with State and local peace officers and maintain a vast fingerprint and identification file that is invaluable in criminal investigations and prosecutions.

The *Immigration and Naturalization Service* administers the immigration and naturalization laws.

Immigration and Naturalization

We are a nation of immigrants. Except for the American Indians, all of us have come here from abroad or are descended from those who did.

Congress Has Power to Regulate Immigration. Under international law, all sovereign states may regulate the crossing of their borders. The Supreme Court has held that this sovereign power, although not expressed in the Constitution, is an exclusive power of Congress. In addition to this international source for the power to regulate immigration, Congress may lean on its expressed power to regulate foreign commerce — people being classed as commerce.

The Immigration and Naturalization Service administers the laws regarding the entry and naturalization of aliens. The basic law today is the Immigration and Nationality (McCarran-Walter) Act of 1952. Of course, other acts contain sections relating to aliens — for example, the Internal Security (McCarran) Act of 1950 — and those provisions are also enforced by the Service.

Through the first hundred years of our national history, immigration was generally encouraged. There were vast and uninhabited stretches of the frontier West to be filled. But, by the 1880's, the open frontier was becoming a thing of the past.

Beginning with the Chinese Exclusion Act of 1882,[2] Congress began to clamp down on immigration. Many groups were excluded in the next several years. They included the feeble-minded, anarchists, paupers, and other people of undesirable characteristics.

The flood of immigration continued, running over 1,000,000 a year in the first years of this century. In 1921, Congress began limiting immigration on the basis of national origin as well as on personal grounds. Finally, the National Origins Act of 1929 set the basic pattern for the present system of control.

---

[2] This law was intended to stem the flow of coolie labor to the Pacific Coast. Because of their lower standard of living the Chinese could afford to work for less than white laborers, especially in the mines and on the railroads. By 1924 all Orientals had been excluded except for temporary visits. World War II brought a slight relaxation in the Oriental exclusion policy; but until 1952 only limited numbers of Chinese, Filipinos, and natives of India were admitted.

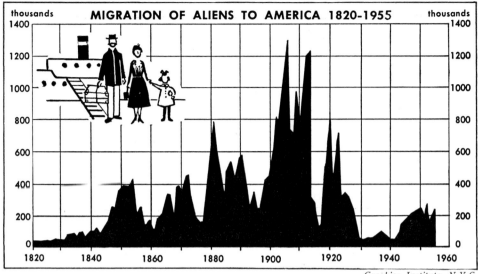

thousands 1400

thousands 1400

Graphics Institute, N.Y.C.

No alien ineligible for citizenship may enter the United States, except for temporary purposes. All aliens who are allowed to enter to remain and to become citizens come in as *quota* or *nonquota* immigrants. Many *nonimmigrants* are admitted each year, for temporary stays.

Undesirable Aliens Banned. The list of undesirables now takes up five pages in the *United States Code.* It includes the feebleminded, the insane, epileptics, chronic alcoholics, drug addicts, vagrants, beggars, stowaways, paupers, tuberculars and carriers of other contagious diseases, criminals, immoral persons, polygamists, adults unable to read any language, those who advocate the forcible overthrow of our government, and members or former members of communist or fascist parties.

The Quota System. Despite the exclusion of various groups after 1882,

the number of immigrants continued to rise. So, after World War I, Congress began placing restrictions on mere numbers. Each country outside the Western Hemisphere has been assigned a *quota* — the number of immigrants that may be admitted from that country each year.[3] Quotas are alloted to each country in the same proportion to which the different nationalities contributed to the population of the United States as of the 1920 census. The grand total of all quota immigrants admitted each year is now limited to the total of 154,657, but

---

[3] An immigrant's nationality for determining under which nation's quota he enters is determined by his place of birth rather than by his residence. Thus one born in Germany but entering the United States from Great Britain is admitted under the German quota. The Immigration and Nationality Act of 1952 eliminated the entire Oriental exclusion policy and extended the quota system to all parts of the Far East, as well as the rest of the world.

no nation has a quota of less than 100. Under this system Great Britain naturally has the largest quota, 65,361; Germany is second with 25,814, other quotas ranging on down to the minimum 100 for such countries as India and Ethiopia.

Nonquota Immigrants. In addition to the 154,657 quota immigrants, thousands of others enter the United States each year outside the quota restrictions. No quota restrictions are placed on persons born in the Western Hemisphere; but they must meet the personal standards required of an immigrant. Other nonquota immigrants include alien wives or husbands of American citizens, resident aliens returning from a brief visit to their native countries, ministers who intend to preach their religion in this country, and the alien children of American citizens.

Congress sometimes relaxes the bars for certain groups or persons. This was done for " war brides " after World War II. The Displaced Persons Act of 1948 and 1950 allowed the admission of 415,744 refugees from war-torn Europe. Between 1953 and 1956 Congress authorized the admission of another 214,000 persons, mostly iron-curtain refugees; and over 35,000 refugees from revolt-torn Hungary were admitted in 1957.

Nonimmigrants. Each year thousands of aliens come to the United States as nonimmigrants — that is, for temporary purposes. Students, tourists, businessmen, and newspapermen from other countries are examples. By special act, Congress

IMMIGRATION TO AND MIGRATION FROM THE UNITED STATES

COUNTRIES	1940		1950	
	INWARD	OUTWARD	INWARD	OUTWARD
Germany	21,520	1,978	128,592	1,309
Canada	10,806	769	21,885	2,267
England	5,850	998	10,191	2,919
Italy	5,302	1,534	12,454	1,636
West Indies	2,675	1,300	6,206	3,190
France	2,575	542	4,430	1,125
Mexico	2,313	4,584	6,744	1,257
Hungary	1,902	136	190	27
Belgium	1,713	61	1,429	237
South America	1,105	1,004	3,284	2,873
Czechoslovakia	1,074	39	946	97
Greece	811	261	1,179	588
Eire	749	322	4,837	372
Poland	702	81	696	106
All others	11,569	7,582	46,124	9,595
Total	70,666	21,191	249,187	27,508

granted the late Sister Elizabeth Kenny, the Australian nurse famed for her infantile paralysis work, the right to enter and leave the United States at will.

Aliens in the United States. About 2,800,000 aliens now live in the United States; some 200,000 immigrants and 600,000 nonimmigrants come here each year.[4] In nearly all respects these people enjoy the same great civil liberties that citizens do. In many States certain professions (such as law, medicine, and dentistry) are closed to them, and in some States they cannot own such weapons as rifles. In a few States their right to own property is very severely restricted, and many defense industries will not employ aliens. A few States deny them unemployment compensation. But, generally, they may attend the public schools, make contracts, use the courts, own property, enter most businesses — in short, do most of the things any citizen may do. Of course, they cannot vote or hold most public offices, but they must pay taxes. When an alien becomes a citizen, he gains all of the rights and assumes all of the responsibilities of that cherished status.

How Immigrants Enter the United States. Every alien immigrant seeking to enter the United States must go before an American consul and obtain from him a visa establishing his apparent right to en-

Wide World Photo

HUNGARIAN REFUGEES

In late 1956 and early 1957 Hungarian refugees, who had fled their native country during the 1956 revolts, were admitted to this country as nonquota immigrants. Again the United States was the refuge of the oppressed.

ter the United States, subject to a further examination at the port of entry. Consuls deny visas to aliens who are legally inadmissible to the United States. Some few immigrants are turned back on arrival at our " ports of entry " by immigration officials.

A steamship line which knowingly or carelessly brings an alien who is not admissible is required to return the alien to the port where he boarded the ship. An alien from Brazil once was rejected for insanity. Brazil would not take him back because he was not a citizen of Brazil. The ship carried him back and forth for years, until his condition improved.

---

[4] Aliens of all ages must register with the Justice Department during the first thirty days in each year.

Deportation. A citizen cannot be deported. But an alien may be forced to leave for a variety of reasons. Illegal entry is the most common cause. Aliens who enter with falsified passports or sneak in by plane or ship or at night are usually persons of low moral code. Having entered illegally, they are considered a menace and are deported. In times like these, immigration and other federal officers are especially concerned with foreign agents who may slip in.

"Wadies," Mexicans who wade or walk across the border, present a peculiar problem. Many are attracted by higher farm wages here, and they must be rounded up periodically — sometimes hundreds of miles from the border. It is not at all uncommon for many of the very same wadies to be deported several times in the same month.

Any alien who commits a crime involving moral turpitude, or violates narcotics laws, or commits practically any other felony (not a minor crime) may be deported. Lately, the Justice Department has been moving against many alien gamblers and racketeers in order to deport them.

Finally, any alien may be deported who teaches or advocates the forcible overthrow of the Government of the United States, or who belongs to an organization which does, the communist party, for example. We have no use for those who would come here to enjoy our liberties while working at the same time to overthrow those liberties.

The Alien Record a Good One. Through the years, the record of the alien population has been quite good. According to FBI records, for example, the crime rate for aliens is well below that for citizens. Because those who are admitted must meet the high standards set by law, they many times become among the very best of our citizens.

Naturalization of Aliens. One of the functions of the Immigration and Naturalization Service is to keep records of immigration and to see that those who desire citizenship may be naturalized according to law.

Three Ways of Becoming Citizens. All persons born in the United States,[5] and subject to the jurisdiction thereof,[6] are citizens of the United States and of the State wherein they reside. Inhabitants of acquired territory are usually naturalized *en masse.* Congress determines who shall become naturalized and provides for the naturalization of individuals by the judicial process described below.

Who May Become Naturalized. The Immigration and Nationality Act of 1952 wiped out the ban against naturalization of most Orientals. Any person who comes as a legal immigrant is now eligible to become a natu-

---

[5] Children born abroad to United States citizens who have once resided in the United States are natural-born American citizens. Children born abroad, one of whose parents is a citizen, must live in United States territory for at least five years between ages 14 and 28 or lose their citizenship. See chart, page 253.

[6] See Amendment 14, note, and page 253.

CITIZENSHIP CEREMONY

New citizens take the oath of allegiance to the United States at ceremonies in a New York baseball park. On this day, the first observance of Veterans' Day (1954), some 48,000 men and women became citizens throughout our land.

ralized American citizen. The naturalization of both parents [7] naturalizes the children under sixteen if living in the United States. The naturalization of husband or wife does not automatically naturalize the other.[8]

---

[7] If one parent is naturalized before the other, the children become citizens only upon the naturalization of the latter.

[8] An alien woman or man must now become naturalized independently of husband or wife, but if the one is a natural-born or naturalized American citizen the other need not file a " declaration of intention " and need reside in the United States only three years before " filing petition."

Today American citizenship is neither acquired nor lost by marriage. Until 1922 an

In What Courts. One may become naturalized in a United States alien woman became an American citizen by marriage to an American citizen; and an American woman lost her citizenship by marriage to an alien. An American woman who thus lost her citizenship can regain it as soon as the naturalization examiner satisfies the judge that she was once a natural-born citizen of the United States.

Any person born in the United States who lost his or her United States citizenship by naturalization in a foreign country but was readmitted to the United States for permanent residence prior to March 3, 1931, and is eligible to citizenship, may become naturalized in the United States in as short a period as six months. Aliens in the armed forces may also be naturalized in as quickly as six months.

District Court or he may be naturalized in any State or territorial court of record having jurisdiction of cases in which the amount in controversy is unlimited.

Filing Declaration of Intention. Although he is not required to file one, an alien at least 18 years of age may file a declaration of intention to become an American citizen with the clerk of one of the above courts. This declaration contains facts for identification, and an intention to renounce all allegiance to any foreign state and to become a United States citizen.

Filing Petition. After five years' residence in the United States (or three years if the alien is married to an American citizen), including six months in the State, the applicant files his petition for citizenship with the clerk. He states that he is not opposed to organized government, that he is not a polygamist, and that he renounces his allegiance to his former country.

Witnesses. When the petition is filed, two American citizens must testify to the clerk of the court that they have known the petitioner to have resided continuously in the United States during the last five years, to have been of good moral character and to be attached to the principles of the Constitution of the United States. If part of the five years has been spent in another country, the petitioner might file depositions from other witnesses to cover that period.

Examination. Formerly the judge conducted the examination. Now a United States District Judge may appoint a naturalization examiner. The examiner questions the applicant and witnesses. He learns whether an applicant speaks English, has a reasonable knowledge of the Constitution and Government, and fulfills all other requirements for citizenship. He then reports what he finds, with recommendations, to the District Judge. The examiner may also perform this service for State judges.

Granting Citizenship. In not less than thirty days after filing the petition the applicant goes before the judge. The judge may ask a few questions or he may ask many. When he is satisfied that the applicant meets the standards the law requires, he administers the oath of allegiance. The new citizen will then be given his certificate of citizenship signed by the judge.

Loss of Citizenship. Despite the popular impression, a person cannot lose his citizenship upon being convicted of an ordinary federal or State crime. Some of the *privileges* of citizenship, especially the right to vote, are often denied felons. Under no circumstances may a State deny one his American citizenship.

Under federal law, the only crimes for which citizenship may be lost are the following: treason, attempting or conspiring with others to overthrow the government by force, bearing arms against the United States, evading the draft in time of war, or desertion from the armed forces.

HOW CITIZENSHIP IS ACQUIRED

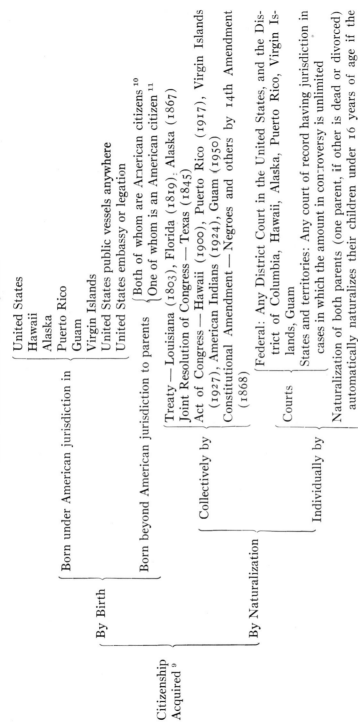

Citizenship Acquired[9]

By Birth
- Born under American jurisdiction in
  - United States
  - Hawaii
  - Alaska
  - Puerto Rico
  - Guam
  - Virgin Islands
  - United States public vessels anywhere
  - United States embassy or legation
- Born beyond American jurisdiction to parents
  - Both of whom are American citizens[10]
  - One of whom is an American citizen[11]

By Naturalization
- Collectively by
  - Treaty — Louisiana (1803), Florida (1819), Alaska (1867)
  - Joint Resolution of Congress — Texas (1845)
  - Act of Congress — Hawaii (1900), Puerto Rico (1917), Virgin Islands (1927), American Indians (1924), Guam (1950)
  - Constitutional Amendment — Negroes and others by 14th Amendment (1868)
- Individually by
  - Courts
    - Federal: Any District Court in the United States, and the District of Columbia, Hawaii, Alaska, Puerto Rico, Virgin Islands, Guam
    - States and territories: Any court of record having jurisdiction in cases in which the amount in controversy is unlimited
  - Naturalization of both parents (one parent, if other is dead or divorced) automatically naturalizes their children under 16 years of age if the children are residing permanently in the United States.

[9] See 14th Amendment.
[10] At least one of the citizen parents must have resided in the United States or an outlying possession at some time.
[11] The citizen parent must have resided in the United States or an outlying possession for at least 10 years, 5 of them after age 14. Such child must live in the United States continuously for at least 5 years between ages 14 and 28.

Expatriation. A native-born citizen may be expatriated (voluntarily or involuntarily lose citizenship) by comitting the crimes listed above, also by (1) taking an oath of allegiance to a foreign state, (2) formally renouncing United States citizenship, (3) serving in the armed forces of or holding any governmental post under a foreign state, (4) voting in a foreign election, or (5) if a child, by the naturalization of a parent to a foreign state.

Denaturalization. It is much easier for a naturalized citizen to lose his citizenship. His citizenship may be revoked by the federal courts if it can be shown that he obtained it through fraud or that he took the oath of allegiance with mental reservations. He may lose it if he establishes a foreign residence within five years after his naturalization, or if he joins a subversive organization within that period. And, of course, he may lose it for the same reasons for which a native-born citizen may be expatriated.

WHAT THIS CHAPTER IS ABOUT

We maintain a huge defense force to (1) protect us against foreign attack and (2) to discourage attacks. Serving in the nation's defense is one of the citizen's major responsibilities.

Defense is a national function, though the States may keep militias. Congress, with its " war powers," and the President, as Commander-in-Chief, control the armed forces.

The Department of Defense is headed by the Secretary of Defense. He is assisted by the Joint Chiefs of Staff and the Armed Forces Policy Council. The Department includes the three noncabinet departments of Army, Navy, and Air Force.

The armed forces carry out the orders of the President and protect and defend the nation.

The Army is especially responsible for operations on land, the Navy (including the Marines) on the seas, and the Air Force over both land and sea.

Selective service " drafts " eligible young men for military service. Many people favor (and many people oppose) Universal Military Training as the solution to our country's military manpower problem.

The Atomic Energy Commission controls the military and other development of atomic energy in the United States.

The Justice Department, headed by the Attorney-General, investigates and prosecutes federal crimes, advises the Government on legal matters, and administers the federal courts and prisons. It also administers the immigration and naturalization laws.

QUESTIONS ON THE TEXT

1. What are the major " war powers "?
2. Who is the Commander-in-Chief?
3. What three departments are subordinate to the Defense Department?

4. What are the major functions of each of these three?
5. Under what service is the Marine Corps located?

6. Between what ages may a young man be drafted? For how long? Who may be deferred?

7. Give the central argument for and against U.M.T.

8. What is the function of the Atomic Energy Commission?

9. List three functions of the Attorney-General.

10. Why are we a " nation of immigrants "?

11. On what bases does Congress have the power to regulate immigration?

12. List five classes of undesirable aliens.

13. What is the quota system?

14. Distinguish between nonquota immigrants and nonimmigrants.

15. May a citizen be deported?

16. What are the three ways in which individuals may acquire United States citizenship?

17. What courts have jurisdiction to naturalize?

18. Distinguish between *expatriation* and *denaturalization*.

PROBLEMS FOR DISCUSSION

1. Rockets and atomic bombs necessitate what changes in methods of defense? Is infantry now more important or less important than formerly? Cavalry? Navy? Air Force? Distant naval base? Distant air base? Coast Guard? An international police force?

2. Do you agree that the best way to keep out of another world war is to prevent the war? By what methods can we help prevent it?

3. " Because of its traditions and the nature of its government, it is always difficult for a true democracy to make clear to a dictator that at some point in his aggression he must face the firm resistance of free nations. Four times the democratic nations waited too long to preserve the peace. Had the Kaiser known that Britain would take the invasion of Belgium as a cause of war between herself and Germany; had the arrogance of Mussolini in invading Ethiopia been met with other than ineffective sanctions; had the Japanese entry into Manchuria been countered in 1931 with strong determination by the United States and Great Britain; had Hitler's first tentative steps in the Saar and in the Ruhr been firmly opposed — can there be doubt of the effect upon the rising tempo of their boldness? "

What bearing does this statement of the first Secretary of Defense, James Forrestal, have upon present conditions?

THINGS YOU MIGHT DO

1. Stage a debate or class forum on the question: " *Resolved,* That the Congress should enact a system of Universal Military Training."

2. Ask a qualified veteran and/or present member of the armed forces to address the class on his (or her) experiences in the service.

3. Several students might investigate and report on the criticisms of the Immigration and Nationality Act of 1952.

4. Ask a naturalized citizen to address the class on his (or her) experiences in obtaining citizenship.

5. Prepare an essay on the subject " What It Means to Be an American."

WORDS AND PHRASES YOU SHOULD KNOW

Alien	Fission	Nonimmigrants
Atomic Energy Commission	Immigration	Nonquota immigrants
Commander-in-Chief	Joint Chiefs of Staff	Quota system
Denaturalization	Militia	ROTC
Draft	Mothballing	Selective service
Expatriation	National Guard	U.M.T.
FBI	Naturalization	War powers

SELECT BIBLIOGRAPHY

ATWOOD, ALBERT W., " Immigrants Still Flock to Liberty's Land," *National Geographic*, November, 1955.

BALDWIN, HANSON W., " Is the Navy Obsolete? " *Saturday Evening Post*, August 11, 1956.

CARR, ROBERT K., and others, *American Democracy in Theory and Practice*, Chapters 13, 34. Rinehart, 1955.

HARVEY, FRANK, " Those Half-Pint A-Bombers! " *Saturday Evening Post*, November 5, 1955.

" Immigration and the American Ideal," *Current History*, November, 1955, entire issue.

KNEBEL, FLETCHER, " The U.S. Has a Defense against Atomic Attack," *Look*, May 3, 1955.

——, " J. Edgar Hoover, the Cop and the Man," *Look*, May 31, June 7, 1955.

PARSON, MAJOR NELS A., " Guided Missiles in War and Peace," *U.S. News*, January 20, 1956.

RYAN, CORNELIUS, " I Rode the World's Fastest Sub," *Collier's*, April 1, 1955.

SHALETT, SIDNEY, " How to be a Crime Buster," *Saturday Evening Post*, March 19, 1955.

SPIERS, AL, " The Case of the Lunch-Hour Bandit," *Saturday Evening Post*, August 28, 1954.

" The Keeper of the Nation's Secrets," *Newsweek*, February 13, 1956.

" The U.S. Air Force," *Time*, March 5, 1956.

" These Choices Are Open to Draft-Age Youths," *U.S. News*, April 27, 1956.

THOMPSON, CRAIG, " America's Strangest Island," *Saturday Evening Post*, July 7, 1956.

" What to Do About the Draft? " *Life*, May 14, 1956.

" Why Kidnapers Always Get Caught," *U.S. News*, September 7, 1956.

> Neither snow, nor rain, nor heat, nor gloom of night stays these couriers from the swift completion of their appointed rounds.
>
> — *Inscription on the New York Post Office*

★

Chapter 14

THE POST OFFICE AND THE DEPARTMENT OF THE INTERIOR

THE POST OFFICE DEPARTMENT

A Huge Business. The federal agency with which most Americans are most familiar and the one with which they most often come into contact is the Post Office Department. It is by far the Government's biggest business enterprise, and it is a public monopoly.

Some indication of the size of the Department's operations can be seen in these facts:

Its more than 500,000 employees handle some 60,000,000,000 pieces of mail a year — more mail than is handled by all of the other postal systems of the world combined. The annual postal income amounts to more than $2,500,000,000 a year.

The mail routes cover some 2,250,-000 miles — or ninety times the distance around the earth at the equator. The postmen use 27,000 government-owned or -rented vehicles.

There are today some 37,500 post offices. The Department sells some 23,000,000,000 stamps each year and handles nearly 1,000,000,000 " special service " transactions — such as registering and insuring mail and issuing money orders.

Then, too, the Department performs many other " odd jobs." It manufactures and repairs locks and mailbags, sells internal revenue stamps indicating tax payment on property transfers, sells the migratory bird stamps that are attached to hunting licenses, and distributes the flags used to drape the coffins of deceased veterans.

The *Postmaster-General* is the head of this tremendous and far-flung operation. The office was created in 1775, when Benjamin Franklin became the first Postmaster-General under the Continental Congress. Franklin had been appointed Co-Deputy Postmaster-General of the colonies by the English government in 1753.

Article I, Section 8, of the Constitution gives Congress the power to " establish post offices and post roads." The First Congress continued the office of Postmaster-General in 1789 — with seventy-five post offices under him.

Departmental Organization. The Deputy Postmaster-General is the chief adviser and assistant to the Postmaster-General.

The bulk of the work of the Department is carried on through its five bureaus, each headed by an Assistant Postmaster-General: Post Office Operations, Transportation, Finance, Facilities, and Personnel.

Postal inspectors keep tabs on the condition of the postal system and enforce the postal laws of the United States.

Postmasters are graded into classes (1st, 2d, 3d, 4th) according to the receipts of the office in their charge.

Those of the first three classes are appointed by the President and Senate for a four-year term. Although the Civil Service Commission examines applicants for the post and the President appoints from among the three highest, the appointment is quite a " political plum." The appointment usually goes to some faithful party worker as a " reward " for services rendered. The Hoover Commission and several other groups have strongly urged " taking the post office out of politics."

Fourth-class postmasters, postal clerks, letter carriers, and other postal employees are appointed under civil service rules by the Postmaster-General, and they enjoy permanent tenure.

Postal Rates. Congress sets the rates charged for the carrying of various kinds of mail. Many factors and pressures are present in each decision.

Originally, the charge for carrying a letter was based on the distance and the number of pages involved. A little over 100 years ago it cost a dollar to send a four-page letter from Boston to Charleston, South Carolina. Today a three-cent stamp will carry a letter anywhere in the country or the territories.

Letter (first-class) and parcel post (fourth-class) mail rates are set at or a little above actual cost.

The six-cent stamp on an air mail letter does not cover the costs of handling. Air mail has always been carried at less than cost, and this practice was important in the encouragement of aviation in the United States. Subsidies are paid to the private airlines which carry this mail and produce a significant portion of their income.

Cheap air mail saves valuable time for individuals and business. For instance, in one mail a Chicago bank returned enough checks to New York to save $1700 — the interest for a single day.

Several million pieces of mail are carried free, including that sent by the blind, the widows of former Presidents, servicemen overseas, and agri-

258

U.S. Post Office Department

EARLY MAIL TRUCK

The Post Office Department was using trucks like this one about 1910. As new equipment and methods become available, the Department discards the old as quickly as congressional appropriations allow.

cultural colleges and experiment stations (farm bulletins and information). The mail of Congressmen (under the "franking privilege") and of federal agencies is carried "free" — but the Congress appropriates an annual sum for the Post Office to cover most of the cost of this service.

Newspapers, periodicals, and books are carried at a reduced rate in order to encourage education, the dissemination of information, and literature, the arts, and science. Because of the difficulty of financing a newspaper in a rural community, any newspaper is distributed free within the county in which it is published at offices which do not have letter carrier service.

Village and rural free delivery (R.F.D.) service was provided by Congress, so that those who live outside cities and towns might have the same services as those who live in the more populous communities.

Other services, in addition to carrying the mail, are performed by the Post Office. These include the services we noted on page 257 and special delivery, cash-on-delivery (C.O.D.), and postal savings services and the selling of savings bonds and stamps. The postal service has also carried bil-

Chapter 14. THE POST OFFICE AND INTERIOR DEPARTMENTS   259

lions of dollars' worth of gold from New York and Philadelphia to the Government's vaults at Fort Knox, in Kentucky.

Each year the Division of Philately sells some $2,000,000 worth of stamps to collectors. No one knows how many of the nation's 12,000,000 stamp collectors buy stamps for their albums at local post offices. But, since most of these stamps are not used on mail, the Department realizes a tidy little eighty-five per cent profit on their sale.

The Postal Deficit. Until the middle of the last century, the Post Office Department was expected to pay its own way or even make a profit.

Since 1852, however, service and not profit has been our postal policy. This year the postal deficit amounts to approximately $600,000,000.

The large volume of mail carried free or at reduced rates is the major cause of this loss. Many people feel that the Post Office should pay for itself, and they advocate higher postal rates to accomplish this. But those who benefit from reduced or free postage and those who believe that the postal system should be operated for service and not profit, are opposed to an increase.

Prohibited Articles. In addition to parcels beyond a certain size and weight, many articles are exclud-

LOADING A DC-7

The volume of air mail carried increases every year. This makes possible a low air-mail postage rate and fast dependable service for letters of business and friendship.

U.S. Post Office Department

Unit III. THE EXECUTIVE DEPARTMENT

ed from the mails — for example: poisons, explosives, intoxicating liquors, live animals and other things dangerous to the mail or the postal employees; concealable firearms except to dealers and officers; libelous, treasonable, or obscene matter, lottery tickets or other prize schemes dependent upon chance; and fraudulent schemes.

Fraud Orders. When any person or firm attempts to procure money or property through the mails by fraudulent schemes, or schemes of chance, the privileges of the mails are withdrawn from the offender.

If the Postmaster-General decides that a business is fraudulent, he issues a " fraud order " to the local postmaster and to the person accused, whereupon the postmaster stamps the word " fraudulent " upon all letters addressed to the accused and returns them to the writers either direct or through a Dead Letter Office if they must be opened for the return address.

The most vicious type of frauds include the so-called work-at-home scheme and the sale of nostrums represented to be cures of disease.

Some years ago a fraudulent firm under the pretentious name of the National Mail Order Brokerage Exchange mailed letters from Minneapolis offering a $4.50 silk petticoat for ten cents in silver, on condition that the purchaser notify five friends of the offer and request each one of them to do likewise. More than 500,000 orders arrived at the Minneapolis office. The perpetrator received only about 300 dimes before a Fraud Order routed him. It cost the Government about $20,000 to return the letters to their senders.

It is illegal to use the mails in promoting any lottery scheme. A short time ago a real estate dealer advertised through the mails that he would give a chance on a house and lot to each of the first twenty persons who bought a lot from him. This was construed to be a lottery and for nearly a year his incoming mail was stamped " Fraudulent " and returned to the senders. He was also heavily fined.

THE DEPARTMENT OF THE INTERIOR

The Department of the Interior was created by Congress in 1849. Its principal work is concerned with the management, conservation, and development of the natural resources of the United States. These resources include the public lands,[1] water and

power resources, oil, gas, and other mineral resources, certain forest resources, wildlife, and the national park system.

The Department also has custody of 750,000,000 acres of land in the continental United States, the Caribbean, the Pacific, and Alaska. It promotes mine safety, the protection of fish and wildlife, the preservation of

---

[1] Soil conservation on private lands is administered through the Soil Conservation Service in the Department of Agriculture.

scenic and historic areas, and the reclamation of arid lands in the West, and it manages the federal hydroelectric power systems.

The Interior Department is also responsible for the welfare of some 3,000,000 persons in the territories and of the 343,000 Indians who live on reservations.

The *Secretary of the Interior* heads the sprawling Department. His chief aides are the Under Secretary and five Assistant Secretaries, one each for public land management, water and power development, mineral resources, fish and wildlife, and department management. The principal agencies under the Secretary are the —

> Bureau of Land Management
> Bureau of Reclamation
> Bonneville Power Administration
> National Park Service
> Geological Survey
> Bureau of Mines
> Fish and Wildlife Service
> Bureau of Indian Affairs
> Office of Territories

Bureau of Land Management

The Bureau of Land Management has charge of the survey, management, and disposition of the public lands of the United States, and of the minerals they contain.

Federal Land Policy.   At one time or another, some eighty per cent of the land in the United States has belonged to the National Government, including practically all of the area west of the original States except Texas.

The original States surrendered their public lands to the National Government, which then assumed the States' debts. Other public lands were acquired by conquest or purchase in our westward expansion.

To gain revenue and, more important, to encourage western settlers, much of the public lands were sold at very low prices. Most of this land was sold or given to homesteaders in 160-acre lots. The attraction of cheap lands in the West was a major factor in the geographic and economic building of the United States.

Large tracts were given to railroads as an inducement to build lines across the nation. Much land was given to the States for the support of education and for other purposes.

About 170,000,000 acres remain in unreserved national lands — not including national forests, national parks, and Indian reservations.

Practically all the public land suitable for agriculture has long since been sold. On that remaining, the Bureau (known familiarly in the West as BLM) promotes conservation. Some of the land is reserved for oil, gas, or minerals, some for waterpower sites,[2] and over most of it grazing is now restricted. BLM leases or issues permits for the use of the land it controls.

---

[2] For several years the Government has reserved power sites and subsoil deposits on the lands it disposes of.

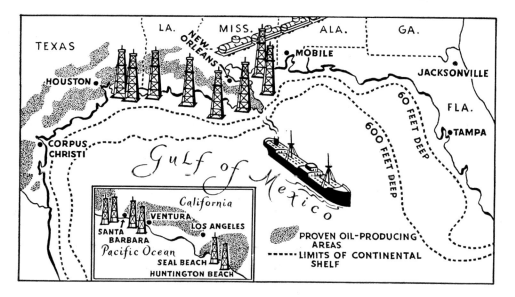

The "Tidelands" Controversy.

In recent years there has been considerable political and legal dispute over the question of State or federal ownership of the so-called "tidelands."

Actually the tidelands, the lands covered by the ebb and flow of the tides, were never in dispute. Everyone agrees that these have always belonged to the States. The dispute involves the *offshore* lands, those reaching out under the sea. In Louisiana, Texas, and California these lands contain rich oil fields.

On two occasions the Supreme Court held that the States did not have title to these lands. Then, in 1953, the Congress granted the coastal States title to the submerged lands out to their "historic boundaries" (usually three miles). The United States has title to the rest of the Continental Shelf.

The dispute continues. Those who favor federal control of the entire offshore area argue that the resources and the revenue from them should belong to all the people of the United States. Those who favor State control argue that the resources and the revenue should belong to the people of the particular State.

Bureau of Reclamation

In large parts of the West successful farming and ranching is all but impossible without an artificial water supply to supplement the limited rainfall.

More than a century ago, Brigham Young and his followers began a startling demonstration of what irrigation can accomplish. Young, traveling with his caravan to Utah, told his Indian scout that he intended to plant a farming community beyond the mountains.

The scout pooh-poohed the idea and offered a thousand dollars for the first ear of corn that was grown.

In July, 1847, these pioneers came from Immigration Canyon into the parched Salt Lake Valley. They unhitched their teams along the little stream now known as City Creek. The same afternoon they unloaded their plows and began breaking the dry desert land. The next day the stream was diverted, the plowed land irrigated, and potatoes planted. This was the beginning of modern irrigation in the West. Today more than 275,000 people live in this Salt Lake Valley region.

The Reclamation Act of 1902. Largely owing to efforts of Theodore Roosevelt, Congress created the Bureau of Reclamation. This act and later acts set aside money obtained from the sale of public lands as a " revolving fund " to be applied to the reclamation of arid lands.

When an irrigation project is completed, the land is sold to farmers in small tracts on easy terms. The money collected from these sales then goes into the revolving fund to be used for additional irrigation projects. For the larger reclaiming projects, Congress appropriates needed additional funds.

Most of the Bureau's projects are small ones which emphasize irrigation. As a measure of what this reclaiming of arid lands can mean, one project alone, in the Yakima Valley in Washington, has produced $76,-000,000 in crops in a single year.

More than 100,000 people now live in an area where once only sagebrush and jack rabbits were found. The entire project represents a federal investment of less than $40,000,000 — all of which is being repaid.

Among many other things, the Bureau is now seeking a practical method for converting salt water to usable fresh water. If one can be found, the benefits to be realized defy the imagination.

Multipurpose Dams. The Bureau has built and is building several huge multi-purpose dams in the West. These dams are " multipurpose " because they provide for several things at once — including hydroelectric power, irrigation, flood control, recreation facilities, and improved navigation.

Several other federal agencies, notably the Army Corps of Engineers, are also involved in dam-building. At times this overlapping has led to a good deal of confusion and political wrangling.

The Boulder Canyon Project and Hoover Dam. The hot semitropical Imperial Valley at its lowest point is 279 feet below sea level. It was originally part of the Gulf of California. But the Colorado River brought down enough mud every year to cover 100,-000 acres a foot deep. When in flood the river was too thick to drink and too thin to plow. So in time it filled the Gulf of California and built up a deltaic ridge, which is now over 100 feet above sea level at the international boundary.

This ridge forms the southern rim of the Imperial Valley. The Colorado River, flowing along it until it turns south to the Gulf of California, was kept out of the low valley by a levee seventy miles long; but as the river became higher each year, there was danger of a break in the levee and of flooding the homes of a hundred thousand people.

The mighty Hoover Dam, completed by the Bureau in 1936, created an artificial lake (Lake Mead) 115 miles long. It now catches the silt that had been raising the level of the river downstream at the levees.

Hoover Dam is the highest ever built by man. It is 726 feet high, 1,244 feet long at the top, and contains 4,400,000 cubic yards of concrete. The mammoth U-shaped structure has eighteen generators with a total capacity of 1,249,800 kilowatts of electricity.

It is the principal part of the Boulder Canyon Project which includes other dams downstream, like the Davis, Parker, and Imperial dams. Together these multipurpose units irrigate large parts of Arizona, New Mexico, and southern California. They also provide water for the whole Los Angeles area, 265 miles from Hoover Dam.

Grand Coulee Dam, located on the Columbia River in eastern Washington, was put into operation by the Bureau in 1942. It is part of the planned development of the whole Columbia River Basin in Oregon, Washington, and Idaho.

Grand Coulee is the largest man-made structure in the world and its power plant is the greatest ever built. Its eighteen generators are capable of producing 2,370,000 kilowatts, and the dam will eventually irrigate more than 1,200,000 acres of once useless wasteland. The flow of water at the dam is five times that at Hoover and can produce five times the power of the American Falls at Niagara.

Many other multipurpose dams have been built and are still being built on the Columbia and its tributaries, including Bonneville, Chief Joseph, McNary, and The Dalles dams.

GRAND COULEE DAM

The primary purpose of this dam is to provide vast quantities of water to irrigate formerly unproductive sagebrush areas. It also provides industrial power and helps control floods.

Bureau of Reclamation

Bureau of Reclamation

CALIFORNIA COTTON

Irrigation has made California one of the leading producing States of fine cotton. This farmer works his well-watered land near the town of McFarland.

Some involve the Bureau of Reclamation and others the Army Engineers. Together they provide irrigation, flood control, navigation aids, and recreational facilities as well as power for the rapidly expanding and power-hungry Pacific Northwest.

The Central Valley Project in California is bringing irrigation and power to a valley 500 miles long and fifty miles wide. The valley already has a population of more than 1,500,000, and its products are worth $1,000,-000,000 a year.

Twenty-four dams and reservoirs are planned for the regulating of the Sacramento and San Joaquin rivers. Shasta Dam, near Redding, is the biggest one now in use. An intricate system of canals helps to distribute the water throughout the lush region.

The Colorado–Big Thompson Project, now nearly completed by the Bureau in northeastern Colorado, is a modern miracle. It will collect water in Granby Reservoir on the *western* slope of the Rocky Mountains, carry it *under* the Continental Divide, and use it for power and irrigation on the *eastern* slope.

Thus, by an intricate system of lakes, canals, reservoirs, tunnels, pumps, and dams, the Colorado–Big Thompson Project will redirect mother nature. Adams Tunnel, the main tunnel under the Rockies, will be the biggest in the world — over thirteen miles long and more than nine feet in diameter.

Hungry Horse Dam, on the Flathead River in Montana, is the third largest in the United States (ranking after Grand Coulee and Shasta). It provides 285,000 kilowatts of power and valuable irrigation and flood control in the Columbia River Basin.

The *total ultimate cost* of all the Bureau's irrigation and power projects comes to approximately $7,100,000,000. Of this amount, nearly ninety per cent is being repaid to the federal treasury through the periodic payments of the water users and the sale of electric power.

The remainder of the total costs involve so-called " nonreimbursable " features of the various projects — such as flood control and navigation work and fish and wildlife protection.

BONNEVILLE DAM PROJECT

The concrete gravity dam and spillway are in the left channel. The powerhouse and ship locks may be seen in the right channel. Fish ladders and locks allow the salmon to avoid the powerhouse.

Bonneville Power Administration

Bonneville Dam stretches across the Columbia River about forty miles east of Portland, Oregon. It was built and is maintained by the Army Engineers, but the power it generates is marketed by the Bonneville Power Administration within the Department of the Interior.

BPA also markets the power from Grand Coulee. Together the two dams produce more than half of all the electricity in the Northwest.

So that the dam would not destroy the multimillion-dollar Columbia River salmon industry, a unique system of " fish ladders " was built along with the dam itself. Salmon swimming upstream to spawn enter a fishway which winds around a hill imitating a real creek. Two fish locks float the fish over the dam, and the salmon then " climb " three fish ladders to get beyond the dam.

Salmon weighing a total of 500,000 pounds have found their way over the dam in a single day. Their migration downstream is fraught with more danger. Many fingerlings wash over the spillways or through the ladders, but others are dashed to death at the powerhouse.

(The Tennessee Valley Authority, an independent federal agency, is discussed in Chapter 39.)

National Park Service

The National Park Service was created in 1916 to promote and regulate the use of national parks and monuments in order to " conserve the scenery and the natural and historic objects and the wildlife therein and to provide for the enjoyment of the same in such manner and by such means as will leave them unimpaired for the enjoyment of future generations."

The Service oversees nearly 200 parks and monuments and many historic buildings, prehistoric sites, and other properties of historic or archeologic significance. Through its Office of National Capital Parks, it also maintains the White House and grounds in Washington.

The Service has charge of an estimated $4,000,000,000 worth of real estate containing some of the most breath-taking scenic beauty in the world. Its domain includes towering snow-capped peaks, glaciers, volcanoes, deserts, giant sequoias over 3500 years old, geysers, cascading waterfalls, caves, and petrified forests. Not the least of its problems are the more than 60,000,000 tourists it plays host to each year. By 1966 this figure is expected to top 80,000,000 a year.

Geological Survey

In 1879 Congress created a still little-known agency, the Geological Survey. It develops and publishes for public use facts about the geographic and geologic nature of the United States.

The Survey has made topographic and geologic maps of nearly half of the country. Their worth cannot be estimated. Because of them we know the heights of mountains, the volume of water which flows in streams, the areas where valuable minerals are most likely to be found beneath the surface, and hundreds of other vital and useful facts.

The varied work of the Survey can best be illustrated by a few examples. A number of years ago the Lackawanna Railroad relocated thirty-four miles of its main line. The chief construction engineer was able to sit in the comfort of his office and run all of the preliminary surveys, and even make the final location for the $21,000,000 improvement, from topographic sheets prepared by the Geological Survey.

A Survey research project found usable quantities of uranium in phosphate rock in Florida. From maps developed by the Survey a mining company discovered zinc deposits worth $100,000,000 in Tennessee. From its glacial maps, building contractors are able to find great stores of excellent sands and gravels, and well drillers are able to locate waters trapped in glacial rubble.

Late in World War II the Japanese

OUR NATIONAL PARKS

Visitors to one of our national parks gather around a campfire. Millions of tourists visit and enjoy our national parks each year.

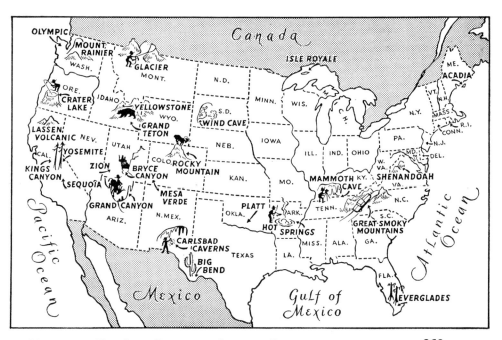

launched some 9000 balloons supposed to drift to our Pacific coast to start forest fires. Less than 300 of them reached this country. By examining only four cupfuls of sand from the ballast, the Survey was able to pinpoint the tiny strip of beach southeast of Tokyo where the balloons were being launched, and the Air Force was able to bomb the launching sites.

Over and over again, the Survey's work has led to rich oil discoveries and other important finds. No wonder its scientists are sometimes called " Uncle Sam's treasure hunters "!

Bureau of Mines

The Bureau of Mines was created in 1910. Its major concerns are with the conservation and efficient development of our mineral and fuel resources and with the improvement of health and safety conditions in the mining industry.

The Bureau has examined thousands of mineral deposits in the United States and the territories. Through its work domestic supplies of such strategic minerals as bauxite (essential to aluminum production) and manganese (essential to steel production) have been made available.

In its Demonstration Plant at Rifle, Colorado, the Bureau has produced gasoline from oil shale at 8.4 cents a gallon. If a practical method to produce it in volume can be found, the United States might become wholly independent of foreign oil, and thus the life of our own oil reserves might be prolonged indefinitely.

Through its mine inspection program the Bureau works to reduce the number of mine deaths, which now run to about 1000 a year. It has the power to order proper safety precautions in mines employing fifteen or more men underground. It also supervises mine-rescue training and investigates the causes of mine fires and explosions.

Fish and Wildlife Service

The Fish and Wildlife Service dates back to 1871. Its two Bureaus (of Sport Fisheries and Wildlife, and of Commercial Fisheries) work to insure the conservation of our wild birds, fish, mammals, and other wildlife.

Many species of wildlife have been saved from complete extinction by the Service — as, for example, the American buffalo. It carries on several programs to control diseased and dangerous animals that prey on farm stock and endanger human life. Its fisheries and game preserves help both sport and commercial interests. Much of the work of the Service is done in cooperation with State and private groups. The Fish and Wildlife Service also works closely with Canadian and Mexican conservation agencies to protect the migratory waterfowl of North America.

Bureau of Indian Affairs

The Bureau of Indian Affairs was first established in 1824 as a part of the old War Department and was shifted to the Department of the Interior when that Department was created in 1849.

Our Indian policy has developed by fits and starts, and many of its earlier pages are none too glorious. Happily, the situation is much improved today.

At first, the National Government treated the Indian tribes much as foreign nations and attempted to deal with them by treaty. As the nation moved westward and the Indians were pushed from their ancestral homes, lands were set aside as " reservations " where the Indians might live by themselves.

Many of the treaties were violated by the thoughtlessness and greed of white men. Even the Congress, and at times the Indians, broke the agreements.

By 1871 Congress stopped making treaties with the various tribes, and our policy soon became one of attempting to school the red man to take a full and complete place in the general population.

But sad experience proved this to be the wrong approach. For example, lands were allotted to individual Indians as private holdings. Most of them were soon squandered or lost to unscrupulous whites. In general, the Indians proved ill-suited to our way of life.

Our Indian policy changed abruptly in 1933. Instead of trying to break down the tribal relationships and wipe out the distinctions between Indians and other people, the aim is now to promote the development of the Indians within the framework of their own culture and their own distinctive way of life.

Of course, many Indians have bridged the gap between the two cultures. Most of them, however, live in tribal communities on reservations under the general supervision of the Bureau of Indian Affairs.

The Bureau has two major responsibilities in its work with the Indians: (1) assisting and encouraging the Indians in the wise and efficient use of their lands and resources and (2) providing public services in education, public health work, and welfare.

The 343,000 [3] Indians under the Bureau's jurisdiction now live on reservations, which total 56,000 acres, mostly in States in the western part of the country.

In carrying out its functions the Bureau describes itself as working " to abolish the need for its own existence." Judging by the way the Indians have developed in the past twenty years or so, the day when the Bureau will no longer be needed may not be too far distant.

---

[3] When Columbus discovered America there were about 846,000 Indians here. By the mid-1800's the total had dropped to less than 250,000.

Office of Territories

The Office of Territories dates back only to 1934. It promotes the economic and political development of the territories Congress has placed under the jurisdiction of the Interior Department. These include the Trust Territory of the Pacific Islands, and Baker, Howland, Jarvis, Canton, and Enderbury islands in the mid-Pacific.

The Office also cares for the mentally ill in Alaska and handles various public works construction in that territory, in Puerto Rico, and in the Virgin Islands. (See Chapter 20.)

WHAT THIS CHAPTER IS ABOUT

The Post Office Department, under the Postmaster-General, is the Government's biggest business enterprise and is a public monopoly. In addition to its main job of carrying the mails, it performs a number of " odd jobs," as, for example, the manufacturing and repairing of its own mailbags and the selling of savings bonds and of stamps to collectors.

Postmasters of 1st, 2d, and 3d class post offices are appointed by the President and Senate, while those of the 4th class are appointed under civil service rules. Many groups advocate " taking the Post Office out of politics."

Postal rates are set by Congress and reflect a variety of pressures. Most types of mail are carried at a loss, thus producing an annual postal deficit. The dispute which centers about the deficit involves the question of whether the Post Office should be run for service or for profit.

The Department of the Interior is concerned with the management, conservation, and development of our natural resources.

The names of the principal agencies under the Secretary of the Interior give an indication of the work of each: Bureau of Land Management, Bureau of Reclamation, Bonneville Power Administration, National Park Service, Geological Survey, Bureau of Mines, Fish and Wildlife Service, Bureau of Indian Affairs, and Office of Territories.

QUESTIONS ON THE TEXT

1. Give three statistics indicating the tremendous size of the operations of the Post Office.

2. Who heads the Post Office Department?

3. What basis is used to determine the class into which each post office falls? How are postmasters appointed?

4. How are postal rates set?

5. How much is the annual postal deficit? What is the major cause of it?

6. List four articles prohibited from the mails.

7. What is the Interior Department's major function?

8. List the principal agencies within the Interior Department and briefly describe the functions of each.

9. What is the " tidelands " dispute about?

10. What is meant by a multipurpose dam?

PROBLEMS FOR DISCUSSION

1. As we have seen, the Post Office is a huge business enterprise owned and controlled by the National Government. Do you think this is proper or should the postal system be operated privately? Why?

2. Some years ago a young man married a wealthy woman in Maryland and then persuaded her to send him to medical school in Philadelphia. She mailed him money at regular intervals, but instead of using it for a medical education, he did nothing but have a good time. Because he had used the mails to request money for a fraudulent purpose from his wife (who later divorced him), he was convicted in United States District Court of using the mails to defraud.

We have seen how the National Government has expanded through its powers to regulate commerce and to tax. Is the power to prevent fraudulent use of the mails likely greatly to increase its powers?

3. How would you expand on this thought: " Conservation is the wise use of our natural resources, not the refusal to use them "?

4. Does the reclamation of arid lands increase or decrease the value of other arid lands which are not irrigated? Does it increase or decrease our national wealth?

THINGS YOU MIGHT DO

1. Write a brief essay on the subject of the postal deficit.

2. Ask your local postmaster to address the class on the work of his office.

3. Stage a class debate or forum on the question of private or public development of our power resources.

4. Various federal reclamation and power projects might be assigned to members of the class for special reports.

WORDS AND PHRASES YOU SHOULD KNOW

Conservation	Multipurpose project	Revolving Fund
Franking privilege	Postal deficit	R. F. D.
Indian reservation	Reclamation	Tidelands

SELECT BIBLIOGRAPHY

FISHER, ALLAN C., and WENTZEL, VOLKMAR, " Everyone's Servant, the Post Office," *National Geographic*, July, 1954.

HORAN, JAMES D., " The Oklahoma Land Rush: Thus the Frontier Vanished," *Collier's*, November 9, 1956.

MARTIN, HAROLD H., " Uncle Sam's Treasure Hunters," *Saturday Evening Post*, July 17, 1954.

" National Parks," *Time*, July 23, 1956.

SCHAEFER, JACK, " The American Indian," *Holiday*, February, 1956.

" The Nation's Biggest Landlord," *Time*, August 23, 1954. Also *Reader's Digest*, November, 1954.

YODER, ROBERT M., " Twenty-Four Million Acres of Trouble," *Saturday Evening Post*, July 3, 1954.

It will not be doubted that, with reference either to individual or national welfare, agriculture is of primary importance.

— *George Washington*

*

Chapter 15

THE DEPARTMENT OF AGRICULTURE

Agriculture is America's basic industry. This has been true ever since the birth of the nation. The first census in 1790 showed that ninety-five per cent of the 3,929,214 people then in the United States lived in rural areas.

Since then, cities and industries have grown, of course. Today 24,-000,000 Americans live on our 5,000,-000 farms. They produce practically all of our food and food for many other people in the world. American farmers provide many of the raw materials used in manufacturing.

Considering the size and the importance of agriculture all through our history, it is not at all strange that the National Government has been so directly concerned with it. As Woodrow Wilson once observed, without the farmer, "every street would be silent, every office deserted, every factory fallen into disrepair."

Departmental Organization

Origins. The history of governmental concern for agriculture dates back to the early colonial period. In 1622, King James I began to promote the growing of mulberry trees and the breeding of silkworms in the colonies. On various occasions Parliament and the colonial legislatures also subsidized other farm products.

As early as 1776, the Continental Congress considered measures to aid agriculture. In his last annual message to Congress in 1796, President Washington urged the creation of boards of agriculture to provide information for farmers.

It was not until 1839, however, that Congress began to develop the present Department of Agriculture. In that year it appropriated $1000 to be used "to distribute seeds, conduct agricultural investigations, and collect agricultural statistics." A single clerk in the Patent Office was directed to administer the program.

In the period of a few short months

274

in 1862, Congress passed three acts of lasting importance to farmers. These were acts (1) creating a Department of Agriculture (though not of Cabinet rank), (2) making grants of 160-acre plots to people who would settle on and develop them (the Homestead Act), and (3) making grants of land to the States for the establishing of colleges of agriculture and mechanical arts (Morrill Act).

From 1862 to 1889 the Department was administered by a Commissioner of Agriculture. Then in 1889 the Congress enlarged the powers and duties of the Department. It was made the eighth Cabinet department, and the Commissioner became the Secretary of Agriculture.

The Secretary of Agriculture. The Secretary, like the nine other heads of the executive departments, is appointed by the President and Senate. His department is often cited as a model of administrative organization and efficiency. Sir Horace Plunkett once wrote that " the United States Department of Agriculture is perhaps the most popular and respected of the world's great administrative institutions."

The Department (often referred to as the USDA) is constantly reorganizing itself in order to improve its operations. Within the past few years practically all of the agencies within it have been re-formed.

The Under Secretary is the Secretary's principal aide in running the 80,000-man Department. Three Assistant Secretaries and the Director of the Agricultural Credit Services head the agencies which do the actual field work of the USDA. The General Counsel is the chief legal officer, and the Administrative Assistant Secretary is responsible for the internal workings of the Department.

The functions of the Department may be conveniently grouped under four broad headings. They are (1) research and education, (2) conservation, (3) marketing, and (4) crop stabilization and credit.

Research and Educational Activities

None of the Cabinet departments makes more use of science than does the Department of Agriculture. Its thousands of scientists make studies and experiments in a wide range of agricultural fields in order to benefit farming in the United States.

The *Agricultural Research Service* conducts most of the physical, biological, chemical, and engineering research done by the Department.

By listing the agencies within the Service we can get some idea of the tremendous scope of its scientific work. The Branches within the Service are those of Plant Pest Control, Plant Quarantine, Animal Disease Eradication, Animal Inspection and Quarantine, Meat Inspection, Field Crops Research, Entomology Research, Soil and Water Conservation Research, Agricultural Engineering

Research, Production Economics Research, Animal Disease and Parasite Research, Dairy Husbandry Research, Animal and Poultry Husbandry Research, Human Nutrition Research, and Home Economics Research. The Office of Experiment Stations is also within the Agricultural Research Service.

Much of the Service's scientific research is conducted at the 12,000-acre Agricultural Research Center at Beltsville, Maryland. A great deal of work is also done at laboratories and experiment stations located throughout the country, in the territories, and in foreign countries. State agencies, private companies, and public and private colleges also work on scientific projects in co-operation with the Service.

The many accomplishments of the Service can be illustrated by the examples described in the next few paragraphs.

By experimenting in the breeding and feeding of livestock and poultry, scientists have found that dairy cows fed on a good grade of alfalfa hay produce milk with five times as much vitamin A in it as do those fed on a good grade of timothy hay. They found that if farmers kept the best breeds of chickens and fed them properly the annual value of egg production in the United States could be increased by $100,000,000.

Several different kinds of insects menace crops, animals, and even persons. One of the methods used to combat those which are brought here from elsewhere in the world is to seek out the pests' native homes and discover their natural enemies. When the white scale of citrus fruits threatened the citrus industry in California, ladybugs were imported from Australia. From California ladybugs were carried to other parts of the country to prey upon aphides and plant lice. One ladybug will eat about 200 plant lice a day.

The Smyrna fig trees in California did not bear fruit until the fly which is the go-between in fertilizing the fig was imported from the Near East.

More than 100,000 kinds of plants and seeds have been brought here from abroad, and many have become quite important in our agriculture. The long-fiber Pima cotton was brought from Egypt and is the basis of the prosperity of the Salt River Valley in Arizona. The navel orange was brought from Brazil and is now one of California's principal crops.

Soil analyses are made so that a farmer can learn the physical and chemical properties of his soil and thus can know what crops are most likely to be successful on it.

Better ways of storing food and cooking it; improvement of such farm machinery as harvesters, hay driers, and flax machines; meat inspection; new and better dairy processing methods; and the fight against the hoof-and-mouth disease are a few more of the hundreds of examples we could list.

But these illustrations should be enough to indicate how valuable the

CROSSBRED CALVES

The Department of Agriculture is developing a superior beef animal for the Gulf Coast area. Such an animal should endure heat well, resist pests, grow rapidly, and thrive on grass. These calves are second-generation one-fourth Brahma and three-fourths Angus.

Agricultural Research Service is to the farmer — and, in turn, how valuable it is to all of us.

The *Experiment Stations Division* dates back to 1888, when the Congress established an experiment station at every land-grant college.[1] The

[1] The so-called " land-grant colleges " are those State colleges established as a result of the Morrill Act of 1862. This and later acts of Congress provided for the granting of land (altogether nearly 11,000,000 acres, much of it very valuable) to the States for the establishing and maintaining of colleges to teach " without excluding other scientific and classical studies and including military tactics . . . such branches of learning as are related to agriculture and the mechanical arts."

Congress now appropriates about one-fourth of the approximately $200,-000,000 these stations spend each year. The rest of the funds come from State and private sources.

The experiment stations conduct thousands of experiments each year, and the USDA co-operates with them through its Office of Experiment Stations. Through bulletins and circulars, which the Post Office carries free, the results of the stations' projects are made available to the farmer.

The *Farmer Co-operative Service* provides research and educational assistance to the three out of every five farmers in the country who belong to farm co-operatives. It aids these farmers with such matters as the organization, financing, membership, and quality problems of their co-operatives.

The *Federal Extension Service* was created in 1914. Together with the States and nearly every county, it provides " beyond-the-classroom " education in the rural areas of America. The Extension Service works through hundreds of specialists stationed at State land-grant colleges and through many more county agents, home demonstration agents, and 4-H Club agents to lend assistance and " know-how " to the farmer and to the farm community. There are more than two million 4-H Club members.

Conservation Activities

As we learned in Chapter 14, the Department of Interior is directly responsible for the conservation of our natural resources. At the same time, by improving farm products and promoting better farming methods, the USDA is, in effect, helping to conserve our natural resources.

Two of the Department's agencies are directly engaged in conservation work: the Forest Service and the Soil Conservation Service.

The Forest Service. No one need be told of the importance of the forests and of wood products to our way of living. Our forests provide natural cover for wildlife. They act as great natural reservoirs to collect rainfall and, by releasing it gradually, help to prevent floods and droughts. They help to hold the soil against erosion by wind and rain.

Over forty per cent of what is now the United States was once covered by forests. But much of this natural wealth has disappeared through the clearing of farm lands and the cutting of timber for fuel and for construc-

tion. Much of it has also been destroyed through man's downright carelessness.

Beginning in 1891, and especially under the leadership of Theodore Roosevelt and Gifford Pinchot, the Congress authorized the setting aside of certain timber lands as national forests.

The Forest Service administers the 152 national forests, which now cover more than 180,000,000 acres in thirty-nine States, Alaska, and Puerto Rico.[2] Its forest rangers are charged with promoting the conservation and best use of our forest lands.

The Forest Service provides fire protection, disease control, and recreational facilities in our public timber lands. Its " smokejumpers " and ground fire crews would be able to

---

[2] About 55,000,000 acres of other forest lands are under the jurisdiction of other federal agencies — especially the Bureau of Land Management, the Bureau of Indian Affairs, and the National Park Service within the Interior Department. State and local governments hold some 40,000,000 acres and about 400,000,000 acres are privately owned.

278

American Forest Products Industries

PRESERVING OUR FOREST HERITAGE

Two lookouts (*black arrows*) have detected a fire in their area. After locating it on a map by means of the Osborne fire finder, they report it by telephone. Within minutes, men and equipment are at work. Smokejumpers (*lower left*) descend near a fire in Montana. Ground fire crews (*lower right*) dig a fire trench to surround and suppress a forest fire in South Carolina.

U.S. Forest Service   U.S. Forest Service

provide even better protection than they do if it weren't for the fact that ninety per cent of all forest fires are caused by man's carelessness.

The forests are under careful management for the permanent production and use of their timber, water, forage, wildlife, and recreational resources. The Forest Service scientifically regulates livestock grazing on its lands and also controls the exploitation of minerals the lands may contain. New trees are constantly planted. Selective logging is practiced to clear out mature trees which would otherwise decay, and to promote the growth of younger trees.

The Forest Service maintains experiment stations and laboratories to conduct research into all phases of forestry.

The Soil Conservation Service. Wasteful and mistaken land-use practices have caused erosion which has practically ruined some 300,000,000 acres of land in the United States (or an area twice the size of the State of Texas). In earlier days farm lands in many parts of the East were "mined out." So long as new and fertile lands could be had to the west, no one seemed to be concerned about "overcropping" and erosion. Once the good lands in the West had been taken up, however, the problems of proper soil care could no longer be ignored.

For many years the Department of Agriculture has attempted to promote soil conservation by educating the farmer in soil-saving practices. In 1935 the Soil Conservation Service was created to assist farmers and ranchers in soil conservation. The principal duty of this agency is to assist farmers in locally organized and locally directed soil conservation districts. There are now over 2700 of these districts.

The Service also administers the paying of subsidies to farmers and ranchers who will undertake supervised soil conservation projects under a broad federal-State program. Soil conservation scientists have helped 1,700,000 farmers and ranchers prepare and put into operation their own conservation projects.

Specific Soil Abuses.[3] Soil abuse today is due mostly to old-fashioned methods of "square farming." Plowing in straight rows uphill and downhill has produced *sheet erosion,* in which the top layer of soil is skimmed off the land and *gullies* are formed that eat away the earth in big chunks, leaving worthless subsoil.

Other abuses include *one-crop farming* which exhausts and ruins the soil, *overgrazing* which destroys the grass and causes erosion, and the *wasteful use* of forests and woodlands.

Rescuing the Soil. The Soil Conservation Service teaches our farmers such things as the following:

(1) *Contour plowing* — "on-the-level-plowing" which follows a contour line around a sloping hill. The level furrows hold the rainfall.

---

[3] We are indebted to *Our Times* magazine for these specific suggestions.

Soil Conservation Service

WASTE

Unchecked, irreplaceable topsoil washes off this farmland every time it rains, even though the slope is very slight — only about three per cent.

(2) *Strip farming* — the growing of different kinds of crops in alternate strips. This blankets the soil better than large fields of a single crop, such as corn. It checks the rush of water and breaks up air currents.

(3) *Terracing* — the use of broad-based ridges thrown up across a sloping hill and following the contour of the slope. This slows down erosion by even the heaviest of rains.

(4) *Gully control* — the planting of trees, shrubs, and grass and the building of check-dams.

(5) *Setting up windbreaks* — planting trees so as to break the force of wind and cut down wind erosion.

Air-Conditioning the Dust Bowl. In the drought-ridden year of 1935,

CONSERVATION

By contour plowing, this farmer preserves his topsoil. Furrows follow contours of the hill and hold the rainfall.

Franklin D. Roosevelt promoted a program to plant 300,000,000 trees from the Canadian border to Texas in an effort to salvage the dust-bowl area.

Some 40,000 windbreaks, each with about twenty rows of trees, some of them as high as a house, now cover the " Shelter-Belt " area. The original plantings were made by the Forest Service, but they are now managed by local farmers in soil conservation districts. The stately string of trees stands as a growing monument to an idea which was once a target of a barrage of doubts and jokes.

These windbreaks help to " condition " the air by slowing down the winds which blew thousands of tons of topsoil halfway across the continent in the early 1930's. Valuable topsoil and moisture are now held in place, the danger of uncontrollable prairie fires is lessened, and insect-eating birds like pheasant and quail are plentiful again.

The planting continues and the trees are cheap, largely a gift from the National and State Governments.

Rural Electrification Administration

When the Rural Electrification Administration was created in 1935, only ten per cent of the farms in the United States were receiving electric power. Today eighty per cent of the nation's farms are electrified. Private utility companies have expanded their service in rural areas during this period, of course. More than half of the farms which now have electricity, however, have it because of the REA.

Electrification in rural areas is promoted by REA loans up to 100 per cent of the cost of a project. These loans are made for rural electric distribution systems, and Congress has provided that, in making such loans, preference must be given to public bodies, co-operatives, and non-profit or limited-dividend associations.

A flat two per cent interest is charged on the loans, and they are repaid in installments over a period of from twenty-five to thirty-five years. More than 1000 REA-financed power systems with about 1,500,000 miles of line serving 4,700,000 farm families are now in operation. By 1958 the Congress had authorized the lending of more than $3,400,000,000 for the rural electrification program.

Loans for wiring, appliances, and plumbing are also made by REA in order to bring some of the taken-for-granted comforts of city-living to our rural population. No loans are made to individuals under this program. Rather, they are made to local rural electrification co-operatives, which may in turn extend credit to individuals for the purchase and installation of wiring, electrical appliances, water pressure systems, and plumbing.

One farm family uses electricity in sixty-seven ways and estimates that it saves the labor of two hired men while increasing the total output of the farm.

Rural telephone systems are now financed by REA, too. Loans are made to telephone organizations, with preference going to existing companies and co-operatives. Unlike the electric programs where the REA makes 100 per cent loans, telephone borrowers are required to provide a portion of the investment themselves. Although the program has been in operation less than seven years, it is already bringing new or more dependable service to approximately 800,000 rural subscribers. Thousands more are being added each month. The REA stands as one of the many examples of how government can help people to help themselves.

Farmers Home Administration

By 1935 forty-two per cent of our farmers had slipped from farm ownership to tenancy. Today only twenty-seven per cent are tenants. The Farmers Home Administration helps to keep the independent farmer solvent and assists tenants in buying farms by extending credit to farmers who cannot get the financing they need at reasonable terms elsewhere.

All loans are made through local offices located at most county seats. A local committee of three persons, at least two of whom must be farmers, decides whether a loan should be granted or not.

Farm ownership loans are made for the purchase of a family-type farm or to improve or enlarge a farm in order to make it an efficient family-type unit. These loans are made for as long as forty years at four per cent interest. The payments may be arranged so that advance installments are paid in good years, thus protecting the farmer against falling behind in the lean years.

Operating loans are made for the purchase of such things as livestock, seed, feed, equipment, and fertilizer. Not more than $20,000 will be lent to any one person. The interest rate is five per cent, and the repayment period can run for as long as seven years.

Other loans are made to insure mortgages, to provide water facilities such as wells and pumps, and for emergency purposes in disaster areas.

The Farm Credit Administration. This agency, outside the Department of Agriculture, is discussed in Chapter 19. •

Marketing Activities

Farming is at best a risky business. One of the things that makes it so is the weather — which is often the farmer's friend, but which can be his mortal enemy, too. Another of the factors which make farming hazardous is the market in which he deals — and over which he has little control.

As farming methods have improved, the annual output of farm products has naturally increased. When the supply of farm products exceeds the demand for them, the farmer suffers unless government steps in to take care of the surplus.

As we shall see a little later, the National Government does step in to take care of at least a good deal of the annual farm surplus. But it also provides aids to help the farmer plan and market his crops in such a way as to avoid surpluses.

The *Agricultural Marketing Service* aids the farmer in the orderly marketing and effective distribution of his products. The Service collects marketing information and releases regular up-to-the-minute reports on crop conditions, prices, and prospects at home and abroad. These releases are made available to the farmer through newspapers, radio, and special bulletins through the mail. Through them, the farmer is able to learn the best marketing times and methods. He is also able to plan ahead in selecting the best crops to plant.

In addition to providing market news, the Service also provides uniform standards for commodities and containers and inspects and certifies farm products to guarantee quality.

As we shall see, the Government buys and stores surplus farm products to protect the farmer's market. That part of the surplus which is used, as in the national school lunch program or in foreign aid, is distributed through the Agricultural Marketing Service.

The *Commodity Exchange Authority* attempts to prevent price manipulations, the cornering of the market in a particular crop, and the dissemination of false or misleading crop and market information. Dishonest traders and food brokers could control the market, with serious injury to the farmer, the retailer, and the consumer, if it weren't for the work of the Authority.

The *Foreign Agricultural Service* is constantly seeking new markets for our farm products abroad. It also represents the Department in all relationships with other agencies engaged in conducting our foreign relations.

With so much of the world hungry and in want and with our current farm surpluses, the work of the Foreign Agricultural Service can be of untold value in promoting our friendships abroad and promoting the cause of world peace.

Stabilizing Farm Prices

Following World War I there was a gradual decline in the general price level throughout the United States. The decline in farm prices was greater than the decline in other fields. Wheat dropped from the wartime price of two dollars a bushel to less than forty cents. Cotton skidded from twenty-nine cents a pound in 1923 to less than six cents in 1933. The farmer found that his income was far below that of his city friends.

The First AAA, 1933. After trying several plans to rescue the farmer in the late 1920's, the Congress passed the first Agricultural Adjustment Act in 1933. The act encouraged farmers to reduce production in order to force prices up. Those who did so were paid a subsidy out of funds collected by a processing tax levied on the commodities which were produced. Thus a tax was levied on each bushel of wheat a miller processed. The proceeds went into a fund to pay farmers a subsidy for the wheat they did not grow.

The law met with considerable public opposition, but it did raise farm prices an average of more than 60 per

284

cent in three years. In 1936 the Supreme Court held the processing tax unconstitutional. It described the tax as " the expropriation of money from one group for the benefit of another " in order to control agricultural production which, added the Court, is within the reserved powers of the States.

The Second AAA, 1938. After attempting for two years to accomplish crop reduction through payments under the soil conservation program, Congress enacted the second Agricultural Adjustment Act in 1938. Essentially, the new law provided what the first one had but without the processing tax.

It also provided for the so-called " ever-normal granary." As Joseph in ancient Egypt stored up grain in years of plenty to use in years of famine, so the new law provides for storing surpluses against future shortages. The second AAA created the Commodity Credit Corporation (CCC) to make loans to farmers to help them carry over their surpluses in government warehouses and elevators for sale in the short years.

World War II suddenly reversed our whole farm problem. Instead of needing to limit farm production, overnight we needed to expand it. Everything possible was done to increase supply.

The present price support program was begun in 1942. To stimulate wartime production the Government guaranteed to farmers a specified minimum price for their crops.

The program has been continued since the end of World War II in order to protect the farmer against a slump like that which he experienced after World War I.

The price the farmer is guaranteed is set in terms of *parity*. That is, he is guaranteed a price that will give him the same purchasing power he had in an earlier and favorable period — a fair price for his products in relation to the things he must buy.

Until 1954 the price support program was a " rigid " one. The actual support figures were set in most instances at a flat (rigid) ninety per cent of parity. In other words, a floor was placed under prices for these crops; a farmer was guaranteed no less than ninety per cent for such basic crops as wheat, corn, and cotton.

The price support law now in effect provides for a " flexible " support program. Under it, various crops are supported at from seventy-five to ninety per cent of parity. The law provides that certain crops *must* be supported by the Government: corn, wheat, rice, tobacco, wool, cotton, peanuts, mohair, tung nuts, honey, and milk and butterfat. Other items may be supported at the discretion of the Secretary of Agriculture. The actual price support figure for each crop is set each year by the Secretary.

The *Commodity Credit Corporation,* which has the authority to borrow up to $14,500,000,000 from the Treasury, maintains the price support program. It either loans the farmer money on his crop, holding it as security, or it makes outright purchases. If it loans the farmer money and the price for his crop climbs above the amount of his loan, he may repay the loan, get his crop back, and sell it at a profit. If the price does not climb, the Government continues to hold his crop indefinitely.

The price support program has piled up huge surpluses in Government warehouses. Today the CCC has millions of tons and billions of dollars worth of butter, dried milk, wheat, cotton, and other farm commodities in storage. The storage costs alone run to an estimated $1,000,000 a day.

Disposing of these surpluses poses a tremendously difficult problem. If they were to be sold here at home, our domestic markets would be flooded and farm prices would be forced down. This would mean that the Government would have to step in and maintain prices through the support program and thus build the surpluses right back up again.

Selling the surpluses abroad could undermine world markets and hurt those friendly nations which produce the same commodities.

Some of the surplus stocks are now being used up in the school lunch program, in aid to the needy, in such State institutions as mental hospitals, in disaster relief, and in the foreign aid program.

The " Soil Bank " Plan, begun in 1956, is intended to reduce the production of crops which are now in surplus. Under the plan, farmers are paid to take land out of the production of these crops and plant, instead, trees and grasses to halt erosion and build up the soil.

WHAT THIS CHAPTER IS ABOUT

Agriculture is America's basic industry. Our 5,000,000 farms produce practically all of our food. The farms also supply many of the raw materials needed in industry and manufacturing.

The Department of Agriculture has been a Cabinet department under a secretary only since 1889, but governmental concern for agriculture dates back to the early colonial period.

The Department's functions may be conveniently grouped under four broad headings. They are (1) research and education, conducted mainly by the Agricultural Research Service, (2) conservation, through the Forest Service and the Soil Conservation Service, (3) marketing aids, mostly through the Agricultural Marketing Service, and (4) credit and price stabilization through the Farmers Home Administration and the Commodity Credit Corporation.

The Rural Electrification Administration is responsible for the making of loans to promote electrification on the nation's farms and rural telephone systems.

QUESTIONS ON THE TEXT

1. How many people live on farms?

2. Why was the year 1862 of particular significance to agriculture in the United States?

3. Who heads the Department of Agriculture? How is he appointed?

4. What is the work of the Agricultural Research Service? Extension Service?

5. What is a land-grant college?

6. Which two agencies in the USDA are most directly concerned with conservation work?

7. How does the Rural Electrification Administration aid the farmer? The Farmers Home Administration?

8. How does the Government aid the farmer in marketing his products?

9. What is meant by *parity*?

PROBLEMS FOR DISCUSSION

1. Erosion removes half a billion tons of our rich topsoil each year. Does this fact concern the farmer alone, or is it a national problem? Why?

2. In your community do you have grasshoppers, Mormon crickets, black stem rust of grains, white pine blister rust, citrus canker, peach mosaic disease, pink bollworm, gypsy moths, Japanese beetles, or Mexican fruit flies? What is being done to eradicate and control these pests?

3. Does the money spent on agricultural research benefit the farmers more than the consumers of farm products who live in cities? In what ways does the city dweller benefit?

4. In cities, industrial workers have been better organized to maintain high wages than farmers, who are largely individualists and scattered. What would happen to farmers if the Government did not give them numerous financial aids? What would happen to city industries that depend upon farm products or farm customers?

5. Electricity on the modern farm not only gives the farmer's wife the conveniences of the city dweller, but it also can help the farmer grind his feeds, milk his cows, and heat and light his poultry houses. For what else does a farmer use electricity?

6. Except in case of specialty farms it is difficult for a small farm to compete with a large mechanized farm, which often is owned by a corporation and backed by capital and efficient management. Do you think the Government should try to preserve the independent farm or should it accept large corporate farms as economically desirable? What are some of the advantages of each type of farm?

7. " The United States has had an economic deficit for more than three hundred years," states a conservationist. By what conservation and constructive measures could we end this practice of wasting more than we replace?

THINGS YOU MIGHT DO

1. Invite your local county agent to describe to the class his work with farmers and 4-H clubs.

2. Write a brief essay or editorial on the reasons why you think the Government should (or should not) provide price supports for basic farm commodities.

3. If there is an REA group in your area, make a report on its operations to the class.

4. List ways in which you think the Government might dispose of its stores of farm surpluses. Bear in mind that the surpluses cannot be used in a way that would flood the market and depress current farm prices.

5. List three specific soil abuses and three recommended ways of correcting or preventing soil abuses. Do you know of any examples of soil conservation?

WORDS AND PHRASES YOU SHOULD KNOW

Commodity	Land-grant college	Stabilization
Erosion	Morrill Act	Subsidy
Homestead Act	Parity	Tenant

SELECT BIBLIOGRAPHY

" ABC's of the New Farm Law," *U.S. News,* June 1, 1956.

" Agriculture: The Closest Thing to the Lord," *Time,* October 24, 1955.

" American Farm Policy," *Current History,* September, 1956, entire issue.

BIRD, JOHN, " They're Inventing the Drudgery Out of Farm Life," *Reader's Digest,* June, 1955.

——, " They Tamed Their Floods," *Saturday Evening Post,* May 26, 1956.

CARR, ROBERT K., and others, *American Democracy in Theory and Practice,* Chapter 29. Rinehart, 1955.

DEROOS, ROBERT, and NEUNS, ALVA, " Forest Fire! " *Collier's,* July 22, 1955.

" Five Billions for Farmers: Where the Money Goes," *U.S. News,* August 10, 1956.

HORNER, WINIFRED B., " How Long Can We Stay on the Farm? " *Saturday Evening Post,* April 14, 1956.

JOHNSON, CLAUDIUS O., *American National Government,* Chapter 20. Crowell, 1955.

KNEBEL, FLETCHER, " Do Farm Price Supports Make Sense? " *Look,* October 11, 1954.

MATCH, RICHARD, " The Story of Wheat: The Story of Civilization," *Reader's Digest,* February, 1955.

MATHEWS, S., and FLETCHER, J., " Beltsville Brings Science to the Farm," *National Geographic,* August, 1953.

MATSUKATA, HARU, " Our Youngest Ambassadors," *Saturday Evening Post,* February 19, 1955.

STROHM, JOHN, " When the Whole Town Pulls Together," *Reader's Digest,* December, 1956.

THRUELSEN, RICHARD, " Too Much Is Our Trouble," *Saturday Evening Post,* June 18, 1955.

U.S. Department of Agriculture, *Yearbook of Agriculture.* Annual; " *List of Available Publications of the USDA.*" Annual.

" What's This ' Soil Bank ' Idea? " *U.S. News,* November 11, 1955.

WOLF, BILL, " A U.S. Animal Quarantine Station, Uncle Sam's Ark," *Saturday Evening Post,* December 3, 1955.

WOLFERT, IRA, " Drama Behind the Crop Forecasts," *Reader's Digest,* August, 1955.

I go for all sharing the privileges of government who assist in
bearing its burden.

— Abraham Lincoln

★

Chapter 16

THE DEPARTMENTS
OF COMMERCE
AND LABOR

THE DEPARTMENT OF COMMERCE

The present Department of Commerce was first created by Congress in 1903 as the Department of Commerce and Labor. Ten years later a separate Department of Labor was created, and the original Department was renamed the Department of Commerce. The Department is charged with promoting our foreign and domestic commerce and with promoting the mining, manufacturing, shipping, and fishing industries, and the transportation facilities of the United States.

Departmental Organization

The Secretary of Commerce. Appointed by the President and the Senate, he usually comes from the ranks of successful businessmen. He is responsible for making the services of his Department available to the business community and the public.

The Secretary's principal aide in running the Department is the Under Secretary of Commerce. An Under Secretary for Transportation is responsible for Commerce's activities in that field. There are now three Assistant Secretaries — one for Domestic Affairs, another for International Affairs, and a third for Administration.

The major units within the Department are the Census Bureau, the National Bureau of Standards, the Patent Office, the Weather Bureau, the Bureau of Public Roads, the Bureau of Foreign Commerce, the Coast and Geodetic Survey, the Foreign-Trade Zones Board, the Federal Maritime Board, the Maritime Administration, and the Civil Aeronautics Authority.

Census Bureau

The Census. A census, taken every ten years, is provided for by Article I, Section 2, of the Constitution. Its primary purpose is to determine each State's population and the national population, so that the seats in the House of Representatives and direct taxes may be apportioned among the States.

The First Census was taken in 1790 and the Seventeenth in 1950. In that period our national population grew from 3,929,214 to 150,697,361. In early 1958 our national population

SCOREBOARD

This exhibit, based on the results of long-term statistics, tabulates the effect of births, deaths, and migration on the population of the United States. It may be seen in the lobby of the Commerce Building, Washington, D.C.

Courtesy LIFE Magazine: © Time, Inc.

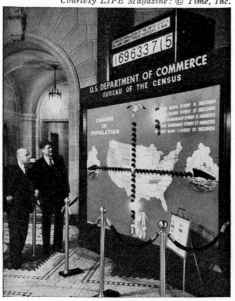

reached 173,000,000 and it is expected to be 228,000,000 in 1975.

Beginning in 1810 the census was broadened to include much more than mere head-counting. Today the extensive records of the Bureau can show our military chiefs how many males are of military age now or will be at some future date; educators, the educational attainments of our population; school boards, how many children will soon be of school age; employers and social workers, how many are unemployed; sociologists, the ages at which different racial and economic groups marry, the number of children reared, and how many families own their homes; legislators, whether more or fewer farmers than formerly own their homes; advertisers and the Federal Communications Commission, how many radio and television sets are in each locality; and economists, the annual income of the people of the States.

The census volumes on manufactures and agriculture are especially valuable to persons interested in these industries. For instance, if a manufacturer of corn cutters, milk cans, or poultry food wants to know where there is a demand for his products, he can learn how much corn is produced and about how many cows and chickens there are in each county in the United States.

From the population figures an advertiser of razors can learn that in Seattle, Washington, there are 2600

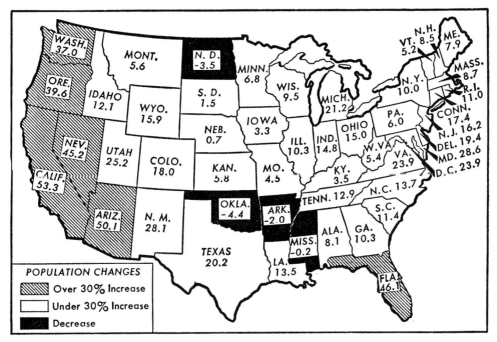

PERCENTAGE CHANGES IN POPULATION, 1940–1950

This map is based on the official United States Census of 1950.
What factors explain the net gain or loss in your State?

POPULATION CHANGES
Over 30% Increase
Under 30% Increase
Decrease

more men than women; and an advertiser of cosmetics that there are 84,100 more women than men in Los Angeles, and 106,000 more women than men in Massachusetts.

The population census is taken every tenth year, but many other periodic censuses are taken, as well; for example, on housing, manufactures, agriculture, mineral industries, business, governmental units, and transportation. In 1958 the Bureau is taking censuses of business, manufactures, mineral industries, and transportation; others are scheduled for 1959.

Millions of our population were born before birth records were universally kept. Such records are important in getting a job, for registering to vote, for draft registration, insurance, passports, establishing citizenship, social security rights, etc. For these people the Census Bureau will consult its records and furnish, if possible, evidence of birth.

The 1950 Census, taken by 140,-000 enumerators, showed a national population of 150,697,361. This was an increase of fourteen per cent over 1940, double the seven per cent increase from 1930 to 1940. The increase was due especially to higher standards of living and a consequently higher birth rate. The census showed the Pacific Coast to be the fastest growing section in the country. The 106 cities with more than 100,000 residents contain nearly three-tenths of all our population. Between 1940 and 1950 the suburbs of the nation's twelve largest cities outgrew the cities themselves as improved transportation facilities enabled more and more families to live outside the limits of the congested urban areas.

National Bureau of Standards

Because of the absolute need for standardized weights and measures, the Constitution (Article I, Section 8, Clause 5) gives Congress the power to "fix standards of weights and measures." Under this power, Congress has legalized the cumbersome English system with which everybody is familiar, and also the simple metric system which the student uses in laboratories.

The National Bureau of Standards. With a staff exceeding 3000, the Bureau occupies buildings on a 68-acre plot in Washington which resembles a scientific college campus. Here the original units of weights and measures are kept, here States get copies for local testing, and here research and standardization centers.

Here everything is tested, from filling-station meters to brick, from steel bridge girders to cups and saucers. Here the Government has developed a system of tests for various materials purchased by the Government, and more than two thousand purchase specifications are continuously revised on the basis of laboratory investigations. Like any thrifty housewife, the Government wants to get good value for its money when it buys things. Hence, the Bureau tests the various articles bought by Government purchasing agents. If it is an automobile tire, how long can it be used? If it is a building material, how strong is it and how well will it resist fire?

To help in designing modern skyscrapers, a model of the Empire State Building in New York was built at the Bureau. The model was placed in a wind tunnel and a gale of wind blown against it. Thus engineers were able to know what strains could be placed on this highest building in the world before construction began.

Tests show that sole leathers first tanned with chromium salts and then retanned with vegetable materials wear from 25 to 75 per cent longer than the ordinary vegetable-tanned sole leathers. The durability of leathers was tested, in the shoes worn by policemen, postmen, soldiers, and others. Then sole leather tests in a resistance-to-abrasion measuring machine were compared with service durability by the volunteers who had worn shoes with soles of the same kind of leather. Such laboratory tests enabled manufacturers to make accelerated tests in 24 hours equivalent to several months' actual wear of shoes.

What mixture of air and gas gives most car miles? The answer becomes a standard for designers of gasoline engines. A thousand industries need such basic data, and to furnish this information is one purpose of the Bureau of Standards.

Within the 20 major and 50 minor buildings of the Bureau, worth $25,-000,000, are found such facilities as a three-story 1.4-million-volt X-ray, an experimental paper mill, a mathematics computation laboratory, and excellent machine shops. The Bureau co-operates with 775 scientific and technical bodies, including the American Petroleum Institute and the Society of Automotive Engineers.

Standard sizing of young girls' clothes on the basis of body measurements has been developed by the Bureau to replace the age basis. When the age basis was used, different garment makers used different measurements for the same age. Height is now the primary guide to size. Weight and girth measurements are secondary guides.

The Bureau contends that adherence to the standard reduces the large volume of returns made by customers for incorrect size and also increases the sales of ready-made garments. To

National Bureau of Standards

HIGH–VOLTAGE

The central column is a generator that can produce a current of 25 milliamperes at 1,400,000 volts. The voltmeter is inside the smaller column (*left*). An X-ray tube is seen at the right. The cancer research made possible by this laboratory ultimately benefits everyone.

arrive at the measurements which provide the best fit for the most persons in each size range, the Bureau followed a study made by the Department of Agriculture in which 150,000 youths were measured.

Patent Office

The Patent Office administers the patent laws enacted under the provisions of Article I, Section 8, Clause 8, of the Constitution. That clause gives Congress the power " to promote the progress of science and useful arts, by securing for limited times to authors and inventors the exclusive right to their respective writings and discoveries."

A *patent* [1] *of invention* is an ex-

[1] A certificate issued to a patentee is called a " letters patent," meaning an open letter. (Latin: pateo, patens, *be open.*)

clusive right granted by the Government to make, use, and sell any new and useful process, machine, manufacture, or composition of matter, or any new and useful improvements thereto, for a limited period — now 17 years by Act of Congress.[2] Patents are also granted for new varieties of certain living plants.

Any American and any foreigner may file an application for a patent by paying $30. An additional $30 is paid if the patent is granted. The applicant for the patent must declare to the Commissioner of Patents that he believes himself to be the original inventor. He must submit with his application a full description of the invention, a drawing in cases that can be illustrated, and a model if the Commissioner requests it. If the examiner approves the application,[3] the patent is valid for 17 years, and it cannot be renewed except by special Act of Congress — something that rarely happens.

If by error the Patent Office grants a second patent for the same inven-

---

[2] The right may be assigned to another person or inherited as other property. If another infringes upon a patent right, the holder of the patent may go to court to restrain the infringer and may sue him for damages as well.

[3] If the patent is refused by the examiner who examines the applicant's claims, an appeal may be taken to the Board of Appeals of the Patent Office, which includes the Commissioner of Patents. If this board also decides against the patent, an appeal may be taken to the Court of Customs and Patent Appeals. If a constitutional question is involved, the case may go to the Supreme Court for final determination.

tion, the owner of the first patent can have the federal courts declare the second patent void. In obtaining a patent an inventor is not required to employ a patent attorney; but a patent attorney is highly desirable, because without skillful preparation of the specifications and claims an application is likely to be rejected. Also a patent attorney knows how to obtain patents in all other countries that reciprocate with us. Of course a fee must be paid to each country.

Among the early important patents are Eli Whitney's cotton gin (1793) and Robert Fulton's steamboat (1809). When the Wright Brothers invented the biplane, they specified every phase of the invention to be protected by the patent. Thomas Edison is credited with more than a thousand patents, including the incandescent light bulb, the phonograph, the carbon transmitter which made the telephone commercially feasible, the motion picture camera, and the sound motion picture.

More than 2,700,000 patents have been issued so far. One recent patent is for stainless steel stockings for women. Although they are still a laboratory curiosity, it is claimed that the steel threads can be woven into stockings as sheer as silk or nylon.

A *patent of design* is the exclusive right of a designer of originality and inventiveness to make, use, and sell any new, original, and ornamental designed article of manufacture. This right holds good for $3\frac{1}{2}$, 7, or 14 years, as the applicant elects. The length of the patent can be extended only by special Act of Congress. The badge of the Daughters of the American Revolution, originally patented in 1891, has been renewed by Act of Congress at the end of each period of 14 years. Examples of patents of design are automobile bodies, fraternity emblems, lighting fixtures, and wallpapers.

A *trade-mark* is a distinctive word, emblem, symbol, or device used on goods actually sold in commerce. These trade-marks identify the manufacturer or seller of the goods. Examples are Kodak, Beauty-rest, Sunkist, Ford, and Coca-Cola.

Any individual or firm that provides service but does not manufacture or sell goods can register a certain mark to identify the particular service.

The power of Congress to protect trade-marks is derived from its power to regulate interstate and foreign commerce. Only marks of articles associated with interstate or foreign commerce, therefore, may be registered in the United States Patent Office.

A trade-mark is registered for 20 years. It may be renewed any number of times. There would be no object in an industry's spending large sums in advertising and using a distinctive trade-mark if others were allowed to imitate it. A trade-mark may be worth a million dollars. Often it is sold as a part of a business or the good name of a business.

CAN YOU IDENTIFY THESE TRADE-MARKS?

Bureau of Foreign Commerce

The Bureau of Foreign Commerce is charged with promoting the foreign and domestic commerce of the United States. It furnishes advice and aid to American businessmen at home and abroad and publishes periodic reports on business activities throughout the world. Businessmen bring many of their practical problems to the Bureau for solution. A cattleman from Texas, a lumberman from Oregon, a farmer from Iowa, an industrialist from Connecticut, all may benefit from the Bureau's detailed information on more than 800,000 foreign firms and individuals engaged in international trade. They may also secure accurate and up-to-date surveys of trade opportunities from the Bureau of Foreign Commerce.

Civil Aeronautics Authority

The Civil Aeronautics Authority is a rather peculiar agency — it performs no functions whatever. But it is made up of two important agencies which do: the Civil Aeronautics Board and the Civil Aeronautics Administration.

The Civil Aeronautics Board. The CAB is an independent agency outside the Commerce Department. Its five members are appointed by the President and Senate. The CAB encourages the development of air transportation, passes on air line route applications, regulates air freight and passenger rates, fixes rates for the carrying of air mail, prescribes safety rules for air travel, and investigates airplane accidents.

Its accident investigations have been responsible for the correction of many errors in plane construction and the preventing of future accidents which might otherwise have taken countless lives.

The Civil Aeronautics Administration. The CAA is within the Commerce Department. It enforces regulations of the CAB, licenses pilots and planes, maintains air navigation aids such as beacons and lights, operates the Washington National Airport, and maps the airways of the United States and the territories.

Weather Bureau

The Weather Bureau provides invaluable services to the American people. Weather observations are made at thousands of places throughout the country and by ships at sea. The Bureau receives countless daily reports of heat, cold, clouds, rain, snow, wind direction and velocity, and similar conditions. From this information well-trained experts are able to forecast weather conditions with a high degree of accuracy.

We could compose an endless list of the ways in which the Weather Bu-

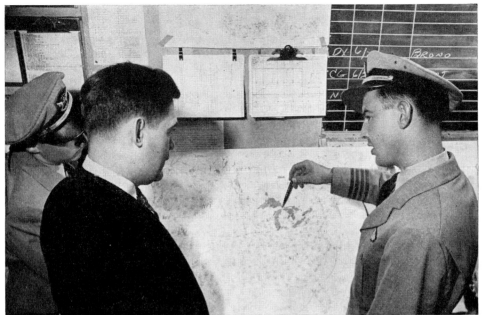

FLIGHT-PLANNING TEAMWORK

Pilot and dispatcher discuss a Weather Bureau map. Radio and tele-
type and the close co-operation of federal and air-line meteorologists
are very important parts of planning an air flight.

reau's services aid people in all walks of life. Daily storm warnings are especially valuable to pilots and fishermen. Frost warnings make it possible for the fruit grower to protect his orchards. Flood forecasts, often a week or more in advance, enable a farmer to save his livestock and other property. They allow cities to prepare for the high water.

Freezing forecasts make it possible for railroads to save perishables in transit and warn motorists to drain their radiators or add antifreeze. Rain forecasts govern planting and harvesting and are watched closely by building contractors.

The Bureau is now able to make general weather predictions in a given locality months and even years in advance.

This newspaper story illustrates some of the value of the Bureau to aviation:

Two passenger planes stood on the runways at Portland recently. One was to go north to Seattle and the other south to San Francisco. From a doorway emerged a man carrying a sheet of paper with certain technical notations. To one pilot he handed an order to gain an altitude of 7500 feet as he headed south, and to the other an order to travel north at a 4000-foot elevation.

Propellers whirled and the planes

Chapter 16. THE DEPARTMENTS OF COMMERCE AND LABOR **297** skimmed the surface of the field, gained altitude, banked and headed in opposite directions. When the control boards in front of the pilots indicated that they had gained their respective levels, both planes found strong tail winds and rode on the wings of the gales into port, making record time.

This apparent aeronautical paradox was the result of careful studies of weather and air currents by attachés to the United States Weather Bureau. Without the information supplied by the observers, discovery of the favorable winds blowing in opposite directions high overhead would have been a matter of chance, with the probability that at least one of the planes would have bucked a head wind instead of being helped on its journey by the great force of nature.

Today daring Air Force and Navy fliers fly into the very heart of a hurricane to aid the Weather Bureau in tracking the storm and warning those in its path.

Coast and Geodetic Survey

The Coast and Geodetic Survey is one of the oldest agencies of the National Government. In 1807 Congress created the Coast Survey. This bureau's task was to make an accurate survey of the coasts of the United States. In 1871 Congress broadened its functions to include the entire country. The present name, Coast and Geodetic Survey, dates from a statute passed in 1878.

The Survey's charts, maps, and other reports are little known to the general public. But they are extremely useful to persons engaged in aviation, radio, engineering, fishing, navigation, construction, and related fields. For example, the Survey's seismological research is extremely valuable in the reduction of damage from earthquakes. Many of the larger buildings and dams in the United States have been designed and built on the basis of this earthquake data.

Foreign-Trade Zones Board

The Foreign-Trade Zones Board establishes and operates " foreign trade zones " in the United States. These zones, known as " free ports " in Europe, are located at or near various American ports of entry. They are small enclosed and policed areas where foreign goods intended for transshipment to other countries may be stored and processed free of customs duties and regulations. Storage and processing facilities are also available for domestic goods destined for export. Of course, any foreign goods stored in these areas but later sold in the United States become subject to customs on the same basis as goods entering the country through normal commercial channels.

Four foreign trade zones, intended to promote foreign commerce, are now in operation. They are located at the harbor areas of the following Atlantic, Gulf, and Pacific coast cities: New York, New Orleans, San Francisco, and Seattle.

298

Federal Maritime Board and Maritime Administration

The Federal Maritime Board and the Maritime Administration are the two agencies of the National Government most directly concerned with our water-borne foreign commerce.

The *Maritime Board* is composed of three members appointed by the President and Senate. Its chairman is also the head of the Maritime Administration. The Board regulates the rates, services, and practices of American vessels engaged in foreign commerce. It also regulates the dock, warehouse, and terminal facilities used in our foreign commerce.

In order to encourage American shipping the Congress provides subsidies for the construction and operation of privately owned vessels. These subsidies not only make it possible for our merchant marine to compete with foreign shipping, but also guarantee that we shall have adequate shipping in case of another war. The subsidies are handled by the Board.

The *Maritime Administration* carries out the rules and regulations of the Board. It investigates shipping conditions, ship construction and safety, and otherwise promotes the interests of our ocean-borne commerce.

During World War II, private concerns built thousands of Liberty, Victory, and other merchant ships in Government-constructed shipyards. The Administration now charters or sells these ships to private operators. It also maintains a national reserve fleet for use in case of another emergency and has four complete shipyards kept up on a stand-by basis as a precautionary measure.

The Administration operates the Merchant Marine Academy at Kings Point, New York, to train young men as merchant marine officers. The actual licensing of officers, pilots, and seamen is handled by the Coast Guard.

Bureau of Public Roads

The Bureau of Public Roads is the principal road-building agency of the National Government. It supervises the construction of roads in the national parks and forests and of other federal roads. And it administers the grants-in-aid which are made to the States for road construction.

Each year the Congress appropriates substantial sums to aid the States in the building and maintaining of a 41,000-mile interstate highway system and thousands of miles of other State, county, and city roads. Before a State may receive these federal grants, the Bureau of Public Roads must approve the plans drawn up by the State highway department, and the State must agree to match the federal funds with money of its own.

The Congress provided for a vast expansion of the road-building program in the Federal Aid Highway Act of 1956. Under it, more than $33,-000,000,000 will be spent on a huge construction and modernization project that will be completed in 1972.

The Act's major purpose is to create a system of straight, safe four-to-eight-lane highways criss-crossing the nation from coast to coast and border to border.

THE DEPARTMENT OF LABOR

As we learned at the beginning of this Chapter, the Department of Labor was established as a separate Cabinet Department in 1913. Congress created it to "advance the public interest by promoting the welfare of the wage earners of the United States, improving their working conditions, and advancing their opportunities for profitable employment."

Departmental Organization

The Secretary of Labor. The Secretary of Labor, who is appointed by the President and the Senate, is responsible for the over-all work of the Department of Labor. His chief assistant is the Under Secretary of Labor, and the day-to-day activities of most of the agencies within the Department are handled by two Assistant Secretaries. There is also an Assistant Secretary for International Affairs and an Administrative Assistant Secretary.

The major units within the Labor Department include the Office of International Labor Affairs, Wage and Hour and Public Contracts Division, Women's Bureau, and Bureaus of Apprenticeship, Employment Security, Labor Standards, and Labor Statistics.

Office of International Labor Affairs

The Assistant Secretary for International Affairs heads the Office of International Labor Affairs, which is concerned with the ways in which labor problems here and abroad affect American foreign policy. Of course, the Office works closely with the Department of State. Thus it is responsible for our participation in the International Labor Organization (the ILO is one of the specialized agencies of the United Nations, which we shall consider in Chapter 40).

This little-known agency also furnishes information and technical help on labor questions to the State Department, other federal agencies, and foreign governments.

In order to encourage international friendship and understanding the Office sponsors an exchange program under which American labor officials go abroad and foreign union representatives come here. With little public notice, the Office works quietly but effectively for world peace.

300

Bureau of Labor Statistics

The Bureau of Labor Statistics is one of the Government's major statistical and fact-finding agencies and has no enforcement or administrative functions. It collects, analyzes, and publishes data on such subjects as employment and unemployment, manpower needs, productivity, housing construction, industrial relations, wages, hours of work, accidents, price trends, costs, and standards of living. Most of the information is voluntarily supplied by thousands of business and labor organizations, economists, private research groups, and by other governmental agencies.

The Bureau is a mine of necessary and useable information on our economy. Among its many services is its file of current labor-management contracts. These provide background information and valuable guides that are often used in the settlement of labor disputes and in the writing of new working agreements between employers and employees.

Wage and Hour and Public Contracts Division

The *Fair Labor Standards Act of 1938* was passed by Congress in order to place a floor under wages and a ceiling over hours of work. That is, it provides a minimum wage and maximum hours for workers in industries *in* or *affecting* interstate commerce. The Act also provides for the regulation of child labor in these industries. The Wage and Hour and Public Contracts Division administers the law.

The minimum wage that may be paid in the industries covered is now set at one dollar an hour, and one-and-a-half times the regular rate must be paid for all work beyond eight hours a day and forty hours a week.

"Oppressive child labor" is forbidden in the production of goods that move in interstate commerce. Oppressive child labor means the employment of any child under sixteen

"BREAKER BOYS"

Boys, some less than twelve years old, once worked in the coal mines of Pennsylvania. Today this is illegal. Many other improvements have been won for all workers, but especially for women and children.

Brown Brothers

years, or under eighteen in hazardous occupations like mining or lumbering. (The statute specifically exempts child actors and those working in agriculture while not legally required to attend school.)

You may recall having read that in 1922 the Supreme Court held an earlier child labor act unconstitutional. In 1941 it overruled the earlier decision and upheld the child labor provi-sions of the Fair Labor Standards Act.

The Division also enforces the Walsh-Healey Act of 1936. That act provides for the inclusion, in every Government supply contract of over $10,000, provisions for a minimum wage (now one dollar an hour), a maximum work-week of forty hours plus time-and-a-half for overtime, and certain welfare provisions.

Other Agencies

The Women's Bureau promotes better wages, working conditions, and employment opportunities for women.

The Bureau of Labor Standards prepares reports on labor standards, advises the Congress and the States on labor legislation and provides information and assistance to business and labor groups.

The Bureau of Apprenticeship develops standards of apprenticeship for the training of skilled workers in industry. Together with State labor offices it attempts to persuade management and labor to accept these standards.

The Bureau of Employment Security aids the States in the administration of the unemployment compensation programs and their employment services.

(On labor unions and the settlement of labor disputes, refer to Chapter 38.)

WHAT THIS CHAPTER IS ABOUT

The Department of Commerce, created in 1903, exists to promote our foreign and domestic commerce and to promote the mining, manufacturing, shipping, and fishing industries, and the transportation facilities of the United States. The major agencies within the Department are the following boards, bureaus, and authorities: Census Bureau, the National Bureau of Standards, the Patent Office, the Weather Bureau, the Bureau of Public Roads, the Bureau of Foreign Commerce, the Coast and Geodetic Survey, the Foreign-Trade Zones Board, the Federal Maritime Board, the Maritime Administration, and the Civil Aeronautics Authority.

The Labor Department, created in 1913, exists to promote the welfare, working conditions, and employment opportunities of American wage earners. The major agencies within the Department are the Office of International Labor Affairs, the Wage and Hour and Public Contracts Division, the Women's Bureau, the Bureau of Labor Standards, the Bureau of Labor Statistics, the Bureau of Apprenticeship, and the Bureau of Employment Security.

QUESTIONS ON THE TEXT

1. What is the major function of the Commerce Department?

2. Why, specifically, does the Constitution require a decennial census? Give two examples of the usefulness of the census.

3. What does the National Bureau of Standards do?

4. What is a patent of invention? A patent of design? A trade-mark?

5. Outline the work of the Bureau of Foreign Commerce; of the Civil Aeronautics Authority.

6. Give three examples of the ways in which the Weather Bureau aids various people in the United States through its forecasts.

7. What is the Coast and Geodetic Survey?

8. Explain what is meant by a " foreign trade zone."

9. Outline the work of the Maritime Board and the Maritime Administration.

10. How does the National Government aid the States in their building of roads?

11. What is the major function of the Labor Department?

12. Outline the major provisions of the Fair Labor Standards Act of 1938.

PROBLEMS FOR DISCUSSION

1. How would you express the thought contained in the quotation from Abraham Lincoln found on page 289?

2. In this chapter we have mentioned several of the services the National Government provides to business and labor. Do you feel that these services *should* be performed by the Government? How many other governmental services to business and labor can you list?

THINGS YOU MIGHT DO

1. Invite someone familiar with the work of one or more of the agencies of the Commerce Department or the Labor Department to address the class — for example, an importer, labor union official, industrialist, State employment service officer, inventor, etc.

2. Through the State highway department, learn as much as you can about your State's road system and the amount and kind of federal help it receives. A report on this material might be presented to the class.

3. Most libraries or local government offices have Census Bureau Reports on file. Prepare a class report on the character of the population in your area based on the Census Reports.

WORDS AND PHRASES YOU SHOULD KNOW

Decennial census
Fair Labor Standards Act
Foreign trade zone
Maritime

Patent of design
Patent of invention
Trade-mark
Walsh-Healey Act

SELECT BIBLIOGRAPHY

" A Boom in People, Too," *U.S. News*, January 6, 1956.

BREAN, HERBERT, " Dead End for the U.S. Highway," *Life*, May 30, 1955.

CARR, ROBERT K., and others, *American Democracy in Theory and Practice*, Chapters 28, 30. Rinehart, 1955.

" How Big Will Your State Be? " *U.S. News*, April 6, 1956.

Interview with C. D. Curtis, Commissioner, U.S. Bureau of Public Roads, *U.S. News*, July 20, 1956.

JOHNSON, CLAUDIUS O., *American National Government*, Chapters 18, 19. Crowell, 1955.

KENNEY, NATHANIEL T., " King's Point: Maker of Mariners," *National Geographic*, November, 1955.

LEEK, JOHN H., *Government and Labor in the United States*. Rinehart, 1952.

MacKAYE, MILTON, " We're Cracking the Secrets of the Weather," *Saturday Evening Post*, September 11, and 18, 1954.

SOCKS, HERBERT, " I Had to Be Heartless," *Saturday Evening Post*, April 2, 1955.

STAPLETON, BILL, " Hurricanes Coming? " *Collier's*, April 15, 1955.

" The Census: More People and Problems," *Newsweek*, August 28, 1950.

THRUELSEN, RICHARD, " Coast to Coast Without a Stop Light," *Saturday Evening Post*, October 20, 1956.

WALL, C. B., " Incandescent Genius," *Reader's Digest*, April, 1954.

" Weather Bad? Don't Blame the Atom," *U.S. News*, March 4, 1955.

" Where Population is Expanding: A Look Ahead to 1965," *U.S. News*, March 4, 1955.

The productivity of our heads, our hands, and our hearts is the source of all the strength we can command.

— Dwight D. Eisenhower

★

Chapter 17

THE DEPARTMENT OF HEALTH, EDUCATION, AND WELFARE

Society would be nearly perfect if everyone had enough food and clothing, adequate shelter, good health, an education, the chance to earn a decent living, and security in old age.

There is not now nor has there ever been such a society. But in the United States we have come closer to this goal than has any other country on earth.

Through the years we have come to believe that one of the proper functions of government is to help in the march toward that goal.

The whole field of social welfare — of conserving our human resources in much the same way as we conserve our natural resources — is a relatively new one for government.

In earlier days, the States and local governments — and even before them, the colonies — did make some provision for the unfortunates in society. This help, though, was mostly the county poor farm and the almshouse.

By and large, the problems of the poor, the sick, and the aged, of the blind, the crippled, and the feeble-minded, were looked upon as private matters.

This same attitude prevailed in relation to such other social problems as sanitation and disease prevention. In those days, even public education was a not-too-common thing.

Of course, the picture is radically different today. Now the States and the National Government spend vast sums on a wide variety of social welfare programs.

The Department of Health, Education, and Welfare (HEW) administers most of the social welfare programs of the National Government.

HEW is the newest of our Cabinet Departments. It was created by Congress in 1953 as the first major reorganization step taken under the Eisenhower Administration, replacing the Federal Security Agency.

The Secretary

The Secretary of Health, Education, and Welfare, like all other Cabinet members, is appointed by the President and the Senate. As head of the Department, the Secretary supervises and directs its operations.

The principal agencies within HEW are the Office of Education, the Social Security Administration, the Public Health Service, and the Food and Drug Administration.

HEW also includes the Office of Vocational Rehabilitation, which works with the States in aiding the mentally and physically handicapped, and Saint Elizabeths Hospital, the Government's mental hospital in the District of Columbia.

Three corporations, which are in part supported by federal funds, are to a limited extent supervised by the Department: Howard University, an institution of higher education for Negroes, located in Washington, D.C.; Gallaudet College, the world's only institution offering higher education especially for the deaf, also in Washington, D.C.; and the American Printing House for the Blind, in Louisville, Kentucky.

The Office of Education

The providing of public education is one of the functions reserved to the States in our federal system. And it is usually regarded as the responsibility of local communities (see Chapters 4, 35). The National Government does have, however, certain promotional programs in the field of education. Congress created the Office of Education in 1867

for the purpose of collecting such statistics and facts as shall show the condition and progress of education in the several States and Territories, and of diffusing such information respecting the organization and management of schools and school systems, and methods of teaching, as shall aid the people of the United States in the establishment and maintenance of efficient school systems, and otherwise promote the cause of education throughout the country.

The Office is headed by a Commissioner appointed by the President and Senate. He is always a distinguished educator with many years of public school experience.

In addition to collecting and publishing factual information about education in the United States, the Office does many other things. It makes special studies of problems facing the schools — for example, how to deal with the especially gifted child.

It administers the funds Congress provides for the land-grant colleges and for vocational education in the States in such fields as agriculture and home economics. It also handles the federal aid given to the various school systems around the country with unusually high enrollment owing to federal projects in their areas.

The Social Security Administration

The Social Security Act of 1935 created an agency now known as the Social Security Administration. The Act itself was the result of the Great Depression which began in 1929.

When it hit, the depression threw millions of people out of work and millions more were impoverished. For example, in 1929 there were some 2,000,000 unemployed workers in the United States. By 1933 the figure had jumped to 13,500,000. In 1935 there were 18,000,000, including children and the aged, who were wholly dependent on emergency relief. Some 10,000,000 workers had no employment other than on relief projects.

Only a few States had done much of anything to meet such a crisis, and even these were utterly swamped. Poverty and need had become nationwide problems overnight.

Under President Roosevelt's New Deal, the National Government spent billions of dollars in direct relief and on public works projects to stimulate employment. But this approach was only a temporary one designed to meet the immediate situation.

What was needed was a permanent, long-range program to help the country right itself and to prevent any such disaster in the future.

The Social Security Act of 1935 was one of the major steps taken in that direction. The law has been amended many times since 1935, and no doubt it will be amended many more times.

The Social Security Administration. Headed by a Commissioner appointed by the President and Senate, this Administration carries out the various aid programs provided under the Social Security Act.

The Administration is composed of four bureaus: the Bureau of Old-Age and Survivors Insurance, the Bureau of Public Assistance, the Children's Bureau, and the Bureau of Federal Credit Unions.

Old-Age and Survivors Insurance. OASI is a long-range insurance plan intended to provide those covered with a minimum income after they reach retirement.

Coverage. All workers, except those whom the law specifically exempts,[1] are required to participate. Today over 70,000,000 people are insured under OASI. Counting those already retired under the program, over 75,000,000 are covered. Including the families of these people, the total reaches 135,000,000.

Financing. The program is financed through payroll taxes. Employees who are covered pay a $2\frac{1}{4}$ per cent tax on the first $4200 of their

---

[1] The few major groups not now covered under OASI include those federal employees who are under the civil service retirement system, those employed by the relatively few State and local governments which have not yet authorized their employees to take part in OASI, those ministers who do not wish coverage, self-employed doctors, and persons with incomes too low to qualify for benefits under the program.

annual income (or a maximum tax of $94.50 a year). Employers pay a like tax of $2\frac{1}{4}$ per cent.[2]

Self-employed people, like a store owner or independent carpenter, pay a tax of $3\frac{3}{8}$ per cent on all income up to $4200 a year (or a maximum tax of $141.75 a year). Self-employed workers pay their social security tax annually — on April 15.

The taxes paid by each person are credited to his account. With the millions and millions of accounts involved, it is easy to see that this is probably the biggest single record-keeping job in the world. All the social security taxes go into an Old-Age and Survivors Insurance Trust Fund in the United States Treasury. This money, now well over $23,000,-000,000, may be invested only in interest-bearing bonds issued or guaranteed by the National Government.

Benefits. Monthly benefits are paid to those who reach retirement age. The retirement age for most is sixty-five, but it is fifty for the permanently disabled and sixty-two for a widow or a dependent mother of a deceased worker.

A complex formula is used to figure benefits: The monthly payment to a retired worker amounts to 55 per cent of the first $110 of his average monthly earnings plus 20 per cent of the next $240 (all rounded off to the near-

est dime). If he is married, his wife will receive, at sixty-five, a monthly sum equal to half of his. Thus:[3]

AVERAGE MONTHLY EARNINGS	MONTHLY BENEFITS AT AND BEYOND AGE 65	
	SINGLE WORKER	MARRIED WORKER
$ 40 or less	$ 30	$ 45
50	32.50	48.80
100	55	82.50
200	78.50	117.80
300	98.50	147.80
350 or more	108.50	162.80

A wife may, if she chooses, begin to receive benefits at sixty-two, but she is paid at a lesser rate than she would be if she waited until sixty-five.

A widow of an insured person receives a survivor's benefit at sixty-two which runs as high as $81.40 a month. If she has one or more children under eighteen, her pension can run as high as $200, regardless of her age.

Of course no one is forced to retire. A person may work beyond sixty-five if he cares to, and he may retire when he wants to. If he does retire and later goes back to work, his benefits are reduced if he earns more than $1200 in a year — but this restriction does not apply if he is over age seventy-two. Anyone seventy-two or older may earn any amount and still receive his full benefit.

Old-Age Assistance. The program of OASI just described is an

[2] The tax on both employees and employers was 1% from 1937 (when the plan went into operation) to 1950, and $1\frac{1}{2}$% to 1954, and 2% to 1957. The rate is scheduled to go up to 4% by 1975.

[3] Congress has raised the benefits under the law five times since it was first passed in 1935.

insurance plan for employed workers. But there were (and are) many old people in need who are not receiving OASI benefits.

In order to encourage the States to provide assistance for these people, the Social Security Act provides for a grant-in-aid system under which the States receive federal funds to help them help the needy aged.

Under the involved formula by which federal grants are made, the National Government provides three-fourths of the first $20 the State provides, plus one-half of the balance up to an overall maximum of $55. In other words, if the State pays an old-age pension of $25 a month, the National Government adds $15 plus $2.50 and the total is $42.50 a month.

Today nearly twenty per cent of our population over sixty-five is receiving aid under this program.

Other Aid Programs. Aid to dependent children, aid to the blind, and aid to the permanently and totally disabled are provided on the same basis as aid in the old-age assistance program; that is, federal grants help the States in their aid programs.

In addition to carrying out these various aid programs, the Social Security Administration carries out studies of special problems and promotes State and local action in the welfare field. For example, it conducts many studies in child welfare — on infant mortality, orphanages, juvenile courts, diseases, and the like — and passes its findings and recommendations on to the States, local governments, and private agencies.

SOCIAL SECURITY SYSTEM

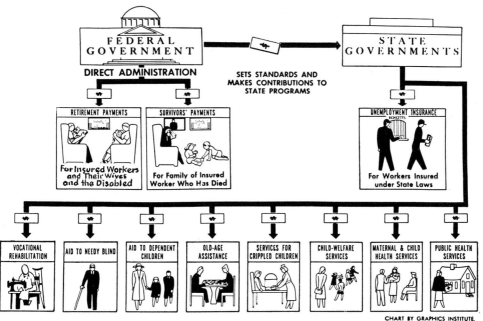

CHART BY GRAPHICS INSTITUTE.

The Public Health Service

A seventeenth-century English author incidentally mentions the fact that every fourth person in a representative audience was horribly disfigured by smallpox. With modern means of travel and commerce we would never be safe from smallpox, cholera, yellow fever, typhoid, and other dreaded diseases were it not for Uncle Sam's efficient family physician — the United States Public Health Service.

The Public Health Service dates from a 1798 act of Congress which created the Marine Hospital Service to care for American seamen. From this beginning, the Service has been expanded to the place where most of the health activities of the Government are centered in its hands.

The Service is directed by the Surgeon-General who is appointed by the President and Senate. He is a commissioned officer with the same rank as the Surgeon-General of the Army. The administrative officers under him are also commissioned, and there is a reserve corps of medical officers who may be called up in time of war or national emergency.

Hospitals. The Public Health Service operates a number of hospitals and other medical facilities. It has sixteen hospitals, twenty-four outpatient clinics and ninety-nine outpatient offices where seamen of vessels of American registry, Coast Guardsmen, and others may receive medical and dental care.

Freedmen's Hospital, in the District of Columbia, is also operated by the Service. It is a general hospital for the treatment of acute medical and surgical conditions, with an extensive system of clinics for outpatients. The hospital also provides internship and clinical experience for the students and graduates of Howard University's College of Medicine.

The National Leprosarium at Carville, Louisiana, cares for hundreds of quarantined leprosy patients, treats them, and carries on research for the prevention of the dreaded disease.

There are two hospitals for drug addicts, one at Fort Worth, Texas, and the other at Lexington, Kentucky. The Service also directs the medical care of federal prisoners and furnishes psychiatric service in federal courts.

Research. Much of the work of the Public Health Service is aimed at discovering the causes and the cure of disease. Several of its officers have lost their lives because of infections contracted in their work.

Research work of the Service has produced many medical triumphs. Its scientists found the cause and cure for pellagra, discovered how to produce a vaccine from ticks to counteract Rocky Mountain spotted fever, and found that rats can carry infantile paralysis.

The National Institutes of Health are the principal research arm of the Public Health Service. Designed to improve health through research and

Courtesy National Institute of Health

HEALTH RESEARCH

The weight and blood changes of rats with folic acid deficiency are studied by researchers at the National Institute for Arthritis and Metabolic Diseases. The results will help those with anemia and other blood disorders.

education, there are now seven Institutes: Cancer, Heart, Dental Research, Mental Health, Neurological Diseases and Blindness, Microbiological, Arthritis and Metabolic Diseases, and Allergy and Infectious Diseases.

The Clinical Center of the National Institutes is a huge medical research center, a 14-story structure with a 500-patient capacity. It is located near Bethesda, Maryland, and took five years and $64,000,000 to build.

It is no ordinary hospital. As the Director of the National Institutes explains: " This is not a hospital. You don't get in just by being sick. You don't get in for medical care.

You get in for research. . . . For the first time in history we shall be able to integrate laboratory and clinical research so that there can be a complete study of the chronic diseases that kill men."

All patients admitted (the first eight were women suffering from cancer) must be volunteers willing to lend themselves to research in their particular illness (cancer, heart diseases, arthritis, mental ailments, rheumatic fever, epilepsy, or dental diseases). Only patients recommended by physicians, hospitals, or medical schools may be admitted. Every step of the treatment is explained to the non-paying patient, and he is free to call off the treatments and leave the Center at any time he pleases.

A fellowship program is provided to train the most promising and brilliant research scientists from this country and abroad. The Public Health Service also works closely with universities and hospitals around the country and finances joint research projects.

The Other Work of the Public Health Service would take at least an entire volume to describe. It administers a program under which the States receive federal grants-in-aid for the training of professional and practical nurses. It makes awards to individual students and to educational institutions in order to encourage the training of persons who will enter the public health field.

The Service is responsible for the health and medical care of those Indians who live on reservations. It is studying ways to combat air pollution. It works with the States and with local communities in the inspection and control of the purity of milk supplies and the handling of food in restaurants. It has drawn up a model milk inspection ordinance which has been put into effect in a number of

States and in cities and counties in other States.

Public Health Service officers inspect and approve all biological products — vaccines, serums, antitoxins, and the like — before they may be shipped in interstate commerce. It maintains physicians abroad who prevent diseased persons from coming to the United States. Ships and planes bound for this country are regularly inspected and often fumigated.

In its fight against bubonic plague the Health Service attempts to destroy all rats found on ocean-going vessels touching American ports. The campaign has been so successful that fewer than one out of twelve ships entering American ports are rat-infested.

The Service works closely with State health agencies in making and enforcing quarantine regulations. Advice and assistance is given freely, and qualified officers are often loaned to State agencies.

It also certifies the drinking water for use on interstate carriers. One of the by-products of this activity is its effect on local officials who do not want to be criticized for providing for the townspeople water not fit for use on trains that make a stop at their towns.

Food and Drug Administration

When foods and drugs are produced in quantity, as ours are today, the consumer has little or no chance to check for himself the quality and pu-

rity of what he buys, except, perhaps, from its effect on his health, which may inform him too late.

Toward the turn of the century a

number of shocking abuses in the food and drug industries were brought to light. Many foods were adulterated and made attractive by the use of poisonous dyes. Misbranding became rather common; for example, canned veal was sold as chicken. Unsanitary practices were followed in packing and canning plants, away from the eyes of the consumer. All sorts and kinds of cures for every known ache and pain flooded the market, and many unsuspecting sufferers put their faith (and money) into useless and often harmful concoctions.

To counteract these conditions, Congress passed the Pure Food and Drug Act of 1906. But this first legislation did not have enough teeth in it or broad enough application. So the Food, Drugs, and Cosmetics Act of 1938 broadened the powers of the Federal Trade Commission to forbid false advertising, and strengthened the enforcement authority of the Food and Drug Administration.

Today controls are applied to foods, drugs, and devices intended to cure disease or " affect the structure or any function of the body " and to cosmetics " rubbed, poured, sprinkled, or sprayed on " the body for " cleansing, beautifying, promoting attractiveness, or altering the appearance." All such goods shipped in interstate commerce are subject to national regulation.

The Food and Drug Administration tests thousands of samples in its laboratories. It has found candy adulterated with clay, peanut hulls in stock feeds, and tartaric acid in lemonade.

Labels must honestly list the ingredients and quantity in a package. Narcotic drugs must be labeled: " Warning — May Be Habit-Forming." Poisonous drugs must be plainly labeled; instructions must be given for their use and antidotes for their misuse.

The work of the Food and Drug Administration, together with that of the Federal Trade Commission (see page 139) and the Department of Agriculture's Agricultural Research Service (see page 273), has saved untold thousands of lives and protected the health and well-being of all our people. And

" U.S. PRIME STEER "
Inspecting and grading meat is just one of the many safeguards used by the Food and Drug Administration to protect the health of the nation's consumers.

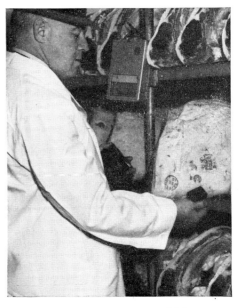

so has the work of similar agencies maintained by the States.

A recent federal court case presents an interesting illustration of the work of the Administration in protecting the public against unscrupulous racketeers. For nearly twenty years a man had been selling a device he called the "Spectro-Chrome." He claimed that it would cure practically any ailment known to medical science. His Spectro-Chrome was, in reality, nothing more than a box containing a strong electric light bulb and several different colored panes of glass. But he had sold over 9000 of them at $90 each!

He claimed that when the light was passed through one of the panes and onto the "patient" it would cure cancer, when passed through another it would cure ulcers, and so on. One defense witness at his trial testified that the machine made calving easier for cows when they were faced to the north during treatment. Another claimed that the machine had actually cured a dachshund of constipation. But several Government witnesses told of many people suffering from serious illnesses who had died while being "treated" by the machine.

One defense witness who claimed that the Spectro-Chrome had cured him of epilepsy suffered an epileptic attack while testifying. He might have strangled to death had not a doctor (who was a Government witness) saved him.

Because the Food and Drug Administration is understaffed and because of public indifference, it is estimated that for every criminal convicted for fraud of this kind two others are at large. Most of those who "get away with it" are petty crooks — selling fakes in a bottle for a dollar or two or such things as adulterated sugar or mislabeled horse meat. These crooks who flaunt the law are still a very real threat to the health and safety of our citizens.

WHAT THIS CHAPTER IS ABOUT

The whole field of social welfare — of conserving human resources in the same sense that we conserve natural resources — is a relatively new one for government.

Most of the social welfare activities of the National Government are administered through the Department of Health, Education, and Welfare. HEW, headed by a Secretary appointed by the President and Senate, is the newest of the Cabinet Departments.

The principal agencies under the Secretary are: the Office of Education, the Social Security Administration, the Public Health Service, and the Food and Drug Administration.

The Office of Education co-operates with the States in the promotion of public education.

The Social Security Administration manages the Old-Age and Survivors Insurance program. OASI is an insurance and retirement program for employed workers financed by contributions from employers, employees, and the self-employed. The Administration also supervises the granting of federal funds to the States for old-age assistance and aid to the blind, to dependent children, and to persons who are permanently and totally disabled.

The Public Health Service is the agency through which most of the health activities of the National Government are handled.

The Food and Drug Administration enforces the laws which prohibit the shipping of adulterated, misbranded, or otherwise dangerous food, drugs, cosmetics, and devices in interstate commerce.

QUESTIONS ON THE TEXT

1. Who heads the Department of Health, Education, and Welfare?

2. What are the four principal agencies within the Department?

3. What are the basic functions of each of these agencies?

4. What national crisis produced the Social Security Act?

5. What is the Old-Age and Survivors Insurance program? How many workers are now covered by this insurance plan?

6. How is OASI financed? How are benefits figured?

7. In what way does the National Government aid the States with their own welfare programs?

8. List three activities of the Public Health Service.

9. Why was the Food and Drug Administration created?

10. How is the consumer protected against misbranded foods?

PROBLEMS FOR DISCUSSION

1. Why do you think it is necessary or unnecessary for government to maintain social welfare programs?

2. If you feel that social welfare is a proper function of government, do you feel that it should be handled by local governments, the States, the National Government, or all three levels? Why?

3. What potential dangers do you see in a too-generous or too-inclusive governmental welfare program? How could those dangers be avoided?

THINGS YOU MIGHT DO

1. Ask your school principal or other school administrator to tell the class in what ways the Office of Education affects education in your locale.

2. From your State's Bluebook and the State Public Welfare Commission (or similar agency), find out the nature and extent of your State's welfare programs.

3. Ask your county and/or city welfare officers to describe their work to the class.

4. List as many of the ways as you can through which governments in the United States promote the public welfare. There are many in addition to the functions suggested in this chapter.

WORDS AND PHRASES YOU SHOULD KNOW

Adulterated
HEW
Grant-in-aid

Old-Age and Survivors Insurance
Social security
Social welfare

SELECT BIBLIOGRAPHY

BENDINER, ROBERT, " The Doctor With 2,300 Patients a Day," *Collier's*, September 30, 1955.

" Bigger Benefits for 75 Million," *U.S. News*, September 3, 1954.

CARR, ROBERT K., and others, *American Democracy in Theory and Practice*, Chapter 31. Rinehart, 1955.

DAVIS, ARTHUR L., " Death in Small Doses," *Saturday Evening Post*, January 21, 1956.

HOBBY, OVETA CULP, " Are You Getting Your Share of Social Security? " *American Magazine*, April, 1955.

JOHNSON, CLAUDIUS O., *American Government*, Chapter 21. Crowell, 1955.

" Latest on Social Security," *U.S. News*, January 7, 1955.

MILLER, HELEN LEE, " Social Security," *Collier's*, May 13, 1955.

PRINGLE, HENRY and KATHERINE, " The Case for Federal Relief," *Saturday Evening Post*, July 19, 1952.

SWARTHOUT, JOHN M., and BARTLEY, ERNEST R., *Principles and Problems of American National Government*, Chapter 25. Oxford, 1955.

" The Older Worker," *Time*, October 19, 1953.

" Things You Need to Know About Pension Changes," *U.S. News*, August 3, 1956.

" Who Gets Pension Gains? " *U.S. News*, July 27, 1956.

YODER, ROBERT M., " Uncle Sam's Big Pay-Off," *Saturday Evening Post*, November 19, 1955.

UNIT IV

ADMINISTRATIVE AGENCIES AND THE TERRITORIES

Horydczak

Federal Reserve System Building

IT IS ALMOST IMPOSSIBLE to comprehend the . . . problems of the Federal Government unless one has some concept of its hugeness and complexity. The sheer size, complexity, and geographical diversion of its operations almost stagger the imagination. As a result of depression, war, new needs for defense, and our greater responsibilities abroad, the Federal Government has become the largest enterprise on earth.

THE HOOVER COMMISSION
Concluding Report, 1949

The happy imagined time when government did not interfere in the freedom of the individual by meddling in business never in fact existed.

— *Carl Becker*

★

Chapter 18

INDEPENDENT REGULATORY COMMISSIONS

The United States Constitution makes no provision for the organization of the Executive Branch under the President.[1]

The Founding Fathers did expect, however, that a number of administrative agencies would be created. They knew that these agencies would be absolutely necessary to enable the President to carry out his constitutional duty to " take care that the laws be faithfully executed." [2]

Since 1789 the Congress has created a tremendous number of executive agencies. As we know, it has created ten Cabinet Departments to assist the President in executing the laws.

Not all of the activities of government have been assigned to these Departments, however. A great many special agencies, outside any Depart-

ment, have also been established. These " independent agencies " deal with activities ranging all the way from such things as transportation and power to public housing and foreign aid.

There are a number of reasons why these various independent agencies have been established outside of the Cabinet Departments. Sometimes special interest groups have persuaded Congress to give an agency independent status. Or, an agency may have been set up as an independent one in an attempt to protect it insofar as possible from partisan politics. Agencies also have been created as independent ones by " accident," without any particular thought to the administrative hodgepodge resulting.

Finally, some agencies are independent because of the nature of the work they do. This is especially true of the so-called " independent regulatory commissions."

In this chapter we discuss three of the independent regulatory commis-

---

[1] Only passing reference is made to " the principal officer in each of the executive departments " and to " the heads of departments." Article II, Section 2, Clauses 1 and 2.

[2] Article II, Section 3.

sions. The more important of the other independent agencies are dealt with at appropriate places elsewhere in the book.[3] In the next chapter we shall discuss those independent agencies which are especially concerned with finance.

The Independent Regulatory Commissions. These commissions are agencies created by Congress especially to regulate certain aspects of the American economy. The most notable ones include the Interstate Commerce Commission, the Federal Communications Commission, and the Federal Power Commission, all three of which are dealt with in this chapter; and the Federal Trade Commission (page 139), the Securities and Exchange Commission (page 338), and the National Labor Relations Board (Chapter 39).

Like the other independent agencies, these commissions are not within any Cabinet Department. Unlike the other independent agencies, however, these commissions are also largely independent of the President.

The President appoints the commissions' members with Senate consent, but they serve long terms (usually seven years). This long term lessens the control a President might exercise over the members. They may be removed

only " for cause " as provided by Congress and not at the President's pleasure (see page 182).

As with other agencies, these commissions have administrative powers to carry out the laws enacted by Congress in their particular fields. Unlike other agencies, they also have what are known as *quasi-legislative* and *quasi-judicial* powers.[4]

Their quasi-legislative powers are exercised when they issue rules and regulations to fill in or spell out details of acts passed by Congress. For example, Congress has provided by law that railroad rates must be " just and reasonable." The Interstate Commerce Commission sets the *actual* rates to be charged in a particular situation.

Their quasi-judicial powers are exercised when they decide disputes arising out of the issuing of rules and regulations. For example, if a railroad feels that a rate is too low or if a shipper feels that a rate is too high, the ICC will hear the case and make a decision, much as a court would. Appeals from decisions made by an independent regulatory commission may be taken to a United States Court of Appeals.[5]

---

[4] The prefix *quasi* is from the Latin, meaning " in a certain sense, resembling, seemingly."

[5] Because the independent regulatory commissions exercise all three of the major functions of government, executive, legislative, and judicial, they provide an exception to the principle of separation of powers. The Second Hoover Commission recommended that most of the functions of these agencies be taken over by regular Cabinet agencies.

---

[3] For example, the United States Tariff Commission, page 120; the Federal Trade Commission, page 139; The United States Information Agency, page 203; the Atomic Energy Commission, page 243; the Housing and Home Finance Agency, Chapter 38; and the Tennessee Valley Authority, Chapter 39.

The Interstate Commerce Commission

When and Why Created. In the early days of railroading the operations of the various lines were simple and local enough for the States to be able to regulate them fairly well. By the latter 1860's, however, the railroads began to extend their lines through many States. Their operations, almost overnight, became " big business " with huge profits at stake.

The National Government had given many of them large tracts of land to encourage the building of lines, and some rail officials used these lands for personal gain. Larger companies squeezed smaller ones out of business and gained monopolies. Especially in the Middle West, farmers and other shippers were charged exorbitant rates, and a few shippers were favored over others.

In some States, the legislatures were actually controlled by the railroads. In others, the legislatures struck back at the railroads by setting rates so low that the lines were in danger of losing money.

These and other similarly unhealthy

CONTROL BOARD

This vast network of rail lines leading into the marshaling yard requires a great deal of careful planning if traffic is to move smoothly and safely. High in the tower, an operator directs the movement of the cars by remote control.

ORE DOCK, DULUTH

The tugboat heads for the loaded ore boat. It will maneuver the larger ship away from the dock and out into St. Louis Bay and the Great Lakes.

conditions finally forced Congress to act. In 1887 it passed the Interstate Commerce Act and created the Interstate Commerce Commission.

Today, the ICC's authority covers not only rail lines but also interstate motor carriers, most water carriers operating between coastal points and on the nation's lakes and rivers, interstate pipelines, except those which carry water and gas, sleeping-car companies, and interstate carriers using routes partly water and partly land. The ICC has, furthermore, the authority to determine the standard time zones in the United States and Alaska. Air transportation is not regulated by the ICC but rather by the Civil Aeronautics Board and the Civil Aeronautics Authority. (See page 296.)

Membership. The ICC is composed of eleven members, who are appointed by the President and the Senate for seven-year terms. The commissioners elect a chairman from among themselves. They are assisted by a large staff of economists, lawyers, and transportation experts.

Powers. The ICC's powers of regulation over rail, land, and domestic water carriers [6] are so great that the

---

[6] *Common carriers* are railroads, ships, busses, trucks, pipelines, taxicabs, airplanes, etc., which carry goods or persons of a general class for pay. *Contract carriers* carry particular goods or persons.

Commission is sometimes called " the nation's transportation czar."

Rate-Setting. The setting of rates is one of the most difficult and important duties of the ICC. If rates are set too low, investors will lose money or at least not receive a " fair return " on their investment. If rates are too high, shippers and the public will suffer.

Carriers are forbidden to charge unjust rates, and they must publish their rates for public inspection. They may not charge more for a short than for a longer haul, except where the Commission considers competition to justify it. For instance, the rail rates from New York to the Rocky Mountain States may be higher than those to the Pacific Coast. If the coast rates were not lower, freight would go by way of the Panama Canal. This would mean that the roads would lose freight that their expensive roadbeds can carry without additional cost.

Carriers may not give rebates to individual shippers or discriminate against particular shippers or localities. Rates charged between two points within a State cannot be so low as to put points outside the State at an unreasonable disadvantage. " Passes " or free transportation may be given only to a very restricted group of persons; for example, present or retired employees.

The ICC is often criticized because it has commonly fixed truck and bus rates higher than necessary in order to permit rail lines to compete with motor carriers. Those who defend the ICC

argue that the railroads are essential to the nation, especially in wartime, and therefore must be kept in a healthy condition.

Securities Regulation. In the past, railroads often " watered their stock." That is, they issued stock, selling it or giving it to existing stockholders, far in excess of the actual value of the road. Thus they could reduce the apparent profit the road made. For example, a road earning a twelve per cent profit might double its stock and thus appear to have earned only a six per cent profit.

While this practice may have benefited some stockholders, it also served as a " justification " for unreasonably high rates and was a hazard to financial stability.

Today, carriers must have the approval of the ICC before issuing stocks and bonds or otherwise borrowing, except for certain short-term loans. In approving or rejecting the issuing of securities, the ICC must be guided by the " public interest."

Service. Common carriers must provide " reasonable service." Before a carrier may begin operations or extend present routes, a " certificate of convenience and necessity " must be secured from the ICC. Thus uneconomic duplication of lines may be prevented or, in the case of motor carriers, the highways may be protected from overcrowding.

The Commission may require a railroad to extend its lines to serve shippers when this seems to be reasonably necessary. Trains may be required to

Railway Age

THE ICC IN ACTION

At one of these hearings, the fare rates you will pay on a train, or the amount you will pay for freight shipments, may be determined.

make automatic stops along certain routes.

Carriers may also be required to cooperate in the interest of shippers. For example, the ICC may transfer rail cars from one company to another in an emergency. This has been done many times to prevent produce from spoiling for lack of cars to transport it to market. Also, the ICC may route rail traffic over other lines if the one receiving it is unable to handle it. It may and often does require the joint use of station and other terminal facilities.

Safety Requirements. The ICC has issued many safety rules which carriers must obey. For example, truck drivers who operate in interstate commerce must be at least twenty-one years of age, in good mental and physical condition, free from such things as drug addiction, and must not drink alcoholic beverages while on duty or drink to excess at other times.

All manner of safety devices are required for carriers. Insurance must be carried to protect property and life. Trucks are forbidden to pick up " hitchhikers." The list of safety precautions carriers must follow is almost endless.

Accounting Procedures. The ICC may require all of the utilities it regulates to keep uniform accounts and render periodic reports to the commission. The ICC also has free access to the carriers' books, so that it may have the information it needs to perform its functions.

The Federal Communications Commission

In most European countries such means of communications as the telephone, telegraph, cable services, radio, and television are government-owned and -operated. In this country, however, we know only very limited government-ownership in these fields.

The National Government maintains communications facilities for its own use, especially in the armed forces. State and local governments do so especially for police purposes, and several States own and operate educational radio and television stations.

Our communications services have been developed largely by private companies and individuals. However, these communications services are subject to a good deal of governmental control.

The Federal Communications Commission. Another of the independent regulatory bodies, the Federal Communications Commission, was created by Congress in 1934. It is composed of seven members appointed by the President and Senate for seven-year terms.

In the Communications Act of 1934 the FCC was given the task of insuring " rapid, efficient, nation-wide and world-wide wire and radio communication service with adequate facilities at reasonable charges."

Telephone, Telegraph, and Cable. The FCC's regulation of telephone, telegraph, and cable services is much like that of the ICC over interstate transportation. The lines or wires are " common carriers." Service must be adequate, rates just and reasonable. Rates can be changed only with Commission approval and must be published for the information of clients.

Certificates of convenience and necessity are required before new lines may be constructed or existing ones extended. Lines may not be abandoned without FCC approval.

The FCC does not have quite as much authority over these services as the ICC has over interstate transportation, however. It has no power, for example, over the securities issued by companies in these fields.

Radio and Television. The regulation of radio and television presents special problems. Not all telephone or telegraph service is interstate in character. Much of it is purely local and subject only to State regulation. Radio and television broadcasting are no respecters of State lines, however. Their waves range far and wide.

The FCC regulates both interstate and foreign broadcasting. Of course, control over foreign broadcasting can extend only to outgoing communications. If objectionable matter is broadcast into the United States, the problem must be handled through diplomatic channels.

The Communications Act specifically provides that radio and television stations are *not* common carriers. Hence, the FCC has no authority to regulate such things as security issues or the rates that may be charged to advertisers.

All radio and television operators must have a license from the FCC in order to go on the air. Licenses are needed for those who operate standard broadcasting stations, amateur radios, police radio stations, aircraft radio systems, and so on.

The license assigns a particular frequency and may impose other limits, too; for example, the hours of use. The useable frequencies are those from about 10 kilocycles to about 30,000,-000 kilocycles. Only the band between 550 and 1600 kilocycles may be used for standard broadcasting.

The Commission distributes licenses, wave lengths, periods of time for operation, and station power among the States and local communities in a way that will provide a " fair, efficient, and equitable distribution of service to each."

When paid matter is broadcast the name of the sponsor must be an-

TRANSCONTINENTAL RELAY

This is one of more than a hundred stations in a radio-relay system from Boston to Los Angeles. Telephone messages, carried by radio microwaves, are received at each tower. They are amplified and sent on to the next tower.

nounced. If a station permits a broadcast by or in behalf of a candidate for office, it must give opposing candidates equal opportunity at the same rates.

It is a federal crime to use indecent language on the air or to give information concerning a lottery or otherwise to defraud the public.

The Federal Power Commission

The Federal Power Commission. Another of the great independent regulatory commissions, the Federal Power Commission, is responsible for carrying out federal regulation of the hydroelectric power and natural gas industries.[7]

The providing of electric power and natural gas service divides rather naturally into three basic steps. These are (1) the manufacture of the product, (2) the transmission of it to the locality where it will be used, and (3) the distribution of it to customers.

It is with the second of these three steps, transmission, that federal regulation and the FPC are especially concerned. The transporting of electricity and natural gas almost always involves interstate commerce.

The manufacturing (producing) step and the distributing (selling) step seldom involve interstate commerce. They are usually local activities and therefore are largely controlled by State and local agencies. However, the FPC must approve (license) the construction of any hydroelectric project on the navigable waters or public lands of the United States. It also regulates the wholesale rates a distributor is charged when he purchases electricity or gas outside the State.

The FPC was originally created in 1920 to regulate the development of hydroelectric power projects on the nation's navigable waters and public lands. Regulation had become neces-

---

[7] Practically all electricity and gas manufactured from fuels are produced in the localities in which they are used. Thus their production, transmission, and distribution seldom involve interstate commerce and federal regulation.

sary in order to insure orderly development and to promote conservation. To these ends, the Commission was given the power to license projects.

Through the years, its powers have been increased, especially over the interstate transmission of electric energy. Natural gas was brought under the Commission's jurisdiction by the Natural Gas Act of 1938. The FPC also regulates the issuing of securities by the electric power and natural gas industries.

The Commission does *not* build dams. Federal dam-building is done mostly by the Bureau of Reclamation, the Army Engineers, and the Tennessee Valley Authority.

WHAT THIS CHAPTER IS ABOUT

The Constitution is notably silent on the matter of administrative organization. In addition to the ten Cabinet Departments, Congress has, for a variety of reasons, created a great many independent agencies. These agencies are located outside any of the regular Departments.

Among the independent agencies is one particular group known as the " independent regulatory commissions." They are not only independent of any Cabinet Department. They are, as well, largely independent of the President.

These commissions have been created especially to regulate certain aspects of the American economy. In addition to administrative powers, they also possess quasi-legislative and quasi-judicial powers.

The Interstate Commerce Commission was created in 1887 to provide sorely needed regulation of interstate railroad transportation. Today its authority also covers interstate motor carriers, interstate water transportation, interstate pipe lines (except those which carry water and gas), sleeping-car companies, and interstate carriers using routes partly water and partly land.

The Federal Communications Commission was created in 1934 to regulate interstate telephone, telegraph, and cable communications, radio, and television.

The Federal Power Commission was created in 1920 to regulate the building of hydroelectric power projects on the nation's navigable waters and public lands. Today its authority also covers the interstate transmission of electric energy and natural gas.

QUESTIONS ON THE TEXT

1. Why did the Founding Fathers expect that Congress would create a number of administrative agencies under the President?

2. Why have some of these agencies been created independent of the Cabinet Departments?

3. What are the *independent regulatory commissions?*

4. In what particular ways are they made largely independent of the President?

5. How do these commissions exercise their *quasi-legislative* and *quasi-judicial* powers?

6. When and why was the Interstate Commerce Commission established?

7. What aspects of interstate transportation are included within its authority today?

8. Why is setting rates one of the ICC's most difficult and important duties?

9. What is a certificate of convenience and necessity?

10. When and why was the Federal Communications Commission created?

11. Are radio and television stations common carriers?

12. When and why was the Federal Power Commission created?

13. What three basic steps are involved in the providing of electric power and natural gas service?

14. With which of these three steps is the FPC most concerned? Briefly explain why.

PROBLEMS FOR DISCUSSION

1. Do you think that the regulation of all transportation should be assigned to the ICC?

2. An Oregon man who used profane language in a radio talk in which he criticized chain stores was sentenced to six months in jail by a United States District Court. Should a young man use profanity to show emphasis and temper, or should he develop a vocabulary that will enable him to express himself within the law? Why?

3. Why are such public utilities as power and light companies almost always monopolies? Does the fact that they are, increase or decrease the need for governmental regulation? Cite local examples, if you can, to illustrate your answer.

THINGS YOU MIGHT DO

1. Stage a class forum or debate on the topic: " *Resolved:* That the present system of commercial broadcasting should be abolished and government-operated radio and television be substituted therefor."

2. Several members of the class might prepare reports on various transportation businesses in your local community.

3. Invite a local radio or television station manager to address the class on the subject of his business.

WORDS AND PHRASES YOU SHOULD KNOW

Certificates of convenience and necessity
Federal Communications Commission
Federal Power Commission
Independent regulatory commissions

Interstate Commerce Commission
Quasi-judicial powers
Quasi-legislative powers
" Watered stock "

SELECT BIBLIOGRAPHY

FERGUSON, JOHN H., and McHENRY, DEAN E., *The American System of Government*, Chapters 25, 26, 27. McGraw-Hill, 1956.

MERRIAM, CHARLES E., and ROBERT E., *The American Government*, Chapters 24, 27. Ginn, 1954.

SWARTHOUT, JOHN M., and BARTLEY, ERNEST R., *Principles and Problems of American National Government*, Chapters 16, 22, 23. Oxford, 1955.

WHITE, LEONARD D., *Introduction to the Study of Public Administration*. Macmillan, 1955.

> Finance is not mere arithmetic. . . . Without sound finance no sound government is possible; without sound government no sound finance is possible.
>
> — *Woodrow Wilson*

★

Chapter 19

FINANCIAL AGENCIES OF THE GOVERNMENT

In Chapters 11 through 17 we discussed each of the ten Cabinet Departments, and in Chapter 18 we considered several of the independent agencies within the National Government.

In the present chapter we shall deal with several other independent agencies. These are agencies which are particularly concerned with the field of finance, its regulation, and its promotion.

The Nation's Banking System

Early History of Banking. In 1791 Congress created the First Bank of the United States. As we saw earlier, its creation was accompanied by one of the most important disputes in our constitutional history. The Bank had been proposed and was favored by Alexander Hamilton and the liberal-constructionists. It was stoutly opposed by Thomas Jefferson and the strict-constructionists.

The First Bank of the United States. The First Bank of the United States was chartered by Congress for twenty years. The National Government held twenty per cent of its capital stock of $10,000,000, and the other eighty per cent was subscribed by private individuals. It had the power to issue notes which circulated as paper money.

With its eight branches located in principal cities, the First Bank proved of great value to both business and the Government. It aided in the collecting of revenue, made loans to the Government, and served as a depository for public funds.

Although many continued to oppose the First Bank after its creation, its constitutionality was not challenged in the courts. When its charter expired in 1811, the Congress simply did not renew it.

The Second Bank of the United States. The financial crisis brought on by the War of 1812 led Congress to charter the Second Bank of the United

States in 1816. It was quite similar to the First Bank but was set up on a much larger scale. Its capital stock was $35,000,000; the division of stock between private holders and the National Government remained the same, however.

The Second Bank had a much more stormy career than its predecessor. The constitutionality of its charter was attacked, but it was upheld by the Supreme Court in 1819 in the famous case of *McCulloch* v. *Maryland*.[1] The Second Bank was not so well managed as the First had been, and it was opposed by State-chartered banks which resented its competition. Andrew Jackson, an ardent foe of the Bank, ended its existence in 1836.

The Period of State-Bank Monopoly. From 1836 until 1863 State banks (*i.e.*, private banks chartered by the States) enjoyed a monopoly of the banking business in the United States, and State banking laws were quite liberal.

Although the Constitution prohibits the States from issuing paper money,[2] the Supreme Court ruled that the States *could* authorize private banks to do so. Some States permitted banks to issue no more notes than they could redeem in gold, but most banks were able to issue any amount

they pleased. Of course, the country was flooded with a bewildering variety of paper money, the value of which ranged all the way from being " as good as gold " to being worth next to nothing, depending upon the bank of issue.

The National Banking System. The chaos created by the lack of any central banking system led to the passage of the National Banking Act of 1863. In it, Congress restored a measure of federal control over banking activities. The new law did not create another Bank of the United States. Instead, it provided for the chartering of private banks under the authority of the National Government.

These " national banks " (*i.e.*, private banks chartered by the National Government) were each permitted to issue notes up to the amount of their capital stock; but these notes had to be secured by federal bonds owned by the bank and deposited with the United States Treasury.

Shortly after the passage of the Act of 1863, Congress imposed a ten per cent tax on all notes issued by State banks. This tax, which drove State bank notes out of existence, was upheld as a valid use of the taxing power by the Supreme Court in 1867.

The new banking system brought marked improvement in banking and currency. The system remained largely unchanged for fifty years, until the creation of the Federal Reserve System in 1913.

Two Systems of Banks Today. There are two principal systems of

---

[1] The case is especially important because in it Chief Justice John Marshall upheld the doctrine of implied powers and ruled that States could not tax the instrumentalities of the National Government. See pages 107–108.

[2] Article I, Section 10, Clause 1.

banks in the United States today: *State* and *national*. State banks are chartered under State law, and national banks are chartered under federal law.

Both kinds of banks are subject to the regulation of the State in which they do business. Both are also subject to federal regulation, except for the relatively few uninsured banks which are not members of the Federal Reserve System.[3]

Of course, State banking regulations vary from State to State. Nevertheless, State and federal authorities co-operate well in safeguarding the public interest without disrupting the American principle of private enterprise. In particular, the creation of the Federal Reserve System in 1913 and the Federal Deposit Insurance Corporation in 1933 has produced considerable uniformity in the regulation and supervision of banks in general to safeguard the funds of depositors everywhere.

All national banks and the majority of State banks do the general business of *commercial banks*. That is, they receive deposits for safe-keeping, accept saving accounts, perform trust functions, use their funds to make loans and investments, and render various other financial services to individuals and to groups.

One group of State banks, however, the *mutual savings banks,* usually restrict their business exclusively to the receipt and investment of small sav-

ings deposits. There are now 524 mutual savings banks, located chiefly in New England and other eastern States. Although they comprise only a small portion of the some 14,300 banks in the nation, they have impressive total deposits that today amount to more than $30,000,000,000.

With the passage of the National Banking Act of 1863, State banks all but disappeared. Most State banks at the time became national banks in order to be able to continue the issuing of notes. Then, as the use of checks increased, as mutual savings banks began to grow, and as trust companies began to do general banking business, the number of State banks began to increase again. Today there are more State banks (about 9500) than there are national banks (about 4650 in 1957).

National banks came into being to provide a sound control of bank note currency. When the currency-issuing Federal Reserve Banks were set up in 1914, national banks lost the power to issue notes. National bank notes are now retired whenever deposited in banks, and there are few of them in circulation today. National banks are today merely federally controlled commercial banks much like the State-chartered commercial banks.

---

[3] A national bank must have the word "national" in its corporate title.

Organization and Functions of National Banks. With the approval of the Comptroller of the Currency,[4] any five or more persons may secure a charter of incorporation for a national bank. They must have a capital stock varying from $50,000 in places of less than 6000 inhabitants to $200,000 in cities of more than 50,000 inhabitants.

These banks receive deposits from individuals and corporations and lend money to individuals and corporations. They must be examined by a United States examiner at least twice a year. They must also make reports to the Comptroller of the Currency at least three times a year — whenever called for.

Insurance of Deposits. All national banks, and State banks which are members of the Federal Reserve System, must insure their deposits up to $10,000. State banks which are not members of the Federal Reserve System, however, may also qualify for this insurance.[5]

Insured banks pay an annual premium in proportion to their average deposits. In return each bank depositor's account is insured up to $10,000. The sign shown on the preceding page is displayed by all insured banks in the United States.

The insurance program is adminis-

tered by the Federal Deposit Insurance Corporation. The FDIC was created when the insurance program was set up by Congress in 1933. It is an independent agency composed of the Comptroller of the Currency and two members appointed by the President and Senate for six-year terms.

No appropriations are made by Congress to the FDIC. Its entire income arises from the insurance premiums paid by insured banks. The Corporation's surplus now amounts to approximately $1,650,000,000.

When a national bank is closed, the FDIC is appointed receiver. A new bank is organized and assumes the liabilities of the closed bank. If stock in the new bank can be sold, the new bank will continue. If not, the assets may be sold to another bank. If neither of these arrangements is possible within two years, the bank will be liquidated (abolished).

Branch Banks. National banks may establish branch banks in their home cities if those cities have 25,000 or more inhabitants. They may also establish branch offices in foreign countries.

Those with $500,000 or more capital may, with the consent of the Comptroller of the Currency, establish branches within the State to the extent that State banks are permitted to create branches.

Examinations. In general, national banks are subject to unannounced examinations by specially trained examiners. These examiners check to see that the banks are in sound condi-

---

[4] Within the Treasury Department, see page 219.

[5] Unsound practices cause a nonmember bank to lose its insurance privilege, a State bank to lose its membership, and a national bank to be closed.

MODERN BANKING

The Chase Manhattan Bank is scheduled for completion by 1960. It is a good example of the type of modern office building going up all over the country. Although banks in smaller communities may not be as grand as this bank in physical appearance, they all provide the same basic services.

tion and that they are being properly run.

Thus, through improved regulation and supervision, our entire banking system has been greatly strengthened in recent decades.

The Federal Reserve System—"Bankers' Banks"

Originally, national banks were entirely separate institutions, with no means of coming to one another's aid in time of crisis. To remedy this situation and give national banks the strength of unity, Congress established the Federal Reserve System in 1913. In 1935 the System was brought more under the control of the National Government.

Organization of Federal Reserve Banks. The United States is divided into twelve Federal Reserve districts. There is one Federal Reserve Bank located in the Federal Reserve Bank city of each district. Each of them is directly supervised by a board of directors. There are also Federal Reserve branch banks.

Member Banks. Every national bank is a member of the Federal Reserve System. As such, it is required to subscribe to the stock of the Federal Reserve Bank of its district. State banks and trust companies may become members by complying with certain conditions of membership.

The Board of Governors of the

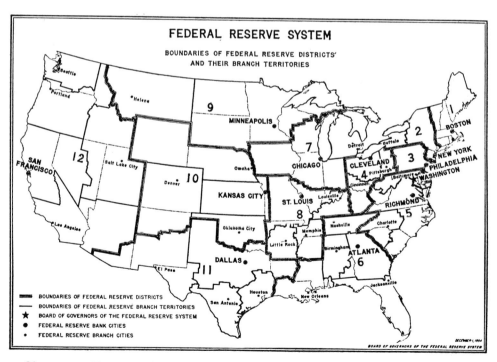

FEDERAL RESERVE SYSTEM
BOUNDARIES OF FEDERAL RESERVE DISTRICTS'
AND THEIR BRANCH TERRITORIES

BOUNDARIES OF FEDERAL RESERVE DISTRICTS
BOUNDARIES OF FEDERAL RESERVE BRANCH TERRITORIES
BOARD OF GOVERNORS OF THE FEDERAL RESERVE SYSTEM
FEDERAL RESERVE BANK CITIES
FEDERAL RESERVE BRANCH CITIES

Federal Reserve System is composed of seven members appointed by the President with the approval of the Senate. Each member of the board serves a single term of fourteen years, one member retiring every second year.

Powers of the Board of Governors. The Board determines the percentage of deposits that member banks must deposit with the district Reserve Banks. If member banks are unwisely lending money for speculative purposes, the Board will curb them by requiring them to place a larger proportion of their deposits on reserve. On the other hand, if constructive business needs more loans, the Board will return a portion of the reserves to the member banks to take care of those needs.

Issue of Federal Reserve Notes. When more money is needed for legitimate purposes, the Board may issue any amount of Federal Reserve Notes through any of the Federal Reserve Banks. Twenty-five per cent of the notes, however, are secured by gold certificates, and the balance either by government bonds or commercial paper.

Determination of Interest Rate. When a businessman borrows money from a national bank or a State bank, he gives his note. If the bank needs money, it can get it from the Federal Reserve Bank by turning over those notes for security. The Board determines the interest rate charged the banks. If industry is slack, the interest rate will be low to encourage borrowing. If a boom is on and speculation is raising prices unduly, the interest rate will be made higher to discourage reckless borrowing and spending.

Interest Rate on Deposits. The Board limits the interest rate that member banks may pay on time and savings deposits. This prevents a reckless bank from paying more than a safely managed bank can afford to pay.

Supervision. The Board supervises Federal Reserve Banks. It can even remove officers of recklessly managed member banks.

Since 1935 the purchase and sale of bonds has become an important function of Federal Reserve Banks. In this way the System exerts another control over the amount of money in circulation. Originally, Federal Reserve Banks lent only to member banks, but now the Reserve Banks may also make loans to individuals and corporations under certain stipulated conditions.

System of Farm Credit Banks

The Farm Credit Administration. The Farm Credit Administration was created in 1933 to co-ordinate the various lending organizations which Congress had created to assist farmers during the years of the depression.

It is an independent agency headed by an officer known as the Governor of the Farm Credit Administration. He is selected by the thirteen-member

Farm Credit Board, a part-time group of advisers to the Governor. The Governor administers the Federal Land Banks and other banks of the Farm Credit system.[6] The country is divided into twelve Farm Credit Administration districts. There is a Federal Land Bank in a centrally located city in each district.

Federal Land Banks. These banks were created in 1916 to give the farmer an opportunity to borrow money on his land at low rates of interest by giving a long-term mortgage. These banks borrow money by the sale of partially tax-exempt bonds on which they pay about 3% interest and then lend it to national farm loan associations at about 4% interest.[7]

Loans are made only for the purchase of land, for its improvement, or for purchase of livestock, equipment, or fertilizers, or to provide buildings on a farm, or to pay off a debt under certain conditions. A loan must not exceed 65% of the normal agricultural value of the farm offered as security.

The amount borrowed must not be less than $100 or more than $200,000. No mortgage shall run for more than forty years, or for less than five except by special arrangement. The loan is repaid in annual or semi-annual installments.

Ten or more farmers who own land may form a national farm loan association, and through this association may borrow money from a Land Bank. The association is liable for the loan made to each of the members. If direct loans are made to individuals, $\frac{1}{2}$ of 1 per cent more interest is charged.

Federal Home Loan Bank System

The Federal Home Loan Bank System. The System was created by Congress in 1932 to provide a credit reserve for savings and home-financing institutions. It serves as a bank from which member institutions can borrow funds with which to meet the home-financing needs in their areas and withdrawals by investors.

There are eleven regional Federal Home Loan Banks located in principal cities across the country. The System is managed by the Home Loan Bank Board. This Board consists of three members appointed by the President and Senate for four-year terms.

The eleven regional Home Loan Banks make loans to savings and loan, building and loan, and homestead associations, savings and co-operative

---

[6] These are *Intermediate Credit Banks* which make loans through various agricultural credit corporations instead of directly to the farmers, and loans to production credit associations which consist of ten or more farmers, and *Banks for Co-operatives* which make loans to agricultural co-operative associations.

[7] The Federal Farm Mortgage Corporation was created in 1934 as an emergency measure to assist farmers who were about to lose their farms because of the depression prices of farm products. The Corporation was authorized to issue partially tax-exempt Government guaranteed bonds, and to lend the proceeds to worthy farmers at a low rate of interest. Many a farm was saved for its owner by this Government corporation.

banks, and insurance companies. These member institutions, of which there are now more than 4400, have total assets of more than $40,000,-000,000. They make loans to home builders. Most of the member institutions are the savings-and-loan type.

Federal Savings and Loan Associations can be organized by a responsible group of citizens applying to the nearest Federal Home Loan Bank. In these associations (banks) individuals may earn interest on their savings; or, if they are good risks, they may borrow money for home financing needs. Deposits in a federal savings and loan association are insured up to $10,000 by the Federal Savings and Loan Insurance Corporation.

(Other federal agencies in the field of home-financing, such as the Federal Housing Administration and the Federal National Mortgage Association, are discussed in Chapter 38.)

Other Federal Loan Agencies

In other chapters we have considered several federal agencies which make loans for various purposes. For example, in Chapter 15 we dealt with the Farmers Home Administration, the Rural Electrification Administration, and the Commodity Credit Corporation.

There are two more independent lending agencies with which we must deal here. They are the Small Business Administration and the Export-Import Bank.[8]

The Small Business Administration. Congress created this lending agency in 1953 to replace the Reconstruction Finance Corporation. It is designed to encourage small businesses by making financial help available to them and by helping them to secure government contracts. This agency is headed by an Administrator appointed by the President with the consent of the Senate.

The SBA has a lending authority of $530,000,000. Of this amount, $305,-000,000 is available for loans to small businesses. Individual loans up to $150,000 may be made to small firms which cannot obtain suitable private financing. Another $125,000,000 of the total is available for the making of disaster loans. The remaining $100,-000,000 is available for governmental projects.

The Reconstruction Finance Corporation. Once the National Government's largest lending agency, the Reconstruction Finance Corporation was abolished by Congress in 1954. The RFC was born in the depression year of 1932 at a time when, because of economic conditions, only the Government itself was able to borrow large sums of money. During its life it made public credit available to large

_____
[8] The United States is also a member of two international lending agencies, the International Bank and the International Monetary Fund. We also make loans to foreign governments through such agencies as the International Cooperation Administration.

Bethlehem Steel Company

GIANT TUNNEL

Financed by the RFC, this 1.73-mile-long tunnel runs between Brooklyn and the Battery, at Manhattan's lower tip. The tunnel is made up of two parallel tubes, each thirty-one feet in diameter and with two traffic lanes.

and small commercial, industrial, and governmental borrowers.

It lent over two billion dollars to banks during the depression, practically all of which has been repaid. Without RFC loans a number of railroads would also have ceased operations in the depression years.

State and local governments received a total of about two billion dollars from the RFC in the same period. The RFC also helped to finance many agencies of the National Government.

Loans were made for such projects as the Metropolitan Water District of Southern California (see Chapter 34), San Francisco bridges, and New York tunnels.

In 1941 Arkansas refunded $136,000,000 of its outstanding 4.4% tax-exempt highway bonds to take advantage of lower prevailing interest rates. Private bankers offered to refinance the bonds at 3.5% interest. The RFC thought the private bank rates too high, bought the bonds at 3.2%, and then resold them at a slight profit. This transaction will save Arkansas about $28,000,000 interest over the life of the bonds.

As World War II approached, the RFC made loans to finance the expansion of war industries. It bought large quantities of rubber, tin, and other raw materials for which we were dependent on overseas supply. During the war it owned and operated several war-born industries.[9] After the war it helped finance reconversion and made large loans to such concerns as Kaiser-Frazer and Northwest Airlines.

In recent years the RFC has been severely criticized by private business and financial competitors. There were disclosures of corruption among a very few RFC employees. Altogether, though, the RFC chalked up an impressive record in its lending operations. Besides the industries it saved in the 1930's and its wartime work, it

---

[9] The Government has since disposed of most of these production activities. For example, the Rubber Producing Facilities Disposal Commission, set up by Congress in 1953, had disposed of most of the Government's synthetic rubber plants by 1957.

paid many millions in interest into the United States Treasury.

The Export-Import Bank. To stimulate foreign trade, which had sagged during the world-wide depression, the Export-Import Bank was created in 1934. It is headed by a five-man Board of Directors appointed by the President and Senate.

The Bank is authorized to lend up to as much as $5,000,000,000. Loans are made to encourage our exporting and importing trade.

During the 1930's, many loans were made to enable other countries to buy in the United States. During World War II, loans were made to China and several Latin-American nations to help stabilize their economies and as part of the Good Neighbor Policy. Following the war, rehabilitation loans were made. For example, the Bank lent to large Italian industries, with the loans guaranteed by the Italian Government. These Italian loans had to be spent in the United States for equipment and machinery.

Among typical recent loans have been one for $12,000,000 to Spain and another for $40,000,000 to Japan to help finance their purchases of raw American cotton.

The Securities and Exchange Commission

Millions of Americans own stock in large and small business concerns. Millions more have loaned vast sums to business concerns by purchasing their bonds. Indeed, it is impossible to see how our huge private-enterprise system could have been financed in any other way.

Among the many honest dealers in stocks and bonds there are always a few dishonest racketeers who attempt to bilk the people. At one point in our history, there were so many fraudulent mining stocks being sold that Mark Twain defined a mine as a " hole in the ground owned by a liar."

Beginning with Rhode Island and Kansas in 1910–1911, the States attempted to regulate the traffic in stocks and bonds. These State laws were known as " blue-sky " laws because they were aimed at dishonest traders who would sell " the bright blue sky above " if they could.

By 1933 every State except Nevada had blue-sky laws, but the stock market crash of 1929 proved them ineffective. The losses suffered by investors because of fraudulent stocks have been estimated at about $25,000,000,000 as the country passed from the boom of the 1920's to the depression of the 1930's.

The Securities and Exchange Commission. Created by Congress in 1934, the Securities and Exchange Commission is composed of five commissioners appointed by the President and Senate for five-year terms.

The Commission's task is that of protecting the interests of the public and investors against fraud and misrepresentation in the securities and financial markets. The SEC administers several laws to accomplish this purpose.

The Securities Act of 1933. Sometimes called the " Truth-in-Securities Act," this act requires a full disclosure of all of the material facts in regard to the issuance of new securities. Thus an investor may have sufficient information upon which to base his judgment before he buys. The law makes it a crime to sell or offer to sell to the public, by mail or in interstate commerce, any security not properly registered with the Securities and Exchange Commission.

Under the Act, the Government does *not* guarantee any security issue or purchase. In effect, however, the law adds to the ancient rule of *caveat emptor* (" let the buyer beware ") the newer rule of *caveat vendor* (" let the seller beware ").

The Securities Exchange Act of 1934. This act was a logical follow-up to the 1933 law. It lays down regulations concerning trading in securities *after* their issuance. All securities listed on the nation's securities exchanges, the best known of which is the New York Stock Exchange, must be registered with the SEC.

The Commission prepares elaborate forms with questions covering whatever it thinks will help the public to understand the real condition of a corporation. For example, it required more than a hundred pages for the Standard Oil Company of New Jersey

PYRAMIDING CONTROL

This graph shows how a relatively small investment, $2,340,900, controlled companies worth $90,000,000. The financier bought the majority of voting stock in holding companies X, Y, and Z. He then used money from the sale of nonvoting stock to buy a majority of voting stock in nine operating companies, A to I.

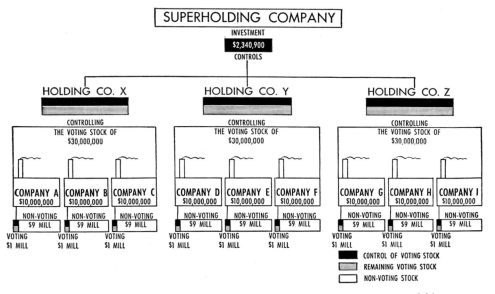

to answer the questions asked by the Securities and Exchange Commission.

The Public Utility Holding Company Act of 1935. This law was brought about by the public utility "holding companies." These were corporations chartered in one State and holding the controlling stock in operating companies scattered around the country. Because of their interstate character, they were able to evade any real State regulation.

This holding company device came to be widely used by electric power and gas companies. Financiers who controlled holding companies claimed that their holding companies promoted large-scale production and greater efficiency. Opponents showed that their very complexity made it possible for shrewd financiers to conceal profits which should rightfully have been used to reduce the price of electricity and gas.

Therefore, in 1935 Congress directed the SEC to require a full and fair disclosure of the corporate structure of holding company systems. The Commission was also directed to eliminate uneconomic holding company structures and to supervise security transactions and other operations of *electric* and *gas* holding companies.[10]

Other acts administered by the SEC include the Investment Company Act of 1940, covering the operations of investment trusts, and the Investment Advisers Act of 1940, covering the operations of investment counselors in relations with their clients. Trading on the agricultural commodity exchanges is regulated by the Commodity Exchange Authority in the Department of Agriculture.

WHAT THIS CHAPTER IS ABOUT

The First Bank of the United States (1791 to 1811) and the Second bank (1816 to 1836) were the forerunners of the system of national banks created by Congress in 1863. Today there are two principal systems of banks in the United States: State banks (private banks chartered by the States) and national banks (private banks chartered by the National Government).

All national banks and most State banks do the general business of commercial banks. One group of State banks, mutual savings banks, restrict their business to the receipt and investment of small savings deposits. National banks are subject to both State and national regulation.

The Federal Deposit Insurance Corporation insures deposits in national banks, in State banks which are members of the Federal Reserve System, and in some nonmember State banks, up to $10,000.

The Federal Reserve System was created by Congress in 1913 to give the nation's banks the strength of unity.

The system of Farm Credit Banks was created by Congress in 1933 to co-ordinate various lending programs intended to aid the farmers.

The Federal Home Loan Bank System

---

[10] The actual *operating* electric and gas companies, as distinguished from the *holding* companies, are regulated by the Federal Power Commission (see pages 327–328).

was created in 1932 to provide a credit reserve for savings and home-financing institutions. These member institutions, now numbering more than 4300, make loans to home builders.

The Small Business Administration was set up in 1953 to replace the Reconstruction Finance Corporation. The SBA is designed to encourage small businesses by making financial help available and otherwise assisting them.

The Export-Import Bank, created in 1934, makes loans to encourage trade by other countries with the United States.

The Securities and Exchange Commission, also established in 1934, is the general policeman for securities trading in the United States.

QUESTIONS ON THE TEXT

1. What was the principal argument which arose over the creation of the First Bank of the United States? Why was it of crucial importance to our constitutional history?

2. Describe the First and Second Banks.

3. Why is the case of *McCulloch* v. *Maryland* so important in our history?

4. What are the two principal systems of banks in the United States today? What is a mutual savings bank?

5. Where may national banks establish branches?

6. What is the Federal Deposit Insurance Corporation?

7. How many Federal Reserve Banks are there?

8. What banks are members of the Federal Reserve System?

9. What powers has the Board of Governors of the Federal Reserve System?

10. What is a Federal Land Bank? Who may borrow? At what interest rate? For what period?

11. Why was the Small Business Administration created? What agency did it succeed?

12. What is the particular function of the Export-Import Bank?

13. What are " blue-sky " laws?

14. Why was the Securities and Exchange Commission created?

15. What is a holding company?

PROBLEMS FOR DISCUSSION

1. During hard times a merchant in a small city will quite likely go to a national bank to borrow money by giving his note. Why is he more liable to get his money now than before the creation of the Federal Reserve System?

2. The Panic of 1907 was caused largely by a hoarding of money. Why is such a situation almost impossible today?

3. Why do you favor or oppose federal insurance of bank deposits up to $10,000?

4. In 1936 private bankers wanted 5 per cent interest for money to refinance Great Northern Railway bonds which were coming due. The Reconstruction Finance Corporation agreed to refinance the bonds at 4 per cent. With this encouragement, the railroad was able to sell its bonds at 4 per cent to its own stockholders and bondholders, thus saving $1,000,000 annually. Why do you favor or oppose such government competition with private banks?

THINGS YOU MIGHT DO

1. The class might visit a local bank and observe its various operations or invite a local banker to address the class.

2. An officer of a local federal savings and loan association, national farm loan association, or other lending institution might also be invited to address the class.

3. A local banker or investment counselor might be invited to discuss the making of investments with the class.

WORDS AND PHRASES YOU SHOULD KNOW

" Blue-sky " laws
Bonds
Caveat emptor
Caveat vendor
Commercial banks
Comptroller of the Currency
Export-Import Bank
Farm Credit Administration
Federal Deposit Insurance Corporation
Federal Home Loan Bank System
Federal Land Banks
Federal Reserve System
Federal Savings and Loan Associations

First Bank of the United States
Holding company
McCulloch v. *Maryland*
Mutual savings banks
National Banking Act of 1863
National banks
Reconstruction Finance Corporation
Second Bank of the United States
Securities and Exchange Commission
Small Business Administration
State banks
Stocks

SELECT BIBLIOGRAPHY

" A Hard Look at Consumer Credit," *Life,* November 21, 1955.

CARR, ROBERT K., and others, *American Democracy in Theory and Practice,* Chapters 27, 28. Rinehart, 1955.

JOHNSON, CLAUDIUS O., *American National Government,* Chapters 17, 18. Crowell, 1955.

ROHLFING, CHARLES C., and others, *Business and Government.* Foundation Press, 1953.

SHIELDS, MURRAY, " No More Depressions? " *U.S. News,* December 23, 1955.

SWARTHOUT, JOHN M., and BARTLEY, ERNEST R., *Principles and Problems of American National Government,* Chapter 18. Oxford, 1955.

" The President's Economic Adviser, Arthur F. Burns, Forecasts the Business Future of America," *U.S. News,* May 6. 1955.

" The Signal Callers for Squeeze on Money," *U.S. News,* September 21, 1956.

" What Tight Money Really Means," *U.S. News,* September 14, 1956, also *Reader's Digest,* December, 1956.

The old imperialism — exploitation for foreign profit — has no place in our plans.

— *Harry S. Truman*

★

Chapter 20

TERRITORIES AND OTHER DEPENDENCIES

The United States emerged from the Revolutionary War as a Union of thirteen States spread along the Atlantic seaboard. By the Treaty of Paris, which officially ended the war in 1783, we also possessed all the territory from the Great Lakes to Florida and west to the Mississippi. But this was only a beginning.

The Louisiana Purchase in 1803, the annexation of Florida in 1819, the annexation of Texas in 1845, the Oregon Treaty in 1846, the cessions from Mexico in 1848, and the Gadsden Purchase in 1853 rounded out the continental United States. Since then, we have added far-flung possessions to our domain. Today, the American flag flies over an insular empire of more than 700,000 square miles.

Powers over Territories

Power to Acquire. The Constitution does not give Congress the *expressed* power to acquire (take possession of) new territory. However, the Supreme Court has held on several occasions that the United States has the same right as any other sovereign state to acquire territory.[1]

---

[1] In 1856 Congress authorized the President to take jurisdiction over guano islands discovered by American citizens. In 1890 the Supreme Court upheld the act when it ruled: "By the law of nations, recognized by all civilized states, dominion over new territory may be acquired by discovery and occupation, as well as by cession or conquest."

The power to make treaties implies the power to gain territory by treaty. The power to make war implies the right to make conquests. The power to admit new States implies the power to obtain territory out of which new States might be made.

Power to Govern. The Constitution *does* give Congress the expressed power to govern the territories of the United States. Article IV, Section 3 provides:

The Congress shall have power to dispose of and make all needful rules and regulations respecting the territory or other property belonging to the United States.

In time of war, the President governs any territory occupied by the armed forces under his powers as Commander-in-Chief.

Classification of Territories. Congress has divided the territories into two classes: *incorporated* and *unincorporated*.

The *incorporated territories* are those that Congress has declared to be *a part of* the United States. Today the incorporated territories are Hawaii and Alaska. All parts of the Constitution — except those that clearly and expressly apply only to the admitted States — apply to these territories of Hawaii and Alaska.

For example, the constitutional requirement that all indirect taxes must be " uniform *throughout the United States*," means that indirect taxes must be levied at the same rates in the two incorporated territories as they are within the forty-eight States.

The incorporated territories are looked upon as capable of governing themselves and on the road to eventually becoming States.

The *unincorporated territories* include all of our other possessions. They *belong to* but are not legally *a part of* the United States.

In some instances it is difficult to draw a sharp distinction between the incorporated and unincorporated territories. As we shall see, Congress has granted a considerable measure of self-government to Puerto Rico, Guam, and the Virgin Islands.

The District of Columbia is not a " possession " or " territory " in the sense that the other areas are. It is a federal district set aside as the site for the nation's capital. But, still, none of these could be said to be on the way toward becoming States.

In the case of our other territories, like the Canal Zone and various Pacific islands, the distinction is clearer. These territories do not govern themselves and are held only for some special reason, usually their strategic location.

Hawaii

The Hawaiian Islands were discovered and explored by Captain Cook, an Englishman, in 1778.[2] The foreign riffraff of explorers and whalers who

---

[2] Though the name did not stick, Cook named the Islands the " Sandwich Islands " in honor of his patron, the Earl of Sandwich. (The Earl was so fond of playing cards that he would not stop to eat. He would have a servant bring him a slice of cold meat between two slices of bread so he

visited the Islands in the next half century acted on the assumption that no laws, whether of God or man, were in force west of Cape Horn. But the coming of the missionaries in 1820

---

could eat while playing. The combination became known as a " sandwich.") At first, Cook was taken as a god by the natives. But the outrageous conduct of his crew emboldened a native to kill him with a dagger.

brought civilization to the natives of the Islands.

Hawaii was ruled by a native monarchy until 1893. In that year a revolution, carried out mainly by Americans, overthrew the government of Queen Liliuokalani and established a republic. In the same year the Islands unsuccessfully sought annexation to the United States.

Hawaii's strategic location and value as a naval base became apparent during the Spanish-American War. So, in 1898, the Congress passed a joint resolution annexing the Territory of Hawaii.

The Territory is in the mid-Pacific, about 2400 miles south and west of San Francisco. It consists of twenty islands, nine of which are inhabited, with a total area of 6435 square miles. According to the 1950 census, the population is 499,794.[3] Of these, those of Japanese descent comprise about a third, white Americans about a third, only two per cent are pure Hawaiian, and the rest are Hawaiians in part, Filipinos, Chinese, Koreans, Portuguese, and others.

Any person born in Hawaii is an American citizen at birth and may enter and leave the continental United States on the same basis as any other citizen. Immigration is regulated under the same laws as the mainland.

Government. Congress passed an Organic Act providing for the government of the Territory in 1900. It was patterned after the laws for the then

Hawaii Visitors Bureau

SUGAR CANE EXPRESS

Much like a toy train, the little " sugar cane express " hauls tons of cut cane to one of the many mills in the Hawaiian Islands. More than a million tons of sugar are grown there each year. Raising sugar is the greatest industry in Hawaii.

Territories of Oklahoma, New Mexico, and Arizona.[4] Under it, all provisions of the Constitution and laws of the United States, except where special exception was made or where they were locally inapplicable, were extended to Hawaii. In effect, the Organic Act is Hawaii's constitution.

The Hawaiian government is divided into three branches — executive, legislative, and judicial.

The *Governor* is the Territory's chief executive. He is appointed by the President and Senate for a four-

---

[3] Hawaii's 1940 population was 423,330.

[4] All of our States were territories before becoming States, except the original thirteen and Maine, Vermont, Kentucky, West Virginia, Texas, and California.

year term and must be a resident of the Islands. He appoints the chief administrative officers with the advice and consent of the territorial senate and exercises the usual powers of a State governor, including the power to veto bills passed by the legislature and separate items in appropriations bills.

The *Legislature* is bicameral. The Senate consists of fifteen members popularly elected for a four-year term. The House of Representatives has thirty members elected for two years. Regular sessions are held biennially and are limited to sixty days. The legislature may enact any law which does not conflict with the Constitution, laws, or treaties of the United States. However, Congress has imposed restrictions on the legislature, especially in regard to financial matters.

The *Judiciary* is actually composed of two court systems: one federal and one territorial. A United States District Court hears all federal cases arising in the Territory. Its two judges are appointed by the President and Senate for six years. The territorial courts, which handle all non-federal cases, consist of a supreme court, five circuit courts, and several local district courts.

A *Territorial Delegate* to Washington is elected by the people for each term of Congress. He sits in the House of Representatives and may debate and serve on committees, but he cannot vote. His salary is the same as that of a Congressman.

Taxation. Hawaiians pay the same federal taxes and duties on goods from other countries that are paid in the forty-eight States. Of course, there is no tariff on goods shipped either way between Hawaii and the mainland. Local taxes are levied by the legislature just as in the States.

Education. Hawaii is at the crossroads of the Pacific and the races meet with practically no conflict. The public schools use only English and are constantly merging the various racial stocks into loyal American citizens.

The Island's economy is largely based on the $250,000,000-a-year sugar cane and pineapple crops. The tourist trade is quite important, too. World War II and the Korean war booms have expanded the economy, but there is still a wide gap of imports over exports.

Statehood? Hawaii has been asking for Statehood since the turn of the century. Since 1937 various Congressional committees have investigated the question on the spot and have all recommended it. The Hawaiians themselves have voted more than two to one for Statehood and they have already drafted a proposed State constitution.

Both major parties are on record in favor of Statehood. With more than half a million people, Hawaii has a larger population than any of our States at the time of admission except Oklahoma. Her commercial and military importance make the "Crossroads of the Pacific" at least as important as some of our States.

Those who oppose Statehood cite

the distance from the mainland and the character of the population as their main arguments. The advocates note the fact that California is closer to Hawaii than it is to most of our Eastern States. Her various mixed races live harmoniously and democratically according to our constitutional principles and customs.

The Hawaiian people demonstrated unquestionable loyalty to the United States in World War II and Korea. Her men have served and are serving with distinction in our armed forces.

The people of Hawaii have amply demonstrated their ability for self-government in the past half-century. Statehood now seems but a question of time. It was nearly granted in 1954: the Senate passed a measure to admit both Hawaii and Alaska, but the House, which had previously passed a bill for Hawaii, refused to agree to Alaska, too. The issue failed in 1955, 1956, and 1957, and is now before Congress again.

Alaska

Alaska is the oldest and largest of our territories. We purchased it from Russia in 1867 for $7,200,000. Because Alaska lies in the same latitudes as Norway and Sweden and much of it is frozen waste, many called it " Seward's Folly " and " Seward's Icebox " (after Secretary of State William Seward who negotiated the purchase).

It wasn't generally realized that those parts of Alaska affected by the Japanese Current have winters more moderate than those in many of our Northern States. Nor was Alaska's great natural wealth known.

The Territory is 586,400 square miles in area, larger than our three largest States combined. The 1950 population was 128,643 [5] — of which number some 33,000 were Indians and Eskimos.

Government. Although the treaty of cession granted citizenship to all

inhabitants, it was not until 1912 that Congress passed an Organic Act for Alaska. Today it is governed much like Hawaii. Its inhabitants pay federal taxes and are subject to other federal statutes as is Hawaii.

The *Governor* is appointed by the President and Senate for a four-year term and has the usual powers of a State governor. He does not have to be a resident of Alaska.

The *Legislature* is bicameral. The Senate consists of sixteen members and the House of twenty-four. The legislature meets biennially for a period of not more than sixty days. Its laws must not conflict with the Constitution, laws, or treaties of the United States or with the Organic Act. Congress may disapprove acts of the Alaskan legislature, but seldom does.

As an example of the restrictions imposed by Congress, neither the Hawaiian nor the Alaskan government may grant a divorce to anyone who

---

[5] Alaska's population increased by 75 per cent over the 1940 census (72,524).

has not lived in the territory for at least two years.

The *Judiciary* consists of one United States District Court organized into four divisions. The judges are appointed by the President and Senate for terms of four years.

A *Territorial Delegate* is elected every other November to represent Alaska in the Congress. Like the delegate from Hawaii, he sits in the House of Representatives, debates, and serves on committees, but has no vote. His salary is the same as that of a Congressman.

Proposed State Constitution. In 1956 the voters of Alaska gave overwhelming approval to a constitution for use if and when Alaska becomes a State. The document was drafted by a convention composed of fifty-five popularly elected delegates representing all parts of the territory. In framing the document the convention gave careful study to the Federal Constitution and to the present State constitutions. Their product has been described by students of government as "one of the finest ever written."

Like the Federal Constitution, the proposed Alaska constitution is short and flexible — those who wrote it had no desire to hamstring the Alaskans of the future.

The proposed constitution provides for only two elected executive officers — the Governor and the Secretary of State. These officers would be chosen together, as a unit, to serve four-year terms. The Secretary of State would succeed to the governorship if that office became vacant. All other executive officers would be appointed by the Governor.

The legislature would be bicameral with a Senate composed of twenty members elected for four-year terms and a House of Representatives of forty members chosen for two-year terms. (A unicameral legislature was seriously considered by the framers.)

The court system would be headed by a Supreme Court with lesser courts to be created by the legislature. The Governor would appoint judges from among persons nominated by a judicial council of representatives of the legal profession and the public.

The minimum voting age would be set at nineteen and local government would be in the hands of boroughs (roughly corresponding to counties) and cities.

The Resources of Alaska are great. It has gold, coal, copper, timber, water power, fish, seals, oil, and many valuable mineral deposits. The canning and salting of fish is a big industry.

The Pribilof Islands are the breeding grounds for the world's largest herd of fur-bearing seals.[6] Because

---

[6] In May of each year the 500-pound bull seals arrive and fight over areas for their harems. In June when the 100-pound cows arrive, the bulls drag as many as possible to their harems and then stand guard over them without food, drink, or rest for several weeks. After a pregnancy of nearly a year, the cows deliver their pups. Then the breeding season follows again. Some 60,000 young bachelors are slaughtered each year by the Fish and Wildlife Service to provide skins for sealskin coats.

the seals were becoming extinct, the United States, Canada, Russia, and Japan entered into a treaty in 1911 to prevent indiscriminate slaughter. The Pribilof herd, under the management of the Fish and Wildlife Service, has increased from 132,000 to more than 3,000,000. Each year enough surplus three-year-old males are taken to produce furs worth $5,000,000.

There is enough spruce and hemlock in Alaska's steep coastal forests to provide a sustained yield of a billion board feet a year. The agricultural resources in the millions of unbroken acres of grasslands and rich valleys have been barely tapped and present a challenge much like that which faced the pioneer settlers of our Far West. Gold is still produced in quantity and oil resources are being explored and exploited.

Alaska's Strategic Location may be seen from a quick glance at a globe. Any future attack on the United States would probably come by long-range bombers and guided missiles across the Arctic. The tip of the Aleutian Island chain is less than a mile from Russian territory.

Effective defense has required bases not only in Alaska, but in northern Canada, Greenland, and Iceland, too. The Alcan highway from the United States to Alaska was built during World War II to reduce the submarine danger. It is now maintained by Canada.

Statehood for Alaska seems farther away than for Hawaii. The Alaskan legislature has unanimously petitioned Congress in favor of it and Alaskan voters have approved it. But opponents feel that Alaska is not nearly as developed as it should be to become a State.

Puerto Rico

The United States took possession of Puerto Rico in 1898 during the Spanish-American War, and acquired it by treaty the following year. The Island lies southeast of the United States on the northeastern rim of the Caribbean Sea. Its area is 3435 square miles and its population in 1950 was 2,210,703. Three-fourths of the population is white; the rest, mulattoes and Negroes.

Government. A new constitution, which was drafted by the Puerto Ricans themselves, went into effect on July 25, 1952, fifty-four years to the day after American troops hauled down the Spanish flag and ran up the Stars and Stripes. Earlier in the year, the constitution had been approved by a popular majority of more than four to one and had then been approved by Congress. (From 1900 until 1952 the Island's basic charter was an Act of Congress. We have told the Puerto Ricans that they may have full independence whenever they want it.)

The convention which drafted the constitution made a careful study of the United States Constitution and of the constitutions of the various States.

As a result, the new document contains many provisions common to constitutions adopted by the States, as well as other provisions which are designed primarily to meet local problems.

Under its new constitution, Puerto Rico is a " commonwealth . . . within our union with the United States of America." The basic relationships between Puerto Rico and the United States remain largely unchanged. Thus, Puerto Ricans are still American citizens. The Island remains within the American tariff system and continues to enjoy free trade with the mainland. Its citizens are still subject to federal law, but they have control over their own internal affairs much as in the States of the Union. For example, Congress no longer has the power to repeal laws made by the Puerto Rican legislature.

The *Governor* is popularly elected for a term of four years.[7] He must be at least 35 years of age, and he must have been, for at least five years preceding his election, a citizen of the United States and a *bona fide* resident of Puerto Rico. The governor is vested with those powers usually lodged with a chief executive under our form of government, including the veto power. He appoints, with Senate consent, the heads of departments in the executive branch. Succession to the governorship falls to the Secretary of State.

The *Legislative Assembly* consists of a Senate and House of Representatives. The Senate has 27 members, two elected from each of the eight senatorial districts plus eleven chosen at large. The House contains 51 members, one elected from each of forty districts and eleven at large. Under a novel provision, whenever one political party gains more than two-thirds of the seats in either house the number of seats in that house may be increased to broaden the representation of the minority party or parties.[8]

Members of both houses are popularly elected for a term of four years and must be both United States and Puerto Rican citizens. A governor's veto may be overriden by a two-thirds vote of the total membership of each house. Although, as we have seen, Congress and the President no longer

---

[7] The system of voting in Puerto Rico is unique, and seems fraud-proof. Voters are required to be in their polling places before one o'clock. At that hour the doors are locked and the voting begins. Each registered voter's name is called in alphabetical order and he receives his ballot and casts his vote.

[8] This provision amounts in effect to a modified form of proportional representation (see page 455). If one party gains more than two-thirds of the seats in either house, but does not gain more than two-thirds of the votes cast for governor, the number of seats at large is increased. This is done by declaring enough candidates of the minor party (or parties) elected to bring its total to 9 in the Senate or 17 in the House, as the case may be. If the dominant party obtains *more* than two-thirds of the votes for governor, enough additional minority candidates (but not exceeding 9 in the Senate and 17 in the House) are declared elected to bring the representation of minority parties as close as possible to the proportion of votes cast for each party in the gubernatorial election.

have the power to void laws passed by the Puerto Rican legislature, these laws must not be contrary to the Constitution, laws, or treaties of the United States.

The *Judiciary* has long since been almost completely Americanized in form, law, and procedure. The Supreme Court is the Commonwealth's highest court. It consists of a Chief Justice and four Associate Justices. They are appointed by the Governor and the Senate and hold office for life or good behavior. The number of justices cannot be changed unless at the direct request of the Supreme Court itself. The lower courts are established by the Legislative Assembly. There is also a United States District Court for Puerto Rico.

A *Resident Commissioner*, elected by the voters every four years, represents the Island in Washington. Unlike the delegates from Hawaii and Alaska, he has no statute right to a seat in the House, but under the House rules he is given the privilege of debate and may serve on committees though he may not vote. He receives the same salary and allowances as a Congressman.

The *Bill of Rights* in the Commonwealth's constitution includes provisions similar to those in the Constitution of the United States and those of the States. In addition, it contains express provisions regarding public education, the conditions of labor, and the protection of private property.

Constitutional amendments may be proposed by two-thirds of the total membership of each house of the Legislative Assembly. They are ratified by a majority of the voters at a general or special election.

The finances of Puerto Rico are not handled like those of the incorporated territories (Alaska and Hawaii). Instead of paying the internal revenue taxes levied by Congress, the local legislature levies these taxes for Puerto Rico, including the income tax. Commodities between Puerto Rico and the United States do not pay tariff duty, but articles entering the United States from Puerto Rico must pay the United States internal revenue tax, and articles from the United States entering Puerto Rico must pay the Puerto Rican internal revenue tax. Articles entering Puerto Rico from countries other than the United States pay the same tariff duties that they would pay if entering the United States. All of these taxes go into the treasury of the Puerto Rican Government.

Tax revenues and federal grants-in-aid come to about $165,000,000 a year. Included in this total are: some $65,000,000 from excise taxes, $60,000,000 from local income and property taxes, a refund of about $17,-000,000 in U.S. internal revenue taxes on rum imported from Puerto Rico, and $20,000,000 in grants-in-aid.

Economic Conditions. Writing in 1897, a high official in Spanish-controlled Puerto Rico had this to say about the Puerto Rican laborer: " With a pale face, bare feet, lean body, ragged clothes, and feverish look, he walks indifferently, with the

THE UNIVERSITY OF PUERTO RICO

The beautiful campus of the University is located at Rio Piedras, a short distance from the capital city of San Juan. Puerto Rico also supports a Polytechnic Institute.

shadows of ignorance in his eyes, dreaming of the cockfight, the shuffle of the cards, or the prize in the provincial lottery."

The masses continue very poor in Puerto Rico but a definite improvement in their lot has been developing, especially in the last few years. Yet the average annual income is only about twenty-five per cent of that per person in the States. Some 2,200,000 people live on the Island, averaging 641 people to the square mile, compared with 50 in the United States. The total population is in-

creasing at the rate of 70,000 each year. Only half of the land is arable and there is little mineral wealth.

The migration of thousands of the Island's people to the continent and to neighboring Spanish-speaking countries is a practical, though temporary, solution to the economic plight.[9]

---

[9] As Puerto Ricans are citizens of the United States they may come here without restriction. In recent years several thousands have come to New York by boat and plane each month. Most of them settle in already overcrowded areas and get jobs in the needle trades, restaurants, as janitors, or in helping crews clean ships.

354   *Unit IV.* ADMINISTRATIVE AGENCIES AND THE TERRITORIES

Some of the facts just cited once led observers to call Puerto Rico " Uncle Sam's neglected stepchild." Today, the child is coming of age. The Island Government, with the backing of Washington, is bringing about a modern " industrial revolution," and a progressive, dynamic Commonwealth is in the making.

" *Operation Bootstrap,*" as it is called, is a concerted effort to free the Island of its economic chains. American businesses are being encouraged to build their new plants in Puerto Rico. As one way of attracting these businesses, the Government grants acceptable businesses an almost complete exemption from Puerto Rican property and income taxes until 1959, with partial exemption from then until 1962. The large population provides a ready labor source and the Government is more than willing to co-operate in every way. A program of hydroelectric development is helping to bring in industry from the United States.

While taxes in the States are going up and regulations are becoming more stringent on the mainland, the Island becomes all the more attractive to American investors. Over 400 new factories have been opened by American and Puerto Rican capital since the program began. Under present plans it is hoped that 150 more will be added each year until 1960.

This recent and rapid expansion has been accompanied by related governmental efforts in other fields, such as education and social welfare. As one observer puts it, the program " has been like a sack of feed set in front of a starving chick." Ten years ago the Island's net income (total amount earned by residents and corporations after taxes and depreciation) was $359,000,000; now it has risen to more than $1,000,000,000 a year. Employment has increased greatly. And the sharp lines between the many poor and the very few rich are being rubbed out by a rising middle class.

Vocational schools have been established and, amazing as it may seem, more than one-fourth of the Island's governmental budget, or some $35,-000,000, is earmarked for education. A great many slums still exist, but a vigorous low-cost housing program is making inroads. Sugar is still the backbone of the Island's agricultural economy, but pineapple, tobacco, and coffee are increasingly important.

The program still has a long way to go, but the goal for 1960 has been set at a $2,000,000,000 net income for the Island — or just twice what it is today. Puerto Rico still has a long way to go, yes. But the future is bright, and this proud Island promises to become, as did the Philippines, a model for other colonial domains around the world.

Guam

The island of Guam in the Marianas was ceded to us by Spain in 1899. It comprises only 206 square miles in all and has a population

(1950) of only 59,498. But it has an importance all out of proportion to its size. Its strategic location makes it invaluable as a naval and air station.

With the exception of the two years that Japan occupied the island in World War II, Guam was governed by the Navy until 1950. In that year Congress passed an Organic Act which makes all Guamanians citizens of the United States.

Guam is still an unincorporated territory. But under the act, it now has a bill of rights, a governor appointed by the President and Senate, and a popularly elected single-house legislature. In addition to these there is a United States District Court for Guam.

Huge naval and military installations are maintained on the island. The area is administered under the Office of Territories in the Department of the Interior.

Trust Territory of the Pacific Islands

The United States Trust Territory of the Pacific Islands consists of three island groups: the Marshalls, the Marianas, and the Carolines. They lie east of the Philippines and include some 98 islands and island clusters with a total land mass of only 687 square miles, a total population of about 55,000 natives, and negligible resources.

The islands were held by Germany until the peace settlements of World War I when Japan received them under a mandate from the League of Nations. The United States conquered them in World War II and in 1947 the islands became a trusteeship of the United States by unanimous vote of the UN Security Council.

The Trust Territory is governed by a High Commissioner under the Secretary of the Interior. He is appointed by the President and Senate.

The area is worthless to us except for defense purposes. Some islands are fortified as naval and air bases, and we have conducted several atomic and hydrogen bomb test explosions in this area.

Other mid-Pacific islands also belong to the United States. Wake, Midway, and Johnston Islands, and Kingman Reef are administered by the Navy. The Interior Department administers Samoa, Baker, Howland, Jarvis, Canton, and Enderbury Islands — the last two jointly with the British. The islands are valuable for aeronautical, naval, meteorological, and radio purposes.

The United States controls, but does not have title to, the Ryukyu, Bonin, and Volcano island groups, and Parece Vela, Rosario, and Marcus Islands in the Western Pacific. All were wrested from Japan in World War II; Iwo Jima in the Volcanoes and Okinawa in the Ryukyus were the scenes of especially bitter fighting. We control these under the Japanese peace treaty and have the right to request a UN trusteeship over them.

PRINCIPAL TERRITORIES	DATE ACQUIRED	PRIOR STATUS	HOW ACQUIRED	AREA (SQ. MI.)	POPULATION (1950)
Alaska	1867	Russian possession	Treaty with Russia, purchased for $7,200,000	586,400	128,643
Hawaii	1898	Independent republic	Annexed by joint resolution of Congress	6,423	499,794
Guam	1898	Spanish possession	Conquest and Treaty, Spanish-American War	206	59,498
Puerto Rico	1898	Spanish possession	Conquest and Treaty, Spanish-American War	7,435	2,210,703
Panama Canal Zone	1903	Panamanian territory	Treaty with Panama, rented in perpetuity for $10,000,000 plus annual payment (now $1,930,000)	553	52,822
Virgin Islands	1917	Danish possession	Treaty with Denmark, purchased for $25,000,000	133	26,665
Trust Territory of the Pacific Islands	1947	Japanese mandate	Conquest in World War II and UN Trusteeship	8,475	54,843
The Philippines (Independence granted July 4, 1946)	1898	Spanish possession	Conquest and Treaty, Spanish-American War	114,830	19,497,700
District of Columbia	1791	Portion of Maryland	Donated by Maryland, accepted by acts of Congress, 1790–91	69	802,178

The Panama Canal Zone

The Panama Canal Zone is a strip of land extending five miles on either side along the famous Canal. A treaty with Panama in 1903 gave us the Zone in return for an original payment of $10,000,000 plus an annual rent which now amounts to $1,930,000. We possess the territory in perpetuity (forever).

The Canal Zone includes the Chagres River, where dams have been built to store water during the rainy season as a supply for operating the locks during the dry season. It also includes all of the lake created by Gatun Dam.

MIRAFLORES LOCKS

The Canal was opened in 1914 and is just a little over fifty miles long. Privately owned vessels pay the United States a toll of $1.20 a ton for passage. This means, for example, a $12,000 toll on a 10,000-ton vessel. Tolls collected in the fiscal year 1957 amounted to more than $40,000,000.

The Zone's population is 52,822 and most of the inhabitants are connected with the operation of the Canal.

During the construction of the Canal, the Zone was administered by a Commission appointed by the President. In 1913, with the work on the Canal nearly completed, Congress authorized the President to appoint a Governor and such other officers as he might find necessary.

Today the President and Senate appoint the Governor for a four-year term. He is usually an Army engineer and administers the affairs of the Zone under the Secretary of the Army. Because there is no local legislature, such laws as operate within the area are either enacted by Congress or take the form of Presidential orders. Because of the President's influence in the governing of the Canal Zone, it has been called a " crown colony."

Organized towns (with no elective officials) and a system of courts have been provided by Congress. There is one District Court with several magistrates' courts (much like justice of the peace courts) under it. Congress has provided for the extension of the Bill of Rights to the Canal Zone.

The Virgin Islands

The Virgin Islands, consisting of St. Croix, St. Thomas, St. John, and fifty-odd other small and uninhabited islands, lie east of Puerto Rico. The total area is only 132 square miles. Christopher Columbus named the island group after Saint Ursula and her 11,000 virgins because the islands were too many to name individually.

We purchased the islands by treaty with Denmark in 1917 for $25,000,-000. They are valuable to us because of their strategic location and the fine harbor at Charlotte Amalie, on St. Thomas.

The 26,665 inhabitants are mostly Negro. Congress extended citizenship to them in 1927. The governor, appointed by the President and Senate, operates under the supervision of the Secretary of the Interior. A bicameral and popularly elected legislature meets at the capital, Charlotte Amalie. A District Court and several lower courts form the territory's judiciary.

The District of Columbia

The Constitution gives Congress the power to " exercise exclusive jurisdiction " over a district " not exceeding ten miles square " which might be donated by one or more of the States as the " seat of government." [10]

The actual location of this district was the subject of stormy debate. Philadelphia, New York, Trenton, Baltimore, and other cities vied for the honor, but none of these was chosen.

In 1791 Congress accepted grants of land along the Potomac River from Maryland and Virginia. A city was then laid out along the Maryland side of the river and the National Government moved there in 1800.[11]

---

[10] Section I, Section 8, Clause 17.
[11] George Washington was inaugurated President and the First Congress met in Federal Hall in New York City in 1789. The temporary national capital was moved to Philadelphia in late 1790 and remained there until 1800.

Under the mistaken notion that it would never be needed, Congress returned to Virginia in 1846 the land she had originally donated. Today the District consists of sixty-nine square miles on the Maryland side of the Potomac.

Government. For most of the period before 1871, Congress permitted Washington to be governed by a locally-elected mayor and council. But corruption and inefficiency became so marked that that government was abolished in 1871. A so-called territorial government existed from 1871–1874. But it was overly zealous and high-handed in the use of its powers to develop the capital, and it piled up an alarming debt.

In 1874 Congress placed the debt-ridden District in the hands of a sort of receivership under three commissioners. The arrangement was supposed to be temporary but became permanent because Congress could not agree upon any substitute plan.

Since 1878 the District of Columbia has been administered by a three-man Board of Commissioners. Two of these are local residents appointed for three-year terms by the President and Senate. The third Commissioner is an engineer detailed by the President from the United States Army to serve for an indefinite period. Other officers are likewise appointed by the President. The three Commissioners direct most of the city departments, such as fire, traffic, police, and public health. They recommend needed legislation to Congress, but Congress is the only legislative body for the District. Thus the Commissioners may act only within limits set by congressional statute.

All bills relating to the governing of the District are considered by committees, usually by the House Committee and the Senate Committee on the District of Columbia, or by the House Committee and the Senate Committee on Appropriations. It is at public hearings of these committees that the people of the District make their views and wishes known. These committees have their hands full, but, unfortunately, most other members of Congress tend to shy away from the problems of the District.

Congress used to appropriate half of the total expenses for the District, but this proportion has been reduced since 1920. The federal payment now amounts to approximately $20,000,000 a year.

This amounts to less than one-tenth of the District's expenditures. This appropriation is made because the Government owns so much tax-exempt property, makes much use of services rendered by District agencies (water, etc.), and wants an especially fine capital city.

The Problem of Self-Government in the District. Since 1874 residents of the District have been denied the right to elect the officials of their local government. Because the District is not a State, they have never been permitted to vote for presidential electors nor are they represented in Congress. It is paradoxical that a republic, proud of its system of representative government, should have " taxation without representation " in its very capital of 802,178 people.

Numerous proposals have been made to rectify this situation. Constitutional amendments and bills on the subject have been introduced in every recent Congress. An amendment would be needed to grant presidential suffrage in the District.[12] But, by statute, Congress could grant home rule and provide for representation by a District delegate (much like the Hawaiian and Alaskan delegates).

Various bills providing for municipal home rule have come close to final passage in recent years. The pro-

---

[12] The United States Constitution provides that each *State* shall choose as many presidential electors as it has Senators and Representatives in Congress. The District of Columbia has no congressmen; therefore it would be unconstitutional for Congress to grant presidential suffrage to the District.

posal with the most support today is one providing for a mayor-council form of government much like that found in many other large cities. Under it, a District Council, Mayor, Board of Education, and Delegate to Congress would be popularly elected. The Council would assume the powers of the present Board of Commissioners and, as well, have local legislative powers, much like those of the Hawaiian and Alaskan legislatures.

At present, if any change is to be made, the plan for home rule appears to have the best possibilities for adoption by Congress. There are a number of municipal associations through which the citizens can express themselves on problems of local government.

The Philippines

The Philippine Republic has been an independent and sovereign state since 1946. But the Islands were an American possession for nearly half a century. The Republic is vitally important to our defense and stands on the very doorstep of Asia as an object lesson in democracy and American intentions.

The archipelago consists of more than 7000 islands with a total area of 115,600 square miles — larger than Great Britain and about the size of the State of Nevada. According to the last census (1950) the population was 19,497,700. It is the only Christian nation in the Orient.

The United States took possession of the Philippines in 1898 during the Spanish-American War. Spain ceded them to us the following year. Almost immediately the United States began preparing the Islands for independence.

Step-by-step, more and more local control over the government was granted. In 1934 Congress passed an act truly remarkable in the annals of colonialism. This Philippine Independence Act directed the Filipinos to draft their own constitution and created the Philippine Commonwealth.

In 1937, Manuel Quezon, the first President of the Commonwealth, said:

The Philippines have been assisted economically and schooled politically by the United States for nearly forty years. No people in history, coming under a foreign flag, have ever been treated so generously.

The 1934 Act promised full independence in ten years. But the Japanese occupied the Islands during World War II. Independence was proclaimed by the United States and the new Philippine Republic on July 4, 1946. Today, as a sovereign state, the Republic is recognized by practically all governments and is a member of the United Nations.

The United States could not just simply step out of the picture with the granting of independence. Three years of Japanese occupation and the fight to retake the Islands had left them shattered.

Three Lions

PLEDGE OF INDEPENDENCE
Philippine citizens demonstrate in favor of independence. This was on the occasion of the visit to Manila of a high American official, before 1946.

Since the end of the war we have spent over $2,000,000,000 to help in rehabilitation. The money has been used to bolster the economy and to build or rebuild hospitals, schools, highways, bridges, and the like. Much of this money also went in the form of back pay to Filipinos who served as guerillas against the Japanese.

Further to aid recovery, Philippine products were admitted to this country duty-free until 1954. Until 1974 the tariff rates are being gradually increased to bring them up to the levels applied to other nations.

The Islands are a vital link in our defense chain in the Pacific. In 1947 we signed a 99-year treaty under which we maintain air, land, and sea bases in the Philippines. We also have a mutual defense pact with the Republic and continue to train the Philippine armed forces. A large detachment of Filipino combat troops fought valiantly under the United Nations command in Korea. In 1954 the Philippines joined with us and six other nations in the South East Asia Treaty Organization against communist aggression.

The Filipinos are not yet on a stable

economic footing. The troubles caused by the communist-led Hukbalahaps (Huks) have been practically eliminated by the late President (and former Defense Minister) Ramón Magsaysay.

But the future is bright. The Filipinos can look back on a decade of progress and forward to the promise of much to come. And the rest of the world can see the Republic of the Philippines as an inspiring example of American intentions and American-style democracy in action.

WHAT THIS CHAPTER IS ABOUT

In addition to the continental United States, we hold a far-flung insular empire of more than 700,000 square miles. Congress has the power to acquire territory because the United States is a sovereign nation and, by implication, because of the war and treaty powers and the power to admit new States. Congress has the expressed power to govern the territories.

Congress has divided the territories into two classes. (1) The incorporated territories (Hawaii and Alaska) are those that Congress has declared to be *a part of* the United States. All applicable parts of the Constitution extend to them and they are considered on the road to eventual Statehood. (2) The unincorporated territories *belong to* but are not *a part of* the United States. These territories are: Puerto Rico, the Panama Canal Zone, the Virgin Islands, Guam, the Trust Territory and several other mid-Pacific islands.

The Philippines, now an independent Republic, were prepared for self-government by the United States. They stand on Asia's doorstep as an object lesson in democracy and American intentions.

The District of Columbia, seat of our nation's capital, is not actually a territory but a federal district provided for in the Constitution.

QUESTIONS ON THE TEXT

1. What authority does Congress have to acquire territory? Govern it?

2. Distinguish between our incorporated and unincorporated territories. Which are incorporated?

3. How and when did we acquire Hawaii? Alaska?

4. Are persons born in Hawaii American citizens? In Alaska?

5. How are the governors of Hawaii and Alaska chosen? The legislatures?

6. By whom are Hawaii and Alaska represented in Washington? How do they compare with a Congressman?

7. Why was Alaska once called "Seward's Icebox"?

8. What are the major arguments advanced for and against Hawaiian Statehood?

9. What are the prospects for Alaskan Statehood?

10. How and when did we acquire Puerto Rico?

11. Describe the Puerto Rican constitution.

12. How is the governor of Puerto Rico chosen? The legislature?

13. What is the novel legislative representation scheme in the Puerto Rican constitution?

14. Why is Guam so important to us? How and when did we acquire it?

15. What three groups of islands constitute the Territory of the Pacific Islands? How and when did we acquire them? How are they governed?

16. How and when did we acquire the Panama Canal Zone? How is it governed?

17. How does the Constitution provide for the District of Columbia? How is the District governed today?

PROBLEMS FOR DISCUSSION

1. The work of the early Christian missionaries from the United States is one of the reasons why there is less racial prejudice in Hawaii than in most places where Orientals and Occidentals mingle. What does the Bible teach regarding the brotherhood of man? What other reasons for the fact that racial prejudice has been a very minor problem in Hawaii can you suggest?

2. The United States has officially informed the Puerto Ricans that they may have full independence whenever they want it. Why have they not asked for it?

3. The latitude of Alaska is the same as that of Scandinavia. Because of this, many say that it is possible for Alaska to attain as high a degree of development. What is your opinion?

4. Article 73 of the United Nations Charter provides in part that those nations with dependent people should guide them toward self-government. In what ways has the United States done this with her territories?

5. Why do you think Congress has denied the residents of the District of Columbia the right to elect local officers? Why do you think Congress has not proposed an amendment to the Constitution providing for congressional and presidential suffrage for the District?

THINGS YOU MIGHT DO

1. Hold a class debate on the question: *Resolved,* That Hawaii (and/or Alaska) should be granted Statehood.

2. Each of our possessions could be the subject of research and a report by various groups of students. Each report could treat of such matters as the history, government, people, culture, education, resources, economy, etc., of the particular territory.

WORDS AND PHRASES YOU SHOULD KNOW

Acquire	Mandate	Trusteeship
Incorporated territory	Territorial Delegate	Unincorporated territory

SELECT BIBLIOGRAPHY

CARTER, HODDING C., " The Case For Hawaii," *Saturday Evening Post,* June 12, 1954.

GRUENING, ERNEST, " Statehood for Alaska," *Harper's,* May, 1953.

MAGSAYSAY, RAMÓN, " The Philippines — Democracy in Asia," *Collier's,* January 7, 1955.

MONRONEY, SENATOR A. S., " Let's Keep It 48," *Collier's,* March 4, 1955.

" Operation Bootstrap," *Life,* May 21, 1956.

UNIT V
THE JUDICIARY
AND CIVIL RIGHTS

Supreme Court Building

TYRANNICAL GOVERNMENTS . . . immemorially utilized dictatorial criminal procedure and punishment to make scapegoats
of the weak, of helpless political, religious, or racial minorities,
and of those who differed, who would not conform and who
resisted tyranny. . . . The rack, the thumbscrew, the wheel,
solitary confinement, protracted questioning and cross-questioning, and other ingenious forms of entrapment of the helpless
or unpopular . . . left their wake of mutilated bodies along
the way to the cross, the guillotine, the stake, and the hang-
man's noose.

JUSTICE HUGO BLACK
Chambers v. *Florida,* 1940

★

Chapter 21

THE NATIONAL COURT SYSTEM

A system of courts is as vital to the successful functioning of government as are the legislative and executive branches. The legislature makes the laws, the executive administers and enforces them, and the judiciary (court system) interprets and applies them.

Creation of the National Judiciary

There was no national system of courts under the Articles of Confederation. The acts and treaties of Congress were interpreted and applied by each State, through its own courts. Each State's courts decided disputes between their own and other States and between their citizens and those of other States.

The result was chaos and confusion. Alexander Hamilton spoke for most of the Founding Fathers when he called " the want of a national judiciary . . . a circumstance which crowns the defects of the Confederation." And, arguing the need for a *national* system of courts, Hamilton added:

Laws are a dead letter without courts to expound and define their true meaning and operation.

Article III, Section 1, of the Constitution creates the national judiciary in one brief sentence:

The judicial power of the United States shall be vested in one Supreme Court, and in such inferior courts as the Congress may from time to time ordain and establish.

Types of Courts Created. Thus the Constitution itself creates only the Supreme Court of the United States. It leaves to Congress the creation of any and all other federal courts. In exercising this power, Congress has created two types of courts:

(1) *The Constitutional Courts* are those that Congress has created under Article III to exercise " the judicial power of the United States." These are the Supreme Court, the Courts of Appeals, the District Courts, and (since 1953) the Court of Claims.

(2) *The Special Courts* do not exercise " the judicial power of the United States." Rather, they have been created by Congress to hear and decide cases that arise under certain of the delegated powers. These are the Customs Court, the Court of Customs and Patent Appeals, the territorial courts, the courts of the District of Columbia, and the Court of Military Appeals.

Constitutional Courts

Jurisdiction. Jurisdiction is the right of a court to hear and determine (try and decide) a case. Under Article III, the federal courts have jurisdiction over a case because of (1) the subject matter involved or (2) the parties involved.

(1) *Subject Matter.* Two classes of cases may be brought into the federal courts because of the subject matter involved: (1) cases arising under the Constitution, laws, or treaties of the United States, and (2) cases of admiralty or maritime [1] jurisdiction.

(2) *Parties.* Six classes of cases may be brought into the federal courts because of the parties involved: (1) cases affecting ambassadors, other public ministers, and foreign consuls, (2) cases to which the United States itself is a party, (3) cases between two or more States, (4) cases between citizens of different States (so-called cases in diverse citizenship), (5) cases between citizens of the same State who claim land under grants from different States, and (6) cases between a State, or its citizens, and foreign states, or its citizens.[2]

Concurrent and Exclusive Jurisdiction. In *some* of the cases we have just listed, the federal courts have *exclusive jurisdiction*. That is, the cases may be heard *only* in the federal courts. For example, cases involving ambassadors, other public ministers, and foreign consuls are within the exclusive jurisdiction of the federal courts. So are such other cases as those involving admiralty and maritime, patent, copyright, and bankruptcy matters.

---

[1] *Admiralty* cases are those that arise on the high seas or navigable waters of the United States.

Maritime cases are those that arise on land but are directly related to the water, *e.g.*, a contract to deliver ship's supplies at dockside.

---

[2] Under the 11th Amendment, adopted in 1798, a State *may not* be sued in the federal courts by a citizen of another State or of a foreign state. A State *may* be sued without its own consent in the federal courts only by another State or a foreign state. If a citizen of the same or another State or of a foreign state wishes to sue a State, he may do so only with that State's consent and only in its own courts. However, a State may bring a suit against a citizen of another State, an alien, or a foreign state in the federal courts.

Unit V. THE JUDICIARY AND CIVIL RIGHTS

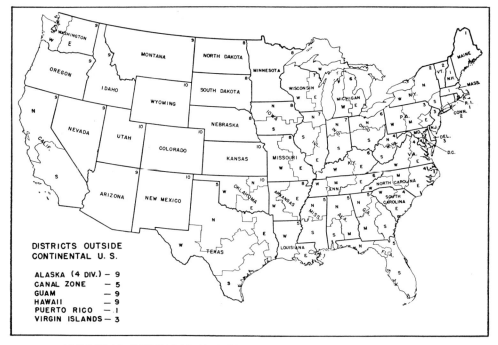

FEDERAL JUDICIAL DISTRICTS AND CIRCUITS

Letters indicate northern, southern, eastern, western, and middle
judicial districts. Numbers indicate judicial circuits.

DISTRICTS OUTSIDE
CONTINENTAL U. S.

ALASKA (4 DIV.) — 9
CANAL ZONE — 5
GUAM — 9
HAWAII — 9
PUERTO RICO — 1
VIRGIN ISLANDS — 3

Some cases, particularly those involving residents of different States, may be heard *either* in a United States District Court *or* in a State court. In such instances, the federal and State courts have *concurrent jurisdiction:* they share jurisdiction. Congress has provided that the District Courts may hear such a case *only* if the amount involved exceeds $3000. In such a case, the *plaintiff* [3] may bring suit in the State or federal court, as he chooses. But, if he brings it in the State court, the *defendant* [4] may have it trans-

ferred to the federal District Court.

Original and Appellate Jurisdiction. A court in which a case is first heard is said to have *original jurisdiction* over it. A court which hears cases on appeal from lower courts is said to have *appellate jurisdiction*.

In the federal court system, the District Courts have only original jurisdiction; the Courts of Appeals have only appellate jurisdiction; and the Supreme Court has both kinds of jurisdiction, though most of its cases come on appeal.

The District Courts. The lowest federal courts, the District Courts, were first created by Congress in 1789. There are ninety-one of them

[3] A *plaintiff* is a person who commences a suit in law against another.

[4] A *defendant* is a person accused or summoned into court who defends himself against the charge.

today. The forty-eight States are divided into eighty-four judicial districts, with one court for each district. Congress has created seven other District Courts for the District of Columbia and the territories.

Each State forms at least one district, but the larger ones include two or more districts. Each district has at least one judge but many have several. Thus New York is divided into four districts and one of them has eighteen judges. By 1958 there were 253 district judges.

District Court cases are usually heard by a single judge. But in a few cases three judges form the court. In these instances, it is said that the court sits *en banc*. They sit *en banc* when an effort is made to have the District Court enjoin (that is, forbid, issue an injunction, an order forbidding) the enforcement of a State law or an order of a State or federal agency.

Jurisdiction. The District Courts have original jurisdiction over all cases that may be heard in the federal courts except those that come under the original jurisdiction of the Supreme Court and those that are heard in the special courts. (The Supreme Court's original jurisdiction and the special courts are discussed later.)

Cases heard in a District Court may be appealed to the Court of Appeals. In a few cases, however, appeals go directly to the Supreme Court: injunction orders issued *en banc,* certain decisions holding acts of Congress unconstitutional, and certain decisions in criminal cases.

The Courts of Appeals. The Courts of Appeals were created in 1891 to relieve the Supreme Court of the large number of cases appealed from the District Courts. These had become so numerous that the Supreme Court was almost three years behind in its business.

The United States is divided into eleven judicial circuits, including the District of Columbia as one of them. There is a Court of Appeals for each circuit. Each Court of Appeals has from three to nine judges (sixty-eight in all) and one justice of the Supreme Court is also assigned to each one.

For example, the Court of Appeals for the Fifth Circuit covers Texas, Louisiana, Mississippi, Alabama, Georgia, Florida, and the Canal Zone. It has seven circuit judges plus Associate Justice Hugo Black of the Supreme Court. It holds its sessions at Fort Worth, New Orleans, Montgomery, Atlanta, and Jacksonville.

Jurisdiction. Congress has greatly limited the types of cases that may go to the Supreme Court as a matter of right. The highest court hears only the more important cases. Of course, this adds to the importance of the Courts of Appeals. They hear appeals from the District Court, the Court of Claims, the special courts, and the independent regulatory agencies, such as the Federal Communications Commission.

Normally, cases are heard by three judges, and a District Court judge is occasionally assigned to sit on cases not appealed from his district.

THE JUDICIAL BRANCH

Supreme Court decisions have shaped history. The present Court, under the leadership of Chief Justice Warren, has handed down many history-making decisions.

The Supreme Court. The Supreme Court is the only court specifically provided for in the Constitution. It consists of a Chief Justice, who is also provided for in the Constitution, and eight associate justices.

Its chief duty is to interpret the Constitution and apply it to cases as they come before the Court. How tremendously important this is to our whole system of government is readily seen when you recall discussions of *Marbury* v. *Madison* (pages 59–60), the informal amendment of the Constitution (pages 72–74), and *McCulloch* v. *Maryland* (pages 107–109).

The Supreme Court is, as Chief Justice Hughes said, " a continuous Constitutional Convention "; the Constitution " means what the judges say it means."

Jurisdiction. The Supreme Court has both original and appellate jurisdiction. That is, some cases are brought directly to the Supreme Court and other cases (most of them) are brought on appeal from the lower courts.

The Court has original jurisdiction in two types of cases: (1) those involving State v. State or the United States v. State and (2) those affecting

Chapter 21. THE NATIONAL COURT SYSTEM   371 ambassadors, other public ministers, and consuls.[5]

The Court has appellate jurisdiction in all other cases it hears.

How Cases Reach the Court. The Supreme Court sits from October to June. During its term hundreds of cases are appealed to it, but only some 100 are actually decided. In the others, the petitions (requests) for review are denied — either because the Court is in full agreement with the decision of the lower court or because no important point is involved.

Cases reach the Court either by *appeal* or by *writ of certiorari. Appeals* are had when one of the parties to the suit petitions the Supreme Court for review. A *writ of certiorari* is an order by the Court directing a lower court to " certify " or send up the complete record in a given case.

The cases come from the highest court in each State, from the Courts of Appeals, and, in a few instances, from the District Courts.

Generally the Court picks and chooses the cases it will hear. Those that it takes are usually ones that involve questions of constitutionality or other grave national questions.

How Cases are Decided. In cases that are reviewed, both parties (the litigants) submit written briefs. These

briefs, which sometimes run to hundreds of pages, set forth the arguments and many times form the basis for the Court's final decision.

Each side is allowed one hour of oral argument during which the justices often interrupt with questions. After the case has been heard, each justice makes up his own mind.

Then, each Friday at noon the justices meet in private conference. They sit around a conference table with the Chief Justice presiding. The late Chief Justice Harlan Fiske Stone thus described what takes place:

At Conference each case is presented for discussion by the Chief Justice, usually by a brief statement of the facts, the question of law involved and with such suggestions for their disposition as he may think appropriate. No cases have been assigned to any particular judge in advance of the Conference. Each Justice is prepared to discuss the case at length and to give his views as to the proper solution of the questions presented. In Mr. Justice Holmes' pungent phrase, each must be able to " recite " on the case. Each Judge is requested by the Chief Justice, in the order of seniority, to give his views and the conclusions which he has reached. The discussion is of the freest character and at its end, after full opportunity for each member of the Court to be heard and for the asking and answering of questions, the vote is taken and recorded in the reverse order of the discussion, the youngest, in point of service, voting first.

On the same evening, after the conclusion of the Conference, each member of the Court receives at his home a memorandum from the Chief Justice advising him of the assignment of cases for opinions. Opinions are written for the most

---

[5] The District Courts also have jurisdiction over suits involving consuls, but not ambassadors or other public ministers. The exemption of ambassadors, ministers, and consuls from suit in State courts applies only to those of foreign governments accredited to the United States. It has no application to those we send to foreign countries.

Unit V. The Judiciary and Civil Rights

part in recess, and as they are written they are printed and circulated among the justices, who make suggestions for their correction and revision. At the next succeeding Conference these suggestions are brought before the full Conference and accepted or rejected as the case may be. On the following Monday the opinion is announced by the writer as the opinion of the Court.

A majority is needed for decision. Some cases are decided unanimously but others find the Court split. Written opinions, which explain the justices' reasoning, accompany each decision. If the decision is not unanimous, dissenting opinions are also written. Concurring opinions are often written, too; in these, one or more of the justices explain why they agree with the majority or the minority but for differing reasons.

The opinions of the Court are not really necessary to a decision. But they serve as valuable " precedents " which are followed in similar cases as they arise in other courts or reach the Supreme Court. Chief Justice Hughes described dissenting opinions as " an appeal to the brooding spirit of the law, to the intelligence of a future day." The minority opinion of the Court today might become its majority opinion tomorrow.

The Court of Claims. It is an ancient principle of public law that a sovereign state cannot be sued against its will. Before the establishment of the Court of Claims in 1855, anyone having claims against the United States could get redress (payment) only by a special act of Congress. Originally created as one of the special courts, Congress made the Court of Claims a constitutional court in 1953. It consists of a chief judge and four associate judges who sit *en banc* in Washington.

Jurisdiction. The Court of Claims handles claims arising out of the Constitution, acts of Congress, regulations of the executive departments, and contracts entered into by the United States.

The awards of this court, unlike those of any other, cannot be paid until Congress appropriates the money to pay them; money is appropriated almost as a matter of course, however.

Occasionally, those who lose cases in this court still manage to convince their Congressmen that they should be compensated. Not long ago, a mink rancher lost a case in which he claimed that low-flying Navy planes had caused several of his female mink to become sterile. He asked $100 a head, but the Government was able to show that any one of several things could have caused the condition; diet, weather, fights, etc. Still, his Congressman introduced a bill that finally paid him $10 for each animal.

Special Courts

The special courts have been created by Congress to exercise jurisdiction only in certain cases. They have no jurisdiction from the Constitution but only that which Congress gives them.

The Customs Court. The Customs Court was created to decide disputes that arise out of decisions made by customs officers. It was first created in 1890 as the Board of General Appraisers, but Congress changed its name to the present one in 1926. Its nine judges, one of whom is the Chief Judge, sit in divisions at the principal ports of entry.

The Court of Customs and Patent Appeals. This court consists of five judges and was created in 1910. It hears appeals from the Court of Customs and has such questions as these to decide: Are golf socks subject to the duty imposed on " wool half hose " or the lower duty imposed on " equipment ordinarily used with golf balls in exercise or play "? Are jew's-harps dutiable as " musical instruments " or " toys "? Are goose livers dutiable as " dressed poultry " or " meats "?

If an examiner in the Patent Office rejects a person's application for a patent, an appeal may be taken to the Board of Appeals within the Patent Office. If the Board upholds the examiner's rejection, further action may then be taken by appealing to the Court of Customs and Patent Appeals.

The Territorial Courts. Under its power to govern the territories of the United States, Congress has established local courts in Hawaii, Alaska, Guam, Puerto Rico, the Virgin Islands, and the Panama Canal Zone. (See Chapter 20.)

The Court of Military Appeals. This court was created in 1950 and consists of a Chief Judge and two associate judges. It is independent as are all other United States courts but is attached to the Defense Department for administrative purposes. It hears appeals from the decisions of the more serious courts-martial (trials of members of the armed forces under an act of Congress, the Uniform Code of Military Justice).

The Courts of the District of Columbia. Congress has created a court system for the District of Columbia. (See Chapter 20.)

The Tax Court. An Agency in the executive branch, this court is not a part of the national judiciary. It is composed of sixteen judges appointed by the President and Senate for twelve-year terms. The court's principal office is in Washington but the judges hear cases throughout the country. It hears appeals from the decisions of tax officers in the Treasury Department.

Judges

Appointment, Term, Salary. All federal judges are appointed by the President and Senate. The Constitution sets out no qualifications, so the President is free to appoint anyone the Senate will confirm. He usually draws his appointees from the ranks of leading attorneys, professors of law, former members of Congress, and the State courts. Often, judges of the Courts of Appeals and the Supreme Court are former District Court judges.

All federal judges are appointed for life or good behavior.[6] They may be removed only by impeachment. As we learned in Chapter 5, only nine federal judges have ever been impeached and four of those were acquitted by the Senate.[7]

Judges of the District Courts and the Court of Customs receive $22,500 in salary a year. Those of the Courts of Appeals, Court of Claims, Court of Customs and Patent Appeals, and Court of Military Appeals each receive $25,500 a year. Associate Justices of the Supreme Court receive $35,000 and the Chief Justice $35,500 a year.

Federal judges who are appointed to hold office during good behavior may resign at age seventy and, if they have served for at least ten years, receive their full salary for the rest of their lives. Or they may retire and receive full salary if they reach age sixty-five and have served fifteen years, or age seventy and have served ten years on the Bench. Retired judges may be called back to active service in the lower courts at any time.

Court Officers

Clerks are appointed by the courts, each having one. They have custody of the seal of the court, keep the records of its proceedings, and are assisted by deputy clerks, stenographers, bailiffs, and such other attendants as are needed.

United States Commissioners are appointed by each District Court in whatever number it needs. They serve four-year terms and issue warrants of arrest, take bail, and determine whether the probability of guilt is sufficient to hold an accused person to answer the charges against him in court.

United States Attorneys and Marshals are not officers of the courts. They serve within the Justice Department.

(For the State judicial systems, see Chapters 29 and 30.)

[6] Except judges of the territorial courts who are appointed for terms varying from four to eight years and judges of the Court of Military Appeals who serve fifteen-year terms.

[7] Judge Pickering of the District Court for New Hampshire was removed for drunkenness in 1803; Judge Humphreys of the District Court for Tennessee, for disloyalty in 1862; Judge Archibald of the Commerce Court, for improper business relations with persons having cases in court in 1913; and Judge Ritter of the District Court for Southern Florida, for bringing his court into scandal and disrepute in 1936. Four other judges have been impeached by the House but acquitted by the Senate. The most famous of these was Associate Justice Samuel Chase of the Supreme Court who was accused in 1804 of " expressing himself too freely in regard to politics." A few District Court judges have resigned to avoid impeachment. One was impeached but resigned before the Senate could try him.

WHAT THIS CHAPTER IS ABOUT

THE NATIONAL JUDICIARY

COURT	CREATED	NUMBER OF COURTS	NUMBER OF JUDGES	TERM OF JUDGES	JUDGES APPOINTED BY	SALARY OF JUDGES
District Court	1789	91	253	Life	President & Senate	$22,500
Court of Appeals	1891	11	68	"	"	25,500
Supreme Court	1789	1	9	"	"	35,000 [8]
Court of Claims	1855	1	5	"	"	25,500
Customs Court	1926	1	9	"	"	22,500
Court of Customs and Patent Appeals	1910 & '29	1	5	"	"	25,500
Court of Military Appeals	1950	1	3	15 yrs.	"	25,500

[8] Chief Justice receives $35,500.

The lack of a national judiciary was one of the most serious weaknesses in the Articles of Confederation. The Founding Fathers corrected this in Article III of the Constitution. There the Supreme Court is provided for and Congress is given the power to create whatever lower courts are needed.

Two types of federal courts have been created: the constitutional and the special. The constitutional courts are the District Courts, Courts of Appeals, Supreme Court, and Court of Claims. The special courts are the Customs Court, Court of Customs and Patent Appeals, territorial courts, courts of the District of Columbia, and Court of Military Appeals.

The constitutional courts have jurisdiction over a case either because of the subject matter or the parties involved. Some cases are within the exclusive jurisdiction of the federal courts while in others concurrent jurisdiction exists with

State courts. Cases first heard in a court are within its original jurisdiction; those heard on appeal are within its appellate jurisdiction.

The ninety-one District Courts hear all federal cases except those within the Supreme Court's original jurisdiction and that of the special courts. The Courts of Appeals hear cases on appeal from the District Courts, the Court of Claims, the special courts, and the independent regulatory agencies. The Supreme Court is the highest court in the land. It generally chooses the cases it will hear from the lower federal courts and the highest State courts. It has original jurisdiction over cases involving ambassadors, other public ministers, and consuls, and over those involving State v. State and United States v. State. The Court of Claims hears cases involving claims against the United States.

The special courts have such jurisdiction as Congress gives them. The Customs Court hears appeals from decisions of customs officials. Appeals from its rulings and from those of the Patent Office go to the Court of Customs and Patent Appeals. The territorial courts and those of the District of Columbia hear cases from those areas. The Court of Military Appeals reviews serious courts-martial decisions. The Tax Court is an independent agency in the executive branch, hearing appeals from decisions of tax officials in the Treasury. Clerks, United States Commissioners, and other lesser officers assist the federal courts.

QUESTIONS ON THE TEXT

1. Name the constitutional courts of the United States. The special courts.

2. The federal courts have jurisdiction over what two classes of cases because of the character of the subject matter? Over what six classes because of the character of the parties?

3. How many District Judges are there and how many districts?

4. The District Courts have jurisdiction over what kind of cases?

5. To what higher courts may appeals be taken from the District Courts?

6. How many Courts of Appeals are there? Who supervises each of the circuits?

7. How many judges has each of the Courts of Appeals?

8. From what courts are cases appealed to the Courts of Appeals? To what court are certain cases appealed from them?

9. Of how many judges does the Supreme Court of the United States consist? When and where does the Court sit?

10. From what courts are cases appealed to the Supreme Court of the United States?

11. In what two classes of cases does the Supreme Court have original jurisdiction?

12. May a question involving the interpretation of the Constitution be taken to the Supreme Court?

13. Of how many judges does the Court of Claims consist? What cases are decided by this court? In what respect does the Court of Claims differ from all other courts?

14. What is the Court of Military Appeals?

15. Who appoints federal judges? For what term? How may they be removed? Under what conditions may they retire on full salary?

PROBLEMS FOR DISCUSSION

1. A woman attempted to pass a fifty-dollar note at Gimbel's store in New York City, but the clerk detected something peculiar about it. The floor detective discovered it to be a twenty-dollar bill with each figure two changed to five. The woman was arrested on the charge of attempting to pass counterfeit money. She was believed to be a " shover " for a band of counterfeiters. In what court was she tried?

2. At a " port of entry " along the Canadian border frog legs were appraised as dressed poultry, there being a tariff duty on poultry but not on frogs. Naturally the importer was dissatisfied with the decision of the appraiser. In what court could he bring suit?

3. The penalty for defacing a letter box is a fine not exceeding one thousand dollars or imprisonment for not more than three years, or both. In what court

would a party accused of this offense be tried?

4. If Virginia should pass a law prohibiting farm hands from working more than six hours a day, the law would probably be unconstitutional. If a sheriff or constable should arrest a farmer for violating the State law and bring him before a justice of the peace for trial, he could claim that the law is unreasonable and contrary to the 14th Amendment of the Constitution of the United States. If the lower courts should decide against the contention, how high could the farmer appeal the case?

5. In 1942, just after the beginning of World War II, all persons of Japanese ancestry — aliens and citizens — were compelled to leave their homes along the West Coast. Those not leaving voluntarily were taken to relocation internment camps. The federal courts declared this action to be constitutional during the war period of great national emergency. In what federal court did a Japanese bring his case? Appealed how high?

6. When the Chicago Canal was dug, connecting Lake Michigan with the Illinois River, the sewage of Chicago was emptied into this Canal. The outlet of the Canal is through the Illinois River into the Mississippi. St. Louis obtains its drinking water from the Mississippi; hence the State of Missouri sued the State of Illinois, demanding that Chicago be prohibited from polluting the accustomed supply of water of St. Louis. The counsel for Illinois had several hundred barrels of harmless bacteria emptied into the stream at Chicago and found that none survived until the water reached St. Louis. In what court did Missouri lose the suit?

7. In 1938 Congress authorized innocent persons convicted in United States courts to bring suit against the United States for damages not exceeding $5000. In what court would such a claim be brought?

8. What court of appeals decided that calf livers were dutiable as " meat " and not as " veal," and that a dollar horn is a " musical instrument " and not a " toy "?

9. Theodore Roosevelt once said: " A judge of the Supreme Court is not fitted for the position unless he is a constructive statesman, constantly keeping in mind his adherence to the principles and policies under which this nation has been built up and in accordance with which it must go on; and keeping in mind also his relations with his fellow statesmen who in other branches of the government are striving in co-operation with him to advance the ends of government. Marshall rendered invaluable service because he was a statesman of the national type, like Adams who appointed him, like Washington whose mantle fell upon him." Do you agree with Theodore Roosevelt? When the Court is interpreting the act for minimum wages, maximum hours, and the exclusion of child-made goods from interstate commerce, is it merely explaining the words of the Constitution or is it performing the function of a statesman?

THINGS YOU MIGHT DO

1. Write a short essay based on this quotation from Chief Justice Hughes:

Democracy will survive only as long as the quick whims of the ma-jority are held in check by the courts in favor of a dominant and lasting sense of justice. If democratic institutions are long to survive it will not be simply by maintaining majority rule and by the swift adaptation to the demands of the moment, but by the dominance of a sense of justice which will not long survive if judicial processes do not conserve it.

2. If possible, one or more students might attend a session of the nearest United States District Court and report their observations of the proceedings to the class.

3. Invite a local judge or attorney to speak to the class on the nature of the law, the legal profession, and our court system.

WORDS AND PHRASES YOU SHOULD KNOW

Admiralty cases
Appeal
Appellate jurisdiction
Concurrent jurisdiction
Concurring opinion
Constitutional courts
Defendant

Dissenting opinion
En banc
Exclusive jurisdiction
Judicial circuit
Judicial district
Judiciary
Jurisdiction
Litigant

Majority opinion
Maritime cases
Original jurisdiction
Petition
Plaintiff
Special courts
Writ of certiorari

SELECT BIBLIOGRAPHY

BROWNELL, ATTORNEY GENERAL HERBERT, " Creeping Justice," *Coronet*, September, 1956.

CARR, ROBERT K., and others, *American Democracy in Theory and Practice*, Chapters 10, 11, 12. Rinehart, 1955.

DABNEY, VIRGINIUS, " He Made the Court Supreme," *Saturday Evening Post*, September 24, 1955.

HUSTON, LUTHER A., " How the Supreme Court Reaches a Decision," *New York Times Magazine*, May 24, 1953.

" Is Justice Breaking Down in U.S.? Shortage of Judges and Money Jams Courts," *U.S. News*, December 24, 1954.

LAWS, JUDGE BOLITHA J., " It Is the Sentence of the Court . . ." *Collier's*, October 14, 1955.

LEWIS, ANTHONY, " Our Extraordinary Solicitor General," *The Reporter*, May, 1955.

MAYERS, LEWIS, *The American Legal System*, Harper, 1955.

RODEBAUGH, EVERETT G., " The Trials I've Seen! " *Saturday Evening Post*, July 25, 1953.

SWARTHOUT, JOHN M., and BARTLEY, ERNEST R., *Principles and Problems of American National Government*, Chapter 15. Oxford, 1955.

VANDERBILT, JUDGE ARTHUR, " Court System Reform a Pressing Problem," *Time*, February 21, 1955.

" What a Court Can Do to Enforce Its Orders," *U.S. News*, September 28, 1956.

> If there is any fixed star in our constitutional constellation, it is
> that no official, high or petty, can prescribe what shall be orthodox
> in politics, nationalism, religion, or other matters of opinion or
> force citizens to confess by word or act their faith therein.
>
> — *Justice Robert H. Jackson*

★

Chapter 22

CIVIL RIGHTS
AND LIBERTIES

We know by heart these hallowed words from the Declaration of Independence:

We hold these truths to be self-evident: that all men are created equal; that they are endowed by their Creator with certain unalienable Rights; that among these are Life, Liberty and the pursuit of Happiness.

The very next line of the Declaration adds these words:

That to secure these rights, Governments are instituted among men . . .

Ours is a democratic government, a government of, by, and for the people. Because it is democratic, our government is a *limited* government. It is not all-powerful; it has *only* those powers the sovereign people have granted to it.[1]

It is in the area of civil rights — the individual liberties of the American people — that government is most severely limited in the United States. In a democracy such as ours, the state exists for the people, not the people for the state. Government is only a means to an end. That end is the good life for all.

Contrast this with the underlying principle of dictatorships where the people exist for the state, not the state for the people. Thus in the Soviet Union no opposition to the dictatorship is tolerated. Even art, music, literature must glorify the state.

Nature of Our Civil Rights

Historical Background. As we noted in Chapter 3, the concept of civil rights is one of those valuable legacies which came to us from England and was so important to the shaping of American government. Over a

---

[1] See pages 40–41.

THE ROAD TO FREEDOM

John Hancock proposed, in Boston, 1788, that the Bill of Rights be added to the Constitution. This was an important milestone in the course of civil liberties.

period of several centuries, Englishmen had fought a continuing struggle to establish individual liberties. The early colonists brought these hard-won freedoms with them to the New World. Indeed, many of the colonists came to the New World in order to find greater personal freedom.

Civil rights took root and flourished in the fertile soil of America. The Revolutionary War was fought to maintain and expand the rights of individuals versus government. Long Bills of Rights were included in the first State constitutions.

The National Constitution, as drafted at Philadelphia in 1787, contained no listing of the basic rights held by people. The outcry this omission raised was so marked that several States ratified the original Constitution only on condition that a Bill of Rights be added immediately. The first session of the First Congress in 1789 proposed the first ten amendments, which became a part of the Constitution on December 15, 1791.

Later amendments, especially the 13th and 14th, have added to the Constitution's guarantees.

The Courts and Civil Rights. In the United States the courts, and especially the United States Supreme Court, stand as the principal guardian of individual liberties. It is the courts which must interpret and apply those parts of the National and State Constitutions that guarantee civil rights. They protect us against arbitrary acts of government and against the unlawful acts of other individuals.

The fact that the courts do stand as our guardians does *not* mean, however, that we as citizens can sit back in assured safety. Nor does the fact that the National and State Constitutions contain lists of basic rights mean that our forefathers have bought and paid for them and that they are ours forever. To continue and to perfect our liberties, each new generation must learn and understand these liberties anew and be willing to fight for them. Eternal vigilance is indeed the price of liberty.

Civil Rights are Relative, not Absolute. Even though basic civil rights are guaranteed to *everyone* in the United States, *no one* has the right to do whatever he pleases. If each person could do exactly as he pleased, he would soon be interfering with the rights of his neighbors. Each person's rights are *relative* to the rights of all.

For example, each person in the United States enjoys the right of free speech, but no person has *absolute* freedom of speech. Thus a man who uses obscene language may be punished by a court for committing a crime.

Liberty, then, must be exercised with due regard for the rights of all others.

Persons to Whom Rights Are Guaranteed. In most of its civil rights provisions the Federal Constitution makes its guarantees to *all persons*. The Supreme Court has often held that the word " persons " includes aliens as well as citizens.

Not *all* rights are extended to aliens, however. For example, the 2nd Amendment forbids the National Government from interfering with the " right to keep and bear arms." Aliens, however, may be and are restricted in this connection.

In 1942, shortly after the beginning of World War II, all Japanese living on the West Coast were evacuated inland. Some 120,000 persons, at least two thirds of whom were *native-born American citizens,* were involved. These people were interned in " war relocation camps " operated by the Government.

The relocation program caused severe economic and personal hardship for many. In 1944, however, the Supreme Court held that the program was legal as a wartime emergency measure.

The action has been criticized ever since. Japanese-Americans fought heroically in the armed forces in World War II, and no single case of *Nisei* (American-born Japanese) disloyalty in the course of the war has ever been found.

Federalism Complicates Our System of Civil Rights. We have, as you well know, a federal system of government in the United States. Federalism affects our system of civil rights in these several ways:

(1) There are some civil rights which are enjoyed against the National Government only.

CIVIL RIGHTS GUARANTEED IN THE FEDERAL CONSTITUTION

AGAINST THE NATIONAL GOVERNMENT	AGAINST THE STATES AND THEIR LOCAL GOVERNMENTS

AGAINST THE NATIONAL GOVERNMENT

1. Writ of habeas corpus not to be suspended except in rebellion or invasion. *Art. I, Sec. 9, Cl. 2.*
2. No bill of attainder. *Art. I, Sec. 9, Cl. 3.*
3. No *ex post facto* law. *Art. I, Sec. 9, Cl. 3.*
4. Treasons specifically defined and punishment limited. *Art. III, Sec. 3.*
5. No establishment of religion. *1st Amendment.*
6. No interference with religious belief. *1st Amendment.*
7. No abridging of freedom of speech and press. *1st Amendment.*
8. No interference with freedom of peaceable assembly and petition. *1st Amendment.*
9. No interference with right of people to keep and bear arms. *2nd Amendment.*
10. No quartering of soldiers in private homes without owners' consent. *3rd Amendment.*
11. No unreasonable searches and seizures; no warrants issued but upon probable cause. *4th Amendment.*
12. No criminal prosecution but upon grand jury action. *5th Amendment.*
13. No double jeopardy. *5th Amendment.*
14. No compulsory self-incrimination. *5th Amendment.*
15. No persons to be deprived of life, liberty, property, without due process of law. *5th Amendment.*
16. Speedy and public trial. *6th Amendment.*
17. Trial of crimes by impartial jury. *Art. III, Sec. 2, Cl. 3; 6th Amendment.*
18. Jury trial of civil suits involving more than $20. *7th Amendment.*
19. Persons accused of crime must be informed of charges, confronted with witnesses, have power to call witnesses, have assistance of counsel. *6th Amendment.*
20. No excessive bail or fines. *8th Amendment.*
21. No cruel and unusual punishments. *8th Amendment.*
22. No slavery or involuntary servitude. *13th Amendment.*

AGAINST THE STATES AND THEIR LOCAL GOVERNMENTS

1. No bills of attainder. *Art. I, Sec. 10, Cl. 1.*
2. No *ex post facto* laws. *Art. I, Sec. 10, Cl. 1.*
3. No slavery or involuntary servitude. *13th Amendment.*
4. No denial of privileges and immunities of citizens of other States. *Art. IV, Sec. 2, Cl. 1; 14th Amendment, Sec. 1.*
5. No denial of equal protection of the laws. *14th Amendment, Sec. 1.*
6. No person to be deprived of life, liberty, property, without due process of law. *14th Amendment, Sec. 1.*
7. Guarantees of freedom of religion, speech, press, assembly. *Through "Due Process" Clause in 14th Amendment.*
8. Guarantee of those freedoms "basic or essential to the American concept of liberty." *Through "Due Process" Clause in 14th Amendment.*
State constitutions also contain provisions guaranteeing rights against the State.

The security of individual liberties, whatever fine declarations may be inserted in any constitution respecting them, must altogether depend upon public opinion, and on the general spirit of the people and of the government. And, here, after all, . . . must we seek for the only solid basis of all our rights.

— ALEXANDER HAMILTON

(2) There are some civil rights which are enjoyed against the States (and their local governments) only.

(3) There are some — a great many — which are enjoyed against both the National Government and the States.

(4) Some of the civil rights enjoyed against the States arise from the National Constitution whereas others arise from the particular State constitution.

As we shall see in a moment, the Supreme Court has lessened the complicated effects of federalism on our system of civil rights through broadening its interpretation of the 14th Amendment.

The Bill of Rights Restricts the National Government Only. The guarantees found in the first ten amendments were originally intended to be, and they still are, prohibitions against arbitrary actions by the National Government. The States are *not* restricted by them.

Take one of the first ten amendments as an example to illustrate the point here. The 2nd Amendment provides as follows:

A well-regulated militia being necessary to the security of a free state, the right of the people to keep and bear arms shall not be infringed.

This means that the National Government may not interfere with the right to keep and bear arms. But the States may and do. For example, it is a crime in most States to carry a concealed weapon without permission to do so.

The 14th Amendment and the "Nationalization" of Civil Rights. The 14th Amendement, added to the Constitution in 1868, provides in part that no State may

deprive any person of life, liberty, or property, without due process of law.

This clause is borrowed from the 5th Amendment. Its primary purpose was to guarantee a fair trial to Negroes accused in State courts. For many years this is exactly the way in which the Supreme Court applied it.

Beginning with a case in 1925, however, the Supreme Court has broadened the interpretation of this clause. The Court has held that the word " liberty " in the 14th Amendment *includes within its meaning all of the provisions of the 1st Amendment.*

In other words, the Court has said that no State may interfere with an individual's freedom of religion, of speech, of press, or of assembly. To do so would be to deprive a person of his " liberty . . . without due process of law " — and this is prohibited by the 14th Amendment.

Does this seem complicated? It is, but it is also quite important. The Supreme Court has, in effect, " nationalized " the basic freedoms involved here. Thus, much of the effect that federalism has on our system of civil rights has been lessened. We now have a much more uniform national pattern of civil rights because of this " nationalization."

It must be remembered, however, that the word " liberty " in the 14th

Unit V. THE JUDICIARY AND CIVIL RIGHTS

SOME HIGHLIGHTS
OF THE
BILL OF RIGHTS

FREEDOM OF RELIGION · FREEDOM OF SPEECH · FREEDOM FROM UNREASONABLE SEARCHES · RIGHT TO ASSEMBLE · RIGHT TO PETITION · RIGHT TO JURY TRIAL AND COUNSEL · RIGHT TO SUMMON WITNESSES · NO ILLEGAL LOSS OF LIBERTY · NO EXCESSIVE BAIL OR FINES · JUST COMPENSATION FOR PROPERTY

Amendment does *not* include within its meaning the other provisions of the Bill of Rights. It includes only those matters the Supreme Court holds are "basic or essential to the American concept of liberty." Just what matters are to be considered basic or essential only the Supreme Court can say.

No Complete Listing of Civil Rights Possible. The National Constitution and the various State constitutions contain a great many provisions in regard to civil rights. Nowhere, though, is there a complete list.

In the National Constitution most of the rights it guarantees are found in the first eight amendments. Others

are found in Article I, Sections 9 and 10, and Article III, Sections 2 and 3.[2] But the 9th Amendment declares:

The enumeration in the Constitution of certain rights shall not be construed to deny or disparage other rights retained by the people.

What are these "other rights retained by the people"? It is impossible to say. As early as 1873 the Supreme Court said that discovering them must be "a gradual process of judicial inclusion and exclusion." The nature and scope of our civil rights are constantly changing as we grow as a people.

[2] You should reread these provisions of the Constitution now and refer to them as we discuss each one.

The Two "Due Process Clauses"

The United States Constitution contains two so-called "Due Process of Law Clauses." In the 5th Amendment the National Government is forbidden to deprive any person of "life, liberty, or property without due process of law." In the 14th Amendment the same restriction is placed upon the States.

Double Meaning of Due Process of Law. When one reads the phrase "due process of law" he usually thinks of due (fair or proper) procedures employed by government. This is what the phrase originally meant. It has come, however, to mean much more.

The Due Process Clause in the 14th Amendment was added to the Constitution to insure justice for former slaves. Fair procedures in court were of little value, though, if a Negro (or anyone else) could be tried under unfair laws. Because of this, the Supreme Court soon held that the guarantees of due process of law require both fair procedure *and* fair law.

Thus due process of law has two meanings, one *procedural* and the other *substantive;* in other words, the *how* and the *what* of governmental action.

Procedural Due Process. From the procedural standpoint, then, due process requires that in dealing with people [3] government must act fairly.

---

[3] Also corporations, because the Supreme Court has held that corporations are "citizens" within the meaning of the Due Process Clause of the 14th Amendment.

A recent California case provides us with a good illustration of procedural due process. A man named Rochin was suspected of selling narcotics in Los Angeles. Three deputy sheriffs went to his home. Finding the outside door open, they entered and then forced open the door to Rochin's room. They found him sitting on the side of a bed. Two capsules were lying on a night stand beside the bed. When asked "Whose stuff is this?" Rochin seized the capsules and put them in his mouth. The officers jumped on him, but he managed to swallow the capsules.

Rochin was handcuffed and taken to a hospital where his stomach was pumped. The two capsules were found to contain morphine. Rochin was convicted of violating the State's narcotics laws. The capsules proved to be the chief evidence against him, and he was sentenced to sixty days.

The United States Supreme Court reversed his conviction in 1952 on the ground that the deputies had violated the 14th Amendment's guarantee of procedural due process. Said the Court:

This is conduct that shocks the conscience. Illegally breaking into the privacy of the petitioner, the struggle to open his mouth and remove what was there, the forcible extraction of his stomach's contents — this course of proceeding by agents of government to obtain evidence is bound to offend even hardened sensibilities. They are methods too close to the rack and the screw. . . .

Substantive Due Process. Substantive due process requires that in dealing with people government must proceed under fair laws. A case from Oregon provides us with a good illustration of substantive due process.

At the 1922 election, the people of Oregon adopted a law requiring that all children between the ages of eight and sixteen who had not completed the eighth grade had to attend *public* schools. Under this law, private schools were practically abolished.

A Roman Catholic school challenged the constitutionality of the act. In 1925 the United States Supreme Court unanimously decided that the law violated substantive due process as guaranteed in the 14th Amendment. The Court held that it " unreasonably interferes with the liberty of parents to direct the upbringing and education of children under their control." It also held that the law denied private schoolteachers and administrators their liberty to make a living in a vocation " long regarded as useful and meritorious."

Conflict of the " Police Power " and the Due Process Clause. Each of our States has among its reserved powers the so-called " police power." [4] The police power is the power of the State to act to promote the public health, safety, welfare, or morals.

Whenever an act of a State (or one of its local governments) is attacked as a violation of the Due Process Clause of the 14th Amendment, the

------

[4] See table on page 388.

defense argues for it as a valid use of the police power. If the Court can be convinced that this is so, it will uphold the act as constitutional.

A Kansas case of several years ago illustrates this situation. In 1881 Kansas outlawed the manufacture or sale of intoxicating liquor, except for medicinal purposes. A man named Mugler was convicted of making and selling beer in violation of the law.

His attorneys argued that he had invested his money in a brewing business when such activity was lawful in Kansas. To deny him the right to operate his business now, they said, would be to deprive him of both liberty and property without due process of law. The United States Supreme Court refused to accept this argument. In 1887 it ruled that prohibition fell within the State's right to regulate in order to promote the public health, safety, morals, and welfare.

One liberty after another has been restricted because legislators and the courts have held health, morals, safety, or welfare of more importance than property.

To promote health, States have been permitted to forbid or restrict the sale of intoxicants and opiates, forbid the practice of medicine without a license, quarantine communicable diseases, require residences to be connected to sewers, and permit officers to seize food unfit for consumption.

To promote morals, States have been permitted to forbid gambling or the sale of lottery tickets, confiscate vehicles used in violating liquor laws,

Conflict between the "Due Process Clauses" and the Police Power

The table presents selected rulings of the United States Supreme Court to illustrate the powers and limitations of the States and of the National Government.

The States:	The National Government:
"... nor shall any State deprive any person of life, liberty, or property, without due process of law." *14th Amendment.*	"No person shall ... be deprived of life, liberty, or property, without due process of law." *5th Amendment.*

Valid Use of Police Power

In the interest of the public good, a State legislature may —	*In territories and indirectly under delegated powers, Congress may —*
HEALTH	**HEALTH**
Forbid child labor; require silver nitrate in the eyes of newborn; limit hours of work for women; quarantine; require compulsory vaccination.	Regulate sale of narcotics (under tax power); require health certificate for all entering the country (under commerce power).
SAFETY	**SAFETY**
Enact traffic regulations; require safety devices for railroads; forbid carrying of concealed weapons.	Require safety devices for interstate carriers (under commerce power).
MORALS	**MORALS**
Forbid sale of alcoholic liquor; forbid business on Sunday; forbid gambling.	Forbid interstate transportation of gambling devices or stolen goods (under commerce power).
WELFARE	**WELFARE**
Restrict use of property through zoning laws; set milk prices and rates for common carriers; compel children to attend school.	Fix prices and wages in wartime (under war powers); set rates for interstate carriers (under commerce power).

Individual Liberties Protected

But a State legislature may not —	*But Congress may not —*
Require all children to attend *public* schools.	Authorize setting of railroad rates so low as to deprive company of fair profit.
Forbid teaching of foreign languages in private schools.	Require unreasonable safety precaution by interstate carriers.
Force child to salute flag, if child's religion forbids such practice.	Make arbitrary discrimination in granting radio and television station licenses.
Require licensed barbers to have four years of college.	Permit racial segregation in schools of the District of Columbia.
Set prices for gasoline.	

forbid the sale of obscene literature, and forbid taverns in certain places.

To promote safety, States have been permitted to forbid the carrying of concealed weapons, require snow to be shovelled from sidewalks, require weeds to be removed from city lots, and require liability insurance for automobiles.

To promote welfare, States have been permitted to restrict reasonably the hours of labor, set reasonable minimum wages, restrict public utilities to reasonable profits, forbid oil and gas wells to be operated in a wasteful manner, and require cedar trees to be cut to protect orchards from cedar rust.

The Right to Freedom and Security of the Person

Every law-abiding person in the United States has the right to be free from physical restraint and to be secure in his person and secure in his home.

Slavery and Involuntary Servitude. The 13th Amendment, added to the Constitution in 1865, prohibits " slavery and involuntary servitude." Today, almost a century after slavery was abolished, there are still occasional cases of it. Only a few years ago a man and a woman were convicted in a United States District Court in Los Angeles for holding a Negro woman in slavery.

The 13th Amendment prohibits more than slavery, however. *Peonage* [5] is also forbidden. Thus a sharecropper cannot be forced to work on the land until he works out a debt to the owner or to a company store. A person may be sued for money damages if he breaks a contract, but he may quit a job whenever he wishes.[6]

The 13th Amendment, however, does not forbid certain forms of involuntary labor. There is a difference between " servitude " and " duty." The Supreme Court held in 1918 that selective service (the draft) is not a violation of the amendment; nor is imprisonment for crime, as the amendment itself declares.

" A Man's Home Is His Castle." Just as a man has a right to physical freedom he likewise has the right to be secure in his home against arbitrary governmental actions. Two of the amendments in the Bill of Rights clearly provide for this security, the 3rd and the 4th Amendments.

The 3rd Amendment forbids the quartering of soldiers in private homes in peacetime without the consent of the householder. It also states that this may not be done " in time of war, but in a manner prescribed by law." This guarantee was written into the Constitution to prevent what had been British practice in colonial days. It

---

[5] *Peonage* is a condition of servitude in which a person is bound to perform a personal service on account of debt.

[6] Except that the courts have ruled that seamen, train crews, policemen, firemen, etc., may be punished for quitting a job and thereby endangering the public.

has had little real importance in our national history.

The 4th Amendment grew out of the British use of " writs of assistance." These were general search warrants under which British officials were able to search persons and homes at any time for any reason. Their use was bitterly resented by the colonists.

The carefully worded 4th Amendment reads:

The right of the people to be secure in their persons, houses, papers, and effects, against unreasonable searches and seizures, shall not be violated, and no warrants shall issue, but upon probable cause, supported by oath or affirmation, and particularly describing the place to be searched, and the persons or things to be seized.

Thus a man's house is his castle. Authorities may not break into his house and gather evidence to be used against him, except with a proper warrant.

Notice that it is only *unreasonable* searches and seizures without a warrant that are prohibited. There are, then, reasonable ones. No warrant is needed when an officer is in " hot pursuit " of a fugitive, even if the man being chased runs into his own house. Nor is a warrant needed when a crime is committed in an officer's presence. And an officer does not need a warrant to search a boat, an automobile, or other " movable scene of crime " which might vanish were he to take the time to get a warrant.

The federal courts will not admit evidence against an accused if that evidence has been obtained through an unlawful search. For example, federal officers searched a Chinese laundry with a warrant describing the laundry and specifying illegal liquor as the object of the search. No liquor was found; but, in a living room off the laundry, dope was found in a baby's crib.

When the laundry-owner was brought to trial in a United States District Court, the case was thrown out. The warrant described only the laundry and liquor, not a room adjoining it and narcotics.

There are literally dozens of other cases like this — cases in which lawbreakers have gone free because, in obtaining evidence, officers have violated the rights guaranteed by the 4th Amendment. Lawbreakers have gone free not because the courts have wanted to be lenient with them, but because any accused person is innocent unless and until he is proved guilty. Guilt must be *fairly* proved. If unfair means may be used to convict a person who has clearly violated the law, what protection has an innocent man wrongly accused of crime?

Every State constitution prohibits unreasonable searches and seizures. Only a few States, though, exclude evidence unlawfully obtained. Most State courts admit evidence regardless of the way in which it is come upon.

There is, then, a difference between the rule followed in federal courts and that followed in most State courts insofar as the admissibility of evidence is concerned. This situation can be illustrated by a recent California case much like the Rochin case. One Mills was arrested by Los Angeles police and federal narcotics agents as he attempted to sell heroin. Just as the officers moved in on him, however, he swallowed the heroin. After he was taken to the station house and charged with both a federal and a State crime, his stomach was pumped. The federal charge was dismissed when he was brought to trial in the United States District Court. There had been no warrant " particularly describing the place to be searched (his stomach), and the . . . things (heroin) to be seized." However, he was tried and convicted in the California courts because they did not follow the federal rule. The stomach pump evidence, although unlawfully obtained, was admitted for use against him. (*Note:* Since the Mills case, the California Supreme Court has ruled that evidence unlawfully obtained *cannot* be admitted in that State's courts.)

The Right to Keep and Bear Arms. The 2nd Amendment, as we saw on page 384, forbids the National Government to infringe upon an individual's " right to keep and bear arms." The right is of only minor significance today. The courts have held that the Amendment applies only to the ordinary arms which were carried by a soldier at the time the Amendment was adopted. It does not apply to sawed-off shotguns, machine guns, blackjacks, and the like. Because the Bill of Rights restricts only the National Government, the States are free to regulate arms as they see fit.

The Right to Freedom of Expression

The right to freedom of expression involves four basic individual liberties: freedom of religion, freedom of speech, freedom of press, and freedom of assembly. These freedoms go to the very core of the democratic process. Democracy could not exist without them.

The 1st Amendment guarantees these freedoms against the National Government:

Congress shall make no law respecting an establishment of religion, or prohibiting the free exercise thereof; or abridging the freedom of speech, or of the press; or the right of the people peaceably to assemble, and to petition the government for a redress of grievances.

The 14th Amendment's Due Process Clause extends these limitations against the States, as we noted on page 384.

Freedom of Religion. The first portion of the 1st Amendment guarantees (1) that there shall be no officially established church in the United States and (2) that there shall be no restriction of personal religious belief.[7]

Separation of Church and State. Our Constitution provides for a complete separation of church and state. Neither the National Government nor

[7] Also, Article VI, Section 3, provides that ". . . no religious test shall ever be required as a qualification to any office or public trust under the United States."

the States may support one, any, or all churches.

However, government has not been unfriendly toward churches and religions in the United States. Practically all church-owned property and contributions to churches are exempt from taxation. Most public officials take an oath of office in the name of God. Sessions of Congress and of most State legislatures are opened with prayer.

It was not until 1947 that the Supreme Court was first called upon to explain the meaning of the " establishment of religion " clause. A New Jersey law permitting public (tax-provided) school bus transportation for parochial school students was challenged as " an establishment of religion."

The Court, by a 5–4 vote, ruled that the law was not an aid to religion. Rather, it held the law to be a safety measure, much like the posting of a policeman at school crosswalks. In reaching its decision, the Court said

The " establishment of religion " clause of the 1st Amendment means at least this: Neither a State nor the Federal Government can set up a church. Neither can pass laws which aid one religion, aid all religions, or prefer one religion over another . . . No tax in any amount, large or small, can be levied to support any religious activities or institutions, whatever they may be called, or whatever form they may adopt to teach or practice religion. Neither a State nor the Federal Government can, openly or secretly, participate in the affairs of any religious organizations or groups and *vice versa.*

Since this decision, two other church-state school cases have been decided by the Supreme Court. These and other cases involving religion and education are discussed further in Chapter 35, pages 631–33.

Freedom of Religious Belief. Everyone has the right to believe whatever he pleases in regard to religion. And if he chooses to believe nothing, that is his right, too.

Like all other civil rights, however, freedom of religion is a relative right. No one has the right to commit a crime in the name of religion. For example, a few years ago the Supreme Court upheld the conviction for fraud of a man who took money from the sick and promised a supernatural cure. It has also ruled that a Mormon may not practice polygamy. And it has ruled that those who for religious reasons oppose military service may nonetheless be drafted; and that a State may make it a crime for one to handle live snakes in the course of a religious or church service.

In recent years several cases in religious freedom have been taken to the Supreme Court by the Jehovah's Witnesses. The Witnesses are active in promoting their beliefs through such devices as handbills and pamphlets, door-to-door campaigning, and phonograph records. In various Witness cases it has been held that " such peddlers of religious thought " cannot be required to buy peddlers' licenses, be discriminated against in the use of public halls and parks, or be punished as " nuisances " for playing phonograph records on the public streets.

392

In the most important of the Witness cases, the Supreme Court in 1943 ruled that no State may require school children to salute the flag, if such an action is contrary to their religious beliefs. The Court said in this case:

A person gets from a symbol the meaning he puts into it, and what is one man's comfort and inspiration is another's jest and scorn.

The quotation introducing this Chapter also comes from this flag-salute case.

Freedom of Speech and Press. The 1st Amendment goes on to provide for freedom of speech and of the press. But what is meant by freedom of speech and press? This is one of the most difficult and delicate questions in the entire field of civil rights.

Nowhere is the fact that civil rights are *relative and not absolute* better demonstrated. No one can have the right to say or to publish anything he pleases.

In normal times freedom of speech and press is restricted to prevent obscenities. No one has the right to *libel* or *slander* another.[8] And no one has the right to use words in a way that will incite a riot. In time of war or other national emergency, freedom of speech and press may be further lim-

Jensen, "The Chicago Daily News"

The constitutional guarantee of a free press makes a democracy such as ours dangerous ground for the growth of any elements of corruption, tyranny, and injustice.

ited in the interests of ensuring the national safety.

The "Clear and Present Danger Rule." It is very difficult to draw a reasonable line between the power of government to protect the public safety and the right of an individual to express himself.

In cases of this sort the Court applies what is known as the " clear and

---

[8] *Libel* (the printed word) and *slander* (the spoken word) involve the using of words maliciously (with vicious purpose) to injure the character or reputation of an individual or to expose him to public contempt, ridicule, or hatred. *The Saturday Evening Post* paid a man $1500 in an out-of-court settlement a few years ago. An article had described him as a " Stalinist busybody." Later the same magazine paid another man $11,000 because it had called him " a communist wrecker in American labor." One of the reasons for the difference in amounts was that one man had been damned in passing, while the other was dealt with at length.

Public officials and candidates for office may be criticized if critics speak of what they know or believe, have only the public interest in view, and speak without malice.

present danger rule." This standard was first laid down by the great Justice Oliver Wendell Holmes in 1919. One Schenck, a Socialist, had been convicted of violating the Espionage Act of 1917. The law forbade anyone to obstruct or engage in a conspiracy to obstruct the war effort. Schenck had been very active in urging resistance to the draft. In upholding Schenck's conviction, the Court said:

The question in every case is whether the words used are used in such circumstances and are of such a nature as to create a clear and present danger. . . .

What constitutes a clear and present danger? Only the Supreme Court can say. The decision must be based on the facts in each particular case.

The recent cases involving the clear and present danger rule have concerned communists and their activities. The most important one was decided by the Court in 1951.

In 1949, after a long and hectic trial, eleven top leaders of the Communist Party in the United States were convicted of violating the Smith Act of 1940. This act makes it unlawful for anyone to teach and advocate the violent overthrow of ordered government in the United States. It also makes it a crime to " conspire to commit " these acts.

The eleven appealed their convictions on the grounds that the Smith Act violates the freedom of speech and press guarantees of the 1st Amendment, and that no act of theirs constituted a clear and present danger to the United States.

The convictions and the act were upheld by the Court of Appeals in 1950. The noted Justice Learned Hand pointed out that the communists' conspiracy created a danger " of the utmost gravity and of enough probability to justify its suppression." In 1951 the Supreme Court also upheld the convictions and the act, declaring:

We reject any principle of governmental helplessness in the face of preparation for revolution, which principle, carried to its logical conclusion, must lead to anarchy.

But, remember, merely to urge one to *believe* something (in contrast to urging him to *do* something) cannot be made illegal. And it was for this reason that, in 1957, the Court upset the Smith Act convictions of fourteen " second-string " Communist leaders.

Picketing. Peaceful picketing is one form of the expression of opinion and as such is protected by the 1st Amendment. The Court has said:

In the circumstances of our times, the dissemination of information concerning the facts of a labor dispute must be regarded as within the area of free discussion that is guaranteed by the Constitution.

Thus peaceful picketing is regarded as lawful, but picketing which is " set in a background of violence " may be prevented. A State may not prohibit the use of pickets who are not themselves employees or former employees of the picketed establishment. But a union may not picket one employer not a party to a labor dispute in order to force him to bring pressure upon a second employer who *is* involved in one.

394

Freedom of Assembly and Petition. The 1st Amendment also guarantees

the right of the people peaceably to assemble, and to petition the government for a redress of grievances.

Of course the Due Process Clause in the 14th Amendment extends this provision against the States as well as the National Government.

The right to assemble and to petition the government is just as essential to the existence of a free society as are the freedoms of speech, press, and religion. Here the right to assemble and discuss public questions is assured. So, too, is the right to organize to secure action, as in political parties and in pressure groups. And here the people are guaranteed the right to express their opinions, favorable and unfavorable, to public officials by such means as formal petitions, letters, lobbyists, and the like.

Like other civil rights, the rights of assembly and petition must be exercised with regard to the rights of others. Notice that it is " the right of the people *peaceably* to assemble " that is guaranteed. Thus mass meetings which become riots may be dispersed by local police. Naturally, no group has a right to assemble to commit a crime.

The right of assembly is further limited, especially in the interests of safety. Thus no group has the right to assemble in a way that will interfere with traffic, or create a fire hazard, or otherwise endanger lives or property. What is protected is the free, lawful, public exchange of opinions and ideas.

The Right to Fair Treatment under the Law

Democracy cannot succeed except where all people are entitled to fair treatment under the law. Here the individual's basic rights fall into one of two classes: (1) those which guarantee fair and impartial treatment to those accused of crime and (2) those which guarantee that the law will not discriminate unreasonably against any person or group.

Fair Treatment for Those Accused of Crime. Both the National Constitution and those of the various States contain numerous guarantees of fair treatment for those accused of crime. As we saw earlier, the 14th Amendment reinforces the guarantees against unfair treatment by the States.

Each of these rights springs from the fundamental belief that any accused person must be treated as innocent until he is proved guilty.

The Writ of Habeas Corpus. A *writ of habeas corpus* is a court order directing that a person being held be brought before the court. The judge then determines whether or not the prisoner is being legally detained. The writ is intended to prevent arbitrary imprisonment.

It is guaranteed against the National Government in Article I, Section 9 of the original Constitution and against the States in their own constitutions. The privilege of habeas corpus may not be suspended, says the Constitution, " unless when in cases of rebellion or invasion the public safety may require it." The writ has been suspended on only one occasion since the War Between the States. It was suspended in Hawaii during World War II, but the Supreme Court declared this action illegal in 1945.

The writ may be used against private persons as well as against public officers. It has been used by a husband to secure the return of his wife who was taken home by her parents, and by a mother to recover her baby mistakenly exchanged for the child of another woman.

Bills of Attainder. A *bill of attainder* is a legislative act which provides for punishment without judicial trial. Both the Congress and the State legislatures are forbidden to pass such a law (Article I, Sections 9 and 10).

The ban on bills of attainder was included in the original Constitution because the British Parliament had passed many of them during the colonial period. They have been quite rare in our own history.

The most recent case arose in World War II. The Congress, in a rider attached to a 1943 appropriations bill, prohibited the paying of the salaries of three government officials whom some suspected of " un-Americanism." The Supreme Court declared the provision unconstitutional as a bill of attainder in 1946.

Ex Post Facto Laws. An *ex post facto* law is a criminal law which is applied to an act committed before the passage of the law and which works to the disadvantage of the accused. Neither the Congress nor the State legislatures may pass such a law (Article I, Sections 9 and 10).

This means, for example, that a State law making it a crime to sell whiskey cannot be applied to a man who sold whiskey *before* the act was passed. But he could be prosecuted for selling whiskey *after* the law was passed.

A law increasing the penalty for murder from twenty years' imprisonment to death could not be applied to a man convicted of a murder committed before the penalty was increased; it could be applied only to one committing a murder after the act was passed.

Notice that only *criminal laws* may be *ex post facto*. A retroactive civil law is not forbidden. Thus an income tax law enacted in November can impose a tax upon one's income for the entire year, including the preceding ten months.

The Right to a Fair Trial. The Bill of Rights contains several guarantees relating to fair trial in the federal courts.[9] A fair trial is guaranteed in the State courts through a State's own constitution and, as we have seen, through the Due Process Clause in the 14th Amendment.

No Double Jeopardy. The 5th Amendment says, in part, that no per-

---

[9] See the 5th, 6th, 7th, and 8th Amendments and also Article III, Section 2, Clause 3. The federal court practice of excluding evidence unlawfully obtained under the 4th Amendment also is intended to guarantee one a fair trial.

son shall be " twice put in jeopardy of life or limb." In ancient times a man could be penalized by taking his life or by cutting off his arm, leg, ear, or some other " limb." Hence the old English phrase " life or limb " was carried into our Constitution.

Today the provision means, in plain language, that once a man has been tried for a crime he may not be tried again for that same crime. However, a few explanations are needed here.

A single act may violate both a national and a State law; for example, selling liquor without a license or peddling narcotics. In such instances the criminal may be tried for the federal crime in a federal court and for the State crime in a State court.

State constitutions also prohibit double jeopardy. A single act, however, may result in the commission of several crimes. If a man breaks into a store at night, steals liquor and later resells it, he can be tried for three separate offenses: illegal entry, theft, and selling liquor without a license.

In a trial in which a jury cannot agree, there is no " jeopardy." It is as though no trial had been held, and the accused may be retried. Double jeopardy, also, is not involved when a case is appealed to a higher court.

Indictment by Grand Jury. The 5th Amendment further provides that in a case involving a " capital or otherwise infamous crime " (*i.e.*, one punishable by imprisonment) a person may be tried only after indictment by a grand jury.

A federal grand jury is a body of from sixteen to twenty-three people. The Supreme Court has held that no person may be barred from grand jury service on grounds of race or color. " Blue-ribbon " juries, though, composed of those whose reputations indicate them to be responsible citizens, are legal.

An indictment is a written accusation and is brought against a person only when a grand jury feels that there is sufficient evidence to warrant a trial.[10] An indictment is not required in cases involving minor crimes, and a person may waive (put aside) his right to grand jury if he so chooses.

Most States also provide for the grand jury. As early as 1884 the Supreme Court held, however, that California — and any other State, of course — is not required by the 14th Amendment to provide grand jury accusation.

Speedy and Public Trial. The 6th Amendment guarantees a " speedy and public trial." This is intended to guarantee a trial within a reasonable time and to prevent one from languishing in jail while awaiting trial. The trial, though, must not be so speedy that one does not have time to prepare a defense nor so public that mob rule prevents a fair proceeding.

The Supreme Court has thrown out

---

[10] An *indictment* is drawn up and laid before a federal grand jury by a United States prosecuting attorney. The 5th Amendment also permits a *presentment* instead of an indictment. A presentment is a formal accusation made by the grand jury on its own motion.

a number of State convictions in cases where the trials have been *too* speedy or public. These have been held to be violations of procedural due process as guaranteed in the 14th Amendment.

Trial by Jury. A trial by an impartial jury is guaranteed in all federal criminal cases [11] and in civil cases involving $20 or more.[12] Under the common law, a trial jury (also called a *petit* jury) consists of twelve persons. In federal cases the jurors must be drawn from " the State and district wherein the crime shall have been committed." [13]

States may not exclude anyone from jury service on account of race or color, but they need not provide for a jury trial so long as some other means of fair trial is employed.

Right to an Adequate Defense. The 6th Amendment guarantees four particular rights to enable an accused person to present the best possible defense:

In all criminal prosecutions, the accused shall enjoy the right . . . to be informed of the nature and cause of the accusation against him; to be confronted with the witnesses against him; to have compulsory process for the obtaining of witnesses in his favor, and to have the assistance of counsel for his defense.

When States fail to provide any of these things in a given case, the 14th Amendment's guarantee of procedural due process has been violated. Thus

---

[11] Article III, Section 2, Clause 3, and 6th Amendment.
[12] 7th Amendment.
[13] 6th Amendment.

the Supreme Court in 1948 threw out the conviction of a seventeen-year-old boy who had not been advised of his right to counsel in a Pennsylvania court.

Self-Incrimination. According to the 5th Amendment, no person accused of crime may be forced to testify against himself. And this freedom from self-incrimination extends to the husband or wife of the accused.

As the Supreme Court has interpreted this clause, a person may claim the privilege in *any* proceeding where testimony is legally required. It has been used many times in recent years before congressional investigating committees.

Freedom from self-incrimination means that a prosecutor cannot force a person to take the stand and convict himself. The prosecution must prove the charges it makes.

If one carries the plea of self-incrimination too far, however, he may be held in *contempt*. That is, he may be punished by a court for obstructing the lawful processes of government. Many people have been found in contempt for refusing to answer proper questions of congressional committees.

Evidence obtained by wire-tapping is not admissible in federal courts, but that obtained by a detectaphone is.

Most State constitutions also guarantee freedom from self-incrimination, but it is *not* one of the " basic rights " covered by the 14th Amendment. Of course, an involuntary confession, one obtained by such " third degree " methods as beating or starving a prisoner, *does* violate the 14th Amendment's Due Process Clause.

Excessive Bail and Fines. The 8th Amendment declares that " excessive bail shall not be required." Bail, usually in the form of money, is the assurance that an accused person gives that he will appear in court at the proper time. No bail is allowed for those accused of capital crimes (those involving the death penalty).

The 8th Amendment also prohibits " excessive fines." A fine must fit the crime for which it is imposed. The constitutions of the various States restrict the States in a similar way.

Cruel and Unusual Punishment. The 8th Amendment further prohibits " cruel and unusual punishments." What is prohibited here are the barbaric and bloody penalties fancied a few centuries ago — burning at the stake, drawing and quartering, dismemberment, etc. A punishment must not be unreasonably severe in relation to the offense being dealt with. For example, starvation is not permissible, but solitary confinement on bread and water is. So is execution by hanging, electrocution, lethal gas, or shooting.

COLONIAL DUCKING STOOL

The ducking stool was commonly used in colonial times to punish nagging women and those believed to be witches.

The Bettmann Archive

The State constitutions and the 14th Amendment also prohibit cruel and unusual punishments. The Supreme Court in 1879 upheld the Utah practice of execution by firing squad. The flogging of prisoners has also been upheld as cruel *but not unusual* punishment.

Treason. The crime of treason is the only crime which is defined in the Constitution. The Founding Fathers provided a specific definition because they knew that the charge of treason is a favorite weapon tyrants use against political opponents. Examples of its unjust use in recent times are easy to find, in Nazi Germany, Fascist Italy, Franco Spain, and in the Soviet Union and the satellite nations of Europe and Asia.

Treason, says Article III, Section 3, can include but two things: (1) levying war against the United States or (2) " adhering to their enemies, giving them aid and comfort."

The Constitution adds that no one may be convicted of treason " unless on the testimony of two witnesses to the same overt act, or on confession in open court." A penalty for treason can be imposed only on the traitor and not on his family or descendants.

The death penalty was not imposed for treason against the United States until 1942. Four German-born American citizens were sentenced to be hanged for aiding Nazi saboteurs who landed on the East Coast from a German submarine. Even these sentences were later reduced to life imprisonment.

Most State constitutions also provide for treason. John Brown was tried for treason against Virginia and hanged, following his raid on Harpers Ferry in 1859. He is believed to be the only person ever executed for treason against a State.

Equality before the Law. The various rights we have just listed, those guaranteed to persons accused of crime, are a necessary part of the broad right to fair treatment under the law. It is also vital to fair treatment that the law itself does not discriminate unreasonably against any person or group.

The Equal Protection Clause. The 14th Amendment forbids any State to

deny any person within its jurisdiction the equal protection of the laws.

This clause prohibits a State from making *unreasonable* distinctions between different classes of people. *Reasonable* classifications are not only permitted; they are often necessary. For example, those who rob banks fall into a special class and are subject to special treatment under the law. This kind of distinction between classes is a reasonable one. Or, a State may legally prohibit marriage by minors. Or, it may impose a tax on the purchase of cigarettes and thus tax smokers but not nonsmokers.

However, a tax could not be levied only on Chinese laundries. Or, a State could not prohibit all price-fixing " except by farmers." In 1914 Arizona required that not less than eighty per

400

cent of the employees of any firm hiring five or more persons had to be qualified voters or native-born citizens. The Supreme Court declared the law unconstitutional. It discriminated against aliens, depriving them of the equal protection of Arizona's laws.

Most " equal protection " cases have involved Negroes. In 1896 the Supreme Court established the so-called " separate but equal doctrine " when it upheld a Louisiana law requiring the segregation of Negroes in rail coaches. Under this rule, segregation of the races was held not to violate the Equal Protection Clause *if* the separate facilities provided for Negroes were equal to those provided for others.

This rule was later extended to other fields, especially education. In the last several years, however, the Court has been chipping away at the separate-but-equal rule. In an historic 1954 decision, segregation in education was outlawed. Said the unanimous Court: " Separate education is inherently unequal."

The Federal Government is not restricted by the Equal Protection Clause of the 14th Amendment. However, unreasonable discrimination by it is prevented by the Due Process Clause of the 5th Amendment. Thus segregation in education in the District of Columbia was outlawed by the United States Supreme Court under the terms of the 5th Amendment in 1954.

Privileges and Immunities. There are two " Privileges and Immunities Clauses " in the Federal Constitution. Article IV, Section 2, Clause 1 provides:

The citizens of each State shall be entitled to all privileges and immunities of citizens in the several States.

Section 1 of the 14th Amendment declares:

No State shall make or enforce any law which shall abridge the privileges or immunities of citizens of the United States.

We considered these rights when we discussed interstate relations in Chapter 4, pages 63–66.

WHAT THIS CHAPTER IS ABOUT

Because ours is a democratic government, it is limited, not all-powerful. It is most severely limited in the area of civil rights.

Our individual liberties come down to us through centuries of English and American history. Today, the courts stand as the principal guardian of them, but they cannot exist unless we know them and are willing to fight for them when they are endangered.

All civil rights are *relative*. No one has an absolute right to do as he pleases. With minor exceptions, aliens as well as citizens are entitled to civil rights.

The fact that we have a federal system complicates our system of civil rights somewhat, but the effects of this have been lessened by the Due Process Clause of the 14th Amendment.

The provisions of the Bill of Rights apply against the National Government *only*. However, the Supreme Court has held that the provisions of the 1st Amendment are included within the meaning of the word liberty in the Due Process Clause of the 14th Amendment and are thus applied against the States.

This clause has a double meaning: *procedural due process* guarantees fair procedures by government; *substantive due process* guarantees that government will act under fair laws. Corporations as well as persons are protected by the clause.

A State law which can be justified as a valid exercise of the *police power* does not violate the Due Process Clause.

No all-inclusive listing of a person's civil rights is possible, but they involve the following:

(1) *The right to freedom and security of the person,* which includes freedom from slavery and involuntary servitude, from the quartering of soldiers in private homes, from unreasonable searches and seizures; and the right to keep and bear arms (with certain minor restrictions by the States).

(2) *The right to freedom of expression,* which includes freedom of religion, speech, press, assembly, and petition. Freedom of religion includes both the right to freedom of religious belief and a ban on the establishment of religion.

(3) *The right to fair treatment under the law,* which includes (*a*) guarantees to those accused of crime: the writ of habeas corpus, prohibitions against bills of attainder, *ex post facto* laws, double jeopardy, self-incrimination, excessive bail and fines, and cruel and unusual punishments; guarantees of grand jury indictment, trial by jury, speedy and public trial, and an adequate defense; and a specific definition of the crime of treason; and (*b*) guarantees of equality before the law in the Equal Protection Clause and the Privileges and Immunities Clauses.

QUESTIONS ON THE TEXT

1. What is a *limited government?* What is the underlying principle of dictatorship?

2. How do the courts stand as the principle guardian of our individual liberties?

3. Why must civil rights be relative, not absolute?

4. Are aliens entitled to all of the civil rights enjoyed by citizens?

5. In what ways does federalism complicate our system of civil rights?

6. Do the provisions of the Bill of Rights restrict the States?

7. In what sense have certain civil rights been " nationalized "?

8. Where in the Constitution are the two Due Process Clauses found? What are the two meanings of due process? Illustrate them.

9. What is the *police power* of a State?

10. Define *peonage.*

11. Will the federal courts admit evidence which is obtained by an unlawful search and seizure? Give an example of an instance in which a federal officer does not need a warrant in order to make a search.

12. May the States infringe upon the right to keep and bear arms? Why?

13. What rights are provided for in the 1st Amendment? Which amendment extends these rights against the States and their local governments?

14. Where in the Constitution is the National Government forbidden to establish an official church? The States?

15. What is meant by *libel? Slander?*

16. What is the clear and present danger rule?

17. What is a writ of habeas corpus? A bill of attainder? An *ex post facto* law?

18. May a person be tried twice for the same crime?

19. Distinguish between a *presentment* and an *indictment* of a grand jury.

20. Why is an accused person entitled to a speedy and public trial?

21. Which amendment especially guarantees a person the right to an adequate defense in a federal court? A State court?

22. May a person be forced to testify against himself in a federal court?

23. Which amendment prohibits excessive bail or fines and cruel and unusual punishments from being imposed by a federal court?

24. Why is treason strictly defined in the Constitution? How does the Constitution define it?

25. Does the Equal Protection Clause of the 14th Amendment forbid a State to make *any* distinctions between persons?

26. What is the separate but equal doctrine?

27. Where in the Constitution are the two Privileges and Immunities Clauses found?

PROBLEMS FOR DISCUSSION

1. Referring to the Supreme Court, Calvin Coolidge once said: " If its authority should be broken down and its powers lodged with the Congress, every minority body that may be weak in resources or unpopular in the public estimation, also nearly every race and religious belief, would find themselves practically without protection." Can you illustrate this with examples from the daily newspapers?

2. Why couldn't the legislature of your State legally provide that no farm hand work more than five hours a day?

3. Why do you agree or disagree with these words written by Woodrow Wilson? " We have learned that it is pent-up feelings that are dangerous, whispered purposes that are revolutionary, covert follies that warp and poison the mind; that the wisest thing to do with a fool is to encourage him to hire a hall and discourse to his fellow citizens. Nothing chills folly like exposure to the air; nothing dispels folly like its publication; nothing so eases the machine as the safety valve."

4. Explain the saying: " One man's liberty ends where the next man's liberty begins."

THINGS YOU MIGHT DO

1. The Constitution contains a Bill of Rights but no " Bill of Obligations." If it did, what would you have it include?

2. Invite a judge, attorney, newspaper editor, or other well-informed person to address the class on the importance of civil rights in a democracy.

3. Obtain a copy of the Report of the President's Committee on Civil Rights, " To Secure These Rights," from a library or some other source. Class reports

and debates could be built around it.

4. Various provisions of the Bill of Rights could be made the subject of individual class reports.

5. For each of the civil rights guaranteed in the Constitution, draw up three hypothetical cases in which you think the Supreme Court would hold that a person's civil rights have been violated.

6. List the civil rights guaranteed in your own State constitution.

WORDS AND PHRASES YOU SHOULD KNOW

Bail
Bill of attainder
Bill of Rights
Civil rights
Clear and present danger
Cruel and unusual punishments
Double jeopardy
Due process of law
Equal Protection Clause
Establishment of religion
Excessive bail or fines
Ex post facto law
Grand jury
Indictment
Involuntary servitude
Libel
Limited government

Nisei
Peonage
Petit jury
Picketing
Police power
Presentment
Privileges and Immunities Clauses
Procedural due process
Self-incrimination
Separate but equal doctrine
Separation of church and state
Slander
Substantive due process
Treason
Unreasonable searches and seizures
Warrant
Writ of habeas corpus

SELECT BIBLIOGRAPHY

ALSOP, JOSEPH and STEWART, " That Washington Security Curtain,"
  Saturday Evening Post, February 19, 1955.

" A Political Suicide," *Time,* January 24, 1955.

BESS, DEMAREE, " California's Amazing Japanese," *Saturday Evening Post,* April 30, 1955.

BROWNELL, HERBERT, " Shall Doors Be Opened to Spies and Subversives? " *U.S. News,* April 29, 1955.

CARR, ROBERT K., and others, *American Democracy in Theory and Practice,* Chapters 7, 8, 9. Rinehart, 1955.

CORWIN, EDWARD S., *The Constitution and What It Means Today.*
  Princeton, 1954.

GRISWOLD, ERWIN N., *The Fifth Amendment Today.* Harvard, 1955.

HAND, JUDGE LEARNED, " A Plea for Freedom of Dissent," *New York Times Magazine,* February 6, 1955.

HOOK, SYDNEY, " Fallacies in Our Thinking About Security," *New York Times Magazine,* January 30, 1955.

KELLY, ALFRED H., *Where Constitutional Liberties Come From,*
  League of Women Voters, 1954.

KOHLER, JOHN, " The Case of Prisoner No. 16688," *Saturday Evening Post,* July 14, 1956.

MacIVER, ROBERT M., " Group Prejudice in the U.S.," *U.S. News,*
  July 6, 1956.

" Security in a Free Society," *Current History,* October, 1955, entire issue.

UNIT VI
POLITICAL RIGHTS
AND PRACTICE

Horydczak

The Lincoln Memorial

AN ESSENTIAL FEATURE of our form of government is the right of the citizen to participate in the governmental process. The political philosophy of the Declaration of Independence is that governments derive their just powers from the consent of the governed; and the right to a voice in the selection of officers of government on the part of all citizens is important, not only as a means of insuring that government shall have the strength of popular support, but also as a means of securing to the individual citizen proper consideration of his rights by those in power.

JUDGE JOHN J. PARKER
Rice v. *Elmore,* 1947

He serves his party best who serves the country best.
— *Rutherford B. Hayes*

★

Chapter 23

POLITICAL PARTIES
AND POLITICS

If, as we know it to be, the chief characteristic of a democracy is *government by the people,* it should be perfectly obvious that the democratic system is going to work *only* so well as the people themselves are willing to make it work.

Consider Elihu Root's remarks:

Politics is the practical exercise of the art of self-government, and somebody must attend to it if we are to have self-government. . . . The principal ground for reproach against any American citizen should be that he is *not* a politician.

Nature of Political Parties

Definition. A political party may best be defined as a rather loosely knit organization of many people which attempts to control government through the winning of elections and the holding of public office.

It is misleading to be more specific than that. To say, as many do, that the people who make up a political party " are united on the basis of certain common principles which they share with one another " is wrong.[1]

---

[1] Nearly two hundred years ago Edmund Burke provided a classic definition, and many that are given today are simply different ways of saying the same thing. A political party, wrote Burke, is " a body of men united, for promoting by their joint endeavors the national interest, upon some particular principle in which they are all agreed."

Practically all of the members of both of our major parties *do* agree on such basic principles as democracy, the republican form of government, and the greatness of the American way of life. But beyond that, we cannot go.

Many Republicans find that they have very little in common with many other Republicans. And many Democrats find that they have very little in common with many other Democrats. Democrats disagree with Democrats, and Republicans disagree with Republicans on such important questions as high vs. low tariffs, the degree to which governmental power should be centralized in the hands of the National Government, the need for higher or lower taxes, public vs. private power development, and so on.

If everyone agreed upon every public issue, there would be no need for political parties. On the other hand, if no one could agree with anyone else, parties would be impossible. Actually, our political parties are composed of people who, broadly speaking, hold *somewhat similar* views on various public questions.

Functions of Parties. We know from our own history, and from that of other democracies too, that parties are essential to the success of the democratic process. The basic reasons for this can be seen if we examine the major functions parties perform. Among the important things that they do are the following:

(1) *Select candidates and present them* to the electorate (i.e., the voters). This is perhaps *the* major reason why we have parties. There must be some device for sifting out and finding the candidates for public office. And there must be some device for concentrating strength (votes) behind the candidates, especially when we insist on majority rule. Parties are the best device we have yet found to carry out these purposes.

(2) *Select issues and present them* to the electorate There are two sides to every political question, and often more than two. By taking at least some kind of " stand " on one or more issues, the parties and their candidates offer the voters alternatives from which to choose. (As we shall note in a moment, parties do not often take

too firm a stand on the more controversial issues.)

(3) *Inform the voters and stimulate interest* in public affairs. By arguing for its own candidates and stands and at the same time criticizing those of the opposing party, political parties help to inform the people and to stimulate their interest in governmental affairs. Of course, a party tries to inform the voters in the way it thinks they should be informed — but so does the other party. And this usually means that the electorate hears each side of the argument. This " educational " process is carried on in many ways, through pamphlets, signs, public speeches on radio, television, and in person, newspaper advertisements, rallies, conventions, etc.

(4) *Act as a " bonding agent "* to insure the good performance of their candidates. The party stands behind its candidates and its officeholders. In selecting its candidates a party must determine that each one is of good moral character. And it attempts to make those members who are elected to office " toe the line." If it does not do these things, the party itself and its other candidates will suffer at the polls. (Remember, unscrupulous political machines and unqualified officeholders exist only where the voters themselves are not doing their work properly.)

(5) *Act as " watchdog "* over the conduct of public business. This is especially true of the party out of power. Its criticisms of the party in power are intended to convince the

voters that the " outs " should become the " ins," but its attacks also tend to make the " ins " a little more careful of its public charge and a little more responsive when considering the wishes of the people.

(6) *Provide a basis of co-operation* in the conduct of government. In many ways government in the United States is government by party. For example, Congress and the State legislatures are organized and conduct their business on the basis of party, and appointments to executive offices are made on the basis of party. Under the American system of separation of powers, the party is usually the agent through which the legislative and executive branches co-operate with each other.

Party and Pressure Groups Distinguished. A pressure group is an organization formed to promote some particular cause or the interests of some particular group. Thus we have pressure groups which work to promote the interest of business, labor, agriculture, particular professions such as medicine, law, and teaching, the aged, veterans, etc. We have other pressure groups which promote such causes as prohibition, good government, better schools, daylight saving time, etc.

Pressure groups do their work (exert their " pressures ") in a variety of ways, as we learned in Chapter 9. In many of their tactics they are much like political parties — for example, when they support and campaign for particular candidates for office.

By Reg Manning. Reprinted by permission of McNaught Syndicate, Inc.

MUSICAL CHAIRS

There are, however, two very significant differences between parties and pressure groups:

(1) Parties nominate candidates for office; pressure groups do not. (2) Parties are (must be) interested in the whole range of public affairs; pressure groups are usually interested only in the particular public questions that *directly* concern them.

Many people belong to many different pressure groups at one and the same time. For instance, an automobile dealer might belong to a car-dealers' association, a veterans' organization, a parent-teacher group, a particular church, a sportsman's club, the local chamber of commerce, and other groups, too — all of which are in one degree or another pressure groups. (See pages 163 and 484.)

The Two-Party System

There are, of course, two major parties in the United States: the Republican and the Democratic. There are other parties — minor or third parties — which we shall discuss in a moment. Republicans and Democrats, however, dominate the American political scene.

Historical Basis. The Constitution's Framers were opposed to political parties and hoped to discourage their being formed in the new nation. But, as we learned in Chapter 3 (page 48), the hope was a futile one. The debate over the ratification of the Constitution itself provided the beginnings of our first two parties — the Federalists, led by Alexander Hamilton, and the Anti-Federalists, who rallied around Thomas Jefferson.

These first two parties, sharply divided, set the pattern for our two-party system. Although the Constitution makes no mention of parties, they have been quite responsible for the development of our constitutional system and are themselves prime examples of that development. (See pages 72–74.)

The Plurality Requirement. In American elections this requirement is likewise a significant cause for our two-party system. In practically every election in the United States, the only candidate who wins an office is the one who receives the most votes.[2] When there are only two candidates for an office, as there usually are, one or the other is bound to receive a majority of the votes. Thus, from a very practical standpoint, it seems to us wise to limit election contests to two main contenders — and that means to two major parties.

The consequences of the existence of a two-party system are extremely important to our scheme of government.

Similarity of the Two Parties. In the first place, our two major parties are firmly based upon compromise and are moderate rather than extreme in their outlook. In many ways the two major parties are quite like one another.

This fact, that it is often difficult to distinguish one party from the other except by name, is held by many to be a weakness in our political system. Actually, the reverse is true. The similarities are a strength and not a weakness.

Both parties must appeal to practically the same voters. Notice, for example, that we do not have sharp economic division between a rich and a poor class in the United States; we are, essentially, a middle-class people. Nor are there sharp religious, nationality, ideological, language, or other distinctions among us that would serve

---

[2] A candidate may win an election by receiving a *plurality* of the votes — that is, more votes than any one else but not necessarily a majority. A *majority* vote is received when the candidate gets more than half of all the votes cast. Thus a majority is also a plurality, but a plurality is not necessarily a majority.

as the basis for a major party. This, in effect, is what Adlai Stevenson meant when, in congratulating Dwight D. Eisenhower on election night in 1952, he said:

It is traditional for Americans to fight hard before an election. It is tradition also to close ranks after an election. We vote as many, but we pray as one.

This necessity to appeal to the same great mass of voters in order to win an election results in compromise as the essence of each of the two major parties. Neither one can long afford to direct its chief appeal to any one particular group, such as labor, agriculture, or business. Each one must appeal to as many voters as it possibly can, and neither one can afford to offend or neglect any large group of voters.[3]

The Power to Govern. The power to govern, or to organize and conduct government, is placed in the hands of one party or the other under our two-party system, as pointed out in our consideration of the functions of parties on page 408. And this enables the voter to locate the responsibility for governmental actions, either fixing blame or giving credit for them at the polls.

The Multi-Party System. There are some who believe that the two-party system should be scrapped for a multi-party system. Under such a scheme there would be several major and a great many minor parties each based on a particular ideology or class interest, as in many European countries. But we know that the multi-party system leads to instability in government. Thus, since the end of the Second World War, France has had a change in governments on the average of once every five months!

The multi-party system worked so badly in Germany and Italy in the years after World War I that it was unable to prevent the rise of the Hitler and Mussolini dictatorships in those countries.

The One-Party System. In dictatorships, like the Soviet Union today, opposition cannot be tolerated. Thus there are no opposition parties — only one party exists. Perhaps it is more accurate to call a one-party system a " no-party system."

The Two Major Parties

The Democratic party is over 150 years old. It arose during Washington's administration and was known as

[3] And this is what was meant on page 408 when we said that the " parties do not often take *too firm* a stand on the more controversial issues." If they do, they run the risk of offending too many voters on the other side.

the Anti-Federalist party. It was next known as the Republican, then the Democratic-Republican, and now the Democratic party.

In the Anti-Federalist days it stood for strict construction of the Constitution, strong localized government, and private individual liberties. The par-

MAJOR POLITICAL PARTIES IN THE UNITED STATES

Year	(Left Party)	(Right Party)
1789	UNANIMOUS — George Washington	
1793	REPUBLICAN	FEDERALISTS — George Washington
1797		John Adams
1801	Thomas Jefferson	
1805	Thomas Jefferson	
1809	James Madison	
1813	James Madison	
1817	James Monroe	
1821	ERA OF GOOD FEELING — James Monroe	
1825	DEM. REP.	NAT. REP. — John Q. Adams
1829	Andrew Jackson	
1833	DEMOCRATS — Andrew Jackson	
1837	Martin Van Buren	WHIGS
1841		William H. Harrison / John Tyler
1845	James K. Polk	
1849		Zachary Taylor / Millard Fillmore
1853	Franklin Pierce	
1857	James Buchanan	REPUBLICANS
1861		Abraham Lincoln
1865		Abraham Lincoln / Andrew Johnson
1869		Ulysses S. Grant
1873		Ulysses S. Grant
1877		Rutherford B. Hayes
1881		James A. Garfield / Chester A. Arthur
1885	Grover Cleveland	
1889		Benjamin Harrison
1893	Grover Cleveland	
1897		William McKinley
1901		William McKinley / Theodore Roosevelt
1905		Theodore Roosevelt
1909		William H. Taft
1913	Woodrow Wilson	
1917	Woodrow Wilson	
1921		Warren G. Harding / Calvin Coolidge
1925		Calvin Coolidge
1929		Herbert Hoover
1933	Franklin D. Roosevelt	
1937	Franklin D. Roosevelt	
1941	Franklin D. Roosevelt	
1945	Franklin D. Roosevelt / Harry S. Truman	
1949	Harry S. Truman	
1953		Dwight D. Eisenhower
1957		Dwight D. Eisenhower

ty stood unopposed when Hamilton's Federalist party died out in 1816. During Jackson's administration, however, a powerful Whig party arose (1832).

The War Between the States split the Democratic party and made it a minority group. From then until 1932 only two Democrats, Cleveland and Wilson, were in the White House. The depression of 1929, however, brought Franklin D. Roosevelt into the White House for four terms.

Mr. Roosevelt's death in 1945 brought Vice-President Harry S. Truman into the White House to complete the fourth term. Mr. Truman was elected to a full term in 1948, but the 1952 Democratic candidate, Adlai Stevenson, was defeated in the landslide election of Dwight D. Eisenhower.

The Democrats regained control of both houses of Congress in the congressional elections of 1954 and managed to retain that control in 1956 despite the second Eisenhower landslide.

The Republican party of today is the only party that, as a minor party, ever displaced a major party. It was formed in 1854 and elected its first President, Abraham Lincoln, in 1860. Actually, it is the descendant of two earlier parties. The Federalist party, led by Alexander Hamilton during the first years of the Republic, favored a strong National Government, broad construction of the Constitution, and Government aid to business and commerce. When Aaron Burr killed Hamilton in a duel, it was said that he

had shot the brains out of the Federalist party.

The opposition which rose up to challenge Jackson first called itself the National Republican and then the Whig party. It was this Whig party that gave way to the present Republican party. The Republican party dominated the national scene until the elections of 1930 and 1932. Except for a victory in the elections of 1946 (in which the G.O.P. won control of both houses of Congress), the Republicans served as the opposition party from 1933 until 1953. In 1952 and again in 1956 Mr. Eisenhower won the Presidency by overwhelming majorities. Although the Republicans did win control of the Congress in 1952, they lost it to the Democrats in 1954 and were unable to recapture it in 1956 despite the second Eisenhower victory.

Party Membership. The fact that the two parties must make their appeals to exactly the same group of voters is reflected in the heterogeneous membership of each. It is a cross-section of the American population. Catholics, Protestants, and Jews, workers, employers, professional men, farmers, white-collar workers, all the many groups that make up our society are to be found in both parties.

It is true that, for brief periods, the members of certain groups align themselves more solidly with one party than with the other. Thus, the Democratic successes from 1932 until 1952 can be explained in part because of an attraction for the big city-labor vote and the farm vote together with the

Solid South. The three pillars of this uneasy alliance, however, were convincingly shattered in 1952. The Democrats were unable to reassemble the coalition for the 1956 election.

A person is a Democrat, a Republican, an Independent, or a minor party member simply because he chooses so to regard himself. It is as simple as that. (Except, of course, that he must register by party in several States. See page 431.) Membership in either party is purely voluntary. It costs nothing, unless a person wishes to contribute to the party coffers. There are no dues to be paid and no chores to be done unless one wishes to work for the party. Both membership and participation are voluntary.

A variety of factors may cause one to say that he is a Republican or a Democrat. A great many people are one or the other simply because that is what their parents were. The section of the country (as, for example, the South) may have a lot to do with the choice. Material considerations (e.g., " Which party is best for my own pocket? ") determines the choice for many. But, whatever the reason, party allegiance can be changed almost at a snap of the fingers.

A Large Independent Voter Class. The independent voters, those who feel bound to neither party, are extremely important in American politics. They come from every group and switch back and forth between the parties from election to election. For many, the switch is unfortunately made on the basis of mere whim. But for many others, it is the result of a decision made after a careful study of the merits of the candidates and the issues.

All in all, there are probably about 12,000,000 straight-ticket, or so-called " bullet," voters in each party. These are the hard-shell, rock-ribbed party members who will vote for any candidate so long as he bears the party label. (These people are sometimes criticized, but often they are thought of as the heart of party organization.)

The remaining 36,000,000 actual voters (based on some 60,000,000 votes cast in 1956) run the scale from the *almost*-always-straight-party voters to the true independents who go one way in one election and the other way in the next. (The independent, moreover, often " splits his ticket " by voting for Republicans for some offices and Democrats for others.) It is this latter group that usually determines the outcome of national elections in the United States.

Minor Parties

Third parties have flashed and faded across the American political scene. Only one, the Republican party, has ever managed to replace a major party. Some of our minor parties, like the Prohibition party since 1869, have been with us for a long time.

Two Kinds of Minor Parties.
Minor parties in the United States may be readily classed as either a party of the " great idea " or of the " great personality." Thus the Prohibition, the American Vegetarian, the Socialist, and the Socialist-Workers parties center on one theme. They live on one particular issue. The Bull Moose Progressive party of 1912, on the other hand, was built around a single dynamic personality: Theodore Roosevelt. These parties collapse or become impotent when their leader fades from the scene — as did the Bull Moose party when T. R. pulled out after the 1912 elections — or their issue loses its appeal or is taken over by one of the major parties.

The Republican party was originally one of the " great idea " minor parties. It was born in the cause of anti-slavery in 1854. The Whig party failed to embrace the new minor party's burning issue; and so the Whigs passed into oblivion as the Republicans replaced them in opposition to the Democrats.

In a few instances, minor parties have been successful on the State and local level. They have even elected a few members to Congress. They have never succeeded in capturing the Presidency, however.

Importance of Minor Parties.
Even so, minor parties have had a tremendous effect on American politics and the major parties. It was a minor party, the Anti-Masons in 1830, that first hit upon the idea of a national convention for nominating candidates

for the Presidency. Woodrow Wilson won the election of 1912 largely because T. R.'s Bull Moose party took millions of votes that would otherwise have gone to William Howard Taft.

The main value of minor parties has been to introduce new ideas and sell them to the people; and it requires idealists to pay the price of bringing worth-while new ideas to realization Many times minor parties have promoted ideas to the point where the major parties could not ignore them. When this has happened, the major parties have simply taken up the idea, presenting it as their own. Norman Thomas, six times the Socialist party candidate for President, more than once complained that " the major parties are stealing from my platform." So a minor party often pays the price of developing a promising idea, only to have a major party appropriate it when it becomes popular.

A new party is usually more " liberal " or more " radical " than an older party. Occasionally, it becomes a vehicle for deception — as the 1948 Progressive party whose leader, Henry Wallace, did not himself then understand the forces behind his party. Some cannot wait for evolution; they must have revolution. But if new ideas are imposed overnight, if radicals are not willing to work with and to wait for public opinion, then revolution, whether for good or evil, is the price.

In the 1956 elections, in addition to the Democrats and Republicans, several minor parties had candidates for

AMERICAN PARTIES

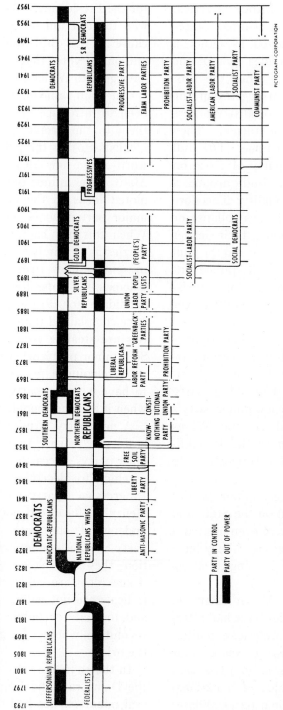

PICTOGRAPH CORPORATION

MAJOR AND MINOR AMERICAN POLITICAL PARTIES

With the exception of the election of 1820, every Presidential election has been contested by two major parties. Notice the growth of minor parties since their beginning in 1829.

416   *Unit* VI. POLITICAL RIGHTS AND PRACTICE

President and Vice-President on the ballot in at least some States, including the States Rights, Constitution, Prohibition, Socialist, Socialist Labor, Socialist Workers, and Poor Man's parties. A few others were not on the ballot in any State but still had candidates. These included the Greenback, Vegetarian, and American Rally parties.

Party Organization

In order to accomplish its main goal, the control of government through the winning of elections and the holding of office, a party must have a workable organization. In underlining the importance of this, Lord Bryce once wrote:

Organization is essential to the accomplishment of any purpose. To attempt to govern a country by the votes of the masses left without control would be like attempting to manage a railroad by the votes of uninformed shareholders, or lay the course of a sailing ship by the votes of the passengers.

National Organization. The general pattern of organization is much the same in both the Republican and the Democratic parties.

The National Convention. The National Convention is the voice of the party on the national level. In the early summer of every fourth year each party holds a convention for formulating its principles and policies into a party platform and for nominating candidates for President and Vice-President. Some months before a presidential election the National Committee of each party meets (usually in Washington) and decides upon the time and place to hold the convention. A number of the larger cities bid for the honor because it means more business for their merchants and helps to advertise their city. The one selected pays a large sum of money to the party treasury.

The Republicans chose San Francisco and the Democrats Chicago for 1956, and the businessmen in each city gave $250,000, free use of convention hall, free television, and numerous other inducements to each party.

When the time and place are determined, the National Committee sends a call to each State Committee naming the time, place, and number of delegates to which the State is entitled. For 1956 the Republican National Committee assigned 1323 delegates to the States, and the Democrats 1372.[4]

---

[4] For 1956 the *Republicans* assigned two delegates for each U. S. Senator, two for each Congressman-at-large (if any), one for each congressional district that cast at least 2000 votes for an Eisenhower elector in 1952 or for a Republican candidate for the House in 1954, an additional one for each district that cast at least 10,000 Republican votes in 1952 or 1954, and six delegates for any State that went for Eisenhower in 1952 or that elected a Republican Senator or governor in 1952 or 1954. The *Democrats'* formula for 1956: to each State the same number of delegates it had in 1952 plus a bonus of four to each State that went for Stevenson in 1952 or that has elected a Democratic governor or Senator since then. Both parties also assigned

PARTY ORGANIZATION

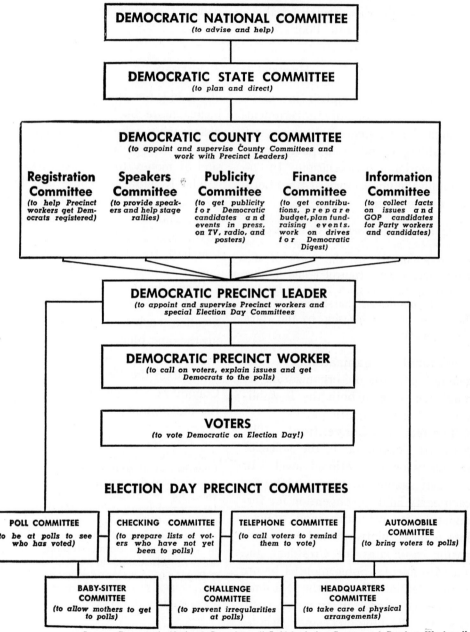

DEMOCRATIC NATIONAL COMMITTEE
(to advise and help)

DEMOCRATIC STATE COMMITTEE
(to plan and direct)

DEMOCRATIC COUNTY COMMITTEE
(to appoint and supervise County Committees and work with Precinct Leaders)

Registration Committee
(to help Precinct workers get Democrats registered)

Speakers Committee
(to provide speakers and help stage rallies)

Publicity Committee
(to get publicity for Democratic candidates and events in press, on TV, radio, and posters)

Finance Committee
(to get contributions, prepare budget, plan fund-raising events, work on drives for Democratic Digest)

Information Committee
(to collect facts on issues and GOP candidates for Party workers and candidates)

DEMOCRATIC PRECINCT LEADER
(to appoint and supervise Precinct workers and special Election Day Committees

DEMOCRATIC PRECINCT WORKER
(to call on voters, explain issues and get Democrats to the polls)

VOTERS
(to vote Democratic on Election Day!)

ELECTION DAY PRECINCT COMMITTEES

POLL COMMITTEE
(to be at polls to see who has voted)

CHECKING COMMITTEE
(to prepare lists of voters who have not yet been to polls)

TELEPHONE COMMITTEE
(to call voters to remind them to vote)

AUTOMOBILE COMMITTEE
(to bring voters to polls)

BABY-SITTER COMMITTEE
(to allow mothers to get to polls)

CHALLENGE COMMITTEE
(to prevent irregularities at polls)

HEADQUARTERS COMMITTEE
(to take care of physical arrangements)

Source: Democratic National Committee. " Guidebook for County and Precinct Workers."

When the call from the National Committee is received, the State committees see that their party delegates are duly elected for the National Convention. In a third of the States delegates are elected by direct primary elections, while in the other States they are chosen in district or State conventions; the delegates-at-large, of course, being chosen at State conventions. The conventions or primary elections that choose these delegates frequently " instruct " them to support a certain candidate for the presidential nomination and to urge that certain policies be included in the party platform.

In the large auditorium decorated with flags, bunting, and pictures of candidates and statesmen of an earlier day, the convention is called to order by the chairman of the National Committee. After the secretary reads the official call for the convention and prayer is offered, the National chairman names the temporary chairman and other officers whom the National Committee has nominated. Unless there is a factional fight, as there was in 1912 in both parties, these nominees are immediately elected by the convention. The temporary chairman is escorted to the chair and makes a lengthy speech in which he assails the record of the opposite party, eulogizes

his own party, pleads for harmony, and predicts victory.

The Committees. Four committees are now formed: (1) Committee on Permanent Organization, (2) Committee on Credentials, (3) Committee on Rules and Order of Business, and (4) Committee on Platform and Resolutions. Each State is entitled to one member on each committee. As the roll of the States is called, the chairman of each State delegation announces the members whom the delegation has chosen to represent that State on the respective committees. After these committees are named, the first session generally ends.

The second session of the convention is usually devoted to receiving the reports of the committees. The Committee on Rules and Order of Business usually recommends the adoption of the rules of the preceding National Convention and of the House of Representatives so far as they are applicable, and recommends a program, or order of business, for the existing convention.

The Committee on Credentials recommends what delegates shall be seated when there is a split in the party and two sets of delegates claim to be the proper delegates, as happened in both parties in 1952.

The Committee on Permanent Organization nominates a permanent chairman and other permanent officers. When elected, the permanent chairman is escorted to the chair and delivers a long speech outlining the issues of the campaign.

---

from one to ten delegates each to Hawaii, Alaska, the Virgin Islands, Puerto Rico, and Washington, D.C. There are as many alternates as delegates in each party. The Democrats permit " fractional " votes: two delegates casting one full vote between them.

Next, the Committee on Platform and Resolutions presents a platform of which a preliminary draft has been prepared by party leaders before the meeting of the convention. In committee a struggle may develop over the wording of the platform, and the debate may be continued on the floor of the convention.

Each party platform contains a statement of its principles and policies. If the delegates cannot agree upon specific problems, noncommittal planks are adopted to avoid offending any large faction of the party. The value of a platform depends upon the party leaders and candidates who indorse it.

Because of the necessity for compromise within the party, the platform is generally intended to attract as many votes as possible while it alienates as few votes as possible. Thus both party platforms have long called for Statehood for Hawaii and Alaska and an Equal Rights for Women Amendment. Sometimes it seems as if some platform promises, like most of the bitter words of the campaign, are forgotten almost as soon as the votes are counted.

Next the convention nominates its presidential candidate. The secretary calls the roll of States alphabetically, beginning with Alabama. As a State is called, its delegates have a right to propose candidates for nomination by long eulogistic speeches. A number of delegates usually second a nomination by similar speeches. After all candidates are placed in nomination, the balloting begins. The secretary again calls the roll of the States, and the chairman of each delegation announces the votes for the entire delegation. The candidate who first receives a majority of all the delegates is nominated. Some State delegations cast their votes as a unit while others split their votes among various contenders.

On the next day, the vice-presidential candidate is nominated. The delegates usually select the presidential candidate's hand-picked choice.

Notification of Candidates. Having nominated the candidates, the convention authorizes its chairman to appoint two special committees, consisting of a representative from each State, to notify the candidates. The committees used to meet the candidates at their homes or where large audiences could assemble, and each candidate would deliver a " speech of acceptance."

In 1932 Franklin D. Roosevelt flew to the Convention and delivered his acceptance speech immediately. Other presidential candidates have followed this precedent or attended the Convention.

Our National Machinery. The National Convention meets only once every fourth year. There must be and is other machinery to conduct the party's business in the campaigns and in the years between conventions.

The *National Committees* of the Democratic and Republican parties consist of one man and one woman from each State and territory. In some States the committeemen are chosen by the direct primary method, in some by a State convention, and in others by the State delegation at the National Convention.

At the head of the National Committee is the National chairman, nominally chosen by the National Committee but really selected on the advice of the presidential candidate. He is the campaign manager, " the headmaster of the machine." For convenience and efficiency the National Committee is divided into subcommittees, such as an executive committee, a finance committee, a committee in charge of the bureau of speakers, a committee in charge of literary and press matters, and a committee in charge of distributing public documents.

Between campaigns the chairman's main job is to keep the machine oiled by raising funds; he replenishes the party's ranks by recruiting new voters and keeping political fences mended.

Congressional Campaign Committees are organized for both the House and the Senate. In the House the Republican Committee consists of one representative from every State having party representation in Congress, and this member is chosen by the Republican representatives from his State. The Democratic Committee includes one representative from each State and territory. States not represented in Congress by a Democrat have a member chosen for them by the committee chairman. Women not members of Congress are often appointed to each committee on the sug-

gestion of a member. The Senatorial Committee of each party is composed of about seven members, who are appointed for two-year terms by the party's leader in the Senate.

These committees are very active, especially in the " off-year " elections, and are assisted by a party staff. They have no official connection with the other party groups, but work in co-operation with them to secure the election of House and Senate party candidates.

State and Local Organization. Many people have the mistaken idea that State and local party organizations are under the direct command and control of the National Committee.

Actually, the party organization in each State is independent of the national organization. Of course, the State organizations usually co-operate with the National Committee, but not always. The influence that the national party organization is able to wield over the various State groups comes about informally — for example, through the use of a President's power to appoint faithful party workers to federal office.

The State Central Committees. These committees vary in composition and power from State to State. The members are chosen by State conventions or in the primaries and usually come from the Congressional or legislative districts or the counties within the State. Their functions are similar on the State level to those of the National Committee.

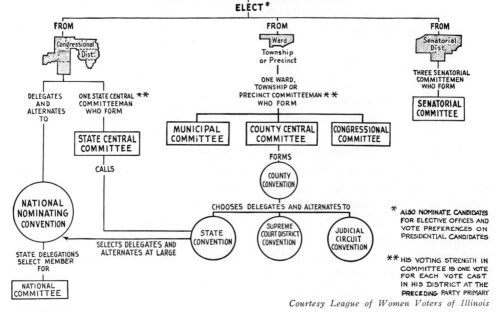

PARTY ORGANIZATION IN ILLINOIS

MEMBERS OF EACH POLITICAL PARTY AT THE APRIL PRIMARIES

ELECT*

FROM Congressional Dist.

DELEGATES AND ALTERNATES TO

ONE STATE CENTRAL** COMMITTEEMAN WHO FORM

STATE CENTRAL COMMITTEE

CALLS

FROM Ward

Township or Precinct

ONE WARD, TOWNSHIP OR PRECINCT COMMITTEEMAN ** WHO FORM

MUNICIPAL COMMITTEE

COUNTY CENTRAL COMMITTEE

CONGRESSIONAL COMMITTEE

FORMS

COUNTY CONVENTION

FROM Senatorial Dist.

THREE SENATORIAL COMMITTEMEN WHO FORM

SENATORIAL COMMITTEE

NATIONAL NOMINATING CONVENTION

STATE DELEGATIONS SELECT MEMBER FOR

NATIONAL COMMITTEE

SELECTS DELEGATES AND ALTERNATES AT LARGE

CHOOSES DELEGATES AND ALTERNATES TO

STATE CONVENTION

SUPREME COURT DISTRICT CONVENTION

JUDICIAL CIRCUIT CONVENTION

* ALSO NOMINATE CANDIDATES FOR ELECTIVE OFFICES AND VOTE PREFERENCES ON PRESIDENTIAL CANDIDATES

** HIS VOTING STRENGTH IN COMMITTEE IS ONE VOTE FOR EACH VOTE CAST IN HIS DISTRICT AT THE PRECEDING PARTY PRIMARY

Courtesy League of Women Voters of Illinois

The Local Units. Party organization varies so widely from State to State that it would be impossible to describe each one here. The typical organization usually follows the lines of the electoral districts. That is, there is usually a party committee for each congressional and each legislative district and for each county, town, borough, precinct, and ward within the State.

In the more populous cities, party organization is also broken down by residential block.

It is in the local party units that the party workers come into the closest contact with the voters themselves. Most young people who are interested in going into politics usually begin at this level, gaining valuable experience "laboring in the party's vineyards." These mostly voluntary and unpaid workers are really the lifeblood of the party.

A Day in a Campaign

Each of the party groups we have just described has one particular job. That job is to elect the party's candidates to office. In doing this, they are most active at campaign time.

Just before his first election to the United States Senate, Senator Paul H. Douglas of Illinois gave this account of one of his typical campaign days: [5]

---

[5] Douglas, Paul H., "*Running* for Office Means What it Says," *New York Times Magazine.* September 5, 1948.

422

Unit VI. POLITICAL RIGHTS AND PRACTICE

White, " *The Akron Beacon Journal* " Haynie, " *The Atlanta Journal* "

" WE CAN GET IT FOR YOU WHOLESALE "   **" BIG THREE "**

My style of campaigning follows this pattern:

I pull up my sound-equipped jeep wagon at a factory gate during a change in shifts, or on a village street, or somewhere else near the main flow of people. I introduce myself to whatever crowd gathers, and then summarize the main theses of the campaign. Afterward I move among the clusters of people to shake hands and to distribute campaign literature which they can read at leisure. In this way I've spoken to about 225,000 people and have shaken hands with over 100,000 of them.

This, of course, is just one side of a day's work. A more detailed view can be grasped from my schedule upon a typical day in the city of Decatur, an industrial community of 70,000:

5:45 A.M. Rise and go to gates of a big machine shop, where I speak to both the night and day shifts as they change.

7:30–9:00. Breakfast with labor leaders.

9:00–11:30. Drive fifty miles into the country and speak in three farming towns.

11:30–12. Speak at lunch hour to 500 foundry workers.

12–12:30 P.M. Speak in railroad shops to 300 employees.

1–2. Lunch with local leaders.

2:30–4. Speak at three factory gates to a total of 600 workers as they come from work.

4–8. Drive thirty miles to Taylorville, speaking twice on the way. Attend dinner of leading party workers, go to the county fair and shake hands with some 250 people and return to Decatur.

8:45–10. Change clothes and speak at meeting of Macon County Women's Democratic League and prepare abstract of speech for the local paper.

10–11. Talk with individuals or delegations who call.

11–12. Handle long-distance telephone calls about details of the next few days' work.

This activity was followed the next day by a 225-mile drive through four farming counties and eight towns, where I spoke to about 2500 people and shook hands with over half of them.

Party Finance

Elections cost money and plenty of it. No one is sure just how much was spent during the last presidential election, but the best estimates indicate about $75,000,000. In other words, approximately $1.25 for each vote cast! And it is safe to assume that the 1960 election will see an even larger amount spent.

Radio and television time, paper, printing, billboards, office furniture, newspaper advertising, hired workers, these and a multitude of other items go into the costs of party operations. Where do the millions of dollars come from?

Source of Funds. Unlike many European parties, our major parties do not collect dues from their members. Our parties depend upon " voluntary " contributions from well-wishers who are interested in the party, the success of its candidates and program, and from those who expect something in return.

The major sources for campaign funds today are (1) individual or family contributors, (2) office-holders and office-seekers, (3) private groups such as COPE (labor's Committee on Political Education), (4) temporary committees formed for the pur-

poses of the campaign such as the Citizens for Eisenhower or the Republicans for Stevenson, and (5) party social functions such as the Jefferson, Jackson, or Lincoln Day dinners, dances, etc.

Regulation of Finances. Congress has attempted to regulate the use of money in any election at which federal officials are chosen.[6] It has done so because the election process is so important in a democracy, because money is so important in elections, and because the line between a political contribution and a bribe can be such a narrow one.

Records of Expenditures. Since 1910 the amounts of national campaign contributions and expenditures of the various parties have had to be filed with the Clerk of the House of Representatives.

Since 1940 the National Committees have been restricted to $3,000,000 each, and individual contributions to $5000; but these restrictions have been evaded by contributions to State

---

[6] Every State also has so-called " corrupt practices acts " which attempt to control money in elections. But, like the federal statutes, they are full of holes and easy to evade.

and local committees and by the direct support of candidates by individuals and various organizations not connected with the party.

Restrictions on Corporations and Unions. Laws enacted by Congress prohibit contributions by corporations or by labor unions to campaign funds used to aid in the election of a President, Vice-President, a Representative, or a Senator. National banks and other corporations organized by authority of any law of Congress are forbidden to contribute to any campaign fund.[7]

Restrictions on Congressmen. The amount of money congressional candidates themselves may spend seeking election is limited by the Corrupt Practices Act of 1925. Candidates for Senator may spend up to $10,000 on their campaigns, candidates for Representative up to $2500. Or the candidate may spend an amount equal to three cents per vote at the last election up to a maximum of $25,000 for senatorial candidates and $5000 for those seeking election as a Representative. Other individuals and groups, however, may and do spend money in behalf of candidates for Congress.

A candidate for Congress must report the receipts and expenditures for his campaign to the Secretary of the

Senate or Clerk of the House within thirty days after an election.

The treasurer of a political committee, or an individual expending $50 or more in two or more States, must file a detailed report with the Clerk of the House annually, quarterly, ten days, and five days before a general election.

Restrictions on Pre-Election Promises or Intimidation. Under the Hatch Acts of 1939 and 1940, it is unlawful in the election of the President, Vice-President, or Congressman for any federal, State, or local administrative official financed wholly or in part by United States funds to offer government work as a reward, or dismissal as a penalty, for a vote or for political activity; or to receive political contributions from persons on relief or on work relief; or to use their authority to affect federal elections.

Restrictions on Activity in Political Campaigns. The officials mentioned in the preceding paragraph (except elective State or local officers) and most federal Civil Service employees are forbidden to take an active part in political campaigns. The U. S. Civil Service Commission tries to enforce the restrictions listed here and in the preceding paragraph.

Restrictions on Contributions to and Expenditures of Campaign Funds. No person or firm entering into a contract with any agency of the Federal Government may make or promise a contribution to a political party or candidate, nor may anyone knowingly solicit such funds.

Bribery, including gifts to influence

---

[7] Besides this federal law prohibiting corporations from contributing, many States prohibit corporations from contributing to State and local elections. The different States have various laws limiting the amount of money a candidate may spend and also specifying for what purposes he may spend it.

voters, is illegal according to the laws of all States.

Newspapers and Other Periodicals must insert the word " Advertisement " at the end of political matter for which pay is received. Otherwise editors or papers would seem to be backing candidates or measures for money — a sort of bribe.

Circulars, and the like, concerning presidential, vice-presidential, or congressional candidates must be signed. Otherwise false statements could be made without anyone being liable.

WHAT THIS CHAPTER IS ABOUT

If democracy is government by the people, it is obvious that democracy is going to work only as well as the people make it work.

A political party is a rather loosely knit organization of many people which attempts to control government through the winning of elections and the holding of office. It is impossible to provide a much more specific definition than this. Except in the very broadest of senses, parties are *not* organizations united on the basis of common principles.

Parties perform six vital functions. These functions are (1) to select candidates and present them to the electorate, (2) to select issues and present them to the electorate, (3) to inform the public and stimulate interest in public affairs, (4) to act as " bonding agents " to insure the good performance of its candidates and officeholders, (5) to act as " watchdog " over the conduct of public business, and (6) to provide a basis for the conduct of government.

Pressure groups are organized to promote a particular cause or interest. Though they do many of the things parties do, they do not nominate candidates and they are usually interested only in a specific portion of the whole range of public questions.

Our two-party system arose from the split over the ratification of the Constitution and is made practically necessary by our plurality-vote election system. Because the two parties must appeal to exactly the same mass of voters, compromise is an essential ingredient in each one.

The Democratic party of today traces its origins directly to Thomas Jefferson and the Anti-Federalists. A little less directly, the Republican party traces its origins to Alexander Hamilton and the Federalist party.

Party membership is not a hidebound matter in the United States. A person is a Republican or a Democrat simply because he thinks he is, although he must register by party in several States. Family background, section of the country, economic status, etc., are factors which influence party choice. Many people are independent, either by whim or by conscious choice.

Minor, or third, parties are one of two kinds: parties of the " great personality " or of the " great idea." They are a valuable force in American politics, especially in prompting the major parties to action.

Each party is organized on the national and the local level. The National Convention stands at the top of the national machinery, but meets only once every fourth year. The National Committee and National Chairman conduct the party's business between conventions. The Congressional Campaign Committees work especially in congressional elections. State and local organization, from the

State central committee down to the local precincts and blocks, is organized on a geographic basis.

The major sources for campaign funds are five in number. They are individual or family contributors, office-seekers and officeholders, temporary campaign committees, private political groups, and party fund-raising social functions.

Congress and the States attempt, but rather ineffectively, to control campaign financing by requiring statements of expenditures and limiting expenditures and contributions.

QUESTIONS ON THE TEXT

1. Restate in your own words Elihu Root's remarks on page 407.

2. What is a political party? Why is it difficult to define in specific terms?

3. List six functions of a political party.

4. Define a pressure group. Give three examples of pressure groups.

5. In what two important ways do pressure groups and political parties differ from one another?

6. What is the historical basis for our two-party system? Why is the plurality requirement in American elections important as a reason for our two-party system?

7. Why are the two major parties not sharply different from one another? Why can neither party long afford to neglect any major group in the electorate?

8. What is a multi-party system? A one-party system?

9. List three factors which might cause a person to become a member of one or the other of the major parties.

10. What are the two kinds of minor parties? Are minor parties of any value in the American political system?

11. Who calls a National Convention? Who determines where it will meet?

12. What is the convention's major purpose?

13. List the four principal committees of the convention. What are the functions of each?

14. Why are party platforms usually broad and general statements rather than specific declarations?

15. What is the National Committee? Of whom is it composed? What are the functions of the National Chairman?

16. Describe a typical State party organization.

17. Why is it necessary to regulate political campaign spending?

18. What are the five major sources for campaign funds?

19. List three specific restrictions which have been placed upon campaign expenditures.

PROBLEMS FOR DISCUSSION

1. What advice would you give to a person who wanted to make politics his career?

2. In Great Britain the party out of power is known as Her Majesty's Loyal Opposition and its leader is paid an official salary. Why has it been said that the phrase " Her Majesty's Loyal Opposition " is " one of the most illustrative terms in the democratic dictionary "? Do you think the leader of the party out of power in the United States should be paid an official salary?

3. After his defeat for the presidency in 1940, Wendell Willkie said: " A vital element in the balanced operation of a democracy is a strong, alert, and watchful opposition. Ours must not be an opposi-

tion against — it must be an opposition for — an opposition for a strong America, a productive America. For only the productive can be strong and only the strong can be free." How would you phrase Mr. Willkie's thought in your own words?

4. Which of the following proposals do you consider to be the most important — pay the costs of political campaigns from public funds; outlaw party organizations; encourage the growth of a third party; compel all citizens to vote; reduce the number of elective offices in the United States? Be prepared to explain and defend your choice.

THINGS YOU MIGHT DO

1. Invite local political party officials and public officeholders to class to discuss their concepts of a political party.

2. Stage a debate or class forum on the question: " *Resolved,* That our two major parties should be completely reorganized so that each one truly reflects sharp differences of opinion in our society."

3. Secure copies of the most recent plat-forms of the Republican and Democratic parties, from party officials, newspaper files, etc. Outline them and discover how they differ from one another, in what ways they are quite similar to each other, and in what ways they are more vague than specific.

4. Discover how the two major parties in your State are organized.

WORDS AND PHRASES YOU SHOULD KNOW

" Bullet " voters
Congressional campaign
   committees
Electorate
Functions of parties
Independent voters

Majority
Minor parties
Multi-party system
National Chairman
National Convention
National Committee
One-party system

Plurality
Political party
Pressure groups
State central
   committee
Two-party system

SELECT BIBLIOGRAPHY

ALSOP, JOSEPH and STEWART, " That's Politics For You," *Saturday Evening Post,* October 4, 1952.

BONE, HUGH A., *American Politics and the Party System.* McGraw-Hill, 1955.

BROGAN, D. W., *Politics in America.* Harper, 1955.

CARLETON, WILLIAM G., " The Triumph of the Moderates," *Harper's,* April, 1955.

JOHNSON, CLAUDIUS O., *American National Government,* Chapter 7. Crowell, 1955.

LUBELL, SAMUEL, " The Politics of Revenge," *Harper's,* April, 1956.

" What's in a Party's Name? " *U.S. News,* September 14, 1956.

" Where Campaign Cash Comes From," *U.S. News,* February 17, 1956.

> Why should there not be a patient confidence in the ultimate justice of the people? Is there any better or equal hope in the world?
>
> — *Abraham Lincoln*

★

Chapter 24

THE SUFFRAGE

A representative democracy such as ours can be successful only if the people take an active part in their own government. And this active participation is seen most clearly in the exercise of the suffrage,[1] in the privilege of voting.

Suffrage not a Right but a Privilege of Citizenship. No one has a "right" to vote simply because he or she happens to be an American citizen. The terms "suffrage" and "citizenship" are not synonomous — are not just different ways of saying the same thing. While it is true that *only* citizens may vote, it is also true that not *all* citizens may vote.

A child born today in Chicago, or anywhere else in the United States, automatically becomes an American citizen at the very instant of birth. But that child cannot vote at the next election, of course. He must wait for at least twenty-one years before exercising the suffrage, even though he is an American citizen during every moment of his life before reaching the age of twenty-one.

There are, then, certain legal requirements in addition to citizenship that must be met before a person is granted the suffrage. Thus it is plain that the suffrage is not a "right" but, rather, a privilege or benefit that the law extends to those citizens who meet the requirements of the law.

Suffrage Determined by Each State. Except for three restrictions placed on the States by the Federal Constitution,[2] each State determines who may vote at both its own and national elections. The restrictions are:

(1) The same persons whom a State permits to vote for members of the most numerous branch of its own legislature must also be permitted to vote for United States Senators and Representatives (Article I, Section 2;

---

[1] The word *suffrage* comes from the Latin word *suffragium,* meaning *a vote,* and is simply the privilege of voting at elections.

[2] The 14th Amendment, Section 2, provides that, except for crime, any State which denies any male citizen over twenty-one the privilege of voting shall have its representation in Congress proportionately reduced. This provision has never been enforced, but after each census, when a reapportionment of representatives is being made, some Congressman calls attention to the provision.

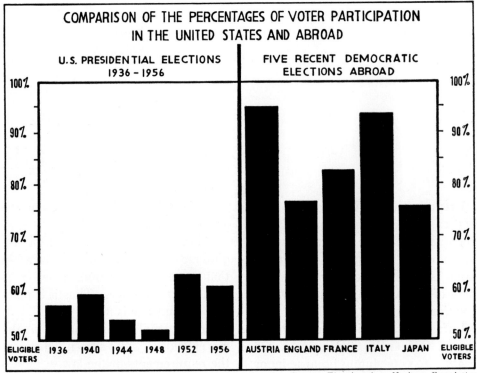

COMPARISON OF THE PERCENTAGES OF VOTER PARTICIPATION
IN THE UNITED STATES AND ABROAD

U.S. PRESIDENTIAL ELECTIONS
1936 – 1956

FIVE RECENT DEMOCRATIC
ELECTIONS ABROAD

ELIGIBLE VOTERS   1936   1940   1944   1948   1952   1956   AUSTRIA ENGLAND FRANCE ITALY JAPAN   ELIGIBLE VOTERS

Source: The American Heritage Foundation

LOOK AT THE RECORD
The American voting record is not one of which we can be especially
proud. Let us hope for improvement in the future.

17th Amendment). This " most-numerous-branch provision " is of little real significance today because, with only minor exceptions, the States commonly permit the same voters to participate in all elections.

(2) No State may deny any person the right to vote on account of race, color, or previous condition of servitude — *i.e.*, slavery. (15th Amendment.)

(3) No State may deny any person the right to vote on account of sex. (19th Amendment.) By the time " woman suffrage " became a part of the National Constitution in 1920, women had already been granted the vote in nearly half the States of the country.

Three Suffrage Requirements Found in All States. Today there are three suffrage requirements imposed by the laws of all States:

(1) *Citizenship*. Each State requires that a person be a citizen of the United States in order to vote. Arkansas, in 1926, was the last State to abolish alien voting, but any State may permit aliens to vote if it chooses to do so.

Unit VI. POLITICAL RIGHTS AND PRACTICE

(2) *Residence.* Each State requires a potential voter to live within the State for a certain period. As the table on pages 432 and 433 indicates, the actual period varies considerably — from six months in some States to as long as two years in others. All States, except Oregon, also require some period of local residence (county, town, or precinct). For example, Nebraska requires State residence for at least six months, forty days' residence in the county, and ten days in the local precinct; Texas requires one year in the State and at least six months in the county.

(3) *Age.* In order to vote one must be at least twenty-one in all States except Georgia and Kentucky where the age now is eighteen. Twenty-one has no special significance. There must be some minimum age, and we have simply followed the old English common law rule of twenty-one as the usual age of majority.

In recent years many, including President Eisenhower, have proposed that the voting age be lowered to eighteen in all states. Those who favor the proposal argue that a person who is old enough to be drafted and to fight for his country is old enough to vote. They also contend that, today, young people at eighteen have usually just completed high school and are more mature and far better informed than were their ancestors at the age of twenty-one. Perhaps some of these young people themselves resent having to wait three years before being able to vote, especially when they consider

some who are legally entitled to cast ballots.

Those who oppose voting by eighteen-year-olds question the maturity and cite the lack of experience of the average person at eighteen. They counter the " old-enough-to-fight, old-enough to vote " argument by claiming that there is no logical parallel between one's *physical* fitness as a soldier and his *mental* fitness as a voter. And they point to the fact that at least half of the approximately 8,000,-000 persons in this age-group will never be old enough to fight because they are female.

Long-established usage, conformity with other age requirements, and inertia seem to indicate that twenty-one will continue to be the minimum voting age in most States. Congress and most State legislatures have considered the problem in recent years. To date, however, only two of the States, Georgia in 1943 and Kentucky in 1955, have made the change. No one has seriously proposed a *maximum* age for voting.

Other Requirements Found in Some of the States. A few other suffrage requirements are found in various States:

(1) *Registration.* All States but Arkansas, North Dakota, and Texas have a registration system to prevent fraudulent voting. In some States all voters must be registered, but other States require registration only by those who live in urban areas.

Without a registration system of some sort it is often difficult to tell

Residence in the State, County, and Precinct

STATE	STATE	COUNTY	PRECINCT
Alabama	2 yrs.	1 yr.	3 mo.
Arizona	1 yr.	30 days	30 days
Arkansas	1 yr.	6 mos.	30 days
California	1 yr.	90 days	54 days
Colorado	1 yr.	90 days	15 days [3]
Connecticut	1 yr.		6 mos. in the town
Delaware	1 yr.	3 mos.	30 days
Florida	1 yr.	6 mos.	
Georgia	1 yr.	6 mos.	
Idaho	6 mos.	30 days	
Illinois	1 yr.	90 days	30 days
Indiana	6 mos.	60 days in the township	30 days
Iowa	6 mos.	60 days	[4]
Kansas	6 mos.	30 days in the township	30 days
Kentucky	1 yr.	6 mos.	60 days
Louisiana	1 yr.	1 yr.	3 mos. [5]
Maine	6 mos.		3 mos. in city or town
Maryland	1 yr.	6 mos.	30 days
Massachusetts	1 yr.		6 mos. in city or town
Michigan	6 mos.	30 days in city or township	
Minnesota	6 mos.		30 days
Mississippi	2 yrs.		1 yr. [6]
Missouri	1 yr.	60 days in county, city or town	
Montana	1 yr.	30 days	30 days
Nebraska	6 mos.	40 days	10 days
Nevada	6 mos.	30 days	10 days
New Hampshire	6 mos.		6 mos. in the town
New Jersey	6 mos.	60 days	
New Mexico	1 yr.	90 days	30 days
New York	1 yr.	4 mos.	30 days
North Carolina	1 yr.		30 days
North Dakota	1 yr.	90 days	30 days
Ohio	1 yr.	40 days	40 days
Oklahoma	1 yr.	6 mos.	30 days
Oregon	6 mos.		
Pennsylvania	1 yr. [7]		2 mos.

[3] Also in city or town 30 days.   [4] 10 days in precinct for municipal elections.
[5] 4 mos. in municipality for municipal elections.
[6] Only 6 mos. local residence (but 2 yrs. in State) required for ministers and their wives.
[7] Only 6 mos. if previously a qualified voter in or native returning to State.

Rhode Island	1 yr.		6 mos. in the town
South Carolina	2 yrs.[8]	1 yr.	4 mos.
South Dakota	1 yr.	90 days	30 days
Tennessee	1 yr.	3 mos.	
Texas	1 yr.	6 mos.	6 mos.
Utah	1 yr.	4 mos.	60 days
Vermont	1 yr.		3 mos. in the town
Virginia	1 yr.	6 mos.	30 days
Washington	1 yr.	90 days	30 days
West Virginia	1 yr.	60 days	30 days
Wisconsin	1 yr.[9]		10 days
Wyoming	1 yr.	60 days	10 days

[8] Ministers and public school teachers need reside in State but 6 mos.
[9] No particular period of residence required to vote for presidential electors.

whether or not a person who claims the privilege is actually entitled to vote. So most States require each voter to " register " his name, address, length of residence, and other facts with a local registration officer.

Most States now have the so-called *permanent* registration system. Under it, the voter remains permanently registered unless he moves, is convicted of a crime or is committed to a mental institution, dies, or fails to vote within a specified number of years or elections. Thus in Oregon, if a voter fails to vote at least once every two years in a county-wide election, he must re-register to vote again.

A few States still have the *periodic* registration system. In some parts of Louisiana a voter must re-register every four years in order to remain eligible. In many parts of New York the voter must sign the registration book annually, and he must sign his name again on election day so that the signatures may be compared and " ghost voting " may be prevented.

(2) *Literacy.* Some sort of literacy or educational test is now required by law in eighteen of the States. In some, it is merely ability to read that is required; in others, to read and write; in still others, to read, write, and " understand " a passage from the State or National Constitution.

The first educational test was adopted by Connecticut in 1855 during the " Know-Nothing " agitation against foreign immigrants. Massachusetts followed in 1857, Wyoming in 1889, Mississippi in 1890, and Maine in 1891. Since then, most of the Southern States have adopted literacy tests, usually with an " understanding clause." [10] Outside the South,

[10] So-called " grandfather clauses " were also inserted in the constitutions of most of the Southern States after the War Between the States. These exempted from the literacy test or other voting qualifications any person, or his male descendants, who had voted in the State prior to the adoption of the 15th Amendment to the U. S. Constitution (1870). All these clauses were abolished by 1915, however, when the Supreme

U.S. News & World Report

ELECTION DAY
The political campaigns are over and the results are in the hands of the voters.

and in addition to the other States already listed, California (1894), Washington (1896), New Hampshire (1902), Arizona (1913), New York (1921), and Oregon (1924) also have some form of literacy test. North Dakota's constitution was amended in 1896 to permit a literacy test but no legislation has been enacted to carry it into effect. In South Carolina property ownership is an alternative to the literacy test.

California's literacy test is rather typical. Each voter is required to be able to " read the Constitution in the English language and write his or her name." Usually the voter's word is taken as proof of literacy although, unless physically handicapped, he must be able to sign his name at registration time.

The New York constitution provides that " no person shall become entitled to vote . . . unless such person is . . . able, except for physical disability, to read and write English; and suitable laws shall be passed by the legislature to enforce this provision."

Court held Oklahoma's — the last to be adopted — in conflict with the 15th Amendment.

Unit VI. POLITICAL RIGHTS AND PRACTICE

Because local election officials did not always administer the law impartially, the legislature gave the power of determining literacy to the State Board of Regents (State Board of Education). Under the New York arrangement a new voter must be able to prove that he has had at least an eighth-grade education or he must present a certificate of literacy issued by the Board of Regents.

The Board has examinations prepared by testing experts and they are given by local school superintendents. Here is a typical examination given to determine literacy:

NEW YORK STATE REGENTS
LITERARY TEST

Read this and then write the answers. Read it as many times as you need to.

" Mary had been waiting for the Fourth of July. It was on this day that her father and mother were going to take her to the park. Because it was a holiday her father did not have to work. Mary had learned in school why we celebrate the Fourth of July. The Declaration of Independence was adopted on July 4, 1776. It was written by Thomas Jefferson. It is called the Declaration of Independence because it declared the thirteen American colonies free from England. The Fourth of July is celebrated as a national holiday by all of the forty-eight states."

(The answers to the following questions are to be taken from the paragraph above.)

1. For what day had Mary been waiting?

2. Where were her father and mother going to take her?

3. Why did Mary's father not have to work?

4. Where had Mary learned why we celebrate the Fourth of July?

5. When was the Declaration of Independence adopted?

6. Who wrote the Declaration of Independence?

7. From what country did the Declaration of Independence declare the thirteen American colonies free?

8. How many states celebrate the Fourth of July as a national holiday?

After all, a large turnout at the polls is of little value if many of the voters do not understand who or what it is they are voting for. And, for just this reason, many people advocate a much higher educational requirement for voting than any State now has.

(3) *Property or Tax Payment.* In the early days of the Republic, property ownership was a common suffrage requirement. This qualification, however, has now all but disappeared.[11] A few States, Michigan and Utah, for example, do allow only property owners to vote in local bond elections. In South Carolina, as we know, property owners need not take a literacy test.

Five Southern States, Alabama, Arkansas, Mississippi, Texas, and Virginia, now require the payment of a poll tax before a person may vote. The law is strictly enforced and the tax, which varies from $1 to $2, usually must be paid well in advance of an election. The purpose of the poll tax originally was to discourage voting by Negroes who could pass the educa-

---

[11] The once-common religious test has completely disappeared in the United States.

tion test, but in recent years most of the Southern States have done away with it.

Groups Generally Barred from Voting. Every State bars certain groups of people from voting. Most States, for example, exclude idiots, the insane, and those in prison. Some States bar forever those who have been convicted of serious crimes like robbery or murder, and a few do not allow voting by anyone who has been dishonorably discharged from the armed forces. Because undue financial pressures might be brought to bear, most States also prohibit voting by those persons on the public relief roles.

Non-Voting. At least 105,000-000 people in the United States are, or could be, eligible to vote. Only about 80,000,000 are registered, however. And in the last presidential election (1956) only about 62,000,000 actually did vote.

Why have we so many non-voters? There are many reasons. Some persons are ill or otherwise handicapped on election day. Others are called out of town unexpectedly. But the chief cause for non-voting is indifference, not caring, and not bothering to in-

" COUNT YOUR BLESSINGS "

Bimrose, " The Portland Oregonian "

Unit VI. POLITICAL RIGHTS AND PRACTICE

form oneself. Perhaps the fact that the indifferent and uninformed often stay away from the polls is to be counted among our blessings. Surely it is not a poll of ignorance that we seek.

Some people do not vote because they oppose all candidates on the ballot and some are perfectly sincere when they say that they do not care who holds public office and guides the nation. But many more do not vote because they are confused by the long ballot found in so many elections in the United States.

The long ballot is a serious problem in American elections. A recent Omaha ballot was over thirteen feet long and contained as much fine print as half an average-size novel. Many voters had to straddle it. A recent Georgia ballot contained over seventy constitutional amendments, many of them highly technical. And a recent Portland, Oregon, ballot listed fifty-two offices and eighteen measures. The voter is justifiably confused under such conditions and many do not vote because they feel they cannot do so intelligently.

In situations like these, along with dozens of others, it seems harmful to good government to ask the voter to attempt to cast an intelligent ballot. Occasionally, a voter will pass up all but the top offices on such a ballot. Once in a while he purposely spoils his ballot — like the wag in Los Angeles who wrote in the names of each of the seven dwarfs for seven judgeships and then voted for Snow White for assessor.

WHAT THIS CHAPTER IS ABOUT

The suffrage is vitally important in a democracy like the United States. It is not a " right " of citizenship but rather a privilege extended by the law to those who can qualify.

Suffrage qualifications are set by each State, subject to three restrictions imposed by the United States Constitution. Each State must permit the same persons whom it allows to vote for members of the most numerous branch of its legislature to vote for United States Senators and Representatives. And no State may deny any person the right to vote on account of race, color, or previous condition of servitude, or on account of sex.

All States now have suffrage qualifications based on three things: United States citizenship, residence in the State for a certain length of time, and age. All States have set the minimum voting age at twenty-one but Georgia and Kentucky, where it is eighteen. Many favor and many are against lowering the voting age to eighteen in all States.

All States but Arkansas, North Dakota, and Texas have some system for the registration of voters. Over one-third of the States also have some sort of literacy or educational requirement. Five States in the South require the payment of a poll tax, but property-ownership has practically disappeared as a suffrage qualification.

Mental incompetents, prison inmates, and certain other groups are commonly barred from voting by the States. Many who are, or could be, qualified to vote, fail to go to the polls, largely because of indifference.

QUESTIONS ON THE TEXT

1. Can you distinguish between *suffrage* and *citizenship?*

2. May a Chinese woman born in the United States vote for presidential electors?

3. What three restrictions does the United States Constitution place on the States in the setting of suffrage qualifications?

4. What three State-imposed voting requirements are common to all the States?

5. What additional qualifications do some States impose?

6. What is the purpose of a registration system? What is meant by the permanent registration system?

7. Why do some States impose literacy qualifications?

8. What is a poll tax? Where is the poll tax still in use?

9. What persons are excluded from suffrage in nearly all States?

10. What are the major arguments advanced for and against lowering the voting age to eighteen?

11. Do any States permit aliens to vote? Could they?

12. What is the major cause for nonvoting? Other causes?

PROBLEMS FOR DISCUSSION

1. Should suffrage be viewed as a right, a privilege, or a duty? Why?

2. Name and discuss the voting qualifications found in your State. What qualifications do you think should be added? Omitted?

3. If your State has an absentee voter's law, make a summary of its provisions. If your State does not have such a law, should one be enacted?

4. In a democracy is education a luxury or a necessity?

5. The strictest literacy test in the United States, the New York State Regents Literacy Test, can be passed by fifth-grade students. If you were preparing them, would you make them easier or more difficult? Why would you favor or oppose requiring all registering to vote to be able to pass a basic American government and current affairs test?

6. In a New England college town a group of college students attended a town meeting for fun and voted to build a town hall six feet wide and two hundred feet long. Because of this type of levity by young people the State constitutions have provisions like the following from the New York Constitution: " For the purpose of registering and voting no person shall be deemed to have gained or lost residence . . . while a student of any seminary of learning." If the student's family lives in the college town, or if he has no other home to which he intends to return, he may vote. In Latin America students play an important part in national politics. Do you think the practice in the United States or in Latin America is the better?

7. Do you favor universal suffrage? H. G. Wells says: " Before he can vote, he must hear the evidence. Before he can decide he must know . . . Votes in themselves are useless things. Men had votes in Italy in the time of the Gracchi. Their votes did not help them. Until a man has an education, a vote is a useless and dangerous thing for him to possess." Should a legislator follow a universal suffrage " public opinion referendum " if contrary to his judgment?

Unit VI. POLITICAL RIGHTS AND PRACTICE

THINGS YOU MIGHT DO

1. Secure a copy of the suffrage laws of your State from the State Bluebook or from local election officials. Compare the requirements with those of other states. Would you recommend any changes? If so, what and why?

2. Stage a debate or class forum on the topic: *Resolved,* That the voting age in all States should be set at eighteen.

3. Discover how many persons voted in your State at the last national, State, and local elections, and what percentage of eligible voters failed to participate. List and discuss as many reasons as you can for non-voting. How might more people be encouraged to vote and to vote intelligently?

4. Write a short report on the registration requirements in your State. Learn how the system is administered and what precautions are taken to insure the accuracy of the registration lists.

WORDS AND PHRASES YOU SHOULD KNOW

Literacy test	Suffrage
Long ballot	" Most numerous branch "
Nonvoter	Registration
Poll tax	Woman suffrage

SELECT BIBLIOGRAPHY

BENDINER, ROBERT, " The Labor Vote — Monopoly or Myth? " *The Reporter,* November 3, 1955.

BONE, HUGH A., *American Politics and the Party System.* McGraw-Hill, 1955.

CLARK, Ex-MAYOR JOSEPH S., " Wanted: Better Politicians," *Atlantic,* August, 1955.

COULSON, ROBERT T., " Let's *Not* Get Out the Vote," *Harper's,* November, 1955.

FERGUSON, JOHN H., and MCHENRY, DEAN E., *The American System of Government,* Chapters 9, 10, and 11. McGraw-Hill, 1956.

GOODMAN, WILLIAM, *The Two Party System in the United States.* Van Nostrand, 1956.

MERRIAM, CHARLES E. and ROBERT, *American Government: Democracy in Action,* Chapters 2, 3, 4, 5. Ginn, 1954.

PENNIMAN, HOWARD, *Sait's American Parties and Elections,* Chapters 25, 26. Appleton-Century-Crofts, 1952.

TURNER, HENRY A., *Politics in the United States.* McGraw-Hill, 1955.

The right of popular government is incomplete, unless it includes the right of the voters not merely to choose between candidates when they have been nominated but also the right to determine who these candidates shall be.

— Theodore Roosevelt

★

Chapter 25

NOMINATIONS AND ELECTIONS

The fact that the election process is all-important to democratic government is so obvious that it hardly needs explaining. In a representative democracy there must be some process through which the people may select those who represent them. The only satisfactory device we know is that of popular election.

The nominating procedure is just as important to democracy as the election procedure. After all, the making of nominations is simply the answering of the question: " Who shall run? " The group which supplies the answer to this question is the group which determines exactly what candidates the voters may choose from at the general election. Nominations, then, should not be underestimated.

Proof of the importance of nominations in the democratic process can be well illustrated with examples from undemocratic, totalitarian dictatorships. In the Soviet Union and the communist satellite countries, candidates for office are commonly elected by majorities of ninety-eight and ninety-nine per cent. The same was true in Fascist Italy and Nazi Germany. The explanation for such overwhelming majorities is to be found in the fact that only one candidate, acceptable to the dictatorship, is " nominated." In such situations the election process becomes a fraud and a sham.

Nominating Methods

There is no single method which is everywhere used for the making of nominations in the United States. Five different methods have been and still are used. They are (1) self-

announcement, (2) the caucus, (3) the delegate convention, (4) the direct primary, and (5) petition.

Self-Announcement. Sometimes called " self-nomination," this is the oldest form of nomination. It was first used in colonial times and is still fairly common in small local elections. Under this method, a person who wishes to run for a particular office — for example, county sheriff — simply announces that fact to his friends or through the local newspapers.

Self-announcement is also used today by dissatisfied and disappointed candidates who have failed to secure a regular party nomination by some other method. These candidates often form "third parties" or run as "independents."

Caucus.[1] Caucus nominations were originally made by small groups of private persons who met informally to decide which candidates they would back at election time. The making of nominations by such a group (caucus) developed in colonial times and was widely used during the last part of the eighteenth century and the beginning of the nineteenth.

One of the earliest descriptions of a caucus can be found in the famous entry in John Adams' diary for February, 1763:

This day learned that the caucus club meets at certain times in the garret of

Tom Dawes. . . . He has a large house, and he has a movable partition of his garret, which he takes down, and the whole club meets in one room. There they smoke tobacco till you can not see from one end of the room to the other. There they drink flip, I suppose, and there they choose a moderator who puts questions to the vote regularly; and selectmen, assessors, collectors, firewards, and representatives are regularly chosen before they are chosen in the town.

The growth of party organizations and demands for more democratic procedures broke down the private or "closed corporation" character of the caucus. It is still used for making nominations for local offices in some parts of the country, especially in New England. It is open to all party members and public notice is given of caucus meetings. In some localities today the caucus is called the *local primary*.[2]

As State governments and then the National Government developed after Independence, it became necessary to make nominations for officers to serve at those levels. The so-called *legislative caucus* developed to meet this need.

This caucus was a meeting of the party's members in the State legislature to name candidates for the governorship and other State-wide offices. By 1800 the *congressional caucus* had been developed to nominate presidential and vice-presidential candidates.

These legislative caucuses were

---

[1] The term "caucus" as used here must not be confused with a caucus in a legislative body. The latter is a meeting of the legislators of a particular party to decide upon questions of legislative organization, committee assignments, upcoming legislation, etc. See page 149.

There are several possible explanations for the origin of the word "caucus." The most likely one is that it comes from the Algonquin Indian word "kaw-kaw-was," meaning "to talk" or "to talk over."

[2] Not to be confused with the *direct primary*, another method of nomination we shall discuss in a moment.

rather practical devices for the making of nominations in early days. Transportation was very difficult, and the legislators were already assembled at a central place.

With the growth of democracy, however, especially under the influence of the newer frontier States, opposition to the legislative caucus grew quickly. It was condemned as a " closed corporation " in which only a very few could participate.

The wave of revolt against the legislative caucus reached its peak in 1824, when the congressional caucus of the Democratic-Republican party nominated William Crawford for the presidency. Crawford was so unpopular that he ran a poor fifth in the Electoral College balloting.

Andrew Jackson and his supporters fought " King Caucus " at every turn. They felt that Jackson had been robbed of the presidency in 1824 by the forces of John Quincy Adams and Henry Clay. In a very short time the caucus died out on national and State levels to be replaced by the delegate convention.

The Delegate Convention. The first national convention to nominate a presidential candidate was held in Baltimore in September, 1831, by the Anti-Masonic party. By 1840 the convention system was used almost everywhere, replacing the caucus for the making of nominations for State and national offices.

On paper, the convention system seems ideal. In a local caucus the party members would choose their party's candidates for local office and at the same time select delegates to a county convention. At the county convention the delegates chosen in the local caucuses would choose candidates for county offices and select delegates to a legislative district convention. At the district convention the delegates chosen at the county conventions would nominate candidates for the legislature and select delegates to the State convention. At the State convention the delegates chosen at the district conventions would nominate candidates for State offices and choose delegates to the national convention. At the national convention the delegates chosen in the various State conventions would then nominate the party's candidates for President and Vice-President.

In theory, the will of the rank and file of the party's members is channelled upward through each of the levels of the convention system. The convention device provides an excellent forum for the compromising of disputes between factions within the party and for the drafting of a party platform.

In actual practice, however, the convention system left a good deal to be desired. It was too open to manipulation by corrupt bosses and others with personal axes to grind. By controlling the selection of delegates in the local caucus and at each step up the ladder of conventions, bosses were able to control the conventions very effectively.

The caliber of conventions at all

levels deteriorated, especially in the latter 1800's. The depths to which some conventions had sunk is shown in this description of the delegates for a Cook County convention held in Chicago in 1896:

Of the delegates those who had been on trial for murder numbered 17; sentenced to the penitentiary for murder or manslaughter and served sentence, 7; served terms in the penitentiary for burglary, 36; served terms in the penitentiary for picking pockets, 2; served terms in the penitentiary for arson, 1; . . . keepers of gambling-houses, 7; keepers of houses of ill fame, 2; convicted of mayhem, 3; ex-prize fighters, 11; poolroom proprietors, 2; saloon-keepers, 265; (public officeholders, 148;) . . . total delegates, 723.

The convention system, which had been hailed as the answer to the evils of the caucus, had proved to be a poor substitute. The better class of people were too often apathetic or disgusted with conventions. They often refused to attend the local caucuses or to serve as delegates.

The great reform movement which swept the country at the turn of the century centered much of its fire on the convention system. It was soon replaced by the direct primary as the principal nominating method.

Conventions, strictly regulated by State law and much improved over those of the latter 1800's, are still used in some States for at least a few nominations. Of course, the convention is still used on the national level to nominate presidential and vice-presidential candidates.

The Direct Primary. A device through which the rank and file members of a party actually choose the party's nominees, the direct primary was first used in Crawford County, Pennsylvania, in 1842. Its use at the local level spread gradually until 1903 when Wisconsin passed the first State-wide direct primary law.

The primary is used in most States for naming most candidates. A few, like New York and Indiana, use it for just a few offices; Connecticut allows its use *only* on demand of a set number of backers of one who lost at a convention but still polled over one-fifth of the convention's votes.

The direct primary is actually an election within a party — an election at which the party members choose the party's candidates for office. Although it is a party nominating election, it is strictly regulated by State law. The State usually sets the date on which the party primaries will be held, most commonly in May or June before the general election in November. Also, the State usually conducts the primary, paying the election officials, using the State's registration lists, furnishing the ballots, and otherwise policing the process.

There are two forms of the direct primary in use today: (1) the *closed primary* and (2) the *open primary*. The details vary from State to State.

(1) The *closed primary* is used in two thirds of the States. It is a nominating election which is " closed " to all except those who are actually members of the party.

CAMPAIGN OF 1828

Andrew Jackson addresses a group of his followers in the hard-fought campaign of 1828. This picture is by Howard Pyle.

In most of the closed primary States, party membership is established when a person registers to vote. When the voter appears at the polls on primary election day his registration is checked and he is then handed the primary ballot of the party in which he is registered.

In some of the closed primary States, especially in the South, party membership is established through the use of the so-called " challenge system." Under this scheme, the voter is usually required to take an oath that he supported the party's candidates at the last general election or that he will support them at the next.

In any of the closed primary States, a person who does not wish to disclose his party preference may still register to vote. He cannot vote in the primaries because they are *party* nominating elections. However, he may still vote in the general election.

(2) The *open primary* is a nominating election in which *any* qualified voter may participate. No one is required to declare his party preference at registration or at any other time. When a person appears at the polling place on primary election day he is handed the ballots of *all* parties holding primaries (usually there are only two, Republican and Democrat). In

444

the privacy of the voting booth the voter then selects the ballot of the party in whose primary he wants to participate.

An interesting variation of the open primary is used in Washington State. It is known as the " wide-open " or " blanket " primary. Under it, the voter is handed only one ballot containing the names of *all* those who are seeking nominations in *each* party. The voter may vote in only one party's primary to nominate candidates for office, or he may switch back and forth among the parties. For example, he may vote to nominate a candidate for governor in the Republican party and a candidate for United States Senator in the Democratic party, and so on down the ballot making one nomination for each office.

Pro and Con. The major arguments advanced *in favor* of the closed primary are: (1) It prevents the members of one party from " raiding " the other party's primary in the hope of nominating weak candidates. (2) It tends to make a candidate more responsible to the party and its members. (3) It tends to make a person more conscious of his duties as a voter because he must choose between the parties in order to participate in the primaries.

The major arguments advanced *against* the closed primary are: (1) It compromises the secrecy of the ballot to the extent that a voter must declare his party preference. (2) It completely excludes the independent voter from the nominating process.

The major arguments advanced *in favor* of the open primary are, in effect, those which are made against the closed primary: (1) It protects the secrecy of the ballot. (2) It permits independents to participate in the primary of their choice.

The major arguments advanced *against* the open primary are: (1) It permits " primary raiding." (2) It tends to make party responsibility much more difficult.

The open primary was the original form of the direct primary. The practice of raiding the other party's primary became so serious in several States that the closed primary system was developed to replace it.

Notice that Washington's " blanket " primary seems to answer the major criticisms made of both the open and the closed primaries.

The " Run-Off " Primary. In most States a candidate needs only a *plurality* of the votes cast in the primary to be declared nominated. However, there are often primaries in which as many as five or six hopefuls file for the party nomination for a single office. Often the winner receives much less than fifty per cent of the votes but still more than anyone else.

In nine States in the South [3] and in Utah, if no candidate receives a *majority* of the votes cast in the primary, a second or " run-off " primary is held

---

[3] Alabama, Arkansas, Florida, Georgia, Louisiana, Mississippi, North Carolina, South Carolina, and Texas. In Virginia a run-off is held only if the second highest person asks for one.

a few weeks later. In the run-off the top two contestants for a nomination face one another, and the winner then becomes the party's nominee.[4]

"*Cross-Filing.*" In California and a few other States a person may run for the nomination to a particular office in both the Republican and Democratic primaries if he cares to. Thus it is possible for a candidate to go into the general election as the nominee of each party and, in effect, be unopposed. Under this arrangement, a candidate *must* win his own party's nomination in order to be able to accept the nomination of the opposing party.

Nonpartisan Primaries. In most States such offices as the State Superintendent of Public Instruction, other school officials, judges, and city and town officers are elected on a nonpartisan basis. In Minnesota and Nebraska, State legislators are also elected on a nonpartisan ballot.

The nominations for these offices are also made on a nonpartisan basis. Those who file for the nomination are not identified as to party on the ballot. The names of the two, or sometimes three, persons who receive the most votes at the primary then go on the general election ballot.

Evaluation of the Direct Primary. The direct primary, open or closed, is a *party nominating election.* It is in-

tended to give the party members themselves a direct voice in the selection of the party's candidates for public office.

It has not proved a panacea for all of the ills of the convention system. It does offer the party voters an *opportunity,* however, to defeat a conspicuously unfit candidate or to nominate a conspicuously well-qualified one.

No primary or general election machinery can take the place of intelligence and public spirit. The direct primary places much of the responsibility for good government squarely upon the shoulders of the voter.

Only a very few people seriously advocate abolishing the direct primary. There are, however, some weaknesses in it that can stand improvement. For example, it often costs a party's candidate a great deal of money to run first in the primary and again in the general election. The primary also adds to the voter's burden. Some primary ballots are so long that the voter is faced with a frightful task. Especially in the closed primary States, the problem of the independent voters needs serious attention.

The Presidential Primary. The direct primary is essentially a nominating election. It is used to select the party candidates for the general election. In nineteen of the States,[5] how-

---

[4] In Iowa and South Dakota, if no person receives at least thirty-five per cent of the votes for a particular state-wide office, the choice of the party's nominee for that office falls to a party's State convention.

[5] In California, Florida, Massachusetts, Nebraska, New Hampshire, New Jersey, Ohio, Oregon, South Dakota, West Virginia, Wisconsin, (and Alaska and Washington,

ever, at least some of the delegates to the national conventions are elected at the primary. This method is known as the presidential primary. Details of the presidential primary laws vary from State to State. In the matter of dates, for example, New Hampshire slated the first 1956 primary on March 13, and California, Montana, New York, and South Dakota the last ones on June 5.

In some States the party voters also express a preference among the party's possible nominees for President. This type of presidential primary is known as the presidential preference primary.

Thus, in Oregon [6] in 1956 the Republican voters expressed a preference for Dwight D. Eisenhower, and all the eighteen delegates they selected were bound to support him in the convention. Oregon's Democratic voters expressed a preference for Adlai Stevenson, and the sixteen Democratic delegates were pledged to his support.

Bimrose, "The Portland Oregonian"

D. C.) *all* delegates are chosen at primaries. In Illinois, Minnesota, New York some are chosen at primaries, some at State conventions. In Pennsylvania some at primaries, some by party committees. In Indiana, Maryland, Montana delegates to State conventions are named at primaries and they in turn choose National Convention delegates. In Alabama all Democratic delegates are chosen at primaries and all Republicans at State convention.

[6] Oregon was the first State to provide for a preferential primary (1910). Its adoption came as a part of the famous Oregon System, designed to accomplish more popular participation in and control of government. The Oregon System included the initiative and referendum, the recall, and the direct primary.

In some of these States only a part of the national convention delegates are selected at the primaries while the rest are chosen at the State convention or by the State executive (central) committee. Thus, the 1956 national convention delegates in New York were selected through both the presidential primary and the convention method in each party. In Pennsylvania they were selected by primary and committee.

A great many people advocate the selection of all national convention delegates through presidential primaries. Others suggest that the conventions be done away with (except to draft platforms) and that the people nominate the major party candidates at a national presidential primary.

Nomination by Petition. There is one other method of nomination in use today, nomination by petition.

Under this method, a candidate for office may be nominated by the securing of a required number of signatures to a nominating petition.

The details of this method vary considerably from State to State, but in most States nomination by petition is the method the law provides for the nominating of independent or minor party candidates. Today this method is being used more and more to make nominations for local offices.

The Election Process

Once the candidates have been nominated for office, they must face the voters at the general election. In most areas in the South and in some northern States like Maine and Vermont, the real contest actually comes in the primaries. Securing the majority party's nomination in these States amounts to almost certain victory on the day the general election is held.[7]

Extent of Federal Control. Nearly all elections held in the United States are held to choose officers for the more than 102,000 units of State and local government. It is quite natural, then, that most of the laws regulating the election process are State laws.

However, the United States Constitution does give to Congress the power to fix the " times, places, and manner for holding elections " of members of the Congress.[8] Congress likewise has the power to " determine the time of choosing " the Presidential Electors and to set the date on which the electoral ballots shall be cast.[9]

As we learned when we discussed Congress and the President, the Congress has set the date for the election of Representatives, Senators, and Presidential Electors as the first Tuesday after the first Monday in November of even-numbered years. Thus in 1956 the national elections fell on November 6th; the 1958 congressional elections will be held on November 4th; and in 1960 the congressional and presidential elections will occur on the 8th of November.

Congress has also required the use of secret ballots and permitted the use of voting machines in elections at which national officers are chosen. The national Corrupt Practices Acts make it a federal crime for one to tamper with elections at which national officers are chosen — and with the primaries in which they are nominated, too.

All other matters concerning national elections and the whole system

---

[7] This is not always true, of course. *E.g.,* Maine's first Democratic governor in two decades, Edmund Muskie, was elected in 1954 and again in 1956. In South Carolina, J. Strom Thurmond won a seat in the U.S. Senate as a write-in candidate against the regular Democratic nominee (but he was re-elected in 1956 as the regular Democratic nominee). Senator Thurmond is the only person ever elected to the Senate as a write-in candidate.

[8] Article I, Section 4, Clause 1.
[9] Article II, Section 1, Clause 3.

448

for choosing State and local officials are dealt with in laws of the individual States.

When Elections Are Held. Most States hold their elections for State officers on the same date Congress has set for national elections — in November of even-numbered years. However, Kentucky, Mississippi, New Jersey, and Virginia hold their State elections in November of the odd-numbered years. Until its constitution was amended in 1957, Maine held its State elections in September of each even-numbered year.

City and other local election dates differ from State to State. Commonly they are held in the spring.

When State and local elections are held on some date other than that set for national elections, many feel that the voters will pay more attention to State and local candidates and issues. Their votes on these are not so liable to be influenced by their Republican or Democratic choices for national office.

How Elections Are Held. For each voting district or *precinct* into which the county or city is divided, the county clerk, city clerk, board of election commissioners, or some other designated official provides a polling place, equipped with voting booths, a ballot box or voting machines, poll books listing the eligible voters, and in most States an American flag.

On election day the polls are open during certain hours — commonly from 8 a.m. to 8 p.m., but in some States longer.

Each polling place is in the charge of judges of election who pass upon a voter's qualifications. The judges are assisted by clerks. They open and close the polls, count the ballots, and certify the results to the proper officials (usually the county board of elections or county clerk).

A " watcher " from each party is permitted to be present at the polling place. He may challenge any person whom he does not believe to be qualified to vote, checks to be sure that as many as possible of his own party members get to the polls, and watches to see that the votes cast are fairly counted.

How Ballots Are Cast. When the voter enters the polling place, he finds himself in a room in which no one else is allowed except election officers, party watchers, perhaps a policeman, and other persons who like himself are casting ballots.

He gives his name, and if it is found in the poll book, he is handed a ballot. He then carries the ballot into an enclosed booth about three feet square. After he marks it, he folds it, leaves the booth, and goes to the ballot box where his ballot is deposited for counting.

In most States the ballot has two perforated stubs at the top, each containing the ballot's number. When the voter is handed his ballot, one of the stubs is torn off. Then when he brings his marked ballot to the ballot box, the other stub is torn off and matched with the one torn off earlier. This practice prevents the so-called

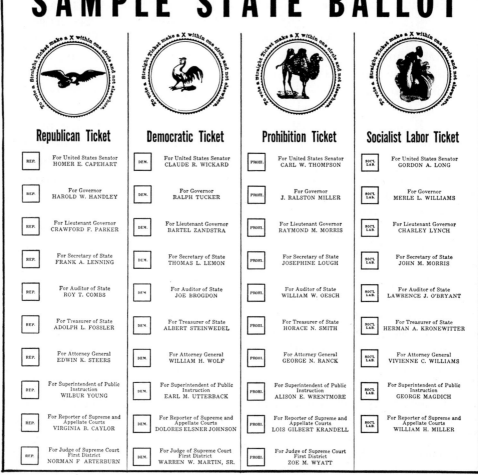

SAMPLE STATE BALLOT

Republican Ticket

REP.	For United States Senator HOMER E. CAPEHART
REP.	For Governor HAROLD W. HANDLEY
REP.	For Lieutenant Governor CRAWFORD F. PARKER
REP.	For Secretary of State FRANK A. LENNING
REP.	For Auditor of State ROY T. COMBS
REP.	For Treasurer of State ADOLPH L. FOSSLER
REP.	For Attorney General EDWIN K. STEERS
REP.	For Superintendent of Public Instruction WILBUR YOUNG
REP.	For Reporter of Supreme and Appellate Courts VIRGINIA B. CAYLOR
REP.	For Judge of Supreme Court First District NORMAN F ARTERBURN

Democratic Ticket

DEM.	For United States Senator CLAUDE R. WICKARD
DEM.	For Governor RALPH TUCKER
DEM.	For Lieutenant Governor BARTEL ZANDSTRA
DEM.	For Secretary of State THOMAS L. LEMON
DEM	For Auditor of State JOE BROGDON
DEM.	For Treasurer of State ALBERT STEINWEDEL
DEM.	For Attorney General WILLIAM H. WOLF
DEM.	For Superintendent of Public Instruction EARL M. UTTERBACK
DEM.	For Reporter of Supreme and Appellate Courts DOLORES ELSNER JOHNSON
DEM.	For Judge of Supreme Court First District WARREN W. MARTIN, SR.

Prohibition Ticket

PROH.	For United States Senator CARL W. THOMPSON
PROH.	For Governor J. RALSTON MILLER
PROH.	For Lieutenant Governor RAYMOND M. MORRIS
PROH.	For Secretary of State JOSEPHINE LOUGH
PROH.	For Auditor of State WILLIAM W. OESCH
PROH.	For Treasurer of State HORACE N. SMITH
PROH.	For Attorney General GEORGE N. RANCK
PROH.	For Superintendent of Public Instruction ALISON E. WRENTMORE
PROH.	For Reporter of Supreme and Appellate Courts LOIS GILBERT KRANDELL
PROH.	For Judge of Supreme Court First District ZOE M. WYATT

Socialist Labor Ticket

SOC'L. LAB.	For United States Senator GORDON A. LONG
SOC'L. LAB.	For Governor MERLE L. WILLIAMS
SOC'L. LAB.	For Lieutenant Governor CHARLEY LYNCH
SOC'L. LAB.	For Secretary of State JOHN M. MORRIS
SOC'L. LAB.	For Auditor of State LAWRENCE J. O'BRYANT
SOC'L. LAB.	For Treasurer of State HERMAN A. KRONEWITTER
SOC'L. LAB.	For Attorney General VIVIENNE C. WILLIAMS
SOC'L. LAB.	For Superintendent of Public Instruction GEORGE MAGDICH
SOC'L. LAB.	For Reporter of Supreme and Appellate Courts WILLIAM H. MILLER

"Tasmanian dodge." This fraudulent scheme involved the stealing of an official ballot before the polls opened or the printing of a counterfeit one. The stolen or counterfeit ballot was then marked the way the political machine wanted an election to go. The fraudulent ballot was next handed to a "floater" or "stinger" hired by the machine. He appeared at the polls and received an official ballot (often by impersonating someone else). In the privacy of the voting booth the ballots were then switched and the fraudulent one dropped into the ballot box. Outside, the machine then marked the newly stolen ballot, handed it to another floater, and continued the process all day. Each floater was paid for switching ballots *after* he brought back a newly stolen one.

BALLOTS

The ballot on page 450 is a so-called "party-column" ballot from the 1956 elections in Indiana (the State where this type of ballot was first used). The one on this page is an "office-group" ballot, from the 1956 elections in Massachusetts (the State where this type of ballot was first used). See page 452.

The Ballot.   During the colonial period and for a good many years after, voting was commonly by voice (*viva voce*). A voter would appear at the polls and in public tell the clerk whom he favored for what office. This encouraged vote-buying and intimidation. It was gradually abandoned by the States in favor of paper ballots.

The first paper ballots were unofficial ones prepared by the voter himself. Then candidates and machines began to print ballots and pay voters to cast them. Even after vote-buying was made a crime, the different parties printed their ballots on different colored paper. Thus the new method was just as public as the old. A vote-buyer, friend, or employer could still know how a person voted from the color of his ballot.

The Australian Ballot.   The Australians devised a secret ballot which found its way to the United States through England. The Kentucky legislature first adopted it in 1888 for use in municipal elections in Louisville, and in 1889 Massachusetts adopted it for all elections. It is used, in slightly varying form, in all States today.

The Australian ballot has three essential features: (1) It is printed at public expense. (2) It contains the names of all the candidates in the election. (3) It is voted in secret.

There are two basic types of the Australian ballot now in use in American elections. They are (1) the " office-group " or Massachusetts ballot and (2) the " party-column " or Indiana ballot.

The Office-Group Ballot.   The office-group ballot is also known as the Massachusetts ballot because it was first used in that State. It is the original form of the Australian ballot and is still used in nearly half the States. Under it, the names of all candidates for a particular office are grouped together under the name of that office.

Originally the names of the various candidates for an office were printed in alphabetical order. In most States today the names are rotated (*i.e.,* the order in which the names appear on the ballot is changed every so many ballots). This is done because there is a psychological advantage in having one's name at the top of the list.

The Party-Column Ballot.   This ballot is also known as the Indiana ballot because it was first used in that State. Today a little over half the States use it. On this type of ballot the names of each party's candidates for all offices are arranged in a vertical column under the party's name. Usually there is a circle at the top of each party's column and, by marking an " X " in the circle, a voter may vote for all of the candidates of that party.

Because the party-column ballot makes " bullet " or " straight-ticket " voting much easier than the office-group ballot does, most students of government oppose its use.

Sample Ballots.   Clearly marked as such, sample ballots are commonly available in most States. In some,

452

they are mailed to all voters before an election or are printed in the newspapers. Of course, these cannot be used for voting, but they do help voters to prepare intelligently for an election.[10]

Voting Machines. Well over half of the States now permit or require the use of voting machines. The voter operates the machine by pulling down a small lever for each candidate he favors. If there are measures as well as candidates to be voted on, he pulls down a small " yes " or " no " lever for each measure, too. Then he pulls a large lever which casts his entire ballot by recording it on a counting tape in the rear of the machine.

Voting machines are rather expensive, costing about $1300 apiece. They soon pay for themselves, however, in time and convenience and because they are virtually fraud-proof. The machines count each ballot as it is cast and thus save the time and money which must otherwise be spent in counting paper ballots. Of course they are most useful in heavily populated areas where a great number of voters must be handled at the polls.

It is impossible for a person to " scratch " (spoil, improperly mark) his ballot. The machine makes it im-

possible to vote for more than one candidate for any office.

The voting machine is sometimes criticized because it has a straight-ticket lever which the voter may pull without bothering with the individual candidate levers. Installing a lock on the straight-ticket lever is a pretty simple matter, however.[11]

A few people claim that voting machines are too complicated and difficult to operate. A few seconds of thought by any voter is usually enough to eliminate this objection.

The Short Ballot Movement. When we discussed the reasons for non-voting, we noted that one reason often given is the long ballot. Ballots in some elections are so long, contain so many names and measures, that even the most conscientious and well-informed voters have difficulty.

Long ballots are often called " bedsheet ballots," and some have been nearly the size of a sheet. The name arose because the voters in Portland, Oregon, were once asked to decide what the exact legal size for hotel bedsheets should be!

The longer a ballot is, the greater is the likelihood of blind or ignorant voting. Blind voting can easily lead to corruption in government.

Theodore Roosevelt put it very well when he said:

---

[10] First in Oregon, and now in about half the States, an official *Voter's Pamphlet* is mailed to all voters before an election. This pamphlet lists all candidates and measures which will appear on the ballot. Each candidate is allowed space to present his qualifications, and the proponents and opponents of each measure are allowed space to present their arguments.

[11] " Write-in " candidates may be taken care of simply by hanging a pad and pencil on the machine. A write-in candidate is someone whose name does not appear on the official ballot. Paper ballots commonly leave space for the writing in of a name other than those printed for each office.

You cannot get good service from the public servant if you cannot see him, and there is no more effective way of hiding him than by mixing him up with a multitude of others so that they are none of them important enough to catch the eye of the average work-a-day citizen.[12]

The average American ballot could be made much shorter if we were to make a number of offices appointive rather than elective. For example, there is little reason why such local officers as the county coroner or surveyor or police chief should be elected. For good government the rule should be: Elect policy-making officers and allow them to appoint those who only administer the policies they make.

The move toward shorter ballots began about the turn of the century and achieved much support in several States. In 1909 the National Short Ballot Organization was formed with

Woodrow Wilson as its first president. Richard S. Childs, its secretary-treasurer, is still active as a leading voice in organizations which promote better government. In 1921 the National Short Ballot Organization became a part of one of these groups, the National Municipal League.

A few States have attained a short ballot. Virginia attained it by five

Virginia Scheme of Elections

1956	1957	1958	1959
President and Vice-President United States Senator United States Representative	Governor Lieutenant-Governor Attorney-General State Delegate	United States Senator United States Representative	Various county and district officials State Senator State Delegate

City elections are held in June. County clerks serve eight years.

methods: (1) longer terms in office; (2) more appointive State and local officials; (3) city-manager government with appointive officials; (4) national, State, and local elections in November of separate years; (5) city elections in June.

In Virginia there are four elections (not including primaries) in four years plus city elections. This makes possible a more careful consideration of each set of candidates and issues.

We have had a short ballot for national elections since 1789. In a national election a voter merely has to choose members of Congress and, every fourth year, a slate of Presidential Electors.

Proportional Representation. PR is a system of voting which attempts to give parties or groups of voters representation in a legislative body according to their actual voting strength.

Several different types of PR are used in different countries of the world. One form of PR, the so-called Hare system, has been and is now used in a few American cities for electing city councilmen. PR was used in New York City from 1937 to 1945 and in Cincinnati from 1924 to 1957.

Under the Hare system several representatives are elected from a single district. The voter marks his ballot by indicating his choices among the candidates. He makes as many rankings as there are representatives to be chosen. For example, if there are nine seats on the city council to be filled, the voter indicates his first through ninth choices among the candidates on the ballot.

The counting process is complicated and difficult and not easily understood by the average voter. First, an " election quota " must be established, that is, the smallest number of votes a candidate needs in order to be elected. The quota is established by dividing the number of ballots cast by the number of candidates to be elected plus one.

For example, take a PR election in which there are nine city council seats to be filled and there are 100,000 votes cast. The quota would be 10,001.

The quota of 10,001 would be reached mathematically this way:

$$10,000 + 1 = 10,001 \text{ quota}$$
$$9 \text{ seats} + 1 = 10 \overline{\smash{\big)}\,100,000} \text{ votes}$$

The ballots are then sorted according to first choices. All candidates having 10,001 or more first-choice votes would be declared elected. Whatever votes they had beyond 10,-001 would be credited to the second choices indicated on each of the ballots involved. This process of transferring votes is carried on until all nine seats are filled. If necessary, the candidates with the fewest number of first-choice votes are eliminated and their ballots distributed according to second choices.

Three major advantages are claimed for PR: (1) It guarantees minority representation. (2) It means that every ballot cast goes to elect someone and is not " wasted." (3) It cuts down the power of small but highly organized machines.

PR is most often criticized because (1) it increases the number of groups or parties in a legislative body and thus promotes instability in government; (2) it is too complicated.

PR is so complicated that few people predict that it will ever be used on any large scale at elections in this country.

The Recall. A recall is an election through which the voters may remove a public official before the end of his completed term. It originated in Switzerland in the nineteenth century and was first adopted in the

United States in Los Angeles in 1903. The first State to apply it to all offices was Oregon in 1908. Today it is available state-wide in twelve of the forty-eight States.[13] Some 2000 cities and counties in over three-fourths of the States also have the recall.

A recall election is brought about through the circulation of petitions. A certain number of registered voters must sign the recall petitions. The required number varies from State to State, but it is usually twenty-five per cent of the number of voters in the district served by the officer involved.

In some parts of the country recalls are not uncommon at the city and county level. They are rare at the State level, however. The only governor ever recalled was Governor Lynn Frazier of North Dakota. He was recalled in 1921. The very next year he was elected to the United States Senate!

WHAT THIS CHAPTER IS ABOUT

Both the nomination and the election process are fundamental to democracy.

Five different methods of nomination have been and are used in the United States: (1) self-announcement, the earliest method used and still known at the local level in many parts of the country; (2) the caucus, developed in colonial times, widely used in the early years of our national history, and used at the local level today in some parts of the country; (3) the delegate convention, which grew up to supplant the caucus in the 1800's and is still used in many sections; (4) the direct primary, which developed at the turn of the century as a substitute for the ills of the convention system and is the most widely used method today; and (5) nomination by petition, used in many local areas.

There are two forms of the direct primary: (1) the closed primary, in which only party members may participate, and (2) the open primary, in which any registered voter may participate. Nonpartisan primaries are used to nominate candidates for nonpartisan offices. Run-off primaries are used, especially in Southern States where a nominee must have a majority of votes for party nomination.

The National Government has only limited control over the election process; it is mostly regulated by State law.

National elections are held on the first Tuesday after the first Monday in November in even-numbered years in every State. Most State elections are held at the same time. Local elections are often held in the spring.

Elections are conducted in precincts, each polling place being supervised by election judges. " Watchers " from each party are usually permitted in the polling place along with the judges, their clerks, and often a policeman.

In all States today the voter casts the so-called Australian ballot, which is of either the office-group or the party-column type. Voting machines are now used in more populous areas of nearly all States.

Most ballots used in American elections are far too long and tend to confuse the voter and lead to blind voting.

Proportional Representation (PR) is a

---

[13] Arizona, California, Colorado, Idaho, Kansas, Louisiana, Michigan, Nevada, North Dakota, Oregon, Washington, and Wisconsin.

complicated system of voting intended to guarantee minority representation in a legislative body. It is used in some American cities today.

A recall election is one at which a public official may be removed from office before his term has expired. It is used state-wide in twelve States and in some 2000 cities and counties in over three-fourths of the States.

QUESTIONS ON THE TEXT

1. Why are nominations just as important to democratic process as are elections?

2. Define briefly the five methods of nomination which have been and are used in the United States.

3. What are the two basic forms of the direct primary? What are the major arguments for and against each?

4. Describe the Washington "blanket primary."

5. What is a run-off primary? A non-partisan primary? Cross-filing? The presidential primary?

6. What has Congress provided insofar as the control of elections is concerned? Why is most control exercised through State rather than federal law?

7. When are national and most State elections held? Why do many students of government favor separating State and local from national elections?

8. What is a " watcher " and what are his principal duties?

9. What is the " Tasmanian dodge "? How do most States attempt to prevent its use?

10. List the three essential features of the Australian ballot.

11. Distinguish between the office-group and the party-column ballot. Which type is favored by most students of government? Why?

12. Why is the use of voting machines usually held to be much better than the use of paper ballots in larger communities?

13. How has Virginia attained a short ballot? What is the danger of a long ballot?

14. What is the purpose of proportional representation?

15. What is the purpose of a recall election?

PROBLEMS FOR DISCUSSION

1. What did the Nazi political scientist Ernst Huber mean when he wrote that " it is not decisive for the character of an elected representative body who possesses the suffrage, but, to a much higher degree, who determines the candidates put up before the electorate "?

2. Explain the following quotation:

" We cannot make the voters all go into politics, but by a drastic reduction in the number of elective offices we can make politics come to the voters."

3. Would you favor or oppose a nation-wide presidential preference primary? Explain your answer.

THINGS YOU MIGHT DO

1. Stage a class debate on the topic: " Resolved, That our State should adopt the open (or closed) primary."

2. Invite your local county clerk or other election officer to address the class on the conduct of elections in your local-

ity. A copy of all of your State's election laws can be secured from the Secretary of State at the State Capitol.

3. Make a list of those State and local officers who are now popularly elected in your State who you think should rather be appointed (if any). Why do you think they should be appointed?

WORDS AND PHRASES YOU SHOULD KNOW

Australian ballot	Nominations	Proportional representation
Bed-sheet ballot	Nonpartisan	Recall
Caucus	Office-group ballot	Run-off primary
Closed primary	Open primary	Tasmanian dodge
Congressional caucus	Party-column ballot	Self-announcement
Convention	Petition	Short ballot
Cross-filing	Precinct	Write-in candidate
Direct primary	Presidential primary	

SELECT BIBLIOGRAPHY

" And May the Best Man Win," Time, Inc., Chicago, 1952.

BEAN, LOUIS H., " The Head, the Heart, or the Pocketbook? " *New York Times Magazine,* October 31, 1954.

BENDINER, ROBERT, " Portrait of the Perfect Candidate," *New York Times Magazine,* May 18, 1952.

BONE, HUGH A., *American Politics and the Party System.* McGraw-Hill, 1955.

" Campaign Buttons Write Our Political History," *Collier's,* October 26, 1956.

CARR, ROBERT K., and others, *American Democracy in Theory and Practice,* Chapters 14, 17, 18. Rinehart, 1955.

HINDERAKER, IVAN, *Party Politics.* Holt, 1956.

MACDONALD, AUSTIN F., *American State Government and Administration,* Chapters 5, 6, 7. Crowell, 1955.

MAULDIN, BILL, " A Cartoonist Goes Campaigning," *Collier's,* September 28, 1956.

PHILLIPS, JEWELL C., *State and Local Government in America,* Chapters 4, 5, 6. American Book, 1954.

POLLACK, JACK H., " How Crooks Steal Your Vote," *Reader's Digest,* September, 1956.

SWARTHOUT, JOHN M., and BARTLEY, ERNEST R., *Principles and Problems of American National Government,* Chapter 8. Oxford, 1955.

TAYLOR, FRANK J., " How to Run for Office," *Saturday Evening Post,* October 29, 1955.

TURNER, HENRY A., *Politics in the United States.* McGraw-Hill, 1955.

Your State's *Election Laws* and sample ballots can usually be obtained from local officials or from your Secretary of State.

UNIT VII
THE STATES

© *Harris & Ewing*

The Jefferson Memorial

THE FEDERAL SYSTEM was created with the intention of combining the different advantages which result from the magnitude and the littleness of nations; and a glance at the United States of America discovers the advantages which they have derived from its adoption. . . . The Federal System rests upon a theory which is complicated, at the best, and which demands the daily exercise of a considerable share of discretion on the part of those it governs.

ALEXIS DE TOCQUEVILLE
Democracy in America, 1838

He that goeth about to persuade a multitude, that they are not so well governed as they might be, shall never want attentive and favorable hearers.

— *Thomas Hooker*

★

Chapter 26

STATE CONSTITUTIONS

Thus far in this book we have been especially concerned with the organization and functions of the National Government. It is the National Government that attracts the most popular attention and headlines. But to a much greater degree than most of us realize, it is the States that most directly affect our daily lives.

Nearly every citizen of the United States is at one and the same time the citizen of a State, and the resident of a county, and of a village, town, township, borough, or city. Practically everything that we do, at any time of the day or night, is influenced or regulated by State law or by the ordinances of local governments (which are created by the State and receive their powers from the State).

In Chapter 4 we discussed the position of the States in the Federal System and you should refresh your memory of that material now. Reread, too, the section on the first State Governments in Chapter 3, pages 39–41.

Definition. A State constitution may be defined as the fundamental law under which a State is organized and the relations of individuals with each other and with the State are regulated.

The State constitution is the supreme law within the sphere of State powers. Its provisions must not conflict with the " supreme law of the land " (the United States Constitution plus the acts of Congress and treaties of the United States). But it is supreme over all other forms of State law — statutes, city and county charters, and local ordinances.

Early State Constitutions[1]

When the thirteen colonies threw off the yoke of British rule in 1776 and became independent States, each

one faced the problem of establishing its own government.

The Continental Congress, on May 15, 1776, advised each of the new States

---

[1] See Chapter 3, pages 39–41.

VIRGINIA CONSTITUTION REVISED
James Madison addresses the Chair at the Virginia Constitutional
Convention of 1829–1830. Other distinguished delegates included
James Monroe and John Marshall.

to adopt such governments as shall, in the opinion of the representatives of the people, best conduce to the happiness and safety of their constituents in particular, and America in general.

Colonial Origins. Even with their faults, most of the colonial charters served as models for the new State Constitutions. Indeed, in Connecticut and Rhode Island the old charters seemed so well adapted to the needs of the day that they were carried over as constitutions almost without change. Connecticut did not adopt a new fundamental law until 1818, and Rhode Island not until 1842.

Adoption of the First Constitutions came about in a variety of ways. The people were given scant opportu-

nity to approve or reject them. In Connecticut and Rhode Island the legislatures made the minor changes in the old charters and no special action by the people was involved in either State.

In 1776 the Revolutionary legislatures in six States — Maryland, New Jersey, North Carolina, Pennsylvania, South Carolina, and Virginia — drew up new constitutions and proclaimed them in force. These documents were not submitted to the voters for ratification.

In Delaware (1776), New Hampshire (1776), Georgia (1777), New York (1777), and Pennsylvania (1789) the constitutions were drafted by conventions specially called by the

462

BAY COLONY CHARTER ARRIVES

The artist shows Governor Winthrop at Salem, 1630. He is bringing the charter of the Bay Colony to Massachusetts.

legislature in the State; but in none of these was the new document submitted for popular approval.

In 1780 a popularly elected convention met and drafted the Massachusetts constitution which was then submitted to the voters for ratification. Massachusetts thus set the pattern of popular participation that has been followed since.[2]

As new States have come into the Union and as the constitutions of the older States have been revised, popular participation has been the rule. All of the State constitutions in existence today were drafted by assemblies representing the people, and most of them have been approved by the people.[3]

Contents of the first State consti-

[2] In 1784 New Hampshire adopted a second constitution and followed the Massachusetts practice of popular election of delegates to a convention and popular ratification of the finished product.

[3] Congress never admits a new State into the Union until the territory desiring to be admitted has framed its constitution. On the admission of some States Congress has passed an act empowering the people of a territory to hold a convention and frame a constitution; on the admission of other States Congress has accepted and confirmed the constitution previously drawn up by a territorial convention. No State may be divided or formed by the union of existing States without the consent of the legislatures of the States concerned and of Congress.

tutions varied greatly in detail, but they had many general features in common, as we saw in Chapter 3. The people were recognized as the sole source for governmental authority and the powers of the new State governments were strictly limited. Seven of the documents began with a lengthy bill of rights and all of them made it clear that the sovereign people had " unalienable rights " that the government must at all times respect.

The separation of powers system was followed in each State and each branch was given powers with which to check the others. With the memory of the royal governors fresh, the legislatures were given most of the authority the State possessed; and high suffrage qualifications were found in each State.

In all but Georgia (until 1789) and Pennsylvania (until 1790) the legislatures were bicameral (two-chambered).[4] At first, only Massachusetts and South Carolina gave the governor the power to veto acts passed by the legislature.

Present State Constitutions

The State constitutions in force today vary widely in details. But compare your own State's document with the six parts common to most:

(1) *A Preamble* which states the general purposes for which the government is organized.

(2) *A Bill of Rights* which lists certain fundamental rights each person has and which government must respect.

(3) *Provisions for the organization of the executive, legislative, and judicial branches* and the powers and duties of each.

(4) *Provisions for local governments* generally outlining their organization and powers.

(5) *Miscellaneous provisions* dealing with such matters as suffrage, elections, revenues and expenditures, education, etc.

(6) *Provision for future change* which outline the amendment process.[5]

Constitutional Amendment

Even the wisest of constitution-makers cannot hope to build for all time. An essential part of any constitution, therefore, is the provision of methods by which the constitutions can be improved upon or altered. Social and economic changes must be accounted for and so must newer and better ways of doing things.

When many changes are to be made, a *convention* is usually called to revise the old constitution or frame a new

---

[4] Vermont, which was admitted as the fourteenth State in 1791, also had a unicameral legislature until 1836. Nebraska, with a one-chambered legislature dating from 1937, is the only unicameral State today.

[5] Most State constitutions also contain a *schedule* — that is, provisions for putting the new document into operation and avoiding conflict with the old one.

one. When only a few changes are involved, the much simpler procedure of partial amendment is commonly used.

Constitutional Conventions. A constitutional convention is an assembly of delegates chosen by the voters to revise an old constitution or to frame a new one. In all States the constitution may be changed by a convention, but in most States it must then be ratified by the voters.

There are usually three popular votes connected with a new or revised constitution: (1) the vote of the people authorizing a convention, (2) the election by the voters of delegates to the convention, and (3) the submission to the people for approval of the constitution framed by the convention.[6]

Missouri Convention of 1943. The Missouri constitution requires a vote every 20 years as to whether a constitutional convention shall be held. In 1942 the people voted " yes "; in 1943 delegates were elected; and in 1945 an entirely new constitution only two thirds as long as the old one was ratified by a two to one majority of the State voters. The new constitution had cost about a million dollars, but it is worth it. The following are some of the changes made in the new constitution:

---

[6] Some States dispense with one or more of these votes; and in 1890 the Mississippi Legislature provided for an election at which delegates were chosen, and when the delegates had framed the constitution they adopted it without consulting the people.

Seventy-odd departments, boards, etc., reduced to fourteen.

Civil Service Merit System introduced in some State institutions.

Cities of 10,000 or more may frame their own charters — " home rule."

State required to support public libraries.

Intangibles (money, stocks, bonds) are taxed on yield instead of on market price and at a rate not to exceed 8 per cent of yield.

Legislature may reduce taxes for 25 years to encourage reconstruction of city slums or reforestation of lands not suitable for farming.

The New York Constitution of 1939 was submitted to the voters in 1938 in nine parts to prevent unpopular changes from defeating the whole constitution. Only six parts were approved.

The Missouri and Georgia constitutions of 1945 and the New Jersey constitution of 1948 are the newest ones. The table on pages 466 and 467 shows when each of the present State constitutions became effective.

Partial Amendment. The partial amendment procedure involves two steps: proposal and ratification. In New Hampshire, amendments as well as revision may be proposed only by a convention. But in the other forty-seven States amendments may be proposed by the legislature, and in thirteen States the people themselves may propose amendments.

Legislative Proposal. The details of legislative proposal vary from State to State. In some States the process is fairly simple, while in a few it is extremely difficult. Both the California constitution of 1879 and the Louisiana constitution of 1921 have been altered some 300 times. The Tennessee constitution of 1870 was not amended once until 1953. In both California and Louisiana the legislature may propose as many amendments as it cares to and ratification is secured by a simple majority of those voting on the measure at the polls. In Tennessee, on the other hand, amendments may be proposed by a majority in each house at two successive sessions of the legislature and must be ratified by a majority of all the people who voted for governor at the most recent election.[7]

AGE OF STATE CONSTITUTIONS

STATE	PRESENT CONSTITUTION BECAME EFFECTIVE IN [8]	STATE ENTERED UNION IN
Alabama	1901	1819
Arizona	1912	1912
Arkansas	1874	1836
California	1879 [9]	1850
Colorado	1876	1876
Connecticut	1818	1788
Delaware	1897	1788
Florida	1887	1845
Georgia	1945	1788
Idaho	1890	1890
Illinois	1870	1818
Indiana	1851	1816
Iowa	1857	1845
Kansas	1861	1861
Kentucky	1891	1792
Louisiana	1921	1812
Maine	1820 [10]	1820
Maryland	1867	1788
Massachusetts	1780	1788
Michigan	1909	1837
Minnesota	1858	1858
Mississippi	1890	1817
Missouri	1945	1821
Montana	1889	1889
Nebraska	1875	1867
Nevada	1864	1864
New Hampshire	1784	1788
New Jersey	1948	1788
New Mexico	1912	1912
New York	1939 [11]	1788
North Carolina	1876	1789
North Dakota	1889	1889

[7] This complicated procedure for amending the Tennessee constitution dates only from a 1953 amendment. The original amendment procedure was much more complicated: amendments could only be proposed by a majority vote in each house at one session and a two-thirds vote in each house at the next session. A few other States have rather complex systems, too — see note 15, page 467.

[8] Several of the State's constitutions were actually ratified a year or more before they became effective: Arizona (1911), Florida (1886), Kansas (1859), Maine (1819), Michigan (1908), Minnesota (1857), New Jersey (1947), New Mexico (1911), New York (1938), Oregon (1857), Pennsylvania (1873), Rhode Island (1842), Utah (1895), Wyoming (1889).

[9] California's constitution became effective July 4, 1879, for purposes of the election of officers, the beginning of their terms of office, and the meeting of the legislature. It became effective for all other purposes January 1, 1880.

[10] The Maine constitution in 1876 and the Vermont constitution in 1913 were rearranged by incorporating the amendments into the text itself.

[11] New York's 1939 constitution includes unchanged many of the articles from the 1895 constitution.

STATE	PRESENT CONSTITUTION BECAME EFFECTIVE IN [8]	STATE ENTERED UNION IN
Ohio	1851	1803
Oklahoma	1907	1907
Oregon	1859	1859
Pennsylvania	1874	1788
Rhode Island	1843	1790
South Carolina	1895	1788
South Dakota	1889	1889
Tennessee	1870	1796
Texas	1876	1845
Utah	1896	1896
Vermont	1793 [10]	1791
Virginia	1902	1788
Washington	1889	1889
West Virginia	1872	1863
Wisconsin	1848	1848
Wyoming	1890	1890

In thirty-four States amendments may be proposed by a single session, but the other thirteen [12] require proposal at two successive sessions. Only simple majority approval is required in each house in nineteen of the States,[13] but a two-thirds majority is needed in another eighteen,[14] while seven States require three-fifths.[15]

A few States limit the number of amendments that may be submitted to the voters at any one election; for example, in Kansas no more than three, and in Kentucky two. In Illinois, no single legislature may propose amendments to more than three articles; in Colorado, to more than six articles. Various restrictions of this sort are found in other States.

Proposal by Popular Initiative. Beginning with Oregon in 1902, thirteen States now provide for the proposal of constitutional amendments by the people themselves.[16] This procedure is known as the *initiative* because the amendments are initiated by the voters. Any individual or group may draft a proposal. If the required number of qualified voters signs an *initiative petition* the measure is then placed on the ballot. By this method the people take a direct part in the amending process.

In Massachusetts 25,000 and in North Dakota 20,000 qualified voters must sign the petition. The other eleven States each require a certain percentage, *e.g.*, eight per cent in Cali-

[12] Connecticut, Delaware, Indiana, Iowa, Massachusetts, Nevada, New York, Pennsylvania, Rhode Island, Tennessee, Vermont, Virginia, Wisconsin.

[13] Arizona, Arkansas, Indiana, Iowa, Massachusetts, Minnesota, Missouri, Nevada, New Mexico, New York, North Dakota, Oklahoma, Oregon, Pennsylvania, Rhode Island, South Dakota, Tennessee, Virginia, Wisconsin.

[14] California, Colorado, Delaware, Georgia, Idaho, Illinois, Kansas, Louisiana, Maine, Michigan, Mississippi, Montana, South Carolina, Texas, Utah, Washington, West Virginia, Wyoming.

[15] Alabama, Florida, Kentucky, Mary-

land, Nebraska, North Carolina, Ohio. New Jersey's 1947 constitution provides for either a three-fifths vote in one session or a majority vote in two successive sessions; Connecticut requires a majority vote of the house in one session and a two-thirds vote of each house in the next; Vermont, a majority of the house and two-thirds of the Senate in one session and a majority of each house in the next.

[16] Arizona, Arkansas, California, Colorado, Massachusetts, Michigan, Missouri, Nebraska, Nevada, North Dakota, Ohio, Oklahoma, Oregon.

fornia, ten per cent in Ohio, Oregon, and Michigan, fifteen per cent in Arizona. As in the case of proposal by the legislature, the details of proposal by initiative petition vary from State to State.[17]

Ratification of Amendments. In every State except Delaware, all amendments, whether proposed by the legislature or by initiative, must be ratified by the voters before they become effective.[18] Proposed amendments are usually placed before the voters at a regular election, but in some States special elections are also called for the purpose.

Generally, approval of a majority of those voting *on the amendment* makes it a part of the constitution. But again there are exceptions.

Minnesota, Mississippi, Oklahoma, and Wyoming require a majority of *all voting in the election,* not just of those who vote on the measure. And, as we saw, Tennessee requires a majority of all voting for governor at the most recent election. Many times amendments have been defeated in these States even though they actually received more " yes " than " no " votes — because many voters fail to vote on the ballot measures.

General Observations

The Need for Reform. In nearly every State there are individuals and groups working for reform in their State's constitution. And most constitutional authorities agree that the need is urgent. Most of the documents are too long and many of them are sadly outdated.

The Problem of Length. The original State constitutions were quite

brief. Their framers intended them as statements of basic principles and organization. They left to the legislature the task of filling in the details as needed.

Thus the longest of the first constitutions was that of Massachusetts. It ran to some 12,000 words; the shortest was New Jersey's at about 2500 words.

Through the years, constitutions have become longer and longer. Rhode Island and Vermont have the shortest today — each less than 6000 words. California's constitution is the longest; it contains nearly 90,000 words and prints up in 200 pages. The Louisiana constitution has some 70,000 words. (The Constitution of the United States, including all twenty-two amendments, contains less than 7000 words.)

---

[17] For instance in Massachusetts before an initiative proposal may be submitted to the voters it first must be approved by one-fourth of all the members of the legislature in joint session at two consecutive legislatures. In Arkansas, the petition must contain signatures of voters from each of fifteen counties; in Nebraska, from each of two-fifths of the State's counties, and in Ohio from each of one-half of that State's counties.

[18] In South Carolina and Mississippi *final* ratification, after a favorable popular vote, rests with the legislature.

Why are the documents becoming longer? The reasons are not hard to find. The people generally tend to distrust the legislature and so write provisions into the fundamental law where they cannot be so easily changed. Pressure groups know that a provision that benefits them is safer in the constitution than in a mere statute. Liquor interests, for example, are often successful in this regard. The result is that State constitutions are cluttered with a great deal of material that could (and should) be handled by ordinary legislation.

Then, too, court decisions can be effectively overridden by constitutional change and this has been done many times. For example, the New York courts declared a workmen's compensation law unconstitutional in 1911. A short time later, an amendment was adopted authorizing such a law.

Two further reasons are important: State and local functions have expanded tremendously in recent years and many new powers and agencies have been called for. Finally, the people have not been stingy in their use of the initiative in the thirteen

JOINING THE UNION

It was a day for celebration when Vermont became the fourteenth State in the Union, March 4, 1791.

States where the initiative is now permitted.

In short, there is an unfortunate failure in nearly every State to distinguish between *fundamental law* (that which should be in the constitution) and *statutory law* (that which ought to be handled through ordinary legislation).

The Problem of Age. If you look again at the table on page 466, you will see that most of our State's constitutions are comparatively ancient. Though most of them have been amended many times, these changes have, more often than not, compounded the clutter in the documents.

Using just one State as a *typical* example, the Oregon constitution was written a century ago, 1857. It has been amended more than 100 times and now contains *two* Articles VII and *eight* Articles XI! Like most of the rest, it is full of statutory material.

The oldest documents in force today are those of Massachusetts (1780),

New Hampshire (1784), and Vermont (1793). From the table on page 466, you can see that eighteen of the States still have their original constitutions, ten have documents at least 100 years old, and thirty of the others were written between fifty and 100 years ago. The average age is about seventy-five years.

The Model State Constitution was drafted by a group of distinguished political scientists and published by the National Municipal League in 1921. It has been revised and improved upon four times since. It is intended to serve as a model and a stimulation for constitutional reform. Several of its provisions, for example the legislative council idea, have had considerable influence in that direction.[19]

If more citizens would study their State constitutions and learn that many improvements — resulting in better and more economical government — could be made, State government would be greatly improved.

WHAT THIS CHAPTER IS ABOUT

The State constitution is the fundamental law under which the State is organized and the relations between individuals and with their government are regulated.

When independence came, eleven of the original States adopted their own constitutions. In Connecticut and Rhode Island the colonial charters continued to serve as constitutions. Generally, the people had little to do with the adoption of the new documents until 1780. In that year, Massachusetts adopted a constitution that was drafted by delegates elected by the voters and ratified by them. Popular participation is now the almost universal rule.

The first State constitutions varied widely in details but had many features in common: the principles of popular sovereignty, limited government, separa-

---

[19] Copies of the latest revision of the Model State Constitution can be obtained from the National Municipal League, 47 East 68th Street, New York City, at 50 cents per copy.

tion of powers and checks and balances, a relatively strong legislature and weak governor, and high suffrage qualifications.

State constitutions today commonly consist of these six parts: a preamble, bill of rights, provisions for the organization and powers of the government, for local governments, for such other matters as suffrage, and for amendment.

The details vary State-to-State but changes in a constitution are proposed in one or more of these ways: by a convention, by the legislature, or by initiative petition. In every State ratification is by popular vote — except in Delaware where the legislature has this power.

Nearly every State constitution is in need of reform. They have grown much too long and are generally outdated. They contain far too much material which should be covered in ordinary statutes enacted by the legislature.

The Model State Constitution of the National Municipal League now serves as a valuable guide to State constitution-makers.

QUESTIONS ON THE TEXT

1. What is a State constitution? How does it stand in relation to the supreme law of the land? In relation to other forms of State law?

2. What new feature of constitution-making did Massachusetts introduce? When?

3. Of what six parts does a State constitution commonly consist?

4. For what purpose does a State decide to assemble a constitutional convention?

5. What part do the voters usually take in making a new constitution?

6. What is meant by *partial amendment* of a State constitution? Describe how it is accomplished in your State.

7. What new way of amending constitutions has developed since 1902? Explain this method.

PROBLEMS FOR DISCUSSION

1. Secure a copy of your State constitution from your Secretary of State. Study its contents and answer as many of the following questions as you can.

　　a. When was it adopted? How many times has it been amended? By what process were the amendments made?

　　b. How long is the document? Does it deal only with the framework of your State government or does it contain regulations of social and economic problems?

2. The State constitution of Massachusetts requires a two-thirds vote in the House and a majority vote in the Senate in two consecutive General Courts before an amendment can be referred to the electorate. The Model State Constitution would require a simple majority vote of a unicameral (one-house) legislature. Which system would you prefer? Why?

3. If State constitutions were abolished, would it make the governments more or less democratic?

4. In a number of State legislatures the cities are not represented in proportion to population because the legislators from the country who now dominate the legislature are unwilling to increase the legislative influence of cities. What effect would the introduction of the constitu-

tional initiative have upon the representation of cities in a State where the city voters are in the majority?

5. How may new States be formed out of old States? (See U.S. Constitution, Art. IV, Sec. 3.) If the legislatures of New York and Illinois were willing to have New York City and Chicago become separate States, do you believe Congress would create new States of these cities? Would the House or Senate of Congress be more favorable? Why?

THINGS YOU MIGHT DO

1. Write a brief history of the drafting of your present State constitution.

2. Draw up an outline of your State constitution. What, if any, changes would you recommend and why?

3. Invite one or more of the State legislators from your area to address the class on the State constitution and ascertain his views in regard to its content and the need, if any, for change.

4. Invite representatives of various groups, labor, agriculture, business, education, etc., to address the class on the same subject.

WORDS AND PHRASES YOU SHOULD KNOW

Convention
Fundamental law
Initiative petition
Statutory law

Model State Constitution
Preamble
Schedule

SELECT BIBLIOGRAPHY

GRAVES, W. BROOKE, *American State Government,* Chapters 1, 2. Heath, 1953.

MACDONALD, AUSTIN F., *American State Government and Administration,* Chapters 1, 4. Crowell, 1955.

——, *State and Local Government in the United States,* Chapter 5. Crowell, 1955.

Model State Constitution. National Municipal League, 1948.

Modernizing State Constitutions. National Municipal League, 1948.

PHILLIPS, JEWELL C., *State and Local Government in America,* Chapters 1, 2, 3. American Book, 1954.

> Lean men there are as legislators, and fat men; tall men and
> short men, bald men and Beaux Brummels, old men and young men,
> sober men and smiling men, modest men and mere men, rich men
> and poor men, college-bred and corn-fed — men there are indeed,
> of every sort and condition.
>
> — *T. V. Smith*

★

Chapter 27

STATE LEGISLATURES

The details of the organization and even the official names of the forty-eight State legislatures vary from State to State. But the basic reason for its existence is everywhere the same: the legislature is the law-making branch; it is charged with the high duty of translating the will of the people into public policy. This it does by making law.

The legislature has been described as "the powerhouse of State government." Through its law-making power it creates the energy which keeps the wheels of State government moving.[1]

The Official Name

What we commonly call the "State legislature" is *officially* known by that title in only twenty-four of the States. In nineteen others it is the "General Assembly."[2] Montana, North Dakota, and Oregon call it the "Legislative Assembly." In Massachusetts and New Hampshire the legal name is the "General Court."

Every State has a bicameral legislature, except Nebraska, and each upper house is known as the "Senate" and this is the name Nebraska applies to its one house. But several titles are used for the lower house. Most of the States call it the "House of Representatives." In California, Nevada, New York, and Wisconsin, however, it is the "Assembly"; in New Jersey the "General Assembly"; and in Maryland, Virginia, and West Virginia the "House of Delegates."

---

[1] Lien, A., and Fainsod, J., *The American People and Their Government*, page 251. Appleton-Century-Crofts, 1934.

[2] These are: Arkansas, Colorado, Connecticut, Delaware, Georgia, Illinois, Indiana, Iowa, Kentucky, Maryland, Missouri, North Carolina, Ohio, Pennsylvania, Rhode Island, South Carolina, Tennessee, Vermont, and Virginia.

A. Devaney, Inc., N.Y.

TEXAS STATE CAPITOL
The majestic dome of the capitol building overlooks the city of Austin, capital of our largest State.

Bicameralism

One House or Two? Nebraska is the only State with a unicameral legislature today.[3] Recently the one-house system has been widely recommended as the best way to strengthen and improve our State legislatures.

---

[3] Georgia until 1789, Pennsylvania until 1790, and Vermont until 1836 had unicameral bodies. In opposing the change to bicameralism in Pennsylvania, Benjamin Franklin quoted the fable of the snake with two heads and one body. "She was going to a brook to drink, and on her way was to pass through a hedge, a twig of which opposed her direct course; one head chose to go on the right side of the twig, and the other on the left; so that time was spent in the contest, and, before the decision was completed, the poor snake died with thirst."

Pro and Con. Bicameralism's supporters claim that one house acts as a check on the other to prevent unwise legislation. Opponents cite numerous examples to show that the theory has not worked out so well in practice. Although the second house fails to pass many bills it receives from the first, the major reason is that they are never even considered; and those that do pass both houses are seldom changed in any way by the second house. The governor's veto, the press, and public opinion have proved a better check against harmful legislation than has bicameralism on the State level.

474

The fact that the bicameral system has worked well in Congress is often cited in support of the system for the State legislatures. But bicameralism in Congress reflects the federal character of the Union, and the States are not federal. In most States both houses represent exactly the same people and interests.

On the other hand, in a single house based on population, cities might so thoroughly dominate that rural interests would be virtually unrepresented. In some States, notably California, a balance of interests has been worked out. In California, the Assembly is controlled by the urban population while the Senate is in the hands of the rural population.

In the complicated structure of a two-house system special interests have a better chance to block popular legislation. Furthermore, the two-house system makes it almost impossible to fix definitely the responsibility for some action.

The Nebraska experiment has not been a cure-all for all the ills of legislatures, but it has worked well thus far. The other States are watching with great interest, and several of them in recent years have been seriously considering making the change. In Nebraska costs have been reduced, greater efficiency of operation has resulted, and fears that " unwise " legislation might result have proved to be unjustified.

Size and Terms

The Senate. The Senate varies in membership from State to State. Delaware and Nevada have the smallest upper chambers with seventeen members. The Senate in Minnesota is the largest with sixty-seven members. In some States one Senator is elected from each county, but most States are divided into senatorial districts of about equal population.

Senators are popularly elected in all of the States — for terms of four years in thirty-two States and two years in the other sixteen.

The Lower House. The membership of the lower house also varies in size among the States. Delaware's House of Representatives is the smallest — with thirty-five members. New

Hampshire has the largest, with about 400 members. In some States one or more representatives are elected from each county or each township, whereas other States are divided into House districts of about equal population.

From time to time the legislatures create new Senate and House districts which correspond to the changed distribution of population. As the cities grow in population, the rural county representatives commonly refuse to increase city representation proportionately for fear that the counties will be controlled by the cities. An especially unfair apportionment is called a " gerrymander," as described on page 85.

In most States it is the constitutional duty of the legislature to reapportion the State, usually every ten years, to take account of population shifts and increases. Short of constitutional amendment or, in some States, the use of the initiative, there is no way to force the legislature to reapportion. And many States have not been reapportioned for several years. For instance, Oregon's legislature ignored the constitutional requirement for more than forty years. Finally, the voters, through an initiative amendment, forced a reapportionment which took effect with the 1955 session.

In some States the people have taken the job out of the hands of the legislature and given it to reapportionment boards, as in California, Maryland, and Ohio. In those States reapportionment is largely automatic and the problem no longer exists.

The rapid growth of cities has caused some States to fear the domination of the whole State through one large city's controlling the legislature. So in Pennsylvania no city is allowed to have more than one-sixth of the senators; and in Rhode Island no town or city may have more than one-fourth of the representatives.

Representatives serve a two-year term in forty-three States. They serve four-year terms only in Alabama, Louisiana, Maryland, and Mississippi. (Remember, Nebraska has no lower house.)

Qualifications and Compensation

Qualifications. Every State constitution requires formal qualifications for membership in the legislature. In most States any qualified voter is eligible. Twenty-one is the minimum age for the House in all States, but some States set a higher age for the Senate. For example, in Texas a State Senator must be at least twenty-six.

A legislator must be a United States citizen but only Maine (five years), Alabama and California (three years), and New Jersey (two years) specify any particular period.

The members must be residents of the State in every instance and, either by law or custom, reside in the district, too.

Compensation. As in the case of Congressmen, what we pay our State legislators is a serious problem. Perhaps it is more serious at the State level, however, because the salaries are generally quite low.

Some people seem to feel that it is payment enough for one to have the honor of sitting in the legislature. A few seem to feel that legislators aren't really worth paying a salary to. But most people seem to be unaware of the problem.

The cold, hard facts are these: it costs money for legislators to live; and it costs money for them to take time away from their normal occupations in order to serve the State. Far too many times, capable and hard-

476

working men and women refuse to run for the legislature for the simple reason that they can't afford the financial sacrifices involved.

From the chart on page 478, you can see the salaries paid in each State. While most legislatures meet for only a few months every other year, the members are called upon to give up time between sessions to serve on committees and to take care of other legislative work.

In addition to the salaries, most States provide some sort of additional allowances. For example, in Alabama they receive $20 a day for subsistence during the session, in Kansas $7 a day for the session, and in Michigan $1000 a year for expenses. In most of the States, though, the additional allowances are only for postage and mileage for a single round trip.

In some States the legislator's pay is set by the constitution, but in most the amount is left up to the legislature itself. Why, then, don't the members simply raise their own pay? The best answer to this question is that they are usually afraid that such a move would be misinterpreted by many people and used as campaign ammunition against them at the next election.

The fairly good salaries now being paid in a few States like California, Illinois, Massachusetts, Michigan, New Jersey, Pennsylvania, and New York are encouraging steps in the right direction.

Legislative Sessions

Annual Sessions. Fourteen States now hold annual sessions.[4] This list has grown in the past few years because more and more it is seen that the work of the legislature cannot be handled best on an every-other-year-for-a-few-months basis.

Biennial Sessions. The other thirty-four States still hold biennial sessions. But the increasing press of State business today has meant that special sessions have become fairly common in most of these States; and so too has the use of *interim commit-* *tees* (those which function in the *interim,* between sessions of the legislature.)

In most States the legislators are elected in November of even-numbered years and take their seats the following January. But a few States select them in the odd-numbered years in order to separate the consideration of State candidates and issues from national ones.

Length of Sessions. As a general rule, sessions are becoming longer and longer. Some State constitutions limit the length of regular sessions to a definite number of days. Others allow no compensation after a certain period. But, again because of the growing volume of State business,

---

[4] Arizona, California, Colorado, Georgia, Kansas, Louisiana, Maryland, Massachusetts, Michigan, New Jersey, New York, Rhode Island, South Carolina, West Virginia.

STATE	ANN. OR BIEN.	LIMIT OF REGULAR SESSION WITH PAY	NO. OF MEMBERS IN SENATE	NO. OF MEMBERS IN HOUSE	TERM OF SENATORS (YEARS)	TERM OF REPRESENTATIVES (YEARS)	SALARY OF MEMBERS [1]
Alabama	Bien.	36 days	35	106	4	4	$10 per diem
Arizona	Ann.	60 days	28	80	2	2	$8 per diem
Arkansas	Bien.	60 days	35	100	4	2	$1200 bien.
California	Ann.	120 days	40	80	4	2	$6000 ann.
Colorado	Ann.	None	35	65	4	2	$3600 bien.
Connecticut	Bien.	Varies	36	279	2	2	$600 bien.
Delaware	Bien.	None	17	35	4	2	$1000 ann.
Florida	Bien.	60 days	38	95	4	2	$1200 ann.
Georgia	Ann.	40 days	54	205	2	2	$20 per diem
Idaho	Bien.	60 days	44	59	2	2	$10 per diem
Illinois	Bien.	6 mos.	58	177	4	2	$5000 ann.
Indiana	Bien.	61 days	50	100	4	2	$1800 ann.
Iowa	Bien.	None	50	108	4	2	$2000 bien.
Kansas	Ann.	None	40	125	4	2	$300 ses'n
Kentucky	Bien.	60 days	38	100	4	2	$25 per diem
Louisiana	Ann.	60 days	39	101	4	4	$7650 bien.
Maine	Bien.	None	33	151	2	2	$1250 ses'n
Maryland	Ann.	90 days	29	123	4	4	$1800 ann.
Massachusetts	Ann.	None	40	240	2	2	$4500 ann.
Michigan	Ann.	None	34	110	2	2	$4000 ann.
Minnesota	Bien.	90 days	67	131	4	2	$4800 bien.
Mississippi	Bien.	None	49	140	4	4	$3000 ses'n
Missouri	Bien.	5 mos.	34	157	4	2	$1500 ann.
Montana	Bien.	60 days	56	94	4	2	$20 per diem
Nebraska	Bien.	None	43	None	2	—	$872.09 ann.
Nevada	Bien.	60 days	17	47	4	2	$15 per diem
New Hampshire	Bien.	None	24	400 [2]	2	2	$200 bien.
New Jersey	Ann.	None	21	60	4	2	$5000 ann.
New Mexico	Bien.	60 days	32	66	4	2	$20 per diem
New York	Ann.	None	58	150	2	2	$7500 ann.
North Carolina	Bien.	None	50	120	2	2	$15 per diem
North Dakota	Bien.	60 days	49	113	4	2	$5 per diem
Ohio	Bien.	None	34	139	2	2	$5000 ann.
Oklahoma	Bien.	None	44	121	4	2	$3275 bien.
Oregon	Bien.	None	30	60	4	2	$600 ann.
Pennsylvania	Bien.	None	50	210	4	2	$3000 ann.
Rhode Island	Ann.	60 days	44	100	2	2	$300 ann.
South Carolina	Ann.	None	46	124	4	2	$1000 ann.
South Dakota	Bien.	60 days	35	75	2	2	$1050 bien.
Tennessee	Bien.	75 days	33	99	2	2	$15 per diem
Texas	Bien.	120 days	31	150	4	2	$25 per diem
Utah	Bien.	60 days	25	64	4	2	$1000 bien.
Vermont	Bien.	None	30	246	2	2	$70 per week
Virginia	Bien.	60 days	40	100	4	2	$1080 ses'n
Washington	Bien.	60 days	46	99	4	2	$2400 bien.
West Virginia	Ann.	60 days	32	100	4	2	$1500 ann.
Wisconsin	Bien.	None	33	100	4	2	$2400 ann.
Wyoming	Bien.	40 days	27	56	4	2	$12 per diem

[1] Most legislators receive additional payments in the form of expense money.

[2] Varies 375–400, as some small towns are not represented at all sessions.

these restrictions are disappearing.

" Budget Sessions." In some of the annual-session States (*e.g.,* California, Kansas, Louisiana, Maryland) the sessions in the even-numbered years are budget sessions. These sessions have been provided for especially to consider fiscal matters; and in some States (*e.g.,* Kansas and Louisiana) *only* such matters may be considered.

Special Sessions. Extraordinary or special sessions are becoming rather common. The State constitutions give the governor the power to call them in every State. And in fourteen of the States the legislature itself has the power to call special sessions if it wishes to do so.

Powers of the Legislature

Of course, you recall the *division of powers* between the National Government and the States under the federal system. The National Government has those powers which are *delegated* to it in the Constitution. The 10th Amendment provides that

The powers not delegated to the United States by the Constitution, nor prohibited by it to the States, are reserved to the States, respectively, or to the people.

Thus the States have the *reserved powers.*

No State's constitution contains a detailed listing of the legislature's powers. Rather, the legislature has those that are not granted to the executive and judicial departments and to local governments and those that the constitution does not specifically deny to the legislature.

To put it another way, the legislature has all those powers not granted elsewhere and which are not prohibited to it in the National or State Constitutions.[5]

This means that *most* State powers are vested in the legislature.

1. *The Bill of Rights* — guarantees such basic civil rights as freedom of religion, press, speech, assembly, jury trial, the writ of habeas corpus, protection against unreasonable searches and seizures, due process of law, etc.
2. Other Parts of the Constitution:
   a. Prohibit special privileges to corporations.
   b. Limit State debts and require regular payment of principal and interest.
   c. Set suffrage qualifications and terms and duties of certain State and local officers.
   d. Lay down certain rules for public education, and public institutions such as prisons, hospitals, colleges, etc.
   e. Provide certain rules for local government and in many States, " municipal home rule."
   f. Place restrictions on the passage of " special laws " — that is, laws applying to a particular person, corporation, or locality (township, county, or city). Legislatures often used to use special laws to penalize or discriminate against larger cities. For example, the Pennsylvania legislature once compelled Philadelphia to build a city hall costing millions of dollars and much larger and more expensive than the city needed or would have provided for itself.

---

[5] The following restrictions are commonly placed upon the legislature by the State constitution:

Because a legislature can enact any laws that are not in conflict with federal law and the State constitution, it is impossible to list the legislature's powers in 1, 2, 3 order.

Examples of subjects on which it legislates are: taxation; appropriations; civil matters such as contracts, real and personal property, inheritances, mortgages, corporations, marriage and divorce; crimes such as murder, burglary, arson, and kidnapping; and the regulation of business, labor, the various professions, agriculture, and so on.

The " Police Power." Every legislature has the so-called " police power." That is, it has the power to legislate to protect and promote the public health, safety, morals, and general welfare of the people. It may do this so long as it does not violate a person's right to life, liberty, or property, without due process of law.

Under this broad power, the legislature passes literally thousands of laws. For example, to protect and promote health it passes quarantine laws, requires compulsory vaccinations, and guarantees pure food and drugs.

For morals, it regulates intoxicating liquors and suppresses gambling, lotteries, and immoral entertainments. For safety, it regulates fireworks, explosives, firearms, industrial working conditions and automobile speeds. You can find dozens of other examples where the legislative " police power " regulates and protects both personal and public welfare.

Executive Powers. The legislature has a good deal of control over the executive branch in each State. It often appoints many of the executive officers. By law it creates most of the agencies within the executive branch and defines their duties. Through its power of the purse it often has life and death say in executive matters.

Judicial Powers. In every State, except Oregon, the legislature has the power to impeach and remove executive and judicial officers.[6] It also defines crimes and provides for their punishment and otherwise controls the work of the courts.

You remember from the last Chapter that the legislature also has various *constituent powers* — that is, powers in connection with the making and amending of the State constitution.

Organization of the Legislature

In most ways the legislatures of the forty-eight States are organized in much the same manner as is Congress (see page 95).

Presiding Officers. The officers of the legislature are quite similar to those in Congress and their duties are about the same. The lower house in

---

[6] Oregon's constitution does not provide for impeachment. But it does provide for the popular recall of any elected State official and that " incompetency, corruption, malfeasance, or delinquency in office may be tried (in court) in the same manner as criminal offenses."

each State elects its own Speaker.[7] Thirty-seven States elect a lieutenant-governor who presides over the Senate, except in Kentucky, Massachusetts, and Mississippi. In these three and the other eleven States the Senate chooses its own President. In actual practice, the majority party caucus really chooses the presiding officers — except the lieutenant-governors, of course.

Other officers, such as clerks, reporters, sergeants-at-arms, and doorkeepers are also chosen by each house and dozens of other employees, like stenographers, are also on hand.

Rules of Procedure. These rules are determined by each house, and each house also judges disputes regarding the qualifications of its own members.

The Committee System. The committee system is very similar to that in Congress, discussed on pages 150–154. Most of the important work of the legislature is done through committees and their sub-committees.

It would be impossible for every member to read, let alone understand, all of the bills introduced. The wide variety of these measures was hinted at when we discussed the legislature's powers. The committees provide for specialization and without them the legislature could not do its work.

Each committee usually deals with a particular subject: taxation, high-ways, health, appropriations, commerce, local government, etc. Members are usually assigned to those committees in which they express an interest and for which their training and experience equip them.

The number of standing committees varies in the lower house from eight in Maine and South Carolina to sixty-three in Georgia and sixty-four in Missouri; and in the Senate from three in Maine and seven in New Mexico to thirty-nine in Iowa and Texas and forty-six in Mississippi. Committees are so numerous in some States that legislators often have no time for much public business they should attend to. Some States have corrected this situation in the past few years. Thus in 1956 the Kentucky legislature reduced committees from thirty-nine in the Senate and seventy-one in the House to eighteen in each chamber. Still, the problem of too many committees continues to plague most legislatures and legislators.

The "pigeonholing" of bills is quite common in State legislatures. A common method of preventing the passage of a bill is to have it referred to the Judiciary Committee, claiming it to be "of doubtful constitutionality." The committee's majority is counted on to pigeonhole the measure. Such a committee is often nicknamed the "graveyard committee."

One of the weirdest examples of pigeonholing occurred in one of our inland States a few years ago. A bill relating to the State mental hospital was referred to the House Committee

---

[7] Unlike the national Speaker, in most States he has the power to appoint the special and standing committee members and preside over the committee of the whole.

on Deep Sea Navigation. Not only was this done in a *landlocked* State, but Congress and not the States has control over deep sea navigation under its power to regulate foreign commerce.

Despite this and other abuses of the committee system, however, committee hearings and reports are an essential part of the legislative process.

In Massachusetts, for example, notice of all hearings is given in the public press, and the committee hearings are well-attended, not only by people who have an ax to grind, but by citizens interested in legislative reforms. All testimony taken is carefully weighed; in fact, the legislature and its committees assume rather a judicial attitude. Petitions are brought before them, testimony given, arguments heard, and the committee generally decides the matter on the basis of all these considerations.

Joint Committees, composed of members from both houses, are being used more and more in several States. The savings made in time and duplication of effort are substantial.

Interim committees, those which meet between sessions, are used in several States to study particular problems and make recommendations to the full legislature — for example on highways or taxation. (See the discussion of Legislative Councils on page 485.)

How Bills Become State Laws

Preparation of Bills. Although most State legislators may have above average intelligence, few of them are trained to prepare bills in clear, unmistakable language [8] or in such a way as to avoid conflict with federal law and the State constitution.

In earlier days, the members who were lawyers or an experienced clerk did the bill-drafting. With the development of lobbying, the lobbyists often did the job for members whose acquaintance and good will they valued.

Today each State has trained assistants who put into proper form the

[8] As an example of what can happen when legislators are not careful, the Oregon House of Representatives recently approved a bill to require the filling in of all abandoned wells — but the bill was so worded as to require the filling of a well *before* it had been dug!

THE COURSE OF A BILL

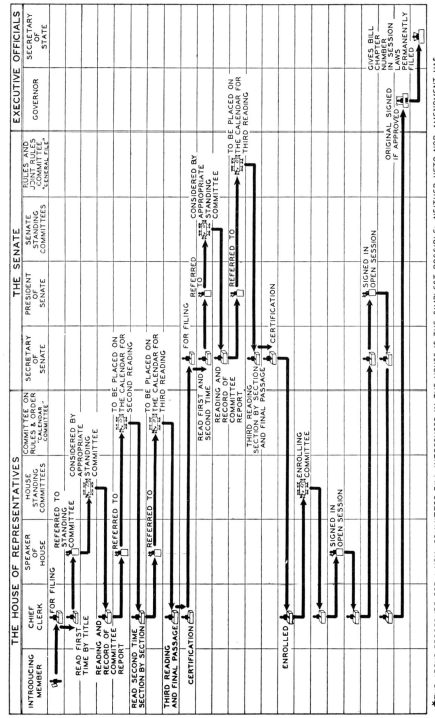

*THE ABOVE PROCEDURE FOR A NON-COMMITTEE BILL INTRODUCED IN THE HOUSE IS THE SIMPLEST POSSIBLE; NEITHER VETO NOR AMENDMENT HAS OCCURRED. IF SUCH A BILL IS INTRODUCED IN THE SENATE, THE SECRETARY OF THE SENATE WOULD PERFORM ESSENTIALLY THE SAME FUNCTIONS AS THE CHIEF CLERK OF THE HOUSE INDICATED ABOVE, AND THE ACTION OF THE HOUSE THEREON WOULD OCCUR AFTER PASSAGE THEREOF BY THE SENATE.

BUREAU OF GOVERNMENTAL RESEARCH AND SERVICES UNIVERSITY OF WASHINGTON.

ideas that members wish to enact into law. These assistants are usually connected with the Legislative Reference Bureau or the Attorney-General's office.

A *Legislative Reference Bureau* is now maintained by over half the States. It is either a division of the State Library or has a library of its own to assist members. Specialists collect reference materials such as court decisions, newspaper clippings, magazine articles, and books on government and its problems, official reports, party platforms, governors' messages, information on other States, and any other material that might be valuable to legislators. Its experts prepare reports, draft bills and generally help the members with legislative problems.

Bills are often prepared by State executive agencies, lobbyists, and private persons and handed to a member to introduce. Just as in Congress, hundreds of " by-request " bills turn up in every session.

Introduction of Bills. Any member of either house may introduce as many bills as he chooses; but important bills are commonly prepared by a committee and introduced by its chairman. In introducing bills the members merely file them with the clerk. Some legislatures prohibit the introduction of bills after the legislature has been in session a certain number of days; others require that bills of a local or private character must be announced in the locality to be affected; and still others require that local bills receive a two-thirds vote of each house instead of simply a bare majority, which is sufficient for public bills.

Passage of Bills. The passage of a bill through the typical State legislature is outlined in the chart on page 483.

On account of the large number of bills introduced at each session of the State legislature it would be impossible for the committees to give consideration to all of them. Therefore those bills which are not introduced by prominent members or backed by influential lobbyists are seldom considered seriously and are usually pigeonholed. Many of the bills that the legislative leaders oppose, but which have public support, are sometimes intentionally reported out of committee too late in the session to be considered on the floor.

Pressure Groups and Lobbyists

The State legislatures, like Congress, are beset by lobbyists and pressure groups. Lobbyists are often given the dignified title " legislative agent " or " public relations counsel." They make a practice of frequenting lobbies [9] or other convenient places for the purpose of persuading legisla-

---

[9] A *lobby* is an anteroom or corridor connecting with the main assembly room, or else a railed-off part of the assembly room itself to which the public is admitted.

tors to vote for or against certain bills.

As was suggested on page 163, lobbyists are sometimes former legislators who still have friends in the legislature, sometimes leaders of organizations, and sometimes high-pressure experts. These lobbyists form an important part of the " invisible government " and extralegal legislative machinery. Their methods are not merely to buttonhole legislators, but to put indirect influences to bear: through friends, letters, telegrams, telephone calls, radio broadcasts, and newspapers and other periodicals. A lobbyist may represent business, labor unions, farm organizations, reform groups, or groups like the liquor interests or gambling interests that are endeavoring to have legal restrictions removed.

Regulation of Lobbyists. For many years, some States have controlled lobbying along the lines set up by Congress in its Reorganization Act of 1946 (page 164). For example, the State of Wisconsin requires all persons employed to lobby at a legislative session to be registered on a legislative docket which is kept by the Secretary of State. The names of the employer and employed must be entered with a statement of the legislation in which they are interested and the terms of employment. The lobbyist is not allowed to enter upon the floor of either house; and his lobbying must be restricted to committees or work properly incidental thereto, to newspaper publications, public addresses, or written briefs delivered to each member of the legislature and filed with the Secretary of State. A detailed statement of expenses must be filed within thirty days of the adjournment of the legislature.

Legislative Councils

A little over twenty years ago, Kansas launched an experiment which has now been copied by nearly two-thirds of the States: the *legislative council.*

As the work of the State legislatures has increased in volume and complexity, the need for more wise planning and leadership has become acute.

The legislative council prepares a law-making program for each session.

Its members, from each house of the legislature, meet several times during the interim period (between sessions), usually under the chairmanship of the Senate or House presiding officer.

It makes detailed studies of State problems, keeps the entire membership of the legislature informed of its work, and generally tries to keep the law-making branch abreast of its work.

Improving State Legislatures

Following the lead of Congress, many of the States are now reorganizing and improving their legislative bodies. Professors of political science and several citizen's committees and private research organizations are helping with the task.

One of the private groups, the Council of State Governments, has prepared a very valuable study entitled *Our State Legislatures*. In summarizing its findings, the report makes these recommendations (which also indicate the scope of the problem):

(1) Restrictions on the length of regular sessions should be removed. Legislatures should be permitted to meet as often and as long as conditions require.

(2) Adequate salaries, sufficient to permit competent persons to serve in the legislature, should be provided. Salaries should be determined by statute rather than by constitutional provision.

(3) Legislative terms of office should be lengthened and staggered to provide continuity in membership.

(4) Skilled and essential full-time legislative employees should be appointed on the basis of merit and should retain their positions regardless of changes in party majorities.

(5) Committees should be reduced in number wherever practicable; and they should be organized with regard to subject matter, equalization of work, and cooperation between the two houses. Permanent and public records of committee action should be kept.

(6) Committees should provide for public hearings on all major bills, with advance notice of time and place.

(7) Legislative councils or interim committees, with adequate clerical and research facilities, should be provided.

(8) Legislative reference services and similar organizations should be established and strengthened in each State.

(9) Legislative rules should limit the time period during which new bills may be introduced in order to prevent congestion at the end of the session.

(10) Legislative rules should be revised wherever necessary to expedite procedure, although with regard for full deliberation and minorities.

(11) The legislature should make suitable provision, by means of a budget, for all of its own expenditures.

(12) Special legislation should be avoided. Claims against the State should be handled by judicial or administrative agencies. Municipal affairs should be regulated by general or optional legislation, or by conferring home rule upon municipalities.

Direct Legislation

Beginning with South Dakota in 1898, several States now permit the voters themselves to take a direct hand in State legislation through the use of the initiative and the referendum.

The Initiative. As we learned in our study of constitutional amending procedures, the voters themselves may initiate (propose) constitutional amendments in thirteen States.[10] In nineteen States[11] they may also initiate ordinary laws.

---

[10] See page 467. The States are: Arizona, Arkansas, California, Colorado, Massachusetts, Michigan, Missouri, Nebraska, Nevada, North Dakota, Ohio, Oklahoma, Oregon.

[11] The foregoing thirteen States plus Idaho, Maine, Montana, South Dakota, Utah, and Washington. The initiative, and the referendum, too, are used in local matters in hundreds of cities and counties, also.

486

The initiative, then, is a device by which an individual or group may propose legislation.

An *initiative petition* is circulated by the sponsors of the measure. This petition must be signed by a certain number of registered voters. The

The *direct initiative* is the most common form. Under it, the proposed law goes *directly* to the ballot to be voted on by the people at the next election.

The *indirect initiative* is found in those States in which the proposal

POPULAR PARTICIPATION IN LAWMAKING

Initiative	*Direct.* (Referred to the voters directly without being submitted to the legislative body.)		Constitutional Statutory
	Indirect. (Referred to the legislative body, and if enacted by this body, reference to the people is unnecessary.)		Statutory only
Referendum	*Mandatory by a constitutional provision* (also called compulsory or obligatory). Examples: State constitutional amendments, bond issues, amendment of home rule charters.		
	Optional with a legislative body (also called voluntary). Examples: A measure passed by a body with legislative power and submitted to the voters for ratification; a proposed law submitted to the voters for advice before action by the legislature.		Submitted for ratification Submitted for advice
	Appeal from a legislative body through popular petition. Example: An unpopular legislative act voted on at a special election called by petition of specified number of voters.		

number required varies from State to State. For example 10,000 signatures are required to propose a law in North Dakota; in Ohio, ten per cent of the registered voters.

When and if enough valid signatures are collected, the measure goes on the ballot or to the legislature — depending on whether the State has the *direct initiative* or the *indirect initiative*.[12]

goes first to the legislature. Then, if the legislature does not enact it, the measure goes to the voters.

Here are some examples of the use of the initiative:

Oregon (1954) approved a measure which repealed laws empowering the State Board of Agriculture to fix minimum milk prices at the producer, wholesale, and retail levels.

California (1950) defeated a proposal to

[12] Ten States have the *direct initiative,* five (Maine, Massachusetts, Michigan, Nevada, and South Dakota) have the *indirect,* and California, Ohio, Utah, and Washington have both.

OREGON STATE CAPITOL

Completed in 1939, the marble building is distinguished by the sheer white central tower. The famous bronze statue of the " Pioneer " stands atop the seventy-five-foot tower.

legalize practically all forms of gambling in the State.

North Dakota (1954) defeated a measure proposing an 11 P.M. closing hour for all places where liquor is sold in the State.

The Referendum. There are three kinds of referenda in use in the various States — the mandatory, the optional, and the popular.

Mandatory Referendum. In every State except Delaware, the mandatory referendum is provided for constitutional amendments. That is, they *must* be referred to the voters and approved by them before they go into effect. In several States, some other measures must also be referred to the people; the calling of a constitutional convention and bond issues are common examples. For instance: in 1957 the voters in Maine approved one amendment changing the date on which the State's general elections are held. Since 1820 Maine had regularly held her elections in September. Beginning in 1958 she will hold her elections on the same day in November as do each of the other forty-seven States. Another amendment approved at the same time provides that, beginning in 1960, the governor's term (now two years) will be increased to four years.

Optional Referendum. If a meas-

488

ure is voluntarily referred to the voters by the legislature, it is said to be an *optional* or legislative referendum. A State legislature is often willing to refer a measure to the people when it is unwilling itself to assume the responsibility for passing it. Here are two examples: in 1938 the voters in Oregon overwhelmingly approved a measure requiring physical and mental examinations for all men and women who apply for marriage licenses. At a special election in 1947 the voters in Oregon overwhelmingly defeated a referred measure which would have provided a State sales tax.

Popular Referendum. This is the type of referendum most often associated with " direct legislation." It is found in twenty-one States — the nineteen which have the statutory initiative (page 486) plus Maryland and New Mexico.

Under it, the people may demand that a measure passed by the legislature be referred to them for final approval or rejection.[13] The demand is made by a petition which must be signed by a certain number of registered voters. The number required varies among the States but is usually between five and ten per cent.

Here are examples:

Oregon (1956) defeated a measure providing for a three-cent sales tax on cigarettes but not on other tobacco products (cigars, pipe tobacco, etc.)

Oregon (1952) approved a measure providing for sale of liquor by the drink in State-licensed restaurants, taverns, clubs, etc.

WHAT THIS CHAPTER IS ABOUT

The details of organization and even the official names of the legislatures vary from State to State. But everywhere its basic function is the same — to make law.

The legislature is bicameral in every State except Nebraska. Bicameralism's supporters claim that one house acts as a check on the other, but its opponents dispute this and add that the governor's veto, public opinion, and the press are the real checks. Bicameralism in Congress reflects the federal character of the Union; but the States are not federal.

The size of the legislature varies considerably from State to State. Senators are popularly elected for four years in thirty-two States and two years in the other sixteen. Representatives are popularly elected for two-year terms in forty-three States and four-year terms in four.

Reapportionment and gerrymandering are problems in many of the States though in a few the matter has now been taken out of the legislature's hands.

All State constitutions require a legislator to be at least a qualified voter and some States set a little higher qualification. Most legislators are seriously un-

---

[13] There are some measures which need to become effective immediately, without waiting the sixty to ninety days in which the people may circulate referenda petitions. These " emergency measures " become effective immediately if the legislature attaches an " emergency clause " to them.

To prevent the legislature from attaching the emergency clause to a measure just to avoid its being referred, some States give the governor the power to veto an emergency clause. Also, one State, Oregon, forbids the emergency clause on any tax bill.

derpaid with the result that many capable people refuse to run for the office. Some sort of additional allowance goes along with the salary in several States.

The increasing pressures of State business have forced most legislatures to hold longer and longer sessions and numerous special sessions. Fourteen State legislatures now hold regular sessions annually while the others still convene biennially.

The legislatures have all those powers not granted elsewhere and not prohibited to them by the National Constitution or that of their own State. They have certain executive and judicial powers; their most important legislative power is the so-called " police power."

The organization of the legislatures is quite similar to that in Congress. So is the legislative process. Lobbyist and pressure group activities, an important element in legislation, are found as much in the State capitals as in Washington, D.C.

Legislative Councils exist in nearly two-thirds of the States. They serve as planning agencies presenting the legislature with a law-making program for the session.

Through the various forms of direct legislation (the initiative and referendum) the people themselves may take an active hand in the making of law that they desire.

QUESTIONS ON THE TEXT

1. By what name is the legislature in your State known? The upper house? The lower house?

2. How many members are there in the upper house of your State's legislature? The lower house?

3. How often does your legislature hold regular sessions? Is the length of the session restricted? Why are more States coming to the annual session?

4. What salary do the members of your legislature receive?

5. What powers does a State legislature have? What are the so-called " police powers "?

6. List three restrictions commonly placed on the legislature's power by a State constitution.

7. Why do the legislatures function through committees? What is a joint committee?

8. What is a legislative reference bureau? A legislative council?

9. What is meant by lobbying?

10. Define: Indirect Initiative. Direct Initiative. Does your State have the initiative? For constitutional amendments or statutes or for both?

11. What are the three types of referenda? Does your State have the type most often associated with direct legislation?

PROBLEMS FOR DISCUSSION

1. Many State constitutions commonly restrict the session of State legislatures to a certain number of days, which means that bills must be passed or rejected because of the calendar rather than after due consideration. Would it not be well for all States to pay their legislators by the year and permit them to prolong the session for as long as need be?

2. About half the States now have voting machines for their legislatures. The Wisconsin Assembly has for some years saved about 125 hours a session by the use of a machine which records the

490

votes of all members in less than a minute instead of ten minutes for a vocal roll call.

When an issue comes to a vote the Speaker turns a key on his desk and proclaims: " Roll call." Thereupon each legislator presses one of three buttons on his desk; and thereby registers either: " Yes," " No," or " Present but not voting." The Speaker inquires: " Has everyone voted? " The Speaker then locks the machine, which produces a photostatic copy of the roll, showing the vote of each individual and the total recorded vote on the issue under consideration.

In the gallery, visible to each member, is the name of each member with a white light (yes) and a red one (no) which flash on at the touch of the button on the member's desk.

The machine cost $12,000 and one electrician is required to operate it.

Do you think all legislatures should use such a machine? Why? Why do you suppose some legislators oppose the use of an electric voting machine?

THINGS YOU MIGHT DO

1. If the legislature is in session, by all means make every effort to visit it and observe it at work.

2. Write a short biography of each of your local State legislators. If at all possible, invite them to speak to the class.

3. Stage a class debate or forum on the question: *Resolved:* That the legislature of this State should become unicameral.

4. Draw up a list of as many arguments for and against direct legislation as you can.

5. Using the recommendations by the Council of State Governments on page 486, discover whether or not each of these would apply in your State. (Consult your local legislators and the State Blue Book.) Brief reports might be written to indicate why these suggestions should or should not be adopted in your State.

WORDS AND PHRASES YOU SHOULD KNOW

Bicameralism	Legislative council	Police power
Initiative	Legislative reference bureau	Referendum
Interim committee	Lieutenant-Governor	Unicameralism

SELECT BIBLIOGRAPHY

DESMOND, STATE SENATOR THOMAS C., " Those Dinosaurs — The State Legislatures," *New York Times Magazine,* January 16, 1955.

LOCKARD, DUANE, " Tribulations of a State Senator," *The Reporter,* May 17, 1956.

MACDONALD, AUSTIN F., *American State Government and Administration,* Chapters 8, 9. Crowell, 1955.

MARTIN, J., " What Those Politicians Do to You! " *Saturday Evening Post,* December 12, 19, 26, 1953.

PHILLIPS, JEWELL C., *State and Local Government in America,* Chapters 7, 8. American Book, 1954.

VELIE, LESTER, Series of Articles in *Reader's Digest,* January–May, 1953.

Energy in the Executive is a leading character in the definition of good government. . . . A feeble Executive implies a feeble execution of the government. A feeble execution is but another phrase for a bad execution; and a government ill-executed, whatever it may be in theory, must be, in practice, a bad government.

— *Alexander Hamilton*

★

Chapter 28

STATE GOVERNORS

Historical Development. The governor in each of our forty-eight States occupies an office which is the direct descendant of the earliest executive office in America. The history of the post dates back to the first colonial governorship, established by the London Company in Virginia in 1607.

Much of the resentment that finally brought on the Revolutionary War was directed at the royal governors, as we noted in Chapter 3. When the first State constitutions were written, the memory of the royal governors was fresh.

It was quite natural, then, that most of the powers granted to the original State governments were given to the legislature. The governor had only rather meager authority. In every State except Massachusetts and New York he was chosen by the legislature. Only in Massachusetts and South Carolina did he have the veto power.

The early State governors are often described as "figureheads." Thus, in addressing the Philadelphia Convention of 1787, James Madison was able to say:

The executives of the States are in general little more than ciphers; the legislatures are omnipotent.

Gradually, however, the people began to realize that the original separation of powers between the legislature and the governor was an unsatisfactory one. The legislature often abused its powers, and the weak governor was unable to check it. So, as new State constitutions were written and the older ones amended, the legislature's powers were lessened and those of the governor were generally increased.[1]

Through the early years of the nineteenth century the power to choose the governor was taken from the legislature and given to the voters. The veto power was granted to the governor,

[1] The title of the best study made of the office of State governor illustrates the evolutionary process through which the position has passed: Lipson, L., *The American Governor: From Figurehead to Leader,* University of Chicago Press, Chicago, 1939.

492

THE ARREST OF ANDROS, 1689

In 1686, King James II combined the colonies of Massachusetts, Plymouth, Maine, Rhode Island, and King's Province (now part of Rhode Island) into a single Dominion of New England under autocratic Governor Edmund Andros. After James was dethroned in 1688, Andros was arrested and his government abolished.

and his powers of appointment and administration were increased.

At the same time, however, new and popularly elected officers, boards, and commissions were also provided for in several States.[2] These executive officers, supposedly within the governor's

[2] As one authority on State government has put it: " Though popular faith in legislative bodies had declined sharply . . . , dispersion of executive power was mute testimony to the persistence of the popular fear of concentrated power." — Phillips, J., *State and Local Government in America,* American Book Company, New York, 1954, page 184.

administration, were actually independent of him. He could exercise no real control over them because they, like him, were elected by the people. Many States are still plagued by too many examples of this development.

The most striking developments in the character of the governorship have taken place only in the past thirty to forty years. Beginning with Illinois in 1917, most States have reorganized the executive branch to make the governor a chief executive in something more than name. Of course, some

States have gone farther than others in the strengthening of the office. In all States, however, the governor is much more important and powerful now than in earlier days — and the trend to a stronger governor continues.

General Consideration of the Office

Selection. Only a few States, New York, for example, still use the convention method to nominate candidates for governor. The direct primary is used today in most States.

In every State the governor is chosen by popular vote.[3] In all but four States the candidate who receives a plurality (more votes than any other candidate) is declared elected. In Georgia, Maine, Mississippi, and Vermont a candidate must receive a ma-

---

[3] In Mississippi each county or legislative district has as many " electoral votes " as it has members of the State House of Representatives. The candidate receiving the most popular votes in a county receives all of that county's electoral votes. In order to win the governorship, a candidate must receive a majority of both the electoral and the popular votes in the State. If no candidate receives both, the choice of a governor falls to the House of Representatives.

GOVERNOR'S INAUGURATION, 1879
The first public inauguration of a governor in Kansas is shown by an old woodcut. The scene is Topeka, the State capital.

jority of all of the votes cast in order to win.[4]

Qualifications. Every State's constitution sets out certain formal qualifications that must be met before a person can be elected governor.

The qualifications provided in the Texas constitution are typical: No person may be chosen governor unless he or she (1) is an American citizen, (2) has lived in the State for at least five years, and (3) is at least thirty years of age. Texas and seven other States [5] also bar atheists from the governorship.

State politics usually impose other " informal " qualifications on a candidate. He must usually live in a populous area, have an acceptable record of accomplishment in politics, business or some other field, be acceptable to the various wings of his party or at least not have made too many enemies, and so on.

Term. Under the first State Constitutions governors were commonly chosen for one-year terms. Today, twenty-nine of the States provide for a four-year term and the other nineteen for two years (see table, page 497).

Nearly half of the States place some limit on the number of terms a governor may serve. For example, in New Jersey and in Oregon no person may serve for more than eight years in any twelve. In Indiana, Pennsylvania, and Virginia a governor may not succeed himself.

Removal. The governor may be removed from office by the impeachment process in every State except Oregon.[6] Only four governors have been impeached and removed since the years immediately following the War Between the States — William Sulzer of New York, 1913; James E. Ferguson of Texas, 1917; [7] J. C. Walton of Oklahoma, 1923; and Henry S. Johnston also of Oklahoma, 1929.

The governor may be recalled from office in twelve States,[8] though only one has ever been so removed. Governor Lynn J. Frazier was recalled in North Dakota in 1921. The next year he was elected to the United States Senate!

Succession. Each of the State Constitutions provides for a successor should the governor die, resign, be removed from office, or be physically

---

[1] If no candidate receives a majority in Georgia or Vermont, the winner is selected by the two houses of the legislature in joint session. If no candidate has a majority in Maine or Mississippi, the governor is chosen by the lower house alone.

[5] Arkansas, Maryland, Mississippi, North Carolina, Pennsylvania, South Carolina, and Tennessee.

[6] In Oregon the governor may be recalled. See note 6, page 479.

[7] " Pa " Ferguson was later " pardoned " by the Texas legislature and immediately announced his candidacy for the governorship. However, the State supreme court held the legislature's action unconstitutional in 1930. Article XV, Section 4, of the Texas constitution provides that any officer removed by impeachment is barred " from any office of honor, trust, or profit " in the State. Most other State constitutions contain a similar clause.

[8] Arizona, California, Colorado, Idaho, Kansas, Louisiana, Michigan, Nevada, North Dakota, Oregon, Washington, and Wisconsin.

unable to carry out his duties. In thirty-seven States there is a lieutenant-governor, and he is first in line to succeed. In eight of the other States [9] the president of the senate takes the governor's chair, and in the remaining three the secretary of state does so.[10]

Most constitutions also provide for a temporary successor or " acting governor " whenever the chief executive is out of the State. Oregon recently had seven " governors " within a period of five days. This happened because the governor was absent from the State for five days and, during that period, several other high officials found it necessary to travel elsewhere, too.

The importance of provisions for succession is tragically illustrated by an airplane crash in Oregon in 1947. The crash took the lives of three of the State's top officials: the governor, secretary of state, and president of the senate.

Compensation. The governor is treated much more generously in the matter of salary than are most other State officeholders. A glance at the table on page 497 will show that the salaries range from $9000 in North Dakota to as much as $50,000 in New York.

In all except ten States the governor is provided with an official residence, usually called the Governor's Mansion, and many States also give him an expense account. For example, in New Jersey the governor's salary is $30,000. In addition to his regular salary, he also receives an expense account of $20,000 and lives in a fine mansion furnished and maintained by the State.

To his salary and other compensation must be added as " income " the honor and prestige that go with the governorship. It is this " prestige income," as well as a sense of public service, that often leads many of our better citizens to seek the office. Many governors have later served in high national office.

About a third of the members of the United States Senate are former governors of their home States (and many Senators later serve as governors). Chief Justice Earl Warren went to the United States Supreme Court from the governor's chair in California. Several Presidents, including Theodore Roosevelt, Woodrow Wilson, Calvin Coolidge, and Franklin Roosevelt, had been governors in their respective States, before going on to the White House.

The Governor at Work

The powers of a State governor can be classified under three major headings: (1) his executive powers, (2) his legislative powers, and (3) his judicial powers. He also performs a great many miscellaneous jobs, as we shall see as we discuss his duties.

[9] Florida, Maine, Maryland, New Hampshire, New Jersey, Oregon, West Virginia, Tennessee (where by law the presiding officer is called " lieutenant-governor ").

[10] Arizona, Utah, and Wyoming.

Most States also provide a certain amount for various expenses, *e.g.*: Indiana, $10,000; Minnesota, $10,000; Nevada, $7200; Oregon, $4800.

STATE	CAPITAL	TERM IN YEARS	ANNUAL SALARY
Alabama	Montgomery	4	$12,000 and residence
Arizona	Phoenix	2	18,500
Arkansas	Little Rock	2	10,000 and residence
California	Sacramento	4	25,000 and residence
Colorado	Denver	2	17,500
Connecticut	Hartford	4	15,000 and residence
Delaware	Dover	4	17,500
Florida	Tallahassee	4	22,500 and residence
Georgia	Atlanta	4	12,000 and residence
Idaho	Boise	4	10,000 and residence
Illinois	Springfield	4	25,000 and residence
Indiana	Indianapolis	4	15,000 and residence
Iowa	Des Moines	2	12,500 and residence
Kansas	Topeka	2	15,000 and residence
Kentucky	Frankfort	4	15,000 and residence
Louisiana	Baton Rouge	4	18,000 and residence
Maine	Augusta	2	10,000 and residence
Maryland	Annapolis	4	15,000 and residence
Massachusetts	Boston	2	20,000
Michigan	Lansing	2	22,500
Minnesota	St. Paul	2	19,000
Mississippi	Jackson	4	15,000 and residence
Missouri	Jefferson City	4	25,000 and residence
Montana	Helena	4	12,500 and residence
Nebraska	Lincoln	2	11,000 and residence
Nevada	Carson City	4	18,000 and residence
New Hampshire	Concord	2	15,000
New Jersey	Trenton	4	30,000 and residence
New Mexico	Santa Fe	2	18,000 and residence
New York	Albany	4	50,000 and residence
North Carolina	Raleigh	4	15,000 and residence
North Dakota	Bismarck	2	9,000 and residence
Ohio	Columbus	2	25,000 and residence
Oklahoma	Oklahoma City	4	15,000 and residence
Oregon	Salem	4	15,000
Pennsylvania	Harrisburg	4	25,000 and residence
Rhode Island	Providence	2	15,000
South Carolina	Columbia	4	15,000 and residence
South Dakota	Pierre	2	13,000 and residence
Tennessee	Nashville	4	12,000 and residence
Texas	Austin	2	25,000 and residence
Utah	Salt Lake City	4	12,000 and residence
Vermont	Montpelier	2	12,500
Virginia	Richmond	4	17,500 and residence
Washington	Olympia	4	15,000 and residence
West Virginia	Charleston	4	17,500 and residence
Wisconsin	Madison	2	18,000 and residence
Wyoming	Cheyenne	4	12,000 and residence

THE GOVERNOR OF A STATE...

Controls the
enforcement
of state laws

Sends messages
to state legislature
suggesting needed laws

Vetoes some bills

Calls special
sessions of
legislature

Appoints certain officials

Pardons criminals

PICTOGRAPH CORPORATION

The Governor's Executive Powers. Many persons seem to believe that the President of the United States and the governor in each of our States can be approximately likened to one another in the nature and extent of their powers of office. This is by no means true.

The United States Constitution makes the President *the* executive in the National Government. Article II, Section 2, declares: " The executive power shall be vested in a President of the United States . . ."

State constitutions, on the other hand, merely make the governor the *chief* or *supreme* executive in State government.

" This distinction," as one authority on State government has said, " is

498

more than a matter of mere terminology." [11] Most State constitutions distribute the executive power among a half dozen or more " executive officers."

For example, Article IV, Section 1, of the Texas constitution provides:

> The Executive Department of this State shall consist of a Governor, who shall be the Chief Executive Officer of the State, a Lieutenant-Governor, Secretary of State, Comptroller of Public Accounts, Treasurer, Commissioner of the General Land Office, and Attorney General.

As we shall see, these other officers are usually popularly elected and thus beyond the governor's direct control. In most States it may be said that the governor is the captain of a Ship of State navigated by a crew which he does not select, and over which he has few powers of command.

Despite this, however, the governor is the one whom the voters hold responsible for the conduct of State administration.

Appointment and Removal Powers. The chief executive's power to appoint and remove those in office under him is, or should be, one of his most important. Practically every State constitution declares that the governor " shall take care that the laws be faithfully executed." He can best do this by being able to appoint those who will work with him and carry out his policies.

As we saw just a moment ago, many

---

[11] Macdonald, A. F., *American State Government and Administration*, page 212, 1955 edition. Crowell.

governors do not have full control over their administrations because of the existence of many other elected executive officers. In recent years, however, the trend in most States reorganizing the State government has been to create new departments headed by administrators appointed by the governor.

By using his appointing power to " reward his friends and punish his enemies," the governor is often able to gain a good deal of legislative support for his various programs.

The concept of civil service appointment on the basis of merit is making steady headway in most States. Of course, this places a new and altogether wholesome limit on the scope of the governor's appointing power.

The governor's powers of removal are severely limited in many States. In only a few can he remove an official at his pleasure. In most he must have legislative approval for removal or at least cite some particular " cause," such as incompetence, neglect of duty, or malfeasance in office.[12] Here again, however, the trend is toward giving the governor wider power. Thus Missouri's new constitution of 1945 provides that " all appointive officers may be removed by the governor."

Supervision of Administration. In taking " care that the laws be faithfully executed," the governor must direct the day-to-day work of the several State administrative agencies.

Many of these agencies are subject to his control and many are not. As we noted above, he is often hamstrung because some agencies are headed by popularly elected officers. Some of the agencies, along with their powers and duties, are established in the State constitution. Moreover, the legislature has the power to create various departments, boards, commissions, and other agencies and to define their functions.

The governor's ability to supervise State administration depends, then, in a very large part on just how much the constitution and the legislature allow him to control the agencies within the executive branch. His ability to supervise the agencies also depends upon the extent of his power to appoint and remove his principal subordinates.

Quite often, when a governor has little formal power to control State administration, he is still able to do so because of his position as party leader and as a representative of all of the people of the State.

Happily, the reorganization movement in several States has aided and is aiding the governor to gain more direct command of his administration.

Law Enforcement. As a part of his executive duties, the governor is responsible for general law enforcement in the State. In its broadest sense, the job of law enforcing is done by all of the State's administrative agencies. For example, the State

---

[12] *Malfeasance in office* is the wrongful performance of an act which the officer had no legal right to perform.

Board of Medical Examiners is enforcing the law when it examines and licenses doctors who wish to practice in the State.

In its particular sense, the governor's overall responsibility for law enforcement involves the enforcing of the criminal law. Once again the governor does not usually have the authority to match his responsibility. His chief legal officer, the attorney-general, is popularly elected in forty-two of the forty-eight States. Most local law enforcement officers, such as the sheriff, constable, coroner, and district attorney, are also elective.

State Police. Several years ago the governor of Pennsylvania sarcastically remarked that he was charged with maintaining peace and order throughout the State (45,000 square miles) with no one to assist him but his secretary and stenographer. Today every State has a State police force or highway patrol to aid the governor in the enforcement of State laws.

In most States the main task of the State police is enforcement of motor vehicle laws. In some States, however, the State police have become the major arm of law enforcement. State police often systematically enforce law in rural areas, supplementing the work of local sheriffs and constables.

Military Powers. Each State's constitution makes the governor commander-in-chief of the State militia. Defense is a function of the National Government, as we saw in Chapters 4 and 13. However, each State has a

militia to maintain peace within the State.[13]

In 1916 Congress provided that each State's militia should consist of all able-bodied males between eighteen and forty-five years of age. The National Guard is the *organized* part of the militia. It is trained by the Regular Army and supported by federal grants-in-aid. In cases of national emergency, the President may call it into federal service as a part of the Army.

When the State's National Guard units are not in federal service they are commanded by the governor. He is assisted by an adjutant-general and commissions its officers.

The National Guard has often been used by a governor to deal with prison riots, strike disturbances, floods, and other emergencies.

In 1954 and 1955 units of the Alabama National Guard were used to help clean up vice-ridden Phenix City after a candidate for State attorney-general had been murdered there.

Financial Powers. As a part of the reorganization of State administration in the past several years, the governor has been given increasing authority over finances. In most States he is now responsible for drawing up and submitting the budget to the legislature. More and more he is being given control over the spending by all State agencies once the legislature has appropriated the money.

This control over spending has

---

[13] See page 232.

"KEEP YOUR GUARD UP"

Men from the 186th Regiment of the Oregon National Guard spend several days a year in weapons training. These guardsmen are on the firing line at Camp Clatsop, Oregon.

helped to make it possible for many governors to achieve a degree of control over administrative agencies which probably they would not otherwise have.

The governor's veto, discussed below, also gives him some control over the amount of money an agency will be given to spend. This control is especially effective in the case of the " item veto."

The Governor's Legislative Powers. The governor is the State's chief executive officer, yet he has three important legislative powers: (1) to send messages to the legislature, (2) to call extra sessions of the legislature,

and (3) to veto bills passed by the legislature.

The Message Power. The value of the governor's power to send messages, that is, recommend, legislation to the legislature, depends largely upon the governor's personality, popularity, and party position. A strong governor is often able to accomplish a great deal by sending messages and addressing the legislature in person. He will use informal political pressures to advance his programs, too.

Extra Sessions. For any reason a governor thinks sufficient, he may call a special session of the legislature. Several governors find special sessions more and more necessary today. They have found that the short biennial session is not adequate to meet the complex problems the State faces. Annual legislative sessions are now held in fourteen States.[14] Longer sessions and improved legislative procedures would help greatly. Fortunately, this need is being recognized in several States.

As an illustration of the special session: Governor Robert Holmes called Oregon's Legislative Assembly into special session late in 1957 to lower the rates levied under the State's income tax law. The former rates were so high that they had brought in some $50,000,000 more than expected. In addition to lowering taxes, the special session spent some of the unexpected surplus to aid local school districts.

The Veto Power. With the single exception of North Carolina, the governor in every State has the power to veto bills passed by the legislature. This power, or the threat of the use of it, is usually the most effective weapon the governor has for influencing the legislature.

When a bill is sent to the governor for his signature he is allowed from three to ten days to act on it.[15]

In thirty-nine States [16] the governor's veto power includes the so-called " item veto." That is, he may veto a specific section or item in a bill without disapproving the entire measure.

The item veto is used many times to check extravagant appropriations. Sometimes, however, the fact that the governor has this power encourages the lawmakers to vote appropriations in excess of revenues and then " pass the buck " for balancing the State budget to the governor. Often, too, the governor finds that the item veto is a useful device with which he may persuade or punish legislators who do not favor his policies and proposals.

The governor does not have an absolute veto in any State; in each the legislature may override him. The size of the vote necessary to override varies among the States, but two thirds of the full membership in each house is the most common requirement.[17]

---

[14] See page 477.

[15] Three days in Indiana, Iowa, Kansas, Minnesota, New Mexico, North Dakota, South Carolina, South Dakota, Wyoming; six days in Alabama, Maryland, Rhode Island, Wisconsin; ten days in California, Colorado, Delaware, Illinois, Kentucky, Louisiana, Michigan, Missouri, New York, Ohio, Pennsylvania, and Texas; and five days in the remaining twenty-two States.

The period allowed after adjournment is

longer in some States. For example, it is twenty days in Oregon and forty-five in New Jersey.

[16] All except Indiana, Iowa, Maine, New Hampshire, Nevada, Rhode Island, Tennessee, Vermont, and of course, North Carolina.

[17] A majority of those present in each house is all that is required in Connecticut; a majority of the full membership, in Alabama, Arkansas, Indiana, Kentucky, Tennessee, and West Virginia; three fifths of the members present, in Rhode Island; three fifths of the full membership, in Delaware, Maryland, Nebraska, and Ohio; two thirds of the members present, in Florida, Idaho, Massachusetts, Montana, New Mexico, Oregon, South Dakota, Texas, Vermont, Washington, and Wisconsin; and two thirds of the full membership, in the remaining twenty-four States.

The Governor's Judicial Powers.
Nearly all of the governors have some power of mercy toward persons accused or convicted of crime. It may be to remit fines, to shorten sentences, to pardon a prisoner conditionally or absolutely, to postpone the execution of a death sentence, or to change a death sentence to life imprisonment. That is, a governor may have all or some of these powers, but they are commonly shared with a board of pardons.

These powers exist in order that the ends of justice may best be served. They impose a heavy responsibility and an awful burden on the governor. In this connection, former Governor Lehman of New York has written that this task

particularly weighed upon me; I felt it most keenly in the cases of men condemned to die. I established a rule that prison wardens must call me personally no more than fifteen minutes before an execution, to establish that no new late evidence had turned up. The knowledge that my word would mean life to a condemned man was deeply perturbing. I never learned to take it " in stride." [18]

A good illustration of the wise use of the pardon occurred recently in New Jersey. A young boy found a rabbit destroying his garden and shot it. He was then arrested for shooting a rabbit out of season. Under the law the judge could do nothing but pronounce a jail sentence. However, the

judge immediately wired the governor requesting a pardon, and it was quickly granted. In this instance then, what would have been a miscarriage of justice was avoided by the governor's power of mercy.

There is always the danger that a governor will use the pardoning power too freely. Mrs. James A. (" Ma ") Ferguson, governor of Texas from 1925 to 1927, pardoned 3737 prisoners during her term. The pardons were issued so thick and fast that several Texas newspapers published daily " pardon columns " and the late Will Rogers remarked that her successor would have to start his term by catching his own prisoners.

When he sends or receives extradition papers for the return of fugitives from justice, the governor is also acting in a judicial capacity (see page 66).

Miscellaneous Duties of a Governor.
Much of a governor's time is taken up by a great many other activities. In every State he is an *ex officio* (that is, by virtue of his office) member of several State boards — for example, a Board of State Institutions. He receives official visitors and welcomes distinguished people to the State, hears persisting job applicants, meets with party leaders, must wade through stacks of documents, signs official papers, and speaks to innumerable organizations and public gatherings.

More and more today's governors are being called upon to help settle labor disputes.

---

[18] Lehman, Herbert, " Albany and Washington — a Contrast," *New York Times Magazine,* September 4, 1950.

Other Executive Officers

In the early part of this chapter we mentioned the fact that in most States the governor must share the control of State administration with several other elected officers. Some States have made good progress in making these officials directly subordinate to the governor by giving him the power to appoint them. However, most authorities agree that there are still far too many of these elected public servants. We deal with the more important ones here.

The Lieutenant-Governor. In thirty-seven of the States [19] there is a popularly elected lieutenant-governor. He succeeds to a vacancy in the governorship and acts as governor whenever the chief executive is out of the State. He presides over the Senate in each of these thirty-seven States except Kentucky, Massachusetts, and Mississippi.

The eleven States without lieutenant-governors seem to have lived well without them. Many urge that the office be done away with, including Governor Crosby of Nebraska who, as lieutenant-governor, wrote an article entitled " Why I Want to Get Rid of My Job."

The Secretary of State. Found in each of the forty-eight States, the secretary of state is popularly elected in thirty-eight of them. He is ap-

pointed by the governor in seven States. Those states are Delaware, Maryland, New Jersey, New York, Pennsylvania, Texas, and Virginia. He is elected by the legislature in Maine, New Hampshire, and Tennessee.

He is the State's chief clerk and records the official acts of the governor and the legislature. He has charge of various official documents, usually administers the State election laws, and keeps the State seal. In several States he also handles automobile and driver licensing and performs a variety of other clerical functions.

Auditor or Comptroller. This officer is found in all of our States except Oregon and Wisconsin, though his title varies. For example he is called the Comptroller of Public Accounts in Texas and the Auditor-General in Pennsylvania.

His particular job is to audit (examine and verify) the accounts of all State officers and agencies which collect and spend public funds. No money may be drawn from the State treasury without a warrant drawn by him. He will not issue a warrant until he is satisfied that the expenditure is in all respects legal. He acts as a " watchdog " over public funds.

Because he is a " watchdog," it is generally held that he should not be an executive officer. Rather, he should be chosen by the legislature. The legislature, however, chooses him in only four States: Maine, New Jer-

---

[19] All except Arizona, Florida, Maine, Maryland, New Hampshire, New Jersey, Oregon, Tennessee, Utah, West Virginia, and Wyoming.

sey, Tennessee, and Virginia. In the other States he is popularly elected. In Oregon and Wisconsin the secretary of state performs the audit functions.

The State Treasurer. The state treasurer is popularly elected in forty-two States. In New Jersey, New York, and Virginia he is chosen by the governor, and in Maryland, New Hampshire, and Tennessee by the legislature.

He receives the State's moneys for safekeeping and pays them out only upon a warrant (order to pay, as a check) from the auditor. A department of finance, like the one which now exists in New York and a few other States, is widely recommended to handle all of the details of State finance.

The Attorney-General. The State's chief legal officer, the attorney-general, is elected in all States but Maine, New Hampshire, New Jersey, Pennsylvania, Tennessee and Wyoming.

He acts as legal adviser to the governor, other State officers, and the legislature and is the State's chief prosecutor. In several States the attorney-general's office also provides bill-drafting services to the legislature.

The Superintendent of Public Instruction. Although known by various names among the States, the superintendent of public instruction has general supervision of the State school systems. He often shares his authority with a board of education. He is chosen by the voters in twenty-five States.

Other Officers and Boards or Commissions. These exist in great number but vary from State to State. A particular function may be performed by a director or a superintendent or a commissioner or by a board or by a commission. The following are typical:

(*1*) *Boards for State Institutions* such as charitable, correctional, mental, or educational institutions.

(*2*) *Boards to Supervise State Functions* such as a board of health, board of agriculture, and highway commission or fish and game commission.

(*3*) *Boards to Supervise Commercial Corporations* such as railway or public utilities commission, banking commission, and insurance commission.

(*4*) *Examining Boards* such as a board of medical examiners and civil service commission.

Administrative Reorganization

As one function after another was added to the work of State governments, offices, boards, and commissions were established in a haphazard fashion, independent of one another, to care for new tasks. The inevitable result was chaos and confusion. Overlapping, duplication, waste, and lack of coordination, sometimes mingled with graft, resulted.

With a great many elected officers sharing the executive powers, many a governor has found himself saddled with the responsibility for the work of officers he could not control and probably never would have chosen himself.

Beginning about 1910 reorganization movements got underway in several States. Illinois was the first State to effect a comprehensive reorganization in 1917, and several other States were quick to follow.

Since then, most States have made at least some changes. Still, a great deal remains to be done in most. The work of the two Hoover Commissions at the national level has prompted so-called " little Hoover Commissions " in several States.

There are certain basic principles of State reorganization, and they have been conveniently summarized by the Council of State Governments:

(1) Consolidate all administrative agencies into a smaller number of departments (usually 10 to 20) organized by function.

(2) Establish clear lines of authority running from the governor at the top of the hierarchy through the entire organization.

(3) Establish appropriate staff (advisory) agencies responsible to the governor.

(4) So far as possible, eliminate the use of boards and commissions for administrative work.

(5) An independent auditor, with authority for post-audit only, should be established.

If more citizens would take an active and an informed interest in State governments and their problems, reorganization would be a relatively simple, and a highly profitable, task.

Interstate Agencies

There are numerous organizations which have been formed to promote interstate relationships, further uniform State action to meet common problems, and help the cause of better government.

The Council of State Governments. COSGO was founded in 1935 and is an organization to which each of the forty-eight States belongs. In each State there is a Commission on Interstate Co-operation usually composed of five administrative officers and five members from each house of the State legislature.

The legislation creating these commissions in each State commonly provides that

The Council of State Governments is hereby declared to be a joint governmental agency of this State and of the other States which co-operate through it.

These Commissions on Interstate Co-operation work with one another through COSGO. A central headquarters is maintained in Chicago, and there are also offices in New York, San Francisco, and Washington, D.C.

COSGO is essentially a research organization, providing information to the States. It has furnished the States

506

INTERSTATE CO-OPERATION

Experimenting with various chemicals to find better methods for the control of water pollution, these chemists are working on a program set up by the six New England states and New York. Similar commissions are active all over the country, using interstate co-operation to find answers to their common problems.

with much factual material and guidance in such matters as interstate compacts, crime control, social security, uniform taxation, milk control, flood control, interstate parks, liquor regulation, conservation, highway safety, sanitation, and similar problems.

It publishes a monthly magazine, *State Government,* and a biennial summary of current material, *The Book of the States,* as well as its reports on the various matters it investigates.

Several other agencies for voluntary interstate co-operation exist. Examples are the American Legislators Association, the Governors' Conference, the National Association of Secretaries of State, the National Association of Attorneys-General, the National Association of State Budget Officers, the National Association of State Purchasing Officers, the National Association of Administrators of the Interstate Compact for the Supervision of Parolees and Probationers, the

Legislative Service Conference, and the Conference of Chief Justices.

COSGO is the secretariat and central clearing house for each of these organizations, and through them State officers can explore common problems and exchange ideas.

The Governors' Conference. In 1908 President Theodore Roosevelt called a Conference of Governors at the White House to consider problems regarding the conservation of the nation's natural resources.

Since then, the various governors have held an annual conference. Meeting at various places around the country, they discuss common problems, promote interstate good will, and exchange experiences. Although few uniform laws have resulted from these gatherings, no doubt they have encouraged a useful exchange of ideas and brought about better interstate cooperation. In recent years, many regional conferences of governors have also been held.

WHAT THIS CHAPTER IS ABOUT

The governor in each of the forty-eight States occupies the oldest executive office in America. The first State governors were given only very weak powers, as a reaction against the abuses of the colonial governors. Most of the powers of the State were given to the legislature.

Gradually, this original separation of powers was changed as the legislatures tended to abuse their powers. The development of the office of governor has been described as " from figurehead to leader." The greatest reforms have come with the reorganization movements of the past thirty to forty years.

All States elect the governor by popular vote, although Mississippi combines the popular vote with a county electoral vote system. Each State constitution sets out certain formal qualifications for office, commonly citizenship, age, and residence. The informal political qualifications are everywhere important.

Governors serve a two-year term in nineteen States and a four-year term in the remaining States. The trend is toward the latter. Nearly half the States place a limit on the tenure of the chief executive.

The governor may be removed by impeachment in all States except Oregon and by recall in Oregon and eleven other States. Few have ever been removed from office. Succession to the office falls to the lieutenant-governor who is found in thirty-seven States, to the president of the senate in eight, and the Secretary of State in three.

The governor's salary ranges from $9000 in North Dakota to a high of $50,000 in New York. Most also have an expense allowance and an official residence provided by the State.

The powers of a governor are usually shared with several other elective officers over whom he has little real control. His executive powers include those of appointment and removal, supervision of administration, law enforcement, command of the militia including the National Guard, and some control over State finance.

His most important legislative powers are those to recommend legislation by messages to the legislature, call special sessions, and (except in North Carolina) to veto bills or parts of them. The governor's judicial powers are those he has in

508

regard to mercy toward prisoners, as for example, the pardoning power.

The governor must also perform many miscellaneous duties, usually of a ceremonial nature. In most States his real power is dependent on his popularity, personality, and political position.

In nearly every State there are several other elected administrative officers, including a lieutenant-governor, secretary of state, auditor, treasurer, attorney-general, and superintendent of public instruction.

Recent years have seen a growing demand for reorganization in the executive branch of State government.

Several intergovernmental agencies, especially the Council of State Governments, exist to promote better cooperation between the States and better government.

QUESTIONS ON THE TEXT

1. Describe the original position of the governor under the first State constitutions.

2. How is the governor chosen in every State?

3. For what term does the governor in your State serve?

4. How might he be removed from office? Who would then succeed?

5. What is the range of governors' salaries? How much is he paid in your State? Is he provided with a mansion? With an expense allowance?

6. Compare the powers of the governor with those of the President of the United States.

7. What is meant by the statement that " the governor is the captain of a Ship of State navigated by a crew which he does not select, and over which he has few powers of command "?

8. What are the governor's chief executive powers? Why is the power of appointment and removal so important?

9. What is the State militia? The National Guard?

10. What are the governor's legislative powers?

11. What is the " item veto "? Does your governor have it?

12. By what vote may the legislature in your State override a veto?

13. What are the governor's judicial powers?

14. Does your State have a lieutenant-governor? What other elected executive officers are there in your State?

15. What are the five basic principles of State reorganization as listed by the Council of State Governments?

16. What is the Council of State Governments? The Governors' Conference?

PROBLEMS FOR DISCUSSION

1. In New Jersey the governor is the only executive officer chosen by the people. The State executive officials are all subordinate to him, and he is responsible for their actions. Would you favor having this arrangement in your own State? Explain.

2. Some people oppose giving the item veto power to the governor. Why?

3. New York State has a police school to train police for any locality. Do you think that all States should maintain such schools? Any New York town may have State police permanently by paying their salaries. Why might these police be superior to police chosen locally?

4. Do you think that the governor in your State is well-paid? Explain.

THINGS YOU MIGHT DO

1. Write a short biography of the governor of your State. (See *Who's Who,* the State Bluebook, etc.)

2. From the State constitution and bluebook, make a list of the executive officers in your State. How are they chosen? What are their powers?

3. If at all possible, invite a State official to visit the class and discuss his work with you.

4. Draw up a list of improvements you feel might be made in the organization of the executive branch of your State's government.

WORDS AND PHRASES YOU SHOULD KNOW

Administration
Council of State Governments
Executive powers
Figurehead
Governors' Conference
Impeachment
Item veto
Judicial powers
Legislative powers

Majority
Malfeasance in office
Militia
National Guard
Plurality
Recall
Reorganization
Separation of powers
Veto

SELECT BIBLIOGRAPHY

BATES, SANFORD, " The Trouble with Prisons is Politics," *Saturday Evening Post,* May 14, 1955.

BOWLES, CHESTER, " Governor's Job as Seen by a Governor," *New York Times Magazine,* July 24, 1949.

DAVIDSON, BILL, " This is a Raid! " *Collier's,* April 1, 1955.

MACDONALD, AUSTIN F., *American State Government and Administration,* Chapters 10, 16, 17. Crowell, 1955.

——, *State and Local Government in the United States,* Chapters 6, 27. Crowell, 1955.

MARTIN, HAROLD, " The Things They Say about the Government! " *Saturday Evening Post,* January 29, 1955.

MURRAY, EX-GOV. JOHNSTON, " Oklahoma is in a Mess! " *Saturday Evening Post,* April 30, 1955.

PHILLIPS, JEWELL C., *State and Local Government in America,* Chapters 9, 10, 13. American Book, 1954.

Copies of your State's *Manual* or *Bluebook* can usually be obtained from your Secretary of State.

> If the lamp of justice goes out in darkness, how great is that darkness.
>
> — James Bryce

★

Chapter 29

STATE COURTS

A *court* is a tribunal established by the State for the administration of justice according to law. Courts settle disputes between private persons and between private persons and government. They protect the rights of individuals as guaranteed in the National and State Constitutions. They determine the innocence or guilt of persons accused of crime. And they act as checks on the executive and legislative branches of the government.[1]

Remember that under our federal system there are two separate and distinct court systems: the federal judiciary and the forty-eight State judiciaries. The federal courts have jurisdiction over certain classes of cases, as we saw in Chapter 21. All other cases are State cases — and these are by far the overwhelming number.

Organization of State Courts

The constitution in each State provides for the judicial branch and usually leaves the detailed organization of the court system to the legislature. Article VII, Section I of the Indiana constitution is quite typical:

The judicial power of the State shall be vested in a Supreme Court, Circuit Courts, and such other courts as the General Assembly may establish.

Justice of the Peace. At the base of the State judicial system, in rural areas and small towns, is the Justice of the Peace. He presides over what is commonly called the Justice Court, and he is usually elected for a short term, commonly two years.

The Justice of the Peace generally has jurisdiction in most misdemeanor [2]

---

[1] In several States courts also perform a variety of *non*-judicial functions. School boards are judicially appointed in some States, for example; and in Tennessee the Supreme Court appoints the Attorney-General. In various States, courts also supervise elections, grant business licenses, administer estates, manage the properties of bankrupts, etc. These administrative functions consume much time and many feel that they interfere with the primary court function — to hear and decide cases.

[2] Crimes are of two kinds: felonies and misdemeanors. A *felony* is the greater crime

Three Lions

JUSTICE'S COURT A HUNDRED YEARS AGO
The informality of the court is captured by the artist, Tompkins H. Matteson.

cases and minor civil cases.[3] To illustrate, a Justice of the Peace often hears such misdemeanor cases as traffic violations, disregard of health ordinances, breaches of the peace, etc. He often hears such civil cases as those involving money demands (seldom over $50 or $100), the ownership of personal property, and wrongs or injuries to property. He generally does not have jurisdiction in such civil cases as those involving title to real estate, titles to office, torts (wrongs) to the person, and like matters of considerable importance.

A Justice of the Peace is also usually empowered to hold preliminary hearings of serious complaints — as, for example, in a murder case. Here his function is much like that of a

and may be punished by a heavier fine and/or imprisonment or death. A *misdemeanor* is the lesser crime involving a smaller fine and/or a short jail term.

[3] A *civil case* is a suit brought by one party against another for the enforcement or protection of a private right, or the prevention or redress of a tort (private wrong). It is distinguished from a *criminal case* which is brought by the State against one accused of committing a crime — a public wrong. The State is not often a party to a civil case, but it always is (as prosecutor) to a criminal case.

512

grand jury — to determine whether sufficient evidence exists to hold the accused for trial in a higher court.

Police or Magistrates' Courts. The lowest courts in urban areas, especially in larger towns and cities, are known as Police or Magistrates' Courts. These courts are much like the Justice Courts, with practically the same jurisdiction. The judges are usually elected and salaries are generally quite low. Like the Justice Courts, the Magistrates' Courts are often criticized because the judges are seldom trained in the law [4] and cor-

ruption and political favoritism are not unknown.

Municipal Courts. In recent years so-called Municipal Courts have been created in practically every larger town and city. They usually have full jurisdiction over all civil

---

[4] Though a local lawyer sometimes does preside over these courts, this is not the common rule. A recent study in California showed that non-lawyer justices included carpenters, ministers, truck drivers, school teachers, real estate agents, contractors, bookkeepers, and druggists (not to mention a wife who held court when her husband went fishing). Several States, including California, have been attempting to remedy this situation. In Missouri, for instance, Justice Courts have been eliminated and replaced with Magistrates' Courts with judges selected from the legal profession.

MUNICIPAL COURT SCENE
The judge asks a question in one of the municipal courts of a large city. Notice that no jury is needed in this trial.

and criminal cases arising within the municipality.

In many of the largest cities the Municipal Courts have been organized into divisions — either on a geographic or on a functional basis. Thus among the five boroughs of New York City there are 28 Municipal Court districts. And in Philadelphia there are five divisions of the Municipal Court: civil, criminal, juvenile, domestic relations, and misdemeanor. Several cities also have other functional divisions such as traffic, small claims, probate, and the like.

More and more cities are organizing their Municipal Courts on this functional basis. They are doing so because the scheme provides for courts which specialize in the major types of controversies heard in Municipal Courts.

Take Small Claims Courts as an example. Many people cannot afford to pay the costs involved in suing for the collection of a small debt. A paper boy can hardly afford to hire an attorney and pay court costs in order to collect a month's subscription due from one of his customers. Or a widow who runs a lodginghouse can hardly afford to sue for a month's room rent. Many small tradespeople have been forced to wipe such small debts off their books or sell them at about one-half to collection agencies.

Small Claims Courts have been created to cover just such situations as these. In them a person can bring his claim at an extremely low cost or at no cost at all. The proceedings are quite informal, the judge usually handling matters without attorneys for either side.

The informality of these courts is illustrated by the court (known as the Conciliation Branch) in Cleveland, Ohio. In this court a landlady brought a claim against a boarder who had set fire to a mattress by smoking in bed. The defendant (the boarder) was willing to pay, but he disputed the amount demanded by the plaintiff (the landlady). The judge phoned a department store, learned the price of the mattress, and the matter was settled immediately.

The Small Claims Divisions of the Municipal Court in New York try cases involving less than $50. In one case a waiter in a spaghetti-house had spilled huckleberry pie and coffee on a customer's trousers. The judge believed the trousers were seersucker. But the customer's wife produced a receipt for $12.50 and said the trousers were " billed as flannel." " God help the dealer's soul," said the judge, as he gave judgment for $7 plus $1.25 costs.

As another of these functional divisions several cities now have Juvenile Courts. These courts usually handle cases involving those under 18 years of age. And often they are (should be) presided over by judges especially trained and interested in minors and their problems. Depending on the facts in a given case, the judge may simply offer good advice, place a minor on probation, levy a fine, or if necessary sentence him to a reform school.

In a very short time one morning the judge of a Juvenile Court handled the following four cases. No. 1 was a fight between two small boys. The mother of the larger boy was present and was directed to go into an adjoining room and whip her boy in the presence of an officer. No. 2 was a young girl brought in by her parents. The girl, agreeing to do better, was directed to return to her home and to report weekly to a woman probation officer. No. 3, a girl who had previously been on probation, was accused of stealing. She was turned over to the State reformatory. No. 4 was a young man who accused a boy of annoying his " place of business," a shoeshine stand. Their statements conflicted. When one referred to a reputable witness, they were ordered to return three days later with the witness.

General Trial Courts. Above the courts so far considered are the general trial courts. They are variously known as County, Circuit, District, Superior, or Common Pleas courts. In over three-fourths of the States the trial court judges are popularly elected, commonly serving a four-year term.

The jurisdiction of these trial courts is quite broad. They exercise both original and appellate (appeal) jurisdiction, and it is here that the major civil and criminal cases are begun. Many minor cases that may also be instituted in the Justice, Police or Magistrates', or Municipal Courts may be (and are) begun in the trial courts. And when appeals from the lower courts are heard in the trial court, a completely new trial is often held.

Cases in the trial courts are usually heard by the judge and a *petit jury* (the trial jury which hears and decides the facts at issue in a case). Criminal cases are presented to the trial courts either by grand jury indictments or by information on motion of district attorneys. (See pages 516–518.)

Intermediate Appellate Courts. In over one-third of the States there are courts of appeal between the trial courts and the highest State court. These intermediate appellate courts have been created in an effort to ease the load of the highest court. Besides their appellate jurisdiction these courts occasionally have original jurisdiction in such controversies as contested elections.

Like the trial courts, these courts of appeal are known by a variety of names.[5] The judges are elected in some States and are appointed in others. In Illinois these appeals courts are composed of Circuit Court judges assigned by the State Supreme Court.

State Supreme Court. As the capstone of the State judicial system stands a Supreme Court, the highest

---

[5] In New York, for example, there is an Appellate Division of the Supreme Court. The highest court in the New York judicial system is known as the Court of Appeals.

court in the State.[6] The justices, ranging from three in Arizona, Nevada, and Wyoming to sixteen in New Jersey, are most often elected by the people. In a few States the justices are appointed by the governor (as in Maine and Delaware) or by the legislature (as in Connecticut, Vermont, and South Carolina).

The State Supreme Court's primary function is to hear appeals from the decisions of the lower courts. It is the final interpreter of the State's constitution and laws.

Appeals may be taken from a State Supreme Court to the Supreme Court of the United States — *but only* when a " federal question " is involved, that is, when the case hinges upon the meaning of a provision of the United States Constitution or a federal statute or treaty. Otherwise, the State Supreme Court is the court of last resort.

The Jury System

A jury is a body of persons selected according to law, and sworn to declare the truth on the evidence laid before it. There are two kinds of juries [7] — the grand jury and the petit (trial) jury.

The Grand Jury. A grand jury is a body of persons summoned into a court to consider the evidence against persons accused of crimes, and to determine whether the evidence is sufficient to justify a formal trial for such persons.

This jury consists of twenty-three jurors or less, according to the State law and the importance of the charges to be investigated. In most States it consists of more than twelve jurors, of whom at least twelve must agree that an accused person is probably guilty, or he cannot be held for trial. In some States the grand jury may consist of as few as six. When it consists of as few as six jurors, five must agree or the accused cannot be held for trial. Sometimes one person is appointed to investigate for the judge.

When a grand jury is impaneled (selected) the judge instructs the jurors to find a *true bill of indictment* (charge) against all persons whom the prosecuting attorney brings to their attention and whom they think probably guilty. He further instructs them to bring a *presentment* (accusation) against any person whom they of their own knowledge believe to have violated the criminal laws of the State within their county. They swear or affirm that they will do so, and retire to the jury room, where they deliberate in secret. Their chairman, appointed by the judge or chosen by themselves, is known as the *foreman.*

---

[6] This court of last resort is known as the Supreme Court in thirty-nine States. But in Connecticut it is styled the Supreme Court of Errors, in Maine the Supreme Judicial Court, in West Virginia the Supreme Court of Appeals, etc.

[7] The so-called coroner's jury is not a real jury.

The prosecuting attorney for the county brings into the jury room witnesses to testify against the accused and usually questions them himself, but after he retires the jurors may resummon the same witnesses and question them further or may have the court summon other witnesses to testify against the accused. Nobody is allowed in the room with the jurors except the witnesses, the prosecuting attorney, and, in some States, his stenographer. All are bound to secrecy.

After all witnesses have been summoned and questioned, the jurors are left entirely alone to deliberate, and when they have completed their finding they proceed to the courtroom and their bill of indictment is read in their presence. The bill is recorded in the clerk's office and the jury is dismissed if the term has expired; or, if the term has not expired, the jury is adjourned until the court needs it again to investigate other accusations.[8]

In peaceful rural counties one grand jury a year is usually all that is needed. In larger urban counties there must either be a number of grand juries or else the same one must sit from time to time for several

months — unless an accusation may be brought by " *information.*"

Information. As a substitute for the grand jury over half the States now permit the use of the information to bring criminal charges. The information is a formal charge brought by the prosecuting attorney. It differs from an indictment only in that it is brought by the prosecuting attorney without grand jury action.

The Petit Jury. A *petit,* or trial, jury is a group of persons summoned into court to hear the evidence on both sides of a case and to decide the disputed points of fact, the judge in most States deciding the points of law. This jury tries both civil and criminal cases. Anyone may usually demand a jury trial if the question of life, liberty, or property is at stake.

The number of petit jurors is usually twelve, but in a number of States a lesser number is sufficient in civil cases and minor criminal cases. In the court of the justice of the peace six jurors or less is the rule, though in several States this court, too, may have twelve jurors.

In nearly one-third of the States an agreement of two-thirds, three-fourths, or five-sixths of the jurors is sufficient for a verdict in civil cases or unimportant criminal cases. In the remaining States a unanimous verdict is required even in cases that are unimportant.

The Grand Jury and the Petit Jury Compared. The same courts that have *grand* juries to *accuse* have *petit* juries to *try* the accused. But

---

[8] It is not uncommon for a State to impose upon the grand jury duties other than the consideration of evidence against accused persons. For instance, they may be required to approve the erection of public buildings and bridges in Pennsylvania, fix the tax rate in Georgia, investigate the sufficiency of the bonds of county officers in Alabama and Tennessee, arrest persons selling liquor contrary to law or arrest intoxicated persons in Vermont.

some courts which do not have grand juries do have petit juries. For instance, in most States, Justices' Courts may use petit juries, though they nowhere have grand juries; and courts which have no criminal jurisdiction have no need of grand juries.

Appellate courts of last resort do not use either grand or petit juries because they are concerned primarily with points of law which have been appealed to them from the lower courts. A grand jury investigates all indictable offenses committed during its existence, and usually hears only accusations. A grand jury seldom hears defenses.

Selection of Jurors. In scarcely any two States are jurors selected in exactly the same manner, but in all they are selected in a similar manner. Once a year, or oftener, some county official [9] or special jury commissioners, appointed or elected as the law prescribes, prepare a considerable list of persons eligible for jury service.

In some States any qualified voter of the county in which the court is sitting is eligible, while in others only taxpayers may serve. In the former States the names can be obtained from the poll books and in the latter from the tax assessors' books. Persons under twenty-one and those over sixty or seventy years of age, criminals, and illiterates are commonly ineligible. In most States other classes of persons, such as State and federal officials, professional men, foremen, firemen, and State militiamen, are not required to serve.

The chosen names are written on slips of paper and placed in a locked jury box,[10] which is usually kept in the custody of the clerk of the court. When the court needs a jury the names are drawn from the box by a designated official, and the sheriff is directed to summon such persons by a writ known as a *venire facias* (you must come). After eliminating the names of those who, for good reason, cannot serve, the judge makes a list of those who can serve and returns it to the clerk. This list is known as the *panel of veniremen.*

Grand jurors are commonly selected in the same manner as petit jurors, but in some States a separate list of names is prepared from which grand jurors are selected. Jurors for the justices' courts are commonly selected by the justice himself.

Many otherwise intelligent people think it " smart " to avoid jury duty. It is one of the most serious mistakes a citizen can make. An accused per-

---

[9] This official is usually the clerk of the court, the sheriff, the judge, or county board of commissioners. In the New England States and in Michigan names of jurors are selected by township (" town ") officers and sent to a county officer.

[10] In New Jersey the chancellor (highest judge) appoints for each county a jury commissioner of the party opposed to that of the county sheriff. These two are commissioners of juries and they select names of eligible persons as in other States, but instead of being put into the jury box the names are numbered consecutively and a piece of metal with a corresponding number is dropped into the box in place of the name.

MONTGOMERY COUNTY COURT HOUSE
Of the thousands of county court houses in the United States, the building at Independence, in Montgomery County, Kansas, is one of the most pleasant and dignified.

son, who may be entirely innocent, can hardly expect justice from a jury chosen from among the least intelligent in the community. Nor can the law be enforced properly if the best people beg off. Jury service is one of the most important obligations a good citizen owes to his society.

Criticisms and Proposed Reforms of the Jury System

No aspect of the administration of justice has come in for more criticism, by both lawyer and laymen alike, than the operation of the jury system. These criticisms are not so much directed at the system itself as at the *operation* of that system. All of the criticisms made do not apply to all juries everywhere, of course. And many times critics are inclined to forget this vital fact: the jury system is intended *first* to protect the innocent and only *second* to convict the guilty.

The jury system developed in medieval England on the theory that a man accused of crime, or involved in a dispute with his neighbor, could expect fairer treatment in his case if the facts were weighed and decided by a group of his neighbors. Thus jurors were selected because of their firsthand knowledge of local persons and events.

Today, however, the situation is completely reversed. Those with firsthand knowledge are excluded from service. In effect, as one student of the jury system has put it, in the attempt to get impartiality " ignorance [of the facts] is made virtually a prerequisite for jury service."

Other weaknesses are pointed to. The process of selecting jurymen is frequently long and tedious with the result that the judge falls far behind his docket of cases. Busy people engaged in important business or professional pursuits are often excused from service. Too often this may mean that better qualified jurors escape service while others less qualified serve. (The extreme here is the " professional juror " — a poisonous parasite in our judicial system.)

Another criticism stems from the fact that many jury verdicts are, in reality, compromises reached in the interest of a formal verdict. And at times a jury's verdict seems to be the result of emotional appeal rather than of unrefuted evidence. Jury tampering has occasionally been known, as has bribery of judges.

These and similar charges against the system have led most authorities to recommend various reforms and a few would even do away with juries. One proposal, already adopted in several States, involves reducing the size of juries from the usual twelve to five or six. A lesser number can, presumably, more readily reach agreement without any greater likelihood of injustice being done.

Another proposal, already adopted in several States, too, involves relaxing the unanimity requirement for jury verdicts. If a substantial majority, say three-fourths, is required, " hung " juries are largely eliminated.

Going to the very heart of the weaknesses charged to the jury system is the suggestion that persons accused of crime, or involved in civil suits, be allowed to waive their right to trial by jury and have their case heard only by the judge. This is now fact in nearly every State in civil suits and misdemeanor cases. About one-third of the States also allow for waiver in felony cases.

Some few critics propose complete elimination of the jury in all cases and the hearing of disputes by a single judge or a panel of three judges. This suggestion assumes, of course, complete impartiality from the bench.

Advisory Opinions

In ten of the States the highest courts will deliver what are known as *advisory opinions*. In all ten, these opinions are made available to the governor and in seven of the ten to the legislature as well.[11]

---

[11] To both the legislature and the governor, in Alabama, Colorado, Maine, Massa-

An advisory opinion makes it possible for the legislature, when considering the passage of a bill, and for the governor, before signing a bill, to secure the high court's opinion as to its constitutionality.

These opinions are advisory only. If the bill is passed and later challenged, the court is free to rule on the measure as it will. But at least some indication of the court's attitude may be had in advance.

Declaratory Judgments

In nearly every one of the States, the various courts will render *declaratory judgments*. These judgments are available *before* an actual case is instituted and are designed to indicate the legal rights of parties to a controversy. Suppose that the owner of a glue factory wants to expand his plant and a neighboring property owner objects. Rather than the one expanding his plant and the other seeking damages in court, both parties may ask the court for a declaratory judgment setting forth the rights of each. This practice has forestalled many actions that might have led to expensive legal entanglements.

Advisory opinions and declaratory judgments are often confused with one another. Advisory opinions are not given in disputes between parties; they are intended only as legal advice to the governor or the legislature. And an advisory opinion is in no sense binding, not even upon the judges who render it. But a declaratory judgment is binding between the parties involved.

Legalized Arbitration

The crowded calendars of our courts and the delays and expenses of law suits have encouraged the settlement of business disputes by *arbitration*.

Courts are necessary in *all* criminal and domestic-relations cases because the public is concerned, and in title-to-real-estate cases because the law is complicated.

But simple cases and those where the facts turn on expert knowledge can be decided by specialists in a particular field more quickly and probably more justly than by a judge and jury.

For more than a hundred years the New York Chamber of Commerce has continuously provided for arbitration, and arbitration boards in the motion picture industry annually settle thousands of disputes involving millions of dollars. The American Arbitration Association, with headquarters in New York City, arbitrated 184 dis-

chusetts, New Hampshire, North Carolina, and Rhode Island. To the governor only, in Delaware, Florida, and South Dakota. In other States, the attorney-general, as the State's chief legal officer, performs this task.

COURT HOUSE, SANTA BARBARA, CALIFORNIA

The county court house in Santa Barbara is a beautiful example of architecture in the local tradition.

putes in one year at an average cost of one-half of one per cent of the amount involved. The Association has a panel of about 500 experts in their respective fields who agree to act as arbitrators if called upon when matters are submitted to the Tribunal of the Association.

Trade or commercial organizations often incorporate in a contract provisions for arbitration in case any dispute or claim arises. The contract may (1) specify the number of arbitrators and the method of selecting them; (2) merely refer to the State statute; or (3) provide for following the Rules of the American Arbitration Association. Under these rules attorneys may appear as counsel, but in some trade organizations attorneys are barred from the proceedings.

According to statutes passed by New York, Massachusetts, New Jersey, Pennsylvania, Oregon, California, and Louisiana, an agreement to arbitrate civil disputes, except divorces and titles to real estate, is enforceable just like any other contract. If either party refuses to arbitrate, the courts will compel him to do so. Arbitrators may require the attendance of witnesses and demand that documents be submitted. The award of the arbitrators may be recorded in the same way as a court judgment, and can be collected by the officers of the court. The courts may set aside the award of the arbitrators if partiality, corruption, misconduct, or mistake is found.

WHAT THIS CHAPTER IS ABOUT

A court is a tribunal established by the State to administer justice according to law. The State courts hear all cases not heard by the federal courts, and State cases far outnumber federal ones.

The Justice of the Peace presides over the Justice Court at the base of the State judicial system. He usually hears misdemeanor cases and minor civil cases.

Police or Magistrates' Courts correspond to the Justice courts and are usually found in more populous areas.

Municipal Courts with full jurisdiction over all civil and criminal cases arising in the municipality are found in the larger cities and towns. In the largest cities they are organized into divisions to handle cases of a particular kind (like juvenile cases) or in a particular area of the city.

General Trial Courts, known by a variety of names, stand above the courts so far mentioned. They have original jurisdiction over cases within their district and also hear appeals from lower courts.

Intermediate Appellate Courts, found in over one-third of the States, hear appeals from the general trial courts.

The State Supreme Court is the capstone of the State judicial system. Except for cases which may be appealed to the United States Supreme Court, it is the court of last resort and it is the final interpreter of the State constitution.

Most State judges are elected.

There are two kinds of juries. The grand jury determines whether or not the evidence is sufficient to hold the accused for trial. The petit jury hears a case and decides questions of fact. An information may be filed by the prosecuting attorney, as an alternative to the grand jury, in over half the States. Jurors are selected in a variety of ways among the States.

The jury system is often criticized because it sometimes seems to put a premium on ignorance, the selection process is a long one, the better qualified are often excused, verdicts are sometimes compromises in order that a formal verdict can be returned, and emotional appeals sometimes overcome reason and fact.

Several reforms have been proposed and many have been adopted in various States. These include reducing the size of the jury, relaxing the unanimity requirement, and providing the right to waive the right to trial by jury. Some even propose eliminating the jury.

Advisory opinions on the constitutionality of a proposed law are given by the supreme courts of ten States. Declaratory judgments, indicating in advance the rights of parties to a dispute are given by most State courts. Legalized arbitration, settlement of a dispute by a special third party, is becoming common in nontechnical civil cases.

1. What are the duties of a court?

2. What two systems of courts are there in each State?

3. What classes of cases are brought into the federal courts? Into the State courts?

4. Distinguish a civil from a criminal case. A felony from a misdemeanor.

5. What are commonly the lowest courts in a State's judicial system?

6. What special courts do cities commonly have?

7. What is a juvenile court? Explain the need of small claims courts.

8. What is meant by *appellate jurisdiction?*

9. Do judges have any duties other than interpreting the law and deciding cases?

10. What is a grand jury? What is a petit jury? How many jurors commonly compose each? How does a grand jury differ from a petit jury?

11. Does the highest State court have jury trials?

12. Who serve on juries and how are they chosen?

13. What is meant by a *true bill of indictment? Presentment? Foreman? Information?*

14. What is an advisory opinion? What is a declaratory judgment?

PROBLEMS FOR DISCUSSION

1. Why are citizens never justified in resorting to lynch law?

2. Most State judges are elected by the voters. Why do most students of government think it better to have them appointed by the governor or the chief justice or elected by the licensed lawyers in the area in which they are to serve? Is it more important for judges, governors, or legislators to serve long terms?

3. In Idaho a prisoner charged with threatening a man with a revolver was tried and found guilty by a jury composed wholly of women. Should men be tried by men, women by women?

4. A New Yorker kept account of 46 times that he put a penny in a subway vending machine for a penny chocolate and every time the machine failed to work; so he sued the company owning the machine and recovered 46¢ plus $1.25 advanced for a summons. In what court did he sue?

5. Does, or would, the presence of a small claims court in your community help to increase respect for law and government? Do you suppose the newsboy who won a 45-cent suit for a newspaper account became a more patriotic citizen because of his experience with the Small Claims Court?

6. In Virginia in each county the former Justices of the Peace are now replaced by one County Justice appointed by the Circuit Judge. As a practicing attorney, the appointee can hear these minor cases on the side. The appointee is usually an able lawyer very superior to the average Justice of the Peace. Should every State have such County Justices instead of township Justices of the Peace, in your opinion?

7. Give your arguments for or against a law, proposed or in existence, giving legal approval to arbitrated cases in your State. What disputes growing out of the industries of your community would lend themselves to arbitration?

THINGS YOU MIGHT DO

1. Write a short essay or editorial on the importance of jury duty.

2. Invite a local judge, prosecuting attorney, or lawyer to address the class.

3. If possible attend sessions of a court and report on the experience to the class.

4. Construct a chart of your State's court system. Show the organization of each court, how its judges are chosen, and its jurisdiction. (Consult the State constitution, State manual, and local attorneys.)

WORDS AND PHRASES YOU SHOULD KNOW

Advisory opinion
Arbitration
Civil law
Criminal law
Declaratory judgment
Domestic Relations Court
Felony

General trial court
Grand jury
Indictment
Information
Intermediate appellate court
Justice of the Peace
Juvenile Court

Magistrates' Court
Misdemeanor
Municipal Court
Petit jury
Police Court
Presentment
Small Claims Court

SELECT BIBLIOGRAPHY

BELL, JOSEPH N., " Are Juries Giving Away Too Much Money? " *Reader's Digest,* October, 1956.

GREENBAUM, EDWARD S., " A Plea for Court Reform *Now,*" *New York Times Magazine,* February 27, 1955.

MACDONALD, AUSTIN F., *American State Government and Administration,* Chapter 11. Crowell, 1955.

——, *State and Local Government in the United States,* Chapter 8. Crowell, 1955.

MURTAGH, JOHN M., " I Sit in Judgment," *Saturday Evening Post,* November 7, 1953.

PHILLIPS, JEWELL C., *State and Local Government in America,* Chapter 11. American Book, 1954.

RITTWAGEN, M., " Child Criminals Are My Job," *Saturday Evening Post,* March 27, 1954.

VANDERBILT, ARTHUR, " Overloading Our Courts," *Time,* February 21, 1955.

YODER, ROBERT, " Wisconsin Throws Them Out of Jail," *Saturday Evening Post,* February 4, 1956.

It is the judge's sacred duty to keep the wells of justice pure and to do everything in his power to improve its processes.

— *Judge Harold R. Medina*

★

Chapter 30

CIVIL AND CRIMINAL PROCEDURE

As we learned in Chapter 29, the basic function of the courts is to hear and decide cases. The rules of procedure under which they do so are rather complicated and justice some-times seems to move at a snail's pace. But this is so for a very good reason. Our whole legal system is designed to one great end — to protect the citizen in the lawful exercise of his rights.

Kinds of Law Applied by State Courts

In dealing with the cases that come before them, the State courts apply several forms of law. They apply the United States Constitution, the constitution of the State, and city and county charters. They also apply legislative acts, those of Congress, the State legislature, city councils, and county boards. Then, too, they apply the executive ordinances issued by agencies of the National, State, and local governments. The State courts also apply two other forms of law in cases they hear; namely, *common law* and *equity*.

Common Law. The common law may be defined as " judge-made " law based upon precedent. Contrary to popular belief, most court cases are decided on the basis of common law, rather than *statutory law* (law enacted by a legislative body).

Long before the settling of the thirteen colonies, English judges began to decide cases on the basis of past decisions in similar cases. Through the centuries a vast body of judge-made or common law developed.

Naturally, the common law was brought to America by the English settlers. In America the common law was (and still is being) shaped to American needs. It became the basis for the legal system in each of our states, except Louisiana.[1]

---

[1] Because of the early French influence, Louisiana's legal system is based upon the Napoleonic Code rather than the common law. But gradually the common law has been working its way into Louisiana law.

526

Stare Decisis. The common law has grown through the application of the legal principle of *stare decisis* — that is, the following of the precedents set by courts in deciding similar earlier cases.

Equity.   Equity is a branch of the law which developed alongside the common law. As common law developed, judges became conservative and ceased to create means of obtaining justice as new conditions demanded. They had certain forms, called " court writs," upon which one had to state his case. If he could not state it on one of these forms, he could not bring his case before the court.

Those who were thus barred from the courts appealed directly to the king for justice. The appeals became so numerous that the king created a new court, the Chancery Court, to handle these cases in a conscientious and equitable manner. So there grew up a branch of the law known as *equity* with its own set of principles and writs.

Probably the most important difference between the two forms is that the common law is *remedial* while equity is *preventive*. That is, the common law deals with matters *after* they have happened; equity seeks to *prevent* the doing of a threatened wrong. For example, if your neighbor begins to add a room to his house, you can prevent him from extending it onto your property by securing an *injunction* — a court order enjoining (preventing) him from doing so.

The English brought equity as well as the common law to America. At first the two were administered by different courts. But today only seven States have separate equity (" chancery ") courts. In the other States the same courts administer both forms and in general the procedural distinctions between the two forms are disappearing.

Civil Procedure

A *civil suit* usually involves a dispute between private parties over their respective legal rights and duties. A government is sometimes involved in a civil suit, as for example when a State sues a person or consents to being sued. Usually, however, civil suits are between private persons.[2]

A civil suit may be distinguished

from a *criminal case,* as you will see in a moment, by the fact that in a criminal case the State is always the plaintiff against a person charged with a public offense (crime).

There are two kinds of civil procedure — *law* suits and *equity* suits. For instance, if someone owes you money and refuses to pay, or does injury to your person or property, for example in an automobile accident, or violates a contract, you can sue him at law for money damages.

---

[2] One or both persons may be artificial, *i.e.,* a corporation, such as the General Motors Corporation or the United States Steel Corporation.

If, on the other hand, you want to prevent him from doing some wrong, or if you want him to live up to a contract rather than pay money damages, or if a person who has property in trust for you refuses to pay you the income from it, you can sue him in equity.

In cases at *law* the judge usually has a jury to decide the facts, and the witnesses usually testify in court. But in *equity* cases the judge usually decides the facts himself without a jury, and instead of having the witnesses in court he often appoints a " referee " to hear the evidence and

report it to him in writing. In the following examples, the two kinds of suits are illustrated as they would proceed in Virginia. They would proceed in a similar manner in other States.

Suit at Law. Suppose Mr. A, a passenger, has received bodily injury from a railroad wreck in Albemarle County, say on the Southern Railroad, and brings suit for $5000 damages. Here Mr. A is the *plaintiff* and the Southern Railroad Company the *defendant*. Mr. A will have his lawyer file his claim against the Southern Railroad Company with the clerk of

THE LAWYER FOR THE DEFENSE ADDRESSES THE JURY

The responsibility of deciding the guilt or innocence of the defendant rests with the twelve citizens seated in the jury box.

Harold M. Lambert

Unit VII. THE STATES

the court in Albemarle County. The railroad company will deny A's right to $5000 damages, by a plea, and will have its lawyer represent it in court.

When the judge holds court in Albemarle County a jury will be impaneled unless the lawyers, known as the counsel for the plaintiff and defendant, are willing to dispense with a jury. The judge also must agree to decide the facts of the case, as well as the law, else the jury cannot be dispensed with. If a jury is impaneled it will decide all disputed facts, as, for example, whether Mr. A was in fact injured, to what extent injured, and hence how much damages he should receive. The judge will decide all points of law and instruct the jury as to the law.

After the counsel for each side argues the facts of the case, the judge instructs the jury as to the law and the jury retires to the jury room. After deliberation, if the jury can agree upon the amount of damage done Mr. A, it renders a decision, called a *verdict*. If the jurors cannot agree, it is a mistrial and the case may be tried again.

The judge finally gives *judgment* in accordance with the verdict of the jury. In this case if the judgment is in favor of the plaintiff, the defendant may appeal the case to the Supreme Court of Appeals, because damages exceeding $300 are involved. Or suppose the defendant accepts the decision but fails to make prompt payment of the damages awarded; then the clerk will issue an execution to the sheriff or a constable directing him to levy execution and sell the personal property of the defendant. If there is no personal property the court may authorize the sale of real estate.

Suit in Equity. Suppose X, a farmer, has a fresh stream of water running through his farm and by his house, which he uses to water his stock and which his wife uses for washing clothes. Y establishes a large creamery on the stream above the X farm. The creamery empties greasy water and acids into the stream to such an extent that it produces a stench at the farmer's home, his cattle refuse to drink the water, and it can no longer be used for washing clothes.

X will have his attorney file suit with the clerk of the court to *enjoin* (forbid) Y from emptying the grease and acids into the water, and the clerk will have the sheriff notify Y that suit has been brought. A jury is not needed to decide the facts, and witnesses need not appear in court.[3] A master in chancery, notary public, or justice of the peace gets the counsel for each side together at some convenient time and place to take *depositions* (testimony), which a stenographer records word for word. These depositions are given to the judge. The counsel for the plaintiff and for the defendant argue the points of law and evidence before the judge in court or in vacation (between terms).

---

[3] In some States the evidence would be taken in open court, the lawyers and judge asking questions of the witnesses.

If the judge is not satisfied as to the facts perhaps he will go to the scene, call witnesses before him, or order the master in chancery to make further investigation as to certain facts. With the facts and the law both presented, the judge is prepared to render a decision, which is called a *decree* in equity cases. If the judge decides that the injury to X is as claimed, he will decree that Y must cease emptying grease and acids into the stream.

The court costs of a civil suit such as witness fees, jury fees, and recording fees are usually placed by the court upon the party losing the case. Sometimes some costs are granted with which to pay lawyers, but each party usually has to pay his own lawyers.

Criminal Procedures

A *crime* is any act which is considered so dangerous to the public peace and safety that it is prohibited by law. The law defining a certain act as a crime also sets out the punishment for the crime.

Crimes may be immoral in themselves, like murder or burglary. But other acts are crimes only because they are prohibited by law, like exceeding the speed limit or failing to remove snow from the sidewalk.

Crimes range all the way from minor ones (*misdemeanors*) like traffic violations to the more serious ones (*felonies*) like murder or arson.

Felonies are crimes of a more serious character than misdemeanors. They vary so much from State to State that no general definition of them can be given. But in many States all crimes which are punishable by confinement in a State penitentiary or by death are defined as felonies. The following crimes are almost universally classed as felonies.

(1) *Murder in the first degree* generally means the unlawful, inten-

tional, and premeditated killing of a human being, or such a killing resulting from the commission or the attempt to commit one of the graver crimes such as arson, burglary, or robbery. Such crimes are punished in about a fourth of the States by death, in about half by death or life imprisonment, and in the remaining States by long terms in the penitentiary — usually for life.

(2) *Murder in the second degree* generally means the unlawful, intentional killing without premeditation, or such killing as a result of an attempt to commit some lesser crime. It is punished by imprisonment varying from a minimum of one year in a few States to a maximum of life in many States, and even death in several.

(3) *Manslaughter* is the unlawful killing of another without malice. The killing may be voluntary, as in a sudden heat of passion; or it may be involuntary, in the commission of some unlawful act or a lawful act without due caution. Many States di-

vide manslaughter into two degrees. It is punished by imprisonment for a term ordinarily shorter than that for murder in the second degree. Great discretion is given to the jury or judge.

(4) *Arson* is the act of unlawfully and maliciously burning a building or other property. It is more serious if done at night and most serious if an inhabited dwelling is burned at night.

(5) *Burglary* is the breaking and entering of a dwelling house during the night, with the intent to commit a felony, whether the felony is actually committed or not. The same offense is called *housebreaking* if committed during the day. In some States, the charge of burglary covers illegal entry into other buildings besides dwelling houses.

(6) *Robbery* is the theft of property from the person or in the immediate presence of the victim, accompanied by force or fear.

(7) *Larceny* is simply theft, and *grand larceny* is the theft of property above a fixed value, generally from $25 to $50. In a number of States to steal any amount from the person of another without force or fear is considered grand larceny.

Arson, burglary, robbery, grand larceny, assault with intent to kill, bigamy, perjury, forgery, and embezzlement are commonly punished by a considerable term of imprisonment. Burglary may be punished by death in one State, robbery by death in two States, and arson by death in six States.

Misdemeanors are crimes of a less serious character than felonies and, like felonies, cannot be defined by any general definition which will apply to all States. For instance, in Virginia offenses which are punishable with death or confinement in the penitentiary are felonies; all other offenses are misdemeanors. In the same State the following crimes are misdemeanors and, in general, would be so classed in other States: violation of town or city ordinances, carrying concealed weapons, cruelty to animals, attempting to defraud a hotel-keeper, petit larceny, which is a theft less than a grand larceny, nonsupport of a wife and minor children, permitting a gambling house on one's premises, libel, assault and battery. These misdemeanors are punishable by confinement in jail or by fine. But such misdemeanors as drunkenness without disorder or profanity are punishable by fine only. In such cases if the person who has been fined cannot or will not pay his fine, he may be sent to jail in many States.

Criminal Procedure. *Arrest of Felons.* A private individual may arrest a person to prevent the commission of a felony in his presence, or may, without a warrant, arrest a felon whom he has seen commit a felony, or may even arrest one without a warrant on reasonable suspicion of his having committed a felony, provided a felony has been committed.

An officer of the peace (sheriff, constable, policeman) may do anything a private person may do. He should furthermore pursue a felon who is making

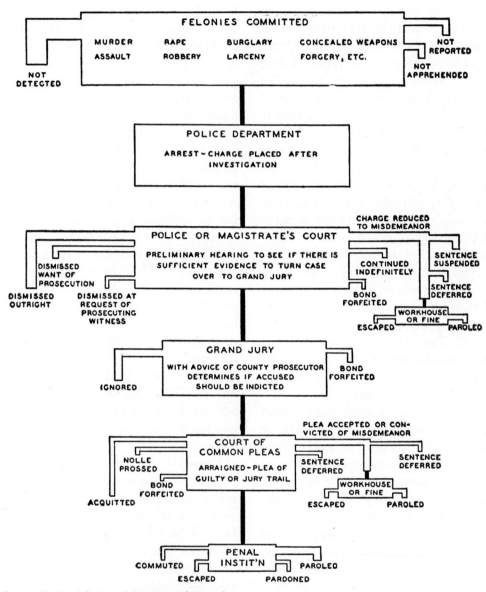

Source: **Cincinnati Bureau of Governmental Research.**

his escape though he has not actually seen the crime committed. If the policeman, constable, or sheriff does not attempt to arrest a felon, the prosecuting attorney will usually take the initiative and have the suspected felon arrested.

The injured party or anyone knowing of the crime may go to a justice of the peace or some other magistrate who has power to issue a warrant and, by taking oath as to the crime, have a warrant issued for the arrest of some designated person, provided the magistrate is satisfied as to the truth of the complaint. The *warrant* is a written document describing the felon, setting forth the offense, and directing that he be brought before some specified magistrate, usually the one who has issued the warrant. A policeman, constable, sheriff, or any other peace officer may make the arrest (" serve the warrant ") and bring the felon before the proper magistrate for trial. In making the arrest the officer may call upon any persons to assist him, may break into a building, or may kill the felon *if necessary*. By " necessary " is meant self-defense or preventing the escape of one who has committed a felony.

Arrest of Misdemeanants. A private person may arrest another without a warrant to quell a breach of the peace in his presence, but he may not arrest one to prevent any other misdemeanor; nor may he arrest one for any misdemeanor already committed. A peace officer may arrest without a warrant for a breach of the peace or any other misdemeanor committed in his presence. If the misdemeanor was not committed in his presence he can arrest only on a warrant. The same magistrates who issue warrants for felons may issue them for misdemeanants, and arrests are made by the same officers in the same manner except that an officer is never justified in killing a misdemeanant fugitive,

though of course he has the right of self-defense.

The Commitment. After the accused is arrested he is brought before the magistrate, usually the justice of the peace, except in cities where there is a special police justice, or in towns in which the mayor has the powers of a justice. If the crime is a misdemeanor the accused is probably tried at once. If the crime is a felony the magistrate gives the accused a preliminary hearing: and when the evidence indicates a probability of guilt, the accused is held for the grand jury, or brought to trial by *information*. If the crime is murder the accused is usually committed to jail, but otherwise, unless his being at large is considered especially dangerous, he is released until the grand jury meets, provided he can give bail.[4]

The Indictment. The *prosecuting attorney*, called State's attorney or district attorney in some States, investigates the evidence against such persons as the committing magistrates have held for the grand jury, or

---

[4] Furnishing bail (Old French *bail* = a guardian) is theoretically putting a man in charge of a private jailer and in effect is the guarantee that an accused person will appear for trial if allowed to go at large. It is usually a sum of money, depending upon the character of the charge, and is determined by a judge or special bail officer. The cash, or other security, may be furnished by a friend or by the accused himself if he possesses the amount required.

Professional criminals often secure bail through one who makes a business of going bail for a fee. And too often the criminal commits another crime while out on bail to secure money with which to pay his bail fee.

against any other persons whose probable guilt has been brought to his attention. If he thinks there is sufficient evidence to convict, he draws up a *bill of indictment,* a written document stating the charge, and has witnesses summoned for the grand jury.

If a certain majority of the grand jury (the majority varies from State to State) thinks there is sufficient evidence to warrant a court trial, the foreman writes across the face of the indictment the words, " a true bill " (of indictment). The indicted person must then stand trial in court. If the prescribed majority does not think that the evidence justifies a trial the words " not a true bill " are used, and the charge is dropped.

The Trial. The Justice Court usually has original jurisdiction in misdemeanor cases. Here the trial is very informal because justices of the peace are not always lawyers and must depend upon what untrained minds can glean from a volume of laws compiled for their use. With few exceptions an appeal may be taken to the county or superior court in criminal cases.

In felony cases sent to the county or superior trial court by the grand jury the prisoner appears in the custody of the sheriff, deputy sheriff, or some like officer who perhaps bears a different title. In misdemeanor cases sent from the grand jury or appealed from a justice of the peace the prisoner need not appear in person. He often prefers to leave his case to an attorney. But a felony case cannot proceed unless the accused person is present.

The prisoner is charged with committing a crime against the State [5] and is prosecuted by the prosecuting (State's) attorney of the county. The clerk of the court reads the indictment or presentment to the prisoner, who pleads " guilty " or " not guilty." If he pleads guilty, and is of a sound mind, the judge usually pronounces the sentence according to the State law, and the case ends. But if he pleads not guilty he is entitled to a trial by jury if he desires it, and in some States one accused of a felony is obliged to stand trial by jury. If the prisoner cannot afford an attorney the judge appoints a lawyer, commonly a young inexperienced one, to defend him. In most States this attorney is paid a small fee by the State.

There are usually about twice as many persons summoned as are needed for the jury, but when the court meets, the counsel may challenge a certain number, which is limited by law, without giving any cause, and the judge will excuse such venire-

---

[5] For a great many acts a person may be proceeded against criminally by the State because he has disturbed the peace of the community generally, and also in a civil action by a person because the latter has been injured individually. If a man libels you by an unlawful malicious publication and thereby injures your good name, you can sue him for money damages; if his libeling you causes a breach of the peace, he has also committed a crime and may be punished by the officers of the State in the name of the State, because the entire State is injured by lawless people who break the peace.

Harold M. Lambert

THE DEFENDANT ANSWERS A QUESTION

Seated in the witness chair, the defendant answers the lawyer's question as the judge behind the bench and the jury in the foreground listen attentively.

men. Then the counsel may challenge any other veniremen for cause, such as relationship to the parties to the suit or for some other reason why they might not be impartial; if it is a murder trial, because they do not believe in capital punishment.[6]

If others are challenged, the judge, in some States, may have the sheriff summon bystanders (*talesmen*), while in other States a new list must be prepared as the former one was and this procedure must continue until the prescribed number of suitable men are *impaneled,* that is, secured to serve.[7]

After the case is opened the wit-

[6] In some States unsatisfactory laws or inefficient judges often permit the lawyers to ask every conceivable question in order to determine whether the jurors hold any opinions which would cause them to be prejudiced in the case. For example, after the Iroquois Theatre fire in Chicago, in which so many people lost their lives, and the Theatre Company was being sued, and the counsel for the company asked the prospective jurors such questions as these: " What paper do you read? Do you believe in card playing?

Dancing? Theatre going? Have you any prejudices against city people? Have you ever had a friend killed in a fire? "

[7] In the $1,219,000 Brink's robbery trial in Boston in 1956, 1621 veniremen were examined and three weeks were needed to complete the jury. 4150 veniremen were called in nine and a half weeks in a murder trial in Indiana in 1878.

nesses for the State and for the prisoner are examined and cross-examined, arguments are delivered by the attorneys for each side, and the judge gives the *instructions* to the jury, explaining the law governing the case. (In Virginia the instructions precede the arguments.)

The jury then retires to consider the evidence in the case and arrive at a decision. If the jury cannot agree, the foreman reports " no agreement "; if the requisite number agree, usually all in an important criminal case, he reports " guilty " or " not guilty." If guilty, the jury usually determines the punishment in its verdict,[8] which is read by the clerk of the court, and the judge pronounces the sentence.

If the penalty is merely a fine, this is paid to the clerk; if more than a fine, the sheriff takes charge of the prisoner, who is taken to jail to serve his term, or until he can be transferred to the penitentiary, executed, or disposed of according to the sentence. If there has been a disagreement (" a hung jury "), the case is either set for a new trial or it is dismissed.

If the verdict has been " guilty," the prisoner may petition for an appeal to a higher court on the grounds that the verdict is not according to the law, or to the evidence, or that some error has been committed in the trial. If the appeal is granted and is sustained the higher court will order the lower court to hold a new trial; but if no error is found the appeal is dismissed and the order of the lower court stands.

Improving Judicial Procedure

We have come a long way in the administration of justice from the " trial by ordeal " days of the Middle Ages. Then, an accused person was subjected to various forms of physical torture. If he emerged uninjured, he was judged innocent of the crime charged.

There are still many things about our judicial procedures that are in need of reform, however. For example, most State court systems lack any particular plan of organizational unity. That is, the structure is often

" jerry-built " with much overlapping and lack of co-operation between the minor, general trial, and intermediate courts. Under the new constitution in New Jersey, the judiciary was completely reorganized to meet this criticism. That State now has only three levels of courts: the supreme court, superior courts, and county courts, all organized into a unified court system.

Another criticism often heard centers around the delay and the cost in obtaining justice. As a common example of what this can mean, take the case of a man badly injured in an automobile accident. He is often forced to settle his claim against the

---

[8] In many States the judge determines the punishment after the jury has determined the guilt.

other party out of court and at a much lower figure than he could win in a suit. Why? Because he must support his family and pay his bills like anyone else. He can't afford to wait for a year, eighteen months, or even longer to win a court award.

Court costs and attorneys' fees make the administration of justice pretty expensive. Persons of moderate means often cannot afford to appeal a case, even though they feel they have been denied justice in a lower court.

Courts *must* insist on precise and exact procedures in order to give the accused every benefit of a fair trial. But occasionally this is carried too far. In a recent Texas case, for example, a man admitted drowning his wife and son. But his conviction and death sentence were reversed on appeal because the indictment was faulty — it did not state that the drownings had taken place *in water!* He was retried three times and finally sentenced to life. Similar instances can be cited in practically every State. Numerous other defects and needed

reforms are constantly cited by bar associations and individual lawyers, judges, and other legal authorities.

Judicial Councils are now found in about three-fourths of the States. Some are much more active than others. Among the most active are those in California, Connecticut, Kansas, Michigan, New York, and Texas. They are usually composed of one or more supreme court justices, judges from the lower courts, the attorney-general, legislators, and professors of law.

The Council usually gathers information, makes studies of particular judicial problems, and recommends needed legislation. In a few States, like California, it has wider powers; for example, to make rules of procedure, transfer judges to courts with crowded dockets, and co-ordinate the work of all the courts in the State judicial system.

Legal Aid Societies and Public Defender Offices have been established in many of the larger cities and counties to provide counsel and advice to those unable otherwise to afford it.

WHAT THIS CHAPTER IS ABOUT

Our whole legal system is designed to protect the citizen in the lawful exercise of his rights. State courts apply several forms of law — the National and State Constitutions, city and county charters, acts of Congress and the State legislature, local ordinances, and executive orders. They also apply the common law and equity.

The common law is judge-made law based on precedent. Most court cases

are decided on the basis of the common law rather than statutory law (that enacted by the legislative body). Equity developed alongside the common law in England and covers those matters not included within the common law. It is preventive while the common law is remedial.

Civil suits involve private parties in disputes over their respective legal rights and duties. Governments are sometimes involved, as in claims cases. In a criminal case the State is always involved as prosecutor against a person charged with a crime.

There are two kinds of civil procedure — law suits and equity suits.

A crime is any act which is considered so dangerous to society that it is prohibited by law. The law also sets the punishment for its commission. Crimes are of two kinds: they may be either misdemeanors (lesser ones) or felonies (greater ones).

There is always room for improvement in our judicial procedures. Some of the most pressing problems revolve about delay, cost, complex organization, and occasional overzealousness.

QUESTIONS ON THE TEXT

1. What various forms of law do State courts apply?

2. What is the common law? Equity?

3. Distinguish between a civil suit and a criminal case.

4. If you sue for a sum of money do you sue *at law* or *in equity?*

5. Explain just how a suit *at law* proceeds. What do you mean by *plaintiff? defendant? verdict? judgment?*

6. Explain just how a suit *in equity* proceeds. What is a *decree?* What are *depositions?*

7. What is a crime? Are all crimes wrong in themselves? If not, why are they considered crimes?

8. Crimes are of what two degrees? What distinguishes them in many States?

9. What is Murder in the First Degree? Murder in the Second Degree? Manslaughter? Arson? Burglary? Robbery? Larceny? Grand Larceny?

10. Who may arrest felons?

11. What is a *warrant?* Is it necessary to have a warrant to arrest a felon? Who serves a warrant? May he call upon bystanders to assist him?

12. May a peace officer without a warrant arrest one who has committed a misdemeanor?

13. Who usually tries a criminal and commits him to jail when he is first arrested?

14. What is meant by the expression *giving bail?*

15. Who draws up bills of indictment to present to the grand jury?

16. Describe a jury trial.

17. What do you mean by *instructions?*

18. By whom is the law governing a case decided? the facts?

19. What is meant by a " hung jury "?

20. Describe a court in session.

21. On what grounds may one petition for an appeal?

22. What legislation is recommended by the National Crime Commission?

23. What is a judicial council?

PROBLEMS FOR DISCUSSION

1. In New York City a thief stole a plume worth $57, but proved that it was marked down to $49.50 the day he stole it; hence his offense was merely a misdemeanor, whereas it would have been a felony if he had stolen goods valued for as much as $50. What crime did this thief commit? Would his crime be the same in every state?

2. In the eighteenth century nearly 200 crimes were punishable by death in England. A death penalty was prescribed for stealing a handkerchief. The people and even the judges ceased believing in the

justice of such laws and did not enforce them. For instance, in one case a man was accused of stealing a sheep. Because it was a ewe that had been stolen, the judge threw the case out of court so that he might not have to pronounce a death sentence. Have any of these technicalities of the law come down to us today even though we do not need them? Why are such technicalities not needed today?

3. Are crimes prevented more by the severity of punishment or by the certainty of punishment? Would you consider it extravagant for the government to spend $100,000 in order to detect and bring a murderer to justice?

4. In Oregon a boy charged with violating the cigarette ordinance was sentenced by the judge to wheel eight tiers of wood from the street into the City Hall. Do you consider that the judge showed wisdom in his sentence? What sentence would you have given?

5. You cannot compel a person accused of a crime to testify against himself according to law. You cannot so much as ask him where he was when the crime was committed. What do you think of this old legal rule? Would you favor compelling the accused to make a statement as to his whereabouts to the justice of the peace before whom he is brought — else assume that he is guilty?

6. In some States persons convicted of murder are put to death by the gallows, in others by the electric chair, in others by lethal gas, in Utah by a firing squad, and in some there is no capital punishment. Which sentence do you think is most likely to reduce crime? Do you feel the States should have the same punishments for major crimes?

7. The late Judge George Shaughnessy of the Municipal Court of Milwaukee heard about 150 criminal cases a month — principally felonies. He was efficient and gave prompt *justice*. One morning a man murdered his wife, and in less than eight hours he was serving his life sentence in the penitentiary.

In Milwaukee the accused are brought to trial by " information " instead of the slow grand jury process; there is no easy bail, so there are no professional bondsmen there; a juror is not disqualified merely because he has formed a tentative opinion about the case; with the consent of the accused, the trial is without jury; and tactics designed to slow up the trial are not permitted.

Criminals know about Milwaukee. A visiting burglar was caught there at midnight. By noon the next day he was on his way to the penitentiary to begin an eight-year sentence, and he thus voiced his disgust to an inquiring reporter: " Tell my pals in Chicago," he said, " to stay out of this man's town! " It is not surprising that the murder rate in Milwaukee was found to be less than that of any other city as large or larger.

If under this system of " prompt justice " it should be discovered that an injustice has been done, is there any redress for the one thus imprisoned? What?

8. Do you agree with the following statement by Judge Shaughnessy? " Speedy trials reduce the upkeep of prisoners in tax-supported county jails. And delay ought to be avoided if only because in our day it has become the refuge of the caught criminal: he realizes far too shrewdly that if his case is continued often enough and long enough, witnesses may disappear or die, important papers and exhibits can be ' lost,' public interest will certainly wear out — and there is a strong chance that the verdict will finally be ' Not guilty! ' "

THINGS YOU MIGHT DO

1. Attend sessions of a local court.
2. Invite a judge, prosecuting attorney, or lawyer to address the class.
3. Follow some prominent court case in the newspapers and note the procedures followed.
4. Hold model court sessions in the classroom.

WORDS AND PHRASES YOU SHOULD KNOW

Bail
Common Law
Counsel
Crime
Decree
Defendant
Deposition

Equity
Felony
Hung jury
Indictment
Injunction
Instructions
Judgment
Misdemeanor

Plaintiff
Precedent
Stare decisis
Statutory law
Talesman
Verdict
Warrant

SELECT BIBLIOGRAPHY

GRAVES, W. BROOKE, *American State Government,* Chapters 16, 17, 18. Heath, 1953.

HOFSTADTER, JUDGE SAMUEL H., " Traffic Jam in the Courts," *New York Times Magazine,* February 21, 1954.

——, " Let's Put Sense in the Traffic Laws," *Saturday Evening Post,* October 22, 1955.

MACDONALD, AUSTIN F., *American State Government and Administration,* Chapters 21, 22. Crowell, 1955.

——, *State and Local Government in the United States,* Chapter 17. Crowell, 1955.

PHILLIPS, JEWELL C., *State and Local Government in America,* Chapters 19, 24. American Book, 1954.

SONDERN, FREDERIC, " Judge Cooper's Remarkable Experiment," *Reader's Digest,* June, 1956.

STREUER, ARON, " New Cure for Congested Courts," *Reader's Digest,* November, 1956.

Copies of warrants of arrest, subpoenas, summons, etc., can usually be obtained from local officials.

Taxes are portions of private property which a government takes for its public purposes.

— *John Fiske*

★

Chapter 31

STATE FINANCE

As we noted in Chapters 7 and 12, raising and spending of money for governmental purposes is vital to the very existence of government. Most of the functions that a government performs involve money.

Just as the costs of government at the national level have risen to astronomical heights, so have the costs at the State and local levels. Governments in the United States now spend more than $100,000,000,000 a year. State and local governments account for over $30,000,000,000 of this huge sum. The annual expenditures of New York City alone total more than $1,300,000,000, or more than the National Government itself spent in any year before World War I. State and local governments receive their income (revenue) from (1) taxation and (2) nontax sources.

Total State and Local Revenues. As you can see from the table on the next page, State tax collections now amount to more than $14,000,000,000 a year. The various local governments now take in just about the same amount each year.

As we shall see when we discuss the nontax revenues, the State and local governments collect yet another $7,000,000,000 a year from this source. So, in all, the total State and local income in the United States today is well over $30,000,000,000 annually.

Because taxes are the chief source of income, we shall study them before

"I just thought of a wonderful way to live within our budget. Let's give up taxes."

By Franklin Folger: distributed by Newspaper Features Syndicate, Inc.

KIND OF TAX	FISCAL 1957	FISCAL 1956
General and Selective Property Taxes .	$ 480,000,000	$ 467,000,000
Sales Taxes:		
General sales	3,291,000,000	3,036,000,000
Alcoholic beverages	568,000,000	546,000,000
Tobacco	553,000,000	515,000,000
Motor vehicle fuel	2,821,000,000	2,687,000,000
Other	1,106,000,000	1,016,000,000
Licenses:		
Motor vehicles and operators . . .	1,366,000,000	1,295,000,000
Corporations	407,000,000	333,000,000
Alcoholic beverages	83,000,000	79,000,000
Hunting, fishing	90,000,000	86,000,000
Other	241,000,000	231,000,000
Net Income Taxes:		
On individuals	1,563,000,000	1,374,000,000
On corporations	984,000,000	890,000,000
Death and Gift Taxes	338,000,000	310,000,000
Severance Taxes	385,000,000	361,000,000
Miscellaneous Taxes	153,000,000	149,000,000
Total	$14,429,000,000	$13,375,000,000

turning to the nontax revenues.

Taxes Defined. Taxes may be defined as charges imposed by a legislative body upon persons or property in order to raise money for public purposes.

Limits on State and Local Taxing Powers

Federal Limitations. There are several important limitations on the taxing powers of State and local governments which arise from the United States Constitution.

(1) *Interstate and Foreign Commerce.* Article I, Section 10, of the Constitution provides that —

No State shall, without the consent of Congress, lay any imposts or duties on im-

542

ports or exports, except what may be absolutely necessary for executing its inspection laws; and the net produce of all duties and imposts, laid by any State on imports or exports, shall be for the use of the treasury of the United States; and all such laws shall be subject to the revision and control of the Congress.

Section 10 also provides that —

No State shall, without the consent of Congress, lay any duty of tonnage . . .[1]

In these two provisions the States are prohibited from taxing interstate and foreign commerce. And the Supreme Court has often held that, because the Constitution gives Congress the power to regulate interstate and foreign commerce, the States are generally prohibited from doing so. (See Chapter 8.)

The States, then, (and their local governments) cannot tax interstate and foreign commerce *as such*. They may and do impose taxes, however, on property, even though it is used in commerce. For example, property taxes are often imposed upon railroad cars, steamships, airplanes, buses, and the like.

(2) *The National Government and Its Instrumentalities.* As we have already seen, the States have been forbidden, ever since the Supreme Court's decision in *McCulloch* v. *Maryland,* 1819, to tax the National Government or any of its instrumentalities. As

___

[1] *Tonnage* refers to a vessel's internal cubical capacity — how much it will hold — in tons of 100 cubic feet each. *Tonnage duties* are duties upon vessels in proportion to their capacity.

Chief Justice John Marshall said, " The power to tax involves the power to destroy." (See pages 108, 122.)

The fact that the States and their local governments cannot tax federal property means that huge areas of land — for example, military reservations — cannot be taxed. The Congress, however, does appropriate money to be used to make " payments in lieu of taxes " (so-called " lulu payments ") to the States to make up for at least some of this.

(3) *The 14th Amendment.* The " Due Process " and " Equal Protection " clauses of the 14th Amendment also limit State and local taxation, as follows:

. . . nor shall any State deprive any person of life, liberty or property, without due process of law, nor deny to any person within its jurisdiction the equal protection of the laws.

For example, taxes may not be levied for any but a public purpose. Some years ago, Topeka, Kansas, agreed to pay a sum of money to a manufacturer if he would locate his new plant there. He did, but when the city levied a tax to pay the money promised, several taxpayers took the matter to court. The case was finally appealed to the United States Supreme Court, which held that Topeka could not levy the tax. It was not for a public purpose and hence was a denial of the taxpayers' property (their money) without due process of law.

Any tax which makes unreasonable discriminations would violate the " Equal Protection " clause. For example, the Supreme Court once upheld a Louisiana law which imposed a tax upon all manufacturers of sugar except those who refined the products of their own plantations. A State, however, could not thus tax Jews, Germans, Negroes, Republicans, or Catholics who manufacture sugar and exempt all others. Such classifications would be unreasonable.

The law in this area is extremely complicated, but the above illustrations should be enough to indicate the general nature of the 14th Amendment's limitations on the taxing powers of State governments and local governments.

State Constitutional Limitations. In addition to the Federal Constitution, every State's own constitution limits the taxing powers of the State and its local governments in one way or another. Indeed, neither the State nor local governments may exercise *any* power not provided for in the State constitution.

The limits imposed by the various constitutions differ widely from State to State. Most of them provide that taxes shall be uniform, that they be collected only within the geographic limits of the unit of government which levies the tax, and that there should be no arbitrary or unreasonable classification for taxing purposes.

Most State constitutions also exempt churches, schools, cemeteries, museums, etc., from taxation. Many fix a maximum property tax rate at so many mills per dollar.[2] Some prohibit the use of certain taxes — for example, a sales tax or an income tax.

Because each State's constitution differs from all of the rest, you should read the tax provisions contained in your own.

Statutory and Charter Limitations. State statutes (laws) and county and city charters also set forth limitations on the taxing powers. Of course, these limitations vary widely from State to State, too.

Principles of Sound Taxation

Practically any tax, taken by itself, can be proved an unfair one. If all of the revenues of a government came from just one tax, such as the sales tax, the income tax, or the property tax, the tax system itself would be grossly unfair. It would hit some much harder than others and some not at all. Yet, each tax that is levied can be defended as *a part of* the general tax system, which aims at a fair taxation for all individuals.

Adam Smith's Canons. Nearly two hundred years ago, in his book *The Wealth of Nations,* the famous English economist Adam Smith laid down four principles of a sound tax system. Most tax experts today cite the same four. They are as follows:

---

[2] A *mill* is one-thousandth of a dollar, or one-tenth of a cent. Thus, for example, if the local property tax rate is fifty mills a man who owns property assessed at $1000 would pay a property tax of $50.

1. The subjects of every state ought to contribute towards the support of the government, as nearly as possible, in proportion to their respective abilities; that is, in proportion to the revenue which they respectively enjoy under the protection of the state.

2. The tax which each individual is bound to pay ought to be certain and not arbitrary.

3. Every tax ought to be levied at the time, or in the manner, in which it is most likely to be convenient for the contributor to pay it.

4. Every tax ought to be so contrived as both to take out and to keep out of the pockets of the people as little as possible over and above what it brings into the public treasury of the state.

Making any particular tax fulfill these requirements of *equality, certainty, convenience,* and *economy* is an almost impossible task. But our problem at the State and the local level, and at the national level, is one of coming as close to these standards as possible in the interests of fairness to all.

Kinds of State and Local Taxes

Aside from the limitations we have just considered, each State may levy taxes as it sees fit. The State legislature determines what taxes the State will impose. The legislature also determines what taxes the units of local government — counties, cities,[3] school districts — may levy.

The General Property Tax. This is the chief source of income for local governments today. It accounts for about eighty-seven per cent of their tax revenues. Once the principal source of State income, it now brings in less than four per cent of the total State revenues.

The general property tax is a direct tax levied on (1) *real property,* that is, land, buildings, and improvements

that go with the property if sold, and/or (2) *personal property,* which is either *tangible* or *intangible.*

Tangible personal property includes all movable wealth which is visible and the value of which can be easily assessed — for example, farm implements, livestock, pianos, television sets, automobiles, and watches. Examples of *intangible personal property* include such things as stocks, bonds, mortgages, promissory notes, and bank

DISTRIBUTED TO 49 cents
CITIES TOWNS SCHOOLS
$
WELFARE PENSIONS CORRECTIONAL INSTITUTIONS HEALTH 16 cents
HIGHWAYS PUBLIC WORKS WATERWAYS 12 cents
SALARIES EMPLOYMENT PUBLIC SAFETY AGRICULTURAL SECURITY etc. 11 cents
PUBLIC SERVICE 5 cents
EDUCATION 4 cents
VETERANS BONUS SERVICE 3 cents

---

[3] State constitutions sometimes grant certain taxing powers to local governments, but this is not common. Local governments usually receive their taxing powers from acts of the legislature or, in the case of " home-rule " cities and counties (see pages 569 and 590), from their charters.

accounts. Because intangibles can be hidden from the tax assessor more easily than tangibles, they are not taxed in some States — or are taxed at a lower rate than real or tangible personal property.

Advantages of the Tax. Two major arguments may be made in behalf of the property tax: (1) Property is protected by government and may logically be required to contribute to government's support. (2) The rates may be easily adjusted to meet the needs of government.

Disadvantages. Three major arguments are presented against the property tax: (1) The property tax is not geared to ability to pay. (2) It is all but impossible, even with the most competent assessors, to assess all property to be taxed on a fair and equal basis. (3) Personal property, especially intangibles, is easily concealed from the assessors. The amount of property a man owns was once a fair measure of his wealth, but this is no longer true. Many people who own very little real estate property might be nonetheless quite wealthy.

Assessment is the process of determining the value of the property to be taxed. This work is usually done by a popularly elected county, township, or city assessor. Only in a few States must the assessor be a trained specialist, and in those States he is usually appointed rather than elected.

Where personal property is taxed, the assessment is made each year. Real property is usually assessed less often, commonly every second or fourth year. The assessor is expected to visit the property and examine it in order to determine its value. In practice the assessment is often made simply on the basis of the previous year's figures, which were arrived at the same way.

Property is usually assessed at less than its true market value. Most property owners seem better satisfied if the assessment is set at, say, one half of its real value. Thus a city house assessed at $5000 may actually be worth $10,000. If the tax rate is set at four per cent (or forty mills [4]), the tax will be $200. In reality, this is the same thing as a two per cent (or twenty mills) tax on the $10,000 house.[5]

Equalization. If one man's property is assessed at a higher proportionate value than another's, there is usually some means of having the injustice corrected. Complaints may be taken to a local board of equalization, to the county board of commissioners, or to the courts, as the law provides. Many States have a State board of equalization which attempts to see that all assessments around the State are as fair and equal as possible.

Collection of the property tax is

---

[4] See note 2, page 544.

[5] Several reasons are advanced for assessing property at a fraction of its actual market value — none of them valid. One is the belief that full assessments mean exorbitant taxes; another is the wish to lessen the share of State or county taxes paid by an assessed area; third, political considerations such as the desire of county or other assessors to be re-elected; fourth, difficulty of making a fair, full-value assessment.

made by the same officer, commonly the sheriff, who collects other local taxes. In some States a tax bill is mailed to the property owner, but in others he must go to the tax collector's (sheriff's) office to learn the amount of his tax.

If the tax is not paid by a certain date, the owner is *delinquent* and a small penalty is added to his tax. If the tax and penalty are not paid within a certain period, the property may be sold for back taxes.

Exemptions. Many kinds of property are often exempted from taxation. Schools, libraries, churches, and government property are good examples.

The Sales Tax. This is the most important single source of State income and now accounts for about sixty per cent of the total.

The sales tax is either *general,* that is, applied to most commodities, or *selective,* that is, applied to certain ones like tobacco, liquor, and gasoline.

Advantages and Disadvantages. The sales tax is easy to collect and is a fairly dependable source of revenue. But, on the other hand, it is *regressive* — that is, it is not geared to ability to pay and falls most heavily upon those with lower incomes.

Thirty-three States now levy a general sales tax, and the rate varies from one to three-and-a-half per cent of the sale price. Most States exempt such items as certain foods, like bread or milk, or all foods, produce sold directly by the farmer to the consumer, newspapers, or sales under a certain amount.

In some States the sales tax applies to all sales, wholesale as well as retail, but it is usually applied only at the retail level.

Purchases Made Outside the State. To prevent the evading of the sales tax by making purchases outside the State, the States impose a use tax on all articles bought outside the State. For instance, Washington State imposes a tax on articles valued at $20 or more brought into the State by its residents. If one buys an automobile outside the State, a license will not be granted until the use tax is paid. Iowa holds mail-order houses outside the State, as well as those within, responsible for the collection of the sales tax on all goods sold to the residents of the State of Iowa.

How Tax Is Collected. In Illinois each retailer pays the tax on his total gross taxable sales, usually adding the tax to the price of the goods. Some States, where the tax on small purchases may be less than a cent, sell small metal tax tokens to merchants, who sell and resell them to customers. Another State, with a three per cent tax, issues a tax card for three cents, which has places to punch small purchases until the total reaches a dollar. Thus, instead of paying a penny tax on each of ten ten-cent purchases, you pay only three cents.

In Ohio retailers are required to collect the tax from the purchasers at the time of sale. The purchasers receive from the retailers tax receipts that the retailers have purchased from the State. As an incentive for the purchasers to take the receipts, the State will redeem them at three per cent of their face value. Churches, lodges, and charitable organizations have boxes into which the receipts can be dropped.

A selective sales tax on gasoline and liquor is now levied in all States. Forty-two States tax tobacco products, and thirty-two have an amusements (admissions) tax.

Most, but not all, selective sales taxes are imposed on luxuries. Gasoline is certainly not a luxury, but the tax on it (running from three to nine cents a gallon) is generally used for road-building purposes. Those who use the roads thus bear a major share of the burden of supporting them.

Because the sales tax provides a steady return, several of our larger cities, many smaller ones, and even some counties now also have general or selective sales taxes or both.

The Income Tax. Levied on individuals and on corporations, this tax yields about sixteen per cent of all State revenues. Thirty-one States use the individual income tax and thirty-three States the corporation income tax. (See the discussion of the federal individual and corporation income taxes, pages 115–118.)

The *individual income tax* rates are usually *progressive* — that is, the higher the income the higher the tax. The rates in most States vary from one or two per cent on the lower incomes to as much as seven or eight per cent. The highest rate is found in North Dakota. The rate there is eleven per cent on all taxable income above $15,-000. Each State allows certain exemptions and deductions in the figuring of the taxable income.

The *corporation income tax* rates are uniform, a certain fixed percentage of income, in most of the States which have the tax. A few States fix their rates on the graduated (progressive) basis. The highest rate is imposed in Oregon: a uniform eight per cent.[6]

Advantages and Disadvantages. The progressive income tax is held to be the fairest form of taxation because it is directly geared to ability to pay. However, if the rates are too high, the tax discourages incentive — and in our private-enterprise system incentive is the goose which lays the golden eggs. The high federal income tax rates force the States to keep their rates relatively low.

Some cities also levy a small income tax. But city income taxes will never be significant revenue producers unless the federal and State rates are drastically lowered. The prospects for this are dim, indeed.

Inheritance or Estate Taxes. Every State except Nevada levies inheritance or estate taxes. As we explained on page 121, an *inheritance tax* is one levied on the beneficiary's share of an estate, and an *estate tax* is one levied directly on the full estate itself.

Whichever the State has, an inheritance or an estate tax, the rate is progressive — the larger the amount in-

---

[6] Oregon, however, does permit a corporation to offset (reduce) its rate by as much as one-half on the basis of property taxes paid.

volved the higher the tax. And the inheritance tax is also *collateral,* the more distant the relationship between the deceased and the heir the higher the rate. Thus a husband's or wife's share would be taxed at a much lower rate than, say, a cousin's share or the share of someone not related to the deceased.

Several States also impose *gift taxes,* as does the Federal Government. (See page 121.)

Business Taxes. A wide variety of business taxes, in addition to the corporation income tax, are imposed in all States and are an important source of revenue.

Capital Stock Taxes. These are taxes levied on the assessed valuation of the total shares of stock issued by a business concern. Once used by all States, over a third of them have now dropped it in favor of the corporation income tax. Some States, however, still have both taxes.

Severance Taxes. Imposed by twenty-seven States, this kind of tax is levied on the removal of natural resources. Those who cut timber, mine minerals, or pump oil or gas are among those who would pay such a tax.

License Taxes. All States require corporations to pay a license tax for the privilege of doing business in the State. Certain kinds of businesses, especially chain stores, amusement houses, bars and taverns, and transportation lines, must also have an additional license to operate. Then, too, individuals who wish to engage in certain occupations must have a license.

Most or all of the States require licenses for doctors, lawyers, dentists, morticians, barbers, plumbers, engineers, chauffeurs, psychiatrists, and a host of others. More and more, local governments are requiring the payment of various business license taxes.

License taxes other than for business purposes are levied in all States today and are a very significant revenue source. The most important of these are the ones required for motor vehicles and motor vehicle operators. All States also issue hunting and fishing licenses and most also require permits to buy alcoholic beverages.

Poll Taxes. A poll tax is levied in Indiana, Maine, Nebraska, New Hampshire, Vermont, West Virginia, Alabama, Arkansas, Mississippi, Tex-

REHABILITATION

In some State prisons inmates are given vocational training to prepare them for jobs when their prison terms are over.

California Department of Corrections

as, and Virginia. In the latter five States the tax must be paid before a person may vote. (See page 435.)

Payroll Taxes. As payroll taxes support the State-federal unemployment compensation program, they are not really *State* taxes. They are paid into the federal treasury and returned to the States as needed. (See page 302.)

Sharing of State Taxes with Local Governments. The fact that the States tax so many sources of revenue makes it impractical for local governments to tap many of these sources.

The States are distributing among their local governments a percentage of various taxes as they are collected or through appropriations by the legislatures. For example, most States do this with the revenues from gasoline taxes and motor vehicle licenses. Where this is done, the State has a good opportunity to apportion the money on condition that local governments use it for certain purposes — school systems, road building and maintenance, police protection, and so forth — according to standards set by the States.

Nontax Revenues

As we said at the beginning of this chapter, the States and local governments receive revenue from sources other than taxation — the so-called nontax sources. The States receive some $4,000,000,000 and the local governments some $6,000,000,000 a year from these sources.

Federal grants-in-aid to both levels account for about $3,000,000,000 of these nontax funds. As we have seen, these grants-in-aid are made for many purposes — old-age assistance, airport construction, highway building, aid to the blind and disabled, and so forth.

Government-operated businesses also return handsome sums. Toll-bridges and toll-roads would be a common example. The State of Washington is in the ferry business. North Dakota markets a flour sold under the brand-name " Dakota-Maid " (which it advertises on the official stationery

of the State). California operates a short railway line in San Francisco.

Seventeen States are in the liquor-dispensing business, selling it through State-operated stores.[7] For several years, Oregon and Washington jointly owned a liquor distillery in Kentucky.

Many cities own and operate their water, electric power, and bus transportation systems. Some cities operate farmer's markets and rent space in office buildings, warehouses, and housing projects, own and operate dams and wharves, and so on.

The profits from these businesses go toward the support of the governments which own them.

---

[7] Alabama, Idaho, Iowa, Maine, Michigan, Montana, New Hampshire, North Carolina, Ohio, Oregon, Pennsylvania, Utah, Vermont, Virginia, Washington, West Virginia, and Wyoming. North Carolina's stores are operated by the counties. Wyoming's liquor monopoly operates only at the wholesale level.

Other nontax sources include such things as court fines, the sale or leasing of public lands, the interest received on State investments, and similar items.

Borrowing may be considered as a source of nontax revenue, too. But, because the debts must be paid back, it is hardly in the same category with the other nontax sources which do not involve borrowing.

States and their local governments often must borrow money for unusually large undertakings, such as public buildings, bridges and highways, and a veterans bonus, that cannot be paid for out of current revenues.

The borrowing is most often done through the issuing of bonds, as is federal borrowing (see page 101). Occasionally, States and local governments do receive direct loans from banks or major insurance companies, but this is not the common arrangement.

State and local bonds are easy to market because the interest from them is not taxed; that is, they are easy to market if the credit rating of the particular government is good.

Many State and local governments have, in times past, borrowed so heavily that they had to default on their debts. Thus most State constitutions very strictly limit the power to borrow. A ceiling is usually placed on the total governmental debt; the denominations in which bonds may be issued, repayment schedules, and interest rates are often prescribed; and other minute details related to borrowing are spelled out in the constitution.

The total State debts now amount to more than $13,000,000,000, and all local governments now owe more than $20,000,000,000.

State Budget Systems

Since California and Wisconsin led the way in 1911, every State has adopted some form of a budget system for the planned and effective control of the use of the State's money and property.

Before the adoption of budget systems, the appropriations made by a legislature and the expenditures made by the various State agencies were handled in a most haphazard manner. More often than not, each individual agency would appear before the legislature's appropriations committees in a dog-eat-dog battle with one another.

No single official or agency in the executive branch was familiar with the entire business of the State. No official or agency reviewed the needs of the various departments of the government, cut them down where necessary, measured them against the funds on hand and the estimated revenues, and then presented a rounded and carefully prepared financial program to the legislature.

Proposals to spend money came forward every year by the thousands. Their chances of adoption were not in proportion to their merit, but rather to the political influences behind them. When the legislature adjourned, no one had any real idea how much had been appropriated or for what. Local pressures, logrolling, and favoritism were all too common. Extravagance, graft, and debt were inevitable.

In several States, the governor was given the power to veto specific items in appropriations bills. All too often, however, this simply meant that the legislature appropriated millions more than there was either revenue or need for. Responsibility was passed to the governor, who then had to reduce appropriations or not reduce them, as he saw fit.

Budget Systems Today. Now all States have some sort of budget system. Of course, the systems vary widely from State to State, and some are much more effective than others.

There are three fairly distinct types:

(1) *Legislative Budget.* In one State, Arkansas, the budget is prepared and presented to the legislature by a joint committee of its own members. This system makes it difficult to locate responsibility for the various items within the budget.

(2) *Board or Commission Budget.* Seven States [8] have a budget board or commission composed of the governor, one or two other executive officials, and a few members of the legislature, or made up of the principal executive officials only.

[8] Delaware, Florida, Montana, North Dakota, South Dakota, Texas, and West Virginia.

(3) *Executive Budget.* The other forty States make the governor himself responsible for the over-all preparation of the budget, usually with the assistance of a budget director or a budget agency or both.

The budget, by whomever framed, is always drawn up to cover a particular period. In most States this means a fiscal period of two years. Most States' budgets are based on a fiscal biennium because the legislatures meet in regular sessions only every other year in most States.

Steps in the Budget Process. Each of the following six steps is involved in the budget-making process. The more effectively each is followed, the better the budget system.

(1) The preparation of the estimates of probable revenues and the funds needed by each agency of the government.

(2) The review of the estimates by a central budget office staffed by trained fiscal experts.

(3) The collecting of the revised estimates and all supporting information into a consolidated financial program (budget) for presentation (usually by the governor) to the legislative body.

(4) Thorough consideration of the budget and the appropriation of needed funds and enactment of necessary revenue measures by the legislature.

(5) Careful supervision of the actual execution of the budget as approved by the legislature.

(6) An independent check (post audit) on the execution of the budget.

Pattern of Expenditures

State Expenditures. About two thirds of all State spending each year goes for the support of four functions: (1) education, about $5,100,000,000, (2) highways, about $4,800,000,000, (3) public welfare, about $2,600,000,-000, and (4) health and hospitals, about $1,500,000,000.

The remainder of the State's expenditures, $6,000,000,000 to $7,000,000,-000 a year, go for such items as the protection of persons and property, correctional institutions, debt retirement and the payment of interest on outstanding bonds, the development and conservation of natural resources, recreational facilities, and general government.

Local Expenditures. Of the approximately $12,000,000,000 now spent by local governments each year, the major expenditures are made for public welfare, public works, schools, and health and hospitals.

WHAT THIS CHAPTER IS ABOUT

Just as the costs of government on the national level have increased markedly in the past few decades, so have those of State and local governments. State tax collections now amount to more than $14,-000,000,000 each year, local tax collections come to about the same amount, and State and local governments together collect an additional $10,000,000,000 from nontax sources.

Taxes are charges imposed by a legislative body upon persons or property to raise money for public purposes. The canons of sound taxation center around the four concepts of equality, certainty, convenience, and economy.

The United States Constitution, each State constitution, State laws, and city and county charters impose a wide variety of limits on State and local taxing powers.

The principal State and local tax sources include the property tax, the general and selective sales tax, the individual and corporation income tax, the inheritance or estate tax, and various business taxes and license taxes.

Nontax revenues come especially from federal grants-in-aid, government-operated businesses, and such other sources as court fines and the sale or leasing of public lands.

Borrowing, which is subject to strict limitation in most States, is only in a sense a nontax source of revenue.

Each State now has a budget system for the planned and more or less effective control of State finances. There are three fairly distinct types of budget systems: the legislative budget, board or commission budget, and the executive budget.

The budget-making process involves six steps: preparation of estimates, review of estimates, consolidation and presentation of the budget, consideration and adoption of the budget, execution of the budget, and a post audit.

States spend about two-thirds of their total annual expenditures of some $20,-000,000,000 on education, highways, public welfare, and health and hospitals. Of the approximately $12,000,000,000 local governments spend each year, most goes for public welfare, public works, schools, and health and hospitals.

1. Approximately how much do *all* governments spend in the United States each year? How much of this is spent by State and local governments?

2. State tax collections now come to how much of each year? Local tax collections?

3. Approximately how much do States and their local governments receive from nontax sources?

4. List four limitations on the States' powers to tax which arise from the United States Constitution.

5. Outline Adam Smith's four principles (canons) of sound taxation.

6. Distinguish real from personal property taxes, intangible from tangible personal property taxes.

7. What arguments may be made for and against the property tax?

8. What is meant by assessment?

9. Distinguish between the general and the selective sales tax. Why is it said that the sales tax is regressive?

10. What two kinds of income taxes are levied by the States?

11. What is the difference between an inheritance and an estate tax?

12. Give the names of two common business taxes.

13. Why are States more and more sharing their tax receipts with their local governments? With what significant consequence?

14. What are the so-called nontax revenues? List two sources.

15. Why is borrowing not a nontax source of revenue in the usual sense?

16. What is the purpose of a budget system? Identify the three types of budget systems used in the States today.

17. Outline the six steps in the State budget-making process.

18. What is a post audit?

19. List the major items for which the States spend money.

20. List the four major items for which their local governments spend money.

PROBLEMS FOR DISCUSSION

1. Until a gambling crackdown by State police, 95 slot machines in the town of Tallulah, Louisiana, provided the bulk of the revenues for the town and for Madison Parish (county). This income for the town and parish ran at about $150,000 a year. With this source Tallulah was able to levy property taxes as low as 70¢ for each $100 valuation. (In New Orleans the rate runs about $10 per $100 for city and parish taxes.)

With this revenue Tallulah (population 3000) was able to cover practically all of its operating expenses. The slot machines had also provided funds for nineteen new school buses, resurfacing of all Tallulah streets at a cost of $110,000, a $26,000 bridge, two football fields each costing about $50,000, a health building, several fire trucks, and a library.

Why would you favor or oppose permitting local governments to finance themselves in this manner?

2. A State is not allowed to tax goods imported from a foreign country until the original package is once sold, broken open, or used. A State may, however, tax goods shipped in from another State as soon as they come to rest — that is, as soon as they are delivered to the person to whom they are addressed.[9]

[9] As suggested on page 131, a State may not exercise its *police powers* for protecting health, morals, safety, and general welfare

When Tennessee legislated against the sale of cigarettes, a dealer attempted to evade the law by having the cigarettes delivered from outside the State in small retail packages. Why did the United States Supreme Court hold that the sale of these packages was illegal? Could Tennessee have confiscated cigarettes brought from without the State in regular-size commercial cartons? Could she have taxed them?

Can boxes of silk from France be taxed by the State in a New York warehouse? Boxes of silk from Paterson, New Jersey, in a Chicago warehouse?

3. Both the United States and many States tax incomes, inheritances, gasoline, motor vehicles, other commodities, chain stores, and various industries at different

until the original package or article imported from abroad or from another State is once sold, opened, or used, unless permitted to do so by the Constitution or by act of Congress. The original package, however, must be one ordinarily used for the shipment of goods.

Originally States could not regulate alcoholic liquors until the original package or jug was open, but now both the Constitution and Congress allow States to exclude intoxicating liquors from their borders or to regulate them as soon as they enter the State for consumption. Congress also permits States to exclude plants or materials likely to spread pests or disease within the State.

rates, which annoys and disturbs business. Moreover, the collection of these taxes by both State and Federal Governments is costly to the governments and troublesome to the persons taxed who have to make two reports instead of one.

Do you think the United States Government alone should collect these taxes and refund to the States an agreed portion of the amount collected according to population? If so, should the rates be the same throughout the country?

4. In 1956 the per capita State taxes collected (meaning the average amount for every man, woman, and child in the State) ranged from $145 in Nevada and $133 in Washington down to $52 in New Jersey. For the ten most populous States the per capita tax was as follows:

New York	$89
California	122
Pennsylvania	90
Illinois	73
Ohio	74
Texas	73
Michigan	103
New Jersey	52
Massachusetts	86
North Carolina	84

What explanations can you give for the great variations in State taxes per capita?

THINGS YOU MIGHT DO

1. Invite your local tax officers (such as the assessor and sheriff) to address the class on their work.

2. Stage a class debate or forum on the question: " Resolved, That our State should abandon (or adopt) the sales tax." (This might be done in connection with other taxes, as well.)

3. Through the State blue book and by information obtained from State and local officers and others, discover the nature of

your State and local taxing and budget systems. A series of class reports might be prepared here. From the same sources, discover how much your State and local governments spend each year and for what purposes. A series of charts might be made to illustrate this material.

4. Outline the provisions which are found in your State's constitution with regard to the regulation of both State and local finance.

WORDS AND PHRASES YOU SHOULD KNOW

Adam Smith's canons
Assessment
Budget
Collateral tax
Corporation income tax
Equalization
Estate tax
Expenditures
Grants-in-aid

Inheritance tax
Intangible property
License tax
Mill
Nontax revenues
Personal property
Progressive tax
Property tax

Real property
Regressive tax
Revenue
Sales tax
Selective sales tax
Severance tax
Tangible property
Tax
Tonnage

SELECT BIBLIOGRAPHY

GRAVES, W. BROOKE, *American State Government*, Chapters 14, 15. Heath, 1953.

KOETHER, G., " Tax Road . . . or . . . Toll Road," *Look,* June 16, 1953.

MACDONALD, AUSTIN F., *American State Government and Administration*, Chapters 18, 19, 20. Crowell, 1955.

——, *State and Local Government in the United States*, Chapters 28, 29, 30. Crowell, 1955.

PATE, JAMES E., *Local Government and Administration*, Chapters 14, 15. American Book, 1954.

PHILLIPS, JEWELL C., *State and Local Government in America*, Chapter 12. American Book, 1954.

State Tax Collections. Bureau of the Census, Washington, D.C. Annual, free.

" Taxes: Reversing a Trend," *Time,* May 16, 1955.

" Will Property Taxes Nip the Housing Boom? " *U.S. News,* March 18, 1955.

" Your Total Tax Bill is Going Up," *U.S. News,* June 1, 1956.

UNIT VIII
LOCAL
GOVERNMENT

Fairchild Aerial Surveys, Inc.

Washington

I BELIEVE that provincial institutions are useful to all nations, but nowhere do they appear to me to be more necessary than among a democratic people . . . How can a populace unaccustomed to freedom in small concerns learn to use it temperately in great affairs?

ALEXIS DE TOCQUEVILLE
Democracy in America, 1838

Unit VIII. LOCAL GOVERNMENT

Local institutions constitute the strength of free nations.

— *Alexis de Tocqueville*

★

Chapter 32

COUNTY AND TOWNSHIP GOVERNMENT

In order to work effectively, a democracy must rest on a firm base of informed citizens. We live in an age when the people's concern with government and public affairs is largely focused on the National Government. This is quite natural. The most important public questions, especially those involving international peace and security, lie within the jurisdiction of the National Government.

This does not mean, however, that we should ignore those governments closer to home. In the last six chapters we were especially concerned with government at the State level. In this and the next two chapters we turn to the various units of local government.

The latest official count (1957) indicates 102,328 different units of government in the United States. One of these is the National Government itself and, of course, there are the forty-eight State governments. Chapters 33 and 34 are devoted to the 17,183 municipalities across the nation. Here we are concerned with the other 85,096 units, all at the local level: the 3047 counties, the 17,198 towns and townships, and the 64,851 special districts (most of which, 50,446, are school districts).

Counties

The county is " most nearly universal of all units of local government." [1] Every State in the Union is divided into counties [2] and, except in New England, they are important units of local government.

Counties serve mainly as judicial districts in our New England States, where the " towns " handle most of the functions elsewhere performed by counties. The functions of rural government are shared by counties and townships in the States extending west

---

[1] These units of local government are called *counties* because similar divisions in England were so called.

[2] In Louisiana the units corresponding to counties are called *parishes*.

from New York and New Jersey to the Dakotas, Nebraska, and Kansas. In the South and West, counties are the predominant units. (See page 562.) Almost every part of the continental United States is located within some

It has often been said, also, that if county governments in the United States have any one principle of organization in common, it is that of confusion. In practically every county, no one person corresponds to a State

AREAS WITHIN CONTINENTAL UNITED STATES
LACKING COUNTY GOVERNMENT

" Independent " cities (34) located outside of designated counties and administering functions elsewhere performed by counties —
   in Maryland: Baltimore city (distinct from Baltimore county)
   in Missouri: St. Louis city (distinct from St. Louis county)
   in Virginia: Alexandria, Bristol, Buena Vista, Charlottesville, Clifton Forge, Colonial Heights, Covington, Danville, Falls Church, Fredericksburg, Galax, Hampton, Harrisonburg, Hopewell, Lynchburg, Martinsville, Newport News, Norfolk, Norton, Petersburg, Portsmouth, Radford, Richmond, Roanoke, South Norfolk, Staunton, Suffolk, Virginia Beach, Warwick, Waynesboro, Williamsburg, Winchester

Unorganized areas (8) bearing county designations —
   in Rhode Island: (county areas with no county government) Bristol, Kent, Newport, Providence, Washington
   in South Dakota: (county areas attached to other counties for governmental purposes) Shannon, Todd, Washabaugh

Federal areas (4) —
   District of Columbia (without county government and operating primarily as a city)
   Yellowstone Park (not organized for local government): area in Idaho, area in Montana, area in Wyoming

county. There are, however, a few areas which lack any county government.

Chaotic Structure. County government in the United States has often been described as " the dark continent of American politics." Despite the importance of county government, the average person knows little and cares less about the government of his own county.

governor or a city mayor. Thus it is extremely difficult to fix the responsibility for lax or inefficient county government. Authority is usually scattered among several elective officers, boards, and commissions. Executive, legislative, and judicial powers are often concentrated in the hands of the same individual or board.

In short, county government is in serious need of reform all over the

Units of Government in the United States

(The material in this table is drawn from a special study made by the U.S. Bureau of the Census as part of the 1957 Census of Governments. The next such study is planned for 1962.)

States	All Governmental Units [1]	Local Governments					School Districts [2]
		Total	Counties	Municipalities	Townships	Special Districts	
U.S. TOTAL	102,328	51,833	3,047 [3]	17,183	17,198 [4]	14,405	50,446
Alabama	617	506	67	318	—	121	112
Arizona	367	116	14	52	—	50	250
Arkansas	1,127	703	75	374	—	254	423
California	3,879	2,039	57 [3]	330	—	1,650	1,840
Colorado	1,666	729	62 [3]	246	—	421	936
Connecticut	384	380	8	33	152	187	3
Delaware	132	116	3	49	—	64	15
District of Columbia	2	2	—	1	—	1	—
Florida	672	604	67	310	—	227	67
Georgia	1,121	922	159	508	—	255	198
Idaho	843	674	44 [3]	199	—	431	168
Illinois	6,510	4,516	102	1,181	1,433	1,800	1,993
Indiana	2,989	1,958	92	544	1,008	314	1,030
Iowa	4,906	1,240	99	942	—	199	3,665
Kansas	6,214	3,073	105	610	1,550	808	3,140
Kentucky	822	600	120	323	—	157	221
Louisiana	584	516	62 [3]	237	—	217	67
Maine	645	636	16	42	471	107	8
Maryland	328	327	23 [3]	149	—	155	—
Massachusetts	573	568	12 [3]	39	312	205	4
Michigan	5,160	1,945	83	498	1,262	102	3,214
Minnesota	6,298	2,833	87	826	1,828	92	3,464
Mississippi	672	592	82	262	—	248	79
Missouri	5,307	2,072	114 [3]	803	328	827	3,234
Montana	1,503	353	56 [3]	123	—	174	1,149
Nebraska	6,658	1,715	93	534	478	610	4,942
Nevada	110	92	17	17	—	58	17
New Hampshire	545	324	10	12	222	80	220
New Jersey	1,217	727	21	333	233	140	489
New Mexico	317	221	32	77	—	112	95
New York	4,189	2,524	57 [3]	611	932	924	1,664
North Carolina	624	623	100	412	—	111	—
North Dakota	3,968	1,969	53	356	1,392	168	1,998
Ohio	3,667	2,498	88	915	1,335	160	1,168
Oklahoma	2,332	688	77	506	—	105	1,643
Oregon	1,526	799	36	213	—	550	726
Pennsylvania	5,073	2,655	66 [3]	991	1,564	34	2,417
Rhode Island	91	90	(3)	7	32	51	—
South Carolina	503	395	46	235	2	112	107
South Dakota	4,808	1,519	64 [3]	306	1,080	69	3,288
Tennessee	560	545	95	255	—	195	14
Texas	3,485	1,692	254	793	—	645	1,792
Utah	398	357	29	210	—	118	40
Vermont	409	392	14	68	238	72	16
Virginia	367	366	98 [3]	228	—	40	—
Washington	1,577	1,105	39	252	69	745	471
West Virginia	362	306	55	219	—	32	55
Wisconsin	5,731	1,972	71	547	1,276	78	3,758
Wyoming	489	242	23 [3]	86	—	133	246

[1] Includes the National Government and the forty-eight State Governments. [2] Excludes local school systems operated as part of State, county, municipal, or township governments. [3] Excludes areas corresponding to counties but having no organized county government. [4] Includes "towns" in the six New England States, New York, and Wisconsin.

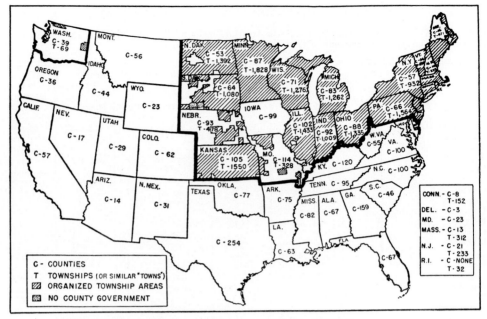

C -	COUNTIES	
T	TOWNSHIPS (OR SIMILAR "TOWNS")	
▨	ORGANIZED TOWNSHIP AREAS	
▨	NO COUNTY GOVERNMENT	

TYPES OF GOVERNMENT IN RURAL AREAS

For the greatest part of the country the county form of government is most common. In New England and to a lesser extent in
other states as far west as the Dakotas and as far south as Missouri,
township government takes precedence.

country. Fortunately, recent years
have seen a slight trend in this direction. The reforms accomplished in
such counties as San Mateo in California, McMinn in Tennessee, and Montgomery in Maryland are notable.
Much more, however, remains to be
done across the nation.

**Number, Size, and Population of
Counties.** There are now 3047 counties in the United States. They vary
in number from 3 in Delaware to 254
in Texas. San Bernardino County,
California, is the largest, embracing
20,131 square miles. The smallest
county in the United States is New
York County (one of the five within
New York City), 22 square miles in

area. Counties also vary widely from
the standpoint of population. Loving
County, Texas, with its 227 residents
has the least population, while more
than 4,500,000 people live in Cook
County, Illinois.

Legal Status of Counties.
" While the county is an agency of the
State, it is likewise a creature of the
State." Thus in 1924 the Supreme
Court of Illinois stated a rule common
to all forty-eight of the States. Coun-
ties are created by the State, are at all
times subject to its control, and may
be abolished by it. For example, the
latest county to be created in the
United States is Los Alamos County,
New Mexico, created by the State leg-

Unit VIII. LOCAL GOVERNMENT

islature in 1949. In the early period of State history this absolute control was largely exercised by State legislatures, but abuses of this legislative power have long since brought about many State constitutional provisions relating to counties. For example, many State constitutions now provide for definite county boundaries, fix the duties of county officials, and designate county seats. Counties are merely administrative subdivisions of the State and have no existence apart from the State.

Functions of Counties

Because counties are creatures of the State, they are responsible for administering State laws and such county laws as the legislature and the constitution permit them to enact.

The functions of counties vary considerably from State to State across the nation. The fairly common ones are to preserve the peace; administer justice; maintain jails or workhouses; record deeds, wills, mortgages, marriage licenses, and other documents; assess property for taxation; collect taxes and expend county funds; issue licenses such as those for hunting, fishing, and marriage; maintain schools; build and repair roads, bridges, drains, and other such public works; administer elections; care for the poor; and protect the health of the inhabitants of the community.

In recent years many counties have also undertaken new functions, especially as populations have increased. These newer functions include such things as establishing parks, hospitals, and airports; providing forest-fire and other fire protection; and engaging in various other activities in relation to agriculture, conservation, the distribution of electricity, water and sewage systems, housing, and zoning.

The ever-increasing demands for governmental services have brought a trend toward more and more State administrative control of most county functions, such as those concerning schools, roads, welfare, taxation, etc.

Structure of County Government

The County Board. There is some kind of county governing body in every State except Rhode Island, where the five counties exist only as judicial districts. This body is usually called the county board, though it is known by at least twenty other titles among the States — county court, board of chosen freeholders, board of supervisors, board of commissioners, fiscal court, police jury, board of revenue, quarter court, etc.

In England the counties were administered by the Quarter Sessions Court of the justice of the peace of the county. Naturally this system was carried to America, and the county governing body of today has descended

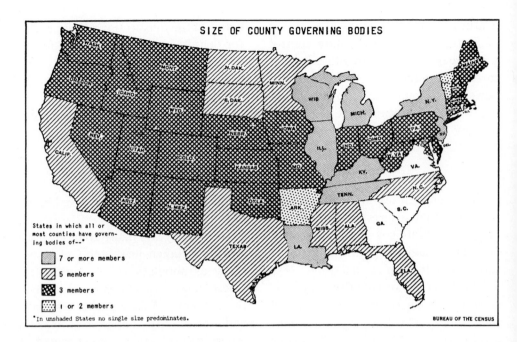

SIZE OF COUNTY GOVERNING BODIES

States in which all or most counties have governing bodies of--*

▢ 7 or more members
▨ 5 members
▩ 3 members
░ 1 or 2 members

*In unshaded States no single size predominates.

BUREAU OF THE CENSUS

from it. In Kentucky, Tennessee, and Arkansas the justices of the peace continue to administer the counties. Since they are elected for definite terms, however, the system is not too unlike that found elsewhere.

The members of the county board, under whatever name, are almost always elective officers serving two- or four-year terms. In a few States, however, the board is appointive. For example, in Connecticut the members are appointed by the State legislature.

Generally speaking, the county boards may be grouped into one or the other of two types. These are the board of commissioners type and the board of supervisors type. The details of each vary widely State to State and even within the same State.

The Board of Commissioners. This is the smaller and more common type of county board. It is found practically everywhere in the South and West and is well known in other sections, too. It has three, or sometimes five or seven, members chosen at large from the entire county.

The Board of Supervisors. This is usually a much larger governing body, ranging in size from fifteen to 100 or more members. Its members are often chosen by the voters from each township in the county, as in New York, Wisconsin, and Michigan. Each member supervises the affairs of his own township, while all act together on county-wide matters.

In most States all counties use one or the other of these two general forms. But in a few States, like Illinois, each county may use whichever it chooses.

Powers. The county board performs both legislative and executive functions, despite the American tradition of separation of powers. Those few legislative powers it has are narrowly defined by the State's constitution and acts of the legislature. The board has the power to tax and to appropriate county funds. More and more, boards are now given some regulatory powers also — for example, to zone the county and to control amusement places, especially where liquor is sold.

The board's executive powers are far more extensive. It does such things as manage county property and finances; maintain jails, courthouses, poor farms and the like; conduct county welfare programs; supervise the construction of public works; and conduct elections.

In nearly every county, though, the board must share its executive powers with other elected officials such as the sheriff, the clerk, and the treasurer. As a result, efficiency and economy are largely impossible.

In most of the States the board does appoint a few, but not many, of the other county officers, such as the superintendent of the poor (welfare officer).

Judicial Officers. In all parts of the country, even in the New England States, the county is an important unit for judicial purposes. Each county has a courthouse and a clerk of the court (who is often the county clerk). Records are kept of the suits brought in the county and of the judgments and decrees of the court.

But less than half of the States have a judge for each county. There is usually a " district " or a " circuit " judge, who holds court in several counties, as we saw in Chapter 29.

In nearly half the States there is a probate judge for each county. His duty is to probate (prove) wills. In the other States the regular judge, the county clerk, or some other officer probates wills.

Except in Rhode Island, each county is served by a prosecuting attorney who prosecutes cases for the county. In some States he serves two or more counties and is often called the district attorney. The exact title of the office varies considerably. If he serves for one county, he is sometimes called the county attorney, State's attorney, or commonwealth attorney; and in some States he is known as the solicitor. In fact, he is sometimes called the district attorney, even though his district consists of only one county.

The Sheriff. Each of the 3047 counties has a sheriff.[3] He is popularly elected in all States except Rhode Island (where he is appointed for an unlimited term).

His main duties are to prevent any breach of the peace; arrest offenders and place them in the jail, of which he or a deputy appointed by him is keeper; attend court and carry out its orders, whether it be to notify witnesses

---

[3] The word " sheriff " comes from *shire-reeve*, meaning " peace officer of the shire." The shire was the Anglo-Saxon name for what became the county (district of a count) after the Norman Conquest in 1066.

or jurors, attend the jury, recover property, collect money, or hang a criminal. He is " the right arm of the judge."

In the performance of these duties he may employ deputies regularly or only in case of emergency; in case of a riot he may summon to his aid the posse — *posse comitatus* (power of the county), which consists of the able-bodied male citizens of the county; and in case of a serious disturbance he may call out the State militia. Since the telephone has enabled a sheriff to communicate with a governor promptly, it is usually the governor who now calls out the militia — the National Guard. Special duties are imposed on sheriffs in the different States. In some of the States in the South and in the West, they act as tax collectors.

The Coroner. In nearly all States the coroner [4] is an officer of the county who holds inquests upon the bodies of persons who are believed to have died from violent or other unlawful means. He empanels a jury, usually of six bystanders, who inquire from witnesses, or even from physicians, chemists, and detectives, as to the probable cause of a death which is known to have resulted or is supposed to have resulted from an illegal act.

If the jury decides that the deceased person has probably met death unlawfully at the hands of a certain person,

---

[4] " Coroner " is the modern spelling of the older word *crowner*. He was appointed by the king and was the crown officer in the shire (county).

the coroner may issue a warrant for the arrest of the accused and commit him to jail to await trial, or he may report the facts to a committing magistrate or the prosecuting attorney as the State law may provide. As a knowledge of medicine and pathology is desirable in the office, several States have replaced the coroner with county medical examiners. Some States have retained the office but prescribed specific qualifications. A study of coroners' reports some years ago did much to prompt the change. Many coroners' verdicts were found to be almost meaningless, and occasionally, even illiterate. Some of the " verdicts ": " Found dead "; " Diabetes, tuberculosis, or nervous indigestion "; " I lerned the man while under the Enfluence of Whiskey or white mule Just willfully drowned himself."

The County Clerk. In half of the States there is a county clerk. He acts as clerk of the court in some States; prepares election ballots and receives election returns, and issues marriage licenses in others; and audits the county accounts, acts as clerk of the county board, and records documents such as deeds, wills, and mortgages in still others. In short, he is assigned various functions of a clerical nature for which there is no specialized officer in the county.

The Register of Deeds. In the more populous States it has been thought expedient to have a special officer to keep the records of such legal documents as deeds and mortgages. It is the duty of the register of deeds to

566

THE COUNTY COURT HOUSE

The court house is an important center of administration at the county level. This handsome court house in Bryan, Texas, is a combination court house and jail.

make exact copies of instruments to be recorded and enter them in indexed books where they may easily be found. As one's title to property often depends upon these records in the register's office, it is very important that no mistakes be made.

The County Auditor. Nearly half of the States have a county auditor, whose business it is to go over the accounts of the other officers of the county, prepare statements of county finances, and issue warrants on the treasurer for the expenditure of county money according to the appropriations made by the county board. Until recently the duties of this office were per-

formed in a very slack manner, but the States are gradually enacting laws for State supervision of local finances. For example, many States require a uniform method of accounting, so that the records can be examined easily by a State accountant or even by a citizen of the county.

The County Treasurer. In every State except Rhode Island, where township officers have charge of local funds, and several Southern States, where the sheriffs or banks perform the duties of county treasurers, there is a county officer to receive and safeguard the county taxes. In a few States there are tax collectors in addition to the treasurer, and in several Southern and Western States collections are made by the sheriff. The treasurer is always placed under bond to insure the State and county against loss from dishonesty or carelessness. He is usually paid a definite salary, but some are paid wholly by commissions on the money handled by them.

The Superintendent of Schools. In nearly every county outside of New England, where public education is administered locally, there is a county superintendent of schools. In most States he is elected by the people, but in some he is chosen by the county school board, by the State school board, appointed by the governor, or otherwise selected. In most States his duty is to conduct teachers' examinations, visit schools to observe and advise teachers, assist district trustees in the selection of teachers and offer other advice, and collect school statistics; and in many States he acts as assistant to the State commissioner of education in a general campaign against illiteracy and indifference to education.

According to a report of the Association of American School Administrators, few people realize the magnitude of the county superintendent's responsibilities. On the average, he has about 150 teachers under his supervision, much of his time must be spent in traveling from place to place, and his best efforts are constantly challenged by problems of finance, buildings and equipment, improvement of the curriculum, school transportation, and the like.

Minor County Officers. Most counties have a surveyor who surveys land for private owners at their own expense, or at the direction of the court when a legal dispute over a land boundary requires it. In some States there is a county engineer instead of a county surveyor. He performs the duties formerly done by the county surveyor, but he also acts as engineer in the construction of roads, bridges, drains, and like improvements.

Southern and Western counties have assessors to determine the value of property to be taxed. In New England and the Central States this is usually done by local assessors. Other usual county officers are a health officer or board and a superintendent or overseer of the poor (now usually known as the welfare officer). The latter officer has charge of the almshouse, poor farm, or hospital of the county, unless the county has substituted cash relief for institutional care.

County-City Duplication

With county and city governments operating over the same area, there is a duplication in functions. This results in unnecessary governmental expenditures and conflict of authority.

To remedy this situation, where the city covers a large part of the county, the boundaries of the city should be made to coincide with the county. The city of San Francisco and the

568

county of San Francisco now cover the same area, and the board of supervisors is the city council.[5]

When a county and city are thus merged, many advantages result. In the first place, only one set of administrative officers is necessary. This makes for efficiency of administration as well as economy in government. In the same way, various municipal employees, such as the police, carry on and complete duties which under the dual system must be handled by two sets of employees. Likewise, responsibility for such matters as good roads, zoning, park systems, and the like become undertakings of a single administration, rather than the divided responsibility of a dual organization.

In a large county the rural population is usually unwilling to be taxed and governed by the urban population, and it will oppose a union when the matter comes up in the legislature.

So instead of extending the city bounds, a number of cities have become independent counties. For example, Denver was made independent of the original county and now constitutes a county in itself.[6] It retained only two of the former seventeen elective county officers, the city officers performing the other county functions. For instance, the duties formerly performed by the sheriff are now cared for by the police department.

Separating a city from the rest of the county is not so satisfactory as extending the city bounds to coincide with the county bounds. As the city population spreads, you soon have a surrounding county thickly settled, usually inefficiently governed, and often corruptly governed. It may plague the city by permitting badly policed roadhouses just beyond the city bounds as well as other nuisances against which the city is zoned.

Reform of County Government

Franklin D. Roosevelt once described county government as " no more fit for its purpose today than an ox-cart would be fit for the task of supplying modern transportation between New York and Chicago." Indeed there are many criticisms of county government. Among those criticisms are the following:

1. There is no one to take full re-

sponsibility because of so many elected and independent officers.

2. This means that local politics, instead of the merit system, too often control.

3. The management of funds and finances is so poor that nearly 2000 of the nation's local governments went into bankruptcy in 1933–1934.

4. The county as a unit is so small,

---

[5] While the county board and city council of San Francisco have merged, unfortunately several of the county and city offices still duplicate one another.

[6] St. Louis, Baltimore, Philadelphia, and all of the class-one cities of Virginia are other good examples of cities which are independent of the surrounding counties.

as a rule, that it does not correspond to the social and economic problems of today.

5. Much confusion exists as to the proper functions of the county, its relation to the State, and its relation to the city.

Many movements are under way for county government reform. The leading movement is the proposal of the county manager plan.

The County Manager Plan. In order to eliminate waste, duplication, and corruption, a few counties in the nation have adopted the county manager plan. The county manager plan is similar to the city manager plan to be discussed in the next chapter.

Under the county manager plan the voters of the county elect the county board which usually consists of three or five members. The board in turn appoints a county manager. It is desirable that the board should appoint a professional public administrator or someone equally well qualified to fill the position.

The county manager appoints his assistants. They handle such matters as finance, welfare, public works, and police. As an experienced administrator appointed for a definite term, receiving an adequate salary and remaining above local politics, he is in a better position than the county board to make wise appointments and to carry on impartially the business of county government.

The county manager system locates responsibility in one person. When something goes wrong the appointed official is definitely responsible and something may be done to correct the matter.

With more appointive and fewer elective officers under the county manager system, the voters are more likely to know something about the candidates for whom they are voting in county elections.

The Need for County Zoning. A man bought some poor land and settled on it with his wife and two children. The unproductive soil yielded him only an aching back and a broken heart. Stranded on the so-called " farm " in which his hopes and meager fortune had been invested, he turned to whatever other source of income he could find. His home was twelve miles from the nearest school; so he wrote to the county school superintendent as follows:

" My wife still has her teaching certificate. Couldn't you give her a job teaching the children at home rather than have them travel 24 miles a day to and from school? If you can't, well, I have a Ford that will run. How about giving me a job driving them back and forth to school? "

The county was legally bound to see that the settler's children had schooling; so the county was saddled with a new expense.

Should people be allowed to move onto land where they can't possibly make a living, and burden the county for schooling and roads? Should not rural areas be *zoned*, that is, have the use of each area restricted according to the most suitable use of the area?

For example, Wisconsin has zoned twenty-four counties and restricted the use of some 5,000,000 acres to forestry and recreation. People already there are not forced to move unless the United States or the local government buys the land, but no newcomers are allowed to move to this low-grade zoned land. Zoning as a feature of city planning will be discussed further in Chapter 34.

Centralizing Tendencies. *State Centralization.* The States are gradually taking over many of the county functions that lend themselves to more efficient centralized administration. School systems and roads are two good examples of this. For example, in most States we still find county roads which are built and maintained by each individual county. Beginning with Virginia and North Carolina, however, the States are assuming responsibility for all roads, and former county roads are now more efficiently maintained as a part of the larger State system.

In the field of education, States are now requiring teachers to have more advanced training, are prescribing minimum wages for teachers, and are increasingly supporting county and district schools.

Federal Centralization. Originally, the Federal Government had practically no direct contact with the local government units. But today, chiefly through grants-in-aid, the Federal Government contributes toward the maintenance of county and township roads. In agriculture it maintains county agents and 4–H Club leaders. In education it has introduced industrial arts, home economics, and ROTC in high schools. It has largely replaced the county poorhouse with Social Security and Old-Age Assistance (see Chapter 17).

Township System

In the study of the township system it is important to know that counties are relatively unimportant in New England except as districts for the administration of justice.

Origin of Town Government in New England. The Pilgrims came to Plymouth, Massachusetts, as a congregation, and very soon (1622) they erected on Burial Hill a meetinghouse, which was used both for public worship and for public meetings. The church and the government were practically one. Sermons were preached on the inside to save souls from perdition, and a cannon was mounted on the outside to save bodies from the Indians. It was at the meetinghouse that the voters met and made their laws directly.

Other congregations from England settled along the coast and established similar governments. As the population of these coast settlements increased, pastors led congregations from them and established themselves elsewhere. The desire to be near the church, the hostility of the savages, the severe climate, and the unsuitableness of the country for large plantations caused the immigrants to form compact communities in New England called " towns."

Town and Township. These communities were called " towns," [7] since they had been so called in England. When it became necessary to survey boundaries between the various towns, the small irregular patches of land which resulted were properly known as " townships " (townshapes).[8] Frontier communities, however, are not very discriminating in their terms. The term " town " was used not only for the cluster of buildings, but the entire township too.

In New England today " town " means a political subdivision of a county which in other parts of the nation is called " township." For the sake of uniformity we shall use the word township when referring to what is called " town " in New England. The early townships were very irregular in shape. They contained an average of not more than twenty square miles.

---

[7] When a clan of our ancestors in northern Europe or England fixed upon some spot for a permanent residence and built a wall around it, the wall was known as a *tun;* in time the space within the wall became known as a *tun,* or *town.* The settlers were called by the clan name, as for example " the Boerings " or " the Cressings "; and the town would be called *Barrington,* " town of the Boerings," or *Cressingham,* " home of the Cressings."

[8] The word *ship,* as here used, comes from the Anglo-Saxon word *scip,* which means shape. Township, therefore, means the shape of a town or the entire bounds of a town.

Powers of New England Townships. For many years the New England townships were undisturbed by the king or parliament of England and exercised such powers of government as are now exercised by a State. They waged war against the Indians, established schools, and as late as the Revolutionary War they appropriated money for war supplies. In fact, they created the States which now control them.

Today they exercise only such powers as the States permit. They have control of most roads, bridges, schools, libraries, poor relief, and taxation for most local purposes. Some townships have charge of such public works and institutions as street pavements, sewers, waterworks, electric light plants, public baths, parks, and hospitals. They also have certain powers to enact police ordinances, such as determining restrictions to be placed on traffic speed.

The Town Meeting. Township laws have always been made in the town meeting. During the first few years the colonists attempted to hold monthly meetings, but this was found to be a cumbersome way to transact business and, as early as 1635, *selectmen* (officers selected by the people) were chosen to administer the affairs of the township during the interval between the assemblies. Thus the government became less democratic (direct rule of the people) and more republican (indirect rule of the people through representatives).

Today the regular meetings are usu-

Free Lance Photographers Guild

A NEW ENGLAND TOWN HALL

In such simple buildings as this one at Chesterfield, New Hampshire, the annual town meeting ensures the vigorous participation of citizens in the affairs of their town government.

ally held in the town hall once a year, but the selectmen may call special meetings. The first Monday in March is a favorite time to have the meetings, but some are held as early as February or as late as April, and Connecticut prefers October. The general nature of the business to be transacted at a meeting must be announced in a *warrant* which is posted in the various parts of the township.

The town clerk calls the meeting to order, usually at nine o'clock, and acts as secretary of the meeting. The first business is the election of the presiding officer, called the *moderator*. In many townships some well-respected citizen is elected year after year as a matter of course. The organization being perfected, the principal township officers are nominated from the floor, but the nominations have frequently been arranged by preliminary party meetings, called *caucuses*. Election is by ballot, and the polls remain open several hours, depending upon the population of the township.

The interesting session of a town

meeting occurs after the balloting — usually in the afternoon, but in a few larger towns not until evening. Each voter has been furnished a printed report of the expenditures for the previous year, and the selectmen make an oral report of what has been done during the year. It is then that the policy for the next year is to be discussed — the real interest for everybody at the meeting.

Nahum Smith may rise and say, " I should like to be informed why the selectmen took the stone from Red Hill quarry instead of Cross Roads quarry, which is nearer." If there is " a rooster in the bag," he is rather certain to crow. It is difficult for a political boss or ring to prosper under this system because any bag containing a rooster must annually or oftener be brought into the presence of the interested parties, and a Nahum Smith is pretty certain to bring at least one crow from the rooster.

Perhaps the cross-questioning of the chairman of the school committee by Jeremy Jones will bring discomfort to the chairman, much to the delight of the boys seated in the rear of the hall. Or the younger blood may advocate a consolidated school or a new high school, which is probably opposed by those farmers who happen to be living a considerable distance from the proposed location.

A few years ago, two towns without a doctor guaranteed a young doctor an income of $5000 a year to settle in their midst and charge $2 for office calls and $4 for every home call no matter how distant it might be from his office.

Township Officers. *Selectmen,* of whom there are three, five, seven, or nine, three being the more usual number, are the principal officers of the township. They are elected by the town meeting, annually as a rule, but in some Massachusetts townships they are elected for three years, one being elected each year.

They issue warrants for holding regular or special town meetings, specifying in a general way the subjects which the citizens desire to have acted upon; lay out highways; grant licenses; arrange for elections; have charge of township property; appoint some of the minor officers; and may act as assessors, overseers of the poor, and health officers. It should be borne in mind that they have no power to determine the tax rate or appropriate money, these functions being performed by the town meeting, and that they have no powers except those conferred by the State or the town meeting.

The town clerk is just as important as the selectmen, and performs many duties which are imposed upon the county clerk outside of New England. He keeps minutes of town meetings, of meetings of the selectmen, and other town records; he records the vote for State and county officers and issues marriage licenses; and he records births, marriages, and deaths. He is elected by the town meeting for only a year at a time, but is usually reelected for a number of years.

Other township officers are the town treasurer, assessors of taxes, overseers of the poor, justices of the peace (township officers in some States), constables, commissioner of roads (under various titles), a school committee (board), and numerous other less important officers. Most of these officers are elected at the annual town meeting. Some years ago the township of Middlefield, in western Massachusetts, had eighty-two voters and eighteen officers.

Difficulties of Township Government. Township government in New England has a noble heritage. Today, however, there are many conditions unfavorable to the town meeting type of government. Ease of transportation and communication is centralizing financial, highway, police, health, and educational powers in the State. The influx of French Canadians and Europeans who are unaccustomed to local self-government adds discord to the town meeting. The growth of factories increased the diversity of interests between the settlement and the surrounding farms. In some places the town meeting has been undermined by the caucus, a preliminary meeting that is held to nominate candidates for office.

The increase in the population of many towns has left the town hall too small for a town meeting. Some of the larger towns are remedying this by a limited town meeting. Brookline, Massachusetts, with a population of fifty-odd thousand, was first to adopt this plan. An act of 1915 divided the town into nine voting precincts and provided for election of twenty-seven members of the limited town meeting from each. Some settlements that have reached an unwieldy size have been incorporated into municipalities, like cities of other sections of the country, and the city council replaces the popular assembly.

Absence of Townships in the South and West. In the Southern and Western States townships cannot be said to exist. In some States the counties are subdivided into one or more sets of districts for one or more purposes. They have no township meetings, and districts other than school districts usually have no power of taxation or of owning property and few, if any, officers independent of county officers. They are simply convenient divisions for performing county functions. Different districts exist for various purposes, such as maintaining schools, roads, justice, and elections. For that reason one kind of district commonly overlaps another kind. The name for the more important of these districts varies from State to State.[9]

---

[9] In North Carolina, South Carolina, Missouri, Arkansas, Montana, and Nevada these districts are called *townships;* in California, *judicial townships;* in Virginia, West Virginia, and Kentucky, *magisterial districts;* in Tennessee, *civil districts;* in Mississippi, *supervisors' districts;* in Georgia, *militia districts;* in Texas, *commissioners' precincts;* in Delaware, *hundreds;* and in the remaining Southern and Western States, *election districts or precincts,* except in Louisiana, where the parishes (counties) are subdivided into *wards.*

County-Township System

Imitation of New England Township Government. Nowhere outside of New England is township government so important as in those six States. In the tier of States extending from New York to Nebraska, however, it is of considerable importance. The northern portions of these States were settled largely by emigrants from New England, who were accustomed to township government. Those who settled the southern portions were from Pennsylvania and the States to the south of the Ohio River and were accustomed to county government. Those accustomed to county government had never attended town meetings and preferred to elect county officers and trust them with all functions of local government.

The result was a compromise. Some functions were assigned to the county and some to the township. In this tier of States the State government preceded the township government and created it. Hence those democratic elements did not develop as they were found in New England, where the township existed first and created the States.

County-Township Conflict in Illinois. When Illinois was admitted to the Union in 1818, the greater number of her citizens were emigrants from the South, who had settled in the southern part of the State. So the State was divided into counties, which were governed by a small board of county commissioners elected at large

in accordance with the Pennsylvania plan.

By 1848 when the second State constitution was framed, New England settlers, or emigrants with New England ideas, had settled in large numbers in the northern part of the State. Thus, in this constitution we find a local option provision which permitted the voters of each county to divide the county into townships whenever the majority should vote in favor thereof. Today 85 of the 102 counties of the State have townships.

Township Officers in the Central States. The New England title of *selectmen* is nowhere found in the Central States. In Pennsylvania, Ohio, Iowa, Minnesota, and the Dakotas their place is taken by a " board of supervisors " or " trustees." In other States there is a well-defined head officer who is assisted, and checked in some matters, by a township board. In New York, Michigan, and Illinois, where this officer is called "supervisor," he is also a member of the county board of supervisors. In Indiana, Missouri, Kansas, and Oklahoma the title of " township trustee " is applied to this officer. The other usual township officers are the clerk, assessor, treasurer, overseer of the poor, overseer of roads, justices of the peace, and constables.

Village Government Weakens Township Government. Townships of the Central States are not only under greater State and county control

576

than New England townships, but as soon as a considerable settlement develops it will obtain a " village " or " town " charter from the State and then exist as a separate government, performing all or certain functions within its boundaries that were formerly performed by the township. In New England many compactly settled communities which would be incorporated independent cities in other States are there a part of the township.

Geographical Townships

Governmental Townships and Geographical Townships. In the preceding sections we discussed townships merely as divisions of territory for the purpose of government, and these are known as governmental or political townships. Divisions of territory for the purpose of surveys are another kind of township and are known as geographical or congressional townships because they are merely bounded by imaginary lines drawn upon the earth in accordance with Acts of Congress.

In States where the geographical townships were surveyed before settlements were made, they were generally used also as governmental townships; but in some localities natural obstacles, such as rivers and mountains, made them unsuitable for purposes of government, and separate areas were created for governmental townships.

Conditions Preceding Geographical Townships. During the colonial period New England and the Southern States developed two very different land systems. In the South as the settlers pushed from Virginia and North Carolina into Kentucky and Tennessee the pioneer selected a fertile piece of land and occupied it. A rude survey was made by a public surveyor or by his inexperienced deputy. The several boundaries or limits of the property were marked by " blazing " the trees with a hatchet, and the survey was put on record in the State land office.

Conflicting patents [10] were not infrequently given for the same tracts, and this confusion produced countless lawsuits. Some of the feuds for which the mountains of eastern Kentucky were once famous are said to have grown out of these disputed land patents and the irregularly shaped pieces of land which lay between the patents. This Southern system, which encouraged initiative and resourcefulness, has been called " indiscriminate location."

In New England the laying out of geographical townships preceded the settlement made during the eighteenth century, and there could be no title to land outside of townships. Square townships were easier to survey in a systematic way than those of any other shape; hence when the land north of the Ohio River, known as the Northwest Territory, was to be surveyed, Thomas Jefferson suggested that it be

---

[10] " Patent " as here used means a written title to land granted by the proper State authority.

surveyed into square townships to make description easier when sold by the government and to prevent disputes as to title. He also had in mind that these square areas would be of convenient size for governmental townships.

Geographical Townships in the West. When Congress was preparing for the government and settlement of this Northwest Territory, the National Government decided that it should be laid out into townships six miles square." [11] An Act of Congress first passed in 1785 applied this system of rectangular surveys to all lands belonging to our public domain. This " Ordinance of 1785 " was the foundation of the American land system, and its leading principles have continued in operation to the present day.

According to the system gradually perfected, north-and-south and east-and-west lines are established. As starting points certain meridians have been designated as *prime meridians.* There are twenty-four of these, the first being the dividing line between Ohio and Indiana, and the last running a little west of Portland, Oregon.

On each side of the prime meridian are subordinate meridians known as *range lines.* These lines are six miles apart and are numbered east and west from the prime meridian. There must also be a *base line* for each survey following a parallel of latitude, and this crosses the meridians at right angles.

[11] The fact that a six-mile square rather than any other size square was adopted by Congress has no special significance.

There are numerous base lines for surveys in different parts of the country. For example, eleven of them cross the State of Oregon.

On each side of a base line are subordinate parallels called *township lines,* six miles apart, and numbered north and south from the base line. Thus these range lines and township lines divide the land into townships six miles square.

The map on page 579 shows the prime meridians and base lines in Ohio, Indiana, and Illinois; that is, in the area between the Ohio and Mississippi rivers. From any prime meridian the tier of townships directly east is called range 1 east (R. 1 E. in Figure 1), and of course other ranges are numbered east and west of that meridian. They are likewise numbered 1, 2, 3, etc., both north and south of the base line. Thus the sectioned township in Figure 1 is township 4 north, range 4 east of the 2d Prime Meridian in the State of Indiana.

This township six miles square is surveyed into thirty-six square miles, which are numbered as shown in Figure 2, and each square mile is called a *section.* Each section is subdivided into rectangular tracts known as halves, quarters, half quarters, and quarter quarters, as shown in Figure 3. Thus if we consider this square mile (Figure 3) as section 1 of Figure 2, we should describe the forty-acre tract starred in Figure 3 as follows: SW$\frac{1}{4}$, NE$\frac{1}{4}$, Sec. 1, T. 4 N., R. 4 E., which means the southwest one quarter of the northeast one quarter of section 1,

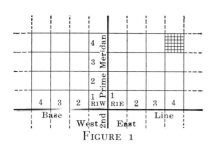

FIGURE 1

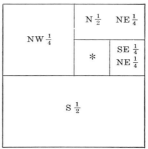

One Square Mile

FIGURE 3

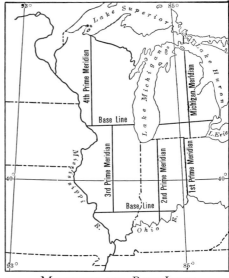

MERIDIANS AND BASE LINES

Six Miles Square

FIGURE 2

township 4 north of the base line in range 4 east of the 2d Prime Meridian in the State of Indiana. So you can readily see that if this tract is to be sold, it is very easy to give an exact description of it in the deed of conveyance[12] without the costly aid of private surveyors.

Special Districts

One other unit of local government must be dealt with before we may turn to municipal government. That is the so-called " special districts " which are found in every State and have been created for the performing of a single governmental function or, oc-casionally, of a few related functions.

By far the most common are the school districts. The first districts for school purposes were set up in New

[12] A deed of conveyance is a contract giving the boundaries of real estate transferred from one person to another.

York in 1812. Of the 64,851 special districts reported by the Census Bureau, 50,446 of them are school districts.

The other special districts, which exist for a wide range of purposes, have developed especially since the depression of the 1930's. They are found usually, but not always, in rural areas. Among the more important are those for the providing of water, sewage, or electrical service; for furnishing police, fire, or sanitary protection; for the construction and maintenance of highways, bridges, airports, swimming pools, or parks; and for such other purposes as soil conservation, irrigation, housing, slum clearance, or reforestation.

The reasons why these districts have been created are many and varied. The principal one lies in the fact that most of the problems with which they deal cover much wider (or smaller) areas than a single county or township. For example, stream pollution might be a problem in each one of the several counties through which a river flows. On the other hand, slum clearance would ordinarily be confined to a rather small section.

In other instances special districts have been formed because local governments could not or would not furnish the services desired — for example, police or fire protection in outlying regions. And in some cases they have been created to keep " politics " out of the picture.

An elected board is usually the governing body for the district, and it commonly has the power to tax and spend to perform the special function for which it was created.

WHAT THIS CHAPTER IS ABOUT

In addition to the National Government and each of the forty-eight State governments, there are altogether 102,328 units of local government in the United States. Of these, 17,183 are municipalities. The rest include 3047 counties, 17,198 townships, and 64,851 special districts (including 50,446 school districts).

The county is found in every State and, except in New England, it is an important unit of local government. The county is mainly a judicial district in New England, shares the responsibilities for local rural government in the northeastern fourth of the country, and is the predominant local unit in the South and West. Only a very few points in the continental United States do not lie within any county.

Legally, counties are creatures of the State and have no existence apart from it. They are responsible for administering State laws and such county ordinances as the legislature and constitution permit them to enact.

Counties vary considerably in size, population, and number from State to State, and the organization of county governments varies almost as widely among the States.

Every county, except the five in Rhode Island, has some form of county governing body, known by a variety of names. Generally there are two types, the smaller and more common board of commissioners and the larger board of supervisors. The board exercises limited legislative and somewhat wider executive powers over county affairs.

The other major offices of county government commonly include the sheriff, coroner, clerk, register of deeds, auditor, treasurer, superintendent of schools, assessor, and surveyor or engineer. A judge and prosecuting attorney may serve several counties at once.

County and city governments often duplicate the functions of one another. In the case of some of the larger cities, the boundaries of the city and county have been made to coincide in order to eliminate needless duplication. Some cities have been entirely separated from any county.

The major reorganization proposed for county government today is the county manager plan. County zoning involves the planned regulation of the use of land within the county.

The States are gradually controlling more and more county functions, and the Federal Government is assisting counties through various grant-in-aid programs.

The town or township is the more important local unit in New England. The township government is usually conducted through an annual town meeting and a small number of selectmen elected at the town meeting. The other township officers include a clerk, assessor, justices of the peace, overseer of the poor, school committeemen, road commissioner, and so on.

Modern transportation and communications, industrialization, and population increase have all worked to outmode townships in many areas. Townships are largely unknown in the South and West. A mixed county-township system exists in the tier of States from New York to Nebraska.

Governmental townships should not be confused with geographic townships. The latter are divisions of territory for the purposes of surveys and land titles.

Special districts have been created in every State for the performing of one or, occasionally, a few governmental functions. School districts are by far the most common among special districts, but they exist for many other purposes as well.

QUESTIONS ON THE TEXT

1. How many units of government are there in the entire country?

2. How many counties are there in the United States?

3. How many States in the Union are divided into counties?

4. Why is county government generally said to be " chaotic "?

5. What is the legal status of counties?

6. List five functions counties commonly perform.

7. Describe the two general types of county boards. Name five officers usually found in a county.

8. What is meant by *posse comitatus?*

9. With what officer have many States now replaced the coroner? Why?

10. How may county-city duplication be remedied?

11. Outline the county manager plan of government.

12. Explain how the New England town or township originated.

13. What does " town " mean in New England? What does it mean in the South and West?

14. What powers do New England towns possess?

15. Explain the work done by a town meeting. What is a town " warrant "?

What is a moderator? What are the duties of the selectmen?

16. What are the benefits of a New England town meeting?

17. How are the various town or township officers selected in New England? For what term?

18. What are some of the difficulties of township government in New England?

19. Explain to what extent the Central States imitated New England township government.

20. Describe the county-township conflict in Illinois. In what region of States are counties least important?

21. In your State, if you have townships, what title is applied to township officers, such as the " selectmen " in New England?

22. Distinguish governmental townships and geographic townships. How did geographic townships come into existence, and why are they useful?

23. Explain how a survey of land is described where geographical townships exist.

24. What is a special district? What particular type is the most common?

25. List four other particular functions special districts have been created to perform. Are these special districts most often found in urban or in rural areas?

PROBLEMS FOR DISCUSSION

1. If you were called upon to recommend to your county board three particular matters which need urgent attention in your county, could you do so? If so, what matters would you list? Why?

2. In Virginia each city of the first class (i.e., the thirty-two listed on page 560) are independent of the 98 counties in the State. Denver, Colorado, is itself a complete county. Which of these two ways of avoiding county-city overlapping do you favor? Why?

3. We now have 3047 counties. Most of them were created before the development of rapid means of communication and transportation. Do you think that your State now has too many counties? Give arguments for and against reducing the number in your State.

4. Why would you favor or oppose the appointment of all county officers except the members of the county board? If you favor appointment, by whom? Explain your answer.

THINGS YOU MIGHT DO

1. Bound the county or township in which you live.

2. Visit the county courthouse. Interview each county officer in order to learn what his functions are. Construct a chart of the government of your county.

3. Invite a member of the county board or other county officer to address the class on the nature of his work or the work of the county in general. If you live in a State in which the township is the more important unit, do the same in regard to township officers.

4. Conduct a debate or class forum on the question: " Resolved, That the county should adopt the county manager system."

5. Write a short essay based on the quotation from de Tocqueville at the beginning of this chapter.

6. If there are any special districts in your area, they could become the subjects for individual reports to the class.

WORDS AND PHRASES YOU SHOULD KNOW

Base line
Board of Commissioners
Board of Supervisors
Coroner
County
County auditor
County clerk
County manager plan
Deed of conveyance

Geographic townships
Ordinances
Patent
Prime meridians
Probate
Range lines
Register of deeds
Section
Selectmen
Sheriff

Shire
Special district
Superintendent of schools
Town
Town clerk
Town meeting
Township
Township lines
Zoning

SELECT BIBLIOGRAPHY

ALDERFER, HAROLD F., *American Local Government and Administration.* Macmillan, 1956.

DESMOND, STATE SENATOR THOMAS C., " The States Eclipse the Cities," *New York Times Magazine,* April 24, 1955.

GRAVES, W. BROOKE, *American State Government,* Chapters 21, 22, 23. Heath, 1953.

LANCASTER, LANE W., *Government in Rural America.* Van Nostrand, 1952.

MACDONALD, AUSTIN F., *American State Government and Administration,* Chapters 14, 15. Crowell, 1955.

——, *State and Local Government in the United States,* Chapters 12, 13. Crowell, 1955.

PATE, JAMES E., *Local Government and Administration,* Chapters 8, 11. American Book, 1954.

PHILLIPS, JEWELL C., *State and Local Government in America,* Chapters 14, 15, 16, 17. American Book, 1954.

The County Manager Plan. National Municipal League, 1950.

A nation is known by the cities that it builds.

— *William Bennett Munro*

★

Chapter 33

VILLAGE AND CITY GOVERNMENT

VILLAGE GOVERNMENT

A village is an organized community in which the population is smaller and the government is simpler than that of cities in the same State. Villages are sometimes referred to as " cities in miniature." They cannot properly be called " cities," yet they are certainly more than " rural."

As people collect in a relatively small area, they soon require such public improvements and services as street lights, sidewalks, fire protection, and a public water supply. Each State permits the people in such areas to form a government distinct from that of the town in New England, of the township in the Middle West, or of the county in the South and West.

In the New England States, villages have been created only in a very few cases. The New England town itself is sufficiently organized to collect the necessary taxes and provide the services that villages provide elsewhere.

These small incorporated centers of population are commonly known as " towns " [1] in the South and West, but in the Middle West they are more generally known as " villages." In Pennsylvania, New Jersey, and Connecticut the English term " borough " is commonly used. For the sake of uniformity, here the word " village " will be used to include towns and boroughs.

How Villages Are Incorporated. Each State, in its constitution or statutes, prescribes the conditions and the manner in which a small community may be incorporated [2] as a village. In Alabama 100 inhabitants are all that are necessary, but a minimum of 200 or 300 is a much more common requirement. Some States further require that the necessary number of persons live within a certain area —

---

[1] Don't confuse the town (village) in the South and West with the New England town (township). See page 572.

[2] *Incorporated* means created into a legal body (artificial person) by the State. The word " incorporate " comes from the Latin *in* (into) and *corpus* (body).

one square mile in New York, for example.

In some States a village may become an incorporated village through a charter enacted by the legislature. However, the usual procedure is for the inhabitants to present to a designated public officer a petition containing a prescribed number of signatures. When this officer (usually a judge) is satisfied that the required conditions are fulfilled, he will declare that the people living within a certain surveyed area are incorporated as the village of X, having such powers as the State grants to its villages. In most States a village may not be declared incorporated until the residents have voted in favor of it at an election called by the officer to whom the petition for incorporation is presented.

Powers of Villages. The few incorporated villages in New England continue as a part of the town (township) for many important purposes such as the providing of roads and schools. They may provide independently for such things as sidewalks, lights, water, sewers, and fire and police protection. In those States which adopted the New England township system, the villages remain a part of the township for certain purposes, but they are more independent than those in New England.

In certain other States, including New Jersey, Pennsylvania, Wisconsin, Minnesota, and the Dakotas, the villages are entirely independent of the township. They perform within the village the functions which the township performs outside, and, of course, the usual village functions, too. In the South and West, the villages (called "towns") are usually included within the county, but as the county is relatively unimportant the village has power to deal with practically all local problems.

Organization of Village Government. *The Council.* Every village has a legislative body which is usually called the council or board of trustees. Its size varies from three to nine members, who are seldom elected for longer than one- or two-year terms.

In every State the council has the power to determine the tax rate (within limits imposed by the State) and to appropriate money for the various needs of the village. Generally, the council can levy special assessments against adjacent properties for such improvements as street paving or sidewalk laying. However, villages often have only very limited power to borrow money and must submit the question of a bond issue to the voters.

The power to pass ordinances varies from State to State and from village to village within the State. Commonly a council may choose certain officers, such as a constable, fire warden, and clerk, and regulate their duties. It may pass certain health and police ordinances; determine the license taxes for movies, peddlers, public vehicles, and other businesses that are licensed; control streets, bridges, and parks; and administer public services owned by the village — for example, the water system.

The Mayor. The principal executive officer in the village is the mayor or, as he is known in some States, the burgess or intendant or warden. He is ordinarily elected for one or two years. He presides over council meetings and usually has the rights of a member. In some villages, however, he merely casts the deciding vote in case of a tie. Only rarely does he have the veto power. His major job is that of enforcing the village ordinances, and in a number of States he also serves as police justice.

Every village has a clerk or recorder, a treasurer or collector, and a police officer ("constable," "marshal," "sergeant," or "bailiff"). Many of them also have a street commissioner, an assessor, and an attorney or solicitor. In the West these officers are usually elected by the villagers. In the other sections of the country they are commonly appointed by the council or the mayor.

Some villages have a justice of the peace and, where the village forms a separate school district, there are school officers, too. Larger villages have such other officers as health, fire, lighting, sewer, and cemetery commissioners.

CITY GOVERNMENT

Meaning of the Term "City." A city is a governmental unit created by the State, with more population and wider powers than a village or town. Each State determines how many inhabitants there must be in a particular area in order for it to become a city. Each State also determines what powers a city may exercise.

In Kansas a community with as few as 200 inhabitants may become a city, but in New York 10,000 inhabitants are required. There are about as many of our forty-eight States which create city governments with less than 2500 population, as there are those which require a greater population, but the United States Bureau of the Census classifies as cities all incorporated places with at least 2500 inhabitants.

Rapid Growth of Cities. When the First Census was taken in 1790, there were 3,929,214 people living in the United States. Of these, only 131,472, or 3.3 per cent of the population, lived in the six cities which had more than 8000 inhabitants. Philadelphia was then the largest city with 42,000 people. New York had 33,000, and Boston had 18,000.

Just nine years before the First Census, Watt had taken out a patent for his double-acting steam engine and thus made large-scale manufacturing possible. Fulton patented his steamboat in 1809 and Stephenson his locomotive in 1829. These made easy the transportation of raw materials to factories and the distribution of manufactured products from the factories. Almost overnight the old home-manufacturing system gave way to factories, population began to concentrate in the budding industrial areas, and cities began to grow.

The invention of a number of farming implements meant that less labor was needed on the farms and that more was needed in the new cities. It also meant that more farms could be operated by fewer people. Thus ever more raw materials were produced to be turned into finished products in the new and increasing and expanding cities.

By the Seventeenth Census in 1950, our urban population had grown to 96,467,686, or nearly two-thirds of our total national population; and the number is well over 100,000,000 today. We are fast becoming a nation of city dwellers. The increase, by decades, of our urban population (persons living in incorporated areas of at least 2500) is shown in the table on this page.

We need hardly add that this shift from a predominantly rural to a largely urban society in the United States is a fact of tremendous significance. Certainly, it makes a knowledge of municipal government essential to the citizen who wishes to keep himself informed in regard to the affairs of his city.

The problems which urbanization has created are found in rural areas only in small degree, if at all.[3] In

rural areas there is some police protection and perhaps fire protection, and there is the need to provide and maintain schools and other public works such as roads and bridges. Even the smaller cities are faced with

GROWTH IN POPULATION

DATE	TOTAL POPULATION	URBAN POPULATION	PER CENT URBAN
1790	3,929,214	201,655	5.1
1800	5,308,483	322,371	6.1
1810	7,239,881	525,459	7.3
1820	9,638,453	693,255	7.2
1830	12,866,020	1,127,247	8.8
1840	17,069,453	1,845,055	10.8
1850	23,191,876	3,543,716	15.3
1860	31,443,321	6,216,518	19.8
1870	38,558,371	9,902,361	25.7
1880	50,155,783	14,129,735	28.2
1890	62,047,714	22,106,265	35.1
1900	75,994,575	30,159,921	39.7
1910	91,972,266	41,998,932	45.7
1920	105,710,620	54,157,973	51.2
1930	122,775,046	68,954,823	56.2
1940	131,669,275	74,423,702	56.5
1950	150,697,361	96,467,686	64.0

problems far more complex and more difficult than those that are found in rural areas.

City governments must see that such services as water, fire protection, police protection, streets, sewers, traffic regulation, transportation, public health activities, parks, and a wide variety of others are provided to its citizens. The larger the city, the more extensive and expensive these services become.

[3] As the nation's cities have grown, so have their suburbs — and in many cases much more rapidly than the cities themselves in recent years. The problems of " suburbanitis " are discussed in the next chapter.

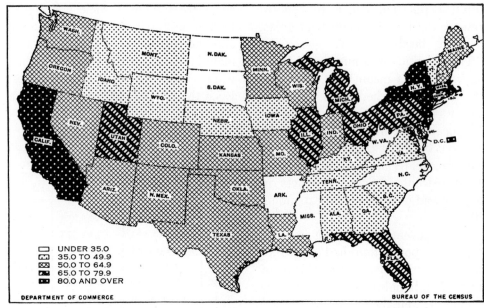

PERCENTAGE OF URBAN POPULATION BY STATES, 1950

UNDER 35.0
35.0 TO 49.9
50.0 TO 64.9
65.0 TO 79.9
80.0 AND OVER

DEPARTMENT OF COMMERCE   BUREAU OF THE CENSUS

City-State Relations

Cities Are Subordinate to the State. Cities, like counties and other units of local government, are created by the State, are responsible to the State, and receive their powers from the State. State control over cities is exercised through the constitution and through acts of the legislature.

In our early history, State constitutions contained few provisions directly relating to cities. Practically all State control was exercised through the legislature. The degree of control the legislature possessed (and in many ways still possesses) over cities is well-illustrated by these words from an 1868 decision of the Iowa supreme court:

Cities owe their origin to, and derive their powers and rights wholly from, the legislature It breathes into them the breath of life, without which they cannot exist. As it creates, so it may destroy. If it may destroy, it may abridge and control. Unless there is constitutional limitation on the right, the legislature might, by a single act, if we can suppose it capable of so great a folly and so great a wrong, sweep from existence all the municipal corporations in the State, and the corporations could not prevent it.

As cities grew in population and multiplied in number, this complete legislative control over cities produced many difficult situations. Legislators were often unfamiliar with the problems of a city, and many of the laws they passed were grossly unfair or

588

impractical. Some legislatures, dominated by members from the rural sections of the State, were suspicious or jealous of cities and sought to restrict their growth by imposing unreasonable burdens on city dwellers and city governments.

Today, in reaction against the legislature's misuse and abuse of its powers, most State constitutions contain a great many provisions concerning municipal government and its problems. These provisions generally relate to such matters as city charters, city officials, elections, council meetings and procedures, taxation and spending, and the classification of cities.

The City Charter. The charter is the city's fundamental law or constitution. Its contents vary somewhat from city to city, but commonly the charter contains the name of the city and a description of its boundaries and declares that city to be a *municipal corporation*.

As a municipal corporation the city has certain rights similar to those of a private corporation. It becomes a legal (artificial) person with the right to sue and to be sued in the courts, to have a corporate seal, to make contracts, and to acquire, own, and dispose of property. It also enjoys the " right of perpetual succession," that is, a complete change in its population through the generations does not affect its status as a legal body.

The charter also provides for other powers of the city, the form of city government, city officers and how they are to be chosen and their duties, city finance, and similar matters.

In colonial days a city usually secured its charter from the colonial governor. After the Revolution, State legislatures took over the function of granting charters, and in a few States each individual city charter is still granted by the legislature.

One of the particular ways that legislatures restricted cities and abused their powers over them was in the granting of charters. Often, for example, those cities which were loyal to the majority party machine in the State received fair and reasonable charters, but others did not. Or, in some States all city charters were almost impossible monstrosities because the rural legislators wanted to restrict the cities.

Broadly speaking, there are five types of city charters. They are as follows:

(1) The *special charter,* like that granted by the governor in colonial days. The legislatures in the few States which still follow this practice may provide a special or separate charter for each city in the State.

(2) The *general charter,* which developed to replace the special charter. Under the special charter arrangement, legislatures were able to penalize particular cities as they saw fit. To correct this abuse, States began to provide a general charter — one for all cities in the State. The general charter soon proved to be as unfair as were the special charters. A charter that was satisfactory for, say, a

small mining community was not at all adequate for a large seacoast city. No State today provides one general charter for all cities in the State.

(3) The *classified charter,* which came about to correct the defects in the special and the general charter systems. Under this scheme, all cities within the State are classified (grouped) according to population, and a uniform charter is granted to all cities within the same class.

The classified charter system is far superior to the special or general charter systems and is used in several of the States. However, it leaves much to be desired. Even within the same population class there may be cities in the State which are vastly different from one another. The governmental problems which face an industrial community of 50,000 population, for example, are usually quite unlike those which face a community of the same size in a farming region.

Often a State will classify cities in such a way that only one city falls into a particular class. For example, there may be only one city in the State with more than 500,000 inhabitants, or there may be only one city with a population between 200,000 and 500,-000. Such classification can amount, in effect, to the old special charter system disguised under another name.

(4) The *optional charter,* which has been used in many States to meet the objections to the three charters above. Ohio began the optional charter system in 1913 by offering its cities a choice of three different char-

ters. Several States soon followed this lead.[4] For example, in Massachusetts all cities except Boston have their choice of five different charters. The cities commonly make their choice of charters by popular vote.

The optional charter system has much to recommend it. It largely overcomes the major objections to the special, general, and classified systems. Still, it does not give full consideration to the peculiar circumstances or the desires of the people in each individual city in the State.

(5) The *home rule charter,* which has come into use because the other charter systems have not satisfactorily solved the problem of providing adequate charters for a number of our cities.

Municipal Home Rule. In several of our States, cities have been given the power to adopt and amend their own charters. This "home rule" may be granted to cities by act of the legislature (statutory home rule) or by the State constitution (constitutional home rule).

Statutory Home Rule. Beginning with Iowa as early as 1858, six State legislatures today grant home rule to some or all of their cities. In

---

[4] At least fifteen States now provide cities with a choice of charters: Idaho, Iowa, Kansas, Massachusetts, Montana, Nebraska, New Jersey, New Mexico, New York, North Carolina, North Dakota, Ohio, South Dakota, Virginia, and Wisconsin. It must be noted that not all States use only one or another of these particular charter systems. Most States use one system for *most* cities, but make use of another system for *some* cities.

Fairchild Aerial Surveys, Inc.

MANHATTAN ISLAND

New York City has five boroughs or municipal centers. They are Manhattan, The Bronx, Queens, Brooklyn, and Richmond. Note the pattern of main streets.

addition to Iowa, the States are Connecticut, Florida, Georgia, Mississippi, and South Carolina.

Home rule granted by the legislature has proved to be unsatisfactory in most of these States because the legislature has been reluctant to give up enough of its control over city affairs. One notable exception to this is Mississippi, however. In that State the legislature has given cities fairly broad control over their own local problems.

Another difficulty with statutory home rule is found in the fact that a legislature might easily repeal the grant at any time.

Constitutional Home Rule. The term " home rule " is commonly used today to refer to the grant of home rule for cities through the State constitution rather than through an act of the legislature. Beginning with Missouri in 1875, twenty-three States now provide for municipal home rule in their constitutions: Arizona (1912), California (1879), Colorado (1902), Louisiana (1946), Maryland.(1915),

PROTECTING THE WATERFRONT

Among the responsibilities of cities and towns is adequate fire protection. This San Francisco fireboat is fighting a big waterfront blaze.

Michigan (1908), Minnesota (1896), Missouri (1875), Nebraska (1912), Nevada (1924), New Mexico (1949), New York (1923), Ohio (1912), Oklahoma (1908), Oregon (1906), Pennsylvania (1922), Rhode Island (1951), Tennessee (1953), Texas (1912), Utah (1932), Washington (1889), West Virginia (1936), and Wisconsin (1924).[5]

In some of these States *any* city

---

[5] Home rule has been used most often by cities in the States of California, Michigan, Minnesota, Ohio, Oklahoma, Oregon, and Texas. In Nevada no city has as yet written its own charter; in Utah only two and in Nebraska only three cities have done so thus far.

may have a home-rule charter; e.g., in Minnesota, Oregon, Michigan, Wisconsin. In most of these States, *only certain* cities may have one. For example, home rule is available to cities of over 10,000 population in Missouri, of over 3500 in California, of over 5000 in Texas, and those with the governor's consent in Louisiana.

The legislature still has at least some control over home-rule cities. These cities are empowered to control " municipal affairs " or are granted " powers of local self-government " by the State constitution.

There are many situations in which something *might* be of purely local concern *or* might be of general State concern; for example, the setting of a speed limit on city streets that are also State highways, or the regulation of a city sewage system which empties into a river flowing through the State. The question of city versus State control in such borderline cases must be settled in the courts, but a few of the newer State constitutions attempt to solve the problem by listing the specific areas in which the cities have exclusive powers.

A home-rule charter may be framed by the city council, by a group of interested citizens, or by a charter convention composed of elected delegates. Once drafted, the charter must be submitted to the city's voters for their approval. Amendments may be proposed by the council and in some cities by initiative petition. They must be approved by the voters before they become a part of the charter.

Altogether, well over 3000 American cities may, if they wish, make their own charters. Nearly 1000 of them have done so. About two-thirds of our fifty largest cities are in the home rule States — not counting Washington, D.C., which has been begging Congress for home rule for years. The major home rule cities include Baltimore, Cleveland, Cincinnati, Dayton, Detroit, Denver, Houston, Kansas City (Mo.), Los Angeles, Philadelphia, Portland (Ore.), and St. Louis.

Changing Municipal Boundaries. As city populations grow the areas around the cities also grow. A city's suburbs or " fringes " often create rather serious problems for the city itself. For example, shacks present fire hazards which might endanger the city itself, septic tanks might pollute the city's water supply, or immoral road houses might complicate the task of the police force in enforcing the law.

Methods for the annexing (adding) of territory to the city are usually provided by the State constitution or by act of the legislature. Compulsory annexation (that is, forcing an area into a city) is rare. Usually, a vote of the residents of the area to be annexed is required. In some States the voters in the city also must vote on the question, but this is not common.

Suburbs often tend to resist annexation, and so most States give their cities so-called *extraterritorial powers* to regulate certain matters such as road houses, sanitation, or fire hazards in the thickly settled areas around the city.

Cities sometimes induce suburbs to come into the city by agreeing not to raise taxes in the annexed area for a certain number of years; or to raise them gradually over a long period.

Forms of City Government

Which is more important: a particular form of government or the men who operate it? Men have argued this question for centuries. In 1733 Alexander Pope penned this famous couplet:

For forms of government let fools contest;
Whate'er is best administer'd is best. . . .

Certainly good men are essential to good government, and good men can make the best of even the worst of forms. But the form is important, too. The better the form of government the more chance there is that capable people will be attracted to public service, and the more the chance that the public will receive the kind of service it wants.

There are three principal forms of city government in America. They are the mayor-council, commission, and council-manager types. No two cities have *exactly* the same governments, of course. Specific details vary from city to city.

The Mayor-Council Form

The mayor-council form of city government is the oldest and still the most widely used type. Its major features are a council to make the laws (*ordinances*) and a mayor with more or less power to enforce them.

The council is almost always unicameral (consisting of one chamber), but it is bicameral in a few cities — Augusta, Maine, for example. There are usually five, seven, or nine members on the council, but there are more in many of the larger cities. Chicago's council is the largest, with fifty members. There are thirty-three councilmen in Cleveland, thirty in St. Louis, seventeen in New York and in Philadelphia, and fifteen in Los Angeles.

The councilmen (sometimes called

National Municipal League

MAYOR-COUNCIL FORM

" aldermen ") are nearly always elected by the city's voters for terms varying from one to four years. The councilmen usually are elected from wards (districts) within the city, but the trend today is toward election at large (from the entire city). Partisan election is still the rule in most mayor-council cities, but an increasing number are turning to the nonpartisan ballot.

The mayor is commonly elected by the voters, too — usually for the same term as the councilmen. He often is not a member of the council but presides over its meetings, votes in case of tie, and may recommend and veto ordinances. The mayor's veto can in almost all of our cities be overridden by a two-thirds vote of the council.

Strong-Mayor or Weak-Mayor Types. The mayor council form is said to be of the *strong-mayor* or *weak-mayor* type, depending upon the powers of the mayor. In the strong-mayor type the mayor is placed at the head of the city administration, usually has the power to hire and fire city employees, prepares the budget, and otherwise has " strong " powers to conduct the city's business — subject to council control, of course.

In the weak-mayor type the mayor has much less power. Sometimes he does not have the veto and cannot appoint or dismiss city officials. He is simply the city's major-domo for ceremonial occasions.

Our larger mayor-council cities are almost all strong-mayor cities. Even so, Los Angeles has had a rather excellent city government for years with a weak-mayor arrangement.

Evaluation. The success of mayor-council government depends in large measure on the popularity and influence of the mayor. Especially in the weak-mayor cities, responsibility for government is hard to fix, as can be seen from the chart on page 594. Leadership is almost wholly lacking.

The strong-mayor form helps to solve the problem of leadership. Still, it is criticized by students of city government for three major reasons. First, whenever the mayor and the council become involved in a major dispute with one another, effective city government is liable to go right out the window. Secondly, the strong-mayor form still relies for success upon the nature of the mayor himself. The third criticism arises from the fact that the mayor-council form is complicated and not often understood by the average citizen. This sometimes makes it possible for a corrupt political machine to control the city. Corrupt machines are pretty much relics of the past, but they are not unknown today.

When New York was in the grip of the famous Tweed Ring in the 1860's and 1870's million of dollars were misappropriated. For example, a city courthouse was designed to cost $250,000. It finally cost $8,000,000! Organizations of aroused citizens can and have defeated bosses and their machines, as the Cincinnati Charter Committee did in the 1920's and as an organization of independents drawn from both major parties did in Philadelphia in 1951. Still, a less-complicated form of city government stands as one of the major protections against corrupt or " invisible " rule.

The Commission Form

Commission government was first tried with success in Galveston, Texas, in 1901. A tidal wave had swept over the island city in 1900 and left it in partial ruins. Nearly 7000 of Galveston's then 37,000 inhabitants were drowned and $20,000,000 worth of property was destroyed. The old mayor-council regime was too corrupt and too incompetent to handle the results of the catastrophe.

The Texas legislature granted Galveston a new charter which provided for the governing of the city by five commissioners with power to make the laws and enforce them. The plan was intended to be temporary, but it proved to be so efficient that it spread to other Texas cities and then to other parts of the country.

In the past few decades many cities have switched from the commission form to the newer council-manager system; commission government is now found in a little over ten per cent of our cities. Among the major cities

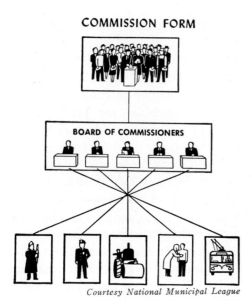

COMMISSION FORM

BOARD OF COMMISSIONERS

Courtesy National Municipal League

using it today are Birmingham, Alabama; Memphis, Tennessee; New Orleans, Louisiana; Omaha, Nebraska; Portland, Oregon; and St. Paul, Minnesota.

The scheme of commission government is rather simple and uncomplicated. Three, five, or seven men are elected " commissioners " (usually there are five). Together the commissioners form the city council; individually they are the heads of the various departments of the city administration. In other words, both executive and legislative powers are centered in this one body.

In some cities the voters and in others the commissioners themselves designate one of the commissioners as mayor. Like the other commissioners, the mayor heads one of the departments; he also presides over council meetings and represents the city on ceremonial occasions. He seldom

has any more authority than his fellow commissioners, and only rarely does he have the veto power.

The commissioners are usually elected for two- or four-year terms from the city at large. Over three-fourths of the commission cities use the nonpartisan ballot, and the commissioners almost always serve as full-time public officials.

The names of the various departments of city government may vary somewhat, but in general their work covers these activities: public affairs, finance, public safety, streets and public improvements, and parks and public property.

Various plans are used to determine which department each commissioner is to head. In most cities, the commission itself assigns its members to particular posts. In some cities, the voters elect commissioners to head specific departments. In a few, the assignments are made by the mayor. The mayor is the commissioner of public safety in nearly all cases.

In its early days the commission form was often criticized because it lacked a system of checks and balances and did nothing to prevent the continuing of a spoils system in city offices and business.

In 1907, Des Moines, Iowa, adopted a charter to help meet these criticisms. Des Moines added the initiative, referendum, and recall, the merit system, and nonpartisan election to the Galveston plan. The improvements of the " Des Moines Plan " stimulated the spread of the commission form. (Des Moines, like many other former commission cities, now has a council-manager government.)

Evaluation. The advantages of the commission government are four: (1) The number of commissioners to elect is small. (2) They can act promptly. (3) They have full power to act and cannot shirk their responsibility by referring an aggrieved citizen to someone else. (4) They are easier to watch than if they were many.

The way to get good government is to give power to a few people and watch those few in order to hold them responsible. The commissioners meet in public, record their votes for the inspection of the public, publish their ordinances in the papers, and issue frequent financial reports.

If they refuse to enact an ordinance which the majority of voters desire, the voters themselves may initiate and pass it (the initiative). If the commission passes an ordinance which the voters do not want, they may have it referred to them and reject it (the referendum). If the commissioners are believed to be dishonest or are in-efficient, a recall election may be called and one or all of the commissioners recalled by electing others to take their places (the recall). Thus we get government for the people by a few who are responsible directly to the people.

In one sense, however, the commission plan violates the principle that policy-makers should be elected by the people and that administrators should be appointed. In the commission plan, the people should and do elect their representatives as councilmen to make the city laws. These same councilmen also administer the laws. Efficient experts to enforce laws and administer a city, however, should not be subject to those political influences and residential restrictions which control elective positions. Such experts are usually best secured through executive appointment.

The commission plan, moreover, does not locate responsibility as well as the manager type. It often creates five little governments as each commissioner attempts to draw as much of the money and authority as he can to his own department.

The Council-Manager Form

Council-manager government was born in Staunton, Virginia, in 1908. The Staunton city council, acting under a charter provision allowing it to appoint new officials as needed, created the post of " general manager " in that year. The general manager's chief duty was to shake up the inefficient and old-fashioned city administration in order to provide Staunton with an efficient city government. The council gave him full charge of the city departments and the power to hire and dismiss all city employees.

The first city charter specifically providing for a council-manager government was granted by the South

COUNCIL-MANAGER FORM

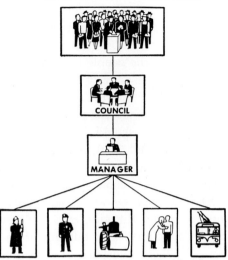

Courtesy National Municipal League

Carolina legislature to the city of Sumter in 1912. Under its new charter Sumter elected three exceptionally capable men as its first three councilmen; one was a planter, another a banker, and the third a lawyer. They advertised for a manager and hired a man from another State.

The new manager brought efficiency and a number of economies to Sumter's government. For example, many of the fine old trees lining the city's streets were being choked out by mistletoe which hadn't been removed because of the great cost involved. The manager knew that mistletoe has a time and place value, however. He had it cut from the trees and then sold it in the North for enough to cover the entire cost of the project.

Dayton, Ohio, was the first large city in the country to adopt the council-manager plan. The residents of

Dayton had long been disgusted with their inefficient city government. Just as a tidal wave in 1900 had brought commission government to Galveston, so a disastrous Miami River flood brought council-manager government to Dayton in 1913. Acting under Ohio's constitutional home rule amendment of 1912, Dayton adopted a new city charter by an overwhelming vote.

The council-manager plan spread with the publicity Dayton gave it. Today it is found in more than 1500 cities. The largest are Cincinnati, Ohio; Dallas and Ft. Worth, Texas; and Kansas City, Missouri.

Council-manager government is really a modification of the commission plan. Essentially, it consists of a strong council and a weak mayor with a manager appointed by the council. The manager has responsibility for city administration, is usually appointed for an indefinite term, and is held accountable by the council at all times.

In effect, this scheme leaves the responsibility for policy-making where it belongs, in the hands of elected councilmen and mayors. It places the responsibility for administration in the hands of a trained and nonpartisan expert.

Evaluation. The council-manager plan has the unqualified backing of students of government. It clearly locates responsibility; " if anything goes wrong you know whom to hang." It makes possible the separation of politics and administration and, because the more time-consuming functions are performed by the city manager, prominent and well-qualified residents are able to run for the *part-time* job of councilman.

Council-manager government promotes efficiency. The city manager of Saginaw, Michigan, found forty-two full-time bridge tenders who did nothing but raise and lower drawbridges an average of twice a week to allow barges to pass. He reduced the number of tenders to seven by having police cars speed to bridges when they needed to be raised for an occasional barge.

The few criticisms sometimes advanced against the council-manager plan are in almost every instance not criticisms of the system at all, but in reality are criticisms of the individuals involved in its operation.

Only a handful of cities which have once adopted the plan have later abandoned it, the chief ones being Cleveland, Ohio, and Houston, Texas. Today cities are switching to it in ever-increasing numbers.

Legal Liabilities of Cities

As we have said, cities are creatures of the State; they are a part of the State. As such, they enjoy the same immunity from suits that States do.

Generally speaking, a city may not be sued (is not liable) when it is engaged in a purely *governmental function,* unless State law specifically permits a suit. Thus a city is not usually liable for wrongs committed by such city employees as policemen, firemen, or public health officers.

For example, if a fire truck crashes into a car on its way to a fire, the city cannot be held for damages. Or, if a school child becomes infected because a city health officer used an unsterile needle in vaccinating him, the city is not liable. Or, if a policeman is unnecessarily violent, the city cannot be sued.

Of course, city employees may be sued as individuals. For example, a policeman who is negligent in operating his motorcycle and runs down a pedestrian may be held for damages by the injured party.

When a city is engaged in a *nongovernmental* or *corporate (business) function,* it may generally be sued. Activities which are commonly held to be nongovernmental include such functions as water, electricity, and gas supply, liquor stores, public markets, and transportation systems. Thus we have the rather strange situation in which, for example, a pedestrian cannot sue the city if he is run down and injured by a fire truck, but he can sue the city if the truck which hits him happens to be from the water department!

WHAT THIS CHAPTER IS ABOUT

A village is an incorporated community in which the population is smaller and the government is simpler that that of cities in the same State. Villages exist to provide essential public services in areas where a relatively small population is concentrated. Village government consists almost wholly of a mayor and council, although their exact names vary somewhat from State to State.

A city is a governmental unit created by the State with more population and wider powers than a village. From our early predominantly agricultural and rural society we have progressed to the point where our society is largely industrialized and urban. Nearly two-thirds of the American people now live in cities.

Cities are creatures of the State. In our early history most State control over cities was exercised through the legislature, but legislative abuse has led to many constitutional protections for cities.

A city's charter is its fundamental law and is granted by the State, either through the legislature or constitutional home rule provisions. Broadly speaking, there are five types of charters: the special, general, classified, and optional charters granted by the legislature, and the home rule charter which is drafted by the city itself. Seven States now provide for home rule by statute and twenty-three by constitutional provision.

City boundaries are extended by the annexation process, and cities are often given extraterritorial powers to deal with certain matters in areas outside their boundaries.

The oldest and most widely used form of city government is the mayor-council form. It is of either the weak-mayor or strong-mayor type, depending upon the powers of the mayor. The weak-mayor type is especially criticized because responsibility is difficult to fix. The strong-mayor type is preferred over it, but still is criticized because it tends to break down when the mayor and the council are at odds. Moreover, it places too much reliance upon the nature of the person who is mayor, and it is too complicated for the average citizen to understand easily.

The commission form of city government originated in Galveston, Texas, in 1901 and spread across the country, though its use is declining today. It consists of elected commissioners who collectively form the city council and individually head the various departments of city administration. Commission government has much to recommend it. It still makes it difficult to locate responsibility, though, and it violates the principle of separation of powers.

The council-manager form of city government originated in Staunton, Virginia, in 1908 and was popularized by Dayton, Ohio, where it was adopted in 1913. It is now found in over 1500 cities, and more cities are adopting it each year. Essentially, council-manager government consists of an elected mayor and council to make policy and an appointed manager to administer that policy. It is backed by students of government as the best of the three forms of city government.

Generally, cities may not be sued when engaged in governmental functions but are liable to suit when engaged in non-governmental functions.

QUESTIONS ON THE TEXT

1. What is a *village?* Where are small incorporated places so named? Where are they known as *towns? Boroughs?*

2. What does the term *town* mean in the New England States?

3. What are the usual powers of vil-

lages? Give a general description of village government.

4. How does a city differ from a town or village?

5. What per cent of the American people lived in cities in 1790? What per cent live in cities now?

6. Why have cities grown so rapidly?

7. What is a city charter? Describe briefly the five types.

8. What is meant by " home rule "? Does your State constitution provide for it?

9. What does *annexation* mean? Why do most cities have certain *extraterritorial* powers?

10. Why is the question of the form of a government important?

11. What are the three principal forms of city government in America? Which is the most common?

12. Distinguish between the weak-mayor and the strong-mayor types of mayor-council government. What are the principal grounds on which the form is criticized?

13. Describe the commission form of city government. Where did it originate and why? What improvements did Des Moines make in the original plan?

14. What are the advantages of commission government? What is the major criticism made of it?

15. Describe the council-manager form of city government. Where did it originate and why? How was a natural catastrophe important to its spread?

16. Why is the council-manager form so widely recommended by students of government?

17. May a city be sued for damage done while performing a *governmental* function? List three such functions of cities.

18. May a city be sued for damage done while performing a *nongovernmental* function? List three such functions of cities.

PROBLEMS FOR DISCUSSION

1. Do you think that every city should be permitted to frame and adopt its own charter?

2. What sort of training do you think a city manager should have? If your city does not have council-manager government, do you think it should?

3. As soon as an accident is reported on the streets of San Francisco, a white police car speeds to the scene to collect evidence while it is still " hot." Does this " traffic court on wheels " work to the advantage of the more innocent party or the reckless driver? Do you think that your city should (if it does not) have a similar arrangement?

4. Would a city be liable to suit in most States in the following situations?

(a) A policeman lost his temper when arresting a drunken driver and broke the latter's arm.

(b) The motorman of a city-owned and city-operated street railway started his car too soon and injury resulted to a passenger boarding the car.

(c) The city ambulance carrying a patient to a quarantine station drove recklessly and smashed a private car.

(d) Typhoid fever was contracted from city water because of carelessness on the part of the city employee in charge of the reservoir.

(e) A Chinese restaurant was destroyed by a gang of ruffians because the police were sympathetic with the gang and did not give vigorous protection.

THINGS YOU MIGHT DO

1. Obtain a copy of your city charter and discover the exact organization of your city's government. What powers does the Council have? The Mayor? What improvements, if any, do you think could be made in your city's government?

2. Make a list of the provisions of your State constitution which relate to cities. What changes, if any, would you propose here?

3. Stage a class forum or debate on the question: "*Resolved,* That our city should be made legally responsible for any negligent act by any of its employees."

4. Invite the mayor, a councilman, or the city manager (if there is one) to address the class on the government of your city, some of its problems, and his particular job.

WORDS AND PHRASES YOU SHOULD KNOW

Annexation
Borough
Charter
City
Classified charter
Commission government
Council
Council-manager
  government

Extraterritorial powers
General charter
Governmental functions
Home rule
Incorporate
Mayor
Mayor-council
  government
Municipal

Municipal corporation
Nongovernmental or
  corporate functions
Optional charter
Special charter
Strong-mayor type
Town
Village
Weak-mayor type

SELECT BIBLIOGRAPHY

ADRIAN, CHARLES R., *Governing Urban America.* McGraw-Hill, 1955.

BROMAGE, ARTHUR, *Manager Plan Abandonments.* National Municipal League, 1954.

CAMERON, FRANK, " He Hunts Firebugs," *Saturday Evening Post,* September 19, 1953.

DEXTER, KARL, " A New Deal in the Old Firehouse," *Reader's Digest,* October, 1956.

" Ex-Mayor," " Are You *Sure* You Want an Honest Mayor? " *Collier's,* October 30, 1954.

HENDERSON, HARRY, " Call for Mr. Emergency! " *Reader's Digest,* October, 1956.

MACDONALD, AUSTIN F., *American State Government and Administration,* Chapter 13. Crowell, 1955.

——, *State and Local Government in the United States,* Chapters 9, 10. Crowell, 1955.

Story of the Council-Manager Plan. National Municipal League, 1954.

WALKER, H., " Cities Like Worcester Make America," *National Geographic,* February, 1955.

Unit VIII. LOCAL GOVERNMENT

> Men come together in cities in order to live; they remain together in order to live the Good Life.
>
> — *Aristotle*

★

Chapter 34

CITY AND VILLAGE PROBLEMS

A city exists to provide services to its residents. The range of the services a city provides, day in and day out, covers a much broader field of activities than the average citizen generally realizes. For most of us, the city enters every waking and even every sleeping moment of our lives to an almost incredible extent. Most of its functions are so familiar that we often take them for granted.

It would be impossible to compile a complete list of all of the functions which our cities perform. Consider, however, some of the things that most or all of them do: provide police and fire protection; build and maintain streets, sidewalks, street lighting systems, bridges, tunnels, parks, swimming pools, golf courses, libraries, hospitals, schools, correctional institutions, homes for the aged, airports, public markets, and auditoriums; furnish such health and sanitation services as disease prevention and rubbish and garbage collection and disposal; operate water, light, gas, and trans-portation systems; and regulate traffic, building practices, and the rates and services of public utilities. Then, too, many cities manage public housing projects, clear slums, conduct city "clean-up" campaigns, maintain youth camps, keep docks and wharves, and operate tourist attractions.

Several cities, large and small, have built their own hydroelectric power dams. A growing number of them now operate profitable farms in connection with their sewage disposal plants.

Nearly all of our large and many of our smaller cities issue an annual report, a summary of the city's condition and the activities of its government over the past year. It is no wonder that many of these reports are really good-sized books.

In carrying out its many tasks a city often faces a number of serious problems. In this chapter, we point up some of the more important of these and indicate ways in which some of our cities have met them.

THE PUBLIC WELFARE

The public services offered by large cities are tremendously varied. This moble unit helps to fight tuberculosis by providing free chest X-rays for the people of New York City.

City Planning

Most American cities have, like Topsy, " just growed." With only a few exceptions, most of our cities have developed without plan, haphazardly and with no eye to the future. The narrow and crooked streets of the original Boston are said to have followed cow paths. The streets in most of our early cities were considered wide enough if two horse-and-wagon teams could pass one another.

The results of this shortsightedness have been unfortunate and are all too obvious. In many cities the busiest downtown streets are much too narrow. Main thoroughfares are sometimes too close together and often too far apart. Adequate parking space is a constant problem. There are often too few parks and other recreation areas, and those that do exist are far too small. Such public buildings as schools, police and fire stations, and hospitals are many times very inconveniently located and difficult to find.

Planning Commissions. Fortunately, more and more of our cities have today recognized the need for city planning. That is, they recognize the need to correct past mistakes in city development and the values that can come from orderly growth in the future. Today nearly ninety per cent of all cities over 500,000 population have permanent city planning commissions.

Washington, D.C., began and has remained a planned city. Its basic plan was drawn up before a single building was erected. When Congress decided in 1791 to locate the national capital on the Potomac River, President Washington sent to France for Major Pierre-Charles L'Enfant. L'Enfant, an engineer, had served in the Continental Army during the Revolution and was now given the task of laying out the new city.

He laid it out on a grand scale with adequate parks and beautiful circles, with parallel streets named according to the alphabet and with those running at right angles numbered, and with houses numbered 100 to the block. Twenty-one avenues were provided to shorten distances by cutting diagonally through the city, with trees and shrubs at intersections. The streets were made purposefully wide, and plenty of space was left for government buildings.

The National Capital Planning Commission guides the development of the city today.

Philadelphia also began as a planned city. It was first laid out by William Penn in 1682 much in the fashion of a checkerboard. Penn's simple scheme called for two main thoroughfares crossing one another at right angles, with an open place at the point of intersection, and with other lesser streets crisscrossing the pattern at regular intervals. In Penn's plan, the City of Brotherly Love was to cover some two square miles.

The city has long since outgrown its founder's plan. It is now the third largest city in the United States and sprawls over 130 square miles with a population of more than 2,000,000. Much of its growth has been haphazard, without plan, and inevitably resulted in congestion. The city's problems were compounded by the fact that for seventy-five years it lay in the grip of a corrupt political machine thrown out by the voters only a few years ago.

Today Philadelphia is engaged in a vast and popular plan of self-improvement. Whole blocks of buildings are being torn down to be replaced by beautiful parks, modern highways, and business projects. As a part of this program, the Pennsylvania Railroad's ancient Broad Street Station, in the heart of the city, was torn down. To celebrate the razing, the 103-piece Philadelphia Orchestra played a requiem in the train shed, and its conductor, Eugene Ormandy, led a large and enthusiastic crowd in the singing of *Auld Lang Syne*.

Many other large cities have gained

CITY PLANNING, LARGE SCALE

Members of the Philadelphia City Planning Commission staff examine a part of their model of downtown Philadelphia. A proposed apartment house development is seen in the right foreground.

and are gaining through wise city planning. Pittsburgh has accomplished a modern miracle by eliminating the industrial smog which only a few years ago blanketed its downtown area so completely that street lights often had to be turned on by 10 o'clock in the morning. The Golden Triangle, Pittsburgh's business district, is being rebuilt, and so are the areas around it, with modern skyscrapers and landscaped parks with six stories of underground parking.

In Dallas, Houston, and Seattle, new expressways and one-way street systems have eased downtown traffic congestion. San Francisco, Los Angeles, and other cities have put in underground garages with beautifully planned and kept parks right on top of them in the middle of the busiest districts.

The accomplishments in these and other cities are largely the result of the efforts of public-spirited citizens, many of them prominent business people. The larger insurance companies have lent cities a real hand in recent years. They have replaced slums with vast and modern housing projects, " cities within cities," in such communities as New York, Los Angeles, and Newark. Parkchester, Peter Cooper Village, and Stuyvesant Town in New York City, the smaller Parklabrea in Los Angeles, and the Parkfairfax in Alexandria, Virginia, for example, all are creations of the Metropolitan Life Insurance Company.

A good many smaller cities are now solving their problems through intelligent long-range planning. Of course, some cities are still stuck in their own quagmire, but tremendous progress has been and is being made. There is much hope for the future of many of our downtown city areas.

Municipal Zoning

Zoning. The practice of dividing a city into a number of districts (zones) and regulating the kinds of property and the uses to which it may be put in each is called *zoning*. Zoning is really one phase of the broader problem of city planning. Many cities, especially smaller ones, have zoning ordinances and yet do not have an overall plan for city growth. Every city in the United States over 100,000 population is zoned — except Houston, where it has been rejected by popular vote.

One would be surprised to find a bathtub in a parlor or a piano in a kitchen. It seems just as absurd for American cities to have allowed stores to crowd in at random among private dwellings, or factories and public garages to elbow in among neat retail stores or well-kept apartment houses, or tall and bulky office buildings to rise so closely crowded that the lower floors become dungeon-like and unsatisfactory for human use. Such conditions added to the always present fire hazards of congested communities.

At first, courts would not allow city councils to restrict the use of private property except in case of such well-recognized nuisances as pig pens, glue factories, tanneries, slaughterhouses, forges, gas works, oil tanks, powder magazines, and the like. We inherited the right to regulate the location of these nuisances in the common law of England.

The developing science of sanitation taught us that there were many nuisances which we had not formerly recognized. With the spread of culture, ugliness hurt the eyes as noise had hurt the ears or odors the nose. In time, the courts began to recognize new nuisances and gradually permitted more and more regulation of private property as a proper exercise of the police powers. Boston, for example, was allowed to limit the height of buildings. Then Los Angeles was allowed to exclude brickyards from residential districts. Roanoke, Virginia, was allowed to require buildings to be erected at a specified distance back from the street.

A MODERN FREEWAY

To prevent traffic congestion thoroughfares are being built all over
the country. The Hollywood Freeway handles 300,000 vehicles a day.
During the rush hours more commuters use it than use the public
transportation systems of any large city.

It has been the practice of real estate dealers in establishing suburban plots to sell the lots subject to certain restrictions on their use. These restrictions are incorporated in each deed of conveyance. It was not until 1926, though, when the United States Supreme Court upheld the zoning ordinance of Euclid, Ohio, that cities have known definitely that it is legal to plot a whole city into zones in which there are restrictions as to the height and size of buildings, the percentage of the lot that may be occupied, the size of yards and courts, the location and use of buildings, and the use of land for trade, industry, residence, or other purposes.

The purposes of zoning are well stated in the following ten points set forth by the Boston City Planning Board:

1. Zoning divides the city into districts, according to the most suitable and valuable uses for each district, based on existing conditions and future needs, and regulates the location and use of new buildings.

2. Zoning makes provision for *general business districts* in suitable locations in which industrial plants may not impair the business environment.

3. Zoning chooses suitable land for *industrial districts* where the best of transportation facilities by rail, water, and highway may be secured and fac-

tories may easily expand without tearing down expensive buildings.

4. Zoning provides *unrestricted districts,* suitable places for those heavy industries such as stockyards, boiler works, coke manufacture, and other industries that would be objectionable elsewhere.

5. Zoning regulates the *heights of buildings* appropriate to their use, so as to provide an equitable distribution of light and air for all, minimizes overcrowding of people, and relieves traffic congestion.

6. Zoning provides *local business districts,* conveniently located near residential neighborhoods, where stores will be concentrated instead of being scattered everywhere.

7. Zoning protects the comfort, convenience, and quietness of *residential districts* by excluding stores, public garages, laundries, factories, and other business and industrial uses.

8. Zoning establishes *uniform building lines* in residential districts to assure an equal amount of light and air and access for all residences.

9. Zoning provides adequate light and air by *side and rear yards* around every building in the suburban residential districts and establishes the *percentage of area of a lot* that may be occupied by buildings.

10. Zoning preserves the home character of single and two-family residence districts by segregating types of residences into appropriate districts.

Zoning Ordinances Must Be Reasonable. We are aware of the fact that the 14th Amendment to the United States Constitution prevents States (*and cities*) from depriving a person of his life, liberty, or property without due process of law. Nearly every State constitution contains the same provision.

Obviously, zoning deprives a person of the right to use his property for certain purposes. For example, if an area is zoned to permit only single-family residences, a man may not build an apartment house or a service station on his property in that zone. Zoning also sometimes reduces the value of a particular piece of property. A choice corner lot might be much more valuable with a grocery store on it than with a house.

Even though zoning may at times deprive one of his property, however, the key question is " Does it do so *without due process of law?* " That is, is it *unreasonable?*

The question of reasonableness is one for the courts to decide. For example, courts have held that zoning ordinances which require that buildings which are higher than a particular height must be torn down, are unreasonable deprivations of property.

So long as a city can show that its ordinance is a reasonable exercise of its *police power,*[1] it will be upheld. For example, ordinances which require the moving of such nuisances as

---

[1] The *police power* is the power of the State (and its local governments, including cities) to regulate in the interest of the public health, public safety, public morals, or the general welfare. See pages 387–389.

slaughterhouses, glue factories, and stables have been upheld as reasonable exercises of the police power.

Excess Condemnation. In the United States, if land is needed for public use, the city may have it condemned through the *right of eminent domain*.[2] To take land for streets, parks, public-building sites, bridge heads, and the like is clearly to take it for public purposes. It may be desirable though, in connection with a public improvement, for a city to acquire more land than is actually needed for the immediate purpose.

If land for a new city hall is acquired in a congested district, for example, it may be desirable that the city take some unsightly property near by in order to have the new structure set in favorable surroundings. It also may be desirable to resell the excess land under restrictions that will insure the attractiveness of the district. This is the regular procedure in Europe.

In many American cities, however, the constitutions, laws, and courts stand in the way. Some States have amended their constitutions, though, and their courts now permit " excess condemnation." City planning with an eye to the beautiful as well as the serviceable is becoming possible.

"Suburbanites" and Metropolitan Districts

" Suburbanitis." Most of our larger cities are suffering from what has been called " suburbanitis." They are literally bursting at the seams. Between 1940 and 1950, the populations of the nation's 168 largest cities increased by some 6,000,000. Their suburbs (areas immediately outside) increased by 9,000,000, or one-and-a-half-times as much!

Between 1940 and 1950 Los Angeles' population grew about thirty per cent while that of many of its suburbs grew *over 100 per cent.* Chicago gained only seven per cent while its suburbs increased thirty-two per cent. The suburbs of each one of the nation's twelve largest cities grew faster than the cities themselves. And this suburban growth is continuing.

The United States Census Bureau lists six major reasons which have caused people to move from the city to the near-by countryside: (1) fast and economical means of transportation, (2) noise and overcrowding in the cities, (3) the attractions of a home with a little ground and fresh air around it, (4) newer schools and safer playing conditions for children, (5) more and more industrial building on the outer fringes of cities, and (6) higher city taxes.

This shift to the suburbs has created a great number of problems for cities. Among the most important are (1) the loss of many of the more

---

[2] The *right of eminent domain* is the power any government has to take private property for a public use. A fair price must be paid to the owner.

610

Unit VIII. LOCAL GOVERNMENT

MODERN TOWN PLANNING

The chairman of a special citizen's committee in Tarrytown, New York, reports to the town trustees. The committee's work resulted in the adoption of an up-to-date building code.

able and civic-minded who might otherwise be helping the city to solve its problems, (2) the loss of tax revenues the cities would otherwise collect from suburbanites who work in the city, and (3) the dangers from the growth of illegal activities just beyond the city's boundaries.

Many of these areas resist annexation; most of the residents moved to the suburbs to get out of the city and are not anxious to rejoin it. In some cities sales taxes are used to try to gain revenue from suburbanites who

shop in the city, but in many situations this has only encouraged the further growth of suburban shopping centers and branches of downtown department stores. In some places, this spreading out has meant that neighboring cities have grown together like Siamese twins.

Metropolitan Districts. The residents of these suburban areas face many common problems, too, such as water supply, sewage disposal, police and fire protection, transportation, and city planning. Duplication of functions by city and city, or city and county, is wasteful and at times even dangerous. More than one fire has burned on while neighboring fire departments quibbled over which was responsible for fighting it.

To meet these problems, some States have taken the control of certain functions away from the cities and counties and vested them in specially created metropolitan districts. Over 150 of these districts are now in existence. The boundaries of these areas commonly disregard city and county lines.

These metropolitan districts are most often established for a single purpose — for example, park development in the Cleveland Metropolitan Park District and sewage in the case of the Chicago Sanitary District.

There is no reason, though, why a district's authority cannot be expanded to include other functions. The Boston Metropolitan District began as a sewage district in 1889. To-day it controls sewage, water supply, and park development and has duties in connection with planning the development of the District as a whole. There is also a rapid transit commission for the District. Boston itself accounts for only about one-third of the District's total population, and the District now includes some forty municipalities.

Dade County, Florida, has undertaken the nation's most ambitious approach to metropolitan problems. In 1957 its voters approved the first home-rule charter to be specifically designed " to create a metropolitan government." Under it, a county-wide metropolitan government is responsible for such area-wide functions as fire and police protection, providing an integrated water, sewer, and drainage system, zoning, expressway construction, and the like. Miami and the other twenty-five cities in the county continue to perform the strictly local functions.

Traffic Congestion

A few minutes on any street in the downtown area of any of our larger cities, and many of our smaller ones, is enough to convince one that traffic congestion is a major municipal problem. The amount of time lost and the inconvenience that is caused by traffic congestion cannot be accurately measured. However, it has been estimated that traffic congestion today costs the residents of New York City more than $1,000,000 a day and the residents of Philadelphia at least $400,000 a day!

Here are some of the things which have been done around the country to help solve the problem. Perhaps something quite similar has been or is being done in your community.

The old Erie Canal was abandoned, and the city of Rochester turned the bed into a subway for passengers and freight, then built an avenue over it.

Denver, Seattle, and now several

612

other cities have fixed traffic lights at some of the busiest intersections to flash red four ways at once. With traffic stopped in all directions, this " scramble " system permits pedestrians to cross intersections every which way and has speeded up both street and sidewalk traffic.

A few cities have now followed the lead of Providence, Rhode Island, with *three-way* streets. On these, traffic inbound for the city uses the lanes on each side while outbound traffic uses the middle.

Portland, Oregon, and many other cities now prohibit parking on certain downtown streets during all or part of week-days. One-way grid-systems, with every other street being one way in the same direction, are now common in many cities.

Cleveland, Chicago, and Boston have established huge parking lots well away from the downtown shopping areas with bus service to shuttle people downtown and back.

New York elevated the downtown continuation of Riverside Drive and also provided for fast traffic along the East River. It built the George Washington Bridge over the Hudson, the Holland Tunnel and the Lincoln Tunnel under the Hudson, and the Battery-Brooklyn Tunnel. It has built a union bus terminal to connect with the Lincoln Tunnel to handle Jersey commuters and thus relieve traffic jams in midtown New York City; on the roof of the terminal, parking is provided for 500 cars. Private capital has built a garage for

Conrad, " The Denver Post "

several thousand cars on the old Hippodrome site. The 1939 World's Fair parking field was reopened with space for 3000 cars. From there commuters ride to the city's center on fast trains or by subway.

There are over 200 miles of expressways (freeways) in Los Angeles which permit cars to move free of cross streets and stop lights. The Dallas Expressway permits a through traveler to go from one end of the city to the other in a matter of minutes.

San Francisco relieved congestion in front of the Municipal Ferry, where the electric cars from all parts of the city converge and circle, by digging a tunnel for through traffic under the circle. It has built two enormous bridges to span the harbor and the Golden Gate. Los Angeles has pedestrian tunnels under dangerous streets adjacent to schoolhouses.

San Francisco built an underground

**MODERN VIADUCT —
TOWARD ALASKA**

This new two-level highway in Seattle, Washington, relieves vehicular congestion downtown and speeds through traffic.

garage beneath Union Square in the heart of the city. Pittsburgh's Mellon Square Park, in the Golden Triangle, conceals a layered parking garage for 1000 cars under an acre of trees, flowers, lawns, and fountains.

Seattle has constructed a two-level viaduct to allow through traffic to skirt the downtown business area. One-way traffic on each level may travel up to 45 miles an hour and the downtown jam caused by through traffic has been eased. Boston is also

contemplating a gigantic expressway and is considering a 2000-car garage under its historic Common. In St. Louis work has begun on two of three expressways designed to encircle and bisect the city.

Fort Worth is contemplating a " dream city " in which the pedestrian will be " king." Under the proposed revamping, the city's business district would be encircled by an expressway which would seal its streets off completely to all automobile and truck traffic. Commuters would park their cars in garages off the expressway and walk into the downtown area or ride in slow-moving pneumatic-tired trains. Stores and offices would be served by trucks traveling in underground tubes. The traffic-freed streets would then become park-like malls.

Like so many other cities, booming Atlanta has found its narrow streets inadequate to carry the present-day traffic load. An expressway running north-south through the city is nearly completed. One skirting the city and at least one more within the city are being planned.

These and similar projects in our major cities — and in many of the smaller ones, too — are helping to meet the problems of downtown congestion. But it is only too obvious that much remains to be done.

Public Utilities

A public utility is an enterprise which, though privately owned, serves the public, makes use of public property, and is a natural monopoly.

Electric power, gas, and water companies, telephone systems, and bus and street railway lines are good examples of public utilities within a city.

It is, almost always, economically unsound for two concerns to compete in the business of providing these public services. For example, it would be well-nigh ridiculous to have two competing sets of telephone lines running down the same street. So these public utilities are made monopolies through State law and city ordinance.

Because public utilities are officially created monopolies, there must be some legal check to prevent them from abusing their privileges. A *public utilities commission* (sometimes called a *public services commission*) regulates such matters as rates and quality of service. The larger cities sometimes have commissions of their own. More often, State commissions regulate city utilities as well as those elsewhere in the State. Regulation by State agencies is more common because the utility often extends beyond the city's boundaries, the activities of the commission can be expensive, and a State-wide agency is less likely to be prejudiced in favor of a particular local utility.

Municipal Ownership. Ownership by cities is increasing steadily in the United States, and we accept it as a matter of course in most instances. Public ownership of roads, bridges, water systems, and sewers are excellent examples which are taken for granted. The public school systems have been publicly owned for so long that few people think twice about the fact now.

Municipal ownership *and operation* usually go hand in hand, though this is not always the case. Cincinnati owns a small railway and Philadelphia owns its local railway system and a gas plant, but these are leased to private operators.

There are more than 2000 publicly owned power and light systems, most of them serving the smaller municipalities. More than two-thirds of all our cities over 100,000 population own their own airports, including the new Greater Pittsburgh Airport which is larger than New York's La Guardia and Washington's National airports combined. While most city transportation systems are privately owned, outstanding cities like New York, Cleveland, Chicago, Detroit, San Francisco, and Seattle own their own. New York collects some 7,000,000 fifteen-cent fares each day from subway passengers.

Those who favor public ownership claim that private ownership usually means poor service and often involves rate-gouging and graft. *Opponents* of public ownership claim that it results in poor service because of the lack of individual initiative and that it invites political corruption.

The truth of the matter seems to be that cities with capable public-spirited citizens who are willing to donate their services usually make a good showing with public ownership where all profit is for public benefit. Where such capable people are lacking, however, private ownership, where the stockholders demand efficient management and public utilities commissions safeguard the people, is probably the best solution.

Water Systems. In 1907, when Los Angeles had a population of only 200,000, the city had sufficient vision to spend $25,000,000 on a water system. It brought water 250 miles — 54 miles through mountains and 150 miles across deserts. The gravity of the water supplied 120,000 horsepower of electrical energy through five power plants, and reclaimed 150 square miles of arid lands near the city. Each year this watered garden yielded products of a value equal to the cost of the entire water system. This water controlled by Los Angeles forced most of the surrounding suburbs to become a part of the city. The water has made possible the growth of the city from 200,000 to more than 2,000,000 population.

In Los Angeles there is almost one car for every two people. This expansion in transportation has enabled the population to spread over a wide area. This necessitates an enormous quantity of water to maintain green lawns and grow shrubbery and shade trees in such a dry climate. It is estimated that it requires about 125 gallons of water per day for a tree — as much as the average per capita consumption.

To keep the water supply ahead of the population, the city has built a series of dams at the mouths of the great canyon basins along the way. In these, water is stored during the wet season and allowed to pass through the power plants uniformly. If a break occurs along the pipe line, no waste results. The water is stored in the reservoir just above, and the lower reservoirs keep the power plants running and supply the city. One reservoir, completed in 1925, is about 300 feet in height, and another beautiful one completed the same year overhangs the very edge of Hollywood. There is a canyon full of water right at the edge of the city which will take care of any emergency.

Still looking ahead, Los Angeles, with other cities forming the Metropolitan Water District of Southern California, voted a $220,000,000 bond issue for a billion-gallon-a-day water supply, with the Colorado River as the source. The RFC helped finance this project by buying a portion of the bonds.

Sewage Disposal. Most cities no longer contaminate streams by sewage. In Baltimore, for instance, sewage is siphoned from one tank to another, then flows through a revolving screen, is sprayed into the air by thousands of small fountains, and is filtered through stone and sand. The filtrate flows into Chesapeake Bay as pure as the water in the city reservoirs. As the water falls from the filtration beds into the bay, it is used to generate electricity by which the disposal plant is operated. Pasadena uses the filtrate of its treated sewage to water a city farm which produces oranges, walnuts, grain, and

HIGHWAY EMERGENCY

Keeping roads open at all times requires constant vigilance and quick action. The collapse of this conveyor belt over a vital artery in New York City receives the immediate attention of highway department engineers and heavy emergency equipment.

hay. Many other cities have similar systems.

Wharves. New Orleans owns nearly all of its water front, and the State of California has long been developing the water front of San Francisco. Greater New York now owns 349 of its 577 miles of water front.

Los Angeles, whose center is twenty-one miles from the coast, has a water frontage of forty miles, a large part of which is improved. The city also owns a forty-eight-mile railway which prevents any railroad company from monopolizing the wharves.

The cities located on the Great

Lakes, on the other hand, own very little of their wharfage. Although the United States has spent more than twenty million dollars improving and maintaining a thirty-foot channel for the harbor of Galveston, the wharves are almost all privately owned.

Free foreign trade zones are areas where imports can be stored and re-shipped to a foreign country without paying United States tariffs. Before the war there were forty-three such zones in Europe.

Congress authorized such zones in 1934, and New York established a fenced-off, policed zone of ninety-two acres. Here importers can hold goods for seasonal demands, new markets, determining of import quotas, or other reasons. If goods are shipped out to United States consumers, all regular import requirements must be met. Goods may be processed if no basic changes are made. Swiss watch movements, for instance, are put into United States watch cases and re-shipped abroad. Other foreign trade zones are now in operation in New Orleans on the Gulf, San Francisco and Seattle on the Pacific Coast.

Civilian Defense

Atomic and hydrogen bombs and long-range bombers have made cities the prime targets in any future war. New York's Civilian Defense Commission predicts that an atomic ex-plosion a half-mile above Union Square would lay waste to the city for two miles in every direction. The Empire State and Metropolitan Life buildings, Peter Cooper Village and Stuyvesant Town, Rockefeller Center and Times Square, the Holland and Queens tunnels, Pennsylvania and Grand Central stations, the Metro-politan Opera House, and many schools, universities, and hospitals — all would lie among the wreckage.

Fire, explosions, flying debris, and broken gas and water mains and tele-phone and electric wires would add to the chaos and devastation.

New York City has made great strides in preparing for such an at-tack. Police and firemen, medical teams and rescue squads, and main-tenance and evacuation crews are be-ing trained and equipped for possible action. Mobile aid stations and kitchens, river fire pumps and heavy clearing equipment, shelters and other facilities are being readied.

Many other cities and States are following New York's lead. The Fed-eral Civil Defense Administration ad-vises and gives financial aid to them. The task is tremendous. Given the frightful possibilities, however, it is a task that no city can ignore.

WHAT THIS CHAPTER IS ABOUT

Cities exist to provide services and the range of city activities is enormous. Most cities have developed haphazardly and with no eye to the future. More and

618

more of our cities have recognized the need for city planning, however. Zoning, which is one phase of city planning, is widespread. Some cities without an over-all city plan do utilize zoning. Zoning ordinances must be reasonable, that is, they cannot deprive one of his property without due process of law.

The rapid growth of suburbs, "suburbanitis," has created many problems for cities and for the outlying areas, too. More than 150 metropolitan districts have now been created to encompass both cities and suburbs.

Traffic congestion, a major city problem, has been and is being met in a wide variety of ways in cities around the nation.

Public utilities are officially created monopolies regulated by State and sometimes city public utilities commissions. Municipal ownership of utilities is growing in the United States. Those who favor it claim that it tends to prevent graft, rate-gouging, and poor service. Those who oppose it claim that it fosters corruption and stifles individual initiative.

Civilian defense is a tremendous task but one which no city can afford to ignore today.

QUESTIONS ON THE TEXT

1. List ten major services which all or most cities provide today.

2. What is *city planning?* Why has it become so necessary in most cities?

3. Who planned Washington, D.C.? Describe its basic scheme.

4. Describe William Penn's plan for the original Philadelphia. What happened to it?

5. What is *zoning?* Why have nearly all large cities found it absolutely necessary? What do we mean when we say that a zoning ordinance must be "reasonable"? What is *excess condemnation?*

6. What is "suburbanitis"? What six causes for it has the Census Bureau listed? Give two major problems it has created for cities. What is a *metropolitan district?*

7. Describe four ways in which some of our cities have attempted to relieve the problem of traffic congestion.

8. What is a public utility? Give two common examples. Why are they regulated by States and cities?

9. What are the major arguments for and against public ownership?

10. Describe the Los Angeles water system.

PROBLEMS FOR DISCUSSION

1. If you were zoning your city, where would you permit residences only? Where would you locate schools? Churches? Hospitals? Retail stores? Garages? Filling stations? Factories? Stockyards? Taverns?

2. Assume that one half of a block is zoned for residences only and that the other half, facing another street, permits garages. The street on which garages are permitted is widened and cuts off so large a portion of the front of a garage that the owner cannot make it pay. He asks to extend that garage back 100 feet into the half of the block in which garages are forbidden. The residents protest, one claiming that the sale of his property at a nice profit would be called off if the garage is permitted to extend. If you were on the city council (or board

of zoning adjustments), how would you vote?

3. Practically all of our larger and many of our smaller cities face acute parking problems. Suburban branch stores have been established by many large department stores — in order to reach more customers *and also* because many people refuse to shop in downtown stores because of the severe parking problem. In Los Angeles a number of stores have parking lots in the rear and have placed main customers' entrances there. Drive-in banks, restaurants, laundries, theaters, and even post offices are becoming more and more common every day. Office buildings with inside parking lots and large municipally-owned parking lots are also common. If your city has a parking problem, how is it being met?

THINGS YOU MIGHT DO

1. Invite a member of your local planning commission or some other city official to address the class on the plans which have been drafted to guide the future growth of your city.

2. Invite the manager of the local Chamber of Commerce or some prominent businessman to discuss the views of businessmen on such matters as your city's future, zoning, etc.

3. Several students might prepare specific reports on various city functions such as the regulation of public utilities, steps which have been taken to relieve traffic congestion, the operation of such city-owned utilities as the water system, etc.

4. Draw up a list of specific things you would do to relieve present or future traffic congestion in your city.

5. Stage a class forum or debate on the subject: "*Resolved*, That our city should own and operate (a particular utility)."

WORDS AND PHRASES YOU SHOULD KNOW

City planning
Eminent domain
Excess condemnation
Federal Civil Defense Administration
Metropolitan districts

Monopoly
Public utilities
Public utilities commission
" Suburbanitis "
Zoning

SELECT BIBLIOGRAPHY

" Can the Big Cities Come Back? " *U.S. News*, July 19, 1957.

CHASE, STUART, " Zoning Comes to Town," *Reader's Digest*, February, 1957.

" Cities As Long As Highways," *U.S. News*, April 5, 1957.

MORRIS, JOE ALEX, " How to Rescue a City," *Saturday Evening Post*, August 18, 1956.

" Our Changing Cities," *Newsweek*, September 2, 1957.

PERRY, GEORGE SESSIONS, " Can This Man Clean Up New York? " *Saturday Evening Post*, November 12, 1955.

REICHLEY, JOHN, " Philadelphia Does It," *Harper's*, July, 1957.

" Why People Move Out of Cities," *U.S. News*, August 10, 1956.

UNIT IX
THE BETTERMENT
OF SOCIETY

The Iwo Jima Memorial

OUR GOVERNMENT today is very different in structure and in operation from that envisioned by the Founding Fathers. From a number of small semi-autonomous agricultural States, we have become a highly industrialized far-flung nation. We have become a world power with interests and responsibilities throughout the globe.

As we have grown as a nation, so have we grown as independent States; and government today — each of our governments — is a large social and economic mechanism designed to serve and operate for the welfare of the people.

THE HOOVER COMMISSION
Report, 1949

Unit IX. THE BETTERMENT OF SOCIETY

I think with you, that nothing is of more importance for the public weal, than to form and train up youth in wisdom and virtue. Wise and good men are, in my opinion, the *strength* of a state far more so than riches or arms.

— *Benjamin Franklin*

★

Chapter 35

PUBLIC EDUCATION

Education a Governmental Function. Education is often described as the " bulwark of democracy." To be successful, our form of government must be based upon an enlightened citizenry. Therefore, the providing of free, tax-supported schools is regarded as a proper governmental function everywhere in the United States today.

This has not always been true, however. In colonial days and up through the early years of the nineteenth century, education was generally regarded as a church or family concern. The first public school in America was founded at Dedham, Massachusetts, in 1644, and in 1647 Massachusetts provided for the first public school system. The 1647 law required any town having fifty families to provide an elementary school, and those towns with 100 or more families were also required to build a secondary school.

That early Massachusetts law was especially intended to make it possible for everyone to be able to read and understand the Bible. The idea that public schools should be provided for the sake of general education did not take hold until many years later.

Today, although there are many fine private schools, over ninety per cent of the nation's pupils attend public schools.

Education a State and Local Function. The field of education lies within the reserved powers of the States. The Constitution of the United States makes no mention of the subject.

Even so, the National Government does enter the field in a variety of ways. Beginning with the Northwest Ordinance of 1787, Congress granted huge tracts of land, altogether some 70,000,000 acres, to the States for the support of education. Congress has also appropriated hundreds of millions of dollars for a host of educational matters. Examples are the support of land-grant colleges, scientific research, vocational education in the high schools, educational benefits for veterans, the school-lunch programs, and school construction in

SCHOOL DAYS

A young student recites from the first American textbook as Noah Webster, the author, listens to the recitation.

those areas in which the local population has been swelled because of military or other heavy federal activities.

The United States Office of Education, discussed on page 308, collects information on education and its problems and furnishes expert advice to State and local school officials. The National Government also maintains schools in some places, such as on army posts and Indian reservations. And it maintains the Military Academy at West Point, the Naval Academy at Annapolis, and the new Air Force Academy at Colorado Springs.

Still, the providing of education is primarily a State and local function. In most States it is essentially a local function.

Education a Huge Enterprise

Public education is the largest single enterprise the States and their local governments engage in today. Measured in terms of public money spent, it ranks right after national defense in the list of all governmental activities. The States and their local governments now spend approximately $12,000,000,000 a year on education.

Enrollment. Today *nearly one-fourth* of all of our people attend school. There are more than 43,000,000 students enrolled in the nation's public and private schools and colleges. Some ninety per cent of these, or about 38,000,000, attend public schools.

Approximately 31,000,000 children are enrolled in the nation's elementary schools, and over 8,000,000 students now attend high schools. About 3,500,000 go to college.

The school population has been increasing by leaps and bounds in recent years. In 1950 there were only some 30,000,000 students enrolled in all of our schools and colleges. More than 1,350,000 children become of school-age each year! By 1959–1960, the United States Office of Education predicts, total grade and high school enrollments will climb to 46,000,000.

Every State in the Union now has some form of compulsory school attendance law. These laws usually require attendance by all between the ages of six and sixteen.

Teachers. There are now some 1,250,000 public school teachers in the United States. Yet, this number falls far short of those actually needed. The United States Office of Education reports that in the fall of 1957 the nation's schools opened their doors with 135,000 fewer teachers than the *minimum* felt necessary for adequate instruction and supervision.

As the babies grow up —

The increase is felt in grade schools ...

Children in kindergarten and elementary school—

1950	21.4 million
1955	27.1 million
1960	32.3 million
1965	33.7 million

... then in high schools

Children in high school—

1950	6.6 million
1955	7.9 million
1960	9.8 million
1965	12.5 million

... then in college

Enrollment in colleges and professional schools—

1950	2.3 million
1955	2.5 million
1960	3.0 million
1965	3.8 million

... and by draft-age boys

18 to 24-year-olds—

1950	8.0 million
1955	7.6 million
1960	8.3 million
1965	10.3 million

Reprinted from "*U.S. News & World Report*," December 31, 1954. © 1954 United States News Publishing Corporation.

This shortage of teachers is created only in part by the fast-rising school population. The attractions of better salaries and working conditions in other fields has lured many away from the teaching profession.

Schools and Classrooms. There are about 160,000 elementary and 30,000 high schools in the country.[1] How

[1] There are more than 1850 institutions of higher education, too. More than 600 of these are operated by States or cities. See page 629.

much the land and buildings involved are worth can only be guessed at, but $10,000,000,000 is probably a low estimate.

Despite this tremendous investment, we have a critical nation-wide shortage of schools and classrooms that has often been termed a national disgrace. The United States Office of Education reports that sixty per cent of the nation's classrooms are over-crowded and that one of every five pupils attends school in a building that does not meet even minimum fire safety requirements. For lack of adequate classroom space, an estimated 700,000 must attend school in shifts. We need 100,000 new classrooms a year in order to meet the overcrowding problem. The total cost of new construction needed right now is set at at least $6,000,000,000.

Public School Administration

Each State constitution makes the State responsible for the providing of a system of free public schools. Acting under this authority, the State legislature decides by law what particular governmental unit within the State is to be charged with the administration of the schools. The particular unit chosen varies greatly from State to State.

Local Units. Some degree of central control is reserved by law to the State government, but the regulation of school affairs is left chiefly to local units. Four principal local units are now used:

(1) *The town or township system* is common in New England and is also used in Indiana, New Jersey, Pennsylvania, and West Virginia. This system places all the schools within its limits under one authority, usually a small board chosen by the voters.

(2) *The county system* is used especially in the Southeastern States from Maryland to Louisiana and in New Mexico and Utah. Usually there is a county board of education and a county school superintendent to manage all schools within the county. In some places, city schools are included within the county system, but in others they are separate units with their own boards and their own superintendents.

(3) *The district system* is used in over half the States. The districts are often quite small and include a single city or village or rural area. Thousands of these districts are only a few square miles in area and include only a few families. An elected board is usually the governing authority for the school system.

(4) *The consolidated district system* is really a modification of the original district system. In many States these have been created to consolidate (combine) the many rural schools into a few larger centrally located schools. The consolidated district must not be *too* large, however, or else the cost of transportation and

Fitz von Grossmann Architects, Milwaukee

NICOLET HIGH SCHOOL, MILWAUKEE

As the population grows, the old, wooden schoolhouse is becoming overcrowded and inefficient. Modern school buildings like this one are planned for efficiency, comfort, and expansion.

the wear and tear of travel are too great.

The Trend to Larger Units. In the past several years, most States have considered and many have passed school district reorganization laws. The result has been a sharp decrease in the total number of local school units, a gradual shift to fewer and larger units. There were 108,579 districts in 1942 and 67,346 in 1952; there are less than 50,000 today.

State Supervision. Each State has a Superintendent of Public Instruction (sometimes called the Commissioner of Education), and forty-

two of the States also have a State Board of Education.[2]

The State superintendent is chosen by the voters in twenty-six States. In six[3] he is appointed by the governor, and in the other sixteen[4] he is appointed by the State board.

The superintendent, or the board

---

[2] All except Illinois, Maine, North Dakota, Rhode Island, South Dakota, and Wisconsin.

[3] New Jersey, Ohio, Pennsylvania, Rhode Island, Tennessee, and Virginia.

[4] Arkansas, Colorado, Connecticut, Delaware, Idaho, Iowa, Maine, Maryland, Massachusetts, Minnesota, Montana, New Hampshire, New York, Texas, Utah, and Vermont.

Chapter 35. PUBLIC EDUCATION

working through him, supervises the school systems in the State in accordance with the general school laws of the State.

Only one State, Delaware, has thus far reorganized its school system to provide for a single, centralized State-wide unit. There the local school districts exist only as administrative units to carry out the policies of the State Board of Education. (Wilmington and a few other cities do retain local school boards, but they are still subject to the supervision of the State Board.)

In practically all States the current trend is in the direction of more and more State control over the local units. This can be seen especially in such matters as the training, licensing, and examination of teachers, the setting of minimum salary scales for teachers, compulsory school attendance laws, the providing of textbooks, funds, and buildings, and the widening of the list of courses which must be offered.

School Finance

As we noted, public school expenditures now run about $12,000,000,000 a year. This is only a little more than the amount we spend on tobacco and about equals what we spend on liquor each year in the United States.

In colonial days, when education was not generally regarded as a public function, it was supported by the churches and the parents of the few who attended schools. When Massachusetts created the first public school system in 1647, it provided for the taxing of those parents who sent their children to school. As the concept of public schools grew, however, so did the notion of their support through general taxation.

When Ohio was admitted to the Union in 1802, the National Government began the practice of granting lands to the States for the support of education. The States have likewise set aside huge tracts of their own public lands for the same purpose.

As the support of schools through taxation developed, it developed on a local basis. For many years public schools throughout the country were supported almost entirely through the local property tax. Considering the country as a whole, the property tax is still the largest single source for school support.

In the past twenty to thirty years, however, the States have been taking on an increasing share of the burden. Today the States as a whole contribute about $3,000,000,000, or about thirty per cent of the total spent, to their local school systems. In Delaware, with its centralized school system, approximately ninety per cent of all school funds come from the State. Among the other States, the proportion the State provides varies all the way from about sixty per cent to less than twenty per cent.

Each State makes some attempt to distribute its school support funds to

628

the various local districts in a way that will help to equalize the financial burdens of education among the local units.[5]

Higher Education

Nine colleges which still exist were founded under church influence before the Revolutionary War.[6] Altogether there are now more than 1850 colleges, junior colleges, universities, and professional schools. More than 600 of these are public institutions, supported by States or cities.

Forty-five States have established one or more public institutions of higher education. The State University of New York is not one institution, but a unified system consisting of several smaller State-supported schools. Pennsylvania co-operates with three private universities (Temple, Pennsylvania, and Pittsburgh), and New Jersey maintains a similar arrangement with Rutgers.

The National Government makes a grant to each State for the support of *land-grant colleges*.[7] These State Colleges were first provided for by Congress under the Morrill Act of 1862. The States have received a total of 11,000,000 acres for the support of these schools, which specialize in agricultural and mechanical education. (See page 277.)

Junior colleges are increasing throughout the country. There are some 525 of them, including about sixty in California alone. They usually offer the first two years of college work and make it possible for many students to continue their education while remaining at home.

Adult education is becoming more widespread in the United States. Classes in vocational and cultural subjects are being offered for adults by both public and private schools and colleges. Some of these classes are taught in the school buildings at night while others are offered by correspondence. The extension divisions of many State Universities are especially active in adult education, offering courses in a great many subjects in communities across the State. The people who take these courses do so for a variety of reasons — many to gain a high school or college diploma, some to learn a particular skill, and others merely to improve themselves.

---

[5] The various apportionment bases used are: (1) taxes-where-paid, (2) total population, (3) school-age population, (4) average daily attendance, (5) aggregate days attendance, and (6) number of teachers employed. Some States use a combination of two or more of these schemes, and a few leave the whole matter to the discretion of the board of education.

[6] Harvard (1636), William and Mary (1693), Yale (1701), Princeton (1746), King's, now Columbia (1754), University of Pennsylvania (1759, reorganized 1779), Brown (1764), Rutgers (1766), Dartmouth (1769).

[7] Three States (New Jersey, New York,

Vermont) distribute this money to various private colleges within the State.

Proposed Federal Aid to Education

Surveys of the educational systems in the forty-eight States indicate quite clearly that, despite their general calibre, there are a number of areas in this country in which the educational opportunities and the facilities available are far from what they should be. This variation in quality occurs both within each and among the various States.

In large part it is caused by the uneven geographic distribution of wealth: some areas are wealthier and some are poorer than the national average. Obviously, the wealthier an area is, the more it has available to spend on its schools. A number of recent studies show that the income of the total population in relation to the total school enrollment (*i.e.*, the income per pupil) in some States is as much as four to five times as high as it is in some other States.

This uneven distribution of wealth, together with the current shortages in teachers and classrooms, plus the rapid rise in school enrollments, has caused many persons and groups to advocate a vastly expanded program of federal aid to education.[8]

President Eisenhower called the White House Conference on Education in late 1955 to consider the present condition of the nation's schools, their needs, and the steps that should be taken to meet those needs.

Following the Conference's strong recommendations, the President urged Congress in 1956 to enact legislation to provide federal grants-in-aid to help the States to meet their school construction needs.

The legislation was defeated by a fairly close vote in the House of Representatives in 1956. The House rejected the proposal by an even closer vote after the President resubmitted it in 1957. The issue is before the Congress once again.

The chief opposition to new federal aid for education comes from those persons and groups who fear that it will inevitably lead to federal control over the educational systems of the States, and especially over the subject matter to be taught. Some people also argue that there is no need for such aid because, they say, each of the States can afford to do the job without it and will do so once the need and importance of it is realized.

Another barrier to the enactment of aid legislation has arisen because of a dispute among the supporters of federal aid: between, on the one hand,

[8] We have noted several times that in the American federal system the field of public education is one of primary concern to the States and their local governments. At the same time, we have also noted that the National Government does play a significant role in the field through a variety of programs, some of them dating back for a century and more. See, especially, pages 57, 306, and 623–24. In the light of this existing federal participation, it is quite unrealistic to discuss, as some do, the proposals *for the expansion* of federal aid as though they involved a new and radical departure from current practice.

those who feel that it should be given only to *public* schools and, on the other hand, those who argue that it should also be extended to parochial and to other private schools. Still another obstacle to passage comes from another dispute among the supporters of federal aid: over the question of whether such aid should or should not be granted to the school systems in those States which continue to maintain schools segregated on the basis of race.

The opposition is intense and the future of this proposal seems dim at best.

Religion and Education [9]

Separation of Church and State.

The 1st Amendment to the Constitution provides: " Congress shall make no law respecting an establishment of religion, or prohibiting the free exercise thereof." This provision is extended to the States through the 14th Amendment and the various State constitutions.

The prohibition of laws respecting " an establishment of religion " thus creates what is commonly called a " wall of separation between church and state " in the United States. This wall of separation does not, however, as the Supreme Court has said, make religion and the state opposed or indifferent to each other. It means, rather, that neither the States nor the National Government may establish or actively promote any church.

There is a close relationship between education and religion — each is directed toward the betterment of man. This relationship can be illustrated with a brief reference to Thomas Jefferson and Horace Mann. Jefferson was directly responsible for the 1st Amendment, and he had previously written the Statute for Religious Freedom in Virginia by which the Church of England was disestablished, thus separating church and state. However, Jefferson was not disinterested in religion and once compiled the sayings of Christ from the Bible. He thought that they should be taught in every school in the land. This compilation was later published as a congressional document popularly known as *Jefferson's Bible.*

Horace Mann, father of the American public school system, also favored the separation of church and state. Like Jefferson, he too appreciated the value of religion. In judging the value of school systems, he wrote: " Do they cultivate the highest faculties in the nature of childhood — its conscience, its benevolence, a reverence for what is true and sacred? Or are they only developing upon a grander scale the lower instincts and selfish tendencies of the race? "

Supreme Court Rulings.

The direct application of the doctrine of the separation of church and state in education did not come before the

[9] See Chapter 22, " Civil Rights and Liberties."

Court until 1947. A few prior cases had bearing on the problem, but not directly.

In 1925 the Court declared unconstitutional an Oregon law which compelled all children between eight and sixteen to attend *public* schools, thus stopping attendance at private and parochial schools. This, said the Court, was a deprivation of property without due process of law and thus in violation of the 14th Amendment.

In 1930 a Louisiana law authorizing the use of public funds to supply " schoolbooks to the school children of the State," including not only public school children but also private and parochial school children, was upheld. The Court said that " the school children and the State alone are the beneficiaries," and not the schools the children attend.

A case in 1934 involved two students suspended by the University of California because of their refusal to take part in the compulsory ROTC program. They had refused on religious grounds. They claimed that the suspension deprived them of their " liberty " as guaranteed in the 14th Amendment. The Court was not sympathetic to their argument. It held that while their liberty undoubtedly included the right to object to military training on religious grounds, " California has not drafted or called them to attend the University."

In 1947 the Court faced the first clear-cut case involving education and " an establishment of religion." The issue was State aid for a church-supported school. A New Jersey law providing public, tax-provided, school bus transportation for parochial school students was challenged as " an establishment of religion." In a 5-4 decision the Court held that the New Jersey law was not an aid to religion. Rather, the law was held to be a safety measure much like the posting of a policeman at school crosswalks.

The so-called " released-time " programs have been the subject of the latest important church-state-school cases. Released-time programs involve the release of students on school time to attend classes in religious instruction. The classes are taught by private teachers employed by religious groups — not by the State, of course. The student may attend these religious classes or remain in school, as he chooses.

In the first released-time case, in 1948, the Court held invalid the Illinois released-time statute. It was, said the Court, " an establishment of religion " because the public school classrooms were used for the purpose of religious instruction.

In a 1952 case, however, a New York released-time law was upheld on grounds that instruction was held off schoolgrounds and, hence, no school (tax-provided) properties were used for the purpose.

Moral Training Essential. The little red schoolhouse lacked just about every material and academic tool. It often had one thing, though, for which neither money nor degrees can compensate — moral purpose.

Because the Supreme Court has outlawed the conduct of formal religious instruction in public school buildings and because courses in ethics are now seldom given, it becomes doubly imperative that the importance of high moral character be brought home to the student through the teaching of such courses as literature and the social studies.

WHAT THIS CHAPTER IS ABOUT

Because an enlightened citizenry is essential in a democracy, public education is regarded as a proper governmental function everywhere in the United States. It is the largest single function the States and their local governments engage in today.

Nearly one fourth of all our people, 40,000,000, attend school and the school population is increasing by leaps and bounds. We have a critical nation-wide shortage of both teachers and classrooms.

Except in Delaware, school administration is chiefly a local matter. Four principal local units are used for school administration. They are (1) the town or township system, (2) the county system, (3) the district system, and (4) the consolidated district system. The current trend is toward larger units and more State control.

The States now spend some $12,000,-000,000 a year on schools. The largest single source of school revenue is still the local property tax, but States are assuming an increasing share of the burden. Some propose federal aid to education to help the States meet their obligations.

There are now some 1850 institutions of higher education, over 600 of them supported by States or cities.

The wall of separation which the 1st and the 14th Amendments create between church and state prevent any State from directly aiding church-supported schools.

QUESTIONS ON THE TEXT

1. Why is public education essential in a democracy?

2. Where was the first public school in America founded? When?

3. Why is education within the reserved powers of the States? List four ways in which the National Government nonetheless enters the field of public education.

4. What is the total school enrollment today? How many of these are enrolled in public schools?

5. What two critical shortages have we in education today?

6. List the four principal local units of public school administration. Which one is used in your locale?

7. List three examples of the trend toward more State control over local school units.

8. How much do we now spend on public education annually?

9. Why do some favor and some oppose federal aid to education?

10. How many institutions of higher education are there in the United States? How many of these are publicly supported?

11. What is meant by separation of church and state in the United States?

12. Why are education and religion so closely related?

13. May States require children to attend only public schools? Why?

Chapter 35. PUBLIC EDUCATION

14. May States provide textbooks for private and parochial as well as public school students? Why?

15. May a State provide school bus transportation for parochial school students? Why?

16. What is a "released-time" program? Is it constitutional?

PROBLEMS FOR DISCUSSION

1. The Policies Commission of the American Association of School Administrators has recommended the operation of elementary schools on a year-round basis. Schools would be open six days a week, with attendance on Saturdays for extra-classroom activities being optional. Proportionately better pay and a month off for vacations would be provided for teachers. Each school would operate a camp to supplement classroom work, and pupils would be promoted at any time that their teacher found them qualified. By operating the schools three additional months each year the youth would get through sooner and thus make the buildings available for the now-increasing grade-school population. Why do you favor or oppose this recommendation?

2. Henry Adams wrote: "They know enough who know how to learn." The poet Milton: "As good almost kill a man as kill a good book: who kills a man kills a reasonable creature, God's image; but he who destroys a good book kills reason itself." About 300 B.C., Ptolemy I, King of Egypt, wanted to study geometry without first mastering the thirteen parts of Euclid's *Elements*. He asked for a short cut, but Euclid replied, "There is no royal road to geometry." (Often misquoted: "There is no royal road to learn-

ing.") Discuss each of these quotations in turn.

3. In many high schools it is customary for either the class in government or the graduating class to go to Washington to see Congress in session and visit the various departments, the Library of Congress, Mount Vernon, and other places of interest. The cost is usually defrayed by a school entertainment. Could the graduates of several high schools in your county arrange to take this trip together? If they already do, discuss the arrangements.

4. Taxpayers at a recent meeting called to reduce expenses brought up several arguments in support of their wishes to reduce school taxes. One speaker said that the State and local governments are overburdened with school charges. Since education is a matter for those who can afford it, he continued, let everyone take as much schooling as he can pay for in private institutions.

Another taxpayer complained that there are too many fads and frills in the school system. If the schools were to return to the "three R's," he argued, school expenses would be reduced greatly.

What is your attitude toward each of these arguments? If you were the school superintendent, how would you answer the two taxpayers?

THINGS YOU MIGHT DO

1. Invite your principal or other school official to describe local and State-wide school organization and administration to the class.

2. Stage a class forum or debate on the topic: " *Resolved*, That the Congress should appropriate money to the States for the support of public education."

634

3. Prepare a constitution for the government of your school or discuss the one already in force.

4. Is the compulsory education law enforced in your community? If not, by what means do you think it could be enforced? Or, do you think it should be enforced?

WORDS AND PHRASES YOU SHOULD KNOW

Consolidated district system
County system
District system
Horace Mann
Jefferson's Bible
Junior college

Land-grant colleges
Northwest Ordinance of 1787
Parochial schools
Released-time program
Separation of church and state

Superintendent of Public Instruction
Town or township system
United States Office of Education

SELECT BIBLIOGRAPHY

CLARK, NEIL M., " High School Kids Hit the Road," *Saturday Evening Post,* May 14, 1955.

" Education in Crisis," *Current History,* September, 1955, entire issue.

HENDERSON, HARRY, " Why Close Schools in Summer? " *Collier's,* June 22, 1956.

KEATS, JOHN, and BROWN, HERBERT, " Are the Public Schools Doing Their Job? Pro and Con," *Saturday Evening Post,* September 21, 1957.

KIRK, GRAYSON, " Three Additional R's of Education," *Vital Speeches,* August 1, 1954.

KRASTIN, A., " Don't Tell Me Teaching's a Soft Job," *Saturday Evening Post,* May 8, 1954.

LIPPMANN, WALTER, " Shortage in Education," *Atlantic,* May, 1954.

MACKAYE, MILTON, " How to Humanize a Scientist," *Saturday Evening Post,* April 23, 1955.

MORSE, ARTHUR D., " Bay City Beats the Teacher Shortage," *Collier's,* November 11, 1955.

RICKOVER, ADMIRAL H. G., " Let's Stop Wasting Our Greatest Resource," *Saturday Evening Post,* March 2, 1957.

ROGERS, V., " Textbooks Under Fire," *Atlantic,* February, 1955.

SMITH, BEVERLY, " Earl Warren's Greatest Moment," *Saturday Evening Post,* July 24, 1954.

STOWE, LELAND, " What You Need Nowadays to Get Into College," *Reader's Digest,* July, 1957.

SUTHERLAND, A., " Segregation and the Supreme Court," *Atlantic,* July, 1954.

" To All on Equal Terms," *Time,* May 24, 1954.

" When Real Crush Hits Colleges," *U.S. News,* September 23, 1955.

No government demands so much from the citizen as Democracy and none gives back so much.

— *James Bryce*

★

Chapter 36

MAKING DEMOCRACY WORK

On many of the pages in this book we have used the word *democracy*. Indeed, it would be impossible to write or to talk or to think about government in the United States without using the word.

On several of these pages we have had occasion to spell out the nature of democracy in particular respects. In Chapter 2 we gave it a brief definition and contrasted it with dictatorship. At the beginning of Chapter 4 we emphasized two of its most important characteristics: popular sovereignty and limited government. In Chapter 22 we examined the most important area in which our democratic form of government is limited, the area of individual liberties. Again, in Chapters 23, 24, and 25 we dealt with another of the basic features of a democratic system: popular participation in the governing process. There have been a great many other references to democracy as we have gone along.

In this chapter we inquire into the nature of democracy again and attempt to discover at least some of the ways in which we, as citizens in this great democracy, can help to make democracy work.

All too often many of us are inclined to take the existence of our democratic form of government for granted. Too often we forget that others before us established our democracy and passed on to us a working system. Our job is to *keep* that system working and, if possible, improve it. In order to do this we must be sure that we understand its basic meaning.

Democracy Defined. As we said on page 22, a democracy is that form of government in which supreme (sovereign) power rests in the people, in which the people rule.

Democracy is not a modern concept in the sense that it was invented only a generation or two ago. The word itself comes down to us from the Greek *demos*, the people, and *kratos*, rule or authority. The Greek word *demokratía* means, literally, popular rule.

636

Read these words by Thucydides, the Greek historian and philosopher who lived from 471 to 401 B.C. Notice how apt they are for today:

Because in the administration it hath respect not to the few but to the multitude, our form of government is called a democracy. Wherein there is not only an equality amongst all men in point of law for their private controversies, but in election to public offices we consider neither class nor rank, but each man is preferred according to his virtue or to the esteem in which he is held for some special excellence: nor is any one put back even through poverty, because of the obscurity of his person, so long as he can do good service to the commonwealth.

The wording is perhaps unusual by our standards today, but the thought is not by any means.

We are forever indebted to Abraham Lincoln for the immortality he gave to his definition of a democracy in his Gettysburg Address in 1863: " government of the people, by the people, for the people." [1] Nowhere

Bimrose, " The Portland Oregonian "

SO MUCH TO BE THANKFUL FOR

In a land little touched by the disaster of modern war, the ruthlessness of dictators, and the uncertainty of shifting governments, we have reason to stop, to think, and to be thankful.

is there a better, more concise definition of democracy. Notice, though, that it is the *second* of the three phrases that distinguishes a democracy from any other form of government. All governments are *of* the people. Even dictatorships are sometimes *for* the people. But only a democracy is *of, for,* and *by* the people.

Democracy or Republic? Often, we use the word *republic* or the phrase *republican form of government* as a synonym for democracy.

Actually, a democracy may be either a *direct* one or an *indirect* one. A *direct democracy* is one in which

---

[1] It does not detract from Lincoln's greatness one whit to note that others before him had used much the same words. For example, in the famous Webster-Hayne debate in the United States Senate, on January 26, 1830, Daniel Webster described our governmental system as " the people's government, made for the people, made by the people, and answerable to the people." William H. Herndon, Lincoln's friend, law partner, and biographer, visited Boston in 1858 and, while there, heard Theodore Parker's address in the Music Hall on July 4. He carried a copy of Parker's speech back to Springfield. In his *Abraham Lincoln*, vol. 2, p. 65, he notes that Lincoln marked with a pencil these words from Parker's speech: " Democracy is direct self-government, over all the people, by all the people, for all the people."

the will of the people is translated into public policy (law) directly and immediately through mass meetings of the citizenry. Obviously, a direct democracy is practicable only in relatively small communities where it is physically possible for the people to assemble in a given place and where the problems of government are relatively few and simple.

Direct democracy does not exist on a national level anywhere in the world today. However, the old New England town meeting and the *Landsgemeinde* in five of the smaller Swiss cantons are excellent examples of direct democracy in action.[2]

We are most familiar with *indirect* democracy, that is, *representative* democracy. In a representative democracy the will of the people is translated into public policy through a relatively small group of persons chosen to represent the people as a whole. These representatives are responsible for the day-to-day conduct of government and are held accountable to the people, especially through periodic elections.

The words *republic* or *republican form of government* mean the same as indirect or representative democracy. Thus James Madison wrote in *The Federalist*, No. 39, in 1788:

... we may define a republic to be ... a government which derives all its powers directly or indirectly from the great body of the people, and is adminis-

[2] In a limited sense, lawmaking by the initiative petition is also an example of direct democracy.

tered by persons holding their offices during pleasure, for a limited period, or during good behavior.

Regardless of the words which are used to describe it, remember that *above all else* in a democracy any and all authority for governmental action *must* come ultimately from the people. As we have said so often,[3] this concept of the people as the only source for the powers exercised by government is known as the doctrine or principle of *popular sovereignty*.

Recall, too, that popular sovereignty is accompanied in a democracy by the doctrine of *limited government* — the doctrine that government may do *only* those things which the sovereign people have given it the power to do.

Fundamental Equality of All Men. Democracy is based upon the belief that " all men are created equal." This does not mean that all men are physically or mentally equal. Nor does it mean that all men shall share equally in the material things of life. It does mean that all men possess the same rights to " life, liberty, and the pursuit of happiness " without regard to race, color, religion, or economic or social status. It means that no man is privileged over another before the law. It means that each man is free to develop himself to his fullest extent.

Peoples' Capacity for Self-Government. Democracy is based upon the belief that the people as a whole can govern themselves more wisely

[3] See especially page 54.

Unit IX. THE BETTERMENT OF SOCIETY

THE UNITY OF DEMOCRACY

This handshake between Senators William Knowland on the left, leader of the Republican forces, and Lyndon Johnson on the right, Democratic majority leader of the Senate in the 85th Congress, symbolizes the basic unity upon which our democracy is founded.

than can one or a few. When the government is popularly controlled, the rights and interests of individuals are more jealously guarded than they are under a dictatorship. Benevolent despots, who claim to know what is best for the people, do not feel acts of misgovernment as immediately as do the people. When governmental power is held by all of the people, no few can benefit at the expense of the many. This is what Lincoln had in mind when he said: " You can fool all of the people some of the time and some of the people all of the time, but you can't fool all of the people all of the time."

Good Sportsmanship Essential. If a democracy is to be a success, its citizens must have a sense of good sportsmanship. This means that they should be good losers and generous winners.

Adlai Stevenson demonstrated fine sportsmanship in conceding his defeat by Dwight Eisenhower in the 1952 presidential election. The following words are from his concession speech:

The people have rendered their verdict and I gladly accept it. It is traditionally American to fight hard before an election. It is equally traditional to close ranks as soon as the people have spoken. That which unites us as Americans is far greater than that which divides us as political parties. We vote as many but we pray as one. With a united people, with faith in democracy, with common concern for others less fortunate around the globe, we shall move forward with God's guidance toward the time when his children shall grow in freedom and dignity in a world at peace.

Fruits of Democracy Ripen Slowly; Roots Grow Deep. True, our democratic government with its checks and balances cannot act as promptly as twenty-four-hour dictatorships, but it has compensating advantages. The fruits of a democracy ripen slowly and are not spectacular, but their roots grow deep and promote contentment and permanency. A dictatorship goes up like a rocket, but comes down like the stick.

Democracy a Challenge. Our forefathers have given us our democracy — a system of government under which we may govern ourselves through representatives of our own choosing. It is a system which depends upon us — upon us, the people — for its very life. Because it is government by the people, government by us, it can be no better than we, the people, are willing to make it.

Democracy then is a challenge. It is a challenge to *all* of us, not just to " the other fellow," and not just to all of us *some* of the time. If we are to maintain and enjoy and develop our democratic system, we must meet this challenge. We must work to make democracy work, to make democracy live.

Personal Liberty. Our whole concept of democracy rests squarely on a recognition of the dignity and worth of the individual. We believe that " *all* men are created equal." No one man or group of men stands above the rest.

If *all* men are equal and all enjoy the same rights, it is obvious that each man cannot enjoy *absolute* or *complete* freedom. In his actions, each man must take account of the rights of all other men. Each man may do as he pleases only so long as he does not infringe upon the rights of others to do as they please. If each man could do absolutely as he pleased, first chaotic anarchy and, finally, rule by the strong would result. In other words, each man's liberty is relative to the liberty of the whole.

Liberty can be absolute only in a state of complete anarchy. On the other hand, the *control* of liberty can be absolute only in a totalitarian state where all individual liberty has been done away with.

Drawing the line between what an individual may or may not do is an extremely difficult task. Yet, the problem lies at the very core of the meaning of liberty in a democracy. Man desires both authority and freedom. The authority of a government must be adequate to the needs of society, but it must not be such as to restrain the individual beyond the minimum necessary to the general welfare of all.

The true meaning of liberty in a democracy is found in the old saying: " Personal liberty ends where public injury begins."

Obedience and Respect for Law. As citizens of a democracy we enjoy many privileges. We are free to live our lives without unduly harsh and arbitrary restrictions. We may speak our thoughts freely, worship as we please, and hold our property free from the fear of confiscation or invasion.

The liberty we enjoy, however, is a liberty under law. Like any form of government, democracy is dependent upon law and the enforcement of that law for its very life. We pride ourselves on the part we have in the making of the laws under which we live. Are we as ready to accept the responsibilities these laws place upon us? Are we willing to obey the law? And much more significant, are we willing to *respect* the law?

There is a marked difference between obedience to law and respect for law. No goverment can exist unless there is obedience to law. In a dictatorship obedience is usually rooted in the fear of the results of disobedience. In a democracy, however, obedience may be rooted, and much more firmly, in respect for law.

Respect for law is a much deeper thing than obedience to law. It implies an attitude of mind which comprehends the importance and the necessity for law and the relationship of each individual to it. Test yourself. Imagine that you are driving an automobile down a country road. There is no one in sight for miles in any direction when you come upon a stop sign. Would you stop or would you drive on through? Or, imagine a situation in which you find that you can, if you want to, steal $1000 and no one would ever know that you did it. What would you do?

Respect for law acknowledges, too, a responsibility to obey the law whether or not one approves of a particular law. There is perhaps some question as to whether democracy can be as effective as dictatorship in enforcing obedience to law. It should be far more successful in promoting respect for law, however. Out of respect for law grows an obedience far more effective than any slavish compliance imposed at gun-point.

We must work to build respect for law until it becomes a national virtue. If this can be accomplished, the continued success of our democratic system will be assured. Ready compliance with the requirements of the Selective Service Acts in both World War I and World War II and in the Korean war, in sharp contrast to the violent opposition to the draft in the War Between the States, is an encouraging example.

Decisions of the courts, even of the Supreme Court of the United States, do not always command popular approval. In a democracy we have the privilege of choice in the making of laws. No one, however, has a privilege of choice in the obeying of laws once they are made.

President Harding once made our point very well when he said:

Laws, of course, represent restrictions upon *individual* liberty, and in these very restrictions make liberty more secure. For the common good, the individual surrenders something of his privilege to do as he pleases, and so organized society is possible. It is successful just about in proportion as laws are wise, as they represent deliberate and intelligent public opinion, and as they are obeyed. Civilization had to travel a long way before it came to be commonly accepted that even an unwise law ought to be enforced in orderly fashion, because such enforcement would insure its repeal or modification, also in orderly fashion, if that were found desirable.

I do not see how any citizen who cherishes the protection of law in organized society may feel himself secure when he himself is the example of contempt for law. Clearly there is call for awakened conscience and awakened realization of true self-interest on the part of the few who will themselves suffer most when reverence for law is forgotten and passion is expressed in destructive lawlessness. Ours must be a law-abiding republic, and reverence and obedience must spring from the influential and the leaders among men, as well as obedience from the humbler citizen, else the temple will collapse.

Crime a Major Problem. Democracy is clearly dependent in part on the extent to which its citizens obey the law of the land. Yet crime is on the increase in the United States. J. Edgar Hoover, chief of the " G-men," estimates the cost of crime in the United States at about $20,000,-000,000 a year. Our tax bill because of crime amounts to more than $130 a year for every man, woman, and child in the country. We have some 12,000 murders annually, and 600,000 persons are sent to jail each year.

In one recent year, the Federal Bureau of Investigation reported 1,686,-670 major crimes committed in the United States. This means that an average of 4621 major crimes were committed each day during that year. On an average day, 247 persons were killed or assaulted, 150 persons were robbed, 467 cars were stolen, 1034 places were burglarized, and 2679 thefts were committed. Or, to put it another way, the F.B.I. says that a major crime was committed every 18.7 seconds during the year. Over 2,500,-000 major crimes were committed in 1957.

The crime tide has been swelling in the United States since the beginning of this century. And the most discouraging feature is the fact that an increasing per cent of crimes are committed by the young — in many cases mere children.

F.B.I. Director Hoover recently said:

The nation is facing a potential army of 6,000,000 criminals and an ever-increasing wave of lawlessness which is feeding the criminal ranks with a never ending supply of recruits. Our homes and our lives are daily threatened by this vast army. Law enforcement today is facing one of its most gigantic tasks. The army of criminals is ten times greater in number than the students in our colleges and universities. And for every schoolteacher in America, there are more than seven criminals.

Juvenile crime has increased at an alarming rate in recent years. In one recent year alone 115,940 persons below the age of 21 were arrested:

AGE	NUMBER ARRESTED
15 and younger	7,223
16	9,311
17	15,216
18	25,926
19	28,912
20	29,352
	115,940

To list the major causes of crime is a relatively simple matter. They include the following: poverty; broken homes; physical and mental defects; such unhealthy influences as obscene and sordid pulp magazines; the desire for " adventure "; the illegal and indiscriminate sale of narcotics, liquor, and firearms; antiquated laws and lax enforcement; corruption in public office; and all too often the lack of adequate religious, educational, or parental training. Recognizing these causes, however, is only the first step toward their elimination.

In a speech to representatives of the press President Hoover pointed out that the press plays a dominant part in creating the attitude of the individual to the law:

It is almost final in its potency to arouse the interest and consciousness of our people. It can destroy their finer sensibilities or it can invigorate them. If instead of the glamour of romance and heroism which our American imaginative minds too frequently throw around those who break the law, we would invest with a little romance and heroism those thousands of our officers who are endeavoring

Bimrose, " The Portland Oregonian "

THE STORY BEHIND THE HEADLINES

A proper understanding of the background of youthful lawbreakers is one of the first steps in the fight to remedy a frightening situation.

to enforce the law, it would itself decrease crime. Praise and respect for those who properly enforce the laws would help.

Speaking to a Law Enforcement Officers' Conference, President Truman called for local, State, and federal co-operation in the war against crime, and added:

Above all, we must recognize that human misery breeds most of our crime. We must wipe out our slums, improve the health of our citizens, and eliminate the inequalities of opportunities which embitter men and women and turn them toward lawlessness. In the long run these programs represent the greatest of all anti-crime measures.

Organized Crime. The investigations of the special Senate Crime (Kefauver) Committee brought into sharp public focus the widespread existence of organized crime in the United States. The gambling syndicates, organized traffic in narcotics, prostitution, tax evasion, and other organized criminal activities exposed by the Committee could not exist without public indifference and official laxity or complicity.

Many States have created so-called " Little Kefauver Committees," and reform movements have accomplished much in several cities. Crime abhors the light of public scrutiny.

Much remains to be done, however. J. Edgar Hoover has said that organized crime could be eliminated in the United States within forty-eight hours by vigorous law enforcement at the local level. Through perjury, tax-evasion, and deportation proceedings the Federal Government is acting against many criminals who have escaped State action for other illegal activities.

In its report to the Senate, the Kefauver Committee made several recommendations for combatting crime. It proposed giving the Securities and Exchange Commission more authority to expose the infiltration of legitimate business by criminal elements. It proposed placing all wire services transmitting gambling information under the supervision of the Federal Communications Commission.

The Committee favored requiring all who admittedly profit from locally outlawed activities, such as gambling, to file complete financial statements along with their tax returns each year. This would enable the Internal Revenue Service to collect millions in taxes that now go unpaid.

The Committee also favored the creation of a permanent Federal Crime Commission. This body would carry on a continuing investigation of organized criminal activities. It would report directly to Congress and provide information to all national, State, and local law enforcement agencies.

As Senator Estes Kefauver emphasized, this " filth on America's doorstep " can be effectively eliminated only with the active backing of citizens at the local level across the nation.

Informed Citizenry Essential. Democracy in the United States involves more than government by the people through elected representatives. In a very real sense, our democracy is government by public opinion. Indeed, the major task of our elected representatives is the translation of the popular will into public policy.

It is obvious that government by public opinion, democracy, works best when the opinions held by the public are *informed* opinions. And, clearly, it is the duty of every citizen to keep himself informed on public affairs.

Keeping informed may not always be an easy task, but it is an essential one. Corrupt political machines and selfish interests breed on public apathy. Democracy flourishes on citi-

"DON'T MESS WITH IT, MAC. IT'S RUNNIN' SWELL — I GUARANTEE YUH."

GOVERNMENTAL MACHINERY

CITIZEN

CORRUPT POLITICIAN

Courtesy " The American City Magazine "

zen interest and enlightenment. In keeping informed, it is important to distinguish propaganda from fact and partisan argument from objective analysis, even though the propaganda or the partisan argument may happen to support one's own point of view.

Unfortunate though it may seem, there is seldom any clear-cut yes-or-no, black-or-white, right-or-wrong solution to public questions. Usually there are good features to every side of an argument. The proper solution to most public problems lies somewhere between the extremes of argument. And this fact makes it necessary for the conscientious citizen to examine all sides of an issue.

There are a great many sources of

information available. Newspapers, magazines, books, and radio and television commentaries are ready at hand. (Naturally, they should be used with care to insure the closest possible approach to unbiased fact.) And there are many nonpartisan groups formed especially to provide citizens with objective information on public affairs. Among these groups are outstanding organizations like the National League of Women Voters, the Fair Campaign Practices Committee, and the National Municipal League. And there are several local groups, *e.g.:* The Seattle Municipal League, the City Club of Chicago, the Commonwealth Club in San Francisco, and the Citizens Union of New York City.

We surely can agree with the late H. G. Wells: " Before he can vote, he must hear the evidence. Before he can decide he must know. . . . Votes in themselves are useless things."

Active Participation in Public Affairs. Citizenship in a democracy carries with it certain definite and important obligations. Some of these duties are obvious — paying taxes and serving in the nation's defense, for example. Other obligations are not always so clear. In the long run, however, they are just as important because they go to the very heart of the democratic process. We have just discussed one of these less obvious duties, that of keeping informed on public affairs.

Another of these obligations is active participation in public affairs. It does little or no good for a person to keep himself informed only to do nothing with the information. Many people are scornful of politics and politicians. There is a positive point of view, though, to be taken here. Politics, like water, can rise no higher than its source. In the United States that source is the people.

Certainly there have been and are corrupt political machines in some parts of the nation. There has never been, however, a corrupt machine that could succeed in the face of an informed *and an active* citizenry.

How can a citizen participate? In a variety of ways. He can make his influence felt by intelligent voting. He can join and work with groups working for better government. He can participate in public meetings and forum discussions. He can write to his elected representatives and other public servants and call on them in person. He can work with the political party of his choice. He can run for and serve in public office. And each of these suggestions in turn suggests other ways in which the average citizen can make his influence felt — that is, make democracy work. Multiply the one citizen by the many, and you have an extremely potent force for good in American politics.

Under its new city charter, Philadelphia began a unique experiment, which is being tried in some other large cities also. One department in the city government, the Mayor's Office for Information and Complaints, has been established solely for the purpose of answering questions and handling complaints from the city's 2,000,000 residents.

This office is no politician's trick to influence the voter. It handles some 700 problems a day. When it first began operating, it was widely publicized in the city newspapers, and some 400,000 taxpayers received " invitations-to-complain " along with their monthly sewer and water bills.

Questions and complaints are phoned in, mailed in, or brought in in person. All sorts and kinds of problems have been handled promptly. Their variety is interesting and astonishing, covering such items as a complaint that a traffic light was obscured by the branches of a tree; a request for a bit of soil from Independence Square for a soil map of the United States; a complaint that trucks were driving on and breaking sidewalks along a narrow street; a request for advice on where to go with a marital problem; complaints about firetraps, dirty alleys and broken fences, gambling, street brawls, and irregular trash collections. Thus Philadelphia is bringing City Hall closer to the people and giving them a real, down-to-earth opportunity to participate in public affairs.

Several other cities, including Houston, Texas, have now established " gripe offices " similar to Philadelphia's.

The Over-Burdened Voter.

The most obvious way that a citizen can participate directly in public affairs is by going to the ballot box. Hence, except on the score of his ignorance or indifference, we need not shed too many tears for the uninformed nonvoter. As long as he remains uninformed, he is doing a service by staying away from the polls.

The uninformed citizen who *does* vote presents a much more serious problem, however. He is rendering a distinct disservice to himself and to our democracy. He, like the nonvoter, is failing in the performance of one of his duties as a citizen. Still, his ballot counts for just as much as one cast by a conscientious and informed citizen.[4] Making these people

see the error of their ways is an important step toward helping to make democracy work more effectively.

The Long Ballot. Intelligent voting is a " must " in making democracy work. Yet, all too often, even the conscientious citizen finds this a well-nigh impossible task. The task seems impossible because he finds that he must mark a ballot containing so many offices that he cannot even name the candidates, let alone decide intelligently among them.

Woodrow Wilson once pointed to this situation when he said:

[4] As amazing as it may seem, a former governor of Oregon bought space in several newspapers in the State just before a recent election to advise voters to vote " no " on any and all ballot measures on which they were uninformed.

I vote a ticket of some thirty names, I suppose. I never counted them but there must be quite that number. Now I am a slightly busy person, and I have never known anything about half the men I was voting for on the ticket that I voted. I attend diligently, so far as I have light, to my political duties in the borough of Princeton — and yet I have no personal knowledge of one half of the persons I am voting for. I couldn't tell you even what business they are engaged in — and to say in such circumstances that I am taking part in the government of the borough of Princeton is an absurdity. I am not taking part in it at all. I am going through the motions that I am expected to go through by the persons who think that attending primaries and voting at the polls is performing your whole political duty.

The voter can perhaps vote intelligently for President, Congressmen, governor, legislators, mayor, and a few other offices. But when he is asked to decide between candidates for such offices as county coroner, treasurer, surveyor, clerk, animal hides inspector, public weigher, prosecuting attorney, registrar of elections, registrar of deeds, and dog catcher, he is at a loss.

Twenty, forty, even sixty offices are regularly filled at elections in the United States. Is it any wonder, then, that sometimes fictitious characters are elected to office? Or that party machines are able to elect men to office simply because their names happen to be similar to those of prominent people? Or that one city treasurer was recently re-elected even though he had run off with several thousands of dollars in city funds six weeks before the election?

There seems to be no valid reason for the popular election of so many public officials. The number of elective offices probably can be cut down with no harm whatever to the democratic process. Indeed, the end result would seem to be only improvement, for the voter can then become the master of his ballot. As matters now stand, most voters either do not vote for the minor offices or simply vote a straight ticket blindly hoping that the party has put up a good slate of candidates.

A few States, like New Jersey, New York, and Virginia, have come to the rescue of the over-burdened voter. And so have a great many cities, especially those with council-manager government. They have done it by providing for the appointment rather than the election of non-policy making officials.[5] In most State and county elections, however, the ballot is still overloaded with far too many elective offices.

---

[5] They have followed the general rule that policy-making officials should be elected and thus held responsible to the voters for their acts while those who do not *make* but only *execute* policies as determined by elected officials should be appointed. For example, a county registrar of deeds does not make public policy, he simply carries out policies as laid down by State law and the county board. He should be appointed, then, by the county board and be responsible to it for his performance. The county board, in turn, should be responsible to the voters for the actions of the registrar of deeds and all other officers of the county administration.

WHAT THIS CHAPTER IS ABOUT

Democracy is that form of government in which sovereign power rests in the people, in which the people rule. Democracy is not a new concept, but nowhere is there a better, more concise definition than Lincoln's " government of the people, by the people, for the people." It is the second phrase, " by the people," that is especially important.

In American usage, the word " democracy " refers to *indirect* or *representative* rather than *direct* democracy. The word " republic " and the phrase " republican form of government " are for us synonymous with representative democracy.

Democracy is based upon the equality of all. It is based upon the belief that the people can govern themselves much more wisely than can one or a few; and it is based upon the concept of good sportsmanship.

Democracy is a challenge, not to a few, not to " the other fellow," but to all.

The true meaning of personal liberty in a democracy is found in the drawing of a proper balance between license and unbridled authority. Like any other form of government, it can survive only if its citizens obey the law. Respect for law, which is a much deeper thing than mere obedience to law, is the firmest base upon which obedience can rest.

Crime, and increasingly juvenile crime, is one of the most serious internal problems our democracy faces. It needn't be, however. An attack upon the physical causes for crime and an attack upon the human failings which produce crime could solve much of it for us.

An informed public is one of the surest and one of the indispensable requirements of democracy. In order to be truly effective, however, an informed citizenry must also be a participating citizenry. The uninformed and the nonparticipating citizen poses a serious threat to the life of a democracy. Removing the few obstacles to intelligent participation, for example the long ballot, remains one of our serious problems.

QUESTIONS ON THE TEXT

1. What is a democracy?

2. Where did the word originate?

3. What is Lincoln's famous definition of democracy? Why is the second phrase of his definition especially important?

4. Distinguish between *direct* and *indirect* democracy. What is a representative democracy? A republican form of government?

5. What do we mean when we say that democracy is based upon the fundamental equality of all men?

6. Describe the nature of personal liberty in a democracy.

7. How is obedience to law usually secured in a dictatorship?

8. Why is respect for law a deeper thing than obedience to law?

9. What are the major causes for crime in the United States?

10. How, according to J. Edgar Hoover, could organized crime be eliminated in the United States within forty eight hours?

11. Why is an informed citizenry so essential to the success of democracy?

12. How can the average citizen take an active part in public affairs? Why is the doing so one of the most important obligations of citizenship?

13. What is the long ballot? Why is it a serious problem?

1. Comment on this statement by Judge Learned Hand:

" What then is the spirit of liberty? I cannot define it; I can only tell you my own faith. The spirit of liberty is the spirit which is not too sure that it is right; the spirit of liberty is the spirit which seeks to understand the minds of other men and women; the spirit of liberty is the spirit which weighs their interests alongside its own without bias; the spirit of liberty is the spirit of Him, who nearly 2000 years ago, taught mankind that lesson it has never learned, but never quite forgotten: that there may be a kingdom where the least shall be heard and considered side by side with the greatest."

2. President Truman's Committee on Civil Rights puts the argument for freedom as we know it in these words:

" In a free society there is faith in the ability of the people to make sound, rational judgments. But such judgments are possible only where the people have access to all relevant facts and to all prevailing interpretations of the facts. How can such judgments be formed on a sound basis if arguments, viewpoints, or opinions are arbitrarily suppressed? How can the concept of the market place of thought in which truth ultimately prevails retain its validity if the thought of certain individuals is denied the right of circulation? "

How would you apply this statement in the current problems of communism and loyalty?

3. Explain the following quotation from Abraham Lincoln:

" Let every man remember that to violate the law is to tear up the charter of his own and his children's liberty."

4. " The law of loyalty is simpler than the law of gravitation. It is this: We love not those who do most for us, but those for whom we do most. Not gratitude but sacrifice begets loyalty. God never did a better thing for the children of men than when he threw Adam and Eve out of the Garden of Eden and told them to hustle for themselves." — Dr. George Barton Cutten.

Do you agree that loyalty comes from sacrifice rather than from gratitude? Explain your answers.

THINGS YOU MIGHT DO

1. Invite your local judge, district attorney, chief of police, or sheriff to address the class on the subject of the causes and remedies for crime in your area.

2. Write an essay or an editorial on this comment by Bernard Baruch: " Every man has a right to his own opinion, but no man has a right to be wrong on his facts."

3. From the Bluebook or Official Manual of your State or some other source, secure the returns for the various offices in the 1952 and/or 1954 elections in your State. What conclusions can be drawn from the number of people who voted, the number who voted for the various offices, the indications of straight- and split-ticket voting, and so on? What efforts are being made or have been made to shorten the ballot? What elective offices in your State do you think should be made appointive, if any? How does a short ballot help the conscientious voters?

WORDS AND PHRASES YOU SHOULD KNOW

Demos
Democracy
Direct democracy
Indirect democracy
Kefauver Committee
Kratos

League of Women
 Voters
Limited government
National Municipal
 League
Obedience to law

Popular sovereignty
Representative democracy
Republic
Republican form of gov-
 ernment
Respect for law

SELECT BIBLIOGRAPHY

ALEXANDER, RUTH, " Are We Too Soft on Young Criminals? "
 Reader's Digest, October, 1956.

BANNING, MARGARET C., " Let's Stop Maligning American Youth,"
 Reader's Digest, August, 1956.

BLOOM, MURRAY T., " Civic Watchdogs in High Heels," *Reader's
 Digest,* June, 1957.

BRECHER, RUTH and EDWARD, " Why Judges Can't Sleep," *Saturday
 Evening Post,* July 13, 1957.

CLENDENEN, RICHARD, and BEASER, HERBERT W., " The Shame of
 America," *Saturday Evening Post,* January 8, 15, 22, 29, February 5, 1955.

GERTZ, ELMER, " Clarence Darrow, an American Legend," *The Progressive,* May, 1957.

GLUCKERT, EUGENIE, " This Cop Leads a Double Life," *Reader's
 Digest,* December, 1956.

HIGHET, GILBERT, " Man's Unconquerable Mind," *Reader's Digest,*
 August, 1954.

LEIBOWITZ, JUDGE SAMUEL, " Why Law Fails to Stop Teen-Age
 Crime," *U.S. News,* January 14, 1955.

LIPPMANN, WALTER, " The Decline of Western Democracy," *Atlantic,* February, 1955.

——, " The Adversaries of Liberal Democracy," *Atlantic,* March,
 1955.

——, " Our Need for a Public Philosophy," *Atlantic,* April, 1955.

MARTIN, JOHN B., " The Making of a Killer," *Saturday Evening
 Post,* March 26, 1955.

——, " The Town That Reformed," *Saturday Evening Post,* October 1, 1955.

MAULDIN, BILL, " Today's Teen-Agers: ' What Gives? ' " *Collier's,*
 January 21, 1955.

MOSES, ROBERT, " Why I am a Conservative," *Saturday Evening
 Post,* February 11, 1956.

" Our Juvenile Jungles," *Newsweek,* August 19, 1957.

YODER, ROBERT M., " They Get Caught in Their Own Traps," *Saturday Evening Post,* October 15, 1955.

Government is a trust, and the officers of the government are trustees; and both the trust and the trustees are created for the benefit of the people.

— Henry Clay

★

Chapter 37

GOVERNMENT SERVICE AS A CAREER

There are about 7,400,000 civilian government workers in the United States today. The National Government employs some 2,300,000, not counting those in uniform. The States and their local governments employ another 5,100,000 persons. Only a relative handful of these are elected to office. Most of them are appointed.

It is upon the shoulders of these appointees, the " civil servants," that most of the burden of day-to-day government rests. The quality of these employees determines in very large measure the quality of government. No matter how wisely legislators may determine policy, the people cannot benefit unless policy is properly and successfully executed. For, as Woodrow Wilson once noted, the administration of governmental policy is " government in action."

It is obvious, then, that the hiring of qualified men and women for the public service — that is, hiring them on the basis of merit — is among the most important problems government faces. In this chapter we deal mostly with the civil service in the National Government. Capable and qualified public servants, however, are equally important to the success of government at the State and the local levels.

Growth of the National Civil Service

A Good Beginning. As the first President of the United States, George Washington knew that the success or failure of the new government under the Constitution would depend in large measure upon those whom he appointed to office. He declared his policy to be that of appointing to office " such persons alone . . . as shall be the best qualified." He demanded that his appointees be loyal to the Constitution. He held no idea,

652

though, that they be loyal to him personally or even to those who supported him politically.

As political parties developed, Washington's successors began to give weight to political considerations in the making of appointments. John Adams followed Washington's policy rather closely. He insisted on competence, but he did see that none of his political enemies were appointed to office.

When Thomas Jefferson entered the White House in 1801, he found most of the positions in the Government held by men who were his political and personal enemies. Although he agreed in principle with Washington's concept of " fitness for office," he combined it with " political acceptability " and replaced many of the Federalists with his own Democratic-Republicans. Even so, not many offices were involved. When the national capital was moved to the new city of Washington in 1800, there were only about 1000 federal employees all told. The Treasury Department employed sixty-nine persons; War, eighteen; Navy, fifteen; and State and Post Office, nine each.

Jefferson's immediate successors, James Monroe, James Madison, and John Quincy Adams, found little occasion to remove anyone for partisan reasons, though they did require party loyalty as a qualification for appointment.

Andrew Jackson and the Spoils System.

By the latter 1820's the number of federal employees had risen well into the thousands. When Andrew Jackson came to the Presidency in 1829 he dismissed large numbers of office holders and replaced them with his own supporters.

Jackson is often cited as the father of the " spoils system," the practice of giving offices and other favors of government to those who have supported the party.[1] This is not altogether fair. Jefferson had laid its foundations in the National Government in 1801, and it was widely practiced in many of the States and larger cities long before Jackson became President.

Jackson looked upon his appointing policy more as a " democratic " one than as a system for rewarding friends and punishing enemies. In his first message to Congress he explained and defended his program on four grounds. He held that (1) since the duties of public office were essentially simple, any normally intelligent person was capable of holding office, (2) there should be a " rotation in office " in order that a wider number of persons might have the privilege of serving in the Government, (3) long service by any person would promote tyranny and intolerance, and (4) the people are entitled to have the party they had chosen control all of the offices of government from top to bottom.

Whatever Jackson's high purposes and " democratic " concepts may have

[1] The famous words " To the victors belong the spoils of the enemy " were first uttered by William L. Marcy on the floor of the United States Senate in 1832.

been, there were others who saw the spoils system as a means for building and holding power. For the next half-century the spoils system held sway. Every change in administration brought a new round of rewards and punishments and, as governmental activities and agencies increased, so did the value of the spoils.

Able and competent persons were squeezed out of the public service or, more often, refused to " soil their hands " by entering it. Efficiency was mostly an idle dream of a few reformers. Huge profits were made on public contracts at the people's expense. Much of the nation's natural wealth was literally stolen. Political power was centered in the vast horde of officeholders and the many others who owed their livelihood to the party in power.

The Movement for Reform. Congress made feeble attempts to correct matters in 1851 and 1853. It required several thousand clerkships to be filled on the basis of examinations given by department heads. This minor reform produced no significant results, however; nor did an 1871 law which established the first national civil service commission and introduced the idea of *competitive* examinations.

Able men pressed for major reform. Civil service reform was debated in every session of Congress after 1865. Men like William Cullen Bryant and Carl Schurz spoke out for it, and leading journals like *Harper's Weekly* and *The Nation* took up the cry. Groups like the National Civil Service Reform League,[2] which was founded in 1881, fought for it.

It finally took a tragedy to change talk to action. The assassination of President James A. Garfield in 1881 by a disappointed office-seeker roused the nation. Garfield's successor, President Chester A. Arthur, pushed reform measures vigorously, and Congress passed the Civil Service Act in 1883.

The Pendleton Act. The Civil Service Act, better known as the Pendleton Act, established the basic pattern of the national civil service. Its major principles are still in effect today. It created the *United States Civil Service Commission* which is an independent agency under the President. The Commission is composed of three members appointed by the President and Senate, not more than two of whom may be from the same political party.

The act divided the administrative employees of the Government into two groups: (1) those in the *classified* and (2) those in the *unclassified* service. The power to determine under which of these two services most agencies were to operate was given to the President.

Appointment to a position under the classified service was to be made on the basis of merit. Merit was to be determined on the basis of competitive

---

[2] Renamed the National Civil Service League in 1945, this group is one of the most influential organizations promoting the merit system at all levels of government today.

Unit IX. The Betterment of Society

CIVIL SERVICE REFORM

After the Pendleton Act established the civil service, applicants for positions in classified government agencies had to take competitive examinations. In this old picture applicants are being examined in the New York City Custom House.

and " practical " examinations given by the Civil Service Commission. The Commission was required to draw up lists (*registers*) on the basis of examination standings, and appointments were to be made from the registers. The act also directed that, insofar as possible, appointments to the classified service should be made on a geographic basis. The number of employees from a particular State was to correspond approximately to that State's proportion of the total national population. After a six-months' probationary period an employee was to become a permanent member of the civil service and be removable only for cause (" the good of the service ").

Under the act, employees were forbidden to participate actively in politics, and Congressmen and others were forbidden to attempt to influence the Commission in regard to the employment of any person. The act established a system of preference for any honorably discharged war veteran and especially for disabled veterans and the widows of veterans. Finally, the act specifically exempted from its operations any person appointed to office by the President with the consent of the Senate.

Extension of the Classified Service. Originally, the Pendleton Act applied to only about 14,000 of the then 110,000 workers of the National Government. Gradually, the various Presidents have extended the ranks of the classified service.[3]

There were many fits and starts, adding to and removing from the classified service, in the administrations of Presidents Cleveland, Harrison, and McKinley. Theodore Roosevelt, who had headed the Civil Service Commission under Presidents Harrison and Cleveland, was a firm believer in the merit system, however, and had the courage to carry out his convictions. He shifted more than 115,000 positions from the unclassified to the classified service.

Later Presidents have followed T.R.'s example, and today approximately ninety per cent of all federal employees are covered by the merit system.

Congress has had a major hand in extending civil service coverage in recent years, too. In 1939 it required all State and local governments to follow a merit system in all agencies receiving grants-in-aid under the social security system. Many federal grant-in-aid programs now carry this stipulation. Under the Ramspeck Act of 1940 the President was given the authority to place *all* federal employees under the classified service except those in a few agencies such as the Tennessee Valley Authority and the Federal Bureau of Investigation. (TVA and the FBI have their own separate merit systems.)

How Civil Service Operates

The United States Government is the largest single employer in the world, and the problems of the civil service system are immense. Abraham Lincoln once likened his task as personnel appointer to that of a landlord who was so busy showing prospective renters (office-seekers) what was to be had in one wing of the building that he had little time to put out the raging fire (a war) in the other wing.

Lincoln was speaking in a day when there were only some 50,000 government workers all told. Today, the *annual turnover* in federal jobs is ten times that number, or about 500,000. In other words, some 500,000 employees (about twenty per cent of the total) resign their positions or otherwise leave the government service each year.

The Changed Emphasis in Civil Service. The primary goal of those who led the movement for civil service reform was the elimination of the spoils system in the selecting of government personnel. As this goal has come closer and closer to being actual

[3] The term *civil service* is often used quite loosely to mean just the *classified service*. Correctly, the civil service includes *all* government workers except the very few at the topmost level of the administration.

A. Devaney, Inc., N.Y.

THE WORLD'S LARGEST OFFICE BUILDING
Although many of the more than 25,000 workers in the Pentagon
are military personnel, the majority are civil service employees.

fact, the emphasis in civil service has shifted. Today we are not so much concerned with eliminating politics from the selection process; this has been largely accomplished. Today the primary concern is centered in the task of securing the best available and most qualified persons and in improving in other ways the efficiency and standards of service.

Position Classification. An effective government personnel program must be firmly based upon a logical system of *position classification*. That is, it must be based upon a breakdown of the service into related classes or groups of positions. Under this ar-

rangement, all the positions with similar duties and responsibilities are grouped together into a single class. For example, all clerk-typists are put into a single class regardless of the agency in which they work. Their jobs are essentially the same in all government agencies.

Position classification is necessary to the handling of the other basic problems of the personnel system: recruitment, appointment, pay, promotions, retirement, etc. For example, the exact nature of a particular job to be filled must be known in order that the best available person can be sought to fill that job.

Recruitment. Too often the average person thinks of a government worker in terms of file clerks and typists or mailmen, messengers, telephone operators, and janitors. Of course, the Government employs thousands of people for these jobs. The civil service also includes nearly all of the occupations which are found in private life, including doctors, dentists, lawyers, chemists, botanists, biologists, physicists, engineers, economists, sociologists, political scientists, social workers, teachers, skilled mechanics, carpenters, plumbers, electronics technicians, draftsmen, photographers, nurses, psychologists, and so on. Altogether more than 2000 different occupations are included in the civil service.

How does the Government go about the important task of attracting people to its ranks? Announcements of examinations are usually posted in public buildings, especially in post offices. Announcements are also placed in the classified advertisements sections of newspapers and sent to schools and radio and television stations. Until recently, however, most applicants for federal jobs learned of their opportunities more by chance than through any real effort on the part of government. There has been improvement in the past few years, but still more could be done to dramatize available job opportunities.

Application. When a person does learn of an opening which interests him, he must fill out an application form. Forms are available at nearly every post office in the country. Form 57 is the most common one, covering most applicants for federal positions. A simpler form is now used for the lowest range of jobs, and the higher and more skilled ones (e.g., physicist, doctor, lawyer) usually involve additional forms.

Form 57 asks for such data as the applicant's name, age, address, date and place of birth, height, weight, sex, etc. It does not ask the applicant's race or religion. There can be no discrimination in federal employment on these grounds. The form also calls for a list of the jobs the applicant has previously held and the reasons why he left each. It also asks for a list of the organizations to which the applicant has belonged, to weed out anyone who has belonged to any subversive organization.

Examination. If a person's application meets the requirements set for the job he is seeking, he is notified when and where to take an examination. The Civil Service Commission uses two general types of examinations. They are called (1) *the assembled* and (2) *the non-assembled.*

The assembled examination is used for most federal positions. Its name comes from the fact that all of the candidates in a particular area are " assembled " in a given place at a given time for the examination. It is a practical test designed to discover a person's particular qualifications for a particular job. The written questions are usually objective ones: true-false, matching, and multiple-choice.

If the job requires a special skill such as typing, this skill is also tested.

The non-assembled examination is commonly used for the higher positions. The applicant for one of these posts is seldom required to report at any special place. Indeed, he doesn't really take an " examination " at all. Rather, he is ranked on the basis of his training, experience, and accomplishments. He may be asked to write a report or an essay on some topic, thus placing the emphasis on thought and originality.

Entry into the federal service today is regarded as more than the taking of a temporary job. It is looked upon as the beginning of a permanent career with promotion through the ranks to higher posts. In line with this, the whole civil service testing program now lays more stress on general all-round ability than it has ever done before.

The Register. All those who make a passing grade (70 on most examinations) have their names placed on a *register*. The register is a list of persons eligible for appointment to a particular position. Each person is ranked on the register according to merit; the person scoring highest on the examination is ranked first, the second highest is ranked second, and so on.

Appointment. The Civil Service Commission does *not* appoint anyone to a federal job — except the employees of the Commission itself. Appointments are made by the agency in which there is a vacancy.

In the past the Civil Service Commission maintained centralized registers for the entire range of government positions covered by the merit system. This led to a good deal of confusion and delay, however. For example, the names of the top persons on a particular register might be under consideration in several agencies at once. Today separate registers are kept for many agencies. Only the more common positions, such as clerk and stenographer, are now kept on central registers. An appointment must be made from among the three highest persons on the appropriate register.

Veterans' preference in civil service appointments dates from the original Pendleton Act. An automatic five extra points on an examination are given to any honorably discharged veteran. A total of ten points is added to the score of a disabled veteran, the wife of a disabled veteran unable to work, or the unremarried widow of a veteran. Some federal jobs, such as messengers and guards, are reserved especially for veterans.

Well over half of all federal jobs are now held by those with veterans' preference. Nearly all State and local civil service systems also give preference to veterans in appointments.

The granting of this privilege to those who have served their country can be easily justified. Notice, however, that it is a slight departure from the principle of appointment on the basis of individual merit.

Geographical distribution in the making of appointments also complicates the process somewhat. Ever since the Pendleton Act, the number of persons in the civil service from any State is supposed to bear a close relation to that State's share of the total national population. Thus, if a State has six per cent of our total population, approximately six per cent of the total number of federal workers must come from that State. This geographic barrier often complicates the appointing process and hardly promotes the hiring of workers on the basis of merit alone.

Probation. After his appointment, the civil servant must serve a period of probation (trial period) up to six months. If by the end of this period the employee is found suitable, his appointment becomes permanent. If his superiors find him unsuitable, he may be dropped.

Temporary appointments may be made without examination for the filling of short-term jobs. In periods of national emergency, government employment usually rises quite rapidly. Temporary appointments are often made to meet the sudden demand for workers.

Compensation. In the lower grades of the civil service the pay scales compare rather well with those paid in private life. The same cannot be said for the higher grades, however.

There are two main compensation schedules in use today.[4] One is the so-called Crafts, Protective, and Cus-

todial Schedule. It is divided into ten basic grades. The starting salaries range from $1945 a year for a person in the grade CPC–1 to a starting salary of $5715 in the CPC–10 grade. Within each grade there are a series of increases which may be had on the basis of length of service and demonstrated ability.

The other salary schedule is known as the General Schedule. It covers the responsible positions and those which require more education and general background. The beginning salaries range from GS–1 at $2690 a year to GS–18 at $14,800 a year. In all except the GS–18 grade, salary increases within the grade are available.

An employee does not necessarily start his government career at the very bottom of one or the other schedule. Remember that under the position classification scheme each job is classed according to its nature, including classification for pay purposes. Thus a particular job which involves some little training and responsibility might be ranked as GS–9. A person appointed to that job would then begin at a salary of $5440 a year.

The present salary schedules were set by Congress in 1955, providing for sizeable increases. Many argue the general level is still too low.

Government can never hope to compete with private industry on a dollar-for-dollar basis in the upper grades. For example, an agency head who is paid $14,800 a year might well be able to make $20,000 or $25,000 or more outside of government. How to at-

---

[4] There are separate pay schedules for a few groups of federal employees, especially postal workers and foreign service personnel.

Unit IX. The Betterment of Society

tract and keep the better people for the higher jobs is a major headache in the civil service system.

Other Compensation. Nearly all federal employees work a forty-hour, five-day week. They are paid extra for overtime or are allowed to make up for overtime work with time off when the workload is lighter.

Each federal worker is allowed twenty six days a year for vacation purposes. If he cares to do so, he may accumulate his vacation leave up to a total of sixty days. Of course, he does not have to work on such national holidays as Christmas, Thanksgiving, and the Fourth of July. The Government also has a rather generous sick-leave plan for its employees. They are allowed one-and-a-half days a month for this, and sick leave may be accumulated to a total of ninety days. Then, too, there is a pension system to which both the government employee and the Government make contributions.

Promotion. The question of promotion is an extremely important one to the civil service worker. If he knows that his chances for promotion are good, his morale and efficiency are likely to be much higher than if he knows that they are not.

As we know, there is an opportunity for promotion within each salary grade. These promotions are made largely on the basis of seniority (length of service). Every employee is also rated on the basis of efficiency by his superior, and merit does play a part in these promotions.

Merit plays its biggest part, however, in the promotion from one job to a higher one. When there is a vacancy in a higher position, it naturally goes to the person who has best demonstrated his abilities.

The ambitious and hard-working person who makes government his career can expect promotion because, remember, merit is the underlying theme of the classified service.

Government Employees and Unions

As we shall see in the next chapter, private employers are required by law to allow their workers to join unions and bargain collectively if they choose to do so. Logically, the Government must and does grant the same rights to its own employees.

The first union of government employees, the National Association of Letter Carriers, was formed as early as 1889, but its activities were severely restricted by executive order.

In 1912 Congress specifically permitted unions of federal employees and since then many such groups have sprung up.

The early government unions were *craft* unions. That is, they were organized on the basis of particular kinds of jobs; for example, the National Association of Letter Carriers or the Railway Mail Association. In addition to postal employees, most of the other craft workers also, such as carpenters, electricians, and plumbers, in the National Government are unionized today.

In the last several years a number of *industrial* unions (those of broader scope) have also developed. Today the National Federation of Federal Employees (an independent union), the American Federation of Government Employees (AFL), and the United Federal Workers (CIO) all claim sizable membership. The several postal workers' unions still contain the largest number of organized federal workers.

These unions of federal workers exist for the same reasons unions exist in private industry. Their major purpose is to promote the interests of their members. They cannot bargain quite as effectively as private unions may, however, because wages, hours, and working conditions in government are set by Congress. Thus these unions must spend much of their time in lobbying activity in order to promote their interests.

The most important difference between the public employee unions and private unions arises in the right to strike. The Taft-Hartley Act of 1947 specifically prohibits strikes by government workers.[5] The national health and safety must be protected against sudden walkouts. Another important difference arises in the fact that no government employee may be forced to join a union in order to get a job or to retain one. In other words, both the *closed shop* and the *union shop* are prohibited in the federal service.

The Problem of Loyalty

Throughout our history the American people have had the right to expect and demand that each and every public employee be loyal to the United States. The threat we face from international communism has made the whole matter of loyalty more urgent in recent years than ever before.

A "loyalty-review program" was begun by President Truman in 1947. It was drastically revised by President Eisenhower in 1953 and is now a "security-risk system." No one may be employed by the National Government unless such employment is "clearly consistent with the interests of national security."

All employees or applicants for federal jobs are screened to prevent subversion and infiltration. When a sensitive position (one vital to the nation's security, as in the State Department) is involved or when "derogatory information" is turned up, the FBI makes a thorough "field investigation" of the person concerned. Less elaborate investigations of prospective employees are made by the agency involved or by the Civil Service Commission.

---

[5] Before 1947 federal workers who went on strike could be prosecuted for such acts as obstructing the mails or conspiring against the government.

662

A person may be judged a " security risk " on several grounds. Membership in or sympathy with the communist party, communist front groups, or other totalitarian organizations makes one a " security risk " under the Eisenhower program. So does close association with known or suspected communists. Drunkards, sex deviates, anyone who is for any reason subject to blackmail or any other pressures, and a host of other persons with defects in their backgrounds cannot be hired or remain in the government service.

Before an employee may be dismissed, the charges against him must be stated in writing. He may demand a hearing before a security board, but the witnesses against him need not appear at his hearing nor may they be cross-examined by the accused. Indeed, they may be wholly anonymous. In all cases, the final decision is in the hands of the head of the agency involved.

The whole loyalty-security program is the subject of intense controversy. At one extreme are those who insist upon an exaggerated standard of loyalty, too often one in accord with their own peculiar definition. At the other extreme are those who insist that the danger we face has been grossly exaggerated for political reasons. In between are the great number of people who are genuinely concerned about the problem and seek an adequate program that will protect the government and at the same time protect the civil rights of federal employees.

WHAT THIS CHAPTER IS ABOUT

Some 7,000,000 civilians work for governments in the United States. Most of them are appointed, not elected, and the day-to-day operation of government is largely in their hands. Some 2,300,000 of these civil servants are employed by the National Government.

George Washington inaugurated " fitness for office " as a qualification for federal employment, but in later administrations " political acceptability " became a qualification, too. Andrew Jackson brought the full-blown " spoils system " to the National Government. Although he conceived it as " democratic," others saw it as a means of power. The spoils system reigned supreme until the assassination of President Garfield in 1881 brought about the passage of the Pendle-

ton Act (1883). This law is still the basis of our civil service merit system.

The Pendleton Act created the United States Civil Service Commission and divided federal employees into two groups: the classified service and the unclassified service. The President determines into which of these two most agencies fall. Today about ninety per cent of all federal employees are within the classified service (covered by the merit system).

Whereas the original emphasis in civil service reform was on eliminating the spoils system, today it is on the securing of the best possible employees. The civil service is based upon position classification. Recruitment for the wide range of federal jobs has not been as effective as it could be, though there has been some improvement within recent years. An applicant for a civil service job takes either an assembled or a non-assembled examination given by the Commission. If he passes, his name is placed on a register from which appointments are made. Veterans' preference and geographic distribution are required in appointments. Appointees serve a brief probationary period before becoming a part of the permanent civil service.

Compensation is based upon the particular grade (GS or CPC) that one's job falls into. The lower grades are relatively well paid, but the Government cannot hope to compete with private industry for the services of top administrators. Overtime, vacation, sick leave, and retirement are also provided for. Promotion comes on the basis of seniority and because of merit.

There are several government-employee unions, but a federal worker may not strike, nor be forced to join a union.

The threat of international communism has made the whole matter of the loyalty of public employees more vital now than ever before in our history.

QUESTIONS ON THE TEXT

1. Approximately how many persons are employed by all governments in the United States? How many are employed by the National Government?

2. What was George Washington's standard for appointment? How did John Adams and especially Thomas Jefferson modify it?

3. What is the " spoils system "? On what four grounds did Andrew Jackson justify it?

4. Why is it not altogether fair to call Jackson the father of the spoils system?

5. What event finally prompted the passage of the Pendleton Act of 1883?

6. Distinguish between the *classified* and the *unclassified* service within the civil service system.

7. Approximately how many federal workers are now covered by the merit system? Who has the power to determine which jobs are in the classified service?

8. Explain the Ramspeck Act of 1940.

9. What was the original goal in civil service reform? To what has the emphasis shifted today?

10. What is meant by *position classification?* Why is it important?

11. Distinguish between the two general types of examinations given by the Civil Service Commission.

12. What is a *register?*

13. Does the Civil Service Commission appoint federal employees?

14. What types of preference are allowed to veterans?

15. What are the two main compensation schedules in the National Government called?

16. On what two bases are promotions in the classified service made?

17. May government employees join unions? May they strike?

18. Why is the loyalty of federal workers more important today than ever before?

PROBLEMS FOR DISCUSSION

1. Do you think that federal workers should be hired because of particular practical skills or because of their broad general background? Would your an-

Unit IX. The Betterment of Society

swer depend upon the particular job for which a person was being hired?

2. In what ways might government make a civil service career more attractive to young people?

3. Do you believe that civil service employees who are not engaged in some work vital to the nation's health or defense should be permitted to strike against the government?

THINGS YOU MIGHT DO

1. Various students in the class might make a survey to discover how many federal employees work in and around your own community.

2. Discover whether or not your city has a civil service system for its employees. If so, what are its major features? If not, do you think that it should?

3. From various periodicals, class reports might be prepared on the loyalty-security program of the National Government. (*The Guide to Periodical Literature* would be most useful.)

WORDS AND PHRASES YOU SHOULD KNOW

Accumulate	Non-assembled	Security risk
Assembled examination	examination	Seniority
Civil service	Pendleton Act	Spoils system
Classified service	Position classification	Unclassified service
Crafts, Protective, and	Probation	United States Civil
Custodial Schedule	Ramspeck Act	Service Commission
General Schedule	Recruitment	Veterans' preference
Merit	Registers	

SELECT BIBLIOGRAPHY

BURNS, JAMES M., and PELTASON, JACK, *Government of the People,* Chapters 18, 27. Prentice-Hall, 1957.

CARR, ROBERT K., and others, *American Democracy in Theory and Practice,* Chapter 25. Rinehart, 1955.

" Hoover Commission: How to Keep Good Men in Government Jobs," *U.S. News,* February 18, 1955.

KNEBEL, FLETCHER, " Bureaucrats Are People," *Look,* May 14, 1957.

RANDALL, CLARENCE, " A Good Word for Washington: A Businessman Finds Cheering Surprises in Government Work," *Life,* April 4, 1955.

U.S. Civil Service Commission, *Role of the Civil Service Commission in Federal Employment.* 1955.

———, *The Way to a Job in Government.* 1954.

" What Top Men in Government Get Now," *U.S. News,* August 3, 1956.

" Why Businessmen Resist Jobs with Government," *U.S. News,* August 9, 1957.

Every citizen wants to give full expression to his God-given talents and abilities and to have the recognition and respect accorded under our great traditions. Americans want a good material standard of living — not simply to accumulate possessions, but to fulfill a legitimate aspiration for an environment in which their families may live meaningful and happy lives. Our people are committed, therefore, to the creation and preservation of opportunity for every citizen, opportunity to lead a more rewarding life. They are equally committed to the alleviation of misfortune and distress among their fellow citizens.

— Dwight D. Eisenhower

★

Chapter 38

SOCIAL LEGISLATION

A number of important factors have combined to make the United States the greatest nation on earth. Certainly, one of the most important of these is our democratic form of government. Another is our private-enterprise economic system. The fact that our country is blessed with tremendous natural wealth is very important to our position, too.

The American people have been and are the most important factor in our greatness. And the people are our major asset.

In other sections of this book, especially in Chapter 17, we have dealt with various ways in which govern-

ment acts to promote the general welfare, the general well-being, of the people. In this chapter we consider three particular areas in which government so acts: health, housing, and labor.

As you read bear these two thoughts in mind: (1) Any governmental program, to be truly successful, cannot be intended to benefit or pamper the few; it must be directed toward the benefit of society as a whole. (2) In each of these three fields — health, housing, and labor — there is extensive room for debate, and many of our most heated domestic disputes arise in them.

Conservation of Health

The general health of the American people has improved steadily over the past fifty years or so. Where white

male children in 1900 could expect to live, on the average, forty-eight years, those born today have an av-

666

MALARIA CONTROL

Constant attention to public health problems by federal, State, and local agencies is effectively helping to eliminate health hazards and lengthen life.

erage life expectancy of over sixty-eight years. The infant death rate now stands at an all-time low in the United States. The rate now stands at about twenty-nine deaths under one year of age for every 1000 live births.

This marked improvement in the nation's health can be seen in other statistics. In 1900 some three million people, 4.1 per cent of the total population, were over sixty-five years of age. By 1958, over fourteen million people, 8.4 per cent of the total population, were over sixty-five.

Tremendous strides in medical and scientific research have been and are constantly being made. The once-great killers, like typhoid fever, scarlet fever, and smallpox, are now largely conquered. The new " wonder drugs " and new methods of treating and preventing diseases have done much to lengthen the life span. The fact that scientists are now able to nurture human skin in a bottle is just one indication of the amazing advances that have been made in medical research.

But, while the nation's health is

steadily improving, it is quite obvious that much still remains to be done. During World War II about five million men were rejected for selective service because of physical or mental defects, and nearly one out of every three is being rejected today.

Approximately 1,500,000 persons die in the United States each year.[1] According to federal health authorities, 325,000 of these deaths could be prevented each year through the medical knowledge and skill we now possess. Sickness and accidents take a terrific economic toll. Today it is estimated that the nation loses 4,300,-000 man-years of work each year through bad health and $27,000,000,-000 in national wealth annually because of sickness and partial or total disability.

Two Serious Problems. Scientific progress has made available new drugs and advanced techniques which have sharply reduced the number of cases and the severity of many illnesses. Still many cases of preventable or curable diseases go unattended. Why? The individual, through indifference, negligence or ignorance may be partly responsible. There are some reasons beyond the individual's control. These include in addition to possible financial limitations, such factors as:

Shortage of Medical Personnel. There is a very serious shortage of doctors, nurses, dentists and other

---

[1] There are now more than 4,000,000 live births registered each year.

trained personnel. There was one doctor for every 636 persons in 1900. Today the ratio is one for every 750. It is estimated that we shall need 254,000 doctors by 1960; yet, as matters now stand, we shall have only 212,000. Today we have only eighty per cent of the number of doctors needed.

The problem is further complicated by the fact that the nation's doctors are not evenly distributed. For example, New York has one doctor for every 500 persons, but Mississippi has only one for every 1500. Doctors, like anyone else, prefer to settle in the wealthier and more comfortable areas. As a result, there is a marked shortage of doctors in the poorer and in the rural areas.

Because of the general population increase (and especially the increased number of older persons), the demands of the armed forces and other governmental agencies, and the increase in the number of families who can now afford at least some medical care, the shortage of doctors and other trained medical personnel is alarming. More doctors must be trained, and they must be persuaded to practice in the rural and the poorer areas.

Several possible solutions have been advanced. The medical schools (both State and private) might well be expanded, and many are expanding. Many suggest a government scholarship program for medical students who agree to practice for a certain number of years in areas where doctors are urgently needed. It has also been suggested that medical students' expenses could be met through loans, either by the State or National Government or privately, to be repaid on a long-term installment basis. Some form of health insurance would go a long way toward solving the problems of the number and the distribution of doctors, too.

Shortage of Hospitals. About 1000 of the counties in the United States possess no adequate hospital facilities. There is a severe shortage of general, mental, and tuberculosis hospitals that meet approved standards. Many of our hospitals are overcrowded as well as understaffed. As with doctors, hospitals are generally concentrated in the higher-income sections of the country.

To help meet this problem, Congress passed the Hill-Burton (Hospital Survey and Construction) Act in 1946. It established a grant-in-aid system for the construction and expansion of hospitals and public health facilities. Under this law the National Government puts up one dollar for every two from the State. In many communities the necessary State money has been raised through private fund campaigns. By 1958 over 2000 projects, costing over $1,000,-000,000, were under way or had been completed. This program has furnished a wonderful example of what people, acting locally, can do to solve civic problems.

Mental Diseases. About a half million persons are now patients in State-operated mental hospitals. Un-told thousands more suffer from mental disorders. Mental and nervous diseases are the largest single reason for selective service rejections and by far the most important cause for medical discharges from the armed forces.

Every State maintains at least one mental hospital. But many of these mental institutions are aptly described as " snake pits." Overcrowded and understaffed, they too often treat their patients as prisoners. Inadequate and even cruel treatment and neglect are not uncommon. The rate of recovery in many of these hospitals is little higher than it was fifty years ago.

These revolting conditions were brought to light all over the country a few years ago. The resulting wave of public indignation forced much-needed reforms. Here again, much remains to be done.

Prevention of Disease. When people believed that disease was a " humor " in the blood, they waited until the malady appeared and cured it with medicines — or at least tried to cure it. Now that we know most of our prevalent diseases to be caused by bacilli (germs), we know it is possible to prevent them if the bacilli are kept from our systems.

For instance, if the parasites causing the hookworm disease had been understood in the United States before Doctor Stiles of the United States Public Health Service identified them in 1902, and not allowed to spread, the millions of victims of the disease would have escaped. Fortunately this disease can now be easily prevented or

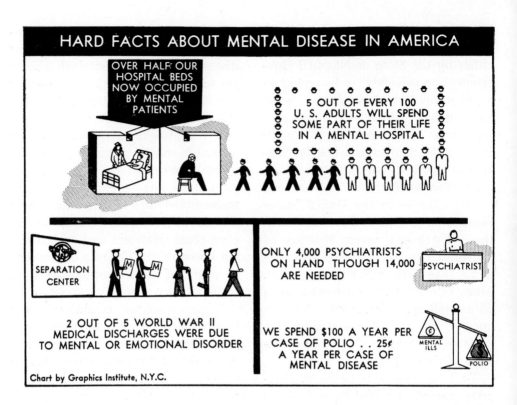

HARD FACTS ABOUT MENTAL DISEASE IN AMERICA

OVER HALF OUR HOSPITAL BEDS NOW OCCUPIED BY MENTAL PATIENTS

5 OUT OF EVERY 100 U. S. ADULTS WILL SPEND SOME PART OF THEIR LIFE IN A MENTAL HOSPITAL

SEPARATION CENTER

ONLY 4,000 PSYCHIATRISTS ON HAND THOUGH 14,000 ARE NEEDED

PSYCHIATRIST

2 OUT OF 5 WORLD WAR II MEDICAL DISCHARGES WERE DUE TO MENTAL OR EMOTIONAL DISORDER

WE SPEND $100 A YEAR PER CASE OF POLIO . . 25¢ A YEAR PER CASE OF MENTAL DISEASE

MENTAL ILLS

POLIO

Chart by Graphics Institute, N.Y.C.

cured, and State and county health boards are co-operating with public schools to eradicate it. Again, if we have the water and milk supply free from typhoid bacilli, and screen against the flies which carry these germs, we are not likely to contract typhoid fever. Individuals living in cities, especially, cannot know whether the water and milk supplies are pure or whether the hotels are sanitary. So States and cities must have officers to inspect the milk supply, water supply, food supplies, hotels, and restaurants.

While the major purpose of private medicine is the treatment and cure of diseases, the major purpose of public health officers and agencies is the pre-

vention and eradication of diseases and their causes. Generally, the States and local governments have restricted their public health activities to disease prevention, to research, and to public information. They have entered the field of direct treatment only where epidemics are threatened or where prevention is possible only on a large-scale basis, as, for example, in combatting tuberculosis.

Today, States and cities maintain laboratories for the examination of water, milk, and other foods; they conduct annual examinations of school children and even of adults; they regulate vaccination; they inspect meat shops, soda fountains, hotels, tenements, factories, and the premises of

670

residences; they disinfect places where contagious diseases have existed; and they maintain health stations, hospitals, pesthouses, sanatoriums for consumptives, and recreation grounds for all persons.

Citizens were at one time slow to realize that it is cheaper to pay taxes for the prevention of disease than to pay doctors' bills and hospital bills for their care. National, State, and local governments are co-operating in public health work today. More than $70,000,000 in federal grants-in-aid go to State and local health agencies each year. And everyone agrees that this amount is still far below what is badly needed.

Health Insurance Programs. The United States Public Health Service reports that on any winter day there are six million people in the United States who are kept away from school or work by illness. It has found that there is almost twice as much illness among families with less than $2000 a year income as among families with more than $6000 income. Illness usually strikes those least able to afford adequate medical care.

Public clinics and hospitals are supported by all of the larger cities or counties. Along with many church hospitals, these are maintained especially for the poor and underprivileged. The cost of care in private hospitals is necessarily high and can be best afforded only by those in the upper income groups. When a prolonged illness strikes a member of a

lower-middle income family the financial pinch is often extreme.

Today many doctors, public officials, and interested private groups are seeking a fair method to provide adequate medical care to all on the basis of need. There has been an increasing demand for some form of group medicine or health insurance.

The Group Clinic Plan. Under this plan the clinical staff is composed of several physicians on a full-time basis. Subscribers pay a small monthly fee. The Stowe-Lipsett Clinic in Oakland, California, is an example of this type. It provides its subscribers with hospitalization for forty-five days, with physicians' and surgeons' services, a clinical psychologist, X-ray and laboratory tests, and ambulance service. Subscribers' dependents pay reduced rates for services if they are not themselves members.

The Closed-Staff Plan. In this plan all the subscribers living within a certain area are treated by one physician. The Transport Workers Union of New York City operates a plan of this sort. The city is divided into districts. Within each district there is a general practitioner treating union members who live in his district besides maintaining his own private practice. The union pays the doctor a salary. Specialists, druggists, and opticians are also available within the plan.

The Free-Clinic, Private Practice Plan. The subscriber to this plan may choose his doctor from a large panel of doctors who have agreed to participate in the plan. Doctors are paid according to the type and amount of services rendered, and they retain their private practices. Under this plan, as in the two above, the subscriber makes a small monthly payment. The various medical societies favor this plan, if any.

The Blue Cross Hospital Plan. Blue Cross is by far the most popular of all the forms of voluntary health insurance. The American Hospital Association passes on all organizations wishing to use the name Blue Cross. Associated Hospital Service of Philadelphia illustrates the general pattern. It is a nonprofit corporation under the supervision of the State Insurance Department. The governing board is composed of an equal number of representatives of the hospitals, the medical society, and the general public. The subscribers pay a small fee, and the Hospital Service pays the hospitals within the plan a flat rate per day which covers bed and board for a limited number of days. Special hospital services are covered similarly.

Many insurance companies operate prepaid health and accident insurance programs.

State Medicine. In recent years many citizens have proposed some form of compulsory national health insurance. The major proposal was made by President Truman. Under his plan, insured persons and their families would receive medical care from doctors of their own choice. The costs would be paid from a fund raised through a special tax on payrolls and on the income of the self-employed.

Great Britain has had a similar program since 1948. There the National Health Service Program provides " free " medical care " from the cradle to the grave."

Our Veterans Administration is an outstanding example of state medicine.[2] The VA employs some 15,000 doctors and dentists and provides free medical care to all the more than 20,000,000 veterans if they (1) have service connected disabilities or (2) cannot afford to pay for private treatment (liberally interpreted).

President Eisenhower has proposed a modified health insurance program. His plan is often referred to as the " federal health *reinsurance* plan." Under it, private health insurance programs would be encouraged to widen their coverage through charging lower premiums and offering greater benefits. The National Government would underwrite (insure) these groups against any losses involved.

Those who favor some plan of state medicine argue:

1. Almost a third of those examined for military service in World War II were rejected because of physical disabilities.

2. On any winter day there are six million people kept away from school or work by illness.

---

[2] See also the discussion of the activities of the United States Public Health Service, pages 312–314.

3. The nation is short of doctors and nurses and hospital facilities. Many rural areas have no medical facilities other than the family medicine chest.

4. Many people cannot afford the high cost of medical services today. Their health, and the nation's health in the event of contagious diseases, is endangered.

Those who oppose any plan of state medicine argue:

1. It would destroy medical free enterprise, and therefore the incentive to maximum efficiency of doctors would be lost.

2. Political bureaucrats probably would administer such a system.

3. It would standardize medical service at a low level.

4. With free care those with imaginary ailments would pester the doctor.

While a great many people favor some form of Government health insurance program, many others are opposed to any such arrangement. The evidence of the need for more and better medical care is overwhelming. Most of the disagreement centers about the *proper method* to be used in meeting the need.

It remains to be seen whether the solution finally takes the form of a compulsory or a voluntary insurance plan, or is governmentally or privately administered. No matter what decision is reached we must take care to see that individual initiative within the medical profession is preserved. Individual initiative is the mainspring

of progress in our civilization, and, in this, the medical profession is no exception.

Liquor. Liquor, and especially the excessive use of it, has been condemned throughout history. The ancient Mosaic Law provided that a glutton and a drunkard should be stoned to death. Shakespeare wrote:

Oh God, that men should put an enemy in their mouths to steal away their brains!

Abraham Lincoln said:

Liquor might have defenders, but no defense. Whether or not the world would be vastly benefited by a total and final banishment from it of all intoxicating drinks, seems to me not an open question.

Dr. Charles Mayo, the noted physician and surgeon, said:

You can get along with a wooden leg, but you can't get along with a wooden head. The physical value of a man is not so much. Man as analyzed in our laboratories is worth about ninety-eight cents.[3] Seven bars of soap, lime enough to whitewash a chicken coop, phosphorus enough to cover the heads of a thousand matches, is not very much, you see. It is the brain that counts, but in order that your brain may be kept clear you must keep your body fit and well. That cannot be done if one drinks liquor.

Liquor Regulation. Since the repeal of the 18th Amendment, which had provided for nation-wide prohibition, the sale and use of liquor has been regulated by the States. The 21st Amendment provides:

---

[3] Dr. Mayo's figure is based on pre-World War II prices.

The transportation or importation into any State, Territory, or possession of the United States for delivery or use therein of intoxicating liquors, in violation of the laws thereof, is hereby prohibited.

The National Government has done little to enforce this constitutional provision. It does make it legal, however, for States to enforce prohibition laws by excluding liquor from outside sources.

One of the major problems the States face in liquor regulation arises from the fact that outright prohibition or too-drastic restriction tends to encourage illegal use.

Liquor laws vary considerably from State to State. Mississippi and Oklahoma have State-wide prohibition. Most of the other States permit cities or counties to vote themselves dry (*local option*).

In seventeen States liquor may be sold in its original package only by State-operated stores.[4] In some of these, the States sell to bars as well as to private persons. In the other States, liquor may be sold by private persons licensed by the State.

Altogether, liquor is legally sold in nearly half a million licensed places in the United States, and we spend more on it each year than we do on public education.

Public Housing

Low-Rent Housing a Government Problem. When mechanical inventions and immigration flooded our cities with laborers from the farm or from European cities, investors built solid blocks of houses to rent to them. Profit was the main thing. Open-air spaces, sanitary plumbing, and conveniences were neglected. These slums breed disease, immorality, and crime. How slums encourage crime is illustrated by the following extract from a pamphlet called " Crime," published by the University of Chicago Press:

Slum conditions of themselves might not create grumbling and dissatisfaction if the slum families had no means of knowing how differently other people lived. But only a few blocks away from the miserable tenements, shop windows blaze with their tempting displays of jewelry, furs, and expensive clothes. Only a few blocks away are the homes of the rich, who can afford all the good things of life. All this contrasts sharply with the grime and sweat and filth of the cheap, dingy rooms of the poor and with their strenuous efforts to keep body and soul together. . . . We shouldn't be surprised at the number of youngsters in the slums who become lawbreakers. The marvel is that slums don't produce many more criminals.

Where private capital is not sufficient to build homes for low-income groups, the Government helps in such undertakings.

---

[4] The seventeen monopoly States are listed on page 550. Most of these permit beer and wine to be sold by the bottle through other outlets such as taverns and grocery stores.

CITY HOUSING UNIT

This attractive housing development in Boston, Massachusetts, is similar to many being built in cities all over the country. With Government aid, city housing authorities can successfully fight slum areas and provide low cost housing for middle- and low-income families.

The Federal Government and Housing. According to the last complete federal census, sixty-four per cent of the total population now live in urban communities. The city-dwelling population has increased by more than twenty million since 1940. All of these people have housing of some sort or other, of course. In many cases, though, this housing is far from adequate.

Home building fell off drastically during the 1930's. So the Federal Government assumed an active role in the promotion of adequate housing facilities. Congress passed several laws to help home owners with the maintenance and mortgages on homes built before the Depression. Then the Government began to encourage the building of new homes. This was done mainly by guaranteeing loans for new home construction and by making grants-in-aid to local communities for the elimination of slum areas.

World War II aggravated the housing problem, especially in defense production centers. To help relieve the pressures of housing war workers, the Government financed and built several housing projects all over the country. Some of these were permanent housing projects, but many of the temporary ones are still in use.

At the end of the war it was estimated that some twelve million new homes were needed to meet the pent-up demand. The prosperous postwar years brought even more demand and the nation's appetite for new housing has not yet been filled.

The greatest need is for adequate housing within the reach of low- and middle-income families. It is estimated that the average family can afford to buy a house costing about twice the family's annual income. Under present conditions, then, a family with income less than $3000 does not face too-happy home-owning prospects.

The Housing and Home Finance Agency. This agency is the overall organization responsible for the principal housing programs of the Federal Government. It is headed by an administrator appointed by the President and Senate and now includes the Federal National Mortgage Association, the Federal Housing Administration, and the Public Housing Administration. The Agency also administers the Federal Flood Insurance Act passed by Congress in 1956.

The Federal National Mortgage Association. This agency is often abbreviated FNMA and called "Fanny May." Financing of new homes

and mortgages is usually handled by banks, building and loan associations, and other private groups. In order to turn their investments into cash, these private institutions often sell their holdings. The FNMA aids private investors by buying these "second mortgages" and, if possible, it later resells them to other private lenders.

The FNMA has an operating capital of $4,300,000,000 and has bought and sold billions of dollars worth of mortgages since it was created in 1938. In the last several years most of its operations have been concerned with providing housing for veterans and farmers.

The Federal Housing Administration. The FHA is the best-known of the Government's housing agencies. The FHA itself does not build homes, nor does it lend money for home construction. It *guarantees* home mortgages and home improvement loans on one- to four-family dwellings built by private persons or companies. The *actual* loans are made by banks or other private lenders. The FHA guarantees loans up to as much as ninety-seven per cent of the appraised value of the property.

Congress sets the precise formula under which the FHA may guarantee loans. And it changes the formula from time to time in accord with the demands for housing and the state of the nation's economy. At present (1958), the FHA will insure ninety-seven per cent of the first $13,500 of a home mortgage. It will also insure eighty-five per cent of the next $2500,

676

and seventy per cent of the remainder, up to a top price of $20,000.

The maximum interest rate on mortgages for either new or existing homes is five-and-one-fourth per cent plus one-half per cent for insuring that the loan will be repaid. Fire insurance must be carried on all homes bought with FHA help, and a home must meet FHA standards in order to qualify for this aid. Loans must be repaid in monthly installments, but the repayment period may run as long as thirty years.

Let us illustrate how your hometown bank may lend money at a low interest rate because the loan is insured through the FHA. Any person of good reputation and sufficient income to justify buying, let us say, a new home worth $9000, including the lot, may borrow ninety-seven per cent of the cost from his local bank. In other words, he could borrow $8730. He would have to make a down payment of $270. The loan would be repaid in monthly installments over as long as thirty years. Or, a home valued at $12,000 would require a down payment of $360 and one worth $20,000 would require a down payment of $1980. And, a home worth $15,000 would require a down payment of $630. FHA will also guarantee loans for remodelling and for other home improvements.

The work of the FHA in encouraging home building is supplemented by that of the Federal Home Loan Banks which make credit available to local institutions engaged in home financing

(see pages 337-338). The Veterans Administration also guarantees liberal home loans to veterans of World War II and the Korean war.

The Public Housing Administration. The PHA is the other principal housing agency of the Federal Government. While the FHA is intended to encourage private building and home ownership by helping people to help themselves, the PHA is directly engaged in the providing of public housing.

The basic task of the Public Housing Authority is the administration of a low-rent housing program. Under this program the PHA makes direct loans to city, county, and State governments for the construction of low-rent housing projects. The Government pays annual subsidies to these local housing authorities in order to provide below-cost rents. Tenants in these projects are limited to citizens with low incomes.

To illustrate, a city housing authority (with the approval of the city council) prepares a plan for a low-rent housing project near a large defense plant. It then applies to the Public Housing Administration for an annual subsidy (not exceeding forty years) so that the city can build and rent dwellings to the needy for twenty per cent less than the prevailing rents in the area. If the PHA approves the details of the plan, the actual construction begins.

The housing project is financed by issuing low interest rate tax-exempt bonds, which are paid off with the rents and the annual Government subsidy. Veterans and those moved out of slum clearence areas (provided only they have low incomes) are given a priority.

The PHA is also engaged in the management and sale of wartime housing projects, many of which have been sold to cities at a very low price. It also administers various veterans' housing projects, and it now administers farm-labor camps previously under the supervision of the Department of Agriculture.

As in the case of many of the other services provided by the Government today, the question of private enterprise versus Government subsidization arises here. But one interesting aspect of all of this is often overlooked in the housing field. As matters now stand, the Government, in many cases, assumes practically all of the financial risks involved and private lending agencies and construction companies are able to make whatever profit there may be in the situation.

We are still quite a distance from solving the housing problem in the United States. Much remains to be done by both the Government and private housing interests before the situation is corrected.

Labor

The Development of Labor Unions. In our early history, when the nation's economy was relatively simple, most people worked for themselves. Those who did work for others normally bargained with their employers on an individual basis. That is, the details of the labor contract, under which one man agreed to work for another in return for certain wages, hours, and other working conditions, were settled by an employer and an employee as a personal, face-to-face arrangement between two people well known to each other.

The coming of the industrial revolution, with the factory system and mass production, brought a drastic change to this employer-employee relationship. Especially after the 1860's small employers gave way to large scale corporations. Where the demand had once been for the services of " Tom Smith, skilled mechanic," it had now become a demand for " fifty precision machinists." Labor met the development of the power of corporate industry with organizations of its own.

Union organization in the United States goes back almost to the days of the Revolution. Before 1800 mechanics and artisans in a few of the larger cities had joined together in local unions. The industrialization of the 1830's spurred local union growth, but unionization gained real momentum in the years following the War Between the States. There were a number of attempts to combine local unions into national groups during the 1850's and 1860's.

678

LABOR UNITY

Secretary of Health, Education, and Welfare, Marion B. Folsom, shakes hands with George Meany and Walter Reuther, president and vice president of the newly merged AFL–CIO.

The Knights of Labor. Formed in 1869, the Knights of Labor was the most successful of these early national unions. The Knights attempted to organize men and women of every craft, creed, and color and included both skilled and unskilled workers. By 1886 the organization reached its peak membership of some 700,000. It advocated such things as the prohibition of child labor, progressive income and inheritance taxes, government ownership of railroads, and equal pay for men and women.

The Knights began to decline in 1886 for a number of reasons. Several disastrous and unsuccessful strikes discouraged many members. The union contained locals and individual members with widely differing views and was often torn by internal strife. The bloody Haymarket Riot in Chicago in 1886 produced splits within the union that threatened to destroy it completely. Several large unions, especially the Railroad Brotherhoods, refused to join the Knights of Labor. By 1917 the union had dissolved.

The American Federation of Labor. In 1881 a group of union officials, socialists, and dissatisfied members of the Knights of Labor organized the Federation of Organized Trades and Labor Unions. It was organized as a union of skilled workers in particular crafts. The Federation and the Knights became intense rivals and in 1886 the Federation called upon all unions not members of the Knights of Labor to join together for protection against the Knights. Thus, in 1886, the American Federation of Labor was born out of the Federation of Organized Trades and Labor Unions. This new organization soon dominated the field.

The A.F. of L. was formed as a federation of *craft unions*. A craft union is one which is composed only of those workers who possess the *same* craft or skill; for example, a plumbers union, a carpenters union, or an electricians union.

The Congress of Industrial Organizations. The development of mass production industries in the United States created a large class of industrial workers not skilled in any particular craft. Many of these workers have been and are organized into *industrial unions*. An industrial union is one which includes *all* workers, skilled or unskilled, in a single major industry. The United Auto Workers and the United Steel Workers are examples of industrial unions.

Some of the members of the A.F. of L. were dissatisfied with their federation because it made no room for these newer unions. However, a majority of the craft unions opposed the admission of unions composed of unskilled workers. After a long and bitter fight over the question of admitting industrial unions, a group led by John L. Lewis was expelled from the A.F. of L. in 1938. Lewis and his followers then established the Congress of Industrial Organizations.

The Merger of the A.F. of L. and the CIO. After nearly two decades of existence as separate and rival national unions, the A.F. of L. and the CIO combined into one huge labor organization in December of 1955.

The merger was accomplished in New York when the A.F. of L. and the CIO, each meeting separately in annual convention, approved the step and then met together in the first national convention of the new body.

The official name of the new grouping is the "American Federation of Labor and Congress of Industrial Organizations." Its first president is George Meany, former head of the A.F. of L. Walter P. Reuther, the last president of the CIO, is one of twenty-seven vice-presidents of the AFL–CIO. He remains, nevertheless, a powerful voice in organized labor.

The huge AFL–CIO holds a national convention to shape policies every two years. In the period between conventions, it is governed by an executive council composed of nineteen leaders from the old A.F. of L. and ten from the CIO.

The AFL–CIO now consists of 141 affiliated unions (109 from the A.F. of L. and 32 from the CIO.)

Union Membership Today. The Labor Department reports that some

18,500,000 workers belong to American labor unions.[5] The AFL–CIO has a membership of nearly 17,000,000. (When the merger occurred in 1955, the A.F. of L. had about 9,600,000 members and the CIO 6,000,000.) Some 1,500,000 workers belong to various independent unions, the largest of which are the United Mine Workers with a membership of about 500,000 today and the Brotherhood of Railroad Trainmen with more than 200,000 members. By 1958 there were more than 67,000,000 persons in the national labor force. Thus only a little over one-fourth of our national labor force is unionized.

Government Regulation of Labor-Management Relations. Government has an obvious interest and obligation in the maintaining of industrial peace. A dispute between a small employer and one or two of his employees over wages, hours, and other conditions of employment is quite important to the parties directly involved. The results of such a dispute may have widespread consequences, but they seldom do. Still, the rights of each party must be protected.

A labor dispute which involves a large employer and hundreds or thousands of employees can and frequently does have a tremendous effect upon the health or the safety of the entire nation.

Collective Bargaining. This is

---

[5] Including more than 1,000,000 who work outside the United States, most of them in Canada.

the cornerstone upon which the American system of labor-management relations is laid. It is the negotiating between an employer and his organized employees (as a group rather than individually) to determine the terms of a labor contract. It takes place when representatives of management and labor sit down to work out an agreement which sets forth the wages, hours, and other conditions under which workers are to be employed.

Collective bargaining is a two-way street. Management makes its proposals for a contract to govern employment. Labor makes its proposals, too. The two sides then bargain (discuss and compromise) with one another in order to reach an agreement satisfactory to each side.

Early Governmental Regulation. The right of workers to organize and bargain collectively is now recognized by all States and the National Government. In their early days, however, unions were commonly regarded with suspicion and disfavor. The common law, inherited from England, held combinations of workers to be criminal conspiracies. Unions were never declared to be illegal as such, but organized efforts to gain higher wages or better working conditions were often prosecuted as conspiracies.

The Supreme Court of Massachusetts pioneered the change in governmental attitude in 1842. It recognized the legality of unions and upheld their right to strike.

Through the latter part of the nineteenth century and into the early decades of this one, government tolerated rather than encouraged and protected union organization. Unions were legal and they were permitted to pursue their objectives, but only through what were then regarded as " lawful " means.

An employer was generally free to oppose unions, and the law paid little attention to his methods. " Yellowdog " contracts were common. These were contracts in which, as a condition of his employment, a worker agreed not to join a union. Company police and labor spies were used, and many workers who favored unions were " black-listed." As a last resort, company unions were formed to stall the growth of legitimate labor unions.

Injunctions [6] were often used to break strikes. Courts held union attempts to enforce contracts to be violations of the Sherman Antitrust Act.

Growth of Labor Strength. Unions continued to grow despite opposition. As they grew, so did their political power through the votes of union members. Especially after 1900 labor's political power came to be reflected in legislation passed by the Congress.

In the Clayton Act of 1914 unions were specifically exempted from the provisions of the antitrust laws. New legislation designed to protect the workingman, in regard to wages,

hours, and other working conditions, began to be enacted.[7]

The depression of 1929 brought widespread unemployment and hardship. It was followed by a wave of new labor legislation, especially after 1933 and inauguration of the New Deal. The Norris-LaGuardia (Anti-Injunction) Act of 1932, the Wagner (National Labor Relations) Act of 1935, and the Fair Labor Standards Act of 1938 are often referred to as " labor's bill of rights." These acts made collective bargaining standard practice, placed a number of restrictions upon employers, and otherwise strengthened the hand of organized labor.

The Taft-Hartley (Labor-Management Relations) Act of 1947 was passed by Congress to provide a fairer balance between management and labor.

Federal Regulation Today. Three particular acts form the base of national regulation of labor-management relations today: the Norris-LaGuardia Act of 1932, the Wagner Act of 1935, and the Taft-Hartley Act of 1947.

The *Norris-LaGuardia Act of 1932* severely restricts the power of the federal courts to issue injunctions in labor disputes. Before an injunction may be issued it has to be shown that every effort has been made to settle the dispute peacefully, that specific unlawful actions have been threatened,

---

[6] An *injunction* is a court order which prevents (enjoins) one from doing something which would injure the personal or property rights of another.

[7] The major federal legislation relating to working conditions is discussed on this and the next two pages.

and that local police officers have not furnished needed protection. The act also provides that no one may be prevented from joining a union, striking or urging others to strike, or engaging in other normal union activities.

The *Wagner Act of 1935* specifically recognizes the right of workers to organize and bargain collectively. Employers in any industry engaged in interstate commerce are required to bargain with the unions a majority of their employees favor. The act lists certain " unfair labor practices " which employers may not commit.

The *NLRB.* The Wagner Act created the *National Labor Relations Board* as an independent regulatory agency to administer the act's provisions. The NLRB was given two broad functions: (1) to conduct elections among employees to determine which, if any, union they favored as their bargaining agent, and (2) to enforce the unfair labor practices provisions of the law.

The unfair labor practices listed in the Wagner Act are quite broad. Employers are especially forbidden: (1) to refuse to bargain collectively with recognized unions, (2) to interfere in union organization, (3) to attempt to influence or pressure an employee in regard to union membership or activity, and (4) to discharge or otherwise punish an employee for union membership or activity. The act contained no similar list of restrictions against workers or unions. The act was the subject of intense criticism as soon as it was passed.

Most of its opponents accepted the basic principle of collective bargaining, but it was widely criticized because it gave unions and union leaders great power without making them responsible for the ways in which they used it. It did not protect employers against unfair union practices, it allowed a union to establish control and even ruthless domination over those workers who did not favor that union, and it placed no limits on union officials in their dealings with members of the union.

The law was also criticized as promoting such unjustifiable practices as union refusal to permit the use of new labor-saving machines and methods and as promoting " featherbedding." Featherbedding is the practice of forcing an employer to hire labor he does not need.

The *Taft-Hartley Act of 1947* was passed as an attempt to meet the weaknesses of the Wagner Act. It was not actually a brand-new labor law. Rather, its provisions are in the form of a series of amendments to the 1935 law. The Taft-Hartley Act carries on the basic principles of the Norris-LaGuardia and the Wagner Acts, but modifies portions of them in an effort to balance the power of labor and management.

The 1947 Act increased the size of the NLRB from three to five members and created a general counsel to prosecute cases involving unfair labor practices before the Board.

The unfair labor practices listed in the Wagner Act were expanded to include restrictions on the activities of unions. Like employers, unions may not refuse to bargain collectively, and they are forbidden to coerce an employee or force an employer to coerce an employee disliked by the union.

Unions may not charge excessive or discriminatory fees or attempt to force an employer to accept featherbedding. So-called "secondary boycotts" are prohibited. That is, unions are forbidden to strike against one employer in order to force him not to do business with another employer who is involved in a labor dispute. Also, unions may not strike to force an employer to deal with one union when the NLRB has certified another as the employee's bargaining agent. Strikes against the National Government are absolutely forbidden.

Unions and union leaders are made legally responsible for their actions. They may be sued for damages which result from unfair labor practices.

Union leaders must make periodic reports of union finances to the union members and to the Secretary of Labor. They must file sworn statements with the NLRB that they are not affiliated with the Communist Party or any other group that advocates the violent overthrow of government in the United States. Failure to file either the financial reports or the noncommunist affidavits bars a union from using the NLRB to protect its rights under the labor laws.

The Closed Shop and the Union Shop. A *closed shop* is one in which only union members may be hired. A *union shop* is one in which employees must join the union within a short time after being hired.

The Taft-Hartley Act outlaws the closed shop. A union shop is permitted only if a majority of the workers agree to it. (Some States have so-called "Right-to-Work" laws which prohibit both closed *and* union shops.) No union may refuse to admit a person nor may one expel a member except for nonpayment of union dues.

The Cooling-Off Period and Injunctions. When a contract expires or a union wishes to change an existing contract, a strike cannot be called except with sixty days' notice. This "cooling-off period" allows time for continued bargaining.

The Taft-Hartley Act created the *Federal Mediation and Conciliation Service* to aid labor and management to reach agreements.

In the case of a strike which endangers the national health or safety the President, acting through the Attorney-General, may seek an eighty-day injunction to halt the walkout. The NLRB may secure an injunction to prohibit unfair labor practices.

Political Contributions. No union may contribute to any political campaign fund. Union funds belong to all of the members, and many may not agree with the union's leaders on political matters. Of course, any member may contribute if he cares to do so, and several groups of union members, like the CIO's Political Action Committee, do back candidates partial to labor's views.

WHAT THIS CHAPTER IS ABOUT

Our people are our greatest asset. Government acts in many ways to promote their general welfare. Here we are especially concerned with governmental action in the fields of health, housing, and labor.

The general health of the American people has improved steadily through the years, but there are still many areas in which improvement is needed. We have a serious shortage of doctors and other trained medical personnel and of hospitals. Mental diseases and their treatment also present a serious and ever present problem.

While the major purpose of private medicine is the treatment and cure of diseases, the major purpose of public health services is the prevention and eradication of diseases and their causes.

The high costs of medical care have brought about a demand for some form of group medicine or " health insurance." There are four major private plans in operation today: the group clinic plan, the closed-staff plan, the free-choice private practice plan, and the Blue Cross hospital plan.

National, State, and local governments provide medical care and hospitalization for many today, especially veterans and the poor. Many propose and many oppose some form of national health insurance.

Liquor, and especially its excessive use, has been condemned throughout history. In the United States liquor regulation is almost wholly a State and local matter. Regulation varies greatly among the States.

The National Government aids in the providing of housing through a variety of programs. The Federal National Mortgage Association aids private home-financing institutions through the buying and selling of second mortgages. The Federal Housing Administration aids home building by guaranteeing loans made on the purchase of new or existing homes. The Public Housing Administration administers federal housing projects and makes loans to State and local governments for constructing their own housing projects.

Labor unions existed in the United States before 1800, but their real growth began with the industrial revolution. About 18,500,000 workers today belong to organized labor unions. The combined AFL–CIO has nearly 17,000,000 members while about 1,500,000 belong to independent unions. Thus a little over one-fourth of the approximately 67,000,000 employable persons belong to unions today.

In their early years unions were commonly regarded with suspicion and disfavor. Through the latter nineteenth century and the early years of this one, government tolerated but did little to protect and encourage them.

Despite opposition, unions continued to grow and as they did they gained political power through the votes of their members. Three particular acts form the base of federal regulation of labor-management relations today: the Norris-LaGuardia (Anti-Injunction) Act of 1932, the Wagner (National Labor Relations) Act of 1935, and the Taft-Hartley (Labor-Management Relations) Act of 1947.

QUESTIONS ON THE TEXT

1. What is the life expectancy of a white male child born today? What was the life expectancy of a white male child born in 1900?

2. How many people are over age sixty-five in the United States today? How many were there in 1900?

3. What is the rate of selective service rejections for both physical and mental causes?

4. Approximately how many persons are born and how many persons die each year in the United States?

5. List two of the suggestions which have been made to solve the problem of the shortage of medical personnel.

6. What is the National Government doing to aid in hospital construction?

7. What are the four principal types of private group medicine plans?

8. Describe the health insurance plan recommended by President Truman. Describe the one recommended by President Eisenhower.

9. Under which amendment to the United States Constitution are the States responsible for liquor regulation? What is *local option?*

10. Why do governments assist private capital in building houses?

11. How does the FNMA aid private lending institutions in their home-financing activities?

12. On what terms does the FHA aid the financing of the purchase of new homes? The financing of the purchase of existing homes?

13. What is the principal function of the PHA?

14. How did the industrial revolution cause a drastic change in the employer-employee relationship in the United States?

15. What are the two principal labor unions in the United States today? When was each founded? How many members has each?

16. Approximately how many workers now belong to organized labor unions?

17. What is *collective bargaining?*

18. What is an *injunction?* How was the injunction once used to combat unionism?

19. What three federal laws form the base of national regulation of labor-management relations?

20. What is the National Labor Relations Board?

PROBLEMS FOR DISCUSSION

1. Many labor unions are now demanding a guaranteed annual wage for their members. That is, they are demanding that employers guarantee fifty-two weeks of work, or wages, to their workers each year. Wage guarantee plans are not new. Procter & Gamble Co., Geo. A. Hormel & Co., and the Nunn-Bush Shoe Co. have had such plans in operation for a number of years. What arguments can you see for and against guaranteed annual wage plans?

2. Can you express this quotation from Abraham Lincoln in your own words? Do you agree with it? " Property is the fruit of labor; property is desirable, is a positive good in the world. That some should be rich shows that others may become rich, and hence is just encouragement to industry and enterprise. Let not him who is houseless pull down the house of another, but let him work diligently and build one for himself, thus, by example assuring that his own house shall be safe from violence when built."

3. If your community has a housing shortage, what factors do you think responsible? How is it being met?

Unit IX. The Betterment of Society

THINGS YOU MIGHT DO

1. Invite a local public health officer to address the class on the nature of his work.

2. If possible, the class might visit a local hospital and State mental institution.

3. If possible, the class might visit a near-by manufacturing plant and observe its operations. Representatives of management and labor could be asked to discuss their problems with the class.

4. Through your local police, discover the ways in which the use of liquor is regulated in your community. Is liquor a serious problem in local law enforcement?

WORDS AND PHRASES YOU SHOULD KNOW

American Federation of Labor
Blue Cross hospital plan
Closed shop
Closed-staff plan
Collective bargaining
Congress of Industrial Organizations
Craft union
Featherbedding
Federal Housing Administration
Federal Mediation and Conciliation Service
Federal National Mortgage Association
Free-choice, private practice plan
Group clinic plan
Group medicine
Hill-Burton (Hospital Survey and Construction) Act
Health insurance
Housing and Home Finance Agency
Industrial union
Injunction
Knights of Labor
Local option
National Labor Relations Board
Norris-LaGuardia (Anti-Injunction) Act
Prohibition
Public Housing Administration
State medicine
Taft-Hartley (Labor-Management Relations) Act
Union shop
Wagner (National Labor Relations) Act

SELECT BIBLIOGRAPHY

" Big Labor's Big Money," *Newsweek,* April 8, 1957.

BRECHER, RUTH and EDWARD, " Patients on Parole," *Saturday Evening Post,* March 26, 1955.

DETZER, KARL, " This Union Found the Best Way to Raise Wages," *Reader's Digest,* February, 1957.

FREEMAN, SILER, " Special Report: The Guaranteed Annual Wage," *Collier's,* September 30, 1955.

HEALY, PAUL F., " Big Labor's Big Boss," *Saturday Evening Post,* June 23, 1956.

MEANY, GEORGE, " What Organized Labor Wants," *Fortune,* March, 1955; also *Reader's Digest,* June, 1955.

MILLER, LOIS M., " Facts About Mental Illness," *Reader's Digest,* May, 1955.

" Who Lives Longest and Where? " *U.S. News,* July 5, 1957.

Nothing is so galling to a people, not broken in from the birth,
as a paternal or, in other words, a meddling government.

— *Thomas B. Macaulay*

*

Chapter 39

GOVERNMENT
IN THE ECONOMY

A busy America is a prosperous America, and we are a busy people. Our standard of living is the highest the world has ever known. The standard is high for a number of reasons. Our knowledge and ability, our skilled workers, technical equipment, and natural resources, have made it so.

We also have an economic system which promotes such a standard. *Capitalism* may be defined as an economic system in which the ownership and management of productive wealth are in the hands of private enterprisers.[1] These enterprisers (*entrepreneurs*, capitalists) hire labor and compete with one another to provide goods and services at a profit.

As we have said, our capitalistic system is often referred to as the free enterprise or private enterprise system. Competition is its lifeblood. Those who are most successful under it are usually those who are able to

provide the best possible product or service at the lowest possible cost.

The fact that ours is a system of *private* enterprise does *not* mean, however, that government has no part to play in it. Quite to the contrary, governments at all levels in the United States play a most direct role in our economy. Many of the pages of this book are devoted to examples of this.

In this chapter, we are especially concerned with re-emphasizing, or tying together, the ways in which government participates in the economy. Basically, it does so in two ways: (1) by acting as regulator and (2) by acting as servant.

As we discuss the activities of government under these two main headings, bear one thought in mind constantly. Remember that most Americans agree that government's place in the economy should be strictly limited to those matters which it is felt are best handled by society acting as a whole rather than through the efforts of each of us acting individually. We

---

[1] You might well reread the discussion of our economic system on pages 24–28.

subscribe to the concept of government which Abraham Lincoln expressed when he said:

The legitimate object of government is to do for the community of people whatever they need to have done, but cannot do so well for themselves in their separate and individual capacities.

As a people we reject the idea that the state is the source of economic prosperity. We believe that to look too much to government is to kill the goose that lays the golden egg. Government is only a tool which must be properly used — as a referee and a helper, not a master and a crutch.

Government as Regulator

From all we can learn from history, it appears that defense against outside attack was the major reason why primitive man first organized a government. Next to defense, the regulation of the people's relationships with one another ranks as government's oldest function. All governments, from the earliest to those of the present day, have attempted to prevent one person or group from doing certain things to others.

At first, government acted to prevent persons from committing crimes, such as murder, theft, arson, and assault. As the centuries passed, the concept of governmental regulation expanded to include more than criminal matters, as, for example, man's economic relationships with his fellows.

Indeed, as we learned in Chapter 3, the need for a strong central government to regulate commerce between the States was the primary reason for the calling of the Constitutional Convention at Philadelphia in 1787. The Founding Fathers were bent upon creating a National Government with power enough to bring order out of the chaos of the times.

Today all three levels of government in the United States are engaged in the regulation of our economic life.

The word " regulation " as it is used here can and does mean many things. Government regulates in the sense of complete prohibition — for example in those " local option " communities where the liquor business is completely prohibited. Government also regulates in the sense of restriction but not complete prohibition — for example, State regulation of public utilities. Government regulates, too, in the sense of promotion — for example, national regulation of navigation in order to promote interstate and foreign trade.

Each level of government regulates in these three ways: to prohibit, to restrict, and to promote.

Increased Economic Regulation. Economic regulation by the National Government has increased tremendously since 1789, and especially in the past hundred years. One chief explanation for this can be found in the increasingly complex nature of American business. The development of mass production methods and the corporation have revolutionized the

Courtesy *United States Steel Corporation*

STOCKHOLDERS MEETING

A small group of stockholders applaud at the annual meeting of a large corporation. With the growth of industry in our country, ownership has passed from the hands of the few into the hands of the millions who own stock.

character of our economy within the short space of a hundred years.

Modern American industry is no longer based, as it once was, upon small shops. A century and more ago in nearly all businesses the owner was the board of directors, general manager, and foreman all rolled into one. He dealt directly with himself as the sole stockholder. The few employees and customers with whom he dealt he knew personally.

Today, the actual owners of an industry, the corporation stockholders,

seldom even know the name of the plant manager, let alone the members of the board of directors. They never have any contact with the foremen or workers. Their contacts with the customers occur only when they themselves happen to purchase one of the corporation's products.

Today, production (i.e., the providing of goods and services) goes through an exceedingly complex pattern of advertising, shipping, handling, and wholesale and retail selling far different from the relatively simple arrangements of a century ago. It involves a maze of relationships among stockholders, directors, managers, office personnel, skilled and unskilled workers, middlemen, retailers, and consumers.

These conditions have seemed to make governmental regulation necessary. This governmental regulation is intended to insure a reasonably smooth and stable economy. It is also intended to protect the consumer and the smaller businesses against unfair exploitation by the larger concerns.

Another major cause for the growth of national regulation has been the increasingly interstate character of American business. In the case of many firms, local and State control cannot possibly be adequate. This is so because the firms' operations involve not just one locale but most or all of the entire country.

Take, for example, a corporation which manufactures automobiles. It is probably owned by stockholders who live in all forty-eight States. Its raw materials come from many different States and involve the work of a large number of persons in those

THE FACT OF THE MATTER

A prime factor in our fight against world communism is our sound economy and growing industry. Our system of free enterprise, based on a vigorous and healthy competition, has given us the highest standard of living in the world. Against this evidence of powerful well-being, the communist prophecy of the collapse of capitalism has been proved both false and foolish.

Cartoons by Roy Justus in " The Minneapolis Star "

States. The company may have assembly plants located in various parts of the country. It sells its products in all forty-eight States through a nation-wide system of distributors.

Effective regulation of an operation like this cannot be accomplished at the State level. If there is to be regulation, most or all of it must come at the national level.

Economic Regulation by the States. National regulation is conducted on a broad scale; it is nation-wide in scope. Thus it tends to overshadow the importance of State regulation in the average person's mind. However, State regulation is quite extensive and significant. Just as the demand for national regulation has grown through the years, so has the demand for State control. As a matter of fact, the States are more directly involved in economic regulation today than is the National Government.

This fact may be illustrated in a number of ways. As just one way, trace a typical day in the life of an average person. Begin with the moment that person awakes and carry through to the time when he goes to bed. You will be amazed at the almost numberless ways in which economic regulation by the State affects each activity. For example, the alarm clock which awakens John Q. Citizen might have cost him a certain fixed price be-cause of the State's " fair-trade " law. The eggs he has for breakfast were probably graded and inspected according to State law before being shipped to the local grocery store. And so it goes, step-by-step, right through his day. When he finally turns off his bedroom light at night he stops the electric current. That current, its production, distribution, and sale is stringently regulated by the State.

Economic regulation by *local governments* is also quite extensive and important. Like national and State regulation it has increased markedly, too. In tracing Mr. Citizen's typical day, there are many points at which local regulation affects his activities. For example, the city zoning ordinance might well determine the location of the place where he earns his living. It might also determine the general type of house in which he and his neighbors in that part of the city live.

What goods may be bought and sold and what other business activities may be conducted on Sundays are often regulated by local ordinances called " blue laws." Cities and counties often limit the weight of vehicles that may cross the bridges on their streets and roads. These few examples should be enough to illustrate our point. They can be multiplied over and over again.

Government as Servant

Governments today do a great deal more than regulate the economy.

They also provide a wide range of services within the economy.

"Socialism" and Services. Many of our most heated political debates today revolve about the extent to which services ought to be provided *socially*. That is, they involve the question of how much should be undertaken by society acting as a whole through government, rather than privately by each individual for himself or by some other individual or group for profit.

Government Aids to the Economy. It would take at least a book to detail the ways in which government promotes or aids our economy, just as it would take at least as much space to spell out the many ways in which government polices it. Indeed, as we said earlier, many of the pages of this book have been devoted to many specific instances of each.

The history of governmental services to aid the economy goes back to the very beginnings of government in America. We noted (page 34) that the first representative legislature in the New World met at Jamestown, Virginia, in 1619. Among other things, it passed laws to aid the farmers of the colony. Our postal system, a great boon to business, traces its ancestry back to the system the British maintained in the colonies. Benjamin Franklin was appointed postmaster at Philadelphia in 1737 and became Co-Deputy Postmaster-General of the British Colonies in North America in 1753. He became the first Postmaster-General under the Continental Congress on July 26, 1775.

Aids by State and Local Govern- *ments*. Under the American federal system, the States and their local governments provide many services which are of direct benefit to the economy. One of the most obvious illustrations of this is the building of the streets and roads over which much of our commerce travels. There are many others, too.

A number of States and cities are today attempting to liberalize their tax laws in order to encourage industrial concerns to locate plants in their areas. Our State colleges and universities conduct extensive research programs to aid agriculture and business within their respective States.

Every State maintains a number of agencies charged with the promotion of a particular segment of the economy within the State. For example, one of the many such agencies in the State of Oregon is the Dairy Products Commission. It exists in order " to increase the consumption of dairy products " and " to publicize and diffuse reliable information showing the importance of the use of milk, cream, and other dairy products."

Aids by the National Government. The Framers of the Federal Constitution expressly provided for several services to be performed by the National Government. For example, Article I, Section 2, Clause 3, in the Constitution provides for the decennial census. We noted some of the ways in which the census serves the business community. Several services are provided for in Article I, Section 8. Clause 4 provides for " uniform laws on the subject of bankruptcies," Clause 5 provides for a uniform standard of weights and measures, Clause 7 provides for the postal system, and Clause 8 provides for our whole system of copyrights and patents.[2]

Recall that the changes which have taken place in the national economy in the last hundred years or so have caused the people to look more and more to the National Government for regulation of the economy. For exactly the same reason the people have looked more and more to Washington for aids to the economy. Most of these have been provided for by Congress acting under the Commerce Clause.

The federal services which are made available to groups within our economy are many and varied, as we have already seen. The farmer is aided through the many programs of the Department of Agriculture. Direct aid to business is provided by such agencies as the Census Bureau, the National Bureau of Standards, the Bureau of Foreign Commerce, the Maritime Administration, the Coast and Geodetic Survey, and the Patent Office, all within the Commerce Department. Invaluable services are also rendered by such agencies as the Bureau of Mines and the Geological Survey in the Interior Department.

Even a brief survey must include a mention of the many financial agencies which make credit available, such as the Small Business Administration, the Export-Import Bank, the Farm Credit Administration, and the Commodity Credit Corporation. Then, too, there are the services of such important agencies as the Federal Housing Administration, the Federal National Mortgage Association, and, of course, the Post Office.

Government in Business. No government in this country is directly engaged in business to the extent many European governments are. Still, a number of the services our governments furnish are of such a nature that the agencies which perform them are virtually business concerns.

The extent to which our governments do engage in business is a little surprising in view of our tradition of private enterprise. The list of businesses actually conducted by the National Government and by the State and local governments is an impressively long one.

Some instances of government in business have been with us so long and are so familiar to us that we seldom give them a second thought. Examples of these include the national postal system, State toll roads and toll bridges, and city water and light systems.

Other instances of public businesses are not nearly so well known. In considering State finances we noted such State-operated enterprises as North Dakota's flour business and Washington's ferry system.[3] In considering

---

[2] Trade-marks are provided for by Congress under the commerce power (see page 295).

[3] See page 550.

the functions which cities perform we listed such municipal enterprises as the local railway system in Philadelphia.[4]

The number of federal business enterprises is indeed large. As a proprietor, the National Government owns, buys, and sells vast amounts of real estate and other property. For its own consumption, it produces quantities of guns, ammunition, and other defense articles; it maintains the Government Printing Office, the world's largest printing and publishing plant; it manufactures mailbags and mailboxes, stamps, money, and prison-made goods; and it operates hospitals, arsenals, dock facilities, courthouses, post offices, and many other public buildings.

Many of the Federal Government's business activities are in the area of general commercial competition. In the field of transportation it operates the Alaskan Railway, the Panama Canal, and the Military Air Transport Service. In the power field it produces, distributes, and sells great quantites of electricity and is now beginning to provide atomic power.

As a manufacturer, it produces and sells such things as fertilizers and steamships. As a landlord, it maintains recreational facilities in the national parks, and it sells timber in the national forests and leases public lands for grazing purposes. Then, too, it operates credit agencies for business, agriculture, and other interests, and it acts as an insurance agent for bank deposits and farm crops and has a huge old-age insurance program.

Why Governments Are in Business. There are several reasons why our National, State, and local governments are engaged in these many business enterprises. In the first place, there are some undertakings that have seemed so huge that they were beyond the capacity of private corporations. Instances of this would certainly include some of the major dams constructed by the National Government, such as Bonneville, Grand Coulee, and Hoover.

Secondly, some functions have seemed so closely related to the public welfare that it appears desirable that they be undertaken publicly, as in the case of the postal service or the production of atomic energy. Third, some projects cover such broad areas and involve such overall planning that it seems they should be undertaken by government. Examples of this include large-scale slum clearance and housing projects by States and cities, or such regional development programs as that in the Tennessee Valley, which we shall look at in a moment.

Fourth, some privately conducted activities necessary to the public have proved unprofitable for private business, and government has had to step in and assume their conduct. This process, known sometimes as " ashcan socialism," can be seen in many city-operated transportation systems.

Finally, government has often found itself in business because of its ownership of vast amounts of property of

---

[4] See page 615.

many kinds. This is true, for example, in the case of the sale of public timber on federal or State lands or the operation of State and local toll roads or toll bridges.

Still, even with these explanations for the wide range of governmental business undertakings, it must be remembered that as a people we favor the least possible extension of public ownership in the field of commercial activities.

The Tennessee Valley Authority

The Tennessee Valley Authority was established in 1933. It is an independent agency within the executive branch of the National Government. Measured by any standards, it is one of the major illustrations of government participation in business in the United States.

TVA grew out of a World War I project producing nitrogen for explosives at Muscle Shoals on the Tennessee River in Alabama. At the end of the war the Government owned a project which consisted of some 2300 acres, two nitrate plants, a powerhouse, and Wilson Dam.

Throughout the 1920's a controversy raged as to what should be done with this rather sizable investment. There were many who proposed that it be sold to private interests, and at one point it nearly went to Henry Ford. Others, led by Senator George W. Norris of Nebraska, urged that the project be expanded to become a huge federal multipurpose program for the entire region of the Tennessee River Valley. Bills which would have begun such a plan were vetoed by both Presidents Coolidge and Hoover.

Finally, in 1933 the first session of the Congress under the Roosevelt New Deal passed the Tennessee Valley Authority Act. The broad purposes and functions of TVA are stated in the law:

To improve the navigability and to provide for the flood control of the Tennessee River; to provide for reforestation and the proper use of marginal lands in the Tennessee Valley; to provide for the agricultural and industrial development of said valley; to provide for the national defense by the creation of a corporation for the operation of the Government properties at and near Muscle Shoals in the State of Alabama, and for other purposes.

Thus Congress provided for the " orderly and proper physical, economic, and social development " of an entire region. This region, the Tennessee River Valley, embraces some 41,000 square miles and parts of seven States — Tennessee, Kentucky, Virginia, North Carolina, Georgia, Alabama, and Mississippi.

TVA is headed by a three-man Board of Directors appointed by the President and Senate for nine-year terms. Its operations are under the supervision of a General Manager responsible to the Board. Its program includes power development, flood control, and navigation work. Its ac-

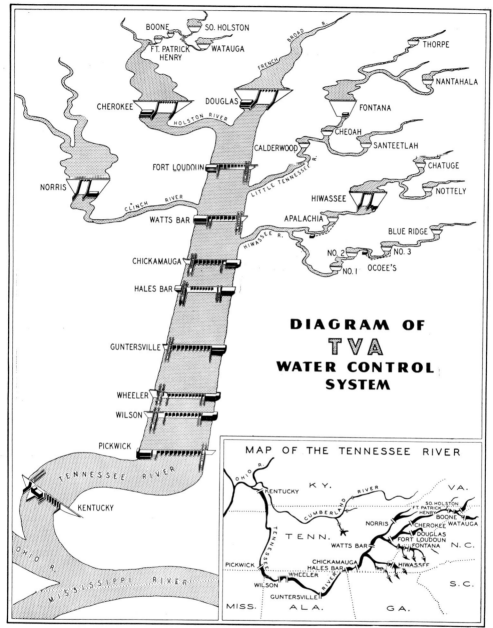

BOONE SO. HOLSTON
FT. PATRICK WATAUGA
HENRY
BROAD R.
THORPE
NANTAHALA
FRENCH
CHEROKEE DOUGLAS FONTANA
HOLSTON RIVER
CHEOAH
CALDERWOOD SANTEETLAH
FORT LOUDOUN CHATUGE
NORRIS LITTLE TENNESSEE R. NOTTELY
CLINCH RIVER HIWASSEE
WATTS BAR APALACHIA
HIWASSEE R. BLUE RIDGE
CHICKAMAUGA NO. 2 NO. 3
NO. 1 OCOEE'S
HALES BAR

DIAGRAM OF
TVA
WATER CONTROL
SYSTEM

GUNTERSVILLE

WHEELER
WILSON

PICKWICK

TENNESSEE RIVER
KENTUCKY

OHIO R.

MISSISSIPPI RIVER

MAP OF THE TENNESSEE RIVER

OHIO R.
KENTUCKY KY. RIVER VA.
SO. HOLSTON
FT. PATRICK
CUMBERLAND HENRY BOONE
NORRIS CHEROKEE WATAUGA
TENN. DOUGLAS
FORT LOUDOUN
WATTS BAR FONTANA N. C.
PICKWICK CHICKAMAUGA HIWASSEE
HALES BAR
WHEELER S. C.
WILSON
GUNTERSVILLE
MISS. ALA. GA.

Tennessee Valley Authority

TVA

The Tennessee River development under the Tennessee Valley Authority exemplifies multiple-purpose planning. Among its activities are navigability and flood control of the river, reforestation, and agricultural and industrial development of the river valley.

tivities also involve reforestation, soil conservation, fertilizer production, agricultural experimentation, the development of recreational facilities, and the encouragement of private industrial growth in the Tennessee Valley.

TVA has had a tremendous effect upon the Valley and upon the lives of its 4,000,000 residents. There is now a nine-foot channel which makes the Tennessee River navigable from its mouth, where it empties into the Ohio River at Paducah, Kentucky, upstream 630 miles to Knoxville, Tennessee. There are nine enormous dams on the main stem of the Tennesse River and a series of power and storage dams on its tributaries and the near-by Cumberland.

There have been no floods in the Valley since the completion of the storage system, and the flood pressures on the Ohio and Mississippi have been reduced. The per capita income of the residents of the region has risen sharply since the advent of scientific farming and plentiful electric power. Approximately ninety per cent of the Valley's farms now have electricity, compared to less than four per cent before 1933. A great deal of new industry has been attracted, and wide areas, once denuded, have now been reforested. The food-freezing industry owes much of its rapid growth to experimental work done by TVA.

TVA has been the subject of bitter argument from its beginning. The Supreme Court found the whole TVA program constitutional in 1936. It held the original Muscle Shoals project valid under the war powers. The later projects were ruled constitutional as a proper exercise of the power to regulate interstate commerce. The sale of surplus electric power in competition with private industry — a major sore point today — was upheld under Congress' power to dispose of property belonging to the United States.

Little criticism is directed against the quality of TVA's administration. No one disputes its tremendous accomplishments. The attacks have centered especially upon wholesale government participation in what are traditionally private fields. Many people, including Presidents Roosevelt and Truman, have proposed similar arrangements for the Columbia and Missouri river valleys. On the other hand, a number of people have urged the sale of TVA and all its facilities, which they condemn as " creeping socialism," to private interests.

TVA is financed through appropriations by Congress. Some additional funds come from the sale of power and fertilizers and from the Authority's severely limited power to issue bonds. A number of critics contend that it is unjust to spend tax moneys from the entire nation for the benefit of one particular region. TVA's supporters reply that actually the program is of benefit to the entire country, not just the Tennessee Valley. They cite as one example of this the providing of the large quantities of power consumed by the atomic energy works at Oak Ridge, Tennessee.

The St. Lawrence Seaway and Power Project

The St. Lawrence Seaway and Power Project, a dream for so long, is now on the way to becoming actual fact. It involves the construction of a series of locks to link the Great Lakes with the Atlantic Ocean and a power project to produce more energy than is now produced at Boulder Dam and only a little less than that produced at Grand Coulee.

Since the beginning of this century Congress had considered various proposals for joint United States-Canadian development of the St. Lawrence. It had been recommended by every President since Warren Harding. The Senate rejected a treaty for construction in 1934, and an executive agreement on the matter was disapproved by Congress in 1941.

Finally, in 1953, at President Eisenhower's urging, Congress gave New York State the right to build the power project in co-operation with the Province of Ontario, and in 1954 it authorized joint United States-Canadian construction of the Seaway.

Work on the Seaway was begun in the spring of 1955, and it will be opened to its first traffic by 1959. The Seaway will give us a vast new 8000-mile seacoast and make seaports of such inland cities as Buffalo, Chicago, Cleveland, Detroit, Milwaukee, and

INLAND SEAWAY

The completion of the St. Lawrence Seaway and Power Project in the next few years will open a vast region to the Atlantic and provide the Northeast with a substantial increase in its power supply.

Reprinted from " U.S. News & World Report." May 14, 1954
© 1954 United States News Publishing Corporation

SEAWAY:

1,600-mile all-water route from Duluth to Montreal
Seven locks between Montreal and Lake Ontario
COST: To U.S., 91 millions; To Canada, 182 millions

POWER PROJECT:

Dams near Ogdensburg and Massena, N.Y.
Powerhouse at Massena
Power output: 1.9 million kilowatts, enough for needs of city of 2.4 million
COST: To State of New York, 300 millions; To Province of Ontario, 300 millions

Toledo. Some 50,000,000 tons of cargo will pass through the Seaway each year, or nearly twice that now going through the Panama Canal. Iron ore from Labrador and South America will be an important part of the inbound cargo.

Seventeen locks are required to overcome the 600-foot drop in the water level between Lake Superior and the Atlantic. Nine of these already exist. Deep-draft ocean-going vessels now navigate the 1000 miles up the St. Lawrence to Montreal, and similar ships ply the Great Lakes from Duluth, Minnesota, or Ogdensburg, New York. Thus the only major construction required is in the 120-mile stretch of the river between Montreal and Ogdensburg.

The power project involves the construction of dams and a hydroelectric power plant at the International Rapids between Massena, New York, and Cornwall, Ontario. The New York State Power Authority is the official agent of the United States in constructing the power project in cooperation with the Ontario Hydro-Electric Power Commission.

The project will produce more than 12,000,000,000 kilowatt-hours of energy a year. This energy is to be divided between New York and Ontario, and New York must make a " fair share " of its power available to neighboring States within economical transmission distance. New York's half of the power produced will add about ten per cent to that now available to practically all of New England and the eastern two-thirds of New York.

The total cost of the Seaway is estimated at $448,000,000. Of this, the United States' share is to be $143,-000,000. Tolls on our portion of the Seaway will bring in some $6,000,000 a year — a sum expected to meet all operating expenses and eventually pay the United States' share, as well.

The total cost of the power project will be $600,000,000. New York's share will be met out of the proceeds from the sale of the power produced.

WHAT THIS CHAPTER IS ABOUT

Our economic system, capitalism, is one of the important factors which contributes to our high standard of living. Capitalism, or as it is often called, the free enterprise or private enterprise system, is based upon competition. Enterprisers hire labor and compete with one another to provide goods and services at a profit.

Even though our economic system is based upon *private* enterprise, government at all levels does play a large role in the economy. Basically it does so in two ways: (1) as regulator and (2) as servant.

As a people, we firmly believe that government's place in the economy must be a strictly limited one.

Regulation is one of government's most ancient functions. Economic regulation in America dates from early colonial days. The need for adequate regulation of interstate commerce was the primary reason for the calling of the Constitutional Convention of 1787. Each level of government today regulates to prohibit, to restrict, and to promote.

Economic regulation has increased especially in the past hundred years because of the industrial revolution and because of the increasingly interstate character of American business. The role of government as servant in the economy, which also goes back to colonial times, has likewise expanded tremendously in the past century. Just as all three levels of government regulate, they also provide many services (aids) to the economy.

All three levels of government are directly engaged in a number of business enterprises, too. They are for a variety of reasons: because of the very size of the undertaking involved, because of its peculiar relation to the public welfare, because of its geographic scope, because of features making it economically unprofitable for private enterprise, or because of the fact of government ownership of vast amounts of many different kinds of property.

The question of the extent to which government *should* engage in business directly is at the core of many of our most heated political debates today.

The Tennessee Valley Authority, created in 1933, is one of the major examples of government in business. The St. Lawrence Seaway and Power Project, a dream for half a century, is now on its way to becoming reality.

QUESTIONS ON THE TEXT

1. What factors have contributed to our high standard of living?

2. Define *capitalism*. What other terms are often used in place of it?

3. In what two basic ways does government participate in our economy?

4. To what extent do most Americans believe government should participate?

5. Give an example of economic regulation by each of the levels of government in the United States.

6. Why has national regulation especially increased in the past century?

7. Give an example of aid to the economy by each of the three levels of government in the United States.

8. Give an example of direct participation in business by each of the three levels of government in the United States.

9. Give four reasons why government is engaged in business enterprises.

10. When was TVA created? From what original project did it develop?

11. How is its Board of Directors chosen? What is the General Manager?

12. Parts of what States are included within the TVA system?

13. What are TVA's broad purposes and functions as outlined in the Tennessee Valley Authority Act?

14. Describe TVA's accomplishments. On what particular ground is its financing often criticized?

15. By whom is the St. Lawrence Power Project being built? Where?

16. By whom is the St. Lawrence Seaway being built? Where is the major construction work being done?

17. What is the estimated total cost of each of these?

18. What will be the effect of the completed Seaway upon our Middle West?

PROBLEMS FOR DISCUSSION

1. A corporation is owned by its stockholders. As a rule, however, these stockholders have little real control over the management and policies of the corporation. Effective control is actually in the hands of a board of directors or other

small group. To what extent do you think that separation between the ownership and the actual control of the modern corporation tends to undermine the principle of individual initiative as the basis for our industrial economy?

2. Do you believe that it is fair that the National Government provides subsidies to various groups, such as farmers, shipowners, airlines, and newspapers, when these supports are financed from taxes which are levied on the entire population? Explain.

3. Can you explain what Adlai Stevenson meant when he said that the American economy has shown " socialism to be obsolete and communism a stagnant pool of violence and reaction "?

THINGS YOU MIGHT DO

1. Make a list of as many examples as you can of the ways in which economic activities in your area are regulated by the National Government, by your State government, and by your local government.

2. Make a similar list of the ways in which these three levels of government aid the economy of your community.

3. Make a list of as many publicly conducted business enterprises as you can in your community. Which, if any, of these do you feel should be conducted privately? Why?

4. Write a brief essay or editorial on the importance of competition to our economic system.

5. If possible, have one or more local businessmen explain to the class the ways in which government regulates and aids his or their particular businesses.

WORDS AND PHRASES YOU SHOULD KNOW

" Blue laws "
Capitalism
Corporation
Entrepreneurs
Industrial revolution

Tennessee Valley Authority
Initiative
Private enterprise
Production
Regulation

St. Lawrence Power
Project
St. Lawrence Seaway

SELECT BIBLIOGRAPHY

BARLOW, MARVIN J., " The Coming Battle of the St. Lawrence," *Harper's*, September, 1957.

BAUM, ARTHUR W., " World's Busiest Waterway," *Saturday Evening Post*, June 4, 1955.

GALLAGER, A. J., " Your Job: Where Does It Come From? " *The Freeman*, April, 1955; also *Reader's Digest*, May, 1955.

" Seaports of Midwest," *U.S. News*, June 1, 1956.

SLICHTER, SUMNER H., " In Defense of Bigness in Business," *N.Y. Times Magazine*, August 4, 1957, and *Reader's Digest*, November, 1957.

" The President's Economic Adviser Forecasts the Business Future of America," *U.S. News*, May 6, 1955.

" Uncivil Civil Servant," *Time*, May 28, 1956.

" Who Gets the Big Subsidies? " *U.S. News*, May 4, 1956.

> The United Nations stands as the living sign of all people's hope for peace.
>
> — *Dwight D. Eisenhower*

★

Chapter 40

THE UNITED STATES AND THE UNITED NATIONS

Two world wars have clearly taught us that we do not and cannot live isolated from the rest of the world. In a great many ways, we live in " one world " whether we like it or not.

The fact that this is " one world," that our own peace and security is directly related to what happens anywhere on the globe, can be demonstrated in several ways.

For example, man's inventiveness has made the world a neighborhood. It took the *Mayflower* sixty days to make its difficult way across the Atlantic in 1620. Today the trip is a half-day's comfortable journey by air.

Wars and political upheavals in any part of the world vitally affect the interests of the United States and the American people. Three times in this century we have become involved in war thousands of miles from home.

Economic events abroad are often felt quite directly in America. A reduction in the price of Australian wool, a coffee shortage in Brazil, or a shutdown in the oil fields of Iran are reflected in our domestic markets almost at once.

In these and other ways, then, we live in " one world." In some ways, however, we do not. Our world is largely divided into two armed camps, with the communist dictatorships on one side and the free democracies on the other. World War III remains a dreadful possibility — a war in which, as Winston Churchill has said, we could only be " victorious on a heap of ruins."

We know that it is essential that we and our friends maintain armed forces adequate to our defense and to the keeping of the peace. We also know that the only sure way to prevent another war is to eliminate the causes for war. To this end, the United States took the lead in creating, and today wholeheartedly supports, the United Nations. As we learned in Chapter 11, working for a lasting peace through the UN is one of the basic cornerstones of American foreign policy.

Birth of the United Nations

The United Nations Declaration. On January 1, 1942, less than a month after the United States entered World War II, the twenty-six nations then at war with the Axis Powers met in Washington, D.C., and signed the Declaration of the United Nations. In it, each nation pledged an all-out effort to win the war and promised not to seek a separate peace. Thus the words " United Nations " were first used. Later in the war, twenty-one other states signed the Declaration.

Steps toward International Organization. In 1943 both houses of Congress passed by overwhelming majorities resolutions approving United States participation in a postwar international organization to guarantee world peace and security. In a high level meeting which took place at Moscow that same year, Secretary of State Cordell Hull pledged American co-operation in establishing " at the earliest practicable date a general international organization for the main-

TOWARD THE FUTURE
Dominated by the imposing Secretariat building, the small cluster of United Nations buildings in New York City stands as a symbol of hope for people the world over.

Unations

Unit IX. The Betterment of Society

tenance of international peace and security."

In 1944 representatives of the governments of the United States, Great Britain, China, and Russia met at Dumbarton Oaks, an estate just outside Washington, and drafted a general plan for such an organization. The Dumbarton Oaks proposals were widely discussed here and abroad. Then, in February, 1945, President Roosevelt, Prime Minister Churchill, and Premier Stalin met at Yalta and called for a United Nations Conference on International Organization to meet in San Francisco on April 25, 1945.

The San Francisco Conference. Delegates from fifty nations met at San Francisco and over a period of two months hammered out the United Nations Charter. Although a good deal of spade-work had already been done, the conference faced many serious problems. On several issues the Soviet Union stood on one side and the United States and Great Britain on the other. On June 26, 1945, however, the delegates met and unanimously approved the United Nations Charter.

The Charter Adopted. The United States, by a vote of 89–2 in the Senate, was the first to ratify the Charter. It became effective on October 24, 1945, after approval by the United States, Great Britain, France, China, Russia, and twenty-four other states. In a short time all fifty of the charter members had ratified, and the first meeting of the UN General Assembly was held in London in January, 1946.

The United Nations Headquarters. The home of the United Nations has been permanently fixed in the United States. John D. Rockefeller, Jr., gave the UN an $8,500,000 six-block tract on the East River in New York City. The Congress authorized a $65,000,000 construction loan, and the UN Headquarters was officially opened in 1951.

The United Nations Charter

Purposes. The Charter begins with an eloquent preamble proclaiming that the UN exists in order " to save succeeding generations from the scourge of war," and Article I declares the organization's purposes to be the maintenance of international peace and security, the development of friendly relations among all nations, and the promotion of co-operation and justice in solving international problems.

Membership. The United Nations consists of the fifty nations which met at San Francisco plus any other " peace-loving states " admitted by the General Assembly upon the recommendation of the Security Council. There are now eighty-two members of the organization. The General Assembly can expel a member if the Security Council recommends it.

Organization. Six " principal organs " are established by the United

ORGANS OF THE UNITED NATIONS

PRINCIPAL ORGANS

SPECIALIZED AGENCIES

INTERNATIONAL LABOUR ORGANIZATION
FOOD AND AGRICULTURE ORGANIZATION OF THE UNITED NATIONS
UNITED NATIONS EDUCATIONAL, SCIENTIFIC & CULTURAL ORGANIZATION
INTERNATIONAL CIVIL AVIATION ORGANIZATION
INTERNATIONAL BANK FOR RECONSTRUCTION AND DEVELOPMENT
INTERNATIONAL MONETARY FUND
UNIVERSAL POSTAL UNION
WORLD HEALTH ORGANIZATION
INTERNATIONAL TELECOMMUNICATION UNION
INTERNATIONAL REFUGEE ORGANIZATION
INTER-GOVERNMENTAL MARITIME CONSULTATIVE ORGANIZATION — Preparatory Committee
INTERNATIONAL TRADE ORGANIZATION — Interim Commission
WORLD METEOROLOGICAL ORGANIZATION

TRUSTEESHIP COUNCIL

SECURITY COUNCIL

GENERAL ASSEMBLY

SECRETARIAT

ADMINISTRATIVE COMMITTEE ON COORDINATION

INTERNATIONAL COURT OF JUSTICE

ECONOMIC AND SOCIAL COUNCIL

MILITARY STAFF COMMITTEE
COMMISSION FOR CONVENTIONAL ARMAMENTS
ATOMIC ENERGY COMMISSION

UNITED NATIONS INTERNATIONAL CHILDREN'S EMERGENCY FUND

Subcommissions

Employment and Economic Stability
Economic Development

Statistical Sampling

Freedom of Information and of the Press
Prevention of Discrimination & Protection of Minorities

COMMISSIONS

ECONOMIC AND EMPLOYMENT
TRANSPORT AND COMMUNICATIONS
FISCAL
STATISTICAL
POPULATION
SOCIAL
NARCOTIC DRUGS
HUMAN RIGHTS
STATUS OF WOMEN
ECONOMIC COMMISSION FOR EUROPE
ECONOMIC COMMISSION FOR ASIA AND THE FAR EAST
ECONOMIC COMMISSION FOR LATIN AMERICA

REGIONAL ECONOMIC COMMISSIONS

UN Presentation 947. 2 rev.

Official United Nations Photo

Unit IX. The Betterment of Society

Nations Charter. These six are the General Assembly, the Security Council, the Economic and Social Council, the Trusteeship Council, the International Court of Justice, and the Secretariat.

Other Major Features. The " sovereign equality " of each member-state is recognized in the Charter, and the UN is expressly forbidden " to intervene in matters which are essentially within the domestic jurisdiction of any state." Each of the members also pledges that the UN will ensure that *nonmembers* will also act in accord with the Charter at least insofar as is " necessary for the maintenance of international peace and security."

Several provisions of the Charter relate to the methods of peaceful settlement of disputes between nations and for the use of armed force to stop a conflict or deal with a threat to the peace. Article 51 guarantees to each member the " right of individual and collective self-defense " in case of an attack upon it. Thus the door is left open for such regional defense alliances as the North Atlantic Treaty Organization.

Amendments may be proposed by a two-thirds vote of the Assembly and must be ratified by two thirds of the UN members (including the Big Five, which are the United States, Great Britain, the Soviet Union, France, and China), according to their own constitutional processes. Thus, because the Charter is a treaty, the United States Senate would have to agree to any amendments to it. A general conference to revise the Charter — in effect, a constitutional convention — may be called by a two-thirds vote of the Assembly and seven votes of the eleven members of the Security Council.

Having briefly sketched the main features of the Charter, we can now turn to the organization and functions of its six principal organs.

The General Assembly

Membership and Voting. Each member of the UN is represented in the General Assembly. Thus the Assembly has eighty-two members today. Each nation may send as many as five delegates, but each state has only one vote. Most important decisions require a two-thirds vote of the members present and voting.

Sessions. Regular sessions of the Assembly begin in September of every year. Special sessions may be called by the Secretary-General at the request of a majority of the UN's members or at the request of the Security Council. (See page 709.)

Powers. The Assembly is often referred to as " the world's town meeting." It has the power to discuss any matter within the scope of the Charter [1] and to make recommendations to

---

[1] Except matters that are being currently considered by the Security Council. This limitation is intended to prevent any confusion that might be caused if both the Assembly and the Council were to consider the same matter simultaneously.

the Security Council and to the member-states. It elects the nonpermanent members of the Security Council, the judges of the International Court of Justice, the members of the Economic and Social Council, part of the membership of the Trusteeship Council, and the Secretary-General. In addition to these duties, it supervises much of the work that is done by the other UN organs.

The Assembly also has the power to draw up the annual budget for the entire world organization and to apportion among each of the members the share each is to pay. Of the total UN budget for 1957, some $49,000,000, the United States paid $16,361,000.

The Security Council

Membership. The Security Council consists of eleven members. Five of them are permanent and six are nonpermanent. The five permanent members are the so-called Big Five — the United States, Great Britain, the Soviet Union, France, and China. The six nonpermanent members are elected by the General Assembly for two-year terms.

Voting and the Veto. On *procedural* questions (i.e., routine or relatively unimportant matters) the Charter provides that decisions may be taken by an affirmative vote of any seven of the eleven Council members. On more important actions (*substantive* matters) the Charter also requires at least seven affirmative votes, but the seven affirmative votes *must* include the votes of each one of the five permanent members.

Thus on important questions, the Council may take action only if each one of the Big Five agrees. If one of them does not, no action may be taken. Each of the Big Five, then, has a *veto power* over Council action.

Because of the veto power, the Security Council can function effectively only when the Big Five co-operate with one another. The Soviet Union has used the veto eighty-two times since the UN was founded; France has used it four times, the British twice, Nationalist China once. The United States has not yet used it.

Sessions. The Security Council is in continuous session, and each member must be represented at the UN seat at all times.

Powers. The Council is the particular UN agency intended to maintain peace and deal with cases of aggression. It has the power to settle disputes between nations. If peaceful negotiation will not accomplish this, the Council may call upon all UN members to sever diplomatic relations with the offender. Or it may impose economic sanctions; that is, ask all members to refuse to trade with the state involved. Or, it may ask all members to cease any and all communications with that state.

As a last resort, the Security Council may call upon all members to take military action against the aggressor, as was done when the North Korean communists invaded South Korea.[2]

Military Staff Committee. Composed of the Chiefs of Staff of the Big Five, this committee is provided for in the Charter. Its functions are to advise the Security Council on matters of disarmament and the use of military force. All UN members are required to make armed units available for use by the Security Council. To date, however, these units have not been activated because of disagreements among the Big Five.

The Council, the Assembly, and Actions Against an Aggressor. Those who framed the Charter clearly intended the Security Council as the organ to take action against an aggressor whenever such action became necessary. But, as we have seen, the Security Council may be paralyzed by a veto cast by any one of the Big Five; the Council can act only when one of the Big Five does not object.

Because of this (and because of the frequent Russian use of the veto), the United States proposed and the General Assembly adopted the " Uniting for Peace " Resolution in late 1950. Under its terms, whenever the Council cannot act in a case in which

there " appears to be a threat to the peace, breach of the peace, or act of aggression," the matter may be considered by the General Assembly immediately. The Assembly may *recommend* that the member states take steps, including military action, to preserve or restore peace.

This measure, in effect, revised the original scheme of the UN. It gave to the Assembly, as well as the Council, the power to act to maintain international order. Remember, *there is no veto power in the Assembly.*

The Suez Crisis. When the Israeli-Egyptian war broke out anew in late 1956, Britain and France invaded Egypt. They took control of the Suez Canal in an effort to keep that vital lifeline open to shipping.

The Security Council could not act in the matter because of British and French vetoes. The Assembly, acting under the 1950 Resolution, took over and soon secured a cease-fire. It then created the UN Emergency Force, an international police force, to supervise the truce. By 1958, a permanent settlement providing for the future of the Canal had not been reached and the UN Emergency Force was still on duty.

The Economic and Social Council

The Economic and Social Council is an eighteen-member body designed to

---

[2] When, on June 27, 1950, the Security Council called upon all UN members to aid the South Koreans to repel the communists, the Soviet delegate was boycotting the Council and so was not present to veto the action.

attack the causes of war and improve standards of living around the world. Its members are chosen by the General Assembly for three-year terms.

It does its work by making studies and recommendations and calling international conferences in the cultural, economic, educational, scientific, social, and health fields.

Specialized Agencies. There are several so-called " specialized agencies " which are not actually within the UN, but are supervised by it. These agencies work through the Economic and Social Council.

The major specialized agencies are the *International Labor Organization* (ILO), which works to promote the health and welfare of workers every-where; the *World Health Organization* (WHO), to improve the health of all peoples; the *Food and Agriculture Organization* (FAO), to increase and improve food production; the *United Nations Educational, Scientific, and Cultural Organization* (UNESCO), to provide for the international exchange of information in all fields; and the *International Bank* and the *International Monetary Fund*, which are discussed in detail later in this chapter, on pages 714–715.

The Trusteeship Council

The Trusteeship Council promotes the interests of those people who live in the nonself-governing territories in the world, as for example, such dependencies as Wake Island, Bermuda, or the " trust territories." The " trust territories " are those placed under UN " trust " and now include (1) those areas which nations now hold under mandate from the old League of Nations, (2) those that were taken from the enemy in World War II, and (3) others voluntarily placed under the trusteeship system.

The Trusteeship Council consists of the Big Five and any other nation administering a trust territory plus an equal number of other members as elected by the General Assembly. The Council receives reports from all nations having nonself-governing territories (including trust territories), oversees the administration of the trust territories, and generally encourages self-government in all of the world's dependent areas and peoples.

(See the discussion of the United States Trust Territory of the Pacific Islands, page 356.)

The International Court of Justice

The International Court of Justice is the judicial arm of the United Nations. It consists of fifteen judges chosen for nine-year terms by the General Assembly and the Security Council. No two of the judges may come from the same country.

The Court holds regular sessions at The Hague in the Netherlands. Only states (both members and nonmembers of the UN, but not individuals) may be parties in cases before the Court. It deals with cases involving the interpretation of treaties, questions

710

in international law, and any other legal matters brought before it, and decisions are made by a majority vote of the Court.

The Court may give an advisory opinion on any legal question when requested by the General Assembly, the Security Council, or other UN organs, with the consent of the General Assembly.

The Secretariat

The Secretariat is the " civil service branch " of the UN. It is headed by the Secretary-General who is appointed by the General Assembly upon the recommendation of the Security Council. Its 3000-odd employees come from most of the member-states.

The Secretary-General has a wide variety of functions. He is responsible for the administrative work of the principal organs of the UN, except for the International Court, and he prepares annual reports to the General Assembly of the working of the UN. One of his most important duties is to bring to the attention of the Security Council any matter which is, in his opinion, a threat to international peace and security.

As a part of its routine administrative duties, the Secretariat provides the secretarial and translation services so important to the functioning of the UN, keeps records, makes studies of the functioning of the UN, publishes reports, provides press, radio, and television facilities, sees that visitors are received courteously and efficiently, and handles official communications between the world organization and states.

The Charter requires that all treaties made between nations be recorded with and published by the Secretariat. If a treaty is not reported to the Secretariat, it is not considered as having any standing in international law.

The United Nations in Action

Not Perfect, but Helpful. The church hasn't eliminated all sin, the schools haven't eliminated all ignorance, and the United Nations hasn't eliminated all war. All three of these institutions, however, are more than worth what little we have put into them.

The United Nations was formed to promote world peace. Yet the whole world spends less on the United Nations each year than the United States alone spent in one day in World War II, or less than the City of New York spends each year on garbage collection!

In its short life the UN has not brought an end to world tensions and the threat of a third world war. Because of this, some say that the UN is a failure. But these people often overlook a most important fact: *the UN is not a world government.* Like water which can rise no higher than its source, the UN can be no more effective than its members make it.

It is easy to overlook the many accomplishments of the UN during its brief existence. Among other things, the UN prevented the Soviet Union from seizing the oil fields of northern Iran. It halted an Arab-Jewish war in Palestine and helped to establish the new state of Israel. It helped settle the Dutch-Indonesian war and establish the new United States of Indonesia. It was instrumental in settling the Berlin blockade dispute and stopped the fighting between India and Pakistan over Kashmir.

When, in June, 1950, the Security Council called upon " all members to render every assistance " in meeting the North Korean attack upon South Korea, sixteen nations responded. *For the first time in history, an international organization met aggression with armed force.*

The UN brought an end to the fighting in Egypt in late 1956 and forced the withdrawal of the Israeli and Anglo-French forces from Egyptian soil. The UN Emergency Force, *the first international police force in history,* has been guarding the truce ever since. It has been widely proposed that UNEF be made a permanent force available for the UN's use whenever trouble flares anywhere on the globe. Several disputes have been settled by the International Court. For example, when a British ship was sunk by an Albanian mine in the Adriatic Sea, the two states went before the court. The British won damages and a dangerous incident was closed.

Much has been done by the specialized agencies, whose work may seem unspectacular, yet is very important. International peace can hardly become a lasting reality when millions of the world's people are hungry, lack shelter, suffer from disease, and live in ignorance. The World Health Organization stopped a cholera plague in Egypt and is working to control malaria in India and Pakistan. The Food and Agriculture Organization defeated a chestnut tree blight in Italy and has sent agricultural experts to aid people in several countries. The International Refugee Organization has given aid to more than 1,500,000 displaced persons, and the United Nations Educational, Scientific, and Cultural Organization is attacking illiteracy all over the world, helping to build new schools and to restore schools destroyed by war.

The mere fact that nations face one another in open forum before the world is significant in itself. World public opinion can be a powerful force. When a nation is in the wrong, the rest are already united to defend the right — as in Korea and Egypt.

The United Nations and Atomic Energy

Ever since its founding, the UN has wrestled with the problem of the international control of atomic energy. The need for such control is obvious.

712

Man, as Albert Einstein once noted, now has the knowledge with which to wipe himself off the face of the earth.

In August, 1945, in order to end World War II, the United States dropped the first atomic bombs on Japan. The first bomb fell on Hiroshima August 6. A second bomb hit Nagasaki three days later. The Hiroshima bomb caused an explosion equal to that of 20,000 tons of TNT. The blast, flash burn, fires, and falling débris killed 78,150 people, injured 37,425, and left 13,083 missing. Many of the injured later died of radiation sickness. At least 170,000 others were reported ill, homeless, hungry, or indigent. The bombing levelled some five square miles of Hiro-

Bimrose, " The Portland Oregonian "

" CRAZY MIXED UP KID "

To the cartoonist the world in this age of atomic power presents a sorry spectacle, not knowing what to do or where to turn.

shima. The Nagasaki blast was equally severe, leaving 73,884 dead.

Since then, because of the threat of another war, the United States has been stockpiling bombs and other atomic weapons more destructive than the bombs dropped on Japan. President Eisenhower has declared that the United States stockpile of atomic weapons, which, of course, increases daily, exceeds by many times the explosive equivalent of the total of all bombs and all shells that came from every plane and every gun in every theater of war through all the years of World War II.

The Soviet Union also has been producing and stockpiling atomic bombs since 1949. In 1952 the United States completed its first explosion tests of a hydrogen bomb. In 1953 the Russians claimed to have produced an H-bomb. Atomic scientists have told us that a single H-bomb could destroy New York City or any other of the world's great cities.

Soon after the end of the war with Japan, the United States announced its willingness to share its atomic secrets with the rest of the world, provided adequate and enforceable international safeguards against destructive use could be established.

Early in 1946 the UN created an Atomic Energy Commission, now known as the Disarmament Commission, to work out such safeguards. Bernard Baruch presented the American plan for international control. The Baruch Plan called for an International Atomic Development Authority with broad powers to own and control all atomic production and materials. The Russians, however, refused to agree to its provisions for strict international inspection and enforcement. They proposed, instead, a plan calling for only limited supervision and inspection.

After two years of deadlock and 220 meetings, and noting that the Soviet bloc would not agree " to even those elements of effective control considered essential from the technical point of view," the Commission adjourned indefinitely. Late in 1953, however, the General Assembly instructed the Disarmament Commission to make another attempt, this time by having " the powers principally involved . . . seek, in private, an acceptable solution."

Then, on December 8, 1953, President Eisenhower made a dramatic speech to the Assembly. He called for the creation of an International Atomic Energy Agency " to lead the world out of fear and into peace." He proposed that all nations possessing atomic materials make continually increasing contributions from their stockpiles to this agency, a sort of " bank of fissionable materials."

Through these contributions the destructive power of the world's atomic stockpiles would be gradually cut down. As a result, the prospects for peace would be considerably improved. Of equal importance, the Atomic Energy Agency would use its stockpiles to encourage worldwide scientific investigations into the apparently limitless peacetime uses of atomic energy.

The Eisenhower " atoms-for-peace " plan was debated inside and outside the UN for nearly three years.

A charter for the Agency was finally framed by an 82-nation conference in October, 1956. Enough states had ratified the document to bring it into force on July 29, 1957.

The IAEA's basic purpose is to promote the peaceful use of atomic energy. It is intended to be a world center for that purpose, supplying fissionable materials and technical help to nations seeking them for peaceful ends. Rigid controls are to be set up to insure that no aid it provides will be used for warlike purposes.

The IAEA held an organizational meeting at its Vienna headquarters in October, 1957.

Both the United States and Russia have already pledged contributions from their stockpiles of atomic materials to the world pool of the IAEA for use in peacetime scientific investigations.

The International Bank for Reconstruction and Development

The International Bank for Reconstruction and Development. This specialized agency of the UN, usually called the World Bank, was founded at the United Nations Monetary and Financial Conference held by forty-four nations at Bretton Woods, New Hampshire, in 1944. The World Bank now has sixty members.

The Bank's powers are vested in a Board of Governors, composed of one governor from each member country. This Board meets once a year to review the Bank's operations. The responsibility for the Bank's general operations is in the hands of sixteen Executive Directors, chosen by the member countries, and a President, chosen by the Directors. The Bank's headquarters are in Washington, D.C.

The Bank has an authorized capital of about $9,000,000,000, and it makes loans to member governments for such productive purposes as reconstruction of war damage, power plants, transportation systems, and irrigation programs. It also promotes the investment of private capital around the world.

The World Bank's first loan was one for $250,000,000 to France to aid reconstruction and additional industrialization. The second was for $195,000,000 to the Netherlands to repair war damage and restore production. By 1958 the Bank had made more than 175 loans, amounting to a little over $3,000,000,000, to more than forty member countries and their territories.

To obtain funds to lend governments, in addition to the capital stock provided by the members, the Bank issues bonds. By 1958 the Bank had issued over $900,000,000 in bonds of which over $700,000,000 were issued and sold in the United States.

The International Monetary Fund. The Fund, with now sixty members, was also established by the Bretton Woods Conference. Its purpose is to encourage world trade and prosperity through stabilizing the value of the currencies of the member nations.

If all nations agree to accept one another's currency at particular known values, commercial relationships are much more easily conducted than would be the case if the values were constantly changing. For example, trade between the United States and Great Britain is made more certain because both we and the British, through the Fund, have agreed that the British pound is worth $2.80 in terms of the American dollar.

All the nations which are members of the Fund have agreed not to change the value of their money without the consent of the World Bank. Thus the kind of world-wide confusion which followed the financial panic of 1929 will not occur again.

Following the panic of 1929, Japan lowered the value of its yen, so that prices other nations would have to pay for Japanese goods would be low and other nations would be encouraged to buy from Japan. Then the British devalued the pound, the United States the dollar, the French the franc, the Germans the mark, and most other countries their money, too. Confusion and uncertainty in world trade was the inevitable result.

American Loans. Our loans to foreign governments cannot be repaid except in gold, commodities, or services. During the depression of the 1930's the Congress created the Export-Import Bank to make loans to foreign governments to encourage them to buy from us. During World War II and since that conflict, the Bank has made loans for a wide range of purposes.

The largest loan we have ever made to any government was one for $3,750,000,000 to Great Britain in 1946. It is being repaid over a fifty-year period at two per cent interest.

No matter to whom we lend, Congress has provided that loans may only be repaid in gold, in commodities, or in services such as water transportation or storage. Because we export about twice as much as we import, it is difficult to see how some of our foreign loans can be repaid. However, we continue to give or lend money to other nations for the following reasons:

(1) So their people won't be in want and thus easy prey to our foes.

(2) To help them to recover from a war they helped us to win.

(3) To help keep them as friends in case another war should come.

(4) To promote their buying of American goods.

(5) To build up credits for the day when we might have to import oil or other raw materials which could become short in the United States.

As We Face the Future . . .

Ours is a nation which was born in revolution and with the Declaration of Independence as our national birth certificate. Today, as then —

We hold these truths to be self-evident: that all men are created equal; that they are endowed by their Creator with certain unalienable Rights; that among these are Life, Liberty and the pursuit of Happiness. That to secure these rights, Governments are instituted among Men, deriving their just powers from the consent of the governed; . . .

In one sense, the American Revolution ended in October of 1781, when Lord Cornwallis surrendered to General Washington at Yorktown. But in another and very real sense, the American Revolution has never ended. It is, rather, a continuing endeavor on our part to build the best possible life on earth, for *all* men and for *each* man.

In the course of this unending effort to preserve our rights and improve our condition, we have faced, and have overcome, many critical challenges. Some of these challenges have involved what seemed at times to be insurmountable odds. They have been, as Thomas Paine described them, " times that try men's souls."

Today we also face challenges. Not the least of these are: (1) How can we best find a just and lasting peace? and (2) What are the most effective ways in which we can promote democracy and defeat international communism?

These, and the problems that will

arise in the years ahead, will be overcome, too. That is, they will be overcome *if* we always remember that we are the heirs to a system of government and a way of life which must depend for its very existence upon what we, as a people and as individuals, are willing to do.

The future is in our hands; it will be whatever we choose to make of it. Because the future is ours to shape as we will, because ours is a government by the people, each one of us is charged with a grave responsibility. What will you do to meet that responsibility? How well and how hard will you work to carry on what has been " thus far so nobly advanced "?

WHAT THIS CHAPTER IS ABOUT

We do not and we cannot live isolated from the rest of the world. In many ways, whether we like it or not, we live in " one world." We live also in a world threatened by a third world war. The United States took the lead in founding, and today wholeheartedly supports, the United Nations in order to preserve peace in the world and prevent war by eliminating its causes.

After much preliminary spadework the UN was organized and its Charter drafted at the San Francisco Conference in 1945. It now has eighty-two members, and its permanent seat is in New York City.

The Charter proclaims the UN's purposes to be the maintenance of international peace and security, the development of friendly relations among all nations, and the promotion of international co-operation and justice. Membership is open to all " peace-loving states."

The Charter forbids the UN to interfere in the domestic affairs of any member. It contains several provisions relating to the peaceful settlement of disputes between nations and the use of military force. The General Assembly or an international conference may propose amendments to the Charter, and these, to be adopted, must be ratified by two-thirds of the members, including the Big Five.

The General Assembly is composed of all of the members represented equally. Essentially, it is the " town meeting of the world."

The Security Council consists of the Big Five and six nonpermanent members. Its powers are mainly related to the maintaining of peace and the dealing with cases of aggression. Each of the Big Five has the veto power. The Soviet Union has used the veto often to prevent UN action.

The Economic and Social Council is an eighteen-member body designed to attack the causes of war and improve standards of living around the world. The specialized agencies function under it.

The Trusteeship Council, composed of the Big Five and any other nation administering a trust territory plus an equal number of other states, oversees the administration of trust territories and encourages self-government for the various dependent peoples of the world.

The International Court of Justice is the judicial arm of the UN. Its fifteen judges hear cases involving international disputes and give advisory opinions to other UN organs.

The Secretariat, headed by the Secretary-General, is the civil service arm of the UN.

The World Bank makes loans to nations; the International Monetary Fund works to promote trade and prosperity by stabilizing the world's currencies.

The UN has wrestled with the fateful problem of international control of atomic energy since its founding. President Eisenhower's "atoms-for-peace" plan may be the key to the problem.

The UN is criticized by some because we still live in an unsettled world, but all too often the organization's many accomplishments are overlooked. It is, as President Eisenhower has said, " the living sign of all people's hope for peace."

QUESTIONS ON THE TEXT

1. Why is it possible to say that, in a variety of ways, we live in "one world" and, at the same time, to say that we do not?

2. What was the United Nations Declaration?

3. What are the UN's basic purposes?

4. Where is the permanent UN seat located?

5. When and where was the UN Charter drafted?

6. Describe the organization and duties of the General Assembly. The Security Council. The Economic and Social Council. The Trusteeship Council. The Secretariat.

7. Explain the voting procedure and the veto power in the Security Council.

8. What are the specialized agencies of the UN?

9. What is the Eisenhower "atoms-for-peace" plan?

10. Give three illustrations of the accomplishments of the UN.

11. What are the World Bank and the International Monetary Fund?

PROBLEMS FOR DISCUSSION

1. Why do you agree or disagree with the following statement: "The United Nations is a failure. It is falling apart — let it. No rational person really expected it to work anyway. If it fails, then we can put our effort and our money into pursuing our own national interests."

2. In presenting the American plan for international control of atomic energy, Bernard M. Baruch made the following remarks. Discuss them in class.

" We are here to make a choice between the quick and the dead. That is our business. Behind the black portent of the new atomic age lies a hope which, seized upon with faith, can work our salvation. If we fail, then we have damned every man to be the slave of fear. Let us not deceive ourselves. We must elect world peace or world destruction.

" Science has torn from nature a secret so vast in its potentialities that our minds cower from the terror it creates. Yet terror is not enough to inhibit the use of the atomic bomb. The terror created by weapons has never stopped man from applying them. For each new weapon a defense has been produced, in time. But now we face a condition in which adequate defense does not exist.

" Science, which gave us this dread power, shows that it *can* be made a giant to help humanity, but science does *not* show us how to prevent its baleful use. . . . We must provide the mechanism to assure that atomic energy is used for peaceful purposes and preclude its use in war."

3. For years it has been proposed that the strategic straits and canals of the world be placed under international control.

Such waterways as the Straits of the Bosporus and Dardanelles, the Kiel Canal, the Panama Canal, the Strait of Gibraltar, and the Suez Canal are involved in such proposals. Locate each of these on a map of the world and explain why they are " strategic." What do you think of the internationalization proposals?

4. Our Government insisted upon the veto power when the UN was founded,

and we do not want it abolished now. Why?

5. Why can it be said that the UN can succeed only if the United States and the Soviet Union are willing to permit it to?

6. Many people favor the creation of a world government as the only real and permanent solution to the problem of lasting peace. Why do you favor or oppose their position?

THINGS YOU MIGHT DO

1. Keep a magazine and newspaper clipping file of the work and accomplishments of the UN.

2. Stage a class debate or forum on the question: " *Resolved*, That the United States should withdraw from the United Nations."

3. Write an editorial or short essay giving the reasons why you think the UN

should or should not concern itself with social and economic problems.

4. Secure a copy of the UN Charter and draw up an outline of its provisions.

5. Read as many articles as you can which propose and as many as you can which oppose world government. Draw up a list of the major arguments pro and con.

WORDS AND PHRASES YOU SHOULD KNOW

" Atoms-for-peace " plan
Big Five
Devalue
Disarmament Commission
Economic and Social Council
General Assembly
International Court of Justice

International Monetary
    Fund
Procedural questions
San Francisco Conference
Secretariat
Secretary-General
Security Council

Substantive questions
Trusteeship Council
Trust territory
United Nations
    Charter
Veto power
World Bank

SELECT BIBLIOGRAPHY

Bess, Demaree, " The Battle Over Atoms-for-Peace," *Saturday Evening Post*, November 16, 1957.

MacArthur, General Douglas, " Can We Outlaw War? " *Reader's Digest*, May, 1955.

Niebuhr, Reinhold, " The UN Is Not a World Government," *The Reporter*, March 7, 1957.

" The United Nations and One-Worldism," *The Freeman*, March, 1955.

U.S. State Department, *The United Nations Today*. Washington, annual.

" Will U.N. Last Another 10 Years? " *U.S. News*, June 24, 1955.

" World Bank: Bearer of Light," *Time*, June 25, 1956.

Bury me on my face; for in a little while everything will be
turned upside down.

— Diogenes

———————STOP THE PRESSES!———

Every effort is made in each edition of this book to present the subject of
American Government in the most up-to-date and accurate manner possible.
The subject is by no means a static, unchanging thing, however. While its
basic nature is fixed and lasting, many of its aspects change as we continue
to develop and perfect our governmental system.

On this page and the following one you will find a number of last-minute
additions, changes, and corrections which, for reasons of time, could not be
included in the main body of the text itself.

THE EFFECTS OF SPUTNIKS I AND II

At the year's end, the after-effects
of the Russian launchings of earth
satellites dominated much of the
American scene. It seemed clear that
the United States continued to possess
more than adequate military power
either to deter, or, if necessary, retaliate effectively against, Soviet aggression. (*Pages 8–9, 208–209, 231–242.*)

But the significant Russian achiev-
ment had, as President Eisenhower
put it, forced a " critical re-examina-
tion of our entire defense position."
The U.S.S.R. had demonstrated that
it had made far greater scientific and
technological advances than we had
generally assumed. (*Page 9.*)

Steps were being taken and plans
laid to insure that the admitted Soviet
lead in satellite and missile development was only a brief and temporary
one. Among the important consequences:

Our own satellite and missile programs were speeded drastically and reorganized. The President appointed
a Special Assistant for Science and
Technology to assist him in prompting
the work. (*Pages 9, 178–179, 232–
233.*)

Steps were taken to inject new vigor
into the NATO alliance and to promote greater cooperation among its
fifteen members in the development
and use of missiles and nuclear and
other advanced weapons. (*Page
211.*)

Indications were that defense expenditures would be increased to at
least $40,000,000,000 in 1958. (*Page
218.*) Widely held hopes for a cut
in the high rate of federal taxation
vanished almost overnight. (*Pages
115, 216–219.*) An increase in the
public debt ceiling seemed certain.
(*Pages 102, 222–223.*) In an attempt

720

to hold the budget within manageable proportions it also seemed certain that various domestic governmental programs would be cut back somewhat.

New emphasis was being placed on scientific and engineering training. New programs of federal aid to education in those fields were being seriously considered, including federal scholarships, subsidies to improve teachers' salaries and provide better school laboratory facilities, and the like. (*Pages 10, 306, 630–631.*) Also being considered were revised Selective Service rules to channel qualified high school and college students into those fields. (*Pages 242–243.*)

All but forgotten in the wake of the satellites was the International Geophysical Year. IGY is an eighteen-month " scientific year " scheduled to last until mid-1958. During IGY most of the nations of the world are promoting intensive scientific investigations of man's physical surroundings, above and below, as well as on the earth's surface. It is intended that each nation's findings will be shared with all. The Russian satellites, and the projected American satellites, too, were originally conceived as one aspect of this international project. The extensive polar investigations in the Antarctic are another part of the many-faceted IGY undertaking.

Pages 243, 299: The Atomic Energy Commission and the Maritime Administration announced late in 1957 the letting of the contract for building the *Savannah*, the world's first nuclear-powered merchant vessel.

Page 274: The Census Bureau reported that by 1957 the nation's farm population had declined to 20,396,000. This represented a drop of nearly 5,000,000 since the 1950 census. Thus the urban trend is continuing.

DOCUMENTS OF OUR LIBERTIES

THE MAYFLOWER COMPACT

In the name of God, Amen. We whose names are under writen, the loyall subjects of our dread soveraigne Lord, King James, by the grace of God, of Great Britaine, Franc, and Ireland king, defender of the faith, etc., haveing undertaken, for the glorie of God, and advancemente of the Christian faith, and honour of our king and countrie, a voyage to plant the first colonie in the Northerne parts of Virginia, doe by these presents solemnly and mutualy in the presence of God, and one of another, covenant and combine our selves togeather into a civill body politick, for our better ordering and preservation and further-ance of the ends aforesaid; and by vertue hearof to enacte, constitute, and frame such just and equall lawes, ordinances, acts, constitutions and offices, from time to time, as shall be thought most meete and convenient for the generall good of the Colonie, unto which we promise all due submission and obedience. In witnes whereof we have here-under subscribed our names at Cap-Codd the 11. of November, in the year of the raigne of our soveraigne lord, King James, of Eng-land, France, and Ireland the eighteenth, and of Scotland the fiftie fourth. Anno: Dom. 1620.

THE DECLARATION OF INDEPENDENCE

In Congress, July 4, 1776
THE UNANIMOUS DECLARATION OF THE THIRTEEN UNITED STATES OF AMERICA

When in the Course of human events, it becomes necessary for one people to dissolve the political bands which have connected them with another, and to assume among the Powers of the earth, the separate and equal station to which the Laws of Nature and of Nature's God entitle them, a decent respect to the opinions of mankind requires that they should declare the causes which impel them to the separation.

We hold these truths to be self-evident, that all men are created equal, that they are endowed by their Creator with certain un-alienable Rights, that among these are Life, Liberty and the pursuit of Happiness. That to secure these rights, Governments are in-stituted among Men, deriving their just pow-ers from the consent of the governed; That whenever any Form of Government becomes destructive of these ends it is the Right of the People to alter or to abolish it, and to institute new Government, laying its founda-tion on such principles and organizing its powers in such form, as to them shall seem most likely to effect their Safety and Happi-ness. Prudence, indeed, will dictate that Governments long established should not be changed for light and transient causes; and accordingly all experience hath shown, that mankind are more disposed to suffer, while evils are sufferable, than to right themselves by abolishing the forms to which they are ac-customed. But when a long train of abuses and usurpations, pursuing invariably the same Object evinces a design to reduce them under absolute Despotism, it is their right, it is their duty, to throw off such Government, and to provide new Guards for their future security. — Such has been the patient suffer-ance of these Colonies; and such is now the necessity which constrains them to alter their former Systems of Government. The history

722

of the present King of Great Britain is a history of repeated injuries and usurpations, all having in direct object the establishment of an absolute Tyranny over these States. To prove this, let Facts be submitted to a candid world.

He has refused his Assent to Laws, the most wholesome and necessary for the public good.

He has forbidden his Governors to pass Laws of immediate and pressing importance, unless suspended in their operation till his Assent should be obtained; and when so suspended, he has utterly neglected to attend to them.

He has refused to pass other Laws for the accommodation of large districts of people, unless those people would relinquish the right of Representation in the Legislature, a right inestimable to them and formidable to tyrants only.

He has called together legislative bodies at places unusual, uncomfortable, and distant from the depository of their Public Records, for the sole purpose of fatiguing them into compliance with his measures.

He has dissolved Representative Houses repeatedly, for opposing with manly firmness his invasions on the rights of the people.

He has refused for a long time, after such dissolutions, to cause others to be elected; whereby the Legislative Powers, incapable of Annihilation, have returned to the People at large for their exercise; the State remaining, in the meantime, exposed to all the dangers of invasions from without, and convulsions within.

He has endeavored to prevent the population of these States; for that purpose obstructing the Laws for the Naturalization of Foreigners; refusing to pass others to encourage their migration hither, and raising the conditions of new Appropriations of Lands.

He has obstructed the Administration of Justice, by refusing his Assent to Laws for establishing Judiciary Powers.

He has made Judges dependent on his will alone for the tenure of their offices, and the amount and payment of their salaries.

He has erected a multitude of New Offices, and sent hither swarms of Officers to harass our People and eat out their substance.

He has kept among us in times of peace, Standing Armies, without the Consent of our Legislatures.

He has affected to render the Military independent of, and superior to, the Civil Power.

He has combined with others to subject us to a jurisdiction foreign to our constitutions, and unacknowledged by our laws; giving his Assent to their acts of pretended legislation:

For quartering large bodies of armed troops among us;

For protecting them, by a mock Trial, from Punishment for any Murders which they should commit on the Inhabitants of these States;

For cutting off our Trade with all parts of the world;

For imposing taxes on us without our Consent;

For depriving us, in many cases, of the benefits of a Trial by Jury;

For transporting us beyond Seas, to be tried for pretended offenses;

For abolishing the free System of English Laws in a neighboring Province, establishing therein an Arbitrary government, and enlarging its Boundaries, so as to render it at once an example and fit instrument for introducing the same absolute rule into these Colonies;

For taking away our Charters, abolishing our most valuable Laws, and altering, fundamentally, the Forms of our Governments;

For suspending our own Legislatures, and declaring themselves invested with Power to legislate for us in all cases whatsoever.

He has abdicated Government here, by declaring us out of his Protection, and waging War against us.

He has plundered our seas, ravaged our Coasts, burned our towns, and destroyed the lives of our people.

He is at this time transporting large armies of foreign mercenaries to complete the works of death, desolation and tyranny, already begun with circumstances of Cruelty and perfidy scarcely paralleled in the most barbarous ages, and totally unworthy the Head of a civilized nation.

He has constrained our fellow-citizens, taken captive on the high seas, to bear Arms against their Country, to become the executioners of their friends and Brethren, or to fall themselves by their Hands.

He has excited domestic insurrection among us, and has endeavored to bring on the inhabitants of our frontiers the merciless Indian Savages whose known rule of warfare is an undistinguished destruction of all ages, sexes, and conditions.

In every stage of these Oppressions We have Petitioned for Redress in the most humble terms. Our repeated Petitions have been answered only by repeated injury. A Prince whose character is thus marked by every act which may define a Tyrant, is unfit to be the ruler of a free people.

Nor have we been wanting in our attentions to our British brethren. We have warned them, from time to time, of attempts by their legislature to extend an unwarrantable jurisdiction over us. We have reminded them of the circumstances of our emigration and settlement here. We have appealed to their native justice and magnanimity and we have conjured them by the ties of our common kindred to disavow these usurpations, which would inevitably interrupt our connections and correspondence. They, too, have been deaf to the voice of justice and of consanguinity. We must, therefore, acquiesce in the necessity which denounces our Separation, and hold them as we hold the rest of mankind — Enemies in War; in Peace, Friends.

We, therefore, the Representatives of the United States of America in General Congress Assembled, appealing to the Supreme Judge of the world for the rectitude of our intentions, do, in the Name and by the Authority of the good People of these Colonies, solemnly publish and declare that these united colonies are, and of right ought to be, Free and Independent States; that they are Absolved from all Allegiance to the British Crown, and that all political connection between them and the state of Great Britain is, and ought to be, totally dissolved, and that, as Free and Independent States, they have full Power to levy War, conclude Peace, contract Alliances, establish Commerce, and do all other Acts and Things which Independent States may of right do. And for the support of this Declaration, with a firm reliance on the protection of Divine Providence, we mutually pledge to each other our Lives, our Fortunes, and our sacred Honor.

JOHN HANCOCK

New Hampshire
JOSIAH BARTLETT
WILLIAM WHIPPLE
MATTHEW THORNTON

Massachusetts Bay
SAMUEL ADAMS
JOHN ADAMS
ROBERT TREAT PAINE
ELBRIDGE GERRY

Rhode Island
STEPHEN HOPKINS
WILLIAM ELLERY

Connecticut
ROGER SHERMAN
SAMUEL HUNTINGTON
WILLIAM WILLIAMS
OLIVER WOLCOTT

New York
WILLIAM FLOYD
PHILIP LIVINGSTON
FRANCIS LEWIS
LEWIS MORRIS

New Jersey
RICHARD STOCKTON
JOHN WITHERSPOON
FRANCIS HOPKINSON
JOHN HART
ABRAHAM CLARK

Pennsylvania
ROBERT MORRIS
BENJAMIN RUSH
BENJAMIN FRANKLIN
JOHN MORTON
GEORGE CLYMER
JAMES SMITH
GEORGE TAYLOR
JAMES WILSON
GEORGE ROSS

Delaware
CÆSAR RODNEY
GEORGE READ
THOMAS M'KEAN

Maryland
SAMUEL CHASE
WILLIAM PACA
THOMAS STONE
CHARLES CARROLL OF
  Carrollton

Virginia
GEORGE WYTHE
RICHARD HENRY LEE
THOMAS JEFFERSON
BENJAMIN HARRISON
THOMAS NELSON, JR.
FRANCIS LIGHTFOOT LEE
CARTER BRAXTON

North Carolina
WILLIAM HOOPER
JOSEPH HEWES
JOHN PENN

South Carolina
EDWARD RUTLEDGE
THOMAS HEYWARD, JR.
THOMAS LYNCH, JR.
ARTHUR MIDDLETON

Georgia
BUTTON GWINNETT
LYMAN HALL
GEORGE WALTON

THE ARTICLES OF CONFEDERATION

To all to whom these Presents shall come, we the undersigned Delegates of the States affixed to our Names send greeting

Whereas the Delegates of the United States of America in Congress assembled did on the fifteenth day of November in the year of our Lord One Thousand Seven Hundred and Seventy-seven, and in the Second Year of the Independence of America, agree to certain articles of Confederation and perpetual Union between the States of Newhampshire, Massachusetts-bay, Rhodeisland and Providence Plantations, Connecticut, New York, New Jersey, Pennsylvania, Delaware, Maryland, Virginia, North-Carolina, South-Carolina and Georgia in the Words following, viz.

Articles of Confederation and perpetual Union between the States of Newhampshire, Massachusetts-bay, Rhodeisland and Providence Plantations, Connecticut, New York, New Jersey, Pennsylvania, Delaware, Maryland, Virginia, North Carolina, South Carolina, and Georgia.

ARTICLE I. — The stile of this Confederacy shall be, " The United States of America."

ARTICLE II. — Each State retains its sovereignty, freedom, and independence, and every power, jurisdiction, and right, which is not by this Confederation expressly delegated to the United States, in Congress assembled.

ARTICLE III. — The said States hereby severally enter into a firm league of friendship with each other, for their common defence, the security of their liberties, and their mutual and general welfare, binding themselves to assist each other against all force offered to, or attacks made upon them, or any of them, on account of religion, sovereignty, trade, or any other pretence whatever.

ARTICLE IV. — The better to secure and perpetuate mutual friendship and intercourse among the people of the States in this Union, the free inhabitants of each of these States, paupers, vagabonds, and fugitives from justice excepted, shall be entitled to all privileges and immunities of free citizens in the several States; and the people of each State shall have free ingress and egress to and from any other State, and shall enjoy therein all the privileges of trade and commerce subject to the same duties, impositions, and retrictions as the inhabitants thereof respectively; provided that such restrictions shall not extend so far as to prevent the removal of property imported into any State to any other State of which the owner is an inhabitant: provided also that no imposition, duties, or restriction shall be laid by any State

on the property of the United States, or either of them.

If any person guilty of, or charged with treason, felony, or other high misdemeanor in any State, shall flee from justice, and be found in any of the United States, he shall upon demand of the Governor or Executive power of the State from which he fled, be delivered up and removed to the State having jurisdiction of his offence.

Full faith and credit shall be given in each of these States to the records, acts, and judicial proceedings of the courts and magistrates of every other State.

ARTICLE V. — For the more convenient management of the general interest of the United States, delegates shall be annually appointed in such manner as the legislature of each State shall direct, to meet in Congress on the first Monday in November, in every year, with a power reserved to each State, to recall its delegates, or any of them, at any time within the year, and to send others in their stead, for the remainder of the year.

No State shall be represented in Congress by less than two, nor by more than seven members; and no person shall be capable of being a delegate for more than three years in any term of six years; nor shall any person, being a delegate, be capable of holding any office under the United States, for which he, or another for his benefit, receives any salary, fees or emolument of any kind.

Each State shall maintain its own delegates in a meeting of the States, and while they act as members of the committee of the States.

In determining questions in the United States, in Congress assembled, each State shall have one vote.

Freedom of speech and debate in Congress shall not be impeached or questioned in any court, or place out of Congress, and the members of Congress shall be protected in their persons from arrests and imprisonments, during the time of their going to and from, and attendance on Congress, except for treason, felony, or breach of the peace.

ARTICLE VI. — No State without the consent of the United States in Congress assembled, shall send any embassy to, or receive any embassy from, or enter into any conference, agreement, alliance or treaty with any king, prince or state; nor shall any person holding any office of profit or trust under the United States, or any of them, accept of any present, emolument, office or title of any kind whatever from any king, prince or foreign state; nor shall the United States in Congress assembled, or any of them, grant any title of nobility.

No two or more States shall enter into any treaty, confederation or alliance whatever between them, without the consent of the United States in Congress assembled, specifying accurately the purposes for which the same is to be entered into, and how long it shall continue.

No state shall lay any imposts or duties, which may interfere with any stipulations in treaties entered into by the United States, in Congress assembled, with any king, prince, or state, in pursuance of any treaties already proposed by Congress to the courts of France and Spain.

No vessel of war shall be kept up in time of peace by any State, except such number only as shall be deemed necessary by the United States, in Congress assembled, for the defence of such State or its trade, nor shall any body of forces be kept up by any State in time of peace, except such number only as, in the judgment of the United States, in Congress assembled, shall be deemed requisite to garrison the forts necessary for the defence of such State; but every State shall always keep up a well-regulated and disci-

plined militia, sufficiently armed and accoutred, and shall provide and constantly have ready for use in public stores a due number of field-pieces and tents, and a proper quantity of arms, ammunition, and camp equipage.

No State shall engage in any war without the consent of the United States, in Congress assembled, unless such State be actually invaded by enemies, or shall have received certain advice of a resolution being formed by some nation of Indians to invade such State, and the danger is so imminent as not to admit of delay till the United States, in Congress assembled, can be consulted; nor shall any State grant commissions to any ships or vessels of war, nor letters of marque or reprisal, except it be after a declaration of war by the United States, in Congress assembled, and then only against the kingdom or state, and the subjects thereof, against which war has been so declared, and under such regulations as shall be established by the United States, in Congress assembled, unless such State be infested by pirates, in which case vessels of war may be fitted out for that occasion, and kept so long as the danger shall continue, or until the United States, in Congress assembled, shall determine otherwise.

ARTICLE VII. — When land forces are raised by any State for the common defence, all officers of or under the rank of Colonel shall be appointed by the Legislature of each State respectively by whom such forces shall be raised, or in such manner as such State shall direct, and all vacancies shall be filled up by the States which first made the appointment.

ARTICLE VIII. — All charges of war, and all other expenses that shall be incurred for the common defence or federal welfare, and allowed by the United States in Congress assembled, shall be defrayed out of a common treasury, which shall be supplied by the several States, in proportion to the value of all land within each State, granted to or surveyed for any person, as such land and the buildings and improvements thereon shall be estimated according to such mode as the United States in Congress assembled, shall from time to time direct and appoint.

The taxes for paying that proportion shall

be laid and levied by the authority and direction of the Legislatures of the several States within the time agreed upon by the United States in Congress assembled.

ARTICLE IX. — The United States in Congress assembled, shall have the sole and exclusive right and power of determining on peace and war, except in the cases mentioned in the sixth article — of sending and receiving ambassadors — entering into treaties and alliances, provided that no treaty of commerce shall be made whereby the legislative power of the respective States shall be restrained from imposing such imposts and duties on foreigners, as their own people are subjected to, or from prohibiting the exportation or importation of any species of goods or commodities whatsoever — of establishing rules for deciding in all cases, what captures on land or water shall be legal, and in what manner prizes taken by land or naval forces in the service of the United States shall be divided or appropriated — of granting letters of marque and reprisal in times of peace — appointing courts for the trial of piracies and felonies committed on the high seas and establishing courts for receiving and determining finally appeals in all cases of captures, provided that no member of Congress shall be appointed a judge of any of the said courts.

The United States in Congress assembled shall also be the last resort on appeal in all disputes and differences now subsisting or that hereafter may arise between two or more States concerning boundary, jurisdiction or any other cause whatever; which authority shall always be exercised in the manner following. [In the original, a passage appears here as to the method of constituting commissioners to decide such contests.]

The United States in Congress assembled shall also have the sole and exclusive right and power of regulating the alloy and value of coin struck by their own authority, or by that of the respective States — fixing the standard of weights and measures throughout the United States — regulating the trade and managing all affairs with the Indians, not members of any of the States, provided that the legislative right of any State within its own limits be not infringed or violated — establishing and regulating postoffices from one State to another, throughout all the United States, and exacting such postage on the papers passing thro' the same as may be requisite to defray the expenses of the said office — appointing all officers of the land forces, in the service of the United States, excepting regimental officers — appointing all the officers of the naval forces, and commissioning all officers whatever in the service of the United States — making rules for the government and regulation of the said land and naval forces, and directing their operations.

The United States in Congress assembled shall have authority to appoint a committee, to sit in the recess of Congress, to be denominated "a Committee of the States," and to consist of one delegate from each State; and to appoint such other committees and civil officers as may be necessary for managing the general affairs of the United States under their direction — to appoint one of their number to preside, provided that no person be allowed to serve in the office of president more than one year in any term of three years; to ascertain the necessary sums of money to be raised for the service of the United States, and to appropriate and apply the same for defraying the public expenses — to borrow money, or emit bills on the credit of the United States, transmitting every half year to the respective States an account of the sums of money so borrowed or emitted, — to build and equip a navy — to agree upon the number of land forces, and to make requisitions from each State for its quota, in proportion to the number of white inhabitants in such State; which requisition shall be binding; and thereupon the Legislature of each State shall appoint the regimental officers, raise the men, and clothe, arm, and equip them in a soldier-like manner, at the expense of the United States; and the officers and men so clothed, armed, and equipped shall march to the place appointed, and within the time agreed on by the United States, in Congress assembled; but if the United States, in Congress assembled, shall, on consideration of circumstances, judge proper that any State should not raise men, or should raise a smaller number than its quota, and that any other State should raise a greater number of men than the quota thereof, such extra number shall be raised, officered, clothed, armed, and equipped in the same manner as the quota of such State, unless the Legislature of such State shall judge that such extra number cannot be safely spared out of the same, in which case they shall raise, officer, clothe, arm, and equip as many of such extra number as they judge can be safely spared, and the officers and men so clothed, armed, and equipped shall march to the place appointed, and within the time agreed on by the United States, in Congress assembled.

The United States, in Congress assembled, shall never engage in a war, nor grant letters of marque and reprisal in time of peace, nor enter into any treaties or alliances, nor coin money, nor regulate the value thereof, nor ascertain the sums and expenses necessary for the defence and welfare of the United States, or any of them, nor emit bills, nor borrow money on the credit of the United States, nor appropriate money, nor agree upon the number of vessels of war to be built or purchased, or the number of land or sea forces to be raised, nor appoint a commander-in-chief of the army or navy, unless nine States assent to the same; nor shall a question on any other point, except for adjourning from day to day, be determined, unless by the votes of a majority of the United States, in Congress assembled. [Passage follows, stipulating publication of journal of proceedings.]

ARTICLE X. — The committee of the States, or any nine of them, shall be authorized to execute, in the recess of Congress, such of the powers of Congress as the United States in Congress assembled, by the consent of nine States, shall from time to time think expedient to vest them with; provided that no power be delegated to the said committee, for the exercise of which, by the articles of confederation, the voice of nine States in the Congress of the United States assembled is requisite.

ARTICLE XI. — Canada acceding to this confederation, and joining in the measures of the United States, shall be admitted into, and entitled to all the advantages of this Union: but no other colony shall be admitted into the same, unless such admission be agreed to by nine States.

ARTICLE XII.— (This article states that bills contracted by Congress in pursuance of this confederation shall be deemed a charge against the United States, for payment whereof " the said United States and the public faith are hereby solemnly pledged.")

ARTICLE XIII. — Every State shall abide by the determinations of the United States in Congress assembled, on all questions which by this confederation are submitted to them. And the articles of this confederation shall be inviolably observed by every State, and the Union shall be perpetual; nor shall any alteration at any time hereafter be made in any of them; unless such alteration be agreed to in a Congress of the United States, and be afterwards confirmed by the Legislatures of every State.

And whereas it hath pleased the Great Governor of the World to incline the hearts of the Legislatures we respectively represent in Congress, to approve of, and to authorize us to ratify the said articles of confederation and perpetual union. Know ye that we the undersigned delegates, by virtue of the power and authority to us given for that purpose, do by these presents, in the name and in behalf of our respective constituents, fully and entirely ratify and confirm each and every of the said articles of confederation and perpetual union, and all and singular the matters and things therein contained. And we do further solemnly plight and engage the faith of our respective constitutents, that they shall abide by the determinations of the United States, in Congress assembled, on all questions which by the said Confederation are submitted to them; and that the Articles thereof shall be inviolably observed by the States we respectively represent, and that the Union shall be perpetual.

In witness whereof we have hereunto set our hands in Congress. Done at Philadelphia in the State of Pennsylvania the ninth day of July in the year of our Lord one thousand seven hundred and seventy-eight, and in the third year of the independence of America.

[The signatures]

THE CONSTITUTION OF THE UNITED STATES
OF AMERICA

Recommended by the Philadelphia Convention, September 17, 1787; ratified by the ninth State (see Article VII) June 21, 1788; in effect, April 30, 1789

Preamble [1]

We, the people of the United States, in order to form a more perfect Union, establish justice, insure domestic tranquillity, provide for the common defence, promote the general welfare, and secure the blessings of liberty to ourselves and our posterity, do ordain and establish this Constitution for the United States of America.

ARTICLE I

LEGISLATIVE DEPARTMENT

Section 1. Two Houses

All legislative powers herein granted shall be vested in a Congress of the United States, which shall consist of a Senate and House of Representatives.

Section 2. House of Representatives

1. The House of Representatives shall be composed of members chosen every second year by the people of the several States, and the electors in each State shall have the qualifications requisite for electors of the most numerous branch of the State legislature.[2]

2. No person shall be a Representative who shall not have attained to the age of twenty-five years, and been seven years a citizen of the United States, and who shall not, when elected, be an inhabitant of that State in which he shall be chosen.[3]

3. Representatives and direct taxes [4] shall be apportioned among the several States which may be included within this Union, according to their respective numbers, which shall be determined by adding to the whole number of free persons, including those bound to service for a term of years, and excluding Indians not taxed, three-fifths of all other persons.[5] The actual enumeration shall be made within three years after the first meeting of the Congress of the United States, and within every subsequent term of ten years, in such manner as they shall by law direct. The number of Representatives shall not exceed one for every thirty thousand,[6] but each State shall have at least one Representative; and, until such enumeration shall be made, the state of New Hampshire shall be entitled to choose three, Massachusetts eight, Rhode Island and Providence Plantations one, Connecticut five, New York six, New Jersey four, Pennsylvania eight, Delaware one, Maryland six, Virginia ten, North Carolina five, South Carolina five, and Georgia three.[7]

4. When vacancies happen in the representation from any State, the executive authority thereof shall issue writs of election to fill such vacancies.

---

[1] The Preamble is of no legal force. It is an introduction to the main body of the Constitution. It assists in interpreting the clauses that follow by indicating the intentions of the Framers.

[2] " Electors " means voters. Each State must permit the same voters to vote for United States Representatives as it permits to vote for the members of the larger house of its own legislature. In 1913 the 17th Amendment extended this requirement to the qualification of voters for United States Senators.

[3] In addition to these formal qualifications, political custom also requires that a Representative reside in the district in which he is elected. The first woman to serve in the House of Representatives in Washington was Miss Jeanette Rankin. Miss Rankin was elected from the State of Montana in 1916.

[4] The income tax is a direct tax expressly permitted by the 16th Amendment, which was adopted in 1913.

[5] The phrase refers to slaves and was superseded by the 13th Amendment and the 14th Amendment.

[6] Under the latest census (1950), there is one Representative for approximately every 345,000 people.

[7] This clause of the Constitution is a temporary one.

5. The House of Representatives shall choose their Speaker [8] and other officers; and shall have the sole power of impeachment.[9]

Section 3. *Senate*

1. The Senate of the United States shall be composed of two Senators from each State [chosen by the legislature thereof] [10] for six years; and each Senator shall have one vote.

2. Immediately after they shall be assembled in consequence of the first election, they shall be divided, as equally as may be, into three classes. The seats of the senators of the first class shall be vacated at the expiration of the second year; of the second class, at the expiration of the fourth year; and of the third class, at the expiration of the sixth year; so that one-third may be chosen every second year; and if vacancies happen by resignation, or otherwise, during the recess of the legislature of any State, the executive thereof may make temporary appointments until the next meeting of the legislature, which shall then fill such vacancies.[11]

3. No person shall be a Senator who shall not have attained to the age of thirty years, and been nine years a citizen of the United States, who shall not, when elected, be an inhabitant of that State for which he shall be chosen.

4. The Vice-President of the United States shall be President of the Senate, but shall have no vote, unless they be equally divided.

5. The Senate shall choose their other officers, and also a President *pro tempore,* in the absence of the Vice-President, or when he shall exercise the office of President of the United States.

6. The Senate shall have the sole power to try all impeachments. When sitting for that purpose, they shall be on oath or affirmation. When the President of the United States is tried, the Chief Justice shall preside; and no person shall be convicted without the concurrence of two-thirds of the members present.[12]

7. Judgment in cases of impeachment shall not extend further than to removal from office, and disqualification to hold and enjoy any office of honor, trust, or profit, under the United States; but the party convicted shall, nevertheless, be liable and subject to indictment, trial, judgment, and punishment, according to law.

Section 4. *Elections and Meetings of Congress*

1. The time, places, and manner of holding elections for Senators and Representatives, shall be prescribed in each State by the legislature thereof: but the Congress may at any time, by law, make or alter such regulations, except as to the places of choosing Senators.[13]

2. The Congress shall assemble at least once in every year, and such meeting shall be on the first Monday in December,[14] unless they shall by law appoint a different day.

Section 5. *Powers and Duties of the Houses*

1. Each House shall be the judge of the elections, returns, and qualifications of its own members,[15] and a majority of each shall constitute a quorum to do business; but a smaller number may adjourn from day to day, and may be authorized to compel the attendance of absent members, in such manner, and under such penalties, as each House may provide.

2. Each House may determine the rules of its proceedings, punish its members for disorderly behavior, and, with the concurrence of two-thirds, expel a member.

3. Each House shall keep a journal of its proceedings, and, from time to time, publish the same, excepting such parts as may, in their judgment, require secrecy; and the

---

[8] Although the Constitution does not require it, the Speaker is always a member of the House.

[9] " To impeach " means to bring an accusation against someone. The House impeaches (accuses) and the Senate tries in impeachment cases.

[10] Replaced by the 17th Amendment in 1913. Senators are now popularly elected.

[11] Changed by the 17th Amendment in 1913. The governor appoints a successor to serve until the voters fill the vacancy at an election.

[12] Those who object, for religious reasons (e.g., Quakers), to the taking of an oath are permitted to " affirm " rather than " swear."

" Two thirds of the members present " must be at least a quorum. A quorum (the required number present in order to conduct business) is 49 in the Senate and 218 in the House.

[13] In 1842 Congress required that Representatives be elected from districts. Delaware, Nevada, Vermont, and Wyoming have only one Representative each. In 1872 Congress required that Representatives should be elected on the Tuesday following the first Monday in November of even-numbered years. Maine is the only State made an exception to this rule. It elects in mid-September and some view its elections as a political barometer. Hence the expression " As Maine goes, so goes the nation."

[14] Changed to January 3rd by the 20th Amendment in 1933.

[15] This provision permits either house, by a majority vote, to refuse to seat a member-elect.

yeas and nays of the members of either House, on any question, shall, at the desire of one-fifth of those present, be entered on the journal.

4. Neither House, during the session of Congress, shall, without the consent of the other, adjourn for more than three days, nor to any other place than that in which the two Houses shall be sitting.

Section 6. *Privileges of and Prohibitions upon Members*

1. The Senators and Representatives shall receive a compensation for their services, to be ascertained by law, and paid out of the treasury of the United States. They shall, in all cases, except treason, felony, and breach of the peace,[16] be privileged from arrest during their attendance at the session of their respective Houses, and in going to, and returning from, the same; and for any speech or debate in either House, they shall not be questioned in any other place.[17]

2. No Senator or Representative shall, during the time for which he was elected, be appointed to any civil office under the authority of the United States, which shall have been created, or the emoluments whereof shall have been increased during such time;[18] and no person, holding any office under the United States, shall be a member of either House during his continuance in office.

Section 7. *Revenue Bills, President's Veto*

1. All bills for raising revenue shall originate in the House of Representatives; but the Senate may propose or concur with amendments as on other bills.

2. Every bill which shall have passed the House of Representatives and the Senate, shall, before it become a law, be presented to the President of the United States; if he approve, he shall sign it, but if not, he shall return it, with his objections, to that House in which it shall have originated, who shall enter the objections at large on their journal, and proceed to reconsider it.[19] If, after such reconsideration, two-thirds of that House shall agree to pass the bill, it shall be sent, together with the objections, to the other House, by which it shall likewise be reconsidered, and, if approved by two-thirds of that House, it shall become a law. But in all such cases the votes of both Houses shall be determined by yeas and nays, and the names of the persons voting for and against the bill shall be entered on the journal of each House respectively. If any bill shall not be returned by the President within ten days (Sundays excepted) after it shall have been presented to him, the same shall be a law, in like manner as if he had signed it, unless the Congress, by their adjournment, prevent its return, in which case it shall not be a law.

3. Every order, resolution,[20] or vote, to which the concurrence of the Senate and House of Representatives may be necessary (except on a question of adjournment), shall be presented to the President of the United States; and before the same shall take effect, shall be approved by him, or, being disapproved by him, shall be repassed by two-thirds of the Senate and House of Representatives, according to the rules and limitations prescribed in the case of a bill.

Section 8. *Legislative Powers of Congress*

The Congress shall have power:

1. To lay and collect taxes, duties, imposts, and excises,[21] to pay the debts, and provide for the common defence and general welfare, of the United States; but all duties, imposts, and excises, shall be uniform throughout the United States;

2. To borrow money on the credit of the United States;

3. To regulate commerce with foreign nations, and among the several states, and with the Indian tribes;

4. To establish a uniform rule of natu-

---

[16] *Treason* is strictly defined in Article III, Section 3. A *Felony* is any serious crime. *Breach of the peace* means any indictable offense less than treason or a felony; hence this exemption from arrest is of little importance today.

[17] This privilege of speech and debate extends to committee rooms and to the official publications of Congress like the *Congressional Record*, but not to outside speech or publication.

[18] " Emolument " means compensation for service; salary or fees. After President Taft appointed Senator Philander C. Knox as Secretary of State in 1909, it was found that during Knox's Senate term the salaries of Cabinet officers had been increased. Congress solved the problem by reducing the salary of the Secretary of State to its former figure.

[19] The President must veto the entire bill; he does not have the " item veto."

[20] Concurrent resolutions do not have the force of law and so are not sent to the President. Neither are those joint resolutions which propose amendments to the Constitution.

[21] For the meaning of these terms, see pages 118–120 in the text.

ralization, and uniform laws on the subject of bankruptcies,[22] throughout the United States;

5. To coin money, regulate the value thereof, and of foreign coin, and fix the standard of weights and measures;

6. To provide for the punishment of counterfeiting the securities and current coin of the United States;

7. To establish post offices and post roads; [23]

8. To promote the progress of science and useful arts,[24] by securing, for limited times, to authors and inventors, the exclusive right to their respective writings and discoveries;

9. To constitute tribunals inferior to the Supreme Court;

10. To define and punish piracies and felonies, committed on the high seas, and offences against the law of nations;

11. To declare war, grant letters of marque and reprisal,[25] and make rules concerning captures on land and water;

12. To raise and support armies; but no appropriation of money to that use shall be for a longer term than two years;

13. To provide and maintain a navy;

14. To make rules for the government and regulation of the land and naval forces;

15. To provide for calling forth the militia to execute the laws of the Union, suppress insurrections, and repel invasions;

16. To provide for organizing, arming, and disciplining the militia, and for governing such part of them as may be employed in the service of the United States, reserving to the States respectively the appointment of the officers, and the authority of training the militia, according to the discipline prescribed by Congress;

17. To exercise exclusive legislation in all cases whatsoever, over such district (not exceeding ten miles square) as may, by cession of particular States, and the acceptance of Congress, become the seat of the government of the United States, and to exercise like authority over all places, purchased by the consent of the legislature of the state in which the same shall be, for the erection of forts, magazines, arsenals, dock-yards, and other needful buildings; — And

18. To make all laws which shall be necessary and proper [26] for carrying into execution the foregoing powers, and all other powers vested by this Constitution in the government of the United States, or in any department or officer thereof.

Section 9. *Prohibitions upon the United States*

1. The migration or importation of such persons, as any of the States, now existing, shall think proper to admit, shall not be prohibited by the Congress prior to the year one thousand eight hundred and eight; but a tax or duty may be imposed on such importation, not exceeding ten dollars for each person.[27]

2. The privilege of the writ of *habeas corpus* [28] shall not be suspended, unless when, in cases of rebellion or invasion, the public safety may require it.

3. No bill of attainder, or *ex post facto* law,[29] shall be passed.

4. No capitation, or other direct tax, shall be laid, unless in proportion to the *census* or enumeration hereinbefore directed to be taken.[30]

---

[22] For explanation of bankruptcy, see page 102.

[23] " Post " comes from the French *poste* meaning mail; " post roads " are mail routes such as turnpikes, rivers, canals, streets, mountain paths, airways, etc.

[24] Our system of patents, copyrights, and trademarks is based on this clause.

[25] *Marque* is a French word meaning " boundary." " Reprisal " is from the French word *représaille,* which means retaliation. Hence, originally " letters of marque and reprisal " were licenses to cross the boundary into an enemy country to capture or destroy. As used here it means a commission authorizing private citizens to fit out vessels (privateers) to capture or destroy in time of war. They are forbidden in international law by the Declaration of Paris, 1856, of which the United States is a signatory nation.

[26] *Necessary* does not mean absolutely or indispensably necessary, but rather appropriate. This is the so-called *necessary and proper clause* or *elastic clause.* It has made it possible for the courts to extend the meanings of other clauses in the Constitution.

[27] Temporary provision.

[28] A *writ of habeas corpus* is directed by a judge to any person detaining another, demanding that person to produce the body of the person detained in order to determine whether such person is rightfully or wrongfully detained. Such person may be a prisoner in jail, an inmate of an insane asylum, or any person detained contrary to law, even by another private person.

[29] A *bill of attainder* is a legislative act which inflicts punishment without a judicial trial. See Art. I, Sec. 10, and Art. III, Sec. 3, Cl. 2. An *ex post facto* law is any criminal law which operates retroactively to the disadvantage of the accused. See Art. I, Sec. 10.

[30] See note 4, page 728 and the 16th Amendment. In 1895 the Supreme Court held taxes

5. No tax or duty shall be laid on articles exported from any State.

6. No preference shall be given by any regulation of commerce or revenue to the ports of one State over those of another; nor shall vessels bound to, or from, one State, be obliged to enter, clear, or pay duties, in another.

7. No money shall be drawn from the treasury, but in consequence of appropriations made by law; and a regular statement and account of the receipts and expenditures of all public money shall be published from time to time.

8. No title of nobility shall be granted by the United States; and no person holding any office or profit or trust under them shall, without the consent of the Congress, accept of any present, emolument, office, or title, of any kind whatever, from any king, prince, or foreign state.

Section 10. *Prohibitions upon the States*

1. No State shall enter into any treaty, alliance, or confederation; grant letters of marque and reprisal; coin money; emit bills of credit;[31] make anything but gold and silver coin a tender in payment of debts; pass any bill of attainder, *ex post facto* law, or law impairing the obligation of contracts, or grant any title of nobility.

2. No State shall, without the consent of the Congress, lay any imposts or duties on imports or exports, except what may be absolutely necessary for executing its inspection laws; and the net produce of all duties and imposts, laid by any State on imports or exports, shall be for the use of the treasury of the United States; and all such laws shall be subject to the revision and control of the Congress.

3. No State shall, without the consent of Congress, lay any duty of tonnage,[32] keep troops, or ships of war, in time of peace, enter into any agreement or compact with another State, or with a foreign power, or engage in war, unless actually invaded, or in such imminent danger as will not admit of delay.

---

on income from real or personal property to be direct taxes and declared the Income Tax Act of 1894 unconstitutional.
[31] " Bills of credit " means paper money.
[32] *Tonnage* is a vessel's internal cubical capacity in tons of one hundred cubic feet each. *Tonnage duties* are duties upon vessels in proportion to their capacity.

ARTICLE II

EXECUTIVE DEPARTMENT

Section 1. *Term, Election, Qualifications, Salary, Oath of Office*

1. The Executive power shall be vested in a President of the United States of America. He shall hold his office during the term of four years, and together with the Vice-President, chosen for the same term, be elected as follows:

2. Each State shall appoint, in such manner as the legislature thereof may direct, a number of Electors, equal to the whole number of Senators and Representatives, to which the State may be entitled in the Congress; but no Senator or Representative, or person holding an office of trust or profit, under the United States, shall be appointed an Elector.

3. The Electors shall meet in their respective States, and vote by ballot for two persons, of whom one, at least, shall not be an inhabitant of the same State with themselves. And they shall make a list of all the persons voted for, and of the number of votes for each; which list they shall sign and certify, and transmit, sealed, to the seat of the Government of the United Sates, directed to the President of the Senate. The President of the Senate shall, in the presence of the Senate and House of Representatives, open all the certificates, and the votes shall then be counted. The person having the greatest number of votes shall be the President, if such number be a majority of the whole number of Electors appointed; and if there be more than one, who have such majority, and have an equal number of votes, then, the House of Representatives shall immediately choose, by ballot, one of them for President; and if no person have a majority, then, from the five highest on the list, the said House shall, in like manner, choose the President. But in choosing the President, the votes shall be taken by States, the representation from each State having one vote; a quorum for this purpose shall consist of a member or members from two-thirds of the States, and a majority of all the States shall be necessary to a choice. In every case, after the choice of the President, the person having the greatest number of votes of the Electors shall be the Vice-President. But if there should remain two or more who have equal votes, the Senate shall choose from them, by ballot, the Vice-President.[33]

---

[33] Superseded by 12th Amendment, 1804.

4. The Congress may determine the time of choosing the Electors, and the day on which they shall give their votes; which day shall be the same throughout the United States.[34]

5. No person, except a natural-born citizen, or a citizen of the United States at the time of the adoption of this Constitution, shall be eligible to the office of President; neither shall any person be eligible to that office, who shall not have attained to the age of thirty-five years, and been fourteen years a resident within the United States.

6. In case of the removal of the President from office, or of his death, resignation, or inability to discharge the powers and duties of the said office, the same shall devolve on the Vice-President, and the Congress may by law provide for the case of removal, death, resignation or inability, both of the President and Vice-President, declaring what officer shall then act as President, and such officer shall act accordingly, until the disability be removed, or a President shall be elected.[35]

7. The President shall, at stated times, receive for his services a compensation, which shall neither be increased nor diminished during the period for which he shall have been elected, and he shall not receive, within that period, any other emolument from the United States, or any of them.

8. Before he enter on the execution of his office, he shall take the following oath or affirmation:

" I do solemnly swear (or affirm), that I will faithfully execute the office of President of the United States, and will, to the best of my ability, preserve, protect, and defend the Constitution of the United States."

Section 2. *President's Powers*

1. The President shall be Commander-in-Chief of the army and navy of the United States, and of the militia of the several States, when called into the actual service of the United States; he may require the opinion, in writing, of the principal officer in each of the executive departments upon any subject relating to the duties of their respective officers,[36] and he shall have power to grant reprieves and pardons [37] for offences against the United States, except in cases of impeachment.

2. He shall have power, by and with the advice and consent of the Senate, to make treaties, provided two-thirds of the Senators present concur; and he shall nominate, and, by and with the advice and consent of the Senate, shall appoint ambassadors, other public ministers, and consuls, judges of the Supreme Court, and all other officers of the United States whose appointments are not herein otherwise provided for, and which shall be established by law; [38] but the Congress may by law vest the appointment of such inferior officers, as they think proper, in the President alone, in the courts of law, or in the heads of departments.

3. The President shall have power to fill up all vacancies that may happen during the recess of the Senate, by granting commissions which shall expire at the end of their next session.

Section 3. *President's Powers*
(continued)

He shall, from time to time, give to the Congress information of the state of the Union, and recommend to their consideration such measures as he shall judge necessary and expedient; he may, on extraordinary occasions, convene both Houses, or either of them, and in case of disagreement between them, with respect to the time of adjournment, he may adjourn them to such time as he shall think proper; he shall receive ambassadors and other public ministers; he shall take care that the laws be faithfully executed, and shall commission all the officers of the United States.

Section 4. *Impeachment*

The President, Vice-President, and all civil officers [39] of the United States, shall be re-

---

[34] Congress has set the date as the first Tuesday after the first Monday in November of every fourth year.

[35] For the order of succession following the Vice-President, see page 176 and the 20th Amendment, 1933. Note that the Constitution does *not* provide that the Vice-President shall become President, but only that " the powers and duties of said office . . . shall devolve upon " him. Since 1841, custom has dictated that the Vice-President shall become President.

[36] This clause is the only authority in the Constitution for the President's Cabinet. There is no act of Congress which makes a department head a member of the Cabinet.

[37] A " reprieve " is the postponing of the execution of a sentence. A " pardon " is legal (but not moral) forgiveness. The President may grant reprieves or pardons in federal cases.

[38] For a discussion of the President's powers of appointments and removals, see page 181.

[39] *Civil officers* subject to impeachment include all officers of the United States who hold

moved from office on impeachment for, and conviction of, treason, bribery, or other high crimes and misdemeanors.[40]

ARTICLE III

JUDICIAL DEPARTMENT

Section 1. Courts, Terms of Office

The judicial power of the United States shall be vested in one Supreme Court, and in such inferior courts as the Congress may from time to time ordain and establish.[41] The judges, both of the Supreme and inferior courts shall hold their offices during good behavior, and shall, at stated times, receive for their services a compensation which shall not be diminished during their continuance in office.

Section 2. Jurisdiction

1. The judicial power shall extend to all cases, in law and equity,[42] arising under this Constitution, the laws of the United States, and treaties made, or which shall be made, under their authority; to all cases affecting ambassadors, other public ministers, and consuls; to all cases of admiralty and maritime jurisdiction;[43] to controversies to which the United States shall be a party; to controversies between two or more States, between a State and citizens of another State,[44] between citizens of different States, between citizens of the same State claiming lands under grants of different States, and between a State, or the citizens thereof, and foreign states, citizens, or subjects.

2. In all cases affecting ambassadors, other public ministers and consuls, and those in which a State shall be a party, the Supreme Court shall have original jurisdiction.[45] In all the other cases before mentioned, the Supreme Court shall have appellate jurisdiction, both as to law and fact, with such exceptions and under such regulations as the Congress shall make.

3. The trial of all crimes, except in cases of impeachment, shall be by jury;[46] and such trial shall be held in the State where the said crimes shall have been committed;[47] but when not committed within any State the trial shall be at such place or places as the Congress may by law have directed.

Section 3. Treason

1. Treason against the United States shall consist only in levying war against them, or in adhering to their enemies, giving them aid and comfort. No person shall be convicted of treason unless on the testimony of two witnesses to the same overt act, or on confession in open court.

2. The Congress shall have power to declare the punishment of treason, but no attainder of treason shall work corruption of blood, or forfeiture except during the life of the person attainted.[48]

ARTICLE IV

RELATIONS OF STATES

Section 1. Public Records

Full faith and credit shall be given in each State to the public acts, records, and judicial proceedings of every other State. And the Congress may, by general laws, prescribe the manner in which such acts, records, and

---

their appointments from the National Government, high or low, and whose duties are executive or judicial. Officers in the armed forces are not civil officers; neither are Senators and Representatives so considered. Instead of the impeachment process, either house of Congress may expel one of its own members by a two-thirds vote.

[40] A majority of the House of Representatives may impeach any civil officer of the United States whom they consider for any reason to be morally unfit for his position.

[41] For the organization of the federal court system, see Chapter 21.

[42] For the meaning of *equity*, see page 527.

[43] *Admiralty jurisdiction* includes cases involving prizes seized in time of war, and criminal and civil suits which arise on the high seas or navigable waters. *Maritime jurisdiction* has reference to such matters as contracts, claims, etc., connected with maritime operations — e.g., a contract on land for ship supplies. Admiralty jurisdiction is given by the locality of the act; maritime, by the character of the act.

[44] Modified by 11th Amendment, 1798.

[45] *Original jurisdiction* means the right of hearing and determining a case in the first instance. *Appellate jurisdiction* means the right to hear cases appealed from inferior courts.

[46] Jury trials are guaranteed in federal courts only. States could abolish jury trials.

[47] If a crime is committed on the sea, the accused is tried by the United States District Court of the district where the prisoner is landed.

[48] During the War Between the States an act was passed by Congress according to which all Confederate army or navy officers should forfeit their property. A certain piece of real estate in Virginia belonging to a Confederate naval officer, Forrest by name, was seized by the government and sold by legal proceedings to one Buntley. Buntley sold it to Bigelow. After the death of

proceedings shall be proved, and the effect thereof.

Section 2. *Rights in One State of Citizens of Another*

1. The citizens of each State shall be entitled to all privileges and immunities [49] of citizens in the several States.

2. A person charged in any State with treason, felony, or other crime, who shall flee from justice, and be found in another State, shall, on demand of the executive authority of the State from which he fled, be delivered up, to be removed to the State having jurisdiction of the crime.[50]

3. No person held to service [51] or labor in one State, under the laws thereof, escaping into another, shall, in consequence of any law or regulation therein, be discharged from such service or labor, but shall be delivered up on claim of the party to whom such service or labor may be due.

Section 3. *New States, Territories*

1. New States may be admitted by the Congress into this Union; but no new State shall be formed or erected within the jurisdiction of any other State, nor any State be formed by the junction of two or more States, or parts of States, without the consent of the legislatures of the States concerned as well as of the Congress.

2. The Congress shall have power to dispose of and make all needful rules and regulations respecting the territory or other property belonging to the United States; and nothing in this Constitution shall be so construed as to prejudice any claims of the United States, or of any particular State.

Section 4. *Protection Afforded to States by the Nation*

The United States shall guarantee to every State in this Union a republican form of government, and shall protect each of them against invasion; and on application of the legislature, or of the executive (when the legislature cannot be convened), against domestic violence.

ARTICLE V

PROVISIONS FOR AMENDMENT

The Congress, whenever two-thirds of both Houses shall deem it necessary, shall propose amendments to this Constitution, or, on the application of the legislatures of two-thirds of the several States, shall call a convention for proposing amendments, which, in either case, shall be valid, to all intents and purposes, as part of this Constitution, when ratified by the legislatures of three-fourths of the several States, or by conventions in three-fourths thereof, as the one or the other mode of ratification may be proposed by the Congress: [52] provided that no amendment which may be made prior to the year one thousand eight hundred and eight shall in any manner affect the first and fourth clauses in the ninth section of the first Article; [53] and that no state, without its consent, shall be deprived of its equal suffrage in the Senate.

ARTICLE VI

NATIONAL DEBTS, SUPREMACY OF NATIONAL LAW, OATH

1. All debts contracted and engagements entered into, before the adoption of this Constitution, shall be as valid against the United States under this Constitution, as under the Confederation.

2. This Constitution, and the laws of the United States which shall be made in pursuance thereof, and all treaties made, or which shall be made, under the authority of the United States, shall be the supreme law of the land; [54] and the judges in every State shall be bound thereby, anything in the constitution or laws of any State to the contrary notwithstanding.

3. The Senators and Representatives be-

Forrest his son and rightful heir claimed it, and obtained it because treason cannot " work corruption of blood or forfeiture except during the life of the person attainted." See Art. I, Sec. 9, Cl. 3.

[49] For *privileges and immunities,* see note 70.

[50] This section provides for what is known as *interstate rendition* or *extradition.* Although the Constitution here says the fugitive " shall . . . be delivered up " the Supreme Court has interpreted it to read " *may* . . . be delivered up." Governors sometimes refuse to return a fugitive.

[51] *Person held to service* refers to slaves and, since the 13th Amendment was adopted in 1865, the section has been of no importance.

[52] Note that this Article provides two methods for the proposing and two methods for the ratifying of constitutional amendments — or, in effect, *four* ways.

[53] Temporary provision.

[54] The Constitution is supreme over any other form of law in the United States. If an act of the Congress and a treaty conflict the courts accept the one most recently enacted or ratified. State law always must yield to any form of federal law in cases of conflict.

fore mentioned, and the members of the several State legislatures, and all executive and judicial officers, both of the United States and of the several States, shall be bound, by oath or affirmation, to support this Constitution; but no religious test shall ever be required as a qualification to any office or public trust under the United States.

ARTICLE VII

ESTABLISHMENT OF CONSTI-TUTION

The ratification of the conventions of nine States shall be sufficient for the establishment of this Constitution between the states so ratifying the same.

Done in Convention, by the unanimous consent of the States present, the seventeenth day of September, in the year of our Lord one thousand seven hundred and eighty-seven, and of the Independence of the United States of America the twelfth. *In Witness* whereof, we have hereunto subscribed our names.

Attest: WILLIAM JACKSON, *Secretary*

GEORGE WASHINGTON
President and Deputy from Virginia

New Hampshire
JOHN LANGDON
NICHOLAS GILMAN

Massachusetts
NATHANIEL GORHAM
RUFUS KING

Connecticut
WILLIAM SAMUEL JOHNSON
ROGER SHERMAN

New York
ALEXANDER HAMILTON

New Jersey
WILLIAM LIVINGSTON
DAVID BREARLEY
WILLIAM PATERSON
JONATHAN DAYTON

Pennsylvania
BENJAMIN FRANKLIN
THOMAS MIFFLIN
ROBERT MORRIS
GEORGE CLYMER
THOMAS FITZSIMONS
JARED INGERSOLL
JAMES WILSON
GOUVERNEUR MORRIS

Delaware
GEORGE READ
GUNNING BEDFORD, JR.
JOHN DICKINSON
RICHARD BASSETT
JACOB BROOM

Maryland
JAMES MCHENRY
DAN OF ST. THOMAS JENNIFER
DANIEL CARROLL

Virginia
JOHN BLAIR
JAMES MADISON, JR.

North Carolina
WILLIAM BLOUNT
RICHARD DOBBS SPAIGHT
HUGH WILLIAMSON

South Carolina
JOHN RUTLEDGE
CHARLES COTESWORTH
PINCKNEY
CHARLES PINCKNEY
PIERCE BUTLER

Georgia
WILLIAM FEW
ABRAHAM BALDWIN

[Rhode Island sent no delegate to the Constitutional Convention.]

AMENDMENTS

Amendment 1 [55]

Freedom of Religion, of Speech, and of the Press: Right of Petition

Congress shall make no law respecting an establishment of religion, or prohibiting the free exercise thereof; or abridging the freedom of speech, or of the press; or the right of the people peaceably to assemble, and to petition the government for a redress of grievances.

[55] The first ten amendments, the Bill of Rights, went into effect on December 15, 1791. They restrict only the National Government — *not* the States. However, since 1925 the Supreme Court has applied the provisions of the 1st Amendment to the States through the " due process clause " of the 14th Amendment.

Amendment 2

Right to Keep Arms

A well-regulated militia being necessary to the security of a free state, the right of the people to keep and bear arms shall not be infringed.[56]

Amendment 3

Quartering of Soldiers in Private Houses

No soldier shall, in time of peace, be quartered in any house, without the consent of

[56] Like the rest of the Bill of Rights, this amendment applies only to the National Government. A State may restrict the right to keep and bear arms as it sees fit. Many States pro-

the owner; nor, in time of war, but in a manner to be prescribed by law.

Amendment 4
Search Warrants

The right of the people to be secure in their persons, houses, papers, and effects, against unreasonable searches and seizures, shall not be violated; and no warrants shall issue, but upon probable cause, supported by oath or affirmation, and particularly describing the place to be searched, and the persons or things to be seized.[57]

Amendment 5
Criminal Proceedings

No person shall be held to answer for a capital,[58] or otherwise infamous, crime, unless on a presentment or indictment of a grand jury, except in cases arising in the land or naval forces, or in the militia, when in actual service, in time of war, or public danger; nor shall any person be subject, for the same offence, to be twice put in jeopardy of life or limb; nor shall be compelled, in any criminal case, to be a witness against himself; nor be deprived of life, liberty, or property, without due process of law; [59] nor shall private property be taken for public use, without just compensation.[60]

Amendment 6
Criminal Proceedings (continued)

In all criminal prosecutions, the accused shall enjoy the right to a speedy and public trial, by an impartial jury of the state and district wherein the crime shall have been committed, which district shall have been previously ascertained by law; and to be informed of the nature and cause of the accusation; to be confronted with the witnesses against him; to have compulsory process for obtaining witnesses in his favor; and to have the assistance of counsel for his defence.

hibit the carrying of concealed weapons, the owning of pistols, etc.
[57] This guarantee against "unreasonable searches and seizures" is discussed on page 390.
[58] A "capital crime" is any crime punishable by death.
[59] For the meaning and significance of *due process of law,* see page 386.
[60] Under the *power of eminent domain,* the government has the right to take private property for public use. This clause places a restriction on that power.

Amendment 7
Jury Trial in Civil Cases

In suits at common law,[61] where the value in controversy shall exceed twenty dollars, the right of trial by jury shall be preserved; and no fact, tried by a jury, shall be otherwise re-examined in any court of the United States than according to the rules of the common law.

Amendment 8
Excessive Punishments

Excessive bail shall not be required, nor excessive fines imposed, nor cruel and unusual punishments inflicted.

Amendment 9
Unenumerated Rights of the People

The enumeration in the Constitution of certain rights shall not be construed to deny or disparage others retained by the people.

Amendment 10
Powers Reserved to States

The powers not delegated to the United States by the Constitution, nor prohibited by it to the States, are reserved to the States respectively, or to the people.

Amendment 11 [62]
Suits against States

The judicial power of the United States shall not be construed to extend to any suit in law or equity, commenced or prosecuted against one of the United States by citizens of another State, or by citizens or subjects of any foreign state.[63]

Amendment 12 [64]
Election of President and Vice-President

1. The Electors shall meet in their respective States, and vote by ballot for President

[61] For the meaning of common law, see page 526.
[62] This amendment was adopted in 1798.
[63] The officers of a State can be sued in some cases, and this practically amounts to a suit against a State.
[64] This amendment was adopted in 1804 and supersedes Art. II, Sec. 1.

and Vice-President, one of whom, at least, shall not be an inhabitant of the same State with themselves; they shall name in their ballots the person voted for as President, and in distinct ballots the person voted for as Vice-President; and they shall make distinct lists of all persons voted for as President, and of all persons voted for as Vice-President, and of the number of votes for each, which lists they shall sign, and certify, and transmit, sealed, to the seat of the Government of the United States, directed to the President of the Senate; the President of the Senate shall, in the presence of the Senate and the House of Representatives, open all the certificates, and the votes shall then be counted; the person having the greatest number of votes for President shall be the President, if such number be a majority of the whole number of Electors appointed; and if no person have such a majority, then, from the persons having the highest numbers, not exceeding three, on the list of those voted for as President, the House of Representatives shall choose immediately, by ballot, the President.[65] But in choosing the President, the votes shall be taken by States, the representation from each State having one vote; a quorum for this purpose shall consist of a member or members from two-thirds of the States, and a majority of all the States shall be necessary to a choice. And if the House of Representatives shall not choose a President, whenever the right of choice shall devolve upon them, before the fourth day of March next following,[66] then the Vice-President shall act as President, as in case of the death, or other constitutional disability, of the President.

2. The person having the greatest number of votes as Vice-President, shall be the Vice-President, if such number be a majority of the whole number of Electors appointed; and if no person have a majority, then, from the two highest numbers on the list, the Senate shall choose the Vice-President; a quorum for the purpose shall consist of two-thirds of the whole number of Senators; a majority of the whole number shall be necessary to a choice.

3. But no person constitutionally ineligible to the office of President shall be eligible to that of Vice-President of the United States.

---

[65] Only two Presidents, Thomas Jefferson in 1801 and John Quincy Adams in 1825, have been chosen by the House of Representatives.
[66] Changed to January 20th by the 20th Amendment, 1933.

Amendment 13 [67]

Slavery

Section 1. Abolition of Slavery

Neither slavery nor involuntary servitude, except as a punishment for crime, whereof the party shall have been duly convicted, shall exist within the United States, or any place subject to their jurisdiction.

Section 2. Power of Congress

Congress shall have power to enforce this article by appropriate legislation.

Amendment 14 [68]

Civil Rights: Apportionment of Representatives: Political Disabilities, Public Debt

Section 1. Civil Rights

All persons born or naturalized in the United States, and subject to the jurisdiction thereof, are citizens of the United States and of the State wherein they reside.[69] No State shall make or enforce any law which shall abridge the privileges or immunities of citizens [70] of the United States; nor shall any State deprive any person of life, liberty, or property, without due process of law, nor deny to any person within its jurisdiction the equal protection of the laws.

Section 2.[71] Apportionment of Representatives

Representatives shall be apportioned among the several States according to their respective numbers, counting the whole number of persons in each State, excluding Indians not taxed. But when the right to vote at any election for the choice of electors for President and Vice-President of the United

---

[67] This amendment was adopted in 1865.
[68] This amendment was adopted in 1868.
[69] This clause was primarily intended to make Negroes citizens, but it has much wider application. " And subject to the jurisdiction thereof " excludes children born to foreign diplomats in the United States and to alien enemies in hostile occupation.
[70] A complete list of the *privileges and immunities* citizens enjoy has never been given, but basically it means that a State may not discriminate against a citizen from another State simply because he is a nonresident.
[71] This section has never been enforced; some jurists argue that it has been superseded by the 15th Amendment.

States, Representatives in Congress, the executive and judicial officers of a State, or the members of the legislature thereof, is denied to any of the male inhabitants of such State, being twenty-one years of age, and citizens of the United States, or in any way abridged, except for participation in rebellion or other crime, the basis of representation therein shall be reduced in the proportion which the number of such male citizens shall bear to the whole number of male citizens twenty-one years of age in such State.

Section 3. *Political Disabilities*

No person shall be a Senator or Representative in Congress, or elector of President and Vice-President, or hold any office, civil or military, under the United States, or under any State, who, having previously taken an oath, as a member of Congress, or as an officer of the United States, or as a member of any State legislature, or as an executive or judical officer of any State, to support the Constitution of the United States, shall have engaged in insurrection or rebellion against the same, or given aid or comfort to the enemies thereof. But Congress may, by a vote of two-thirds of each House, remove such disability.

Section. 4. *Public Debt*

The validity of the public debt of the United States, authorized by law, including debts incurred for payment of pensions and bounties for services in suppressing insurrection or rebellion, shall not be questioned. But neither the United States nor any State shall assume or pay any debt or obligation incurred in aid of insurrection or rebellion against the United States, or any claim for the loss or emancipation of any slave; but all such debts, obligations, and claims shall be held illegal and void.

Section 5. *Power of Congress*

The Congress shall have power to enforce, by appropriate legislation, the provisions of this article.

Amendment 15 [72]

Right of Suffrage

Section 1. *Right of Negro to Vote*

The right of citizens of the United States to vote shall not be denied or abridged by the

United States or by any State on account of race, color, or previous condition of servitude.

Section 2. *Power of Congress*

The Congress shall have power to enforce this article by appropriate legislation.

Amendment 16 [73]

Income Tax

The Congress shall have power to lay and collect taxes on incomes, from whatever source derived, without apportionment among the several States, and without regard to any census or enumeration.

Amendment 17 [74]

Senate, Election, Vacancies

The Senate of the United States shall be composed of two Senators from each State, elected by the people thereof, for six years; and each Senator shall have one vote. The electors in each State shall have the qualifications requisite for electors of the most numerous branch of the State legislatures.

When vacancies happen in the representation of any State in the Senate, the executive authority of such State shall issue writs of election to fill such vacancies: Provided, That the legislature of any State may empower the executive thereof to make temporary appointment until the people fill the vacancies by election as the legislature may direct.

This amendment shall not be so construed as to affect the election or term of any Senator chosen before it becomes valid as part of the Constitution.

Amendment 18 [75]

National Prohibition

Section 1. *Prohibition of Intoxicating Liquors*

After one year from the ratification of this article the manufacture, sale or transportation of intoxicating liquors within, the importation thereof into, or the exportation thereof from the United States and all territory subject to the jurisdiction thereof for beverage purposes is hereby prohibited.

---

[73] This amendment was adopted in 1913. It modifies Art. I, Sec. 9, Cl. 4.
[74] This amendment was adopted in 1913. It modifies Art. I, Sec. 3, Cls. 1 and 2.
[75] This amendment was adopted in 1919 and was repealed in 1933 by the 21st Amendment.

[72] This amendment was adopted in 1870. It was passed to guarantee the suffrage to Negroes.

Section 2. Concurrent Enforcement

The Congress and the several States shall have concurrent power to enforce this article by appropriate legislation.

Section 3. Conditions of Ratification

This article shall be inoperative unless it shall have been ratified as an amendment to the Constitution by the legislatures of the several States, as provided in the Constitution, within seven years of the date of the submission hereof to the States by Congress.

Amendment 19 [76]

Woman Suffrage

The right of citizens of the United States to vote shall not be denied or abridged by the United States or by any State on account of sex.

Congress shall have power to enforce this article by appropriate legislation.

Amendment 20 [77]

Changing the Time of Convening Congress and of Inaugurating the President and Vice-President

Section 1. Terms of President and Vice-President

The terms of the President and Vice-President shall end at noon on the 20th day of January, and the terms of Senators and Representatives at noon on the 3d day of January, of the years in which such terms would have ended if this article had not been ratified; and the terms of their successors shall then begin.

Section 2. Meetings of Congress

The Congress shall assemble at least once in every year, and such meeting shall begin at noon on the 3d day of January, unless they shall by law appoint a different day.

Section 3. Interim Succession

If, at the time fixed for the beginning of the term of the President, the President-elect

---

shall have died, the Vice-President-elect shall become President. If a President shall not have been chosen before the time fixed for the beginning of his term, or if the President-elect shall have failed to qualify, then the Vice-President-elect shall act as President until a President shall have qualified; and the Congress may by law provide for the case wherein neither a President-elect nor a Vice-President-elect shall have qualified, declaring who shall then act as President, or the manner in which one who is to act shall be selected, and such person shall act accordingly until a President or Vice-President shall have qualified.

Section 4. Congressional Choice

The Congress may by law provide for the case of the death of any of the persons from whom the House of Representatives may choose a President whenever the right of choice shall have devolved upon them, and for the case of the death of any of the persons from whom the Senate may choose a Vice-President whenever the right of choice shall have devolved upon them.

Section 5. Time of Effect

Sections 1 and 2 shall take effect on the 15th day of October following the ratification of this article.

Section 6. Conditions of Ratification

This article shall be inoperative unless it shall have been ratified as an amendment to the Constitution by the legislatures of three-fourths of the several States within seven years from the date of its submission.

Amendment 21 [78]

Repealing National Prohibition, and Prohibiting the Importation of Intoxicating Liquor into States in Violation of Their Laws

Section 1. Statement of Repeal

The eighteenth article of amendment to the Constitution of the United States is hereby repealed.

---

[76] This Amendment was adopted in 1920.

[77] This amendment was adopted in 1933. It is often called the "Lame Duck Amendment" because it shortened the period between the election and actual convening of a Congress and thus eliminated the "lame ducks" — members who had been defeated at the polls but continued to serve for four months, until the new term began in March.

[78] The 21st Amendment was referred to the States by Congress in February, 1933, and ratified by the 36th State in December of the same year. This was the first amendment ever submitted to conventions in the States for ratification. In referring the amendment to the States, Congress gave no instructions as to how the conventions should be called, where, or when. Each State legislature provided for the details of its own convention and paid all of the expenses involved.

Section 2. *Conditions of Transportation or Importation*

The transportation or importation into any State, Territory, or possession of the United States for delivery or use therein of intoxicating liquors, in violation of the laws thereof, is hereby prohibited.

Section 3. *Conditions of Ratification*

This article shall be inoperative unless it shall have been ratified as an amendment to the Constitution by conventions in the several States, as provided in the Constitution, within seven years from the date of the submission hereof to the States by Congress.

Amendment 22 [79]

Limiting Presidential Tenure

Section 1. *Limitation and Exception*

No person shall be elected to the office of the President more than twice, and no person

[79] This amendment was adopted in 1951.

who has held the office of President, or acted as President, for more than two years of a term to which some other person was elected President shall be elected to the office of the President more than once. But this Article shall not apply to any person holding the office of President when this Article was proposed by the Congress, and shall not prevent any person who may be holding the office of President, or acting as President, during the term within which this Article becomes operative from holding the office of President or acting as President during the remainder of such term.

Section 2. *Conditions of Ratification*

This Article shall be inoperative unless it shall have been ratified as an amendment to the Constitution by the legislatures of three-fourths of the several States within seven years from the date of its submission to the States by the Congress.

POPULATION OF STATES

RANK 1930	RANK 1940	RANK 1950	STATE	POPULATION 1940	POPULATION 1950	PER CENT OF CHANGE
1	1	1	New York	13,479,142	14,830,192	10.0
6	5	2	California	6,907,387	10,586,223	53.3
2	2	3	Pennsylvania	9,900,180	10,498,012	6.0
3	3	4	Illinois	7,897,241	8,712,176	10.3
4	4	5	Ohio	6,907,612	7,946,627	15.0
5	6	6	Texas	6,414,824	7,711,194	20.2
7	7	7	Michigan	5,256,106	6,371,766	21.2
9	9	8	New Jersey	4,160,165	4,835,329	16.2
8	8	9	Massachusetts	4,316,721	4,690,514	8.7
12	11	10	North Carolina	3,571,623	4,061,929	13.7
10	10	11	Missouri	3,784,664	3,954,653	4.5
11	12	12	Indiana	3,427,796	3,934,224	14.8
14	14	13	Georgia	3,123,723	3,444,578	10.3
13	13	14	Wisconsin	3,137,587	3,434,575	9.5
20	19	15	Virginia	2,677,773	3,318,680	23.9
16	15	16	Tennessee	2,915,841	3,291,718	12.9
15	17	17	Alabama	2,832,961	3,061,743	8.1
18	18	18	Minnesota	2,792,300	2,982,483	6.8
17	16	19	Kentucky	2,845,027	2,944,806	3.5
31	27	20	Florida	1,897,414	2,771,305	46.1
22	21	21	Louisiana	2,363,880	2,683,516	13.5
19	20	22	Iowa	2,538,268	2,621,073	3.3
30	30	23	Washington	1,736,191	2,378,963	37.0
28	28	24	Maryland	1,821,244	2,343,001	28.6
21	22	25	Oklahoma	2,336,434	2,233,351	− 4.4
23	23	26	Mississippi	2,183,796	2,178,914	− 0.2
26	26	27	South Carolina	1,899,804	2,117,027	11.4
29	31	28	Connecticut	1,709,242	2,007,280	17.4
27	25	29	West Virginia	1,901,074	2,005,552	5.4
25	24	30	Arkansas	1,949,387	1,909,511	− 2.0
24	29	31	Kansas	1,801,028	1,905,299	5.8
34	34	32	Oregon	1,089,684	1,521,341	39.6
32	32	33	Nebraska	1,315,834	1,325,510	0.7
33	33	34	Colorado	1,123,296	1,325,089	18.0
35	35	35	Maine	847,227	913,774	7.9
41	37	36	District of Columbia	663,091	802,178	21.0
37	36	37	Rhode Island	713,346	791,896	11.0
44	44	38	Arizona	499,261	749,587	50.0
40	41	39	Utah	550,310	688,862	25.2
45	42	40	New Mexico	531,818	681,187	28.1
36	38	41	South Dakota	642,961	652,740	1.5
38	39	42	North Dakota	641,935	619,636	− 3.5
39	40	43	Montana	559,456	591,024	5.6
43	43	44	Idaho	524,873	588,637	12.1
42	45	45	New Hampshire	491,524	533,242	8.5
46	46	46	Vermont	359,231	377,747	5.2
47	47	47	Delaware	266,505	318,085	19.4
48	48	48	Wyoming	250,742	290,529	15.9
49	49	49	Nevada	110,247	160,083	45.2
			Total	131,669,275	150,697,361	14.5

GENERAL BIBLIOGRAPHY

They know enough who know how to learn.

— HENRY ADAMS

This General Bibliography is intended for those students and teachers who desire additional, more comprehensive, or more specific references than those given in the Select Bibliography at the end of each chapter. Prices may usually be obtained through local libraries, school superintendents' offices, or direct from the publishers.

There are a number of organizations which publish interesting and informative pamphlets on American government and politics and social and economic problems. For example:

The Foreign Policy Association, 345 East 46th Street, New York 17, N.Y.
The National League of Women Voters, 1026 Seventeenth Street NW, Washington 6, D.C.
The National Municipal League, 47 East 68th Street, New York 21, N.Y.

These and other similar organizations will usually furnish a list of their publications, most of which are quite inexpensive.

The United States Government Printing Office issues a free biweekly list, *Selected United States Government Publications,* which is very useful. All orders for Government publications should be addressed to the Superintendent of Documents, Government Printing Office, Washington 25, D.C.

GENERAL REFERENCE BOOKS

United States Code, containing the general and permanent laws of the United States in force January 3, 1958 (annual supplements).
United States Government Organization Manual 1957–58, listing and describing all agencies of the National Government (yearly editions).
Statistical Abstract of the United States, 1957, containing current and historical facts and figures on practically every phase of American life (annual edition).
The World Almanac, 1958, encyclopedia of information (annual edition by the *New York World-Telegram and Sun*).
Congressional Directory, 1958, containing short biographies of each member of Congress, lists of committees, officers of each house, maps showing congressional districts in each State, and list of all agencies of the National Government with brief summary of duties of each (annual edition).
Rules and Manual of the U.S. House of Representatives, 1958, and *Senate Manual, 1958,* including many useful notes and tables (annual editions).

The Manual, Legislative Handbook, or *Blue Book* of your State, usually containing the State Constitution, brief descriptions of State and local agencies, lists of State and local officers, election returns, historical information, and various other material (usually issued annually and free through your Secretary of State).
Book of the States, containing factual information on and latest developments in State Government (biennial edition with annual supplement by the Council of State Governments).
The following would also be useful in the school library, if funds and space permit their purchase:
Annual Reports of departments and agencies of the National Government.
Readers' Guide to Periodical Literature.
State Code and *Session Laws* or *Legislative Acts.*
The American Yearbook.
The Statesman's Yearbook.
Index to the "New York Times."
United States Census Reports.

JOURNALS, MAGAZINES, AND NEWSPAPERS

Quarterly:
American Political Science Review
Foreign Affairs
Political Science Quarterly
Bimonthly:
American Heritage
Annals of the American Academy of Political and Social Sciences
Headline Series
Monthly:
Congressional Digest
Current History
Harper's
National Municipal Review

Nation's Business
Reader's Digest
State Government
Vital Issues
Semimonthly:
Foreign Policy Reports
The Reporter
State Department Foreign Policy Briefs
Vital Speeches
Weekly:
American Observer
Life
Newsweek
Saturday Evening Post
State Department Bulletin

Time
U.S. News & World Report
Daily:
   New York Times (especially Sunday edition)

As many local newspapers as it is possible to secure.
Radio and television newscasters and commentators as available.

SPECIFIC REFERENCE BOOKS

ABRAHAM, HENRY J., *Compulsory Voting.* Public Affairs Press, 1955.

ADAMS, WALTER, *The Structure of American Industry.* Macmillan, 1954.

ADRIAN, CHARLES R., *Governing Urban America.* McGraw-Hill, 1955.

AGAR, HERBERT, *The Price of Union.* Houghton Mifflin, 1950.

ALMOND, G., *The Appeals of Communism.* Princeton, 1954.

American County — Patchwork of Boards. National Municipal League, 1946.

"American Farm Leaders," *Current History,* June, 1955.

ANDERSON, WILLIAM B., *The Nation and the States, Rivals or Partners?* Minnesota, 1955.

ANSHEN, MELVIN, and WORMUTH, FRANCIS D., *Private Enterprise and Public Policy.* Macmillan, 1954.

BABCOCK, ROBERT S., *State & Local Government & Politics.* Random House, 1957.

BAILEY, STEPHEN K., *et al., Government in America.* Holt, 1957.

BAILEY, SYDNEY D., *British Parliamentary Democracy.* Houghton Mifflin, 1958.

BAILEY, THOMAS A., *A Diplomatic History of the American People.* Appleton-Century-Crofts, 1958.

BAKER, BENJAMIN, *Urban Government.* Van Nostrand, 1957.

BAKER, GORDON E., *Rural Versus Urban Political Power.* Doubleday, 1955.

BAUER, RAYMOND A., *Nine Soviet Portraits.* Viking, 1955.

BEARD, CHARLES A., *An Economic Interpretation of the Constitution.* Macmillan, 1935.

BELOFF, MAX, *Foreign Policy and the Democratic Process.* Johns Hopkins, 1955.

BEMIS, SAMUEL ELIOT, *The United States as a World Power.* Holt, 1955.

Best Practices under the Manager Plan. National Municipal League, 1954.

BIRKHEAD, GUTHRIE S., *The Metropolitan Problem.* National Municipal League, 1953.

BLAUSTEIN, ALBERT P., and FERGUSON, C. C., *Desegregation and the Law.* Rutgers, 1957.

BLOUGH, ROY, *The Federal Taxing Process.* Prentice-Hall, 1952.

BOND, FLOYD A., *et al., Our Needy Aged.* Holt, 1954.

BONE, HUGH A., *American Politics and the Party System.* McGraw-Hill, 1955.

BOTEIN, BERNARD, *Trial Judge.* Simon & Schuster, 1952.

BOWLES, CHESTER, *The New Dimensions of Peace.* Harper, 1955.

BROCKWAY, THOMAS P., *Basic Documents in United States Foreign Policy.* Van Nostrand, 1957.

BROGAN, D. W., *Politics in America.* Harper, 1955.

BUCK, PHILIP W., and TRAVIS, MARTIN B., *Control of Foreign Relations in Modern Nations.* Norton, 1957.

BURNS, JAMES M., and PELTASON, JACK W., *Government By the People.* Prentice-Hall, 1957.

BUSS, CLAUDE A., *The Far East.* Macmillan, 1955.

CAMPBELL, A., *et al., The Voter Decides.* Row, Peterson, 1954.

CARR, ROBERT K., (ed.), "Civil Rights in America," *Annals,* May, 1951.

CARR, ROBERT K., *The Constitution and Congressional Investigating Committees.* League of Women Voters, 1954.

CARR, ROBERT K., *et al., American Democracy in Theory and Practice.* Rinehart, 1957.

CARTER, GWENDOLEN M., *et al., Major Foreign Powers.* Harcourt, Brace, 1957.

CHAMBERLAIN, NEIL W., *Collective Bargaining.* McGraw-Hill, 1953.

CHASE, EUGENE P., *The United Nations in Action.* McGraw-Hill, 1950.

CHASE, HAROLD, *Security and Liberty: The Problem of Native Communists, 1947–1955.* Doubleday, 1955.

CHEEVER, DANIEL S., and HAVILAND, H. FIELD, *Organizing for Peace.* Houghton Mifflin, 1954.

CHENERY, WILLIAM L., *Freedom of the Press.* Harcourt, Brace, 1955.

CHILDS, RICHARD S., *Civic Victories: The Story of an Unfinished Revolution.* Harper, 1953.

CLAPP, GORDON R., *The TVA.* Chicago, 1955.

CLOUGH, S., *The Economic Basis of Our Civilization.* Crowell, 1953.

COFFIN, TRIS, *Your Washington.* Duell, Sloan, 1954.

COMMAGER, HENRY S., *Freedom, Loyalty, Dissent.* Oxford, 1954.

COMMAGER, HENRY S., and NEVINS, ALAN, *The Heritage of America.* Heath, 1949.

"Congressional Elections," *Current History,* October, 1954.

COOK, F., *Principles of Business and the Federal Law.* Macmillan, 1952.

CORWIN, EDWARD S., *The Constitution and What It Means Today.* Princeton, 1954.

——, *The President: Office and Powers.* New York University Press, 1948.

County Manager Plan. National Municipal League, 1950.

CRAVEN, A., *et al., A Documentary History of the American People.* Ginn, 1951.

CUNINGGIM, MEERIMON, *Freedom's Holy Light.* Harper, 1955.

CURTIS, CHARLES P., *Lions under the Throne.* Houghton Mifflin, 1947.

CUSHMAN, ROBERT E., *Leading Constitutional Decisions.* Appleton-Century-Crofts, 1955.

DANIELS, W., (ed.), *Presidential Election Reforms.* Wilson, 1953.

DARLING, EDWARD, *How We Fought for Our Schools.* Norton, 1954.

DAVENPORT, RUSSELL W., *U.S.A., The Permanent Revolution.* Prentice-Hall, 1952.

DAVID, PAUL T., *et al., Presidential Nominating Politics.* Johns Hopkins, 1954.

DEGRAZIA, ALFRED, *The American Way of Government.* Wiley, 1957.

DEHUSZAR, GEORGE B., *et al., Soviet Power and Policy.* Crowell, 1955.

DEWHURST, J. FREDERIC and ASSOCIATES, *America's Needs and Resources, A New Survey.* The Twentieth Century Fund, 1955.

DIMOCK, MARSHAL and GLADYS O., *Public Administration.* Rinehart, 1953.

DIVINE, ROBERT A., *American Immigration Policy.* Yale, 1957.

DULLES, FOSTER R., *America's Rise to World Power.* Harper, 1955.

DULLES, J. F., *Labor in America.* Crowell, 1949.

——, *War or Peace.* Macmillan, 1957.

EBENSTEIN, WILLIAM, *Great Political Thinkers.* Rinehart, 1951.

——, *Modern Political Thought.* Rinehart, 1955.

——, *Today's Isms.* Prentice-Hall, 1954.

EDWARDS, RICHARD A., *The Fourteenth Amendment and Civil Liberty.* League of Women Voters, 1955.

EMERSON, THOMAS I., and HABER, DAVID, *Political and Civil Rights in the United States.* Dennis, 1952.

EWING, C. A. M., *American National Government.* American Book, 1958.

Facts about the Council-Manager Plan. National Municipal League, 1954.

FAINSOD, MERLE, *Government and the American Economy.* Norton, 1950.

FAIRMAN, CHARLES, *American Constitutional Decisions.* Holt, 1950.

FARRAND, MAX, *The Fathers of the Constitution.* Yale, 1922.

——, *The Framing of the Constitution.* Yale, 1913.

FENNO, RICHARD F., (ed.), *The Yalta Conference.* Heath, 1955.

FERGUSON, JOHN H., and McHENRY, DEAN E., *The American System of Government.* McGraw-Hill, 1956.

FINER, HERMAN, *The Government of Great European Powers.* Holt, 1955.

Forms of Municipal Government — How Have They Worked? National Municipal League, 1953.

FRANK, JOHN P., *Cases on the Constitution.* McGraw-Hill, 1952.

——, *Courts on Trial.* Princeton, 1949.

FURNISS, EDGAR S., *American Military Policy.* Rinehart, 1957.

GALBRAITH, JOHN K., *American Capitalism.* Houghton Mifflin, 1952.

——, *The Great Crash, 1929.* Houghton Mifflin, 1955.

GALLOWAY, GEORGE B., *The Legislative Process in Congress.* Crowell, 1953.

GOODMAN, WILLIAM, *The Two-Party System in the United States.* Van Nostrand, 1956.

GOSNELL, HAROLD F., *Democracy: The Threshold of Freedom.* Ronald, 1949.

GOULDNER, A., *Wildcat Strike.* Antioch, 1954.

GRAVES, W. BROOKE, *American State Government.* Heath, 1953.

GRISWOLD, ERWIN N., *The Fifth Amendment Today.* Harvard, 1955.

GROSS, BERTRAM, *The Legislative Struggle.* McGraw-Hill, 1953.

GROVES, HAROLD M., *Financing Government.* Holt, 1954.

GUNTHER, JOHN, *Inside U.S.A.* Harper, 1947.

HAAS, ERNEST B., and WHITING, ALLEN S., *Dynamics of International Relations.* McGraw-Hill, 1957.

HALLE, LOUIS J., *Civilization and Foreign Policy.* Harper, 1955.

HAMILTON, CHARLES, (ed.), *Men of the Underworld.* Macmillan, 1952.

HARDIN, CHARLES M., *Freedom in Agricultural Education.* Chicago, 1955.

——, *The Politics of Agriculture.* Free Press, 1952.

HARSCH, JOSEPH C., *The Role of Political Parties U.S.A.* League of Women Voters, 1955.

HART, HENRY M., and WECHSLER, HERBERT, *The Federal Courts and the Federal System.* Foundation Press, 1953.

HAVEMANN, E., and WEST, P., *They Went to College: The College Graduate in America Today.* Harcourt, Brace. 1952.

HAZARD, JOHN M., *The Soviet System of Government.* Chicago, 1957.

HESSELTINE, WILLIAM B., *The Rise and Fall of Third Parties.* Public Affairs Press, 1948.

HOLCOMBE, ARTHUR N., *Strengthening the United Nations.* Harper, 1957.

HOOK, SYDNEY, *Heresy, Yes; Conspiracy, No!* John Day, 1953.

HOSKINS, HALFORD L., *The Middle East.* Macmillan, 1954.

HUNT, R. N. CAREW, *Marxism: Past and Present.* Macmillan, 1955.

HYMAN, SIDNEY, *The American President.* Harper, 1954.

HYNEMAN, CHARLES, *Bureaucracy in a Democracy.* Harper, 1950.

IRION, FREDERICK C., *Public Opinion and Propaganda.* Crowell, 1950.

JACKSON, JUSTICE ROBERT H., *The Supreme Court in the American System of Government.* Harvard, 1955.

JENNINGS, WALTER W., *A Dozen Captains of American Industry.* Vantage, 1955.

JOHNSON, CLAUDIUS O., *American Government: National, State, and Local.* Crowell, 1955.
——, *American National Government.* Crowell, 1955.
JONES, JESSE H., *Fifty Billion Dollars: My Thirteen Years with the RFC.* Macmillan, 1951.
KALIJARVI, THORSTEN V., et al., *Modern World Politics.* Crowell, 1953.
KELLY, ALFRED H., *Where Constitutional Liberty Came From.* League of Women Voters, 1954.
KELLY, ALFRED H., and HARBISON, WINFRED A., *The American Constitution: Its Origin and Development.* Norton, 1955.
KEY, V. O., *Politics, Parties, and Pressure Groups.* Crowell, 1952.
KNEIER, CHARLES M., *City Government in the United States.* Harper, 1957.
KNEIER, CHARLES M., and FOX, GUY, *Readings in Municipal Government and Administration.* Rinehart, 1953.
KONVITZ, MILTON R., *Bill of Rights Reader.* Cornell, 1954.
LANE, ROBERT E., *Problems in American Government.* Prentice-Hall, 1952.
——, *The Regulation of Businessmen.* Yale, 1954.
LASSWELL, H. K., *National Security and Individual Freedom.* McGraw-Hill, 1953.
LEE, A. McC., *How to Understand Propaganda.* Rinehart, 1952.
LILIENTHAL, DAVID, *Big Business — A New Era.* Harper, 1953.
LIPPMANN, WALTER, *The Public Philosophy.* Atlantic-Little, Brown, 1955.
LIPSON, LESLIE, *The Great Issues of Politics.* Prentice-Hall, 1954.
LUBELL, SAMUEL, *The Future of American Politics.* Harper, 1952.
LYON, LEVERETT S., et al., *Modernizing a City Government.* Chicago, 1955.
MACDONALD, AUSTIN F., *American City Government and Administration.* Crowell, 1956.
——, *American State Government and Administration.* Crowell, 1955.
——, *Latin American Government and Politics.* Crowell, 1954.
——, *State and Local Government in the United States.* Crowell, 1955.
MACDONALD, H. MALCOM, et al., *Outside Readings in American Government.* Crowell, 1957.
MACDOUGALL, CURTIS D., *Understanding Public Opinion.* Macmillan, 1952.
MCDONALD, NEIL A., *The Study of Political Parties.* Doubleday, 1955.
MALONE, DUMAS, et al., *The Story of the Declaration of Independence.* Oxford, 1955.
MANGONE, G., *A Short History of International Relations.* McGraw-Hill, 1953.
MASON, ALPHEUS T., and BEANEY, WILLIAM M., *American Constitutional Law.* Prentice-Hall, 1954.
MATHEWS, JOHN M., *The American Constitutional System.* McGraw-Hill, 1940.
MAXWELL, JAMES A., *Fiscal Policy.* Holt, 1955.

MAYO, H. B., *Democracy and Marxism.* Oxford, 1955.
MAZUR, P., *The Standards We Raise.* Harper, 1953.
MERRIAM, CHARLES E. and ROBERT E., *The American Government.* Ginn, 1954.
METCALF, C. H., *A History of the United States Marine Corps.* Putnam's, 1949.
MILLER, GLENN W., *American Labor and the Government.* Prentice-Hall, 1949.
——, *Problems of Labor.* Macmillan, 1951.
Model County Charter National Municipal League, 1955.
Model State Constitution. National Municipal League, 1948.
MOOS, MALCOLM, *Politics, Presidents, and Coattails.* Johns Hopkins, 1953.
——, *The Republicans: A History of Their Party.* Random House, 1956.
MORLAN, ROBERT L., *Capitol, Courthouse, and City Hall: Readings in American State and Local Government.* Houghton Mifflin, 1954.
MUSTARD, HARRY S., *An Introduction to Public Health.* Macmillan, 1953.
NEUBERGER, RICHARD L., *Adventures in Politics.* Oxford, 1954.
NEUMANN, ROBERT G., *European and Comparative Government.* McGraw-Hill, 1955.
NICHOLSON, HAROLD, *The Evolution of Diplomatic Method.* Macmillan, 1955.
NOBLE, S. G., *A History of Education.* Rinehart, 1954.
O'BRIAN, JOHN LORD, *National Security and Individual Freedom.* Harvard, 1955.
OLIVER, D., *The Pacific Islands.* Harvard, 1951.
ORFIELD, L. B., *Criminal Procedure from Arrest to Appeal.* New York University, 1947.
Our Territorial Government. Hawaii Bureau of Research, 1949.
OXENFELDT, A. R., *Economics for the Citizen.* Rinehart, 1953.
PADOVER, SAUL K., *The Living U.S. Constitution.* Praeger, 1953.
PALMER, NORMAN D., and PERKINS, HOWARD, *International Relations.* Houghton Mifflin, 1957.
PAPENDREOU, A., and WHEELER, J., *Competition and Its Regulation.* Prentice-Hall, 1954.
PATE, JAMES E., *Local Government and Administration.* American Book, 1954.
PELTASON, JACK W., *Federal Courts in the Political Process.* Doubleday, 1955.
——, *Constitutional Liberty and Seditious Activity.* League of Women Voters, 1954.
PENNIMAN, H. R., *Sait's American Parties and Elections.* Appleton-Century-Crofts, 1952.
PETERSON, SHOREY, *Economics.* Holt, 1954.
PFEFFER, LEO, *Church, State, and Freedom.* Beacon, 1953.
PHILLIPS, JEWELL C., *State and Local Government in America.* American Book, 1954.
PINCHOT, GIFFORD, *Breaking New Ground.* Harcourt, Brace, 1947.
POSTON, R., *Democracy Is You.* Harper, 1953.
POTTER, E. B., *The United States and World Sea Power.* Prentice-Hall, 1955.

Pound, Roscoe, *The Development of Constitutional Guarantees of Liberty.* Yale, 1957.

Pratt, Julius W., *America's Colonial Experiment.* Prentice-Hall, 1950.

Randle, C. Wilson, *Collective Bargaining.* Houghton Mifflin, 1951.

Rankin, Robert S., *The Presidency in Transition.* Kallman, 1949.

Ranney, Austin, and Kendall, Willmoore, *Democracy and the American Party System.* Harcourt, Brace, 1956.

Rickard, J. A., and McCrocklin, James H., *Our National Constitution: Origins, Development, and Meaning.* Stackpole, 1955.

Riker, William H., *Democracy in the United States.* Macmillan, 1953.

Roche, John P., and Stedman, Murray, *The Dynamics of Democratic Government.* McGraw-Hill, 1954.

Rodell, Fred, *Nine Men: A Political History of the Supreme Court.* Random House, 1955.

Rohlfing, Charles C., *et al., Business and Government.* Foundation Press, 1953.

Roseboom, Victor, *A History of Presidential Elections.* Macmillan, 1957.

Ross, Alf, *Constitution of the United Nations: Analysis of Structure and Function.* Rinehart, 1950.

Rossiter, Clinton, *Conservatism in America.* Knopf, 1955.

Rostow, W. W., *et al., The Prospects for Communist China.* Viking, 1954.

Russell, John E., *World Population and World Food Supplies.* Macmillan, 1954.

Salisbury, Harrison E., *American in Russia.* Harper, 1955.

Salvadori, Massimo, *NATO: A Twentieth Century Community of Nations.* Van Nostrand, 1957.

Saye, Albert B., *et al., Principles of American Government.* Prentice-Hall, 1954.

Schleicher, Charles P., *Introduction to International Relations.* Prentice-Hall, 1954.

Schwartz, Harry, *Russia's Soviet Economy.* Prentice-Hall, 1955.

Scott, Hugh A., *How to Go into Politics.* John Day, 1949.

Serbein, O., *Paying for Medical Care in the United States.* Columbia, 1953.

Shannon, Fred, *American Farmer Movements.* Van Nostrand, 1957.

Sikes, Pressly S., and Stoner, John E., *Bates and Filed's State Government.* Harper, 1954.

Smiley, Dean F., and Gould, Adrian G., *Your Community's Health.* Macmillan, 1954.

Smith, G., *Conservation of Natural Resources.* Wiley, 1951.

Smith, T. V., *The Bill of Rights and Our Individual Liberties.* League of Women Voters, 1954.

Snider, Clide F., *Local Government in Rural America.* Appleton-Century-Crofts, 1957.

Snyder, Louis L., *Fifty Major Documents of the Twentieth Century.* Van Nostrand, 1955.

Snyder, Richard C., and Furniss, Edgar S., *American Foreign Policy.* Rinehart, 1954.

Stapleton, Lawrence, *The Design of Democracy.* Oxford, 1949.

Steiner, G., *Government's Role in Economic Life.* McGraw-Hill, 1953.

Story of the Council-Manager Plan. National Municipal League, 1954.

Sufrin, Sidney C., and Palmer, Edward E., *The New St. Lawrence Frontier.* Syracuse, 1957.

Swarthout, John M., and Bartley, Ernest R., *Materials on American National Government.* Oxford, 1952.

——, *Principles and Problems of American National Government.* Oxford, 1955.

——, *Principles and Problems of State and Local Government.* Oxford, 1958.

Swisher, Carl B., *American Constitutional Development.* Houghton Mifflin, 1954.

Tate, H. Clay, *Building a Better Home Town.* Harper, 1954.

Ten Broeck, J., *et al., Prejudice, War, and the Constitution.* California, 1954.

Thompson, Warren, *Population Problems.* McGraw-Hill, 1953.

Truman, Harry S., *Memoirs: Vol. I, Year of Decisions* and *Vol. II, Years of Trial and Hope.* Doubleday, 1955 and 1956.

Turner, Henry A., *Politics in the United States.* McGraw-Hill, 1955.

"The United Nations," *Current History,* January, 1952.

"United States Tax Policy," *Current History,* August, 1954.

Van Doren, Carl, *The Great Rehearsal.* Viking, 1948.

Wade, William W., *The UN Today.* Wilson, 1954.

Welch, Joseph, *The Constitution.* Houghton Mifflin, 1956.

Westin, Alan, *The Constitution and Loyalty Programs.* League of Women Voters, 1954.

White, Leonard D., *Introduction to the Study of Public Administration.* Macmillan, 1955.

White, William S., *The Citadel: The Story of the U.S. Senate.* Harper, 1957.

Whitehill, Arthur M., *Personnel Relations.* McGraw-Hill, 1955.

Wilcox, Clair, *Public Policies toward Business.* Irvin, 1955.

Williams, Irving, *The American Vice-President.* Doubleday, 1954.

Wilson, H. H., *Congress: Corruption and Compromise.* Rinehart, 1951.

Wright, David M., *A Key to Modern Economics.* Macmillan, 1954.

Zeller, Belle, (ed.), *American State Legislatures, Report of the Committee on American State Legislatures, American Political Science Association.* Crowell, 1954.

Ziegler, Benjamin N., (ed.), *Immigration: An American Dilemma.* Heath, 1953.

INDEX

Agencies, independent, 319–341
Agreements, executive, 184
Agricultural Adjustment Acts, 113, 284
Agricultural Research Service, 275–277
Agriculture, Department of, 274–285
Air Force, 240–242
Alaska, 83, 205, 349–351
Albany Plan of Union, 36–37
Aliens, admission, 247–250; and civil rights, 382; naturalization, 250–253
Ambassadors, 196–199, 200
Amendments, Bill of Rights, 384–401; federal constitutional, 70–74; state constitutional, 464–468
American Arbitration Association, 522
American Federation of Employees, 662
American Federation of Labor, 679, 680
American heritage, 3, 5, 15
Amnesty, 187
Annapolis Convention, 44
Anti-Federalists, 48, 411
Anti-Masons, 415
Anzus Pact, 210
Appeals, Courts of, 370
Appellate Courts, 515
Appointment, power of, 181
Apprenticeship, Bureau of, 302
Arbitration, to settle disputes, 521
Arizona, 68, 488
Arkansas, 468 fn.
Armed forces, use of, 7–8; president's power, 185, 232; functions, 233
Armed Forces Policy Council, 233
Army, functions and organization, 233–235
Army Engineers, 266
Arrest, 531, 533
Arson, 530
Articles of Confederation, 21, 38, 41, 44, 49
Assemblymen, 34 fn.
Assessment, 546
Atomic bomb, 9, 713
Atomic Energy Commission, 243–244, 713
Attachés, 200
Attainder, Bills of, 396
Attorney-General, state, 505; United States, 244
Auditor, county, 567; state, 504
Authority and liberty, 3–15

Bail, 399, 533
Ballots, 449, 452, 647–648
Baltimore, Maryland, 616
Bankruptcy laws, 102–103
Banks, Federal Home Loan, 337–338; Federal Land, 336–337; Federal Reserve System, 335–336; national, 101, 107, 330–336; state, 331
Baruch, Bernard, 713
Bicameralism, 81–82, 464, 474–475
Bill, how it becomes a law, federal, 155–162; state, 482–484
Bill of Rights, 6–7, 49, 71, 384–401
Bills, congressional, 154–162; state, 481–484
Bills of Attainder, 396
Black, Justice Hugo, 366

Blue Cross, 672
Boards, state, 505
Bonds, government, 102, 223–224
Bonneville Power Administration, 267
Boston, Massachusetts, 613, 614; City Planning Board, 608–609; housing development, 675; Metropolitan District, 612; Tea Party, 37
Boulder Canyon Project, 264, 265
Bretton Woods Conference, 714–715
Budget, federal, 179; state, 551–552
Bull Moose Progressive Party, 415
Bureau of, Apprenticeship, 302; the Budget, 179; Customs, 202, 216; Engraving and Printing, 226; of Foreign Commerce, 202, 296; Indian Affairs, 271; Labor Standards, 302; Labor Statistics, 302; Land Management, 262–263; Mines, 270; the Mint, 224; Narcotics, 227–228; Old Age and Survivors Insurance, 307–308; Prisons, 244–245; Public Roads, 299–300; Reclamation, 263–266; Standards, 104–105, 292–293
Burgesses, 34 fn.
Burglary, 530
Business taxes, 549

Cabinet, 179–180
Calendars, 158–159
California, 158–159, 224, 266, 465–466
Campaign, political, 421–425
Capital stock taxes, 549
Capitalism, 24–25, 688
Caroline Islands, 356–357
Caucus, 441–442; party, 149–150; town, 573
Ceiling prices, 227
Census, 83, 586–587
Census Bureau, 290–292
Central Valley Project, 266
Chancery court, 527
Charter colonies, 35
Charters, city, 589–592
Check and balance system, 41, 68–70
Chiang Kai-shek, 206
Chicago, Illinois, 614, 679
Child Labor, 123, 301–302
Children's Bureau, 307
China, 19, 206–207
Chinese Exclusion Act, 246
Circuit Courts, 515
Cities, population growth, 586–587
Citizenship, granting of, 250–253; obligations, 641–642, 644–648
City, government, 586–599; planning, 603–607; problems, 603–618
Civil Aeronautics Administration, 296
Civil Aeronautics Board, 296
Civil case, 512; procedure, 527–530; rights, 41, 380–401; service, 652–663; suit, 527
Civil Service Act, 654
Civil Service Commission, 181, 654–661
Civilian defense, 618
Claims, Court of, 373
Clay, Henry, 652
Clayton Act, 138–139

National Convention, 417–420, 442–443, 447
National defense, 8–12, 15, 178, 180 fn., 185, 202, 231–244
National forests, 278
National government. *See* Congress *and* Government
National Guard, 232, 233
National Institutes of Health, 310–311
National Labor Relations Board, 683, 684
National Municipal League, 470
National Origins Act, 246
National Park Service, 268
National Security Council, 178, 202, 232
Natural Gas Act, 328
Naturalization, 103, 250–253
Navigation, 132–133
Navy, 235–240
Nebraska, 464 fn., 468 fn., 474, 475
Necessary and Proper clause, 106–107
Nevada, 64–65, 186
New England Confederation, 36
New England town meeting, 23 fn.
New Hampshire, 34, 39, 44, 64, 462, 463, 465
New Jersey, 34, 43, 45, 46, 63, 392, 468, 518 fn., 536
New York City, 604, 612, 613, 618, 704
New York State, 34, 43, 45, 63, 66, 435, 465
New York State Regents Literary Test, 435
Nixon, Richard M., 19, 177
Nominations, methods for, 440–448
Norris-LaGuardia Act, 682, 683
North Atlantic Treaty Organization, 210
North Carolina, 34
North Dakota, 456
Northwest Ordinance of 1787, 623

Office of, Defense Mobilization, 178, 202; Education, 624–626; International Labor Affairs, 300; Territories, 272
Ohio, 67, 468 fn.
Oklahoma, 67
Old Age and Survivors Insurance, Bureau of, 307–308
Open door policy, 206
Ordinance of 1785, 578
Ordinances, by President, 187; city, 594
Oregon, 60, 63, 65, 470, 476, 479 fn., 487, 488, 489, 495, 496, 501, 647; Oregon system, 447, 453
Organic Act, 347, 356
Original Package Doctrine, 131, 144

Pacific Islands, Territory of, 356–357
Panama Canal Zone, 358
Paper currency, 226
Pardoning power, of governor, 503; of President, 187–188
Parishes, 559 fn.
Parity, 286
Parliamentary government, 22
Parole Board, 188, 245
Parties, political, 407–425
Party Whip, 149
Passports, 201–202
Patents, 104, 293–295

Paterson Plan, 46
Pay-as-you-go plan, 116–117
Payroll taxes, 550
Pendleton Act, 654–656
Penn, William, 35, 36
Pennsylvania, 4, 35, 44, 45
Peonage, 389
Persona non grata, 198
Petit jury, 517–518
Petition, direct legislation, 467–468, 486–487; right to, 385
Philadelphia, 4, 38, 44, 605, 646–647
Philippines, 361–363
Philippines Pact, 211
Picketing, 394
Pigeonholing, 156, 481–482
Pittsburgh, Pennsylvania, 606
Plaintiff, 528
Planning commissions, city, 605–606
Platform, party, 420
Plurality, 410
Pocket veto, 163
Point Four Program, 209, 210
Police, courts, 513; power, 609
Political parties, 74, 407–425
Poll tax, 435, 549–550
Polls, 449
Popular initiative, 467–468, 486–487
Popular sovereignty, 40–41, 54, 638
Population, United States, 586–587
Portland, Oregon, 613
Post Office Department, 257–261
Post roads, 103
Postal Service, 103–104
Powers, concurrent, 58, 103; delegated, 56, 57; division of, 56–60; expressed, 56, 57, 90; implied, 57–58, 106; reserved, 57–58
Preamble to Constitution, analyzed, 4–13
Presentment, 397, 516
Presidency, 171–188
President, 162–163; as commander-in-chief, 7, 61, 73, 232, 285; election, 171–176; powers of, 180–188; State of the Union Message, 147
Presidential assistants, 178–179
Presidential government, 21
Press, freedom of, 391, 393
Pressure groups, 163–164, 409, 484–485
Prices, stabilizing of, 284–285
Primary elections, 443–447
Prisons, Bureau of, 244–245
Private enterprise, 24; regulation, 688–695
Privileges and immunities, 65–66, 401
Probation officers, 245
Progressive Party, 415
Prohibition, 673–674
Proletariat, dictatorship of, 26, 27
Property tax, 545
Proportional representation, 455
Proprietary colonies, 35
Providence, Rhode Island, 613
Public Assistance, Bureau of, 307
Public debt, 222
Public Health Service, 202, 310–312, 671
Public housing, 674–678
Public Roads, Bureau of, 299–300
Public School Administration, 626–627

Public utilities, 614–618
Puerto Rico, 351–355
Pure Food and Drug Act, 313

Quasi-legislative powers, 320
Quota system, 247

Railroad Brotherhoods, 679
Ramspeck Act, 656
Randolph, Edmund, 45, 46, 48
Randolph Plan, 46
Rayburn, Sam, 81
Reapportionment Act, 83
Recall, 455–456, 495
Reclamation, Bureau of, 263–266
Reclamation Act, 264
Reconstruction Finance Corporation, 338
Referendum, 71, 487–489
Regional Security treaties, 210–211
Register of Deeds, 566–567
Religion, and education, 631–633; freedom, 392–393; strength in, 11
Removal power, 181, 498
Reorganization Act, 188, 189
Republic, defined, 23, 638
Republican form of government, 60
Republican Party, 413, 414–415
Representative government, 638; in colonial period, 33–34
Representatives, United States. *See* House of Representatives
Reserved powers, 57–58
Resolutions, 155
Reuther, Walter, 680
Revenue, federal, 216–222; state and local, 541–551
Rhode Island, 35, 40, 44, 60, 64, 462, 468, 563
Rider, 155
Rights, Bill of, 6–7, 49, 71, 384–401
Rio Pact, 210
Robinson-Patman Act, 138–139
Rochester, New York, 612
Rockefeller, John D., Jr., 705
Roll-call (record) vote, 160–161
Roosevelt, Franklin Delano, 176 fn., 184, 185, 281, 420, 569
Roosevelt, Theodore, 177, 207, 508
Roosevelt Corollary, 207, 453–454
Royal colonies, 34–35
Rules Committee, House, 152–153, 158, 159
Rural areas, types of government, 562
Rural Electrification Administration, 282

St. Lawrence Seaway and Power Project, 699–700
Sales tax, 547–548
San Francisco, California, 613
San Francisco Conference, 705
Savings Bonds, 102, 223
Schools, public, 623–632; shortage, 625–626; superintendent of, 568
Search warrant, 532
Seattle, Washington, 290–91, 606, 612–14, 618
Secret Service, 219
Secretary of, Agriculture, 275; Commerce, 289; Health, Education, and Welfare, 306;

Labor, 300; State (federal), 194–196; State (state), 504; Treasury, 216
Securities and Exchange Commission, 134, 135, 340–342
Security Council (UN), 708–709
Security-risk, 663
Select committees, 153
Selective Service Act, 242
Selectmen, 572, 574
Self-incrimination, 398
Senate, 87–88; bill in the, 161–162; committee system, 150–154; organization, 147–149; president, 148; in states, 475. *See also* Congress
Senate Crime Committee, 11, 644
Senators, 87–92
Seniority, rule of, 149
Severance taxes, 549
Shays' Rebellion, 7
Sheriff, 565–566
Sherman Anti-trust Act, 137–138, 139, 141
Silver, 224; certificates, 226
Slander, 393 fn.
Small Business Administration, 338
Small Claims Court, 514
Small State Plan, 46
Smith, Adam, sound tax system, 544–545
Smith Act, 394
Social legislation, 666–685
Social Security Act, 307–310
Social Security Administration, 121, 307
Socialism, 25
Socialist Party, 415
Soil Conservation Service, 280–281
South Carolina, 34, 39, 468 fn., 597
Speaker of the House, 147–148
Speech, freedom of, 393
Spoils System, 653–654
Springfield, Massachusetts, 7
Sputnik, I & II, 720–721
Stamp Act Congress, 37
Standards, National Bureau of, 104, 292
Standing Committees, 150
Stare Decisis, 527
State, administrative reorganization, 505–506; banks, 331–332; city-state relations, 588–593; civil rights, 383–401; constitutions, 39–40, 461–470, 544, 545 fn.; courts, 511–522, 526–537; definition, 18–20; division of powers between national government and, 56–60; economic regulation, 692–693; educational supervision, 306, 623–632; election process, 448–456; federal aid, 60–62, 306, 308, 309–312, 550; finance, 541–555; governors, 492–508; interstate and intrastate commerce, 132–138; interstate relations, 63–66; legislatures, 473–489; nominating methods, 441–448; party organization, 421–422; police, 500; public health, 668–673; reserved powers, 57–58; revenues and expenditures, 541–552; suffrage, 429–433
State Department, 194–202
State medicine, plans for, 672–673
State universities, 623–624, 629–630
States, admission to Union, 66–68, 463 fn., 466
Staunton, Virginia, 597
Steering Committees, 150
Stevenson, Adlai E., 639–640

OOR

ALABAMA ARIZONA ARKANSAS CALIFORNIA

GEORGIA IDAHO ILLINOIS INDIANA

MAINE MARYLAND MASSACHUSETTS MICHIGAN

NEBRASKA NEVADA NEW HAMPSHIRE NEW JERSEY

OHIO OKLAHOMA OREGON PENNSYLVANIA

TEXAS UTAH VERMONT VIRGINIA